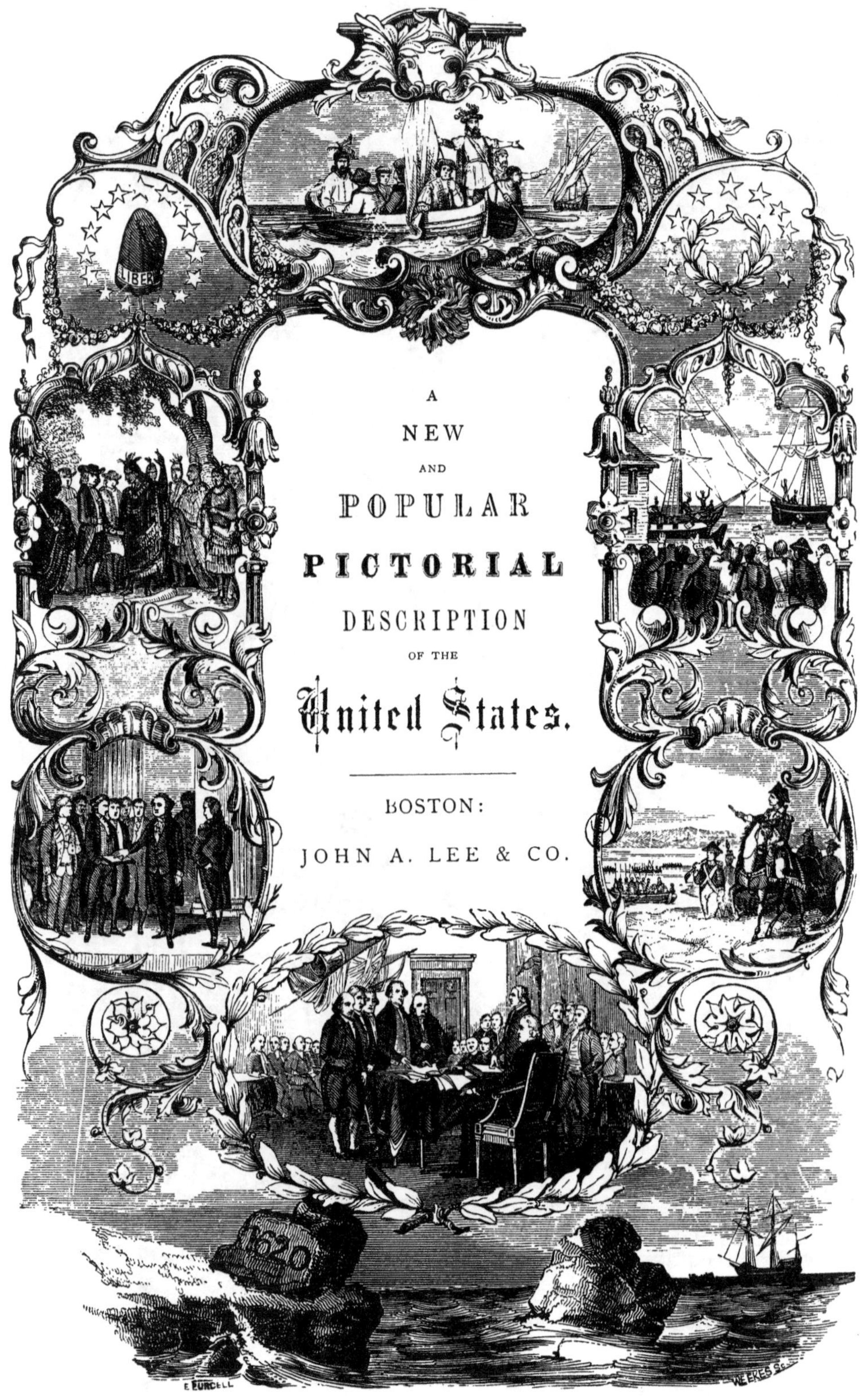
A
NEW
AND
POPULAR
PICTORIAL
DESCRIPTION
OF THE
United States.
BOSTON:
JOHN A. LEE & CO.
1620
E PURCELL
WEEKES Sc

A

PICTORIAL DESCRIPTION

OF THE

UNITED STATES;

EMBRACING THE

HISTORY, GEOGRAPHICAL POSITION, AGRICULTURAL AND MINERAL RESOURCES, POPULATION, MANUFACTURES, COMMERCE, AND SKETCHES OF CITIES, TOWNS, PUBLIC BUILDINGS, ETC., ETC.

INTERSPERSED WITH

REVOLUTIONARY AND OTHER INTERESTING INCIDENTS CONNECTED WITH THE EARLY SETTLEMENT OF THE COUNTRY.

ILLUSTRATED WITH NUMEROUS ENGRAVINGS.

BOSTON:
JOHN A. LEE & CO.,
No. 5 HARVARD PLACE.
1876.

INTRODUCTION.

The history of America has not, like that of the Old World, the charm of classical or romantic associations; but in useful instruction and moral dignity, it has no equal. It is scarce three quarters of a century since this fair and flourishing republic was a colony of England, scarcely commanding the means of existence without the aid of the mother-country, who was herself oppressed by European wars. Our puritan forefathers began in the rough fields of Massachusetts, Rhode Island, and Connecticut, on a broad, comprehensive principle, which has gone forth to fraternize the world. Our history, therefore, like that poetical temple of fame reared by the imagination of Chaucer, and decorated by the taste of Pope, is almost exclusively dedicated to the memory of the truly great. Within, no idle ornament encumbers its bold simplicity. The pure light of heaven enters from above, and sheds an equal and serene radiance around. As the eye wanders about its extent, it beholds the unadorned monuments of brave and good men, who have bled or toiled for their country; or it rests on votive tablets inscribed with the names of the blessed benefactors of mankind.

The puritans of England—the resolute conquerors of the lakes and forests of the New World—occupied, in the first period of their social existence, the depressed position of a European colony; but the spirit of liberty which had led them to these wild regions, and the gifts of a magnificent and fertile nature, were sufficient to prepare them for their high destiny.* This rude apprenticeship lasted more than one hundred and fifty years before the hour of

* We rejoice to see a disposition manifested by the conductors of the secular press, to sanction the great principles of morality and religion, which lie at the foundation of social happiness and national prosperity. We have no confidence in the stability and success of any form of government which does not recognise God "as the Ruler of nations."

"Washington was undoubtedly *the man* of the age in which he lived. He was raised up by Providence for the accomplishment of a most important and difficult work. But wise and gifted as he was, he would never have achieved the sublime results which crowned his efforts, if he had not had the best material the world has ever furnished, for laying the foundation of a government, under whose beneficent influences we have been happy and prosperous. Indeed, the germs of our republic may be traced back long prior to the Revolution. They are seen in the spirit, the intelligence, the probity, the indomitable perseverance, and the piety, of the little band who reached our shores in the May-Flower. It was there, in the solemn compact into which they entered before leaving their frail bark, that we see the incipient steps taken which led on, by a process slow but sure, to the Declaration of Independence. There is nothing that rouses our indignation more effectually, than to hear the miserable prating of some who have yet to learn the rudiments of our true history, throwing out their sneers, and casting contempt upon those to whom they are indebted for their rich privileges, and whose 'shoe's latchet they are not worthy to unloose.' Such a man

"'Is fit for treason, stratagems, and spoils;
The motions of his spirit are dull as night,
And his affections dark as Erebus.
Let no such man be trusted.'"

Philadelphia North American.

change struck; and in the night of the 18th of April, 1775, the cannons of Lexington called a new-born nation to regenerate the world. The people rose as one man, and turning the ploughshare that tilled the soil into a sword to defend it, they threw themselves upon their unjust oppressors, and proclaimed at Philadelphia the immortal principles of self-government, that made tyrants tremble and every generous heart palpitate with joyful hope. At that moment a new name was inscribed on the catalogue of great nations. If not in national importance, it was great by the moral influence it immediately exercised on the world. England, overwhelmed with a debt of one hundred and twenty-eight and a half millions sterling, chargeable with an annual interest of four and a half millions, wished to transfer a portion of the burden to her colonies, and attempted to infringe their rights by the imposition of the celebrated stamp-tax. The colonists admitted the justice of all the members of a confederation contributing, according to their ability, to the support of the common government, since the prosperity of each depends on the security and well-being of all, but declared they could not and ought not share in the expenses of a war with which they had nothing to do, and a luxurious court which was equally repugnant to their repose and American simplicity. At first England affected to acknowledge the right of the colonies to refuse to pay for faults they had no share in committing; but after the pause of a few years, she renewed her attacks under a different form. With equal firmness America repelled the second attempt to violate her liberties; and England, offended at this unexampled audacity, closed the port of Boston, and kindled the flames of a war which doubled her troublesome debt. Then appeared the host of blazing meteors that illumined the path of our Revolution, and now watch in their high spheres over our safety. They broke the chains of thirteen colonies, and offered to the astonished world the most sublime spectacle of ancient or modern times—the fusion of all races, tongues, and sects, in the one political religion of liberty. The Declaration of Independence found thirteen states and three millions of people; now there are thirty-one states, and a population of twenty-five millions. The whole exterior commerce of the republic, at 1780, amounted to about eight and a half millions annually; now our annual exports exceed one hundred and fifty-eight millions, while our internal commerce is valued at five hundred millions per year, without estimating the home consumption.

What a change has the progress of civilization effected on this vast continent during the last two centuries; and what a glorious change to the enlightened mind.* Then a few ill-constructed roads, and the water-courses nature had bestowed, were our only means of intercommunication; now, about ten thousand miles of railway and numerous canals, which embrace, in continuous lines of navigation, thirty thousand miles of lake and river, render the most northern corner of Maine nearer in time to Florida and Mexico than was Boston to Charleston in those days. Steam and the magnetic telegraph have annihilated distance. A few years ago, and the majestic forest spread its wing far and wide, and the Indian was monarch of all he surveyed—traversing its wilds with his spear, or navigating its lakes with his bark canoe. What was once gloomy forests is now beautiful villages and populous cities, teeming with industrious and intelligent inhabitants, ministering to the wants of the mother-country. Our vast prairies are now becoming thrifty farms, and the produce of every climate smiles upon our shores. The application of steam to various purposes has produced wonderful results. America and England are brought withtn a ten-days' voyage, and China will in fifty years be, comparatively, as near as England now is: the whole world will yet be neighbors to each other, and PEACE AND GOOD WILL universally prevail among mankind.

In the preparation of the following work, we have found new reason to admire the rapid progress of our own country in population, the arts, and the various institutions which ac-

* The following passage will realize to our readers the condition of things two hundred years ago:—

"The number of the pilgrims was but one hundred, all told. The bark in which they crossed the ocean was of less capacity than that of one of the craft which navigate our Schuylkill canal. The length of their voyage was the same with that of Columbus, a little more than a century before. The Spaniards had held their 'revels in the halls of the Montezumas' during the greater part of this century. Virginia had been settled a few years, and contained from five hundred to one thousand inhabitants. What we now call New England was regarded as an island—a mistake not corrected in old England so late as the time of an official despatch of Lord North's during our Revolution. They came from England, and our thoughts are naturally turned to the condition of things in England at the time. They had not much glass for their houses, and not a great deal of linen for their persons; no tea or coffee, and but little sugar for their tables, in old England then. They had no science of chymistry or of geology; no knowledge of electricity or of the power of steam; scarcely any manufactures, but very imperfect agriculture, and very little horticulture. Crossbows had scarcely gone out of use in war, and their firearms generally had matchlocks. They had their old baronial establishments, their ruined castles, and deserted monasteries; their magnificent cathedrals, their two great universities, their vast enclosures for parks and preserves. They had monuments of the times of the Druids, and abiding evidence that England, for two centuries, had been a Roman province. They boasted of a constitution; but it existed principally in custom, depending upon uncertain memory, and there were precedents of all kinds—those favoring prerogative greatly prevailing over those in favor of liberty. From the peasant to the prince, the distance was more awful than we can well imagine. For five thousand years the human race had been subject, all the world over, to the dominion of arbitrary power. From the earliest period of recorded time, history had been occupied with the rise and fall of kingdoms and of kings."

company and promote civilization, morals, and religion, as well as national extension, wealth, and power. Great pains have been taken, and expense incurred, to introduce some of the most important, appropriate, and interesting scenes, sketches of character, and other matters embraced in the wide surface of the American Union. In the older states, the historical details offered for a work of this kind are superabundant; and the only difficulty is found in making a selection of periods, and in sufficiently condensing the matter, without reducing it to the form of mere statistics. Respecting the new states, we can assure the reader that the labor of collecting the latest and most authentic information has been very great. We take pleasure in acknowledging our obligations to those benevolent and intelligent friends at a distance who have aided us in collecting the most recent statistics relating to some of the most flourishing parts of our country.

We can not but feel, in looking upon the numerous and important subjects to which the attention of our readers is here directed—as we pass from one portion of the country to another, that they, as well as ourselves, must naturally and almost unavoidably be strongly impressed with several great and salutary reflections. To read the history of any country or people, without permanent benefit, would be to waste time and to abuse one of the most important branches of human knowledge; but to pass over descriptions of our own land, and the history of our own people, without giving them any serious regard, or drawing from them any of those interesting and salutary lessons which they are adapted to supply, beyond almost any other part of the world or portion of the human family, would prove a frivolity of mind, or an insensibility of heart, too great for any author willingly to attribute to the circle of his readers.

We are indeed aware of the extent to which the floods of fictitious writings, at the present day, vitiate the public taste, waste the time, enfeeble the mind, and, alas! pervert the heart; and we find new reason every day to lament the various evils, both mental and moral, which are brought upon individuals and society by that pernicious cause. But still we know full well, that there are those who keep their minds and their hearts free from the contamination, as well as the debilitating influences, of that miserable kind of reading (which deserves not the title of literature), and that there are persons, in all parts of the country, whose native strength of intellect and manly Christian principles have never been subjected to the insidious, injurious, and often ruinous influence of fiction-reading. Heavy responsibility rests upon those who write for the public. Tutors of the world, they may not lightly assume nor thoughtlessly discharge a very important office. Every line found wanting in moral tone should be instantly erased. Incalculable evil may follow its publication—for in that the depraved find countenance, and the young example and encouragement. He is without excuse—nay, he is grossly culpable—who trifles with the welfare of society, or neglects to do good when opportunity is presented. A bad thought uttered in print is not addressed to a single individual, but to the whole community.

While others, though it may be by thousands, devote their leisure hours to subjects of a frivolous and unreal nature, our readers, we would fain hope, will employ them in the more rational and useful task of reviewing the aspect, resources, and history, of their own native land, and the prosperous and powerful nation to which they belong. The materials for such a review we now place before them, in such number and variety as the limits assigned by such a publication permit; and the public will do us the justice to allow that great labor has been bestowed on these pages, and that we have collected an amount of authentic information not easily to be surpassed in importance, variety, and interest, without greatly exceeding the limits to which we have been confined. It has been our constant study to pursue the happy medium between the dry record of facts and dates, and the diffuse and detached descriptions to which the abundance of pleasing topics invited us at every step.

Although four years have not elapsed since the first edition of this work issued from the press, yet a thorough revision of it has been imperatively demanded from the many and extraordinary changes that have, in that brief period, occurred in every section of the country; the most remarkable instance of which is the recent acquisition, discovery of the mineral wealth, and settlement of California, resulting in the addition, without its going through the usual territorial probation, of a new state to the Union upon the very western verge of the American continent. About fifty pages have been added to the original size of the work, comprising a full historical and descriptive account of the above-named new Pacific state, with appropriate illustrations, and of the territories of Minnesota, New Mexico, and Utah. Many important facts have been greatly condensed, and many circumstances of minor consequence excluded for want of room; but we trust that the reader will see that we have, throughout the volume, had in view his own gratification and lasting advantage; and that he will arise from its perusal with the reflection that it has brought him a strengthened mind and an improved heart.

One of the first reflections to which a deliberate survey of our country naturally gives rise, is, that we have a territory vast in extent, varied in surface and climate, embracing numerous and inexhaustible natural treasures, and secured, by its position, from many of the evils to which most other countries are exposed. Without powerful neighbors, jealous of our prosperity, watching our movements, and threatening to interfere in our concerns, as we find most of the nations of Europe, we are left free from apprehensions of such difficulties on all our borders; so that we may choose such objects, ways, and means, as seem good and right in our own eyes.

The general good of the country demands a mutual acquaintance between the citizens in all parts of it. If ignorant of each other's condition, the people of the different states can not feel that high and just regard for each other which is essential to the existence of a strong spirit of brotherhood. The general diffusion of accurate knowledge, respecting all parts of the country, is therefore to be esteemed as an important public object, as it is one of the principal means to secure that great end. While all look with intelligent interest on the progress annually made, in every state and territory, in different branches of improvement, the value of great and good men will be appreciated, and a noble rivalry maintained, from which the whole country will derive advantage.

All history, however, is only useful so far as we are guided by a knowledge of past experience. Rational liberty and the expansive genius of self-government have so far made us united and powerful. To the people who are qualified by correct habits and self-discipline to love and respect the free institutions of our land, liberty is what the sun is to the earth and religion to the soul—light, and life, and infinite progression. Intellectual, apart from moral culture, is, however, to be feared rather than encouraged; it teaches, indeed, how to rear, but is powerless to *perpetuate*. The loss of liberty at Rome was contemporaneous, or very nearly so, with the era of her greatest intellectual achievements. It is not alone a knowledge of their rights that the people require, but *a virtuous appreciation of them.* It was the loss of this public virtue that the elder Cato deplored, when he said to the Roman senate, that it was not by the force of arms, merely, that their forefathers had raised the republic to the greatness it enjoyed in their day, but by things of a very different nature—industry and discipline at home, abstinence abroad, a disinterested spirit in council, unblinded by passion, and unbiased by pleasure.

The preservation of well-regulated freedom should be the prayer of every American citizen; but while honestly desirous of enlarging its circumference, he should take great care lest he admits within the circle the elements of licentiousness. In the present state of society, there is more to be feared from this quarter than from any effort of tyranny. The onward progress of intellect and education has put that down for ever. To those who are united for a good purpose, we would say, look to the constancy and character of the early founders of our republic! While other portions of the earth are slumbering in darkness and debased in crime, let us recall to mind their counsel and example. Let us never forget that it is to an Education, wisely and liberally provided for our people, that America owes her proud superiority. Claiming full exemption from all superstition, we firmly believe that no state can prosper in a long career of true glory, in the disregard of the claims of justice and the injunctions of the Christain religion. A floodtide of apparent prosperity may come, filling for the time the avenues of trade, and satiating the cravings of taste and curiosity; yet, sooner or later it has its ebb, and either cloys with its abundance or leaves the void greater than before. History is a silent but eloquent witness of its truth, and from her undying lamp sheds a stream of unceasing light along our pathway. The fabrics of ancient greatness, built by injustice and consecrated to ambition, are now flitting shadows before us, starting up from behind the broken pillars and falling columns that were reared to perpetuate the genius by which they were wrought.

With such views, the following descriptions of the several states and territories have been written. We shall indeed feel doubly rewarded, if this brief sketch of our great western republic should increase the attachment of our readers to those great principles of equal rights, intelligence, virtue, and peace, in which were laid the foundation of our institutions. In the following pages will be found facts displaying the good principles, sound judgment, and genuine patriotism, of our ancestors, and others of later date, which prove that they have not a few worthy successors. It is an interesting reflection, that each one is a member of this great commonwealth, and that no one is too weak or humble to do something for the public good.

R. S.

Nov., 1851.

MAINE.

NEW HAMPSHIRE.

VERMONT.

MASSACHUSETTS.

CONNECTICUT.

RHODE ISLAND.

NEW YORK.

NEW JERSEY.

PENNSYLVANIA.

DELAWARE.

MARYLAND.

DISTRICT OF COLUMBIA.

VIRGINIA.

NORTH CAROLINA.

SOUTH CAROLINA.

MICHIGAN.

INDIANA.

ILLINOIS.

MISSOURI.

IOWA.

WISCONSIN.

CALIFORNIA.

TERRITORY OF OREGON.

TERRITORY OF MINNESOTA.

TERRITORY OF NEW MEXICO.

TERRITORY OF UTAH.

LIST OF EMBELLISHMENTS.

MAINE.

ALTHOUGH Maine was settled by Europeans several years before any other part of New England, it was not admitted into the Union as a state until 1820. Previously to that period it was a mere territory of Massachusetts, and long bore the title of the "district of Maine." In point of extent, however, and rapidity of growth, it ranks at the head of the eastern states; embracing, between its distant limits of Lower Canada on the north, New Brunswick on the east, the Atlantic on the south, and New Hampshire on the west, an area of 33,223 square miles.

A considerable part of the northwestern division of the state is mountainous, and there are rough tracts and peaks of considerable elevation in some other parts; but in the north the surface is generally even, although the height is considerable, dividing the waters of the St. Lawrence from those emptying into the ocean. The Allegany range, which first appears in Alabama, and traverses all the intermediate Atlantic states, with mountains or hills of different breadth and elevation, is considered as terminating in that cluster of wild and lofty heights which occupy the northwestern counties of Maine; beyond which no ridge is to be found, except that of the greatly rising land in the north just mentioned.

The highest land east of the Mississippi, excepting only Mount Washington, and a few of its neighboring peaks, in the heart of the New Hampshire White hills, is Katahdin mountain, on the Penobscot river, near the centre of this state. It is 5,335 feet high. The other most elevated points are Speckled, Whiteface, Bald, and Saddleback mountains, north of Androscoggin river, and not far from the western boundary of the state.

The rivers of Maine present some striking peculiarities. The surface of the state is divided into unequal parts by the courses of the Penobscot, Kennebec, and Androscoggin, which run nearly south, in directions nearly parallel and equidistant; while, as they approach the sea, a number of smaller streams flow in short courses between them, subdividing the coast into many capes and peninsulas, whose number is still further increased by bays and coves which set up into the land every few miles, and fringe the southern outline of the state along its whole extent of 221 miles, from Kittery point to Quoddy head. The northern part of the map presents countless small streams pouring into the main trunks of the rivers above-mentioned, of which they are the tributaries; while still above them, flowing with a long sweep, from north to east and southeast, the St. John's, the principal stream of the state, encircles the whole, marking out the present northern boundary, till it crosses the eastern boundary, and flows on through the neighboring British province of New Brunswick.

The valley of the Saco embraces 650 square miles, that of the Androscoggin 3,300, the Kennebec 5,280, and the Penobscot 8,200. The smaller streams in the south part of the state, before alluded to, are the Piscataqua, Sheepscot, Damariscotta, Muscongus, Union, Narragaugus, and Machias. The region between the Penobscot and the Kennebec, a distance of fifty miles, is remarkably well supplied with streams and inlets, so that almost every town has a navigable channel of its own.

The soil along the Atlantic border, extending from ten to twenty miles back from the coast, is generally poor, although varying from sand to gravel, clay and loam, producing small crops of grass, Indian corn, rye, &c. The next belt of land, from fifty to one hundred miles wide, is of better quality, and yields, in addition to these articles, wheat, oats, flax, and hemp, as well as most of the northern plants. The tract between the Kennebec and Penobscot is remarkably favorable to grazing, and, when well cultivated, yields forty bushels of corn, and from twenty to forty bushels of wheat, to the acre. Agriculture was greatly neglected for many years, the attention of the inhabitants being almost entirely engrossed, on the one hand, by the cutting of timber in the interior, its transportation to the mills at the falls of the rivers, the sawing and exportation of it to the different ports of the Union and the West Indies; and, on the other hand, by the fisheries along the coast. The increase of population, however, with the rapid disappearance of the forests in the immediate vicinity of streams, together with the diffusion of just views of the importance and methods of agriculture, have produced great and extensive improvements; and the benefits resulting to the state are already incalculably great. Manufactures have also been introduced to a considerable extent, while the mineral resources have begun to be developed, as iron, slate, marble, and especially limestone, which is celebrated for its excellent quality. Literary institutions have been multiplied and well supported, and the common-school system has been placed on a liberal foundation.

Trade is much favored by the nature of the coast and the character of some of the principal rivers; and already great improvements have been made by the construction of roads, railroads, and canals, and the establishment of steamboat lines. The principal ports and places of trade are Portland, Hallowell, Bangor, Calais, Brunswick, and Belfast; and Saco, Machias, and Eastport, have also excellent harbors. The exports are chiefly timber, lumber, dried fish, salt pork and beef, lime, and pot and pearl ashes.

The business of cutting, transporting, and manufacturing timber, includes many laborious operations, and occupies a considerable part of the population. Trees are felled in the winter, drawn by oxen to the nearest water-course, and left upon the ice, marked with the axe in such a manner that they may be recognised by the agents of the owner, stationed on the lower parts of the main river. In the spring, at the melting of the deep snows, the floods carry down the timber with the broken ice; and, after a long voyage, every log is drifted to the falls of the great stream on whose branches it has grown. Here numerous mills are kept in active operation by the powerful currents, which bring down abundant materials to employ them. Above these are long rafts, or floating bridges, called buoys, formed of logs, connected strongly together, and stretched from bank to bank, to stop the floating timber. Men are continually employed with boats, in the spring, in bringing it to the shore as it comes down; and great care is taken to dispose of each stick according to the direction of the owner, whose name is known from the mark. The millers, with their circular saws and other machines, saw whole rafts of logs into millions of planks, boards, shingles, staves, headings, &c.; and vessels, lying at the foot of the falls, readily receive their cargoes of lumber from the doors of the mills, slid down upon their decks and into their holds; and, hoisting sail, steer away for many a distant harbor.

History.—The Jesuits in Lower Canada early began their intercourse with the Indian tribes in Maine, and soon established a mission on the Penobscot, which, according to custom, became a centre of intrigue and of military operations against the New England settlements. It was at length cut off by an expedition from Massachusetts, by which, in a sudden attack, the Jesuit chief, Ralle, was killed. The remnants of the Penobscot tribe are, to this day, chiefly Roman catholics. Previously to the landing in Massachusetts bay, a colony was commenced on the coast of Maine, by Gorges and Mason, under a grant from the council of Plymouth, England, to whom the territory had been granted by King James I., in 1606. The first settlements made, at Damariscotta and a few other points on the coast, were soon abandoned; and few traces are to be found of any of them. Few motives were offered to colonists, to counterbalance the inhospitable nature of the country, the severity of the climate, and the exposure to interference from the Indians and French.

Two or three miles from the road that leads between Linniken's bay and Damariscotta river, where was formerly an Indian burying-place, the remains of cellar-walls and chimneys are found, as also broken kettles, wedges, &c. At the head of the bay are the hulks of two or three large vessels sunk in the water; and on the shore, the ruins of an old gristmill, where the present one stands. On the islands opposite the town, are other ruins, the history of which is unknown, as is also that of those already mentioned. The following interesting facts afford a guide to their origin.

In the year 1605, Captain Weymouth, of Plymouth, in England, returned from an unsuccessful voyage made for the discovery of a northwest passage, bringing with him five American savages, whom he had taken on board in the Penobscot river. Sir Fernando Gorges felt so much interest in these men from a new world, that, to use his own language, he "seized upon" them, and had three of them in his own family for three years; and "this accident must be acknowledged as the means, under God, of putting on foot and giving life to all our plantations." He obtained much information from the Indians, and became, from that time, deeply interested in schemes for the settlement of the New World, and an active member of the Plymouth company.

The first settlement was attempted by Englishmen, on the Kennebec, at the early date of 1609, the same year as that of Jamestown. King James having, by request, granted a patent, in 1606, dividing the coast into North and South Virginia, this part of Maine was embraced in the former, which extended from the 38th to the 45th degree of north latitude. While Gosnold, with Captain Smith for his agent, commenced planting a colony at Jamestown, Captains George Popham and Raleigh Gilbert led another to the mouth of the Kennebec. They landed near the island of Monheagan, a few leagues east of that river, and soon after entered the stream, and stopped at an island near its eastern shore, now forming a part of Georgetown. As Chief-Justice Popham had procured an accurate survey of the river the year before, it is probable that this place was chosen in England, before the sailing of the expedition.

But the history of this colony is short

and melancholy. As it did not arrive until August, there was not sufficient time to complete the necessary preparations for the winter, which set in early and with rigor. A fort was erected, but many arrangements, important to the comfort of the people, could not be made; and, as the ships returned in December, about half of the number embarked in them, apprehending severe sufferings from the cold and the want of food. Part of the buildings and provisions were soon after destroyed by fire; and Captain Popham died before spring. The first ships brought the news of the decease of the chief-justice; and the painful intelligence of the death of a brother rendered it necessary for Captain Gilbert to return to England. The remaining colonists, becoming disheartened, abandoned their enterprise; and, the place being deserted, the Plymouth company did not repeat the experiment.

Gorges, one of the most intelligent and devoted friends of America among the members of the Plymouth colony, endeavored in vain to induce them to send out a second colony. Unwilling, however, to see the object wholly abandoned, he engaged in private enterprises for trading with the natives and fishing; and, in 1616, sent out a party, under the command of Richard Vines, to explore this part of the coast. They penetrated into the country, and were kindly treated; but they found the people suffering from the smallpox, and the hostile attacks of the Tarrantines, a nation east of the Penobscot. They met with the Indians who had been in England, and received special marks of favor from them. On the approach of winter, which they had agreed to spend in the country, they chose a spot on the western side of Saco river, at its mouth. Some of them took up a hundred acres of land on lease from Vines, one of which was for a thousand years, at the annual rent of two shillings and one capon, after the payment of a previous compensation. The lease, partly in Latin, was executed in 1638. A considerable trade was carried on here for some years, the colonists employing themselves both in agriculture and in fishing, besides trading considerably with the savages for beaver-skins, &c.

In the southwestern parts of the state are several scenes of the later and more permanent settlements.

Pegipscot Falls.—Near Lewistown, on the Androscoggin river, is a remarkable cataract, where the current breaks through a range of mountains, and pours over a broken ledge of rocks. The scene is wild and striking, and derives an additional interest from its connexion with the history of a tribe of Indians long since extinct. According to a tradition current in the neighborhood, the upper parts of this stream were formerly the residence of the Rockmego Indians, who inhabited a fine and fertile plain through which the river winds. The situation was remote, and they had never engaged in any hostilities with the whites, but devoted themselves to hunting and fishing. The ground still contains many remains of their weapons, utensils, &c. They were, however, at length persuaded to engage in a hostile incursion against Brunswick, at that time an exposed frontier settlement; and the whole tribe embarked in their canoes to accomplish the enterprise. The stream flows gently on for a great distance, until it approaches very near to the falls; and this was the spot appointed for the night encampment. Night set in before their arrival; and they sent two men forward to make fires upon the banks a little above the cataract. For some unknown reason, the fires were kindled below the falls; and the Indians, being thus deceived concerning their situation, did not bring up their canoes to the shore in season, and were carried over the rocks, and the tribe all destroyed together.

It was along the valley of the Kennebec that the expedition, formed in the winter of 1775–'6, for the capture of Quebec, proceeded. The hardships they endured were very severe, as the country at that time was wholly destitute of inhabitants through almost the whole route, after leaving the seacoast, until approaching the valley of the St. Lawrence. The plan had been formed and adopted while the American army was engaged in the siege of Boston, and General Montgomery was placed at the head of it. Benedict Arnold was among the most active of the officers. After numerous delays, caused by the difficulties of navigation and transportation, cold and hunger, they arrived at the French settlements; but being unable to proceed with desirable rapidity, or to cross the St. Lawrence immediately after reaching its shore, the inhabitants had time to make preparations; and, instead of taking the city by surprise, and at once finding comfortable quarters, they were able only to encamp on the heights of Abraham, after scaling the precipitous shore at Wolfe's cove, with an army between them and the walls. This unfortunate expedition failed, after losing their commander, who was killed in an unsuccessful attempt to gain the lower town by a night attack, and Arnold, with a large division of the forces, who were made prisoners in an assault on the upper town.

The first newspaper in Maine was printed on January 1, 1785. It was called the "Falmouth Gazette and Weekly Advertiser," and published at Falmouth (now Portland), by Benjamin Titcomb and Thomas B. Wait, on a demy sheet. Its name was changed to the "Cumberland Gazette," in 1786. The second was commenced in the same town, in 1790, called the "Maine Gazette," by Benjamin Titcomb, and continued till 1796; at which time there were but three newspapers in Maine, one of them at Hallowell, and one at Augusta. In 1810, there were eight newspapers, and, in 1850, fifty-six.

The first daily paper was begun at Portland, October 13, 1829, and called the "Daily Courier;" and the second, the "Daily Evening Advertiser," in 1831.

York.—There are some pleasant fields about this little place, but its size is insignificant, when compared with the anticipations formed of its destiny at the time of its first settlement; for the ground was laid out for streets, and the divisions of the land still retain much of the regular form given it by the first surveyors. Population, about 3,500

The Nubble is a rocky point, four and a half miles from York, and Cape Neddock lies beyond. While travelling along this dreary country, the road passes the site of an old fort or blockhouse, built before Philip's war. The Agamenticus hills form a range some distance west.

Lower Welles.—There is a little harbor here, defended by a sandbar, with a narrow entrance under a rock; but it is almost dry at low water.

Welles.—The sea often breaks beautifully on the beach, in front of the tavern. Porpoise point is just distinguishable in the northeast, and the view of the sea is fine and refreshing.

Three miles beyond is Breakneck hill, over which falls a small stream, from the height of thirty feet, about forty yards from the path. The old fort was half a mile beyond, or a quarter of a mile from the church. This little fortress was once attacked by five hundred Indians, who at first supposed, as was the fact, that the men were absent from home. The place was, however, very bravely and successfully defended by five women, dressed in their husband's clothes.

Portland.—The situation of this place is remarkably fine, occupying the ridge and side of a high point of land, with a handsome though shallow bay on one side, and the harbor on the other. The anchorage is protected on every side by land, the water is deep, and the communication with the sea direct and convenient. Congress street runs along the ridge of the hill, and contains a number of very elegant private houses. There is also the town-hall, with the market below, and a beautiful church, with granite columns. The steps are fine blocks of granite, six by nine feet, brought from the quarry at Brunswick, twenty-two miles distant.

From the observatory, south and southwest, are seen several distant eminences: among others, the Agamenticus hills; northwest are seen, in clear weather, the lofty ridges and peaks of the White hills in New Hampshire, which are discovered at sea often before the nearer land appears in sight.

Cape Elizabeth is the highland on the

south side of the harbor; and the islands, which nearly close the entrance, are called Bangs's and House islands. Fort Preble stands on the former, and Fort Scammel on the latter. Due east is Seguin lighthouse, which is visible, in clear weather, thirty-two miles distant, at the mouth of the Kennebec. Nearer, and in the same quarter, lie numerous islands of various forms.

The intrenchments on the hill, west of the observatory, belong to Fort Sumner, and part of them were made during the Revolutionary war. Under the bluff, on the water's edge, is Fort Burroughs.

Portland (the former name was Falmouth) was burnt in the Revolutionary war by Captain Mowatt, in the British sloop-of-war Canceau, on the 18th of October, 1775, on the refusal of the inhabitants to deliver up their arms. About one hundred and thirty houses, three quarters of all the place contained, were consumed, some being set on fire with brands, after a cannonade and bombardment of nine hours. The old church is among the buildings saved, and has the mark of a cannon-shot in it. A small part of the hotel belonged to one of the houses not destroyed. There are many fine stores and dwelling-houses in the middle of the town, and the shore is lined with shipping. Pop. 28,000.

Augusta.—This town, the capital of Kennebec county, is fifty-six miles northeast from Portland, and two miles north of Hallowell. It stands on both sides of the Kennebec, forty-seven miles from its mouth, and has a bridge across that river, connecting its two parts. It is a place of some trade, being at the head of sloop-navigation. The situation is pleasant, on the top and sides of an elevation. Population, 9,000.

The statehouse has a front of one hundred and fifty feet, toward the east, with two wings, of thirty-three and fifty-four feet, on a plan somewhat resembling that at Boston; and its position, on Capitol hill, is commanding. It is built of granite, and has eight granite columns, twenty-one feet high, each weighing ten tons. The top of the dome is one hundred and fourteen feet from the ground.

Hallowell is a considerable town, fifty-four miles northeast from Portland, and is a place of much business, and one of the principal in the state. The Kennebec is navigable in vessels of one hundred and fifty tons, and an extensive and productive tract of country is dependent on it. Granite of excellent quality abounds in the vicinity, which is quarried on a considerable scale.

Brunswick.—This town is situated on the left bank of the Androscoggin river, at the Pejepscot falls, which here make an extensive water-power. It contains about six thousand inhabitants, ten churches, two academies, cotton and woollen factories, and is the seat of

Bowdoin College.—The two larger buildings represented in the engraving, are occupied by the students. The three-story building contains the mineralogical cabinet, gallery of paintings, medical cabinet, the library, and lecture rooms. The northerly of the two central buildings, besides rooms for the students, has recitation-rooms, and two spacious apartments for the libraries of two societies. This edifice was erected in place of the one destroyed by fire in 1836. The three-story building is called Massachusetts hall, the large building on the south, Maine hall, the other, North college.

It was after several petitions had been presented to the government of Massachusetts, that, in 1731, a bill was introduced for the establishment of a college in the district of Maine, which was to be called Bowdoin college, after the distinguished governor of that name. It was not built, however, until 1734, during which time Brunswick was chosen as the seat of the college. This act also appointed a board of trustees, which was to consist of thirteen members, and a board of overseers, of forty-five members, who were to regulate the institution. At the same time a grant was made to it of five townships of wild land in the interior of Maine. Immediately after its establishment, Governor Bowdoin's son, honorable James Bowdoin, made to it a donation of a thousand acres of land, and upward of eleven hundred pounds in money. Now the business of the boards was the erection of a suitable building. Accordingly, a meeting

Bowdoin College, Brunswick.

was called at Brunswick, in 1796, for the selection of a location. This town is on a sandy plain, south of the Androscoggin river The plain is slightly elevated, nearly a mile south of the river; and this spot was chosen as the most desirable situation for the college. Although the uninterrupted level of the ground, and the dark green of the pines and firs, render the scenery of Brunswick rather monotonous, yet, by its quiet retirement, it is well adapted for the seat of an institution of learning. Shortly after, the brick building, called Massachusetts hall, was erected, and received the name which it still bears.

The boards assembled, in July, 1801, for the election of a president. The Rev. Dr. M'Keere, from Beverley, Massachusetts, was chosen; and Mr. John Abbott was chosen professor of languages. They were inducted into office on the 2d of September. Also, at this time, eight students were admitted to the institution. The services were performed on a stage which was raised under a grove of evergreens, near to the college. In 1804, Mr. Samuel Willard entered the college as tutor, and the following year Mr. Parker Cleaveland was installed professor of mathematics and natural history. Mr. Bowdoin had given one thousand acres of land toward this professorship.

The first commencement of this college was in 1806, when the honors of the institution were conferred upon seven young men. The name of Richard Goff, Esq., of Boston, stands first on the list of graduates. This was the only commencement at which President M'Keene was allowed to preside, for, in July of the following year, he was removed by death from the scene of his labors.

Eastport, on Moose island, occupying the extreme point of the coast of the United States on the eastern border, is a spot interesting alike for its military importance and its natural features. The ground is rocky, and rises abruptly from the western shore of St. Croix river, to a considerable eminence, which is crowned by the fort, on which waves the first American flag that greets the eye of a traveller from the east, on approaching our country. It is 41 miles east-northeast from Machias, 176 miles east from Augusta, and 279 miles east-northeast from Portland. It contains 2,500 inhabitants.

Moose island, on which Eastport is situated, lies in Passamaquoddy bay, and is four miles long, surrounded by deep water, and connected with Lubec by a ferry, and with Perry by a bridge. The village is in the south part of the island, and is a place of considerable business; the lumber-trade and fishing being carried on with activity.

Bangor.—This city is situated on the west side of the Penobscot, at the head of navigation, on an elevation which commands an extensive view. There is a bridge across the river, 1,329 feet in length; and the place contains a court-house, a jail, seven churches, a bank, two academies, and a population of fifteen thousand. It is thirty-five miles north from Castine, sixty-five northeast of Augusta, and two hundred and twenty-two miles from Boston, with which communication is held by steamboats, touching at Portland, to which latter place rail-road trains run daily. An extensive trade in lumber is carried on at Bangor. The distance from the sea, at Owl's Head point, is thirty miles.

The spot now occupied by the town was in a wilderness only about fifty years ago. The region above, lying in the valley of the Penobscot, and naturally tributary to Bangor, is an area of nine thousand square miles. The water-power is abundant, and applicable to a great variety of machinery. There are few places in the Union which possess greater advantages of this kind. The lumber-trade, which has formed the chief source of business and prosperity, must necessarily decrease; but the clearing of the land will as naturally be accompanied with the extension of agriculture and the increase of its more valuable products, which will of course seek their vent through this town. Navigation is active during the summer-season, and much transportation is performed in the winter in sleighs. The soil in the neighborhood is good for brickmaking

View of Eastport.

Bangor, on account of its rapid growth, as well as its important position, and the beauty of its situation, is the place of the greatest note in the interior of the state. The Kenduskeag enters the Penobscot nearly at right-angles, dividing the town into two parts, and diversifying the surface in the environs with high and picturesque banks. The town appears to great advantage on approaching it from down the valley of the Penobscot, as it is gradually disclosed to view, displaying its numerous clusters of houses spread up the rising grounds and over the more level surface on the summit of the bank. On the northwest side of the town the eminence commands an extensive and charming view, Mount Katahdin appearing in the distance, in clear weather, though more than seventy miles off, its head often capped with snow.

Judge Williamson's History of Maine informs us, that the first settlement was made in this place in the year 1769, when only one family became the inhabitants. A second followed in the course of 1770; and two years later there were twelve families. In 1787, the first public meeting was held, to procure a pastor and a place for public worship; when the Rev. Seth Noble, a whig refugee from Nova Scotia, was appointed, and received his ordination under the shade of an oak-tree. He received a salary of four hundred dollars from the people residing on both sides of the river, and remained there twelve years. He was appointed, in 1791, to procure an act of incorporation from the Massachusetts legislature; and, although the people proposed to call the place Sunbury, the present name was chosen.

The courthouse (now the city-hall) was the first public building erected in the place, in 1812. It was occupied for public worship, as well as for various other public purposes, until 1822. That year the first meetinghouse was built, by the only religious society existing there. The Rev. Harvey Loomis, who was ordained in 1811, officiated in it until 1822, when, having preached a new-year's sermon, on the 2d of January, from the text, "This year thou shalt die," on leaving the pulpit he dropped down dead. Five years afterward the building was destroyed by fire; and, in 1831, a handsome brick edifice was erected in its place.

In 1828, three houses for public worship were commenced, by societies of methodists, baptists, and unitarians, and several others were erected a few years later; and, in 1832, a large courthouse, with county offices, and a jail.

The Theological Seminary has three professors, about fifty students, and a library of seven thousand volumes. The classical and theological course occupies four years. It was instituted, in 1815, to prepare young men to preach the gospel. A tract of five acres of land was given to the institution by Isaac Davenport, of Milton, Massachusetts, on which the present fine building stands. It is of brick, four stories high, and enjoys an elevated and commanding situation. A second edifice, of a similar description, with houses for the professors, was afterward planned. The institution is under the direction of a board of trustees, and has a fund of about a hundred and twenty thousand dollars.

The Bangor House is one of the ornaments of the town. It is constructed on a plan resembling that of the Tremont house in Boston, and was built in 1836.

There is a bridge across the Penobscot, and three across the Kenduskeag. Two of the latter were built by individuals.

The first printing-office was opened in Bangor in the year 1815, by Peter Edes. The first bank was established in 1818; and banks have since been multiplied to supply the demands of the extensive lumber-business and navigation carried on here. The ice interrupts the river-trade during four or five months in the year; but the river is generally open to Frankfort, twelve miles below.

The first railroad in the state was that from Bangor to Oldtown, in Oxford county, twelve miles of which was opened in 1836, at an expense of $250,000.

The market-house is large, and well planned. A rural cemetery, on the plan of that of Mount Auburn, near Boston, was laid out in 1836, two miles from the city, enclosing about thirty acres; of which twenty belong to the public, and the remainder to individuals. A fine greenhouse is connected with it.

In the neighborhood of Bangor, several small manufacturing villages have been founded by capitalists, where large quantities of timber are sawn.

North Bangor.—Here are the mills of the Penobscot Milldam company. It is four miles from Bangor, on the road to Orono, and three miles from—

Lower Stillwater Village, another of these industrious settlements, situated, like the preceding, on the Kenduskeag. The ample water-power at these places admits of a large amount of business.

The population of Bangor experienced a very rapid increase in the course of a few years. In 1793, there were but forty-five rateable polls in the town. In 1800, the population was 277; in 1810, 850; in 1820, 1,221; in 1830, 2,868; in 1840, 8,627; in 1850, 14,441.

Bath, thirty-four miles northeast from Portland, and one hundred and fifty-three northeast from Boston, is situated on the western side of the Kennebec, and occupies a considerable eminence, on a piece of land almost isolated by several arms of the sea, from which it is distant about twelve miles. It is a considerable town, of 8,500 inhabitants, extends along the river a mile and a half, and back from it about three fourths of a mile. The harbor is excellent, and freely admits to its wharves ships of the largest size. There are in the town two banks and five academies. Steamboats communicate daily with Portland and Boston during nearly the whole year.

Castine, the capital of Hancock county, occupies a promontory on the east side of Penobscot bay, and has a good harbor, always open, and accessible to large vessels. It is in latitude forty-four degrees and twenty-four minutes, seventy-eight miles from Augusta, and a hundred and twenty-two east-northeast from Portland. Pop. 2,000.

Houlton is a military post on a small branch of St. John's river, near the line of New Brunswick. It is one hundred and twenty miles north-northeast from Bangor.

Fryeburg, sixty miles northwest of Portland, is remarkable both for its situation and its history. The township, in its extent of six square miles, embraces a rich and beautiful valley, secluded on every side by a wild and mountainous range of country. The Saco river, taking its rise on Mount Washington, and flowing through the notch in the White hills, passes down the valley to Conway, where it finds the termination of the southern range; and then turning abruptly to the east, soon enters the charming meadows of Fryeburg, and performs a serpentine course of no less than thirty-six miles within the limits of the township.

The Indian fort was on a gentle hill at the western side of the village, which commands a view of the Saco valley six miles up its course, and six miles down.

Lovel's Pond is on an isthmus, about one mile southeast from the village, and is memorable as the scene of one of the most severe and disastrous battles in the old partisan warfare against the Indians. The Portland road passes along the western side of the pond, and affords a view of its north end. This was the place of the action. Another road runs very near the north shore; and it is a pleasant ride to the place.

Lovel's Expedition.—In 1725, Captain Lovel undertook a secret expedition through the wilderness against the Pickwaket tribe of Indians. Instigated by the French, they had committed many depredations on the frontier, so that the general court of Massachusetts had offered one hundred pounds each for their scalps. His company consisted of thirty or forty men, many of them accustomed to the life of hardy hunters and settlers, with young Mr. Frye for their chaplain, whose history was somewhat romantic, and from whom this town received its name. They passed up Winnipiseogee lake, Ossipee pond, the Saco, and encamped at the mouth of Mill brook, at the northwest corner of Lovel's pond. It happened that the Indians had gone down the Saco river, and on their return, discovering tracks, pursued them toward Lovel's pond, and, having discovered the encampment, and the way they had gone, removed their packs, and, forming an ambush around the place, fired upon them, on their return, and killed eight men. The white men retreated to the northeast corner of the pond, where is a narrow strip of land, and defended themselves till night; and the remains of the unfortunate expedition returned through the forest, suffering from hunger and fatigue, and some of them from wounds.

Sebago Lake.—This is one of the numerous bodies of water, of different forms and sizes, which spot the surface of Maine, and cover so large a part of it. It has been estimated that, including lakes and rivers, one sixth part of the surface of the state is water. Sebago lake is in Cumberland county, and thirteen miles by twenty in extent, nearly divided by a long cape, which extends from the eastern side, in Raymond, in a southwest direction. No less than five townships lie upon its shores. It receives Crooked river from the north, with the waters of Long lake, which flow into that stream through its outlet. Presumpscut river, which drains Sebago lake from the south, falls into Casco bay, and affords a channel of navigation in boats to Portland.

Moosehead Lake, in Kennebec county, and the source of the east branch of Kennebec river, is sixty miles in length, of an irregular form, and surrounded by a tract of country but little inhabited.

Mount Desert Lighthouse.—Off a part of the coast remarkable for its desolate and forbidding character, and upon a small barren rock, is erected the tall and fine lighthouse depicted in the vignette at the head of this description. One of the spots most dangerous to passing ships, and most destitute of the means of subsistence for shipwrecked strangers, is thus provided with one of those marks for navigators which now occupy every important point along our seaboard, from one extremity of the country to the other.

Mount Desert island, which lies between Union river and Desert sound, is fifteen miles in length, and twelve in breadth. It is in latitude forty-four degrees twelve minutes, and comprises a township of the same name.

With so large a surface as Maine comprehends, such supplies of timber, and such remarkable facilities for procuring, sawing, and transporting it; with so much valuable land cleared and clearing as the forests are removed; together with a population of such energetic character and intelligence, a more rapid increase of numbers, wealth, and power, might be anticipated, if more genial climates and more luxuriant soils did not attract the great masses of emigrants in other directions. In spite, however, of the richness of the western and southern lands, and the softness of the climates in the new states and territories, Maine will probably continue to improve, and to experience a more solid and substantial growth than could be produced by the introduction of a less educated and hardy population.

According to the censuses, taken successively, Maine contained 96,540 inhabitants in 1790; 151,719 in 1800; 228,705 in 1810; 298,335 in 1820; 399,955 in 1830; 501,793 in 1840; and 583,088 in 1850.

Maine has a stringent law for the suppression of traffic in intoxicating liquors. It allows the seizure and confiscation of liquor wherever found, with the exception of places designated by proper authority, where it may be sold for mechanical or medicinal purposes. Those who are discovered with this illicit article of traffic in their possession, are allowed no redress for the loss by the confiscation of their property; and the attempt to try the matter judicially is ineffectual, as the courts are forbidden to entertain suits of this description.

The contrast presented in this state, by a comparison between the present and several past periods of its history, is striking indeed. The most favorable effects resulted from its separation from Massachusetts and erection into a state. Legislation, with the energies of the people, has effected wonders; while commerce, agriculture, manufactures, and education, are annually making advances, which bid fair to continue.

NEW HAMPSHIRE.

THIS state is bounded on the north by Canada, east by Maine, south by Massachusetts, and west by Vermont. Connecticut river forms a part of the northern boundary, and its western shore the whole of the western, the entire breadth of the stream belonging to New Hampshire. Extending from latitude forty-two to forty-five, and having much mountainous surface, the climate is cold, and in some parts severe, although the southern regions, being both low and nearer the ocean, have milder seasons and shorter winters.

The Allegany range, which crosses this state near the middle, though here far distant from its broadest ranges, has its highest peaks in the White hills, whose principal eminences tower above all other peaks this side of the Rocky mountains. In that region are the sources of the principal rivers of the state. The Merrimack rises from the outlet of Winnipiseogee lake, a broad and beautiful sheet of water lying at the foot of the southern eminences of that Alpine region; while the Ammonoosuc, pouring down the steep declivity of Mount Washington, finds its way to the Connecticut; and the Saco, a direct tributary to the Atlantic, after rising within a few yards of the Ammonoosuc, is soon diverted in an opposite channel, and, flowing through the celebrated Notch in the mountains, waters the most Alpine region of New England, before it reaches the manufactories at its mouth, which are moved by its power.

The impediments offered to navigation are not only, in a great measure, counterbalanced by the abundance of valuable water-power afforded by nature, but are obviated by science and art, in the construction of railroads as well as canals, which have been multiplied within a few years, in proportion to the increasing demands created by the numerous manufactories. In all these branches of improvement, New Hampshire has displayed a degree of intelligence and enterprise unsurpassed by any other state, in proportion to her extent and resources, and promises to reap from them long-continued benefits.

A large part of her territory is rendered useless by lofty, wild, barren, and almost inaccessible mountains. The surface, soil, and climate there discourage almost any attempt at cultivation, and in many places entirely refuse a spot for the habitation of man. Immense masses of stone, however, which have been brought down from those regions, by some ancient cause not easily explained, are spread over the surface for seventy or eighty miles south, and have supplied the state with one of the chief sources of its wealth. Blocks of granite and sienite have been cut up for building, and transported to near and many distant places, often at great profit. The New Hampshire stones of these kinds, like those from some of the adjacent states, are known, used, and highly valued, and form the materials in constructing many of the finest edifices in our cities, even to the southern extremities of our country.

The northern extremity of this state is in latitude forty-five degrees eleven minutes, and the southern in forty-two degrees forty-one minutes. The area is 9,280 square miles; and the population in 1850 was 317,864. New Hampshire has the smallest extent of seacoast of all the Atlantic states—only eighteen miles. There is but one good harbor in the state—viz., Portsmouth, where is a navy-yard of the United States. Lying at the mouth of the Piscataqua river, and having a great depth of water, this port is deficient in one very important respect. That river is navigable but a short distance, when it is broken by a fall. The Merrimac has a succession of rapids, which have been canalled and locked all along its course, and render it useful for boat navigation. But its principal value is for manufacturing, in which respect, however, it is one of the most valuable streams in the United States. The largest and most flourishing manufacturing town in the Union, Lowell, in Massachusetts, occupies the most advantageous point on the Merrimac, on the south side, by which it is supplied with abundant water-power.

Lakes.—Winnipiseogee lake is remarkable for its picturesque shores, and numerous and beautiful islands, as well as for the fine scenery which here begins to display itself, offering, to the traveller from the south, the first and distant introduction to the noble features of the White mountains. It is twenty-three miles in length and ten in breadth, measured in the widest part. The water is remarkably clear, and abounds in fish.

Squam Lake, situated north of it, is six miles long and three wide, and lies at the bottom of a deep and narrow valley, surrounded by several mountainous elevations, except on the side where it sends an inlet into Winnipiseogee. Fine trout abound here, which are taken in considerable numbers, and salted for market.

Above these lie Ossipee and Sunapee lakes, which are of inferior size.

Connecticut River.—This is the principal stream of New England, both for size, the rich and populous country through which it passes, and the large meadows which it annually overflows and fertilizes. It rises in the elevated region between this state and Canada, in a pond called Lake Connecticut; and its eastern branch marks the boundary between the two countries, to a point at the distance of one mile from the forty-fifth degree of north latitude. The course of the river is nearly south, and, after separating New Hampshire and Vermont, it flows on through Massachusetts and Connecticut, and falls into Long Island sound at Saybrook. It is navigable in sloops to Hartford, in steamboats a few miles further, and in flat-bottomed boats through Massachusetts to the middle of this state.

Short canals, with locks, are formed round the falls at Enfield, Connecticut, and South Hadley, Massachusetts; but the Farmington canal, with its extension to Northampton in the last-mentioned state, takes off a portion of the trade to New Haven; and much freight, as well

Squam Lake

as most of the travellers, now pass more swiftly along the banks of the stream over the railroads. Several important routes cross Connecticut river at different points; but the principal one is the railroad route from Boston to Albany, through Springfield.

NATURAL CURIOSITIES.—The Notch, Flume, and several objects in the heart of the White mountains, may be termed curiosities, and a remarkable rock in Franconia is noted as such. The profile, when viewed from a particular point, presents a considerable resemblance to the human profile, whence it has received the name of *The Old Man of the Mountains*. The peak rises about one thousand feet above the valley at its base.

HISTORY.—The first settlements were made as stated on page 42, at Dover and Portsmouth, in 1623; and the people voluntarily united themselves to Massachusetts in 1641. But in 1679 the country was constituted a separate colony by Charles II. For many years the frontier villages suffered severely from the hostile incursions of the Indians, usually led or sent against them by the French Jesuits in Canada. Many dwellings were burned in the wars of Philip and France, many lives were lost, and many captives taken to Canada.

The people of New Hampshire bore an active part in the war of the revolution. On the 21st of June, 1788, the convention of the state adopted the constitution of the United States by a vote of fifty-seven to forty-six.

PORTSMOUTH, the principal seaport in New Hampshire, is the capital of Rockingham county. It enjoys a pleasant situation at the mouth of Piscataqua, three miles from the ocean. The harbor, although perfectly shut in by land, is never obstructed by ice. It is fifty-four miles from Boston, and four hundred and ninety-three from Washington. It is connected with the town of Kittery, in Maine, by two bridges, and a third extends to Great island, where is a lighthouse. The navy-yard is on Continental island, on the eastern side of the harbor. There are eight churches, seven banks, two markets, a custom-house, an athenæum, and an almshouse. The population is about ten thousand. The Boston and Portland railroad passes through the town.

The Athenæum, incorporated in 1817, has about five thousand volumes in its library, a cabinet of minerals, and collections in other branches of natural history.

CONCORD.—This town, the capital of New Hampshire, is located upon the Merrimack river, with the principal village upon the western side. It is forty-five miles, west-northwest, from Portsmouth, and seventy-four miles, north-north-west, from Boston by railroad, and sixty-two by turnpike. It has communication, also, with Boston by the Merrimac river and the Middlesex canal, and engrosses the chief trade from the north. Main street, its principal thoroughfare, on which are located most of the public buildings, and the stores and principal places of business, is about two miles in length. A fine intervale lies between the village and the river. Here are the statehouse, state prison, lunatic asylum, also a state institution, county court-house, several banks, twelve churches, and several other public buildings. Concord has about eight hundred and fifty dwelling-houses, and a population of about nine thousand.

The Statehouse, a beautiful structure, appropriately built of granite, is one hundred and twenty-six feet in length, and forty-nine in breadth. It occupies a conspicuous situation, surrounded by a fine park. The view from the cupola is very extensive and picturesque. The halls of the house of representatives and the senate contain several works of art; among which are a portrait of Count Rumford, the founder of the town, after whom it was originally named, and a full-length likeness of Washington (after Stuart) by Walter Ingalls, a native-artist of the granite state, whose lifelike portraits have, both in his own country and abroad, given him a high rank in his profession.

A few years since, but a single railroad extended to Concord; but several roads now radiate from this busy town, and the enterprise of the people, being once awakened to their true interests,

The State House, at Concord.

will not rest till the iron bands, which are drawing the extremes of our wide-spread country nearer and nearer, shall extend to every section of the state, and even to the commercial metropolis of Canada.

MANCHESTER.—This city is one of the youngest but most flourishing manufacturing places in the state. It was commenced with activity, by a large Boston company, about ten years ago, at one of the best sites for water-power on the Merrimac, and has rapidly increased in business. Pop. 20,000. The soil is sandy, and the situation favorable only for the objects for which the town has been built; but the prospects are flattering for permanent and increasing prosperity. The good regulations established in most of the other large manufacturing places in New England, have been, from the first, adopted here, and the results are highly favorable. Precautions are taken to secure comfortable, healthy, and respectable lodgings and accommodations for the work people, or "operatives," of both sexes. Several churches, of different denominations, are erected; schools are abundant; and the agents of the manufactories are men of intelligence and public spirit, who favor all measures for moral and intellectual improvement. A railroad, as in most other instances in towns of this kind, affords its advantages.

Several other towns might be mentioned, in this part of the state, of a similar character, though none of so recent a date, and such rapid and remarkable growth. The various and valuable products of manufacturing skill, constantly yielded by the thousands of industrious hands and busy wheels in these places, find their way to Boston, with but few exceptions; the grand route of transportation being the Lowell railroad, with its extension and branches. It is by this channel that the capital of that wealthy city extends its influence through this part of the country, and brings its profitable returns to the wharves, whence they are transported to distant ports.

There are many agreeable interior towns in the midst of pleasant agricultural regions. The land varies from valleys and level meadows, to swelling and often elevated uplands; but the soil is generally well cultivated, situations healthful and agreeable, and the state of society, in different degrees, refined and intelligent. Considerable diversity is observable, in different parts of New Hampshire, in the character of the population. Portsmouth was, for a time, a seat of no little aristocratic pride, during the period of its existence as a royal colony; and some remains of the feelings of those days may still be found. Large bands of emigrants, of the agricultural classes, who came out from Great Britain and occupied large tracts in the interior, were for a long time found slow in conforming to the habits and institutions which have always characterized those of puritan origin, who constitute the third division of the population.

CHARLESTOWN.—This is a beautiful village on the bank of Connecticut river, and one of the first places occupied, in early times, in the interior of the state. It was included within "Township No. 4" (by which name it was long known), being one of a range of settlements first laid off above the present line of Massachusetts. For many years it was much exposed to Indian depredations, and was defended by a small fort, built of logs, in a spot now crossed by the street, in the southern part of the village. Insignificant as was this little place of defence, it was held by a few men, against a considerable body of savages, during a long and persevering attack.

WALPOLE.—In full view of Connecticut river, this town occupies a fine, commanding situation, on a bold and beautiful hill, which rises abruptly from the shore, three or four miles south of Bellows' Falls. The country in the vicinity presents many striking scenes and beautiful landscapes; the soil is strong and well cultivated, and the village very pleasant. Pop. 2,500.

BELLOWS' FALLS.—Although the village which bears this name is on the western side of the Connecticut, the remarkable descent of the stream from which it has received its name is within the bounds of New Hampshire. There is no other spot along its course which bears so striking marks of the violent operations of nature. An immense mass of the hardest and most solid kind of gray granite has been burst through, and the masses have apparently been torn away in some long passage, while the smoothed surfaces of those which remain indicate the slow but considerable effects of rushing streams, unintermitted for ages. A little above the spot, the water flows in a smooth and gentle current, and spreads out to a considerable breadth; while broad meadows on both sides line its course, and show marks of successive elevations which it formerly maintained at different periods. But just at the falls, the whole stream is confined between two rocks only a few feet apart; while only a portion of the intermediate space is filled by the water, as large masses of granite lie between and divide the current into several parts. The rapidity and force of the descent are extremely great, so that extravagant reports have been made on the subject, especially by a singular writer of past days, Hugh Peters, who gravely published that the water was so much hardened by compression, that a crowbar could not be forced into it!

Salmon, however, used to pass the spot in great numbers, so long as they abounded in the river, and this, like many other waterfalls, was the site of a great Indian fishing-place. The deep pools in the bed of the stream were crowded with them at that season in the spring, when they annually moved up toward the shallow water to deposite their spawn; and large encampments of savages were at that time made upon the banks. Marks still remain, especially in several figures engraved on a smooth, projecting piece of granite, a little below the cascade.

A short canal was commenced, many years ago, to facilitate boat-navigation around the falls. The scenery at the spot is remarkably wild; a mountain rising abruptly from the eastern bank of the river, covered with rocky and forest trees, and casting a deep shadow upon the roaring stream which rushes by at its base. An elevated bridge, which crosses it just below the falls, and affords a near and almost terrific view of the tumultuous scene, gives the place a double interest in the eye of the traveller. The effect of the whole is greatly heightened, by the contrast it forms with the rich and tranquil region which opens to the view above. One of the largest and most fertile tracts of alluvion there spreads out on the river's borders, through which its waters meander in long and graceful curves; and well-tilled and productive fields, covered with the deepest verdure, extend to the borders of the rising grounds, which swell to the wooded uplands.

HANOVER.—This is a remarkably pleasant village, occupying a high level on the top of a considerable ridge of land, in the midst of a wild and sterile tract, which has but few inhabitants. It presents a pleasing aspect; for besides having several streets with a number of neat houses, with court-yards and gardens, there is a large, level public square in the centre, well shaded with trees, and ornamented with some of the finest buildings in the place, especially those connected with the principal literary institution of the state, viz.:—

Dartmouth College.—This was originally a school, founded by the Rev. Mr. Wheelock, for the education of Indian youth for the ministry of the gospel. With a zeal and perseverance fitting the enlightened and noble object, that devoted man surmounted obstacles which it would be difficult to appreciate, to any one not intimately acquainted with the state of the country at the time. Like almost every other attempt made for the extensive and permanent benefit of that unfortunate race, it ultimately failed of success, so far as it related to them. In the course of years, however, it proved useful in an eminent degree; and Dartmouth college has long maintained a highly respectable rank among its kindred institutions. Among its alumni have been found many distinguished men; and its standing and usefulness are likely to rise with the advance of population.

The principal academical buildings

stand on the eastern site of the square, while that of the medical department is a little further north. The houses of the president and professors are neat and handsome structures, and add much to the appearance of the village.

Dartmouth college is supported by funds contributed by individuals at different periods, and lands granted by this state and Vermont. The library of the institution contains about 4,500 volumes, and those belonging to societies of students about 9,000. The corporation consists of the governor and chief justice of the state, the president, ten members elected for the purpose, the councillors of the state, the president of the senate, and the speaker of the house of representatives.

Moore's charity school, a well-endowed institution, is connected with the college.

The following are the names and dates of the presidents of Dartmouth college: Rev. E. Wheelock, D.D., 1769 to 1779; Jno. Wheelock, LL. D., 1779 to 1815; Rev. Francis Brown, D. D., 1815 to 1820; Rev. Daniel Dana, D. D., 1820 to 1821; Rev. Bennet Tyler, D. D., 1822 to 1828; Rev. Nathan Lord 1828.

The annual expense of tuition is twenty-seven dollars; rent, seven and a half dollars; board, from one dollar to one dollar and a half per week.

The course of lectures in the medical college continues fourteen weeks. Four or five lectures are delivered daily. The fees are about fifty dollars.

Haverhill is a town extending along the Connecticut, opposite the Great Oxbow, one of the largest and most fertile tracts of meadow-land on this part of its course. The size of this stream is much smaller here than in the lower part of the state; yet its source is still quite distant; and there are a few points connected with it which may be adverted to in this place.

Connecticut river in this state makes a considerable part of its descent from its headwaters to the ocean level. Lake Connecticut is one thousand six hundred feet higher than Long Island sound; but six hundred of this is reduced in the first twenty-five miles, in which the course is southwest. The next twenty miles, where it runs more southwest, it descends three hundred and fifty feet more. Below this point are two considerable falls, the first of which is at the mouth of White river, and the other is Bellows Falls, which has been described.

The Passumpsic, a considerable branch of the Connecticut, enters it at the foot of Fifteen-mile falls. Nearly two hundred small lakes, or ponds, are formed in different parts of the valley of the Connecticut, two of the largest of which are in New Hampshire, viz., Mascony and Sunapee. The former is seven miles long, and the latter twelve. From the superior elevations in this state, it is not surprising that five of the principal rivers of New England should have their sources within its limits.

The White mountains—those "Alps of New England," as they have been, not inappropriately, called—present numerous attractions to every visiter of taste and science, and are the annual resort of numerous travellers. Winnipiseogee lake, as we have before remarked, lies on the route from the south, and at its outlet is situated one of the most flourishing villages in the state.

Meredith.—This place has the advantage of the water-power of Winnipiseogee river, and lies on the route of the railroad line from Concord northward, which is gradually extended as the stock is taken up, and is designed to extend to Canada. The town has some twenty stores, and its population is about 5,000.

Red Mountain.—This is a conspicuous eminence, occupying a favorable position as a point of view, at the northwest corner of Lake Winnipiseogee, which is a favorite resort of travellers, being easy of access, and commanding a scene of the greatest variety and beauty. The following description was written on the spot:—

"North, the eastern end of Squam lake, and part of a pond lying near it, with the range of the Sandwich mountains behind, stretching off toward the east, with numerous dark-brown peaks, partly cultivated about their bases, and enveloped above with forests, excepting their summits, which are generally divested of verdure. Far beyond these appear several loftier peaks, which might be mistaken for the White mountains, were they visible from this point. An intermediate peak with rocky precipices is White-faced mountain.

"East-northeast, the eye ranges up the spacious valley through which lies the way to the White mountains, and the road which is to conduct the traveller seems diminished to the dimensions of a garden walk. Chocaway, or, as it is familiarly called, Coroway peak, rises on the left; while the noble ridge of the Ossipee mountains begins nearer at hand on the right, and almost overshadows the observer with its enormous size. The sides of these mountains show a beautiful display of farms, interspersed with wood-lots and dwellings, which in many places have encroached far toward the summits, and in others pursue the slope of the fertile uplands to the valley at their feet. Numerous elevations appear at a greater distance, and range themselves in lines to complete the perspective of a most magnificent vista, which finally closes at a ridge, whose shade is reduced by its remoteness to the color of a cloud. A prominent and remarkable mountain, which appears scarcely less distant, is called Pickwaket mountain, and rises by the Saco river, near the place where Captain Lovel fought his well-known battle with the Indians; and the fine valley between is the country passed over in that fatal expedition, in both the approach and the retreat.

"East, the view abuts upon the Ossipee mountains, and no variety is afforded until we turn to the south-southeast. In that direction, and further to the right, the whole surface of Winnipiseogee lake lies charmingly spread out to view, varied by numerous points and headlands, and interspersed with beautiful islands which man despairs to number. Several distant elevations appear, on this side of which the sloping land just mentioned extends for several miles along the shore, with a well-cultivated surface spotted in all directions with large barns and farmhouses, to the very margin of the lake. There numerous points run out far into the water, to complete the labyrinths formed by the islands. Gunstock mountain rises one point east of south, just on the left of which opens the entrance of Merry-meeting bay. The elevated island on the right of that is Rattlesnake island, named from the venomous reptiles with which it abounds; over this the distant land appears high. South by west rises a high hill resembling the Ossipee in the richness of its slopes.

"The southwest and west is agreeably varied with wood-lots and cleared fields, scattered over an undulated surface, which extends for many miles, in some places quite to the horizon, and in others to the broken boundary of tall but distant mountains. In the southwest appear two or three peaks, so far removed that they are almost lost in the blue of the sky. Nearly west are seen several ridges of inferior magnitude, which, approaching as the eye slowly moves toward the left, at length come near the lake, and disappear behind the neighboring mountains.

"Long pond may be distinguished by its shining surface between the west and south, with several other little sheets of water, which lie in tranquillity under the shelter of the hills.

"Winnipiseogee lake is nineteen miles in length, from Centre Harbor to Alton, at the southeastern extremity. Merry-meeting bay lies beyond. Several of the islands are large, and contain good farms and wealthy inhabitants, although only two or three belong to any town, or pay any taxes. Some of their names are Rattlesnake, Cow, Bear, and Moon islands; also, Half-Mile, One-Mile, Two-Mile islands, &c., &c. None of them contain churches; and although they have few school-houses, yet sufficient attention is paid to the rudiments of education to render the children intelligent. Winnipiseogee lake, according to surveys made by Mr. Baldwin in 1825, is five hundred and one feet above the ocean.

"Squam lake lies west from Red mountain, and, like Winnipiseogee lake, abounds not only in islands, but in fish of the finest descriptions."

CENTRE HARBOR.—This is a village situated at the northwest extremity of the lake, in the midst of interesting scenery. The inhabitants are engaged in fishing as well as agriculture, and the place is a favorite stopping-place for travellers. At a short distance rises Red mountain, just spoken of.

CONWAY, six miles.—The view of the White mountains is very fine from this place, presenting a succession of lofty ridges, the most distant of which are the peaks of Mounts Washington, Adams, Jefferson, Madison, Monroe, and Quincy. The most prominent elevation on the right, with two summits, is Kearsarge, or Pickwaket; a level meadow lies in the foreground, with an isolated woody hill in the middle, and the Saco river, which rises on Mount Washington, and flows down a narrow valley, with many meanderings.

The Chalybeate Spring, in Conway, is in a valley, with mountains on every side except the southeast. From near the church, the White mountains are in sight. Two or three miles above, the Saco valley bends to the left, and Ellis's river comes down a narrow vale in front.

A tremendous catastrophe occurred among the White mountains on the night of August 28, 1826. A storm of rain, unprecedented within the memory of the oldest inhabitants, deluged the principal peaks of the mountains, and poured such an inundation upon the valleys and plains below, that it is commonly attributed to the "bursting of a cloud;" although that expression is a very ill-defined one. The effects produced by the flood will remain for centuries.

The inundation was so great and so sudden, that the channels of the stream were totally insufficient to admit of the passage of the water, which, consequently, overflowed the little level valleys at the feet of the mountains. Innumerable torrents immediately formed on all sides; and such deep trenches were cut by the rushing water, that vast bodies of earth and stones fell from the mountains, bearing with them the forests that had covered them for ages. Some of these "slides," as they are here popularly denominated (known among the Alps as "*avalanches de terre*"), are supposed to have been half a mile in breadth, and from one to five miles in length. Scarcely any natural occurrence can be imagined more sublime; and among the devastation which it has left to testify the power of the elements, the traveller will be filled with awe at the thought of that Being by whom they are controlled and directed.

The streams brought away with them immense quantities of earth and sand, which the turbid water deposited, when any obstacle threw it back, in temporary ponds and lakes. The forest-trees were also floated down, frequently, several miles from the places where they were rooted up. The timber was often marked with deep grooves and trenches, made by the rocks which passed over them, during their descent from the mountains; and great heaps of trees were deposited in some places, while in others the soil of the little meadows was buried with earth, sand, or rocks, to the depth of several feet.

The turnpike-road leading through this romantic country was twenty miles in length, but was almost entirely destroyed. Twenty-one of the twenty-three bridges upon it were demolished; one of them, built with stone, cost one thousand dollars. In some places, the Saco river ran along the road, and cut down deep channels.

The Willey house was the scene of a most melancholy tragedy on the night above mentioned, when this inundation occurred. Several days previously, a large "slide" came down from the mountains behind it, and passed so near as to cause great alarm, without any injury to the inmates. The house was occupied by Mr. Calvin Willey, whose wife was a young woman of a very interesting character, and of an education not to be looked for in so wild a region. They had a number of young children, and their family, at the time, included several other persons, amounting in all to eleven. They were waked in the night by the noise of the storm, or more

Centre Harbor, and Lake Winnipiseogee.

probably by the second descent of avalanches from the neighboring mountains, and fled in their night-clothes from the house to seek their safety, but thus threw themselves in the way of destruction. One of the slides, a hundred feet high, stopped within three feet of the house. Another took away the barn, and overwhelmed the family; nothing was found of them for some time; their clothes were found lying at their bedsides. The house had been started on its foundation by an immense heap of earth and timber, which had slid down and stopped as soon as it touched it; and they had all been crushed on leaving the door, or borne away with the water that overflowed the meadow. The bodies of several of them were never found. The last remains discovered were those of a child found in 1846. A catastrophe so melancholy, and at the same time so singular in its circumstances, has hardly ever occurred. It will always furnish the traveller with a melancholy subject of reflection.

Bartlett is a village situated in a rich valley, or intervale, of about three hundred acres, where the view is bounded on every side by near and lofty mountains. There is another intervale among the mountains westward, which, although it contains as much good cleared land, has been converted into a common, in consequence of the difficulty of making a good road to it. Pursuing still the course of the narrow valley, against the current of the Saco, the country is found uncleared, except two or three pretty little meadows, and destitute of inhabitants, excepting only three or four poor families, until arriving at Crawford's farm, seven and a half miles south of the Notch. The water rose in this house two feet in the flood of 1826. This is the place from which visiters formerly began their excursions to the mountains.

Prospect Mountain, one of the principal peaks, presents itself to view a little before arriving at the first Crawford's, with its smooth rounded summit of brown moss, rising several hundred feet above the region of vegetation, and offering an aspect which distinguishes these from the other elevations.

The climate in this narrow valley is still so warm as to favor the growth of various trees, which are scarcely to be found a few miles further north. The forests are here formed of spruce, ash, beech, maple, and sugar-maple; and Indian corn grows well, which will not come to maturity beyond. The orchard contains hundreds of apple-trees. This is one of the principal stopping-places for the sleighs, which pass the mountains in great numbers, during the winter, for Portland, Boston, &c.

Nancy's Hill is a small elevation a few miles north of this place. In 1773 a young woman of respectable connexions, who accompanied a family of settlers to Dartmouth (now Jefferson), set out in the winter to return to Portsmouth, alone and on foot, her lover having promised to meet her there and marry her. There was then no house nearer than Bartlett, thirty miles. Nancy was found by some travellers in this spot, frozen and covered with ice, under a shelter formed of branches of trees, which was the only shelter to be found on the way.

There is a place near the Notch, where the road suffered severe injury. It had been built up against the side of a mountain, on a wall forty or fifty feet high, and about thirty yards in extent, at the expense of five hundred dollars. This whole fabric was swept away by a mass of earth, rocks, and trees, which came from a half a mile up the side of the mountain, rushing down at an angle of forty-five degrees, and precipitated itself into the bed of the Saco, which is nearly three hundred feet below.

The road rises with a steep ascent for a considerable distance before it reaches the Notch, and the traveller observes two cataracts, one pouring down a precipitous mountain at a distance on the west side of the valley, and the other, which is called the Flume, rushing down on the right hand, and crossing the road under a bridge. The scenery is sublime and impressive beyond description. There is also another flume just beyond.

The Notch House, White Mountains.

The Notch is so narrow as to allow only room enough for the path, and the Saco, which is here a mere brook, only four feet in breadth. It is remarkable that the Saco and the Ammonoosuc spring from fountains on Mount Washington, within perhaps sixty yards of each other, though the former empties into the Atlantic, and the latter joins Connecticut river. Another branch of the Ammonoosuc approaches the Saco, in one place, within about six hundred yards. They are both crossed beyond the Notch. The head-waters of the Merrimac rise within about a mile and a half of this place, and run down a long ravine, little less remarkable than that of the Saco.

A road was first made through the Notch in 1785. It was fifty or sixty feet higher than the present turnpike, and so steep that it was necessary to draw horses and wagons up with ropes. The assessment for the turnpike was made in 1806.

Two rocks stand at the sides of this remarkable passage, one twenty, and the other about thirty feet, in perpendicular height. They are about twenty feet asunder, at six or seven yards from the north end, where they open to thirty feet. The part which appears to have been cut through is about one hundred and twenty feet long. A little meadow opens beyond, where is an inn.

Mount Washington.—The ascent of the mountain was formerly a most arduous undertaking, and was very rarely performed; but many ladies are now enumerated among those who have gained the summit. The whole way lies through a perfect forest. The first four miles are over a surface comparatively level; but the last two miles and a quarter are up an ascent not differing much from an angle of forty-five degrees.

The streams of the Ammonoosuc river, which are to be crossed several times, show the ravages of the inundation of 1826.

The ascent of Mount Washington is laborious, and the most arduous exertion will be necessary to attain the summit, which seems to fly before the stranger when he deems it just attained, and to look down in derision from a new and more hopeless height. The first part of the way is through a thick forest of heavy timber, which is suddenly succeeded by a girdle of dwarf and gnarled fir-trees, ten or fifteen feet high, and eighty rods, or about four hundred and fifty yards, broad; which, ending as suddenly as they began, give place to a kind of short bushes, and finally a thin bed of moss, not half sufficient to conceal the immense granite rocks which deform the surface. For more than a mile, the surface is entirely destitute of trees. A few straggling spiders, and several species of little flowering plants, are the only objects that attract the attention under the feet.

The following heights are stated to be those of the different peaks, above the level of the Connecticut river at Lancaster: Washington, 5,350 feet; Jefferson, 5,261; Adams, 5,183; Madison, 5,039; Monroe, 4,932; Quincy, 4,470. Mount Washington is believed to be more than 6,400 feet above the ocean.

In a clear atmosphere (says the "Northern Traveller"), the view is sublime, and almost boundless. The finest part of it is toward the southeast and south. Looking down the valley, through which the road has conducted us, a fine succession of mountainous summits appears for many miles, extending below the bright surface of Winnipiseogee lake.

Toward the southeast, also, the eye ranges over an extent of surface which quite bewilders the mind. Mountains, hills, and valleys, farmhouses, villages, and towns, add their variety to the natural features of the country; and the ocean may be discovered at the horizon with the help of a telescope, although the sharpest sight, perhaps, has never been able to distinguish it without such assistance. In that direction lies Portland, the capital of Maine, and nearer is Lovel's pond.

On the northeast is seen the valley of the Androscoggin river, which abounds in wild and romantic scenery, and was the usual passage by which the Indians, in their hostile incursions from Canada, used to approach the eastern frontier settlements of Massachusetts and New Hampshire. Beyond are the Ktardin hills, near the extremity of Maine.

North, the country is more wild and uncultivated; and Umbagog lake is seen, from which flows the Androscoggin.

West, the nearer view is over a mountainous region, covered with a thick forest, through which an occasional opening is perceived, formed by the farms (or clearings) of the hardy inhabitants. Beyond, the hills are seen to rise from the opposite shore of Connecticut river, the surface of which is everywhere hidden from view, and the summits, rising higher and higher, terminate in the ridges of the Green mountains in Vermont.

Southwesterly is seen the Grand Monadnock.

The Indians knew the White mountains by the name of Agiocochook, and regarded them as inaccessible, or at least represented them as such to white men.

The Lake of the Clouds is a little pond, near the summit of Mount Monroe, of beautiful clear water; it supplies the head stream of the Ammonoosuc river. This little current immediately begins its descent, and dashes in a headlong course of several thousand feet, into the valley near the encampment.

Loose fragments of granite are everywhere scattered over the mountain, with some specimens of gneiss. The granite is generally gray, and at first fine-grained, but grows coarser as we ascend, and is occasionally sprinkled with small garnets. At the summit it frequently contains a little black tourmaline, sometimes in crossing crystals. On the summit, also, some of the granite is tinged with red, although much of it is colored bright-green by lichens, dampened by the humidity of the clouds, and interspersed with thick and soft gray moss. The grain of the coarse granite is elongated; and what strikes the visiter as very singular, is that not a single rock is to be found in its original place—everything bears the mark of removal; and this, taken into view with the precipice on the northern side, seems to indicate that the summit of the mountain has fallen down and disappeared.

The general opinion seems to be that the lofty peak above us is the highest elevation in North America, except Mexico, and some of the Rocky mountains. The inhospitable nature of the climate is such as to forbid all hopes of future improvement; so that the feeling of sublimity, produced by the lonely and desolate character of this desert region, is increased by the reflection that it is destined to be a wilderness for ever.

The only places susceptible of cultivation in the heart of the mountains are the little meadows inhabited by single families, and that at the Notch house; and there the interval of warm weather is so short in the year that few vegetables can arrive at maturity, with all the rapidity of growth which distinguishes such cold regions. Indeed, the shortness and uncertainty of crops, with the expense of keeping stock, &c., would scarcely allow the farmer a support, without the advantages afforded by the thoroughfare, which is particularly great during the winter season. Population, therefore, may extend to the borders of these regions, and increase, as it does, on every side; but it can not pass the limit, because it can not contend with their coldness and sterility.

Various kinds of wild birds and game are to be found in the woods, besides bears, wild-cats, and deer. The moose and the buffalo were formerly abundant among the mountains; and it is scarcely forty years since they were killed in great numbers, merely for their hides and tallow, as the latter still are in the regions beyond the Mississippi. Deer are common in the woods, and frequently are killed by the hunters. Black bears are occasionally seen in the more unfrequented places, but they will always endeavor to avoid a man. A large species of reindeer, known here by the name of the Cariboo, has made its appearance in the White mountains.

The weather is liable to frequent changes in the mountainous region, which is partly owing to the vicinity of the Notch, through which the wind blows almost without ceasing, even when the air is perfectly still at only a short distance from it. From the situation of the mountains, it is impossible that the direction of the wind should vary materially in the valley, and it is therefore, of course, always north or south. During the winter it is often very violent; so that not only the snow is prevented from lying on the path at the Notch, but the surface is swept of everything that a strong wind can remove.

The summits of the mountains are frequently invested with mist when the sky is clear, and those only who inhabit the vicinity are able to tell whether the day is to be favorable for the ascent. The mists sometimes collect in the valleys, and then present some of the most singular and beautiful appearances.

The Shaker Village at Canterbury.—The accompanying engraving affords a view of this settlement of a small and very peculiar sect—the Shakers, or Shaking Quakers, as they are sometimes called. Like their other villages, or "families," as they call their settlements, it consists of a few dwelling-houses and offices, or shops, in which their wares are manufactured, and their seeds and herbs prepared, stored, and sold. Separate habitations, of large size, are appropriated to the different sexes, as their doctrines condemn matrimony, separate man and wife, and break up the real family state from its foundation. Their moral and theological opinions it would be difficult to ascertain, as they keep much aloof and publish but little, while few avow much that is consistent with one another, or even with themselves. The writer speaks from personal knowledge, having held a conference with the leading men of a Shaker village in this part of the country, and tried in vain to learn their whole creed. They only intimated a rejection of some of the doctrines held as fundamental by most American Christian denominations.

Ann Lee, an Englishwoman, the founder of their sect, they regard as a divine person, but differ in their representations of her. She formed the first Shaker settlement at Niskayuna, near Albany, N.Y. She came from England in 1774.

The Shakers first took up their residence in Canterbury in 1782, and formed a society in 1792, under the direction of "Elder" Job Bishop, who died in 1831, aged seventy-one, and was succeeded by Benjamin Whittier. Their religious exercises consist, chiefly, of a peculiar dance, in which both sexes move, in a regular but awkward manner, about a large hall, sometimes whirling round, and uttering inarticulate sounds. Some of them pretend to speak in "unknown tongues," to which no interpreter has ever yet been found. We add the following particulars, relating to this settlement, from a published description:—

This village is located in the north-easterly part of the county of Merrimack, on the main road from Concord to Conway, twelve miles from Concord, on an eminence; at the foot of which, as you approach the village, is a spacious granite watering-trough, from the bottom of which boils a bountiful and never-failing spring, furnished by the society for the accommodation of travellers.

As you approach the village, the first object is the meetinghouse on the right, the only white building in the village, which stands a few rods from the road, at the head of a large open lawn.

On the left stands the trustees' office, a new, spacious, and elegant building of hewn granite and pressed brick, seventy-two by forty feet in size. In this the trustees reside, and transact all the regular business of the family. To this office customers, strangers, and visiters, are to apply, who wish to buy or sell, or for the transaction of any business with the society whatever.

All sales and purchases are made by the trustees, who are the general agents of the society for transacting all their secular matters, and in whom the fee of all the real estate in trust is held.

The total number of dwellinghouses in the society is ten, mostly of wood, painted yellow. There are also many other large and convenient wooden and brick buildings, occupied as workshops; also storehouses and granaries, woodhouses, barns, &c., which are spacious and convenient.

The Shaker Settlement, at Canterbury

The whole number of buildings in the village is about one hundred, many of which are very valuable, composed of the best materials, and built in a faithful and durable manner. Among these are a convenient schoolhouse, one spacious gristmill, two sawmills, three carding-machines, one fullingmill, one triphammer, five mills for sawing firewood, three turningmills, and two tanneries, besides various other machinery. These buildings are all laid out and constructed in a regular, plain, and elegant manner, which gives the village a very fine appearance.

The society own and occupy upward of 2,500 acres of land, which, though stony, is a good deep soil, about 2,000 of which lie in one body, enclosed with good stone wall and cross-fenced with the same materials. Grass, corn, grain, and potatoes, are raised in abundance.

They are industrious, frugal, and temperate. They manufacture many useful articles for sale, which are very neat and durable; such as leather, whips, sieves, tubs, pails, churns, measures, rakes, brooms, trusses, snaths, &c., &c. Their gardens are large, and perhaps the most productive of any in the country. They raise and vend a general assortment of garden-seeds, and spare no pains to furnish those of the best kind. They also collect and prepare a variety of botanical herbs, barks, roots, and extracts, which are prepared in the most faithful manner; the herbs and roots are neatly pressed in packages of a pound, and papered and labelled. All the medicines prepared by them being pure, and gathered in proper season, insure them a very ready sale.

They usually keep about twenty horses, eighty cows, fifteen yoke of oxen, five to six hundred sheep, and other stock in proportion, and cut sufficient hay on their premises for their own consumption. They also annually slaughter forty or fifty swine.

They freely pay their proportion of taxes, and share all the burdens of government, except the bearing of arms, which they deem incompatible with genuine Christianity, being, as they believe, directly contrary to the precepts and spirit of the gospel. So tenacious are they of this fact, that they not only refuse to bear arms, but decline even to receive pensions for their former military services, to which some of them are legally entitled.

Their school will compare well with any in the country. The English language is taught, and partly on the Lancasterian system. They are careful to furnish the school with good books, stationery, &c., so that their scholars, who are disposed, may acquire a good education.

They entirely discard the use of ardent spirits, except occasionally in medical preparations, but drink some cider.

They are temperate and regular in all their habits; their food is plain and wholesome, avoiding all luxuries. They allow eight hours in twenty-four for sleeping.

The society, from its commencement, has gradually increased in number, as well as in good order. At present it consists of about two hundred and forty members.

History.—In 1621 the English Plymouth company granted to John Mason, one of its members, the country between Naumkeag, or Salem, and the Merrimack; and soon after, in the same year, to Mason and Gorges all the lands between the Merrimack and the Sagadahock, extending back to the rivers of Canada. The latter tract was called Laconia. Two years later, two parties of settlers were sent out by "the Laconia company," who began settlements at Portsmouth and Dover. In 1629, Mason took out a new patent for the territory between the Merrimack and the Piscataqua, under the name of New Hampshire. In 1635, the Plymouth company divided New England among their members, before they gave up their charter to the king, and the territory between Naumkeag and Piscataqua rivers fell to Mason.

The first church formed within the present limits of the state dates in 1641. Coos county, including the northern parts of the valley of the Connecticut, was occupied by a few scattered families before 1775; but at the commencement of the revolutionary war, the fear of invasion from Canada drove them all back, and only the return of peace could induce a second and permanent occupation of that region, then a perfect wilderness, difficult of access.

Railroads.—The people of this state have entered with commendable zeal upon several railroad enterprises, which promise to be of permanent advantage to the state.

The Northern Railroad, from Concord to Lebanon, a distance of fifty miles, has been completed the entire distance, and forms, in conjunction with the Vermont Central railroad, a continuous line to Burlington, by way of Montpelier, the capital of Vermont, 210 miles from Boston.

The Boston, Concord, and Montreal Railroad, already incidentally alluded to on page 32, is, as its name implies, intended ultimately to connect the commercial capitals of Canada and New England. It has been opened as far as Warren, and is being rapidly pressed to completion. This road furnishes an easy and rapid conveyance to the White mountains; while the whole line of the route from Meredith village lies through a region so replete with that splendid lake and hill scenery which has given such a world-wide celebrity to New Hampshire, as to render it, for that alone, a desirable route for the admirer of the beauties of nature.

Portsmouth and Concord Railroad.—This is another and most important railroad enterprise. Concord, as indicated by its being the point at which so many railroads meet, is destined to become the great inland freight-dépôt of New England. This renders it important that the commercial capital of the state should possess more facilities of communication with Concord which other sections of country have, particularly as it shortens the communication by railroad with the Atlantic about thirty miles. This road, which is now nearly completed, will make Portsmouth the second port in New England.

There are several other railroads in process of construction, but our limits will not admit a further reference to them.

Education.—Common schools are universal in New Hampshire, as in other parts of New England. Each township is divided into school-districts, which are empowered to build schoolhouses. An annual tax is assessed on the town by the selectmen, and with the avails of it is distributed the income of the literary funds, which is raised by a tax on the capital of banks.

Academies, or high-schools, are scattered all over the state. The oldest are those founded at Exeter in 1781, at Chesterfield in 1790, at Atkinson in 1791, and at Gilmanton and Haverhill in 1794.

Phillips Academy has its name from its liberal founder, John Phillips, LL. D., and has an income of $70,000, with a library of six hundred volumes. The number of pupils is limited to sixty.

The Congregational Theological Seminary at Gilmanton, and the Baptist Academical and Theological Institution at New Hampton, are worthy of particular notice. The latter has had above three hundred pupils at one time.

Learned Societies.—The *N. Hampshire Medical Society* was incorporated in 1791, and holds an annual meeting in Concord on the Tuesday preceding the state election.

The *New Hampshire Historical Society* was incorporated in 1823, and has published several volumes of collections. The annual meeting is on June 17th.

Government.—The legislative power is vested, by the constitution, in a senate and house of representatives, which, together, are styled the General Court of New Hampshire. Every town or incorporated township having one hundred and fifty ratable polls may send one representative; and every three hundred additional polls, one. The senate, consisting of twelve members, is elected by the people in districts. The executive power is vested in a governor, and a council of five members. The governor, council, senators, and representatives, are elected annually by the people on the second Tuesday of March. The general court meets annually (at Concord) on the first Wednesday of June. The right of suffrage is granted to every male inhabitant of age, except paupers, &c. The judiciary power is vested in a superior court and court of common pleas.

View of Burlington.

VERMONT.

This state is distinguished among the other New England states by several marked peculiarities. In situation, it borders, on one side, a foreign country, and on another the grand route of northern invasion, in consequence of which its soil has been exposed to hostile incursions, in the successive wars with the Indians, the French, and the English. Its climate is so cold and healthful as to give hardihood and vigor to the inhabitants; while it possesses so much rich soil, and such abundant water-power and facilities for navigation, as to encourage all the arts of life. Although circumstances retarded the settlement of the country, and led to unfortunate dissensions and conflicting claims for the possession, yet the happy adjustment of all, with New York on one side and New Hampshire on the other, and the erection of Vermont into an independent state, gave an impulse to improvements of every kind, which has produced most extensive and important results.

Extending from forty-two degrees forty-four minutes to forty-five degrees north latitude, and near several lakes, the climate of Vermont would have been rigorous in the winter, even if its surface had not been elevated much above the ocean level; but the Green mountain ridge is of such extent and elevation as to render the cold season very long and quite severe. The longitude is between three degrees thirty-one minutes and five degrees east; the greatest length of the state is one hundred and fifty-seven and a half miles, and the greatest breadth ninety miles. The whole area comprehended within the boundaries is 10,200 square miles.

The Green mountain ridge forms a marked and natural dividing line between the counties of Windham, Windsor, and Orange, on the one side, and Bennington,

Rutland, and Addison, on the other. In all that part of it there is not a single passage to be found wide enough for a road, nor is its long and uniform elevation so much as interrupted by the bed of any stream. Five turnpike roads, indeed, pass it in different places, but they have been constructed at considerable cost and labor, and are very laborious to travel, as they rise and descend the height of the ridge.

In the southern part of Washington county it divides into two ridges, the principal of which borders the counties of Chittenden and Franklin on the east, and the other, known by the name of "The height of lands," strikes off in a northeast direction into the county of Caledonia. This keeps a remarkably uniform elevation, and forms the dividing line between the waters of the Connecticut and the two lakes, Champlain and Memphremagog. The western ridge is cut through by Onion and Lamoille rivers, although its principal summits are the highest in the state. Among these is the Camel's Hump; this ridge constitutes the grandeur of the scenery so much admired along the northeastern side of Lake Champlain.

Mount Ascutney is one of the eminences most celebrated in Vermont, more on account of the beautiful scenery upon which it looks down, and its vicinity to Windsor, one of the principal and most beautiful towns in the state. An excursion to its summit affords many fine views, as it rises abruptly from the borders of the valley of the Connecticut, and the path, in its gradual ascent, opens to the eye many varying landscapes.

Not less than twenty-one rivers have their sources in the Green mountains, of which twelve flow into the Connecticut, and nine into the two principal lakes. From the nature of the country, these streams are necessarily short and small; though in the season of floods, some of them drain off great quantities of water through their rocky channels. No country is better supplied with abundant and pure springs. The water of Vermont is generally good, except along the shore of Lake Champlain, where the rocks are of limestone.

Mineral springs of different kinds are found in several counties. Some are chalybeate, others sulphurous; and some are resorted to by invalids for the improvement of their health.

LAKES.—Lake Champlain extends along nearly the whole western boundary of the state, and forms an important feature in several respects. It affords invaluable advantages of navigation, for it is of sufficient uniform depth for vessels of considerable size, and forms several good harbors; while the canal which connects it with Hudson river offers a direct, safe, and cheap channel of commerce to the city of New York. At the same time, fine steamboats of the largest class daily traverse the lake through its whole extent, on the grand route between the United States and Canada, touching at the principal towns along the shore.

Lake Memphremagog, lying on the boundary line of the United States, has four or five miles of its southern part in Orleans county, Vermont, but its northern and larger portion in Canada. It is about thirty miles long from north to south, and three or four miles wide from east to west. It is about midway between Lake Champlain and Connecticut river. Three small rivers—the Clyde, Black, and Barton—enter the south part of the lake from Vermont. On an island two miles above the line are obtained the celebrated oilstones, for sharpening tools, which are well known throughout our country, and highly prized, being worth half a dollar a pound. Whetstones, for scythes, &c., are obtained in the vicinity of the lake, at the place where the gneiss-rocks pass into mica-slate.

In Lake Champlain are a number of islands, the largest of which are North Hero and South Hero, in the northern part and near the shore of Vermont, to which they belong.

North Hero forms a township of the same name, in the county of Grand Isle. It is twenty-six miles north of Burlington, six west of St. Albans, and contains 6,272 acres. The first settlement was made on this island in 1783. In 1793 the British erected a blockhouse on it, which was given up to the United States in 1796. The soil is good, and there is a small village, four school districts, a courthouse, and a jail, built of stone. The rocks are of limestone.

South Hero is a small island, of 9,055 acres, twelve miles northwest of Burlington, and sixteen southwest of St. Albans. The first settlement was made here in 1784. In the summer season, when the water in the lake is low, a passage can often be made by fording to Chittenden, on the mainland, a sandbar extending the whole distance. The surface is level and the soil good, being formed of limestone, like that of the adjacent shores and islands. Many marks remain in them all of the numerous Indians who formerly resorted to them.

Rivers.—Two or three of the rivers of Vermont, viz., those which cross the Green mountains, being of considerable size, are navigable through most of their course in canoes, and communicating, by a short carrying-place, with the navigable waters of Lake Champlain, were as many principal routes of traffic and of war for the Canadian Indians, on their way to the Connecticut river. When the English first visited the latter stream, they found the savages on its banks, as low down as Hartford, had a trade in furs, &c., with those who inhabited the shores of Lake Champlain and the St. Lawrence, which was carried on by the channels just indicated. At later periods, when the Jesuits, who occupied Montreal and other places in Canada, as lords of the manor, incited and directed the fanaticism of the Indians against the eastern colonies, these same routes were used in the secret, and often unexpected and bloody, incursions which were so numerous in the French wars.

Onion River is seventy miles long. Rising in Cabot, Caledonia county, it runs south, then southwest, and finally northwest, falling into Lake Champlain, passing through Washington and Chittenden counties, five miles below Burlington. The principal branches are Dog, Steven's, North, Mad, Waterbury, and Huntington rivers. Many scenes along the course of the Onion and some of its tributaries are peculiarly wild and romantic. Its highest branch has a fall of five hundred feet, almost perpendicular; and at Bolton is a remarkable chasm, cut by the stream into the solid rocks, sixty feet wide, thirty feet deep, and two hundred and seventy yards long, where the descent is so rapid that the stream rushes through with great rapidity. Four miles below Waterbury is a spot, where a wall of rock rises on one side to the height of one hundred feet, and large fragments have fallen down, and lie in such a manner as to form a bridge. Three quarters of a mile above the falls, an artificial bridge commands a striking view, upon a place where the channel of the river is seventy feet wide and sixty-five feet deep. A fine turnpike-road now leads through the mountains from this stream to White river and Royalton.

This was the principal Indian route to the Connecticut; and many captives, as well as loads of plunder, were in former times carried by this route, from the New England frontier villages, by war parties returning to Canada. The water-power on this river is very great. It is mostly of little depth, as might be expected from its shortness and its small supply of water. It is, however, useful in navigation. Lake vessels can enter the river and sail up five miles, and boats forty.

Two of the earliest and most spirited military measures taken in the revolutionary war were performed by a few men from Vermont, at important points just beyond the bounds of this state. We allude to the surprise of the two great fortresses on Lake Champlain, Ticonderoga and Crown Point. These positions are very peculiar. The lake at these two points, about twelve miles apart, is very narow and crooked; and the two fortresses were so placed as to completely command the passage. The guns, which were numerous and heavy, were mounted on strong walls, scientifically planned by accomplished British engineers, and constructed with great strength, of the limestone abounding along the shores; while deep ditches, in some places cut far down into solid rocks, offered almost insurmountable obstacles to an approach. Lying on the very borders of this state, with some of their outworks actually erected upon the Vermont side of the lake, and owing their capture, as they did, chiefly to Vermont men, a brief description of Ticonderoga and Crown Point may with propriety be here introduced, being extremely interesting to all interested in the war for independence.

Mount Independence is a hill on the Vermont side, of comparatively small elevation east of Mount Defiance, and separated from it by the lake, which has here reduced its size to that of a small river. On a bank just above the water are the remains of a zigzag battery for about forty or fifty guns, running across a little cornfield behind a house, and making five or six angles. The Horse-shoe battery is traceable on an elevation about a quarter of a mile in the rear. A bridge once connected Ticonderoga with Mount Defiance, the buttresses of which are remaining, to the great annoyance of the navigators of the lake. On the west shore (near the stone storehouse), Arnold, when pursued by the British, caused his flotilla to be run on shore. These hulks remain almost as sound as when first stranded. A forty-two pounder is said to have ranged from the Horse-shoe over this channel (now marked by a buoy) and the fortress.

After the revolutionary war, about five hundred cannon were lying about the fortress, lines, &c., many of them as left by the English, with their trunnions knocked off. A twenty-four pounder was taken to the forge at Fairhaven, some years ago, and discharged by the heat, after lying loaded for above twenty years, and a considerable time at the bottom of the lake.

The view from Ticonderoga down Lake Champlain is very pleasant. It abounds, the greater part of the way to Canada, with fine natural scenes.

The Fortress of Ticonderoga.—This famous old fortress, or rather its remains, are overlooked from Mount Independence. An elevated piece of land, gently sloping toward the south, and ending abruptly over a bend of the lake, appears partially covered with trees, and crowned near its extremity with a cluster of broken walls and chimneys.

The old French Lines, where General Abercrombie was defeated in 1758, are the only part of the fortification which was ever the scene of a battle. They commenced on the east side, at a battery of heavy cannon on the shore, about a quarter of a mile south of the ferry. The remains of the breastwork can yet be seen. The lines were drawn in a zigzag; first stretching off to the right, along the side of marshy ground, to a cluster of bushes where was a battery; and then to the left to the verge of a wood, where was another.

Their course may be distinctly traced in this manner across the ridge of land at its highest elevation, over to the brow of a steep bank, looking toward the outlet of Lake George. The woods which now so much interrupt the sight have grown since the evacuation of the fortress, after the revolutionary war.

The fortress is of an angular form, and embraces a large tract of ground, being divided into parts by deep ditches. The walls were originally much higher than at present, being raised by superstructures of logs filled in with earth.

The *Barracks* formed an oblong, and the walls still remain of all except those on the eastern side; their form is plainly distinguishable. The parade is fifty-two and a half yards long, and eight in breadth. The barracks, &c., the walls of which remain on the north, south, and west sides, are built of the rough blue limestone of which the neighboring rocks are formed, two stories high; and these with the chimneys, several of which are standing, are the principal objects seen from a distance. The entrances to this courtyard, or parade, are between the buildings, and quite narrow. By the southern entrance, Ethan Allen entered with his eighty-three raw soldiers when he surprised the fortress on the 18th May, 1775; and on reaching the courtyard and calling on the commander to surrender, the British officer, Captain Deplace, made his appearance at a window and submitted, delivering up three officers and forty-four rank and file. In consequence of this *coup-de-main*, this important place was in the hands of the Americans until the arrival of Burgoyne in 1777.

The troops in the garrison had become loose disciplinarians. A body of men had been despatched from Connecticut to surprise the place, and approached upon the opposite shore, but were unprovided with a conveyance to the intended point of their enterprise. A countryman, who had been in the habit of frequently visiting the fort, was made acquainted with their views, crossed the lake by daylight, went carefully into the fort, and observed in what part of the parade-ground the arms were stacked. Being almost domiciliated by the frequency of his previous visits, he lounged away his time until night approached. He then possessed himself of a large bateau owned by the garrison, and recrossed the lake. Allen, having joined the band, embarked, effected a landing about one mile north of the fort, and proceeded across the meadows, shrouded by the night, and made good their daring enterprise, by threatening the sentry, and taking immediate possession of the firearms, as pointed out by their avant-courier.

The battlements of Ticonderoga first bore the flag of independence. This circumstance should, of itself, render this ruin, so fine in other associations, interesting to the traveller.

At each corner was a bastion or a demi-bastion; and under that in the northeastern one is a subterranean magazine. The cellars south of this, which belonged to the demolished buildings, and are almost filled up, have a room or two with fireplaces still distinguishable.

The Grenadiers' battery is situated on a rocky point toward the east from the main fortress. They were connected by a covered way, the traces of which are distinctly visible.

On a spot formerly occupied as the king's garden Mr. Pell has a fine garden, abounding in the choicest fruits imported from Europe, and transported from the celebrated nurseries of Long Island. Mr. Pell has been a very successful propagator of the locust-tree (*robinia pseudo acacia* of Linnæus), thousands of which are growing on these grounds in the most flourishing manner; here is also the *magnolia grandiflora*, never before cultivated in so high a latitude; the horse-chestnut (*castanea equinus*); and upward of seventy varieties of the gooseberry from Europe. Here, also, we find the beautiful *catalpa*, and the *liriodendron tulipifera*.

On the neighboring Vermont shore, there are still some slight remains of Burgoyne's intrenchments.

From Mount Independence the visiter enjoys, in fine weather, a delightful view of the lake and the surrounding country. On the left is the outlet of Lake George, winding through a dark and narrow valley, and spreading out to embrace an island of the brightest verdure; while more immediately under the eye lies the fortress of Ticonderoga, and the lake, stretching far away to the north.

Mount Defiance rises on the left, about eight hundred feet high, on the summit of which General Burgoyne's troops showed themselves on the morning of July 4th, 1777, with a battery of heavy cannon, which they had drawn up along the ridge by night, and planted in that commanding position, whence they could count the men in the fort. The distance to the summit in a straight line is about a mile, so that the defence of Ticonderoga would have been impossible; and on the firing of a few shots by the British upon a vessel in the lake, which proved the range of their guns, the Americans made preparations to evacuate the place, and effected their retreat to the shore below during the night.

The shores are in this part strewed with the fragments of blue limestone-rock with organic remains.

The immediate shores are generally low all the way to Crown Point, where the lake suddenly turns to the west at a right angle, and, at the distance of a mile, as suddenly to the north again. A low stretch of land covered with a young forest, on the left, conceals the approach to this ancient fortress, which, for position as well as appearance and history, may be called the twin sister of Ticonderoga.

Chimney point is on the north side of the lake, opposite Crown Point, to which is a ferry three quarters of a mile.

The Fortress of Crown Point.—There are several old works thrown up along the shore, with little bays between them. The easternmost one is called the Grenadiers' battery; the middle one is the original old French fort of 1731, and now encloses a garden; and that further west is an outwork to a bastion of the fortress. The fortress is situated about a quarter of a mile back from the shore, and appears much like Ticonderoga from a distance, showing the walls and chimneys of the old barracks, and walls of earth surrounding them. In regard to its plan, however, it is materially different. The fortress of Crown Point was a star work, being in the form of a pentagon, with bastions at the angles, and a strong redoubt at the distance of two hundred and fifty or three hundred yards in advance of each of them. The fortress is surrounded by a ditch walled in with stone, except where it has been blasted into the solid rock of blue limestone (as is the case in many parts, from five to twenty-five feet), and even into quartz-rock which underlays it. Univalve shells are found in the limestone-rock, frequently four inches in diameter. The walls are about twenty or twenty-five feet high, and there is a convenient path running entirely round upon the top, interrupted only by the gates at the north and south sides. Although much shaded by tall sumacs, some fine views are enjoyed in making the circuit, which is not far short of half a mile.

Opposite the north gate is a small ledge of rocks, and, close by, the remains of a covered way to the lake shore. On entering the fortress, the stranger finds himself in a level, spacious area, bounded on the left and in front by long ruinous buildings of stone, two stories high, and the first two hundred and twenty feet long, while the ruins of similar ones are seen on two sides on the right. This parade is about five hundred feet in length. The place was surprised by Colonel Warner in 1775.

The view from the walls toward the north is very fine: looking down the lake, which widens at the distance of two or three miles, you have Chimney point on the right, and two other points projecting beyond the distant peak, called Camel's Hump. Ranges of mountains on the western shore, beginning at the distance of eighteen miles, including Bald peak, gradually approach till they form a near and bold boundary to the lake on the left, scattered with cleared farms and houses, and then stretching away to the south, terminate in the mountain behind. This elevation, although it seems almost as well calculated to command Crown Point as Mount Defiance does Ticonderoga, is not less than four miles distant.

Everything about this old fortress bears the marks of ruin. Two magazines were blown up; the timbers in the south barracks are burnt black; a portion of the shingled roof which remains serves to cover a little hay-mow and the nests of robins; while some of the entrances and other parts are fenced up for a sheepfold. The ground around it is much covered with fragments of blasted rocks, and, particularly at the south, with the ruins of old buildings. The trees which are seen have grown since the evacuation of the place; and on one of the angles is an inscription of the date of the fortress, 1756, when it was constructed on a greatly-enlarged plan, by General Amherst, at an expense of £2,000,000 sterling.

Naval Action on Lake Champlain, in 1776.—After the unfortunate termination of the expedition against Quebec, and retreat of the American troops to Crown Point and Ticonderoga, the British forces under General Carleton began to collect a formidable flotilla at St. John, for the purpose of making their way over the lake. Some of these vessels were constructed at Quebec, or Montreal, in such a manner that they could be taken to pieces, transported over land to the lake, and the parts there united and soon made ready for service. Active preparations were immediately commenced on the part of the Americans to put afloat a sufficient force to meet the enemy, and baffle their movements. General Arnold, who, as is well known, had been a sailor in his youth, was appointed to the command; and, under his direction, a squadron—consisting of two sloops, three schooners, three galleys, and eight gondolas—was in a short time ready to sail. The sloops carried twelve guns, the schooners from eight to twelve, and the galleys and gondolas from three to twelve each.

Having received his instructions from General Gates, who had command of the army in that quarter, he sailed down the lake, and, when within a few miles of the Isle-aux-Tetes, discovered it to be occupied by the enemy. At Windmill point he moored his vessels across the lake, so as to prevent the enemy from passing. The decks of his vessels being very low, Arnold sent a party of men on shore to cut fascines, for the purpose of erecting around them barricades, to prevent their being boarded by superior numbers in small craft. While engaged in this service, they were fired upon by the Indians, and three of their number killed and six wounded. Finding his position too much exposed, he returned eight or ten miles to Isle-la-Motte, and took a more advantageous station. He here received information of the formidable fleet fitting out at St. John; and, deeming it unadvisable to hazard an action where he would be compelled to engage a superior force under great disadvantage, he withdrew still further back, and anchored the fleet in a line between Valcour island and the western shore of the lake.

Early in the morning of the 11th of October, the guardboats gave notice that the enemy's fleet was in sight, off Cumberland head, moving up the lake. It soon appeared advancing around the southern point of Valcour island, and presented a formidable aspect, there being one ship with three masts, two schooners, a radeau, one gondola, twenty gunboats, four longboats, and forty-four boats with provisions and troops. The armed vessels were manned by several hundred chosen seamen. Such an array was enough to convince the Americans that they must rely mainly on their bravery and the advantages of their position. The wind was likewise in their favor, as some of the larger vessels could not beat up sufficiently near to engage in the attack. While the enemy's fleet was coming round the island, Arnold had ordered his three galleys, and a schooner called the Royal Savage, to get under way and advance upon the enemy. On their return to the line, the schooner grounded and was afterward destroyed, but the men were saved.

At half-past twelve o'clock the action became general and very warm, the British having brought all their gunboats and one schooner within musket-shot of the American line. They kept up a heavy fire of round and grapeshot, till five o'clock, when they withdrew from the contest, and joined the ship and schooner, which a head wind had prevented from coming into action.

During the contest, Arnold was on board the Congress galley, which suffered severely. It received seven shot between wind and water, was hulled twelve times, the mainmast was wounded in two places, the rigging cut in pieces, and the proportion of killed and wounded was unusually great. So deficient was the fleet in gunners, that Arnold himself pointed almost every gun that was fired from his vessel. The Washington galley was equally shattered, the first lieutenant was killed, and the captain and master wounded. All the officers of one of the gondolas, except the captain, were lost, and another gondola sunk soon after the engagement. The whole number of killed and wounded was about sixty. The enemy landed a large body of Indians, who kept up an incessant fire of musketry from the island and the opposite shore, but without effecting much injury.

A consultation was held by the officers as soon as the engagement was over, and they agreed, that, considering the exhausted state of their ammunition, and the great superiority of the enemy's force both in ships and men, prudence required them to return to Crown Point, and if possible without risking another attack. The British had anchored their vessels in a line within a few hundred yards of the Americans, stretching from the island to the main, apparently to frustrate any such design. The night was dark, but a favoring breeze blew from the north, and before morning Arnold had passed with his whole fleet through the British line entirely undiscovered. This manœuvre was not less bold in its execution than extraordinary in its success. Arnold himself brought up the rear in his crippled galley, and, before their departure was known to the enemy, they had ascended the lake ten or twelve miles to Schuyler's island. Here they were obliged to cast anchor for half a day, in order to stop the leaks and repair their sails. Two of the gondolas were abandoned and sunk. In the afternoon they set sail again; but the wind had died away in the morning, and it now sprung up from the south, equally retarding the pursuit of the enemy and their own progress.

On the morning of the second day the scene was changed. The Congress and Washington galleys, with four gondolas, had fallen in the rear, all being too much disabled to sail freely. The advanced ships of the enemy's fleet, in one of which was General Carleton, were found to be gaining upon them, under a press of sail, and in a short time were alongside. After receiving a few broadsides, the Washington struck, having been extremely weakened by the loss of men and injury received in the first engagement. The whole force of the attack now fell upon Arnold in the Congress galley. A ship of eighteen guns, a schooner of fourteen, and another of twelve, poured forth an unceasing fire within musket-shot. The contest was kept up with unparalleled resolution for four hours, when the galley was reduced almost to a wreck, and was surrounded by seven sail of the enemy. In this situation, Arnold ran the galley and the four gondolas into a small creek, on the east side of the lake, about ten miles from Crown Point; and as soon as they were aground and were set on fire, he ordered the marines to leap into the water armed with muskets, wade to the beach, and station themselves in such a manner on the bank as to prevent the approach of the enemy's small boats. He was the last man that remained on board, nor did he leave his galley till the fire had made such progress that it could not be extinguished. The flags were kept flying, and he maintained his attitude of defence on the shore till he saw them consumed, and the whole of his flotilla enveloped in flames. There are few instances on record of more deliberate courage and gallantry than were displayed by him, from the beginning to the end of this action.

Being no longer in a condition to oppose the enemy, he proceeded immediately through the woods with his men to Crown Point, and fortunately escaped an attack from the Indians, who waylaid the path two hours after he had passed. The same night he arrived at Ticonderoga. All his clothes, papers, and baggage, had been burned in the Royal Savage at Valcour island. He found at Ticonderoga the remnant of his fleet, being two schooners, two galleys, one sloop, and one gondola. General Waterbury, who commanded the Washington galley, and one hundred and ten prisoners, were returned on parole by General Carleton the day after the last action. The whole American loss in killed and wounded was between eighty and ninety. The enemy reported theirs to be about forty.

Notwithstanding the signal failure of this enterprise, the valor and good conduct of the commander and his officers were themes of applause throughout the country.

Rutland.—This is the capital of Rutland county, and is fifty miles southwest of Montpelier, sixty south of Burlington, and fifty-two northeast of Bennington. The first settlement was made in this township about the year 1770; and in the revolutionary war two small picket forts were built, one near the present courthouse in the east village. Otter creek flows through the township from south to north, and it receives two of its tributaries here, West river and

East creek, on which are several manufactories. Iron, limestone, and clay, are found in different places, the rocks being partly primitive, and partly secondary. Quarries of blue and black marble are wrought in the limestone range which passes from Berkshire county, Massachusetts, through a great part of Vermont. The principal village is in the eastern part, and contains several public buildings, particularly a courthouse.

BURLINGTON.—This town, the capital of Chittenden county, and the chief place of trade in the state, enjoys a fine situation on an excellent harbor of Lake Champlain, from the level of which it rises, up a bold and considerable eminence, making a beautiful display toward the water. The streets present a pleasant aspect, containing many neat and elegant residences, with fine gardens, abounding with flowers and fruits in their season. The inhabitants are distinguished by intelligence, taste, and enterprise, and are extensively engaged in trade, manufactures, and navigation, which is carried on both in steamboats, schooners, and vessels adapted to pass through the Champlain canal to Albany.

The county buildings, academy, bank, and various churches, are the principal public buildings in the town; while the edifices of the Vermont university crown the summit of the eminence. Pop. 5,500.

A manufacturing village, of considerable size, lies one mile and a half northeast from the town, on the bank of Onion river, about five miles from its mouth.

The settlement of Burlington, which was commenced a little before the revolution, was interrupted and delayed by the war, since which, and especially since the opening of the Champlain canal and the establishment of steam navigation on the lake, its increase has been rapid. Limestone and iron ore are obtained in the vicinity, but the soil is generally poor, excepting a rich alluvial tract of land below the falls of Onion river. Southwest of the town hard timber abounds, and pine prevails in a region lying on the northeast. Among the branches of manufacture is that of glass.

The University of Vermont.—This institution, situated at Burlington, was incorporated in the year 1791, but did not go into operation until 1800. The three college buildings are situated on a fine elevation about a mile from the lake, east of the town, commanding a very extensive and agreeable view of both, two hundred and forty-five feet above the water. The first edifice, which was built in 1801, was destroyed by fire in 1824. Two of the present buildings are devoted to the accommodation of students, and the third is used as the chapel and for other public purposes.

The institution is endowed with lands reserved in all the townships, except those granted by New Hampshire, the income of which is increasing, and must hereafter become very large. Money has been furnished by the legislature and by liberal subscriptions.

The corporation consists of seventeen members, including the governor, the speaker of the house of representatives, and the president of the university.

Rev. Daniel C. Sanders was appointed president in 1800, Rev. Samuel Austin in 1816, Rev. Daniel Haskell in 1821, Rev. Willard Preston in 1824, Rev. Jas. Marsh in 1826.

Commencement is held on the first Wednesday in August, and the vacations, one four weeks from that time, and the other eight weeks from the first Wednesday in January. The annual expense for room, rent, and tuition, is twenty-five dollars.

The *Medical Department* of the institution affords lectures during fourteen weeks from the first Monday after commencent, the fees for which are twenty-five dollars, contingent bill three dollars, and graduation fee fifteen dollars.

MONTPELIER, the capital of Vermont and seat of justice of Washington county, is thirty-six miles southeast of Burlington, one hundred and forty northwest of Boston, five hundred and twenty-four north by east of Washington, and one hundred and twenty southeast of Montreal. It stands at the confluence of the two branches of Onion river, and has a remarkably wild and romantic situation, in the midst of high and rugged hills.

The State House, at Montpelier.

It contains the statehouse, a courthouse, the jail, academy, bank, several churches, and a variety of manufactories.

The *Statehouse* is in a fine situation, fronting on State street, from which it is distant three hundred and twenty-five feet. A spacious gateway opens into an ample courtyard, across which leads a pathway of pounded granite, seventy-two feet wide, to three successive terraces, the ascent to which, by a few steps, gradually surmounts the elevation of thirty-two feet above the street. The main building has a front of seventy-two feet, with two wings thirty-nine feet each; making an entire front of one hundred and fifty feet. The main building, including the portico, is one hundred feet deep, and the wings fifty. Six granite Doric columns, thirty-six feet high, and six feet in diameter at the base, support the portico. The walls of granite, from Barre, nine miles distant, are well cut; the roof and dome are covered with copper. The entrance hall is thirty-two by thirty-eight feet, fourteen feet high, with six Ionic granite columns.

The representatives' hall is sixty-seven feet by fifty-seven, and thirty-one feet high. The senate-chamber is oval, forty-four feet by thirty, and twenty-two feet high. The governor's room and other apartments are commodious and in good taste.

The expense of the whole, including the iron railing around the yard, was $132,000, of which the citizens contributed $15,000. Pop. 4,500.

WINDSOR, of which we have spoken before, is one of the most important towns in the state, as well as one of the most beautiful, both in appearance and situation. It occupies a fine piece of ground, which rises, by two graceful swells, from the western bank of Connecticut river, shut in on all sides by superior eminences, especially on the New Hampshire side, where the shore is steep and mountainous, and on the west, where the noble Ascutney, or the Two Brothers, 3,320 feet higher than the ocean, forms the background of the picture. Though about four miles distant, its sides and peak appear near at hand, and add a feature to the scenery which few landscapes can boast.

Windsor is fifty-five miles south of Montpelier, fifty-five northeast of Burlington, ninety-five northwest of Boston, and four hundred and twenty nearly north of Washington. The surface of the township, though hilly, is rich and well cultivated. The first settlement was made here in 1764. The principal street is crooked, but adorned with several handsome public and private buildings, the stateprison in the south part; and a bridge crosses the Connecticut.

BENNINGTON.—This is a frontier town, on the borders of New York, with a hilly surface, rich in iron mines, which supply considerable furnaces and forges. The village stands upon a conspicuous eminence, and contains a court and an academy. The place derives its name from Governor Benning Wentworth, from whom it received its charter in 1749. The settlement was commenced in 1761, by separatists, under Samuel Robinson. They were the first of the inhabitants who resisted the authorities of New York, and drove them from the soil, denying her jurisdiction.

A range of limestone crosses Bennington county, which has been worked for some years, and yields good marble of several different colors and qualities. Some lead is also found.

The *Battle of Bennington* was an action of considerable importance, though fought by a detachment of the British army on the one side, and the militia of Vermont and the neighboring counties of Massachusetts on the other. It was brought about in consequence of General Burgoyne's despatching a strong body of Hessians, under Colonel Baum, to seize a large supply of American provisions collected at Bennington. Burgoyne was at that time—viz., in the summer of 1777—preparing to move down the Hudson for Albany, and was occupied, from July 28 to August 15, in transporting bateaux, provisions, artillery, and baggage, from Whitehall (then called Skeenesbourgh) and Fort George to the Hudson. Many obstacles were in his way, General Schuyler, while on his retreat from Ticonderoga, having thrown trees into Wood creek, and left much to be done in clearing the channel of that stream, and in constructing a log road across the sandy region, for the transportation of the British artillery; while the European troops showed great want of skill in operations so foreign to their habits.

Colonel Baum set off for Bennington with five hundred regular troops, a number of Canadians, above one hundred Indians, and a few tories; while Lieutenant Colonel Brayman took post at Battenkill, with his Brunswick grenadiers, light infantry, and chasseurs, to support him if necessary.

General Stark first received information of the enemy's approach on the 13th of August; but at first was aware only of the small body of Indians, and sent an equal number of Americans to meet them, under the command of Colonel Greg. Near night, however, he was apprized that the force was large, when he called out his whole brigade, and sent an express to Manchester to inform Colonel Warner of the danger, while he ordered the news to be spread in all directions. The next morning he marched, and soon met his advance on their retreat, pursued by the enemy, then only a mile in the rear. The Americans were immediately drawn up for battle; on seeing which, the enemy halted at a commanding position, but made no demonstration of a further advance, thinking it prudent to send back for a reinforcement. Eager for the contest, the American sharpshooters pressed the enemy with skirmishes, and succeeded in killing and wounding about thirty, including two Indian chiefs, without suffering any loss themselves.

To secure a better position, General Stark retired to more favorable ground, about a mile in his rear; and the following day, which was stormy, was spent in skirmishing. The battle began the following afternoon, Colonel Symonds having arrived with some militia from Berkshire county, Mass. The enemy had by this time fortified themselves on a branch of Hoosick river, and were attacked according to a plan adopted by a council of war, which was designed to take them in the rear of both flanks, while an advance was made on their front to occupy their attention. Colonel Nichols, with two hundred men, marched for their left—Colonel Herrick, with three hundred, for their right; while one hundred men marched toward the centre of their line, and two hundred more, under Colonels Hubbard and Stickney, marched against the right. The first two detachments were to unite in the enemy's rear, and then fall upon them together. The Indians fled at the onset, but the rest of the enemy's troops stood their ground for two hours, when, after an unsuccessful attempt by the German dragoons to cut their way through with their swords, all their works were carried, and the whole body, with but few exceptions, were either killed or taken prisoners. Baum received a mortal wound.

The victory was so complete, that the Americans, supposing all was over, began to disperse, when General Stark was apprized of another large force approaching in front. Happily, Colonel Warner arrived at the moment with a reinforcement of Vermont regulars, who, without loss of time, pressed on to encounter the enemy; General Stark soon followed, with all the militia he could muster; and an obstinate engagement ensued, which terminated at sunset, by the rout and pursuit of the invaders. The approach of darkness alone saved the greater part of the fugitives, who left behind two cannon and many wounded and prisoners.

The whole amount of the enemy's loss in these actions was two hundred and seven killed, an unknown number wounded, and about seven hundred prisoners; four brass fieldpieces, twelve base-drums, two hundred and fifty dragoon swords, and four ammunition wagons. The American loss was only thirty killed and forty wounded.

The principal advantage secured by this victory, however, was in the courage with which it inspired the army and the people, who had been exceedingly depressed by the evacuation of the fortress of Ticonderoga, and the undisputed progress of Burgoyne onward toward Albany. The resistance which he met with, a few days after, at Bemis's heights, on the west bank of the Hudson, is supposed to have been rendered more spirited and successful by this great advantage, gained by the Vermont regulars and irregular troops, assisted by their bold and hardy neighbors.

The supreme court has five judges, annually chosen by the legislature. The county courts, likewise, have the same number, two being chosen by the legislature every year in each county, the third and chief being one of the supreme judges on the circuit. The county courts are held twice a year. The justices of the peace, also, are appointed by the legislature.

The first newspaper in Vermont was the "Vermont Gazette, or Green Mountain Newsboy," published at Westminster in 1781 by Judah Paddock Spooner and Timothy Green. Two years after, their press was removed to Windsor. In 1810, the number of newspapers in the state was ten; in 1828, twenty-one; and in 1834, twenty-six.

The Battle of Plattsburgh.—This was one of the most decisive and important engagements in the war of 1812; and like several others which we have noticed, although not fought on the soil of Vermont, was one in which many of the people of this state were engaged, and in the results of which multitudes of them were personally and most deeply interested. Having given the particulars of the naval battle of the same date in our description of New York, and not having had space for the following account of the battle on land, we may with propriety introduce it in this place.

Three points of our extensive country appeared to the English to be fatally vulnerable. First, the outlet of the Mississippi, against which Pakenham was to lead an army of veterans; second, Washington—**the** seat of government—where in August, 1814, General Ross, at the head of his victorious legions, spread fire and sword; and lastly, Lake Champlain—the great highway of invasion to the most densely-populated portion of the Union—where Sir George Provost, renowned for skill and valor on many a battle-field, was to lead the largest division of the formidable troops of Wellington.

On the 4th September, 14,000 troops, with their splendid uniform, and faultless discipline, and admirable bands, and waving banners, and formidable trains of artillery, having crossed the lines and marshalled at Champlain, took up their line of march for Plattsburgh. There was one regiment of these veterans, in which there was scarcely a man who did not bear a wound, and their disfigured faces, and ferocious and determined aspect, reminded one of the hundred desperate charges of the sanguinary conflicts of the peninsular war.

At Plattsburgh about one thousand regular soldiers under the command of General M'Comb, and some seven hundred militia under General Moore, were prepared to oppose the enemy. The nation, saddened and oppressed by the then recent sacking of Washington, and aware of the tremendous force of her formidable foe, looked with deep anxiety and alarm to the issue of the contest at this important point.

On Monday, September 5, 1814, the British army having advanced to Chazy and found the state-road guarded by Colonel Appling's rifle corps intrenched at Dead creek, aided by a troop of horse commanded by Captain Safford and Lieutenant Standish, they crossed to the Beekmantown road, and encamped during the night three or four miles north of the Burdick house at Beekmantown. The militia commanded by General Moore, and composed of Colonel Miller's regiment, a part of Colonel Joiner's regiment, Major Sanford's battalion, and the thirty-seventh regiment, from Essex, spent the night at Beekmantown. Between 9 and 10 o'clock at night, General Moore sent Major R. H. Walworth to the quarters of General M'Comb, who commanded at the forts, with a request that he would send a small body of infantry and a couple of pieces of light artillery, to support the militia in the attack which he intended to make on the British forces on their advance in the morning. Major Walworth arrived at General M'Comb's quarters about midnight, and the general immediately ordered a detachment of two hundred and fifty infantry under Major John E. Wool, who had previously and urgently requested such a command, and two pieces of light artillery under Captain Luther Leonard, to be ready by daylight to start for Beekmantown.

Major Walworth took a party of volunteers from Captain Atwood's company and those of Captains Cochran and Manley, marched rapidly on the bridge, and had just commenced taking off the plank, when the advanced guard of the enemy emerged from the woods within half musket-shot, and fired upon the party taking up the bridge, two of whom, belonging to Atwood's company, were severely wounded and taken prisoners.

Major Walworth and his detachment immediately fell back to the position occupied by Major Wool, who, forming in the highway and flanked by the militia, opened a deadly fire upon the head of the British column, then just in front of Ira Howe's house, and momentarily arrested its progress. Here several of the enemy were killed, and Lieutenant West, of the Buffs, and twenty privates, severely wounded. Very soon the militia broke and mostly retreated in confusion. Many, however, remained with the regulars to contest the ground, inch by inch, and retreat in order.

Meanwhile, General Moore, with the aid of other officers, had succeeded in rallying a portion of the militia, which, being ordered to join Major Wool with his detachment, awaited the approach of the enemy at Culver's hill, about four miles from Plattsburgh. This commanding position was maintained with so much obstinacy as to compel the enemy, after attaining the summit of the hill, to retire to its base with the loss of Lieutenant-Colonel Wellington, who fell while gallantly leading the Third Buffs to the charge. Here, also, Ensign Chapman fell, and Captain Westroff, of the thirty-eighth British regiment, was severely wounded; and here several of Major Wool's men, and Patridge of the Essex militia, were killed. Nor was this position abandoned by Major Wool, until after he had received notice from General Moore that a column of 2,000 of the enemy, advancing on the west Beekmantown road, was gaining on his rear; when the Vermont troops fell back within two miles of Plattsburg. Here Captain Leonard, with two pieces of light artillery, despatched by General M'Comb, arrived to take part in the action; and the fire of the artillery, the regular infantry, and a portion of the militia, literally mowed down the enemy's advancing column.

In front of an overwhelming force, platoon after platoon delivered their fire, and fell back to load and form, in regular succession, contesting every inch of ground, and seizing every favorable point to unlimber their artillery and pour a deadly shower of grape upon the advancing enemy. After repeated contests they were driven across the river, the bridges were taken up in the retreat, a final stand was made on the southern bank of the Saranac, and the enemy driven back beyond the reach of our guns. Forty-five of our men were killed in the retreat; the British had one lieutenant-colonel, two captains, four lieutenants, and more than two hundred men, killed or wounded. Next morning the British, in attempting to cross the river a few miles west of the village, were repulsed by Capt. Vaughan. The enemy were occupied, the four succeeding days, in erecting batteries to play upon the forts, during which there were frequent skirmishes along the river; the gallant Green mountain boys, under the patriotic General Strong, were wafted to our aid by every eastern breeze, swelling our force to upward of three thousand. On the evening of the 9th, one hundred and fifty of our men crossed the Saranac, stormed and took, at the point of the bayonet, a battery defended by four hundred of the enemy, spiked the guns, and made good their retreat, without the loss of a single man. The battle of Beekmantown, the spirited resistance to the enemy's advance, and the burning of the courthouse, &c., north of the river by the hot shot from our batteries, prevented an immediate attack upon the forts, to resist which would have been fruitless.

VIEW OF THE CITY OF BOSTON.

Landing of the Pilgrims.

MASSACHUSETTS.

This state, occupying a leading position among the six eastern members of the Union, in extent, commerce, manufactures, wealth, and population, borders on Maine, New Hampshire, and Vermont, on the north, and Rhode Island and Connecticut on the south; while it is bounded on the east by the Atlantic, and on the west by New York. With the exception of the seacoast, the boundaries of Massachusetts are almost entirely artificial; and, when we cast our eyes over the map, we can discover none of those natural advantages which distinguish most other countries remarkable for prosperity. Massachusetts is a portion of the western continent containing no mines of gold, no long navigable rivers, no broad and fertile plains, not even an accessible supply of timber; and a person unacquainted with the true source of her power and wealth would be at a loss in seeking for it. "A land of hills, and valleys, and fountains of water," as the early explorers represented her, in their favorite scripture language, they had little else to say in praise of the natural features of the country. The coast presents a line of inhospitable rocks and reaches of sterile sand, and the approach is rendered difficult and dangerous by a broad tract of shoals, through which a ship can find its way only by pursuing narrow and intricate channels, by careful sounding.

Harbors.—Massachusetts is distinguished by the number and excellence of her harbors, which will very naturally secure to her a large part of the entire commerce of New England, with the exception of Maine, Rhode Island, and Connecticut.

SHOALS.—Nantucket shoals line the coast for fifty miles, and are forty-five miles in breadth. They are very dangerous, being cut through by numerous channels of different depths, discoverable only by sounding.

ISLANDS.—Several islands of considerable size belong to this state, so situated, and so well provided with headlands for lighthouses, and with harbors for shelter in storms, as to be of important service to the extensive coasting and foreign trade—especially such as are in the vicinity of the shoals.

Nantucket Island is fifteen miles by eleven, and forms, with five smaller islands, a county of the same name. It contains nearly thirty thousand acres. Its inhabitants have long been proverbial for their skill in whalefishing, which was formerly carried on in boats in sight of the shore. They are equally distinguished by their skill and boldness as pilots, many of them spending a considerable part of their lives in sailing about the shoals to pilot ships. The island is thirty miles south of the mainland, sixty southeast of New Bedford, and one hundred south-southeast of Boston. Latitude 41° 15′ 22″, longitude 70° 7′ 56″.

Martha's Vineyard is twenty miles long and from two to five miles broad and lies west of Nantucket. Duke's county is formed of this island and several small ones in its vicinity.

The first settlements were made at Plymouth by the passengers in the May-Flower, the first band of English dissenters, called puritans, who arrived in America. They reached Cape Cod on the 22d of December, 1620, and, after a few days, fixed on Plymouth for their residence, which received its name from the last port in England from which they had sailed. The important consequences which resulted from the arrival of this little band of exiles have invested it with peculiar interest; and the event and its concomitants have been commemorated in numerous writings.

The puritans received this title in derision. They had long been the chief advocates of principles which have since become extensively adopted in this country and elsewhere, particularly civil and religious freedom, and the universal diffusion of learning. Numbers of them had taken refuge in Holland from the persecution they were exposed to in their native land, from the laws which then forbade them to worship God in their chosen manner. But, although treated with kindness by the Dutch protestants, they at length determined to seek a country in which they might rear their children, without exposing them to evil influences or to the loss of their native language. A band of them at length proceeded to England, accompanied by their pastor, the Rev. Mr. Robinson, where, arrangements having been made, after some delay they sailed for America. The part of the coast on which they were landed was farther north than they had intended to reach; but this was probably, in the end, more favorable for their success. The Indians had been almost all destroyed by a fatal disease, so that they found but little opposition among the natives for some years.

The Plymouth colony was followed by several others. Salem was planted in 1628, and Boston in 1630. Most of the settlers being of the same class, a uniform system of laws and habits was established, which was gradually extended, and most of the peculiarities of New England still retain the same character.

These first colonies were the sources or the channels from which the settletlements on the Connecticut, and many of those in New Hampshire and Vermont, derived their impulse and their population, and there we find a general identity of sentiment and society.

The first period in the history of Massachusetts is that between the first settlement and the Pequod war, in 1636, when Rhode Island and Connecticut river had been occupied and exposed to powerful tribes of savages, against whom Massachusetts afforded them aid. Then commenced that active system of mutual support, which often secured the safety of the eastern colonies, and gradually extended to all the colonies from England, and resulted in forming the United States.

View of Boston, in 1776, taken from the road to Dorchester

The second period extends to Philip's war, in 1675, when Massachusetts had several towns on Connecticut river, and had an extensive region to protect at home from a powerful savage combination. The third period may be limited by the close of the last French war, in 1759, when the capture of Canada by the British put an end to the long and disastrous hostilities of France upon the frontiers of the colonies. The fourth period extends to the close of the revolution, and the fifth to the present day.

Early Missions among the Indians.—Rev. John Eliot began to preach to the Indians near Boston in 1646. In 1650 the English "society for the propagation of the gospel in foreign parts," opened a correspondence with the commissioners of the United colonies, and appointed them their agents. Eliot (the apostle to the Indians, as he is often called) had, ere this, been so far successful in his exertions as to feel encouragement, and to inspire the benevolent with hope. He continued his labors several years without reward or expectation of payment; but afterward receiving contributions from gentlemen in England, he was enabled to extend his operations, and to educate his sons at college, the eldest of whom afterward preached to the natives. By his example several other clergymen in the country were encouraged to adopt similar measures. Mr. Bourne and Mr. Cotton acquired the Indian language to qualify them for the task, and preached at Martha's Vineyard, &c.; Mr. Mayhew and his son preached at that island and at Nantucket; while Messrs. Pierson and Fitch followed their example in Connecticut.

Eliot published his Indian translation of the New Testament in 1661, and the whole Bible soon after. The printing was done at the expense of the society for the propagation of the gospel. He prepared also translations of Baxter's Call, psalms, hymns, &c., and composed several works for use in the schools which he established in the Indian villages. Some of the youth were sent to learn Latin and Greek. Several Indian towns were constituted by Massachusetts, and courts established in them, each with one English judge, while other officers were all chosen by the natives.

The first Indian church was formed in 1670, at Natick; the second at Pakemit, now Stoughton, whose first native teacher was named Ahawton. The other Christian or praying towns in the Indian country were the following: Okommakummessit, now Marlborough; Wamesit, now Tewksbury; Nashobah, now Littleton; Mungunkook, now Hopkinton; and there were others in Oxford, Dudley, Worcester, and Uxbridge, and three in Woodstock.

The gospel was thus early made known to the Indians; many of them received it, and it immediately began to produce its natural effects, by introducing civilization with many of its advantages. The people became fixed in their habits and residences, attended to agriculture, began to acquire learning, erected more substantial habitations, and pursued the arts.

In Plymouth colony the success of the early efforts of missionaries among the natives was still more remarkable. About five hundred Indians on Cape Cod, under the care of the Rev. Mr. Bourne, made rapid improvement. About two hundred soon learned to read, and more than seventy to write, and there was a church with twenty-seven communicants, with the Mayhews, at Martha's Vineyard.

PRINTING.—The Rev. Jesse Glover, an English dissenting clergymen, has been called the father of the American press. He embarked for New England in 1638, with his family, and a printing-press which he had purchased with money contributed by himself and his friends, accompanied by a printer, Stephen Daye, whom he had hired. Mr. Glover died on the passage; but the magistrates and elders of Massachusetts encouraged Daye to put the press in operation at Cambridge, where the new-comers took up their residences. In January, 1639, he printed the Freeman's Oath, an almanac, and the Psalms in metre. His first successor, Samuel Green, began to print in 1649, and died in 1702. He had nineteen children, and many of his descendants have been printers.

Government.—The legislative power is vested in a senate and house of representatives, which together are styled *the General Court of Massachusetts.*

The senate consists of forty members, who are chosen annually by the people, by districts, according to population.

The house of representatives consists of members chosen annually by the cities and towns, according to population, every town having 300 ratable polls electing a representative, and for every 450 more, one additional representative. Any town having less than 300 polls, to be represented as many years within ten years, as 300 is contained in the product of the number of polls in said town, multiplied by ten.

The governor is elected annually by the people, and at the same time a lieutenant-governor is chosen.

The governor is assisted in the executive department, particularly in appointments to office, by a council of nine members, who are chosen by the joint ballot of the senators and representatives, from the people.

The judiciary is vested in a supreme court, a court of common pleas, and such other courts as the legislature may establish. The judges are appointed by the governor, by and with the advice and consent of the council, and hold their offices during good behavior.

The right of suffrage is granted to every male citizen twenty-one years of age and upward (excepting paupers and persons under guardianship), who has resided within the commonwealth one year, and within the town or district in which he may claim a right to vote, six months preceding any election, and who has paid a state or county tax.

Railroads.—There are completed and in full operation within the borders of the state of Massachusetts more than twelve hundred miles of railroads. During the year 1850, nearly ten millions of passengers passed over these roads which also transported two and a half millions of tons of freights.—But these many lines of railroad have more than an interior benefit for the state. In conjunction with other railroads beyond the state limits and steam navigation, the city of Boston is connected with thirteen states of the Union, thus introducing the metropolis of the state to a commercial sphere of the utmost importance. The people of Massachusetts have shown a remarkable foresight, energy, and perseverance, in the projection and construction of roads within their own, and in the subscription to the stock of others, in contiguous states, the ultimate benefit of which can scarcely be over-estimated. The money thus appropriated amounts, in the aggregate, to over fifty millions of dollars.

Education.—Common schools were established by law very soon after the foundation of the colony of Massachusetts Bay; and parents, guardians, &c., were required to have their children and wards instructed. Every larger village and town was to have a grammar-school. Education, at least in the rudiments of learning, has always been universal in this state; and the influence of Massachusetts in extending and sustaining institutions of learning in other parts of the country has been great, and not less creditable to her citizens than beneficial to their fellow-citizens of the Union. In the recent improvements in common schools, and some other means of diffusing knowledge, she has been one of the most efficient states; and many of the measures approved and practised by the intelligent friends of learning have been devised or brought into use, or most early or effectually put into practice, within her boundaries. Yet Massachusetts, until 1835, has never had a school fund, and her common schools were wholly supported by the people. A fund was then provided for, limited to one million of dollars.

Every town or district containing fifty families is required to have a school kept at least six months in the year; or, if several schools exist, they shall be kept long enough to equal one school for six months. For those containing one hundred families the requisition is doubled; and for those containing one hundred and fifty families, eighteen months are required.

Massachusetts is therefore justly entitled to a large share of the credit of having given an impulse to the cause of POPULAR EDUCATION. The early settlers of that section of our country were fully sensible of the defects of the English institutions which they had forsaken. That the schools of learning and religion were corrupted, and the fairest hopes overthrown by licentious behavior in those seminaries, was one among the many causes of their emigration from the Old World, and of pledging themselves to the education of their children. In the year 1668, a document was published by order of the government and council of Massachusetts, and addressed to the elders and ministers of every town, in which paper was set forth an earnest desire for the moral and religious instruction of the people, and an appeal to those to whom the instrument was directed, to examine whether the education of youth in the English language was attended to. From the time of the Winthrops and their associates, who labored zealously in this field of usefulness, to the present period, New England has devoted her attention to the promotion of knowledge; and in the industry, integrity, and frugality of her children, now beholds the brilliant results of her perseverance. When we consider that the tide of immigration, which is sweeping before it the forests of the west, takes its rise in the eastern section of the United States, and bears upon its bosom the elements of enrichment—that it is composed, in a great degree, of those who have been enabled to obtain there the rudiments of learning, the first principles of valuable information—ought we not to be grateful to those who have toiled and are still doing all that lies in their power to render the fountain pure and transparent?

Too much can not be done in arousing public opinion on the subject of the education of children. Let the instruction of a child be considered the paramount duty of a good citizen, and then public sentiment will act much more powerfully to produce the results desired than the staff of the officer of police. Public opinion is the best balance-wheel of the machinery of a society constituted as that is in which we live. It must be by promulgating among the people the sentiment of the necessity of education—by arousing their attention to its value—by demonstrating its beneficial results, as not only the best check on the increase of crime, the prevention of pauperism, but also the promoter of public order and private happiness—that we can hope to have education generally diffused. So soon as the people are convinced, we shall have the brilliant object which all should desire to see effected. To produce great results, must be the work of time. The past labors of the people are the best evidences of their devotion to the advancement of learning, and give great hope that the system of education will be laid with a broad and deep foundation, on which the pyramid of the republic's glory and security may rise, and remain an imperishable monument of the benevolence and wisdom of her citizens.

In connexion, however, with the above, we most unhesitatingly assert that mere intellectual improvement is not, or should not be, the exclusive or even the primary object of EDUCATION. Moral and religious principles are infinitely more momentous to the character and interests of the future man than the cultivation of the mind alone, whether we look to the individual himself, or to the influence which he will hereafter exercise upon society. The talented and accomplished scholar may shine in public and social life—may astonish by the depth of his erudition, charm by the graces of his eloquence, or dazzle by the coruscations of his wit; but the truly moral and virtuous man—THE MAN OF PRINCIPLE ONLY—is the centre around which domestic felicity revolves; he only contributes to the real and enduring benefit of society, and his own near and dear connexions. Contemplated in this aspect (and few, we think, will refuse thus to contemplate it), the morality which may be learned from any system of religious opinions that professes to take the Bible for its basis, deserves to be estimated far more highly than even the most extensive acquirements and splendid abilities, if uncontrolled by those motives and principles of action which alone can direct them to the production of solid and abiding advantage. Devoid of these principles, they have been almost invariably found, like sharp and polished weapons in the hands of a lunatic, to inflict a mortal wound upon the possessor, and strike deep at the best interests of society.

"A people, to be truly free, must first be wise and good." This is truly an admirable maxim, and so evident as not to admit of doubt, even if it had not been long since fully demonstrated in the annals of the past. Education is the groundwork of national freedom and civilization —the foundation on which have originated the great and essential improvements of agriculture, the mechanical branches, and the pursuits of science—the main pillars which constitute a nation's power and character. These and the fine arts, which polish and adorn the whole—the beauties of nature, eloquence, and science, with all the social endearments, which refine and embellish society—as well as the higher and more sublime character of those moral and political institutions, which bind together and direct the whole,—are all the effects of that strength and intelligence which education has imparted to the human mind. And when we consider that *ignorance* is the grand cause of vice and crime among the poor—that it contributes to their moral debasement and misery, excluding them from the enjoyment of all rational delight—confining their pastimes and pleasures to mere feats of strength and inebriating hilarity—and how it prevents the mind from expanding for the reception of virtue and morality—we can not but rejoice at the success of all plans for illuminating this darkness, and respect the names and memories of those great and good men who have contributed so largely and freely of their time, influence, and earthly substance, to extend the blessing of a sound and religious education to every son and daughter within the reach of their influence.

Many of the most eminent men of the state and nation were natives or long citizens of Boston. The early clergymen were Cotton, Wilson, the Mathers, Oxenbridge, Norton, Allen, Davenport, Willard, Coleman, Prince, the Eliots, Byles, Thacher, Wadsworth, Pemberton, Callender, Sewall, Cooper, Checkley, Mayhew, Gee, Walter, Condy, Stillman, Chauncey, Lathrop, Howard, West, Belknap, Parker, Everett, Kirkland, Emerson, Buckminster, and Channing. They were eminent scholars, as well as able theologians. We have only room for a few of the distinguished laymen of early times. These were Winthrop, Bellingham, Leverett, Stoughton, Cheever, Bulkley, Dummer, Cook, Brattle, the Sewalls, Belcher, Oliver; and in later periods, Otis, Bowdoin, Samuel Adams, Gridley, Joseph Warren, John Hancock, Richard Dana, Governor Hutchinson, Thacher, Sears, Quincy, Mason, &c. Of these latter individuals especially, many of them made great exertions, and suffered much in various ways, during the war of the Revolution. Several of them were opulent merchants, and they loaned largely of their money to the government for its support. During that period not only was the commerce of this ancient metropolis long suspended and greatly injured, but many of its public and private buildings destroyed. It furnished great numbers of men in various ways in the service of the country; they were obliged to be constantly under arms in times of danger and apprehension. The citizens of all classes—the merchants and mechanics, and the professional men—were zealous advocates of the Federal Constitution in 1788, and afterward the firm supporters of the administrations of Washington and Adams. We learn, from a series of articles, prepared and published by EDWIN WILLIAMS, Esq., of New York, that "the honor of originating a suggestion which afterward led to the organization of the old Continental Congress, and prepared the way for the independence of these United States, was due to the name of SEARS."*

* Colonel ISAAC SEARS, the distinguished character here alluded to, was the originator and leader of the "Sons of Liberty" at the opening of the American Revolution. He seems for a time to have represented the spirit of that revolution more fully than any other person in the city and vicinity of New York. His life has never been written, which, including the doings of the "Liberty Boys," is an interesting and unexplored province of our revolutionary annals. He is often referred to in the correspondence of Washington, Gouverneur Morris, and Messrs. Adams, as

These illustrious worthies of a past age being dead, yet speak to us. We do well to hallow their memories and record their noble deeds. Interesting associations cluster around these great actors in the drama of THE PAST. They belong to the nation; for not the old states merely, but those which sprang into being but yesterday, look upon the glory of the Revolution as a common patrimony. This nation must ever be sensible of the worth of its benefactors, and real merit will soon dissipate the mists of party prejudice. Its effect, like that of a very strong sympathetic feeling running through the people, must be to knit more closely the bonds of national union. It has given freshness to the memory of common efforts in the great national struggle, which must always prove a powerful tie among men who exult in the achievements of a common ancestry. It may have furnished some incense to the vanity imputed to our nation; but this is as dust in the balance compared with the spirit which it indicates and the feelings which it has awakened. Here we may learn useful lessons for the future, from the history of the past.

Let us follow these distinguished men to "old age;" when Nature seemed to demand repose, each had retired to the spot from which the public exigencies had first called him—his public labors ended, his work accomplished, his beloved country prosperous and happy—there to indulge in the blessed retrospect of a well-spent life, and to await that period which comes to all. Did they pass their time in idleness and indifference? No. The same spirit of active benevolence, which made the meridian of their lives resplendent with glory, continued to shed its lustre upon their evening path. Still intent on DOING GOOD, still devoted to the great cause of human happiness and improvement, none of these illustrious men relaxed in their exertions. They seemed only to concentrate their energy as age and increasing infirmity contracted the circle of action—bestowing, without ostentation, their latest efforts upon the state and neighborhood in which they resided. There, with patriarchal simplicity, they lived, the objects of a nation's grateful remembrance and affection—the living records of a nation's history; the charm of an age which they delighted, adorned, and instructed, by their deeds of benevolence, and vivid sketches of times that are past; and, as it were, the embodied spirit of the Revolution itself, in all its purity and force, diffusing its wholesome influence through the generations that have succeeded, rebuking every sinister design, and invigorating every manly and virtuous resolution.

We can not set in too strong a light their history. It awakens the public gratitude for their services; it tells their countrymen to be faithful to their principles, and vigilant in preserving those institutions free and unimpaired, to attain which they sacrificed their ease and safety. These eulogies are in fact the people's testimony to the excellence of our form of government. The veneration paid to such men as ADAMS and JEFFERSON is an acknowledgment of the worth of the political principles which they labored to establish. And when the kingdoms of the Old World are tottering to their foundations, what can be more proper or grateful than the sight of a whole people uniting to testify their love for the government under which they live? In other countries, one half of the nation is employed in preventing the other from pulling the political machine to pieces. HERE, ALL ARE UNITED TO UPHOLD IT.

Of the present distinguished, patriotic, and benevolent citizens of Boston, a long list might be here given, and then not all be mentioned. It has been remarked, and with great truthfulness, that the liberality of her rich men is proverbial from Maine to Missouri, and has secured for that city a name which, we trust, future generations will not only respect, but endeavor to add to its lustre, by imitating such men as the LAWRENCES, DAVID SEARS, the APPLETONS, THOMAS H PER-

rendering important services to the colonies, and is named in the journals of those times as a brave and heroic character. The materials of his biography are yet extant in public and private documents in the city and state of New York, and ought to be collected and preserved, as important sources of history.

Residence of John Hancock, Boston.

KINS, and a host of others, whose coffers are not closed, but who are constantly contributing, by their princely individual donations of ten and twenty thousand dollars, to undertakings of philanthropy and charity—encouraging talent, promoting industry, and fostering the fine arts; thus setting a most noble example to the wealthy of other cities which we could wish more generally imitated. Since the year 1800, over THREE MILLIONS OF DOLLARS have been given in munificent gifts by the citizens of Boston to the cause of education alone.

The first settlers of New England were exceedingly tenacious of their civil and religious rights, and they well knew that KNOWLEDGE was an all-powerful engine to preserve those rights, and transmit them to their posterity. They therefore very early laid the foundation of those FREE SCHOOLS of which all the sons and daughters of New England are so justly proud. Exclusive of infant and sabbath school children, about a quarter part of the population of Boston is kept at school throughout the year, at an annual expense of about two hundred thousand dollars.

Their successors have nobly imitated their bright and patriotic example. Such men are indeed the fathers of the nation, and must ever live in the affections of the people. When time has consigned them to their honored graves, the good they have done will live after them. Future generations will rise up and call them blessed. Their names will fill a niche in the temple erected in every one's memory, to commemorate those who, as they passed along the pathway of life, scattered the seeds of knowledge and morality, which have taken root, sprung up, bearing the most delectable fruits, agreeable to the sight, and of pleasant flavor.

Williams College, at Williamstown, Berkshire county, in the northwest corner of the state, was a public school or academy at its commencement, in 1791, and was incorporated as a college in 1793. It derives its name from its founder, Colonel Ephraim Williams. Besides donations from the state and several individuals, it has received a bequest of fifty-seven thousand dollars from Mr. Woodbridge Little. It is under the charge of seventeen trustees.

The *Newton Theological Seminary*, under the patronage of the baptist denomination, was founded in Newton in 1825, and was incorporated by the legislature the next year. In 1828, a brick building, three stories in height, besides a basement story, eighty-five feet long and forty-nine wide, was erected, at an expense of about ten thousand dollars. Three convenient houses have been since erected for the professors. In the mansion-house are accommodations for the steward's family, a dining-hall, a chapel, and recitation-rooms. The regular course of study occupies three years. There are two vacations of six weeks each—one from the last Wednesday but one in August, the other from the last Wednesday in March. The seminary is about seven miles from Boston, in a very salubrious locality, being beautifully situated on an elevated hill, which commands an extensive prospect of Boston and of the rich country around.

CAMBRIDGE UNIVERSITY.—This institution, which is the oldest in the Union, and the most liberally endowed, was commenced in 1636 by the general court of Massachusetts, who then appropriated four hundred pounds sterling toward the establishment of a college, which was incorporated in 1638, under the title of "Harvard College," in consequence of a legacy left it that year, by Rev. JOHN HARVARD, of £779 17*s.* 2*d.* The state and different liberal donors have since increased its funds to a large amount.

It is situated in the city of Cambridge, three miles west from Boston, and comprises an academical department, as well as those of law, theology, science, and medicine. Each of these five departments is distinct in itself, with its own particular government and body of instructors, each having its separate funds, its own pupils, and its peculiar objects, but all subject to one supreme head.

The buildings of the university are fourteen in Cambridge and one in Boston. Four of the principal buildings are of four stories, for the accommodation of students; two others contain the min-

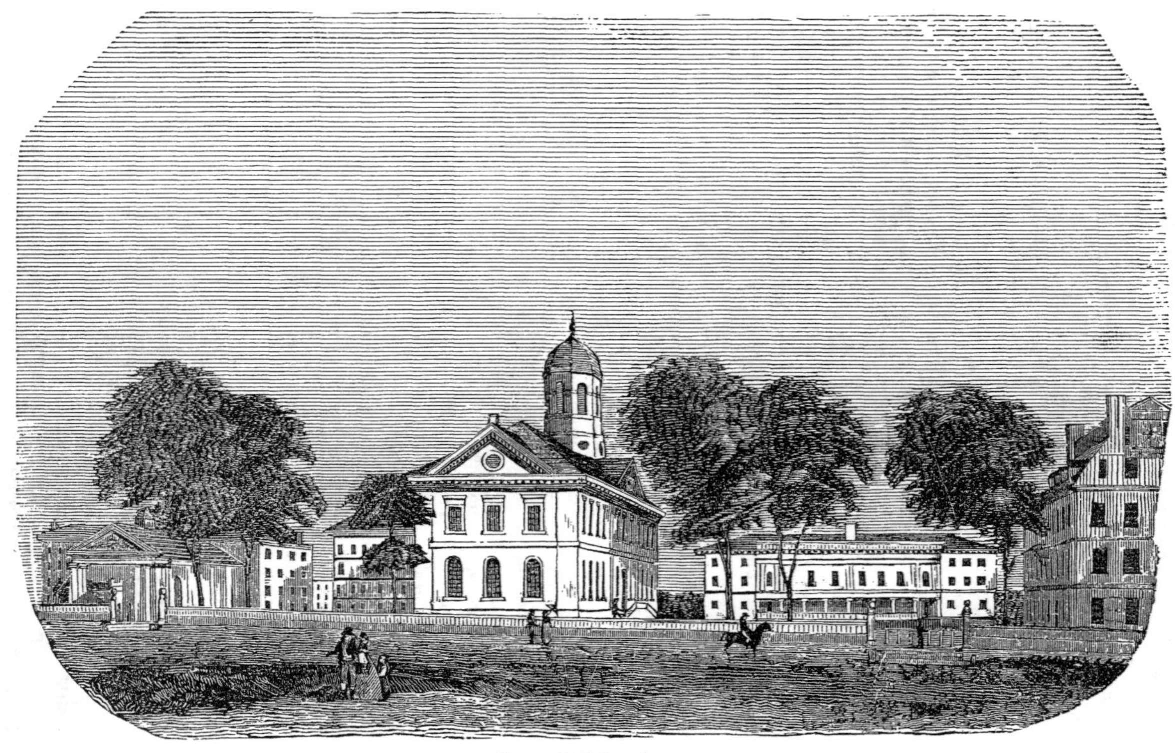

Harvard University

eralogical cabinet, the library, the chapels, &c. Besides these are the halls of law, divinity, medicine, &c. It has an excellent anatomical museum, and a botanical garden of eight acres, richly stored with an extensive collection of trees, shrubs, and plants, both native and foreign. The libraries contain above forty thousand volumes, including those of the several departments. Those belonging to the studies contain about five thousand volumes. The cabinets and apparatus are very valuable. The annual commencement is on the third Wednesday in July.

Cambridge Observatory.—This observatory is situated on a commanding eminence called Summer-house hill, the summit of which is about fifty feet above the plain on which are erected the buildings of the university. This height is found to give from the dome an horizon almost uninterrupted to within two or three degrees of altitude. The grounds appropriated to the use of the observatory comprise about six and a half acres. It is distant nearly three fourths of a mile northwest from University hall, and three and a half miles in the same direction from the statehouse in Boston.

This observatory may be said to owe its existence to the liberality of the Hon. DAVID SEARS, who contributed five thousand dollars for the erection of an observatory tower, five hundred dollars toward the purchase of a telescope, and five thousand dollars more to create a fund, the income of which to be appropriated to the support of the observers, and for other purposes of science.

SEARS TOWER, so called in honor of its founder, whose generous donation is mentioned above, is built of brick, on a foundation of granite, laid with cement. It is thirty-two feet square on the outside, while on the inside the corners are gradually brought to a circular form for the better support of the dome, forming a massive arch. This dome, covering the grand equatorial, is a hemisphere of thirty-two feet interior diameter, formed with stout ribs of plank, and covered externally with copper. There is an opening five feet wide, and extending a few degrees beyond the zenith, which is closed by weather-proof shutters, and worked by means of an endless chain and toothed wheel.

On the lower side of this dome is affixed a grooved iron rail, and on the granite cap of the wall is placed a similar rail: between these grooves are placed eight iron spheres, accurately turned, on which the dome is revolved. The apparatus for moving the dome consists of toothed wheels, geared to a series of toothed iron plates, fastened to its lower section. By means of this, the whole dome, weighing about fourteen tons, can be turned through a whole revolution, by a single person, in thirty-five seconds. In this dome are placed the "Grand Refractor," and one or two smaller instruments. The comet-seeker, a small instrument of four inches' aperture, by Merz, is used from the balconies of the dome. This is the instrument with which the younger Bond has discovered no less than eleven telescopic comets before intelligence had reached him of their having been seen by any other observer. From these balconies a most extensive and beautiful view of the neighboring towns meets the eye—their numerous hills, spires, &c.

On either side of the tower is a large wing. Of these, the eastern is used as a dwelling for the observer; the western, on which is placed the smaller dome, is used for magnetic and meteorological observations. This wing was erected in the years 1850–'51, and adds greatly to the architectural beauty of the observatory. In this dome is placed the smaller equatorial, of five feet focal length, and an object-glass of four and one eighth inches, made by Merz, which is a remarkably fine instrument.

The "Grand Refractor," justly considered second to none in the world, has already become celebrated in the hands of the skilful and scientific director and his assistant, from the many brilliant discoveries which have been made with it. Among these we may particularly mention the new ring and satellite of the planet Saturn. It has also enabled the observers to resolve the principal nebulæ, particularly those in the constellations Orion and Andromeda. The object-glass

Cambridge Observatory, with the Sears Tower.

Grand Refractor, Cambridge Observatory.

was made at the celebrated manufactory of Merz and Mahler, in Munich, Bavaria. Its extreme diameter is fifteen and a half inches, its focal length is twenty-two feet six inches, and its total weight is nearly three tons; yet the friction is so successfuly relieved by the judicious arrangement of wheels and counterpoises, that it could be pointed to any quarter of the heavens by the finger of a child.

A sidereal motion is communicated to the telescope by clock-work, by means of which an object may be constantly kept in the field of view, which essentially aids the observer in delicate examinations of celestial objects.

Besides the grand refractor, the object-glass, &c., the observatory is furnished with many smaller instruments, and a complete set of meteorological instruments, an astronomical clock, and sidereal chronometers.

One of the most ingenious contrivances connected with the observatory is the "observer's chair," invented by the director. By means of this chair, the observer can transport himself to any part of the dome without moving from his seat.

The new method of finding the motion of the earth, by means of a pendulum, has been tried at the observatory, and also by Professor Horsford, at the Lawrence Scientific School.

Lawrence Scientific School.—Practical instruction in the mathematical, physical, and natural sciences, upon a more extended plan than that pursued in the undergraduate department of Harvard, had been a subject of discussion previous to the time of President Everett. In his inaugural address, however, the project of a separate scientific school received its first distinct announcement. About

Lawrence Scientific School, at Cambridge.

this time a vacancy occurred in the Rumford professorship by the resignation of Professor Treadwell. The situation was filled by the election of Professor Horsford, of New York, who soon after his arrival in Cambridge submitted to the corporation a plan for the erection and furnishing of a laboratory for instruction in chymistry and its applications to the arts, contemplating an expense of fifty thousand dollars. This plan, in an able letter from the treasurer, Hon. Samuel A. Eliot, was laid before Hon. Abbott Lawrence.

To this appeal Mr. Lawrence responded in a spirit of munificence altogether unexampled. The gift (of fifty thousand dollars) was accompanied by a letter, proposing, in addition to the erection of suitable buildings, including a laboratory, to found two new professorships, one of zoology and geology, and another of engineering, which, with the Rumford professorships, were to constitute the nucleus of a school for the "acquisition, illustration, and dissemination of the practical sciences."

Soon after the receipt of the donation of Mr. Lawrence, Professor Agassiz, of Switzerland, was invited to the chair of zoology and geology, and at a later period Lieutenant Eustis (of the army) to that of engineering. At the commencement of 1848, the corporation conferred upon the institution the name of "LAWRENCE SCIENTIFIC SCHOOL."

In the summer and autumn of 1849, a laboratory, unsurpassed even in Europe, in its conveniences for practical instruction, was erected and furnished; and in the year following a building was constructed for the temporary accommodation of the departments of zoology, geology, and engineering.

The *Andover Theological Academy* was the first institution of the kind in the country. It was commenced in 1808, having been founded the year before. It is situated in Andover, a pleasant village, in a fine, elevated tract of country, nineteen miles northwest of Boston. The value of the property belonging to it has been stated at four hundred thousand dollars, for which it has been largely indebted to the liberality of its principal donors, namely, John Norris, of Salem; Samuel Abbott, of Andover; and Moses Brown and William Bartlett of Newburyport.

The buildings of the institution consist of a dwelling-house for each of the professors; Phillips hall, of brick, ninety feet by forty, four stories, containing thirty-two rooms for students, built in

1808; Bartlet chapel, an elegant brick building, ninety-four feet by forty, containing a chapel, library, and three lecture-rooms, built in 1818; and Bartlet hall, a handsome brick edifice, one hundred and four feet by forty, containing thirty-two suites of rooms furnished, presented by Mr. Bartlet in 1821. The buildings stand on elevated ground, having a commanding, variegated, and beautiful prospect.

The library of the seminary contains about fifteen thousand volumes. Besides this, there are two other libraries: one, of the Porter Rhetorical Society, containing from two to three thousand volumes; the other, belonging to the Society of Inquiry respecting Missions, containing from one to two thousand volumes. There is an athenæum and newsroom, supported by the students. Annexed to the institution is a commodious mechanic's shop, where the students can exercise themselves in carpentering or cabinet-work. The term is three years. The principal study for the first year is the Bible in its original tongues. The second year is occupied in the study of systematic theology. The third year is devoted to the study of ecclesiastical history, and the composition of sermons. There is also a *Teachers' Seminary* near the institution, which will accommodate two hundred students. It is under the trustees of Phillips Academy and four visiters.

Learned Societies.—The *American Academy of Arts and Sciences* was incorporated in 1780, and has published several quarto volumes.

The *Massachusetts Medical Society* was incorporated in 1781.

The *Massachusetts Historical Society* was established in 1791 and incorporated in 1794, and has published many volumes of collections.

The *American Antiquarian Society* was incorporated in 1812.

The *American Institute of Instruction* was founded in 1831.

Newspapers, &c.—The number of newspapers published in this state before the Revolution (in 1775) was seven, viz., in Boston, the Boston News-Letter, the Evening Post, the Gazette, the Massachusetts Gazette and Postboy; in Salem, the Essex Gazette; in Newburyport, the Essex Journal; and in Worcester (first published at Boston), the Massachusetts Spy. The first daily paper in Massachusetts, was the Boston Daily Advertiser, begun in 1813.

The earliest periodical pamphlets or magazines printed in the state were the following: from 1789 to 1796, the Massachusetts Magazine, or Monthly Museum, which extended to eight volumes; in 1800, the Columbian Phœnix and Boston Review, which ceased after the eighth number; in 1802, the New England Magazine; from 1803 to 1811, the Monthly Anthology, or Boston Review, in ten volumes, edited at first by Phineas Adams, and afterward by Rev. William Emerson, W. S. Shaw, A. M. Walter, James Savage, and others; in 1803, the American Baptist Magazine was begun, which continued under several editors; in 1805, the Missionary Magazine, by congregational clergymen; in 1806, the Panoplist, by Rev. J. Morse and others: these two were united in 1808, and edited by Rev. Jeremiah Evarts from 1810 till 1820, when the Missionary Herald took its place, which is still continued, under the American Board of Commissioners for Foreign Missions. Literary, religious, and scientific publications of this class have since multiplied to such a degree, that we have not room for any further notice under this head. The North American Review, however, must be mentioned, as one of the oldest and most influential publications of the kind in the United States. It was commenced in 1815, forms two volumes annually, and has been edited successively by William Tudor, Jared Sparks, Edward T. Channing, Edward Everett, Alexander H. Everett, &c.

Boston, the capital of this state, is situated on a small peninsula at the head of Massachusetts bay, at the mouth of Charles river, and is the principal city and seaport of New England. The harbor is accessible, large, and well protected by both nature and art. This city contains an uncommonly large proportion of fine buildings, particularly private residences. The finest buildings are of

Boston and Bunker Hill from the east.

whitish granite, brought from the shores of the Merrimack river and Quincy.

Boston, like many other large cities, has been, by common consent, divided into districts, with names indicating the location of each. Thus there are North Boston, West Boston, East Boston, South End, and South Boston. The first section embraces the north end of the city, or all that part lying north of Faneuil hall, and what was the canal, or Mill-creek. This is the oldest part, and formerly had the advantage of the principal trade. The streets here are generally narrow and crooked, and some of them remain much as they were when first constructed, on the model of the old towns in England. The buildings are mostly old, and many are built of wood, and exhibit the different styles of architecture used for a period of more than a century and a half. Except a portion of what was formerly the Millpond, the only spot of land not covered by buildings at present is on Copps hill, and the greater part of this is occupied for a burial-ground. From this hill the British cannonaded the town of Charlestown in 1775, during the memorable battle of Bunker hill. They left a small fort standing on this hill, which remained a favorite resort for the recreation of schoolboys until 1807. The natural situation of this section of the city gives it an advantage over any other part, whether considered as a place for comfortable and healthy residence, or its convenience for trade. The channel of Charles river runs close to the shore, and has depth and width sufficient to accommodate ships of the greatest burden. The spirit of improvement recently awakened in North Boston shows that the citizens begin to appreciate its advantages.

West Boston lies between the common and Canal street, west of Hanover and Tremont streets, and has been recently built. The buildings are principally of brick, erected in a handsome style, and are mostly used as dwellings. The statehouse, hospital, national theatre, courthouse, and jail, are located in this section.

The South End comprises all the peninsula south of Summer and Winter streets, and extends to Roxbury. About one fourth of the buildings in this section are of wood. Those that have been most recently erected are of brick and granite, exhibiting an improved style of architecture. The buildings here, also, are generally occupied for dwellings, except the lower stories of those on Washington street.

South Boston is that section of the city which is separated from the peninsula, or the ancient town, by an arm of the harbor reaching to Roxbury. It contains about five hundred and sixty acres, and, except East Boston, is the newest and most unsettled part of the city. The population has increased rapidly within a few years, and a considerable number of buildings has been erected, chiefly of brick. This once was a part of Dorchester, and embraces the hills known formerly as Dorchester heights, so famed in the annals of the American Revolution. There are two free bridges that connect this with the older part of the city: one is at the South End, near the Neck; the other leads from Windmill point, and was built in 1828.

East Boston is an island, formerly known as Maverick's, Noddle's, and Williams' island. In 1814, the citizens of Boston erected a fort on its eastern extremity, which was called Fort Strong. In 1830, some eight or ten of the most enterprising capitalists of Boston purchased this island, and commenced laying it out into streets and lots, with a view of making it an important part of the city. Among the important improvements in East Boston, we enumerate—first, the introduction of the Cochituate water by the city of Boston; second, the construction of the Grand Junction railroad; third, the construction of the seawall across the basin, thus reclaiming a large quantity of low lands which were hitherto partially covered by the tide-waters. These lands consist of marsh and flats to the extent of about ninety-five acres, lying between Westwood island and the Eastern railroad. The population of East Boston is about twelve or fifteen thousand. It has a deep-water frontage of seventeen thousand feet, and the Cunard steamers have here a wharf.

Old City Hall, State Street, Boston.

The Boston Common.—This is a large and beautiful public square, in the western part of the city, lighted by gas, encircled by an iron fence, and extending down the long and gentle slope of Beacon hill It contains about forty-three acres, exclusive of the malls which surround it, and the botanic garden west of it, the whole comprehending at least seventy-five acres of open land dedicated to the public. In spring and summer, when covered with a coat of verdant grass, and while the numerous fine trees which shade it are in full foliage, the sight is remarkably striking, and can not be contemplated without admiration, as one of the largest and most beautiful public grounds in America. Being slightly relieved by several swells and depressions, it is remarkably well adapted to the manœuvring and encampment of troops, to which it is devoted on days of military display. In the centre of this park there is a beautiful piece of water, known by the name of "*Frog-pond*," of about half an acre in extent, and enclosed by edge-stones of hammered granite. It is now ornamented with a beautiful fountain.

Near this pond, and south of it, stands the celebrated old elm, which for nearly two centuries has triumphed over the heats of summer and the blasts of winter, and under whose shade were formerly held the drumhead courts-martial and the parades of military executions.

Before 1733, rows of trees had been planted on some parts of the common, as, in that year, it was resolved that more should be planted. Since that time the trees have been greatly multiplied, so that the common is at present surrounded with broad and shady avenues, where, on the smooth gravel-walks, thousands of citizens find a favorite retreat from heat, and the enjoyment of a cool breeze, on the summer evenings. The number of elms now exceeds seven hundred; and these are, in some parts, tastefully intermingled with other kinds of trees, lining the numerous shady paths which lead across the grounds around their circuit, or by winding courses up and down the gentle declivities.

On three sides the common is bordered by long ranges of stately mansions, being a favorite part of the city on account of its fine scenery, free air, and retirement. On the west it looks down on Charles river, there spreading out into a wide bay.

The Statehouse.—Overlooking the common from the summit of Beacon hill, on its northern side, stands the statehouse. This elegant and spacious edifice was erected in 1795. The building is seen at a great distance in all directions, and is the principal object visible when the city is first seen by those who visit it. The form is oblong, being one hundred and seventy-three feet in front, and sixty-one feet deep. The height of the building, including the dome, is one hundred and ten feet; and the foundation is about that height above the level of the water of the bay. It consists externally of a basement story twenty feet high, and a principal story thirty feet high. This, in the centre of the front, is covered with an attic sixty feet wide, and twenty feet high, which is covered with a pediment. Immediately above rises the dome, fifty feet in diameter, and thirty in height—the whole terminating with an elegant circular lantern, which supports a pine cone. The basement story is finished in a plain style on the wings, with square windows. The centre is ninety-four feet in length, and formed of arches which project fourteen feet, and make a covered walk below, and support a colonnade of Corinthian columns of the same extent above.

A beautiful statue of Washington, by Chantrey, was procured by private subscription, and placed in the statehouse in the year 1828. The costume is a military cloak, which displays the figure to advantage. The effect is imposing and good; but, instead of confining himself to a close delineation of features, the sculptor, like Canova, has allowed some latitude to his genius in expressing his idea of the character of the subject.

The view from the top of the statehouse is very extensive and variegated; perhaps nothing in the country is superior to it. To the east appears the bay and harbor of Boston, interspersed with beautiful islands; and the distance beyond, the wide-extended ocean. To the

The Boston Common, with the Statehouse in the distance.

north the eye is met by Charlestown, with its interesting and memorable heights and the navy-yard of the United States; the towns of Chelsea, Malden, and Medford, and other villages, and the natural forests mingling in the distant horizon. To the west, is a fine view of the Charles river and bay; the ancient town of Cambridge, rendered venerable for the university, now above two hundred years old; of the flourishing villages of Cambridgeport and East Cambridge, in the latter of which is a large glass manufacturing establishment; of the highly cultivated towns of Brighton, Brookline, and Newton: and to the south is Roxbury, which seems to be only a continuation of Boston, and which is rapidly increasing; Dorchester, a fine, rich, agricultural town, with Milton and Quincy beyond; and still farther south, the Blue hills, at the distance of eight or nine miles, which seem to bound the prospect.

Near the capitol, on the west, is the mansion-house of the eminent patriot the late JOHN HANCOCK, now exhibiting quite an ancient appearance. On the same side, and farther west, rising from the rich foliage which surrounds the spectator in the common, conspicuous among many fine edifices, stands the mansion of the Hon. DAVID SEARS—a gentleman of large landed property, distinguished among those remarkable men of Boston to whom the literature and charities of the country owe so much.

The plan proposed by Mr. SEARS for the enlargement and improvement of Boston, by reclaiming the waste spot of territory back of the public garden, is one so intimately connected with the welfare and growth of that city, that our description of the metropolis of New England would be imperfect without a brief notice of it. We have, when visiting Boston, and realizing its rapid growth and crowded streets, looked upon this immense basin, which, save as a daily recipient of the offal and impurities of streets and dwelling-houses, has long been lying idle (the water-power created by it being a failure, and now disused, and the Water-power Company turning their power into a land-speculation), with a feeling of regret that it could not be handsomely improved, and made to minister to the health, the pleasure, and the comfort of the residents of that beautiful city.

During the year 1849, Mr. SEARS addressed a letter to the mayor and aldermen of Boston, suggesting a plan of improvement of this waste spot, to be effected through an amicable adjustment of the several proprietary interests therein. This proposition of Mr. SEARS led to the appointment of a commission, on the part of the state, to examine into "the tenure of the property, and the rights of individuals, of towns, and of the state therein;" and which may be looked upon as an initiatory or preparatory step to its future improvement. The plan of Mr. SEARS for rendering available and beautifying this basin, can be seen in the diagram on page 83; and its details will be found in the following letter to the state commissioners, which we publish entire, as it embraces extracts from the letter to the mayor and aldermen referred to above, and will give a clearer idea of the proposed improvement than any explanations from us could possibly do:—

"BOSTON, *December* 16, 1850.

"*To the Honorable the Commissioners, &c.*

"GENTLEMEN: Among the questions which may fairly come within your examination, under warrant from the legislature, is the following, viz.: the best plan, having reference to the public, for filling up the Back bay, and making that waste of waters available for useful purposes.

"This subject is distinct from the rights of property, and does not implicate any of those questions which have been so ably argued before you. Yet it is of importance to us all, since it may serve as a starting-point from which the parties interested may hereafter more easily advance to an amicable adjustment; and it is of especial value at this stage of the matter, because the rights of all to the area of land lying between the boundaries of the riparian proprietors of the city of Roxbury and the boundary of the city of Boston being as yet unsettled, a common plan of improvement can be more readily adopted than if said area

The State-House, Boston.

was definitively adjudged to be the property of either.

"In addition to the above, it seems to me that the peculiar tenure of this land—if the original interest of the state is doubtfully merged oy specific grants and easements to various parties—renders it proper that the commonwealth, as sovereign, should still extend over it a protecting arm, and so regulate its future occupation as to make it, as far as is practicable, an ornament to the metropolis, a pride to the city of Roxbury, and a scheme worthy the name and reputation of the state which grants it.

"Under this view of the subject, I have the honor to present to your board, and to make part of your report, a plan similar to that I lately offered for the examination of the mayor and aldermen of the city of Boston, and which I beg you to regard as suggestive only, and as the basis of a more detailed draught, to be worked out by others, for this valuable improvement.

"The principal features of the reservations proposed, and to be ordered by the state whenever the parties in interest—the Boston Water-power Company or others—shall apply for the right to fill up and use for building purposes the abovenamed area of land, are the following, namely: That a pond or lake of water, of not less than twenty-five acres of surface, be for ever kept open for public use and ornament, beginning at a point in the city of Boston where Boylston street, continued, terminates at the boundary line of the city in the receiving-basin of the Boston Water-power Company, and extending in a westerly direction until it reaches the western boundary of the flats claimed by the city of Roxbury: that not less than four public squares, lying within the receiving-basin, and easterly of the boundaries of the above-named riparian proprietors, and southerly and westerly of the Neck-lots and other lands near the boundaries of the city of Boston, of at least six hundred feet by four hundred, be laid out and for ever kept open for ornament and air: that all the principal streets shall be fifty feet wide: that no street shall be less than thirty feet wide: and that the whole shall be drained in a manner to be approved of by the cities of Roxbury and Boston.

"In my letter on the above subject, addressed to the mayor and aldermen of the city of Boston, and dated June 11, 1849, the following suggestions were made, viz.: 'That the Botanic (or public) Garden should be extended some hundreds of feet until it reaches a broad and circular avenue, enclosing within its area from fifiy to seventy-five acres of water: the avenue to be at least one hundred feet wide on the top, and bordered on both sides by elms and other ornamental trees: the water of the lake to be supplied by an aqueduct from the flour and other mills on the cross-dam, and emptied into Charles river by a sufficient raceway: the depth of the lake to be three feet below low-water mark, and with a gravelled bottom: the flats to be filled up to a level with Charles street, and laid out with public squares and other ornamental places, as shown on the plan.

"'This project, if ever carried into effect, will give to the city, at a small comparative cost, a large amount of taxable property; an extensive and beautiful Botanic Garden, terminated by a lake of pure water, equal in size, or larger, than the present Common; and a broad and splendid promenade, not to be surpassed by any in the world.

"'The lake will be in itself an endless source of amusement to the public—a fit place for evening music, for boat-races and aquatic sports in the summer, for skating exhibitions in the winter, and for fireworks and other public displays on the 4th of July and holydays.

"'In the hope that these suggestions may be of service, and if of no other use, perhaps the means of eliciting a more advisable mode of relieving the city of a nuisance, and preparing the way for a more desirable embellishment of her public grounds, I have the honor of laying the plan before you.'

"The same purpose which called forth this letter still exists, and the same wish remains to see this improvement carried out.

"Should the state, as is believed, not contemplate a beneficiary interest in the

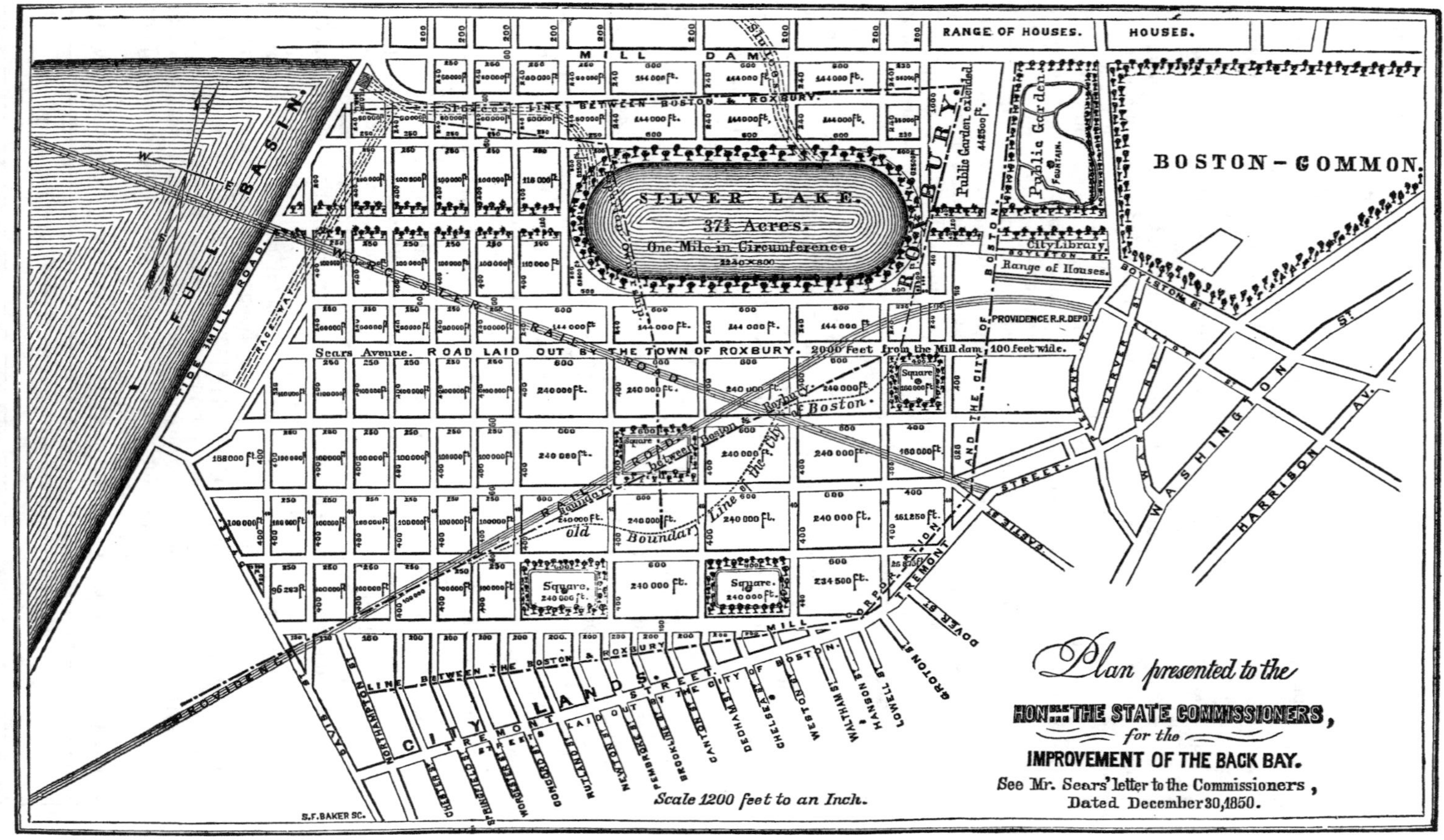
RANGE OF HOUSES.
HOUSES.
MILL DAM
LINE BETWEEN BOSTON & ROXBURY.
FULL BASIN.
TIDE MILL ROAD.
RACE WAY
SILVER LAKE.
37½ Acres.
One Mile in Circumference.
ROXBURY.
Public Garden extended
442500 ft.
Public Garden
FOUNTAIN.
BOSTON-COMMON.
City Library
BOYLSTON ST.
Range of Houses.
PROVIDENCE R.R. DEPOT.
WORCESTER RAIL ROAD
Sears Avenue. ROAD LAID OUT BY THE TOWN OF ROXBURY. 2000 Feet from the Mill dam. 100 feet wide.
LINE BETWEEN THE BOSTON & ROXBURY
AND THE CITY OF BOSTON.
Boundary Line of the City of Boston.
old Boundary Line of the City
Square.
CITY LANDS.
TREMONT STREET LAID OUT BY THE CITY OF BOSTON.
PROVIDENCE
DAVIS ST.
NORTHAMPTON ST.
CHESTER ST.
SPRINGFIELD ST.
WORCESTER ST.
CONCORD ST.
RUTLAND ST.
NEWTON ST.
PEMBROKE ST.
BROOKLINE ST.
CANTON ST.
DEDHAM ST.
CHELSEA ST.
WESTON ST.
WALTHAM ST.
HANSON ST.
LOWELL ST.
GROTON ST.
DOVER ST.
MILL
CORPORATION
TREMONT STREET.
CASTLE ST.
WASHINGTON ST.
HARRISON AV.
CARVER ST.
PLEASANT ST.
Scale 1200 feet to an Inch.
S.F.BAKER SC.
Plan presented to the
HON.BLE THE STATE COMMISSIONERS,
for the
IMPROVEMENT OF THE BACK BAY.
See Mr. Sears' letter to the Commissioners,
Dated December 30, 1850.

matter, but regard its right—be it more or less—only as a means of seeing justice done to the public, then I can not doubt that it will readily approve the principles I have laid down in reference to *a g'neral plan;* and even if it should determine otherwise, still the advantages of a preliminary movement of the kind herein suggested must be obvious to every thinking person who examines it.

"With great respect, I have the honor to be your obedient servant,

"DAVID SEARS.

"Hon. SIMON GREENLEAF, Chairman of Commissioners concerning Boston Harbor and Back Bay."

The advantages which will result from this improvement are incalculable. One benefit to the city will be, the creation of a large amount of taxable property at little or no expense to it, except drains and streets, while it will also benefit individually every real-estate owner, trader, and resident, in Boston. Whatever tends to beautify the city and render it more healthy, has the additional tendency to an increase of population and of business, thereby enabling all to share in the advantages of such a scheme as is now proposed. The water-works which have recently been completed at an immense cost, to furnish an unfailing supply of that important article to the whole population, present a strong inducement to families to move into the city, and will be the means of keeping multitudes from seeking residences in the suburban towns and villages, in preference to the city, as was formerly the case on account of the difficulty of obtaining wholesome water in the latter.

It is characteristic of the Bostonian to feel a just pride in the success of any measure which is designed to adorn his city, and make it more and more truly "the pride of New England." And this project is one that meets with so much favor, that it will undoubtedly at no distant day be adopted, and thus place Boston in the front rank of her sister-cities in point of health and beauty.

The mansion of Mr. SEARS, before referred to, a view of which is on the opposite page, is in a plain, massive style of architecture, but has a light and pleasing effect, being constructed of white granite, and having the front broken by two semi-circular projections, like round towers, extending from the ground to the roof, and affording to the three stories abundant light, and commanding views of the beautiful and extensive scenery spread out around.

In this vicinity are numerous fine and costly dwellings, the residences of distinguished gentlemen—of the princely merchants, the LAWRENCES and APPLETONS—of the eminent lawyers, CHOATE, OTIS, and MASON—of the historian PRESCOTT; and many others. Costly buildings may likewise be seen on the several streets which have, chiefly within the last twenty years, been built up parallel and at right angles with the north line of the common, on the upper slope of Beacon hill; but none surpass, in size or effect, the fine mansion depicted and described.

There are several other edifices on different sides of the common which merit more particular notice than we have room to give them. Park-street church stands on the eastern side, and is one of the oldest churches in the city. The Gothic masonic temple and St. Paul's church, on the south, and other places of worship of different denominations, are seen in the neighborhood, adding variety by their different forms and styles of architecture.

The *Massachusetts General Hospital*, with its two departments—its hospital for the sick and its asylum for the insane—is one of the largest and most important of the charitable institutions of the state. It was incorporated in 1811. It was designed to afford relief to invalids, to reach the necessities of every class of persons, and to yield its benefits at the lowest possible rate. The act of incorporation granted to the hospital a fee simple in the old Province-house estate, on the condition that one hundred thousand dollars was raised within ten years. Special donations for this object, amounting to over one hundred and forty thousand dollars, were made in 1816, and the estates were purchased where the two departments of the institution have been located. Its endowments now amount to about one million of dollars. The hospital for the sick, erected in a spacious enclosure of four acres in Allen street, is

Residence of the Hon. David Sears. Boston Common

one of the most imposing edifices in Boston. The asylum for the insane is beautifully situated on a rising ground within the quiet precincts of the adjoining town of Somerville. Nearly fourteen thousand patients have received the benefits of the former department of the institution, and more than thirty-three hundred have been inmates of the latter. The greatest discovery of the age—the power of producing insensibility to pain—has gone forth from the one; while the humane treatment, and the high professional skill, evinced in the other, have extended its reputation throughout the length and the breadth of the land, and gathered within its walls sufferers alike from the frozen north and the sunny south. One of its earliest and most active advocates was Dr. John C. Warren. He was appointed acting surgeon on its first organization in 1817; and down to the present time, a period of thirty-four years, he has continued assiduously at his arduous post of duty and of honor.

The *New England Institution for the Education of the Blind* is one of the largest and most prosperous establishments of the kind in the Union, and very liberally endowed by public and private donations. It was incorporated in 1829, and in 1833 was presented, by Thomas H. Perkins, with his valuable mansion-house in Pearl street, worth thirty thousand dollars, and by individuals with fifty thousand dollars. The Perkins mansion was subsequently exchanged for the present edifice on Mount Washington, South Boston. Later donations have increased the funds of the institution.

The Customhouse.—This building is located at the foot of State street, between the heads of Long and Central wharves, fronting east on the dock between them, and on the west fronting India street, which is its principal front. The building is in the form of a cross; the extreme length is one hundred and forty feet, extreme breadth ninety-five; the longest arms of the cross are seventy-five feet wide, and the shortest sixty-seven feet. The base of the building is nine feet high, the columns thirty-two feet, entablature ten and two thirds feet, pediment eight and one third feet, and dome at the intersection of the cross twenty-nine feet above that;—making the whole height, from the sidewalk to the top of the dome, ninety feet. The style of architecture is the pure Grecian Doric. Each front has a portico of six fluted Doric columns, thirty-two feet high and five feet four inches in diameter, approached by a flight of fourteen steps, which are equal in height to the base of the building. The walls of the building are composed of sixteen three-quarter columns, four nearly full columns at the corner, all of the same height and diameter as those of the porticoes; and four antæ, thirty-two feet in height, five feet one inch by three feet eight inches at the intersection of the cross. The columns are each in one piece, of highly-wrought granite, costing about five thousand dollars.

The building is founded on about three thousand piles, driven in the most thorough manner; immediately on the heads of these is laid a platform of granite, in the best hydraulic-cement mortar. The large central business-room is sixty-five by sixty-eight feet, and sixty feet high to the skylight of the dome, and is finished in a very elaborate manner in the Corinthian order. There are twelve fluted marble columns, three feet in diameter by twenty-nine feet high, highly wrought out of Egremont marble, having capitals of Italian marble, designed and wrought here, of the most chaste and classic character. The rest of the interior is finished in a plain and simple style, and fireproof throughout, having mostly stone floors, iron doors, &c.

The building is warmed and ventilated by an apparatus, the heating being combined with the ventilation, and effected in part by mechanical means.

Faneuil-Hall Market.—This market is of granite, and has a centre building, seventy-four and a half by fifty-five feet, with wings, extending in all five hundred and thirty-six feet, with a fine façade at each end, with granite columns of single pieces, twenty-one feet high, and weighing each fourteen or fifteen tons. A row of granite buildings on each side, four stories high, for stores, is more than five hundred feet in length.

The Custom House Boston.

Sons of Liberty 1766.

Independence of their Country, 1776.

Faneuil Hall.—This old building, so intimately associated with our revolutionary history, was erected in 1742, by Peter Faneuil, Esq., who presented it to the town of Boston. It was considerably enlarged in 1805, and the following are its present dimensions: length, one hundred feet; breadth, eighty feet; height, three stories; great hall in the second story, used for public meetings, seventy-six feet square, and twenty-eight high; hall for military trainings, in the third story, seventy-eight feet by thirty. The basement story is devoted to stores. A broad staircase, entered from the east front, leads to the second and third stories. The great hall has galleries on three sides, supported by Doric columns; two rows of Ionic columns support the ceiling. Stuart's portrait of Washington, and a portrait of its founder, ornament this fine hall.

The Liberty-Tree.—The above engraving of the Liberty-Tree, so famous in the revolutionary annals of Boston, as it appeared just previous to its destruction by the British troops and tories during the siege of that town, in August, 1775, is copied from a bas-relief representation, placed, by the Hon. David Sears, in a niche of a block of fine buildings which he has recently erected upon the site of an old grove of elms, of which this tree was one. This sculptured representation is placed exactly over the spot where the Liberty-Tree stood. Why can not the patriotic feeling and the provident care, which prompted this act on the part of Mr. Sears, be followed in rescuing from oblivion others of the many localities so interesting and so worthy of being held in perpetual remembrance, from their association with events during the most trying period of our country's history? The silent though no less certainly destructive hand of decay, and the improvements required by the rapid increase of population and settlement, in both country and city, are fast sweeping away every vestige by which the localities so reverenced are recognised; and he who sets up any landmarks by which

Faneuil Hall.

they may be known, as Mr. SEARS has done on the site of the Liberty-Tree, deserves and will receive the grateful thanks of posterity.

The following letter from Mr. SEARS to the mayor and city council of Boston, is so replete with interesting incidents connected with the history of this tree, that we can not repress the inclination to place it on record in the pages of this volume. We take it from a copy printed by order of the city council of Boston, for the use of the members of the city government:—

"BEACON STREET, BOSTON,
Sept. 29, 1849.

"*To the Honorable the Mayor and Aldermen of the City of Boston*:—

"GENTLEMEN: I have the honor to inform you that the old buildings at the corner of Essex and Washington streets have been removed, and that an extensive block of warehouses is being erected in their places, to cover the whole front of my estate on these two streets.

"As this site is somewhat remarkable in the history of Boston—it having sustained, and for more than a century nourished, a splendid American elm, known and venerated as '*Liberty-Tree*'—the present seems a fit occasion to bring it to your notice.

"The tree was supposed to have been planted in 1646, and was cut down by the British in 1775. La Fayette, in his visit to Boston, said, 'The world should never forget the spot where once stood Liberty-Tree, so famous in your annals.'

"In accordance with this sentiment, I have ventured to address this letter to you—to make record of certain facts, and to note the changes connected with this historic corner. And, believing that I shall respond to the general feeling of my fellow-citizens on this subject, I have caused to be sculptured, in bas-relief, a representation of this celebrated tree, with appropriate inscriptions, and have inserted it in that part of the building which fronts on Washington street, and directly over the spot where the tree itself formerly stood.

"The following facts and reminiscences I have gleaned from various authorities—principally from Snow's 'History of Boston,' and from the public records of 1775.

"On the 22d of March, in 1765, the king of Great Britain gave his assent to the stamp-act. This act was extremely odious to the people, and the colonies regarding it as 'taxation without representation,' and therefore 'tyranny,' were determined to oppose it. The citizens of Boston had some time before (in 1761) resisted, upon the same principle, another tyrannous act, called 'writs of assistance;' and the feeling, though somewhat allayed, was still warm in their bosoms, and ready to be brought into action.

"The colonies had earnestly and separately remonstrated against the stamp-act. They looked upon it as the brass collar of servitude to be riveted on their necks, to mark them for the born serfs of George III.; and this they would not submit to. Boston, in particular, showed a strong opposition to the act, and resolved at all hazards to maintain her liberties and the privileges of the charter of Massachusetts; though she well knew that, being no favorite in England, the vengeance of that mighty power would be chiefly turned against her in any contest that might ensue. Her citizens, however, undismayed in their purpose, while they felt that in the coming struggle were staked their property and their lives, did not hesitate to venture both against unlawful oppression. In this sentiment the whole population were united; and the talents, the property, and the religion of Boston stood shoulder to shoulder in the subsequent terrific struggle between might and right. No boastful threatenings marked their course, but on they went as men—cool, determined, and inflexible, straightforward to their end—the independence of their country.

"In the early history of Boston, it appears that 'near the head of Essex street formerly stood a grove of those majestic elms, of the American species, which form one of the greatest ornaments in the landscapes of our country. This grove had obtained the name of Hanover square, or neighborhood of the elms.'

"Under one of these trees, and nearly opposite to the present Boylston market, the people of Boston assembled on the

14th day of August, 1765, and exhibited the first plain evidence of resistance to the oppressive course of their misguided fatherland. A single act of riot—the pulling down of a shed, supposed to have been erected for a stamp-office—marked this meeting, and for a time overshadowed the holiness of their purpose. It proved, however, to be but the intoxication of a moment, and was never repeated.* The building was afterward, with an apology, paid for. The name of 'Liberty-Tree' was then given to this noble elm, and from that time it became 'a sort of idol to the people.' Law and order, charter rights and property, were nourished at its roots, and liberty ripened under its spreading branches. On the 14th of February, 1766, it was pruned in the best manner, agreeably to a vote passed by the 'Sons of Liberty,' an association long before known as a club of gentlemen, united for mutual protection, and to resist oppression, and which first assumed that name, and called upon the patriotic citizens of Boston to join them, in the early part of the preceding December.

"The 20th of February of this 1766 had been agreed upon for burning one of the stamped papers in the principal towns in each of the colonies; and in Boston the ceremony was conducted with great decency and order. It also is recorded that, on the 24th, a vessel having arrived from Jamaica with stamped clearances, the 'Sons of Liberty' immediately sent an order to one of their members to go and demand in their names those marks of creole slavery. The person to whom it was directed went to the vessel, and, being told that the master had gone to the customhouse, followed him there—'when, upon the above order being shown, the stamped clearance was given up. It was then carried to King (now State) street, and publicly burned, a Son of Liberty standing by the paper while it was burning, and shouting to the crowd these words: "Behold the smoke ascends to heaven to witness between the isle of Britain and an injured people!" Three cheers were then given, and in a few minutes every man, woman, and child, retired from the street without the least disorder and in silence.'

"On the 15th of the following May, news was received of the repeal of the stamp-act. The joy of the inhabitants of Boston was great. The bells were rung from every church, and a cannon was fired under 'Liberty-Tree.' The 19th was appointed a day of general rejoicing; 'Liberty-Tree' was decorated with flags and colors, and at the windows of the houses near it were clustered the daughters of our distinguished citizens, dressed in gay attire, and adorned with garlands of flowers. In the evening 'fireworks were everywhere played off—the air was filled with rockets, the ground with beehives and serpents. The gentry gave elegant entertainments, and Mr. Hancock treated the people with a pipe of Madeira.' On the common, the Sons of Liberty erected a magnificent pyramid, illuminated with variegated lamps, and all was bright and joyous. At about midnight, at a signal given, and by beat of drum, the inhabitants quietly retired to their respective dwellings, the lights were put out, and the town was hushed in its usual silence.

"These rejoicings had been ushered in by a subscription for liberating all the poor persons confined in jail for debt, and thus enable them freely to partake of the general joy.

"The ministers of religion also bore their part in these scenes; and the sermons of Drs. Mayhew, Chauncey, and others, were printed.

"In the month of August, 1776, this celebrated tree was cut down 'by the enemies of liberty and America, headed by General Gage.' A party, armed with axes, made an attack upon it, and, after much labor, levelled it with the ground. A Son of Liberty, at Cambridge, gave public notice of its fall, and added these prophetic words: 'But, be it known to this infamous band of traitors, that the grand American tree of liberty, planted

* The Sons of Liberty had no part in the destruction of property at Lieutenant-Governor Hutchinson's house. Their rallying-cries were 'Liberty and Property"—"Law and Order"—but in this case they were overpowered by a mob of misguided men, led on by a rabble of boys and thieves. They always lamented the act as a disgrace cast upon the cause of freedom. —Ed.

in the centre of the united colonies of North America, now flourishes with unrivalled beauty, and bids fair, in a short time, to afford under its wide-spreading branches a safe and happy retreat for all the sons of liberty, however numerous and dispersed.'

"What was then prophecy, has now become history.

"Very respectfully,

"Your obedient, humble servant,

"DAVID SEARS."

The *Athenæum*, in Beacon street, is open daily to strangers introduced by members, and contains a valuable library of about forty thousand volumes, and about fourteen thousand coins and medals. In the rear is the gallery of fine arts, with a collection of statues, paintings, &c. The Massachusetts Historical Society's library is in Tremont street.

THEATRES.—The theatres of Boston are limited in number, and rather ordinary in appearance. They are as follows: 1. The National theatre, corner of Portland and Travers streets. 2. The Boston theatre, formerly known as the Odeon, in Federal street. 3. The Howard Athenæum, in Howard street. Kimball's museum, in Tremont street, is also open for theatrical performances.

BOSTON WATER-WORKS.—The Cochituate aqueduct for the introduction of pure and wholesome water into the city was completed in 1848. The cost of construction was over three millions of dollars. The water is brought in an oval brick aqueduct, above six feet in height, about fourteen and a half miles from the Cochituate lake to Brookline, where it discharges itself into a reservoir of more than twenty acres in extent. From Brookline the water is forced by its own pressure through pipes of thirty and thirty-five inches in diameter, to the two reservoirs in the city. The one on Mount Washington, at South Boston, has a superfices of seventy thousand, and the other on Beacon hill of thirty-eight thousand feet. The latter contains, when full, three millions of gallons. This reservoir enables them to have a fountain on the common, which throws a jet to a great height. The two reservoirs will deliver to the city of Boston ten millions of gallons a day, of the purest and best water, decided by chymists to be equal to that of the Croton of New York.

PUBLIC SCHOOLS.—The educational system of Massachusetts has been noticed on a previous page. The sums spent in the city of Boston alone for public instruction—larger than in all Great Britain—are almost entirely a voluntary offering. The laws of the commonwealth, even as early as 1647, it is true, require the support of public schools in all the towns within its jurisdiction; but *a single* school will meet the demands of the law in most towns; and in Boston itself, three schools and three teachers only would meet the intent of the statute: two of these must be teachers "competent to instruct children in orthography, reading, writing, English grammar, arithmetic, and good behavior;" and the other must be "a master of competent ability and good morals, who shall, in addition to the branches of learning before mentioned, give instruction in the history of the United States, book-keeping, surveying, geometry, and algebra; the Latin and Greek languages, general history, rhetoric, and logic." These three teachers might cost the city, at the present rate of salaries, about four thousand five hundred dollars, with the expense of interest for houses added; in all, perhaps, seven thousand dollars. Instead, however, of being satisfied to fulfil the letter of the excellent law, the citizens of Boston take pride in supporting a Latin school, an English high school, twenty-two grammar-schools, and some two hundred primary schools, with a corps of three hundred and seventy teachers, whose combined salaries amount to a hundred and seventy-five thousand dollars. Add to this a million dollars vested in schoolhouses, besides apparatus and incidental expenses of superintendence, fuel, &c., and the sacrifice of property for the good of posterity stands forth without a parallel in the Union.

Boston Asylum and Farm-School.—In 1813 several gentlemen formed a society for the relief and education of such boys as might be found destitute of parental and friendly superintendence. In February, 1814, an act of incorporation was granted them, and the society was organized, with the title of the "Boston Asylum for Indigent Boys." For many years it was located at the corner of Salem and Charter streets, in the house formerly occupied by Governor Phips. On the 9th of June, 1835, the boys, fifty-two in number, were removed to Thompson's island, which is within the limits of the city, about four miles from the city-hall.

A number of gentlemen in Boston were desirous that an institution should be established there, to which children either already corrupted, or beyond parental control, might be sent without the intervention of a legal conviction and sentence; and in which such employments might be pursued by the children as would make the institution, in the strictest sense, a school of industry. A plan for this object was submitted to a few gentlemen, by whom it was approved and matured; and a meeting was held in the hall of the Tremont bank on the 27th of January, 1832, when a board of directors was chosen. Subscription papers were opened, and twenty-three thousand dollars were soon obtained. In the summer of 1833 following, Thompson's island, containing one hundred and forty acres, was purchased for the objects of the institution; and a building is now completed there, which, besides ample accommodations for the officers of the establishment, is quite sufficient for the charge of more than three hundred children. A suggestion having been made of the expediency of connecting the proposed farm-school with the asylum for indigent boys, conferences were held between the directors of these institutions; and in March, 1835, they were united under the style of the "Boston Asylum and Farm-School."

The objects of the present institution are to rescue from the ills and the temptations of poverty and neglect, those who have been left without a parent's care; to reclaim from moral exposure those who are treading the paths of danger; and to offer to those whose only training would otherwise have been in the walks of vice, if not of crime, the greatest blessing which New England can bestow upon her most favored sons. The occupations and employments of the boys vary with the season. In spring, summer, and autumn, the larger boys work upon the garden and farm. The younger boys have small gardens of their own, which afford them recreation when released from school. In the winter, most of them attend school. Their library contains about five hundred volumes.

Bridges.—Some of the most striking objects in the neighborhood of Boston are the bridges which lead from it to various points. There are no less than seven principal ones, besides several branches. The expense at which they have been constructed, and are kept in repair, is very great; and they furnish great facilities for strangers desirous of making excursions to the surrounding country. The Milldam bridge, or Western avenue, leading to Brookline, is one and a half miles long, and a part of the way one hundred feet wide.

Charlestown was settled in the year 1628. It is the oldest town in Middlesex county, and one of the oldest in the state. It derives its name from King Charles I., the reigning sovereign of England at that time. The Indian name of the settlement was *Mishawam*.

Charlestown is situated on a peninsula, with the harbor on the east; the Mystic river and Chelsea on the north; Charles river on the south; and on the west Somerville, with which it is connected by a narrow strip of land called "*The Neck*." With Malden on the northwest, Charlestown is connected by a bridge 2,420 feet in length, opened for travel on the 23d of September, 1788. A bridge one mile in length leads from the navy-yard due north to Chelsea This was formerly the great thoroughfare from Boston to Salem, *via* Chelsea and Lynn. Now the bridge is used for local travel only, the Eastern railroad being the usual means of conveyance to Lynn, Salem, Newburyport, Nahant, thence to Portsmouth, Portland, &c.

At Charlestown are the stateprison, conducted on the improved plan; Bunker-hill monument; the United States navy-yard, with dry-dock, ship-houses, &c.; and the M'Lean insane asylum.

Bunker-Hill Monument.—On the 17th

of June, 1825, the fiftieth anniversary of the memorable battle of Bunker's hill, the corner-stone of this monument was laid in an angle of the old redoubt on Breed's hill, an inferior eminence behind Charlestown. The base, a mass of fourteen thousand tons' weight, is laid thirteen feet deep, and has six courses of stone to the surface, the first of which is fifty feet on each side. Above this a pyramidal obelisk, thirty feet square, rises tapering, two hundred and thirteen feet four inches on the ground, and fifteen feet at the top. It is composed of eighty courses of stone, each two feet eight inches thick. A winding stone staircase in the inside leads to the summit, whence the view is fine and highly interesting. The whole is built of Quincy granite. The largest block in it is said to be eleven feet long, two broad, and two feet eight inches high, with a weight of ten tons.

After the battle of Bunker's hill, the continental troops were drawn in a more complete line around the town of Boston, which was still in possession of the British, and numerous intrenchments may yet be traced out on most of the hills in the vicinity; but it was not till General Washington had succeeded in occupying Dorchester heights, which command the harbor and town from the southeast, that the British forces embarked in their ships and evacuated the place.

Dorchester heights were occupied on the night of March 4, 1776. Eight hundred men formed the van; then followed carriages, and twelve hundred pioneers under General Thomas, three hundred carts of fascines and gabions, and guns in the rear. Two forts were formed by ten o'clock at night—one toward the city, and the other toward Castle island. Preparations were made for an attack by the British, and for defence by the Americans; but the weather prevented the designs of the former, consisting of ten thousand men, who, after pillaging the town, and providing for the removal of fifteen hundred resident loyalists, embarked for New York, March 17, leaving behind a quantity of ammunition, &c.

Villages.—The vicinity of Boston presents a succession of villages, probably not to be paralleled for beauty in the United States. They are generally the residences of a number of the most opulent citizens during the pleasant seasons, and many of the buildings are fine and expensive. The grounds are also frequently laid out with great taste and highly cultivated; so that no stranger who has leisure should fail to take a circuit through them for a few miles. There are several manufacturing establishments in this vicinity, among which Waltham is conspicuous.

Nahant, fourteen miles northeast from Boston, is a very pleasant and favorite resort during the warm months, being a fine situation, open to the sea, of easy access by land and water, and furnished with several houses for the accommodation of visiters, particularly a large hotel. A steamboat runs thither in the summer, and there is a fine road which passes round the bay, through the town of Lynn (celebrated for the manufacture of shoes), along Lynn beach, and then turns off to the promontory of Nahant, which is a point of rough rocks of considerable elevation.

The passage in the steamboat affords a fine view of Boston bay, with the city; Dorchester heights on the south; Bunker's and Breed's hills on the northwest; and many other very interesting objects. Among the islands which form the defence of the harbor, is that which contains Castle William, besides one or two other fortified ones—Rainsford island, which has the marine hospital, part of it quite elevated, but containing only a few acres; and another on which is the farm-school, an interesting institution for boys. Salt is made in Boston bay, and windmills are sometimes used to pump the water.

The ground near the hotel at Nahant has been laid out and ornamented with taste. The cupola on the top commands a fine water scene; and during the prevalence of a strong wind from the sea, the waves are high and magnificent, breaking wildly against the rocks.

The baths are at a short distance from the hotel, and are quite commodious, furnishing one of the chief attractions of the place.

The *Syren's Grotto* is a remarkable

Bunker Hill Monument.

cavity in the rocks, about a quarter of a mile from the hotel; it has been curiously worn out by the waves. There are several other caverns of a similar character, produced in the course of ages by the constant attrition of the water. The *Spouting Horn* is a hole in the rocks, on the opposite side, where the water is thrown up in the air at particular times of tide. The rocks are of granite, porphyry, epidote, &c., and furnish pebbles of jasper. *Pulpit rock*, on the south, is a singular object; its top is almost inaccessible. The rude shores and the smooth beach can be best examined at lowtide; but those who are fond of sublime scenes should omit no opportunity to visit them when the wind is high, particularly in a moonlight night.

Plymouth.—This place is thirty-six miles south-southeast from Boston. It is highly interesting on account of its history, being the site of the first settlement made by the New England pilgrims, on the 22d December, 1620. A mass of granite rock is still shown, on which those who first landed stepped; it has been divided, and a part of it remains buried near the shore in its natural location, while the upper part is removed into the centre of the village.

A handsome building was erected here in 1820, in which the New England society hold their annual celebrations of that interesting era in the history of the country. Burying hill, which rises near at hand, is the spot where a small fort was erected by the settlers, and where the graves of several of them are still to be found. The banks of the brook south of the hill were the scene of the first conference with Massasoit, a friendly and faithful Indian chief, from whom the name of the bay, and subsequently that of the state, was derived. Manumet point is a promontory on the south side of the harbor; and a small island on the opposite side of it was the spot where the pilgrims first placed their feet on shore in this vicinity, after having previously landed on Cape Cod.

The young and feeble colony suffered extreme distresses here from the severity of the climate (against which they were unprepared, as they had sailed for a more southern region) and the want of provisions. Nothing but the assistance of Massasoit, under the providence of God, preserved them from extinction.

The *Boston and Lowell Railroad*, is twenty-six and a half miles in length. The cars start from North Boston, and pass in view of the ruins of the Charlestown nunnery, on Mount Benedict, which was burned by a mob some years ago on a charge of the ill treatment of some of the nuns. Summit of the road, one hundred and twenty-five feet; maximum grade, ten feet per mile; least radius, three thousand feet. More than one half is straight. It was opened in June, 1835.

This road extends to Concord, from which place, also, several roads, now in process of construction, are to extend to Portsmouth and north into Canada.

Lowell.—Like many other towns in this vicinity, this place has grown from a very small beginning. Thousands of persons now living in the city and surrounding country, well remember when there were not ten men in it. The main canal, which supplies water for turning the machinery of numerous mills on the banks of the Merrimack, was constructed in 1793, simply as a boat and raft channel around the falls. The finest timber in New England was then brought down the Concord and Merrimack, the junction of which rivers takes place at Lowell; and thence, to the ocean, they go by the name of the Merrimack. The construction of this canal soon attracted the attention of capitalists, the result of which was, that one mill after another was erected; and from a little, meager village, Lowell has grown into a powerful city, with vast ranges of magnificent granite and brick factories stretching from river to river, and from street to street, resembling huge towers, and striking the stranger with wonder, surprise, and admiration. The population is about forty thousand.

The value of raw cotton used up here annually is about four hundred thousand dollars; wool, about one hundred thousand dollars. The value of the articles manufactured in all the factories, large and small, is about thirteen

View of Plymouth.

millions of dollars per annum. The amount of money annually paid out to the operatives is one million, eight hundred thousand dollars. The operatives, both male and female, get higher wages than any other persons of their class in the United States, or perhaps in the world. Their intelligence is also greater, and their morals are better. They have two hundred and fifty thousand dollars' worth of stock in the various companies, which they have purchased with their earnings in the mills: thirty thousand dollars in railroad stock, a pretty large amount in bank stock, and two hundred thousand dollars deposited in the savings bank. This money they have made by their industry. Many of them have fine houses. A large number of families are dependent on the earnings of their daughters in these factories. Two nieces of Daniel Webster, and two of Edward Everett, are graduates of these palaces of the poor. The girls publish a periodical of original matter, written entirely by the operatives. Over two hundred young ladies, who labored in these factories and thus earned the money with which they educated themselves, are now instructors of youth, and some of them in the highest female seminaries.

The *Boston and Worcester Railroad*, forty-four and a half miles, extends from the shore of Boston harbor, under Washington street, across the city by a viaduct; over Charles river, on an embankment six hundred and eighty feet long, and through a cut in granite five hundred feet long and thirty feet deep; along Charles river; through Brighton to Needham; and through Natick, Framingham, Westborough, and Grafton, to Worcester, five miles east of which is the summit, five hundred and fifty feet above tide. There is a cut through slate thirty-seven feet deep. Less than one third of a mile on this route is level; maximum grade, thirty feet; least radius, nine hundred and fifty-four feet.

The *Great Western Railroad* (a continuation of the above road) leads from Worcester to Springfield, fifty-four miles, through Charlton, South Brookfield, Palmer, and Wilbraham, and on to West Stockbridge, on the New York line, sixty-two miles further; and thence on to Albany.

The *Boston and Portsmouth* or *Eastern Railroad* extends from East Boston through Lynn, Salem (where is a tunnel under part of the town), Ipswich, and Newburyport (forty miles), to Portsmouth, N. H., fifteen and a half miles. It is continued to Portland, Me., through Wells, Kennebunkport, and Saco; and thence to Bangor, one hundred and thirty-two miles further.

MOUNT AUBURN CEMETERY.—This is the first of the large rural burying-grounds which have since become so common in this country. It occupies a large extent of uneven land, well adapted in form, as well as in the nature of its soil and the abundant and varied growth of forest-trees which it bears, to the solemn and interesting object to which it is devoted. It is surrounded by a strong and high fence, and the front presents a high wall, with a fine gateway of granite. At the entrance, avenues lead off, on either side, through shady groves; and here several of the principal monuments are first presented to view, particularly that of the distinguished phrenologist, Spurzheim, who died at Boston on his visit to the United States. The first interment made at Mount Auburn was that of Hannah Adams, the celebrated writer of the history of the Jews.

The grounds are laid out with great taste, and are gradually filling up with tombs and graves. Many private tombs are seen on every side, constructed in a great variety of styles; and the avenues, roads, and paths, which branch out in all directions, lead the visiter through scenes of great variety, among hills of various elevations, and by the borders of ponds, every step bringing to view some new and sad but appropriate object. Flowers are often mingled with the foliage and shade of funereal trees and shrubs; and many touching emblems and inscriptions are interspersed, on which the mind may dwell with affecting and profitable reflections.

LEXINGTON, Worcester county, is remarkable as the place where the first

Cemetery at Mount Auburn.

blood was shed in the revolutionary war. On the 19th of April, 1776, General Gage sent a body of troops from Boston to seize a powderhouse at Concord belonging to the colony; and the inhabitants were warned of his design by an express despatched by the Hon. Joseph Warren. The militia were called out, but, the alarm subsiding, they were dismissed, with orders, however, to hold themselves in readiness. The enemy unexpectedly made their appearance at half-past 4 o'clock, coming on at a quick step, within a mile and a quarter of the church. The alarm-guns were fired, drums beat, and fifty or sixty militiamen assembled on the parade. The British brigade halted about one hundred and twenty yards from the church to load, and then passing the east end of the building, discovered the Americans, who were ordered at the moment by their commander, Captain Parker, to disperse and take care of themselves, but not to fire. As some of them loitered, the British troops rushed toward them, huzzaing. Major Pitcairn fired a pistol at them when about thirty yards distant, after they had been called "rebels," and ordered them to lay down their arms and disperse. Another officer, who was within a few yards of them, then brandished his sword and ordered the troops to "fire," which was obeyed at the second order; and the fire being returned, it was kept up on the dispersing men until they had all disappeared. Eight were killed and ten wounded. (General Gage falsely stated that the British were first fired upon.)

After the regulars had fired a volley from the green behind the church, and given three cheers, they proceeded to Concord. On their return, being hard pressed by sharpshooters, they burned three houses, a shop, and a barn, killed three more men and wounded one.

Andover is a small village, situated on high ground, twenty miles from Boston. It is remarkable for the Phillips academy and the theological seminary, which are three fourths of a mile east from it, on the summit of the ascent. The buildings belonging to the seminary (which we have before described) make a conspicuous figure from different parts of the surrounding country, and command a view of great extent, bounded on the west by the Temple hills in New Hampshire, backed by the Monadnoc about sixty miles off, and on the south by the Blue hills. A small elevation near by affords a view of the Atlantic ocean, from about Newburyport to Cape Ann, with part of Salem; and in the northwest is a distant peak, which is supposed to be Ascutney, in Vermont.

The academical buildings are distinguished by the names of Phillips hall, Bartlett hall, and the chapel. In the upper part of the latter is a library. The professors' houses are opposite, with a spacious green intervening between the seminary and the street; and there is also a large inn. The academy is not connected with the seminary.

Brookfield.—This was one of the most early settled towns in this part of the country, dating as far back as November 10, 1665; and for several years the only towns in the west were Hadley, Northampton, &c., while there was no white settlement between it and Canada. The stagecoach passes over a long hill in West Brookfield, which commands an extensive prospect, and this is the place where the settlement began. A few yards west of a white house on the north side of the road was a house built for defence, which, though of but little strength, was called the fort. In August, 1675, this place was suddenly beset by several hundred savages. The inhabitants had been imposed upon by the appearance of friendliness shown by the Hassenemesit Indians, and while on their way to their fort, a few miles distant, were ambushed and pursued, so that they barely escaped. The house in which they all assembled was besieged and several times in imminent danger. On one occasion a cart loaded with hemp, &c., and set on fire, was pushed up to the house with long poles, when a sudden shower of rain came up in time to extinguish the flames. The fortunate arrival of Captain Mosely with a small troop of horsemen delivered the inhabitants, and drove away the savages. All the houses having been burned, and the war soon beginning to rage with violence, the settlement was evacuated.

The old well still remains which belonged to the fort or blockhouse; and there is a rock in a wall, on the opposite side of the road, from behind which an Indian shot one of the men who had come out to draw water during the siege.

The present village is at the bottom of the hill, and is pleasantly situated, with several ponds in the neighborhood, which, with the fish and fowl they furnished, were the principal attraction of the savages, who were very numerous in this tract of country. These ponds give rise to the Quabaug river, which, after a course of some miles, takes the name of Chicopee, and joins the Connecticut at Springfield.

Worcester is one of the pleasantest cities in New England. The country around it is rich and variegated, and the dwellings have an air of elegance which does great credit to the taste as well as the wealth of its inhabitants. Brick is extensively used in building. The court-house, bank, &c., stand on the principal street, and east of it the county-house, and the building of the American Historical society; this institution was formed for the purpose of preserving everything relating to the history, traditions, &c., of the country. The state lunatic asylum, conducted on the humane system of moral treatment, is very successful.

Watchusett hills, sixteen miles west-northwest of Worcester, and fifty-two west by north of Boston, are estimated at nearly three thousand feet above the sea, and ascended by an easy path. The spectator looks down on a surrounding scene of wooded mountains, with ponds and farms below them, and a view over cultivated and inhabited regions.

Springfield is a flourishing town, standing at the foot of a high hill, the side of which is ornamented with fine buildings, the residences of some of the wealthier inhabitants, and the top occupied by the United States armory. This establishment occupies a large space of ground, and commands a fine view. The buildings containing the workshops for manufacturing small arms, the arsenal, the barracks, &c., are surrounded by a high wall. The number of workmen required, which is about two hundred and sixty, has a favorable effect on the business and prosperity of the place. About eighteen thousand muskets are made here annually, or sixty a day. The manufactories on Mill river, a little south of the armory, are various, and well worthy of observation.

The town is ornamented with many fine elms and other trees; and there are two very handsome churches. It was originally considered within the limits of Connecticut colony, but at length incorporated with Massachusetts. A tribe of Indians lived for some years on Fort hill; but, being won over to King Philip's party, in 1675, they assumed a hostile air, fired upon some of the inhabitants who were going to their fort, and burned a part of the town.

In 1786, during the rebellion of Shays, he attacked the armory, at the head of a strong party of undisciplined men. General Shepard, who had command at the place, attempted to dissuade them from the attempt, and finally drove them off by firing twice. The first shot over their heads dispersed the raw troops, and the second drove off the remainder (about two hundred revolutionary soldiers), who did not desist until they had lost a few of their men. This was the first check the insurrection received, which was put down without much subsequent trouble.

Wilbraham, seven or eight miles west from Springfield, contains a Wesleyan academy.

West Springfield has a fine street, shaded with large elms, and containing some handsome houses. It is twenty-six miles from Hartford, and about seventeen from Northampton. There is a fine view from the road on the brow of a hill a little north of the town, near a church, which overlooks the river and an extent of country on each side, with Mount Tom and Mount Holyoke in front.

South Hadley Falls.—The village and locks are on the east side of the river.

View of Mount Tom and Mount Holyoke.

The whole fall of the river at South Hadley is fifty-two feet, but at the lower falls only thirty-two. There is a canal two and a half miles long on the east side of the river, cut through a slate-rock for a considerable distance, and in some places very deep. There is a ferry here, which is safe, but the water runs very swiftly.

The Mount Holyoke Female Seminary, at South Hadley, combines a practical domestic education with intellectual instruction.

For several miles before reaching Mount Tom from the south, the road runs along the banks of the river; the river makes an abrupt turn some miles above, running between Mount Tom on the south and Mount Holyoke on the north; and when the scene opens again, it discloses a charming and extensive plain, formed of the meadows on the river's bank, and evidently once the site of a large lake, when the water was restrained by the barrier between the mountains. This plain is one of the richest, and by far the most extensive and beautiful, on the river.

Northampton is situated at the western side of the plain, a mile from the river, and is a favorite place of resort for travellers. It is one of the most beautiful of the New England villages, and is surrounded by a charming country, and lies near to Mount Holyoke, which commands a view of the whole. The streets are irregular, but some of them shady and delightful in summer, being also ornamented with many neat houses. It is a place of much business, and the soil makes valuable farms.

Round Hill is a beautiful eminence just west of the town. On the eastern declivity of the hill stands the house of the Stoddard family, an ancestor of which was a man of talent and influence. In King street, toward the northeast from that spot, stood the house in which President Edwards, senior, lived—President Edwards, junior, and Dr. Dwight were born—and David Brainerd died: his grave is in the burying-ground.

Mount Holyoke is about eight hundred feet high, and there is a good carriage-road for the greater part of the way up. The country southeast, seen from its summit, is undulating, and the soil generally poor; yet several villages are discovered at a distance, particularly South Hadley, which lies immediately below. Southwardly is seen Connecticut river, retiring under the shade of Mount Tom, whitened below by the South Hadley falls, beyond which is the hill at Springfield the river makes several turns, and on the horizon are two very distant peaks, which are supposed to be East and West rocks at New Haven, about seventy miles distant. Northeast is seen Monadnock mountain, in New Hampshire. North, the view is up the charming valley of the Connecticut, bordered by distant ranges of hills and mountains, varied by a few isolated peaks, covered with the richest coat of vegetation, and scattered with villages and innumerable farmhouses. The river makes a beautiful serpentine course from where it first appears at the foot of Sugarloaf mountain and Mount Toby, until it reaches the village of Hadley, which lies in full view; and then taking a bold sweep to the west, and flowing four and a half miles, it returns to the end of that village, only a mile distant from where it first meets it! The whole peninsula is rich and fertile, and covered with cultivated fields of wheat, corn, grass, &c., without being disfigured by fences—and is the richest sight upon the river, particularly when viewed in connexion with the scene immediately below, where the river flows on almost under our feet, and the western shore presents the extensive Northampton meadows, a mile wide; following the current with the eye in the west-southwest, it forms a still more remarkable peninsula, although one of inferior size—the Hockanum bend, being a turn measuring three miles in circuit, while the isthmus was only forty-six rods across. This has been cut through by a flood. In the compass of this view, numerous village spires are seen, with level fields, orchards, and gardens, almost numberless, and the whole scene is bounded with mountainous ridges.

Northampton is seen about west-northwest, with Round hill; and, toward the right, the top of Saddle mountain, in the distance. There are also others, still farther north, particularly Haystack and Bare mountains. More than thirty church steeples may be counted here at one view by taking advantage of different kinds of weather.

In point of history, that part of the Connecticut valley immediately under the eye belongs to the third division of settlements, calling Plymouth and Massachusetts bay the first, and Windsor, Hartford, Wethersfield, &c., the second.

Northampton, Hadley, and Hatfield, were settled in 1653, and remained the frontier posts in this direction till after Philip's war, during which time they suffered severely from constant alarms, and the loss of inhabitants. The Indians who had sold the lands on which the towns were built, had each a spot assigned them within a short distance of the palisades with which the new settlements were surrounded, and lived in peace and good faith until excited by Philip; after which all the towns were at different times attacked by them, and some of them repeatedly. During the French wars, on May 13, 1704, the Indians fell upon a little settlement at the foot of Mount Tom, and killed twenty persons, more than half of whom were children; and a tradition states, though without designating the precise time, that a captive woman was once taken to the top of this mountain and there scalped.

HADLEY was attacked by the Indians while the inhabitants were at church, and was near falling into their hands, when a stranger—a venerable old man—made his appearance, and by his active resistance encouraged them to repel the enemy. It was not known at the time who he was, or whither he went; but there is now little doubt that he was Goffe, one of Charles the First's judges, who was secreted for a length of time in this town. The remains of his coffin, it is believed, were discovered a few years since in the cellar-wall of a house (near the present academy) which was formerly inhabited by one of his friends.

HATFIELD, one mile from Hadley, on the west side of the river, is much devoted to the wintering of cattle raised on the neighboring hilly country. The grass is very fine, and the barns are large; which, with the appearance of the houses, gives the place an air of substantial agricultural wealth. The cattle are bought, stabled, and fatted, whence they are chiefly sent by railroad to Brighton.

AMHERST, situated on elevated ground, is five miles from Hadley, and off the river toward the northeast.

Amherst College, in this town, ranks among the most respectable in New England. The situation occupied by the buildings is pleasant, commanding a rich, extensive, and varied view, partly over the meadows of Connecticut river, with mountains seen in different directions. The retired situation is highly favorable to study and good order, as its elevation and pure air are conducive to health.

The three college buildings, one of which is seen, in all its length, on the right side of our print, are fine, substantial edifices. That which is most distinctly visible is four stories high, with a Doric portico projecting from the middle, and a dome rising from the centre of the roof. Toward the left are the new buildings, lately erected for the cabinet of natural history and the astronomical observatory; while a cluster of dwellings, with a church in the midst, and a number of scattering houses, show the elevated and agreeable situation of the southern part of the village.

Amherst college was founded in 1821, and incorporated in 1825, by act of the legislature of Massachusetts. The Rev. EDWARD HITCHCOCK, long distinguished as the professor of geology, &c., was elected in 1843 as the successor of the president, Dr. HUMPHREY, and ably occupies his station.

There are professors of rhetoric and English literature; mathematics and natural philosophy; chymistry and natural history; Greek and Hebrew; zoology and astronomy; intellectual and moral philosophy; and Latin and French. There are also three tutors, a preceptor in German and French, and a lecturer on political economy.

The libraries of the college and literary societies contain about 15,000 volumes. The college library is accessible to all the students. The north, middle, and south college buildings are capa-

View of Amherst College, with the New Cabinet and Observatory, from the Southwest.

cious, convenient, and situated in a manner highly favorable to appearance.

At the dedication of the new cabinet and observatory, on the 28th of June, 1848, a large number of distinguished men attended, on which occasion due acknowledgments were made to the liberal patrons of the institution, who at different periods had rendered it essential aid from their estates; and gratifying evidence was afforded by a recapitulation of contributions and donations received within a few months, that its character and usefulness are more highly appreciated than ever. The president paid a most appropriate and well-merited compliment to one of the principal benefactors, in the following words: "In the astronomical observatory at Cambridge is a massive tower, called the 'Sears Tower,' which sustains one of the most splendid telescopes in the world. But in the '*Sears Foundation of Literature and Benevolence*'* in Amherst college, we have a more enduring structure." A letter from the Hon. David Sears was read, containing the following paragraphs:—

"It is the peculiar characteristic of Massachusetts to give encouragement to learning, and to cherish her literary institutions. It is a sentiment which has grown with her growth and strengthened with her strength, and almost marks her as a distinct people. From the landing of their forefathers, in 1620, to the present day, her sons—while differing on other subjects—have thought alike on this, and they have reason to be proud of the result.

"The colleges of Massachusetts are aptly called seminaries of learning, for by them the seeds of knowledge, of virtue, of morality, and religion, are sown broadcast through our land. Go where you will, from Maine to Mexico, from Ohio to the Pacific ocean, and much of what you find among the people that is good and honest, intelligent and successful, owes its origin to the loins or education of New England—and principally of Massachusetts. In my humble opinion, our colleges are the great conservatives of the Union, and we are deeply indebted to them for whatever of honest principle and integrity of character exists among us.

"Especially permit me to notice the observatory, and the liberal and enlightened gentleman whose name stands the first on the list of patrons.* I trust that the foundation thus laid by him will hereafter sustain the instruments of modern science to draw from the skies a knowledge of the stars—to demonstrate to men the glory of God, and the magnificence of his works—and show to their wondering minds that 'the thousand brilliant worlds which circle round Him are governed by one law,' and that 'in wisdom he has made them all.'

"I venture to conclude my answer to you, reverend sir, with the following sentiment: Literary talent and pecuniary ability—may their zeal be ever found united in building up the halls of learning, and extending the altars of religion."

The Wood Cabinet is of brick, of an octagonal form, and forty-five feet in diameter, with two lofty stories. It is stuccoed without as well as within, and the two halls which it contains are ornamented with fresco painting. Great care has been taken to render this building secure from fire. The floors are fire-proof; the upper one is supported by four strong iron pillars; and the doors are of iron, weighing nearly half a ton each.

The Lawrence Observatory is an octagonal tower, forty-four feet high and eighteen feet in diameter. It is surmounted by a dome ten feet high, which is so made as to be easily moved round to the right or the left, for the convenience of observers using the telescope. As in the observatory at West Point, &c., the dome rests upon several cannon-balls, placed between large iron hoops, or circular track-ways, which perform the part of wheels.

* It appears that a most liberal individual donation to Amherst college has been made by the Hon. David Sears, of Boston, consisting of real estate in that city, which is estimated by the donor to be of the value of $12,000. This, with $10,000 formerly bestowed by him, is to constitute the "*Sears Foundation of Literature and Benevolence*," which, although for the present it does not yield a large income, yet such are the terms on which it is bestowed, that it must ultimately become of great value to the college.

* Hon. Abbott Lawrence.

The *Sugarloaf* is an isolated hill, of a conical form, about three miles south of Deerfield. The way by which we approach it lies nearly along the old road which led thither through the wilderness in 1675 when it was deserted by the settlers, and Captain Lothrop was despatched, with a body of eighty soldiers and wagoners, to bring off the grain. At the foot of this mountain is the small village of Bloody Brook; and, near the spot where a bridge crosses the stream, Captain Lothrop was ambushed by about eight hundred Indians. The place was a marshy piece of ground; and some traces of the road, which was formed of logs, are still to be seen, running through the fields without crossing at the bridge. The convoy halted at this place, and the soldiers were generally engaged in gathering grapes from the vines which ran on the trees, having left their muskets on the ground, when the Indians fired upon them. Captain Lothrop gave orders that the men should disperse, and fire from behind the trees; but they were all cut off except eight or ten. This massacre was one of the most calamitous which ever occurred in New England, taken into view with the small number of inhabitants at the time; as the company consisted of young men, from the principal families in the eastern towns.

Deerfield.—The meadow near Deerfield was the scene of several skirmishes with the Indians at different times, as the place was a frontier for many years, although it was twice burnt and deserted. In 1704, the period of its last destruction, a large body of Indians, led on by a few Frenchmen from Canada, came upon the town before daylight, and after massacring many of its inhabitants and burning their dwellings, retreated, taking Mrs. Williams a captive to Canada.

The Landing of the Pilgrims at Plymouth, which is represented in the vignette at the head of this description of Massachusetts, is justly regarded as one of the most important events which ever happened on the western continent.

New England was settled by puritans, and still retains much of the spirit and principles of its founders. The puritans were the same men to whom England owed her first emancipation from the tyranny of the Stuart family—the same men whose political principles, sternly asserted, led to the Revolution of 1688, and thus gave to our transatlantic progenitors whatever civil freedom they now enjoy—the same men whose descendants led in the American Revolution of 1776, and thus set an example whose influence, after overturning many ancient dynasties and changing the whole political aspect of Europe, is still felt in the more silent but certain progress of liberal principles, and the wider diffusion of equal rights. John Robinson may be justly regarded as the founder of the sect of *independents* or (as called in New England) *congregationalists.* The most important feature of their ecclesiastical system is the independence of each church or congregation, of all bishops, synods, or councils, and its direct dependence on the Head of the Christian church himself. The preaching of such a doctrine could not but offend the government of England. It drew upon the devoted heads of its disciples the determined persecution of Elizabeth and James, and exasperated the civil war, which, terminating in the dethronement of Charles I., finally gave the ascendency to the puritans.

It was to avoid the persecution of James that the English exiles composing Mr. Robinson's congregation remained for ten years at Leyden. But the same pious views incited them to undertake a more distant migration. They at first cast their eyes upon Guiana, of which Raleigh had given a glowing description, but subsequently decided to seek an establishment in Virginia. Agents were despatched to England, to obtain permission from the king. James, although desirous to promote the increase of the colony which had been planted under his auspices, was unwilling to sanction their religious opinions by taking them under his protection. The utmost he would promise was, to connive at their practices, and refrain from molesting them. After accepting this precarious security, they procured from the Plymouth company a grant of a tract of land, lying, as was supposed, within the limits of its patent; a partnership or joint-stock company was formed, on disadvantageous terms, with certain merchants in London, in order to raise the funds necessary to defray the expenses of emigration and settlement. Two vessels were obtained—the Speedwell, of sixty, and the May-Flower, of one hundred and eighty tons burden—in which one hundred and twenty of their number were appointed to embark from an English port for America. These were to act as the pioneers of the whole congregation. They were destined to figure in the world's history as the celebrated pilgrims of New England.

They sought retirement, isolation, and an opportunity of founding a small community of puritans, where, apart from all the world, their peculiar doctrines could be transmitted from father to son, without attracting the notice of king or bishop. But they had a higher destiny: they were, in fact, to become the most efficient among the founders of a great empire, in which their own principles should flourish for ages after, and a more liberal system of religious freedom should be learned and taught by their descendants.

Robinson and his people devoted their last meeting in Europe to an act of solemn and social worship, intended to implore a blessing from Heaven upon the enterprise in which they were about to engage; and on July 22, 1620, sailed from Delft haven for Southampton—whence, after remaining a fortnight, they sailed for America: but they were compelled by the bad condition of the Speedwell, and the treachery of its captain, to put back twice before their final departure. The Speedwell was abandoned; a portion of the company, who were dismayed at the evident dangers of the voyage, were dismissed, reducing their number to one hundred and one, including women and children. This company were all crowded into the May-Flower, which set sail from Plymouth, September 6, 1620, bearing the founders of New England across the Atlantic.

December 22d, after imploring the Divine guidance and protection, the people landed and commenced a settlement. This day is still celebrated by the descendants of the pilgrims as the anniversary of New England's birth. They gave the town the name of Plymouth, in remembrance of the hospitalities they had received at the last port in England from which they had sailed. Their first operations consisted in measuring out the land to the different families, laying a platform for their ordnance, and erecting habitations. It was not till December 31st that they were able to celebrate the sabbath, with its appropriate exercises, in a house on shore.

The hardships undergone by the people, in exploring the bay and effecting a landing, sowed the seeds of fatal disease; their provisions were scanty; the winter was extremely severe; and the Indians, remembering the kidnapping exploits of Hunt and others, were hostile. More than half the colonists died before spring; and those who retained their strength were hardly sufficient to administer to the urgent wants of the sick and dying. In this employment, no one distinguished himself more than John Carver, the governor. He was a man of fortune, who had spent all in the service of the colony, and readily sacrificed his life in discharging the humblest offices of kindness to the sick. He was succeeded by William Bradford, who was reëlected for many successive years.

Previous to the arrival of the pilgrims in New England, a sweeping pestilence had carried off whole tribes of natives, in the region where they had now settled. The traces of former habitations were apparent, but no Indians were found residing in their immediate vicinity. The spring, which restored health to the colonists, brought them also an agreeable surprise, in the visit of some friendly Indians. The visit of Samoset, whose previous intercourse with the English fishermen enabled him to salute them with "Welcome, welcome Englishmen!" was followed by that of Massasoit, the principal sachem of the country, with whom the celebrated treaty was concluded, which was inviolably observed for more than fifty years, and contributed during that period, more than any other circumstance, to secure New England from the horrors of Indian warfare.

We can not close our description of Massachusetts more appropriately, than by giving biographical sketches of two of her most eminent statesmen. Occupying as they did exalted stations at the extreme points in her history, the impress of their characters has been so strongly marked on the institutions of the state that it will never be effaced. We refer to John Winthrop, the father of the Massachusetts colony, and John Quincy Adams, whose life, from early youth to a ripe old age, was devoted to the service of his country, in its most important offices.

JOHN WINTHROP, FIRST GOVERNOR OF MASSACHUSETTS.—We know of nothing in the history of colonies marked with so many peculiarities, as the first settlement of New England. No others were ever founded for purposes strictly religious. Christian faith gave a tone to society that is still felt throughout the community. The belief of a special Providence directing all matters of government, and ordering its changes, visiting vice with temporal calamities, and giving peculiar aid to right motives, seemed to bring man into more immediate communication with his Maker, and to inspire him with high resolves.* It was in this way that the colonists sustained themselves through the difficulties and dangers which met them at every step, and which it was the daily, constant occupation of their lives to surmount. But for this principle, it would not be easy to understand fully the prevailing character of the early period of their history, and to judge aright of the principles which supported the fathers of New England in their struggles, situated as we are in the midst of ease and prosperity. Indeed the whole character of those who influenced and directed their councils, has never been correctly estimated. By some it has been viewed as a model for the present generation, possessed of every virtue, without blemish or reproach. Others have seen nothing but bigotry, hypocrisy, a spirit of persecution, gloomy superstition, and an absence of the social graces and virtues. Both of these views do violence to human nature, history, and truth. There is a manifest want of justice in deciding upon any portion of history in the abstract, or by views which are obtained in a more refined and cultivated state of society, where questions of natural right are better understood. A more correct judgment may be formed by taking into the estimate the general state of society at the time, and any peculiarities in the combination of circumstances that go to form the aggregate. If we apply this rule to the early settlers of New England, we may lament the severities with which they visited differing shades of opinion and disrespect of authority, the readiness which they manifested to believe that the calamities which befell the erring, and their enemies, were instances of the Divine indignation. We could wish that some things had been otherwise, some we would blot out; but we can not join with those who tread with contempt upon their ashes, and condemn the principal features of their character. They were no common men who guided the sufferers from the vengeance of power to these shores. Virtue was strong; religion found her votaries, who were willing to quit the hearths and altars, the refinement and luxuries of the old world, to erect temples to the Most High in the deep silence of our forests. We can not join in a general condemnation of those who fostered the good institutions that have descended to us; strengthened them against the violence of opposition; planted the seeds of liberty, now in full fruit; and cherished religion, till it became an essential element in the constitution of society. Surely it is some praise that they planted churches in every vil-

* OUR PILGRIM FATHERS.—When our fathers fled from persecution in England, and sought an asylum in this country, they at first depended much upon the supplies of food from the mother country. A company of them having at one time gone to the seashore, after looking anxiously for a vessel which was to bring them corn, and being disappointed, hunger induced them to search among the pebbles for something to satisfy the craving demands of nature.—And sincere was their gratitude to Him who "openeth his hand and satisfieth the desire of every living thing," when they found in the sand a kind of mussel, of which they partook, and found to be wholesome and nutricious. One day, after they had finished a hearty meal of this kind, a venerable old man stood up and returned thanks, by blessing God that he had fulfilled to them the promise made to Zebulon, DEUT. xxxiii. 19: "They shall offer sacrifices of righteousness, for they shall suck of the abundance of the seas, and of treasures hid in the sand."

JOHN WINTHROP,

FOUNDER OF THE CITY OF BOSTON, AND FIRST GOVERNOR OF MASSACHUSETTS.

lage; that, by the system of free schools, established in many towns so early as 1645, and by law in 1648, they sent the kindly influences of learning to the fireside of the humblest citizen; and, to crown all, founded that venerable university, which for two centuries has been the direct source of incalculable good to the people, and may be regarded as, in an important sense, the parent of many of the similar institutions in our land; and all this at a time when the people were few, and, by reason of their poverty, were obliged, for one year, to forbear laying the usual tax.

From a general view of our early history, we are satisfied, that the fathers of New England were upright, intelligent, and pious men, whose main endeavor was to strengthen the colonies they had planted, according to their ability; and that even their errors, in most instances, were the result of good motives, and an ardent desire to promote religion, learning, purity, and all the best interests of the community.

Governor WINTHROP, the subject of this biography, was born at Groton, in Suffolk, England, June 12, 1587; and was descended from an ancient and honorable family. His grandfather was an eminent lawyer, in the reign of Henry VIII., and attached to the reformation. His father was of the same profession, and the governor himself was bred a lawyer, in which character he was eminent for both integrity and abilities. Indeed, he must have had the fairest reputation, for he was appointed a justice of the peace at eighteen years of age.

When the design of settling a colony in New England was undertaken, Mr. Winthrop was chosen, with general consent, to conduct the enterprise. His estate, amounting to the value of six or seven hundred pounds sterling a year, he converted into money, and embarked his all to promote the settlement of New England. When he left Groton he was in the forty-third year of his age. He arrived at Salem with the Massachusetts charter, June 12, 1630.

To no one are we more indebted than to WINTHROP, not only for the manifold good which he did in his own day, but also for the history he has left us of the early transactions in church and state in New England, and especially in Massachusetts. His work, which, as we gather from him, was intended for publication and for posterity, was left by him in manuscript, in three parts. These had all been in the hands of Hubbard, Mather, and Prince, who it seems had derived more assistance from them than they would acknowledge. The first two parts, bringing the history down to 1644, were published at Hartford in Connecticut, in 1790. The third part was discovered in the tower of the old South church in Boston, in 1816. On collating the manuscript of the first two parts with the printed volume, the latter was found to contain many errors; and the whole work has been published by the Massachusetts Historical Society, with the assistance of the legislature of that state; the third part had never before been published. It continues the history down to the time of his death. Much interesting matter, and many important facts, are contained in this part. Of these, are relations of the various discussions between the magistrates and deputies relative to their respective powers; an account of the synod that met at Cambridge to establish the platform of church disciple and government; a defence against the charges which were raised to the prejudice of the colonists, by their enemies, and preferred before the commissioners in England. These all serve to fill up the delineation of the character of the fathers of New England to the middle of the seventeenth century.

The contents of WINTHROP'S "History of New England," are so various, that it is difficult to make an extract that will do justice to the author. But we select at a venture his "little speech," as he terms it. In 1645, when he was deputy governor, he was singled out from the rest of the magistrates, who had acted with him, to defend the legality of his proceedings, in committing to prison certain persons in Hingham, who had been concerned in some disturbance of the peace, and who refused to find sureties for their appearance at court. The day of WINTHROP'S trial came, and he declined taking his seat upon the bench. Speaking of himself, as he does throughout, in the third person, he says: "The day appointed being come, the court assembled in the meetinghouse at Boston. Divers of the elders were present, and a great assembly of the people. The deputy governor, coming in with the rest of the magistrates, placed himself beneath, within the bar, and so sate uncovered. Some question was in court about his being in that place (for many of both the court and assembly were grieved at it). But the deputy telling them, that, being criminally accused, he might not sit as a judge in that cause, and if he were upon the bench, it would be a great disadvantage to him, for he could not take that liberty to plead the cause, which he ought to be allowed at the bar; upon this the court was satisfied."

Winthrop was fully and honorably acquitted of all the charges brought against him. The governor (Dudley) read the sentence of the court. "Then was the deputy governor desired by the court to go up and take his place again upon the bench, which he did accordingly, and the court being about to arise, he desired leave for a little speech, which was to this effect:—

"I suppose something may be expected from me, upon this charge that is befallen me, which moves me to speak now to you; yet I intend not to intermeddle in the proceedings of the court, or with any of the persons concerned therein. Only I bless God, that I see an issue of this troublesome business. I also acknowledge the justice of the court, and, for mine own part, I am well satisfied. I was publicly charged, and I am publicly and legally acquitted, which is all I did expect or desire. And though this be sufficient for my justification before men, yet not so before the God, who hath seen so much amiss in my dispensations (and even in this affair) as calls me to be humble. For to be publicly and criminally charged in this court, is matter of humiliation (and I desire to make a right use of it), notwithstanding I be thus acquitted. If her father had spit in her face (saith the Lord concerning Miriam), should she not have been ashamed seven days? Shame had lien upon her, whatever the occasion had been. I am unwilling to stay you from your urgent affairs, yet give me leave (upon this special occasion) to speak a little more to this assembly. It may be of some good use, to inform and rectify the judgment of some of the people, and may prevent such distempers as have arisen amongst us. The great questions that have troubled the country, are about the authority of the magistrates and the liberty of the people. It is yourselves who have called us to this office, and being called by you, we have our authority from God, in way of an ordinance, such as hath the image of God eminently stamped upon it, the contempt and violation whereof hath been vindicated with examples of divine vengeance. I entreat you to consider, that, when you choose magistrates, you take them from among yourselves, men subject to like passions as you are. Therefore when you see infirmities in us, you should reflect upon your own, and that would make you bear the more with us, and not be severe censurers of the failings of your magistrates, when you have continual experience of the like infirmities in yourselves and others. We account him a good servant, who breaks not his covenant. The covenant between you and us is the oath you have taken of us, which is to this purpose, that we shall govern you, and judge your causes by the rules of God's laws and our own, according to our best skill. When you agree with a workman to build you a ship or house, &c., he undertakes as well for his skill as for his faithfulness, for it is his profession, and you pay him for both. But when you call one to be a magistrate, he doth not profess nor undertake to have sufficient skill for that office, nor can you furnish him with gifts, &c., therefore you must run the hazard of his skill and ability. But if he fail in faithfulness, which by his oath he is bound unto, that he must answer for. If it fall out that the case be clear to common apprehension, and the rule clear also, if he transgress here, the error is not in the skill, but in the evil of the will; it must be required of him. But if the cause be doubtful, or the rule doubtful, to men of such understanding and parts as your magistrates are, if your magistrates should err here, yourself must bear it.

"For the other point concerning liberty, I observe a great mistake in the country about that. There is a twofold liberty, natural (I mean as our nature is now corrupt) and civil or federal. The first is common to man with beasts and other creatures. By this, man, as he stands in relation to man simply, hath liberty to do what he lists; it is a liberty to evil as well as to good. This liberty is incompatible and inconsistent with authority, and can not endure the least restraint of the most just authority. The exercise and maintaining of this liberty make men grow more evil, and in time to be worse than brute beasts: omnes sumus licentia deteriores. This is that great enemy of truth and peace, that wild beast, which all the ordinances of God are bent against, to restrain and subdue it. The other kind of liberty I call civil or federal, it may also be termed moral, in reference to the covenant between God and man, in the moral law, and the politic covenants and constitutions, amongst men themselves. This liberty is the proper end and object of authority, and can not subsist without it: and it is liberty, to that only which is good, just, and honest. This liberty you are to stand for, with the hazard (not only of your goods, but) of your lives, if need be. Whatsoever crosseth this, is not authority, but a distemper thereof. This liberty is maintained and exercised in a way of subjection to authority; it is of the same kind of liberty wherewith Christ hath made us free. The woman's own choice makes such a man her husband; yet being so chosen, he is her lord, and she is to be subject to him, yet in a way of liberty, not of bondage; and a true wife accounts her subjection her honor and freedom, and would not think her condition safe and free, but in her subjection to her husband's authority. Such is the liberty of the church under the authority of Christ, her king and husband; his yoke is so easy and sweet to her as a bride's ornaments; and if, though frowardness, or wantonness, &c., she shake it off, at any time, she is at no rest in her spirit, until she take it up again; and, whether her lord smiles upon her, and embraceth her in his arms, or whether he frowns, or rebukes, or smites her, she apprehends the sweetness of his love in all, and is refreshed, supported, and instructed, by every such dispensation of his authority over her. On the other side, ye know who they are that complain of this yoke, and say, 'Let us break their bands, &c., we will not have this man to rule over us.' Even so, brethren, it will be between you and your magistrates. If you stand for your natural corrupt liberties, and will do what is good in your own eyes, you will not endure the least weight of authority, but will murmur, and oppose, and be always striving to shake off that yoke; but if you will be satisfied to enjoy such civil and lawful liberties, such as Christ allows you, then will you quietly and cheerfully submit unto that authority which is set over you, in all the administrations of it, for your good. Wherein, if we fail at any time, we hope we shall be willing (by God's assistance) to hearken to good advice from any of you, or in any other way of God; so shall your liberties be preserved, in upholding the honor and the power of authority amongst you."

It is a very full evidence of the esteem in which he was held, that, when many gentlemen of character, some of them of noble alliance, were concerned in the same undertaking with him, he, by a general voice, was placed at their head. He says himself, in his excellent journal, which is indeed a treasure to all who revere the memory of their ancestors: "I was first chosen to be governor without my seeking or expectation, there being then divers other gentlemen, who, for their abilities, every way were far more fit."

He was eleven times chosen governor, and spent his whole estate in the public service. His son John, and his grandson, Fitz-John (who was a captain in Col. Reed's regiment at the Restoration in 1660), were successively governors of Connecticut colony, and Wait-Still another grandson, was chief justice of

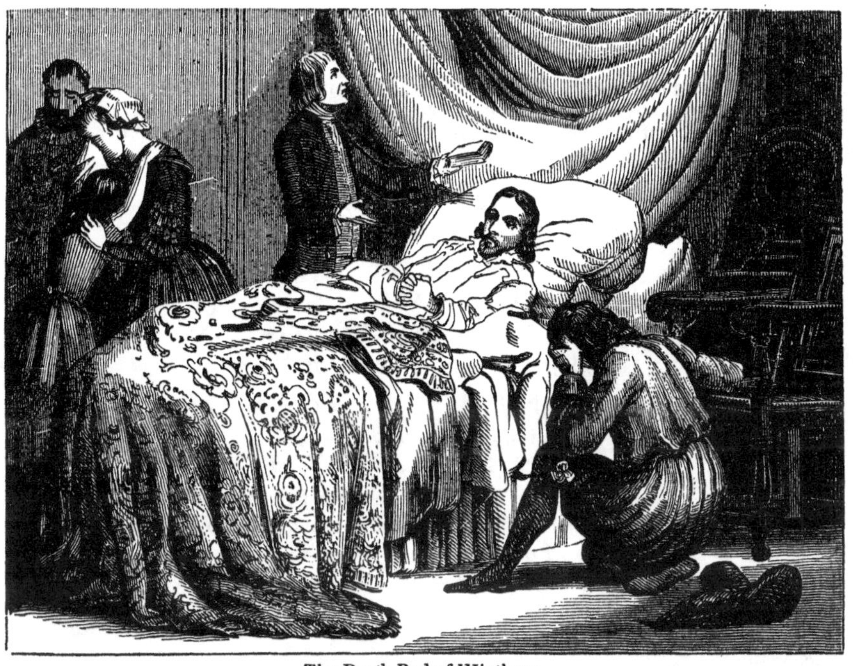

The Death-Bed of Winthrop.

Massachusetts. Stephen, another son of the elder Winthrop, went to England in 1645 or 1646, had the command of a regiment, and succeeded Harrison in his major-generalship, was a member of parliament for Scotland in 1656, and was much trusted by the Protector. The family, in every generation, have occupied high stations, and been deservedly held in great respect. Its character is now most worthily sustained by HON. ROBERT C. WINTHROP, the late distinguished and eloquent speaker of the house of representatives, in the United States' Congress; and the Hon. DAVID SEARS, of Boston. This latter gentleman has been repeatedly a member of the legislature of Massachusetts, as both representative and senator, between the years 1816 and 1851.

Governor WINTHROP died March 26, 1649, in the 62d year of his age, and was buried April 3d, in the northern corner of the King's chapel burying-ground. We may truly say of him, as he finely said of the husband of Lady Arabella Johnson, "He was a holy man and wise, and died in sweet peace." He conducted himself with such address and unshaken rectitude, as to render his character universally respected among his contemporaries, and his memory dear to posterity. In his magnanimity, disinterestedness, moderation, and harmonious character, the father of Massachusetts reminds us of the great "father of his country," and is the only name in our history worthy to stand as a parallel to WASHINGTON.

"His was the upright deed,
His the unswerving course,
'Mid every thwarting current's force,
Unchanged by venal aim, or flattery's hollow reed:
The *holy truth* walked ever by his side,
And in his bosom dwelt, companion, judge, and guide.
But when disease revealed
To his unclouded eye,
The stern destroyer standing nigh,
Where turned he for a shield?
Wrapt he the robe of stainless rectitude
Around his heart, to meet cold Jordan's flood?
Grasped he the staff of pride,
His steps, through death's dark vale to guide?
Ah, no! self-righteousness he cast aside,
Clasping, with firm and fearless faith, the cross of HIM who died,
Serene, serene,
He passed the crumbling verge of this terrestrial scene,
Breathed soft, in childlike trust,
The parting groan,
Gave back to dust its dust—
To Heaven its own."

THE WINTHROP FAMILY TOMB, IN KING'S CHAPEL BURYING-GROUND,

TREMONT STREET, BOSTON.

This ancient Monument originally had inscribed on it the Epitaph which is given below; but it is said that the letters having become nearly obliterated by time, or injured by accident or design, during the Revolution, the stone was replaced by another, wh ch bears the names and ages of the members of the family as follows:—

JOHN WINTHROP,

GOVERNOR OF MASSACHUSETTS,

Died 1649.

MAJOR-GENERAL

WAIT STILL WINTHROP,

Died September 7th, 1717. *Aged* 76 *Years.*

ANN WINTHROP SEARS,

The Wife of DAVID SEARS,

Died Oct. 2d, 1789. *Aged* 33 *Years.*

Here also rest the remains of JOHN WINTHROP, first Governor of Connecticut, [eldest son of JOHN, the Founder of Boston, and first Governor of Massachusetts.] He died at Boston, 5th April, 1676.

FITZ-JOHN WINTHROP, his son, Governor of Connecticut, died at Boston, 27th November, 1707.

THOMAS L. WINTHROP, Lieutenant-Governor of Massachusetts, died 22d Feb. 1840.

STAND TRAVELLER,
And admire ye Tomb,
And to ye Public Tears add your own,
Bewail ye public Loss,
If of ye publick you are part.
This place is a Prince's Court
Rather than a Tomb.
This marble covers dust
Worthy to be enclosed in Gold.
Four WINTHROPS lie buried in this Tomb,
Who were sufficient to enrich ev'n ye four quarters of ye Earth.

He is unacquainted with ye history of New England
Who is ignorant of this Family,
And he has no regard for Universal Virtue
That does not highly value it.
The last of these
here Interr'd
Was WAIT WINTHROP, Esqr
Whose last Honour was this,
That he was Governour of New England,
He was, alas! he was
Of New England, ye glory & Defence,
The Light and Stay.
Major-General of Massachusett's Colony,
Of a noble yet peaceful disposition,
And who for his Country and for Peace could die.
President of ye Council for ye Province,
Whose chiefest care it always was
That ye Commonwealth might receive no damage;
And in whom many died.
Chief Judge,
Who paid an equal regard to Justice & Clemency.
He went thro' ye most honourable
Stations in ye Government,
And adorn'd ye Honours w'ch he bore,
Deserving those he bore not.
A person of ye most undissembled piety
And unspotted probity,
Of an exalted yet a modest Genius.
He placed all things beneath himself,
Himself beneath all men.

Benevolent tow'rds all,
And most so tow'ds ye poor & needy.
Injurious to none not even to enemies;
An enemy to none,
Ev'n tho' highly provok'd.
No unhappy person was by him rejected,
Nor poor one refus'd admittance,
Nor did any go away displeas'd.
He was skillfull in physick,
And being possessed of Golden Secrets,
Indeed more valuable than Gold itself,
And having obtained Universal Remedies,
Which Hippocrates & Helmont never knew,
All that were sick where e'er he came
He freely restor'd to health,
And made almost his whole study of Nature
Subservient to Medicine.
He that under this stone now sleeps in death,
Still lives in ye hearts of thousands
Whose lives he has prolonged.
The merits of WINTHROP with Him
Oblivion shall not bury.
He was born ye 27th day of December 1641,
Died ye 7th day of September 1717,
In ye 76xth year of his age.
They who value Life & still enjoy It,
Wish'd him a Thousand years continuance here,
An age exceeding that of Methusalem.

JOHN QUINCY ADAMS was born in that part of Braintree, now Quincy, near Boston, July 11, 1767—in the midst of that deep, wide, stormy excitement which preceded the separation of the then colonies from the British empire. In the agitation of that period, his father John Adams, bore a leading part; and his mother, a strong-minded woman, worthy of that heroic age, had no thought or feeling that did not sympathize with her husband and her country. The lessons of his infancy were lessons of patriotism and of resistance to wrong. The blood that circled in his veins was alive with the spirit of inflexible opposition to arbitrary power. He was nine years old at the date of the declaration of independence.

Early in 1778, his father, who had been appointed commissioner with Franklin and Arthur Lee, at the court of Versailles, took him to France. Thus early did he become cognizant of public affairs, and particularly of diplomatic business. The elder Adams was training his son for a life of patriotic statesmanship. A treaty having been signed by which France recognised the United States as an independent power, Mr. Adams returned with his son in the same vessel which brought to our shores the first ambassador from France—the first that ever came to us from any foreign power.

Near the close of 1779, John Adams was again sent abroad by Congress, as minister plenipotentiary to negotiate a peace with Great Britain; and again his son John Quincy, then in his thirteenth year, accompanied him to Paris, and thence, a few months afterward, to Holland. The son was placed in school first at Paris, then at Amsterdam. Afterward, while his father continued in Holland, he pursued his studies at the university of Leyden. In July, 1781, Mr. Dana, of Massachusetts, who had accompanied John Adams as secretary of legation, went as minister plenipotentiary from Congress to the empress of Russia; and John Quincy Adams, then just fourteen years old, went with him as his private secretary. A few months afterward he returned to his father in Holland. With his father he went to Paris, where he was present at the signing of the treaty of peace with Great Britain—the act by which the independence of his country was consummated.

At the age of eighteen, his father permitted him to return to this country. He immediately became a student in Harvard college, where he graduated with distinguished honor. He pursued the study of law for three years, having the celebrated Theophilus Parsons for his instructor; and then having been admitted to the bar, he commenced the practice of that profession in Boston.

In 1794, when he was just twenty-seven years of age, he received from President Washington the appointment of minister to the Netherlands. From that time to 1801, he was in Europe, employed by his country in various diplomatic services. Just as General Washington was retiring from office, he appointed Mr. Adams minister plenipotentiary to the court of Portugal. While on his way to Lisbon he received a new commission, changing his destination to Berlin. During his residence of about three years and a half in Berlin, he concluded an important commercial treaty with Prussia—thus accomplishing the object of his mission. He was recalled near the close of his father's administration, and arrived in his native country in September, 1801.

In 1802, he was chosen by the Boston district to the senate of Massachusetts, and soon after was elected by the legislature a senator in Congress for six years, from March 3, 1803. He remained in the senate of the United States, until 1808, when he resigned. While in the senate he received the appointment of professor of rhetoric in Harvard University, an office which he filled with distinguished ability.

In 1809, he was appointed by President Madison, envoy extraordinary and minister plenipotentiary to the court of Russia, where he rendered the most important services to his country. By his influence with that court he induced Russia to offer her mediation between Great Britain and the United States, in the war of 1812, and when the proper time had arrived, he was placed by

Residence of the Adams' Family, Quincy, Mass.

President Madison at the head of five distinguished commissioners to negotiate a treaty of peace, which was concluded at Ghent, in 1814. Mr. Adams was then associated with Mr. Clay, and Mr. Gallatin, to negotiate a commerical convention with Great Britain, and was forthwith appointed minister plenipotentiary to the court of St. James. While in Europe, in 1811, he was appointed associate justice of the supreme court of the United States, which he declined.

Peace being restored, he resided for two years as the representative of his country at the court of Great Britain. At the commencement of Mr. Monroe's administration, in 1817, he was called home to be secretary of state. For eight years in the department of state, he was the guiding mind of that wise, peaceful, and prosperous administration. That memorable administration was perhaps as much the administration of John Quincy Adams as it was that of James Monroe.

In 1825, Mr. Adams was elected president by the votes of the states in the house of representatives, the voting in the electoral colleges having resulted in no choice. Of the measures and policy of his administration, we may not speak particularly. In general they were the same with those which had characterized the administration of Monroe.

Two years after his retirement from the presidency, the people of the congressional district in which he resided, elected him to represent them in Congress. At the commencement of the session in 1831, he took his seat in the hall of the house of representatives, and in that place of honor and of duty, the representative of Plymouth Rock, with generous blood from the May-Flower in his veins, was continued by nine successive elections. It is believed to have been the earnest wish of his heart to die like Chatham in the midst of his labors. It was a sublime thought that where he had toiled in the house of the nation, in hours of the day devoted to its service, the stroke of death should reach him, and there sever the ties of love and patriotism which bound him to the earth. He fell in his seat, on the 21st of February, 1848, attacked by paralysis, of which he had before been a victim. He was removed to the apartment of the speaker, where he remained surrounded by afflicted friends, till the weary clay resigned its immortal spirit two days afterward. "This is the end of earth!" Brief but emphatic words. They were the last uttered by the dying Christian.

In this long career of public service, Mr. Adams was distinguished by faithful attention not only to all the great duties of his stations, but to all their less and minor duties. He was not the Salaminian galley, to be launched only on extraordinary occasions, but he was the ready vessel, always launched when the duties of his station required it, be the occasion great or small. As president, as cabinet minister, as minister abroad, he examined all questions that came before him, and examined all, in all their parts, in all the minutiæ of their detail, as well as in all the vastness of their comprehension. As senator, and as a member of the house of representatives, the obscure committee-room was as much the witness of his laborious application to the drudgery of legislation as the halls of the two houses were to the ever-ready speech, replete with knowledge, which instructed all hearers, enlightened all subjects, and gave dignity and ornament to debate.

In the observance of all the proprieties of life, Mr. Adams was a most noble and impressive example. He cultivated the minor as well as the greater virtues. Wherever his presence could give aid and countenance to what was useful and honorable to man, there he was. In the exercises of the school and of the college —in the meritorious meetings of the agricultural, mechanical, and commercial societies—in attendance upon Divine worship—he gave the punctual attendance rarely seen but in those who are free from the weight of public cares. He has been gathered to his fathers, leaving behind him the memory of public services which are the history of his country for half a century, and the example of a life, public, and private, which should be the study and the model of the generations of his countrymen.

Yale College, Courthouse, &c

CONNECTICUT.

This is one of the small states of the Union, but it has performed a part of much importance to the general interests of the country, in different ways and at different periods. It was not only one of the original states, but contained two of the oldest colonies, having been settled in 1636, sixteen years after the landing at Plymouth.

The boundaries were long unsettled, and, on all its four sides, contesting claims caused agitation and difficulty for years: on the east, with Rhode Island; on the north, with Massachusetts; and on the west, with New York: which three states are now separated from Connecticut chiefly by artificial limits. Having settled several towns on Long Island, Connecticut long extended her jurisdiction across the sound; and the beautiful valley of Wyoming, in Pennsylvania, was once occupied by her, as part of her territory, being included in the royal patent of the colony, which extended to the Pacific ocean.

The limits of the state, as long since finally settled, extend from latitude 40° 2′ to 41° north, and between longitude 71° 20′ and 73° 15′ west. It contains 4,674 square miles.

The soil is generally poor, with some remarkable exceptions, especially on the fertile meadows of Connecticut river.

By a glance at the map, the reader will see that this state is crossed by three principal ranges of high land, from south to north, which give their general direction to the three chief streams—the Connecticut in the middle; the Thames, or Shetucket, in the east; and the Housatonic in the west. Some parts of the hills are rough and of considerable elevation, but scarcely deserve the name of mountains. Most of them consist of granite and other primitive rocks; and to that formation most of the country belongs, except the meadows, which are a rich alluvial soil, annually increased by particles left by the floods, and washed down from the high land by the rains. These lowlands are generally of great fertility—those of the Connecticut, especially, being considered as the best in New England, and equal to almost any other in the United States. The uplands, however, have a soil of but middling quality; yet being divided into small farms, and cultivated by an industrious and intelligent people, they are made more productive than some better lands in less favorable circumstances.

In some parts of the state are small tracts, quite unfit for cultivation; but in many of the roughest and wildest regions are found valuable quarries and mines, many of which are profitably wrought; and the discriminating eye of science has recently recognised some of the rare minerals before discovered in only a few localities in the world.* The greatest treasure of the hilly regions, however, is an immense amount of water-power, afforded by the numerous streams which rush down their declivities, and now give motion to hundreds of mills and thousands of curious machines, which the intelligence of the inhabitants has introduced, or their ingenuity invented. These produce in great numbers the great variety of articles annually manufactured both for home use and for distant markets. Most of these find their way first to the steamboats, or railroad cars, which now keep up an active intercourse with the city of New York, and are thence despatched in different directions, repaying, many times over, the cost of such raw materials as are brought from other regions.

Large steamboats run daily between New York and New Haven, Hartford, Norwich, and Stonington, each communicating with a railroad, and thus affording frequent, rapid, and commodious means of travelling and exportation, scarcely to be exceeded, and highly advantageous to commerce as well as to numerous travellers who are attracted by the beauty of the country. Steamboats of smaller size ply daily between New York and the towns lying along the western part of the sound; while numerous sloops still find employment in the coasting trade. Foreign commerce is carried on to a limited extent; and several vessels from Stonington are engaged in sealing, and more from New London in whaling.

The aspect of Connecticut is generally pleasing to the eye. Its small territory embraces a great variety of natural scenery, everywhere embellished by art, and displaying the evidences of a numerous, intelligent, industrious, ingenious, and prosperous people. The surface is marked by roads running in all directions, and subdivided into thousands of farms of small size; while the flourishing towns and villages which meet the view in great numbers, consist of tasteful and comfortable dwellings, as far removed from splendor on the one hand, as from meanness and poverty on the other. These are evidences of the general degree of comfort and equality which prevails among the people; while the churches and schoolhouses, distributed at short intervals all over the surface, indicate the attachment which the people have always shown for learning and religion.

The facilities and accommodations here offered to travellers, are such as are afforded by the most advanced state of the arts and comforts of life.

In 1818, the state adopted the present constitution, in place of the old charter granted to the colony by King Charles I.

The history of Connecticut under the charter presents a remarkable example of stability and uniformity in government, a parallel to which it would be difficult to find in any country. All the legislative officers, except representatives, were chosen every year by the whole body of freemen, as were the governor, deputy-governor, secretary, and treasurer. The representatives were chosen twice a year by the towns. Many of these various officers, even the higher, held their places till death or advanced age. General Wyllys was elected secretary sixty-three years in succession, including the agitated periods of the stamp-act and the revolution. All ju-

* See the Geological Survey of Connecticut, published in 1839.

dicial officers were appointed annually by the general assembly, and the members of congress by general ticket. Within a period of more than twenty years preceding the adoption of the constitution in 1818, the number of men who lost their places in the assembly and council, in consequence of a loss of popularity, was only two; yet this was a time marked by excitement and violent political parties, embracing the wars of Europe and the last American war.

At the time when the constitution was adopted in the place of the charter, a change took place in the political opinions of the majority of the people; and some of the conflicting views which have since existed in the country, have by turns prevailed in Connecticut. In the meantime, almost every kind of business for which the state is adapted has been carried on with activity, and great exertion made to improve the natural resources; while commerce, the carrying-trade, and the settlement of near and distant regions, have drawn away, either temporarily or permanently, thousands of the people, leaving but a small increase of population to be shown by the census tables.

Exertions were made in different ways for the good of the Indians. For the security of their rights of property, a law was early passed by the legislature in their favor, prohibiting private purchases of land, &c.

The influence of this law was, as may be supposed, most favorable to the Indians. No man being permitted to hold land purchased of them without the authority of the government, all inducement was cut off from unprincipled persons to overreach them, to abuse, destroy, or to drive them away. When land was purchased of the natives, they were generally secured in the possession and permanent enjoyment of such tracts as they wished to reserve; and some of these are still held by their descendants, unalienable without the express consent of the legislature. Officers, called superintendents, are intrusted with the oversight of them, and reports are made by these at every session of the legislature.

Attempts to introduce Christianity among several of the principal tribes were made, in early times, under the authority of the legislature, but with little effect. Their chiefs and head men were generally attached to their pagan systems. Several of the Indians, however, were converts, among whom was Samson Occum, long a distinguished preacher of the gospel. But it appears that no man was found with the zeal and perseverance of Eliot, called the Apostle to the Indians, who displayed such an unconquerable spirit in his prolonged exertions for the instruction and civilization of the Massachusetts Indians. Eliot himself felt so much the duty of having something done for the Indians in Connecticut, that he applied to the legislature and obtained a call for a meeting of the principal men of some of the tribes; but they rejected his offers, and never accepted Christianity as a people.

The history of Connecticut impresses important reflections on the considerate mind.

We have here an authentic account of the foundation of a state on principles of the highest nature, and for the most valuable objects that ever were proposed by any set of men. In this respect the history of all the kingdoms and empires of antiquity sinks into insignificance, and appears deficient in interest, as their origin was owing only to motives of necessity, or the desire of profit or power. The Spaniards, it is true, pretended to have in view the introduction of Christianity into South America; but their real object was conquest, and the history as well as the results of their policy too strongly attests the fact.

The objects and plans of the New England colonies would have been well worthy of our high estimation, even if their experiment had failed or had not been tried. But now, when the proofs of their success are laid before us, and it so far exceeds all anticipation, the mind perceives powerful reasons for attending to this unexampled branch of human history. And the study is recommended by higher considerations than those of mere amusement. The characters developed by the good and intelligent men who are presented, are useful subjects of contemplation; the high value which they set on religion and learning, on private virtue and public faith, lead us more justly to appreciate and more warmly to admire them; while the disinterestedness of their lives tends to make us better, wiser, more active, and more useful, in every sphere and in all situations in life.

Considerable improvement has been made in agriculture in this state within a few years. Agricultural societies have diffused knowledge, encouraged experiments, and favored the introduction of improved implements and methods. Trade, manufactures, and the learned professions (as they are perhaps improperly called), have diverted attention too much from that business which is so highly honorable and affords ample room for the application of science. Improvements might probably be introduced in agriculture, which would furnish the state with a larger supply of grain than it now raises, and prevent the necessity of making the present large annual importations. Wheat has suffered greatly ever since the year 1777 from the Hessian fly, which derives its name from the fact that it first commenced its ravages on that important crop during the year when the Hessian troops came to the country.

Silk has been made with success in Connecticut for many years, though on a limited scale. The cultivation of the white mulberry-tree was introduced into Mansfield in 1760. In 1783 the assembly offered for ten years a bounty of ten shillings, lawful money, for every hundred white mulberry-trees planted, and threepence for every ounce of silk manufactured. In 1735 the American silk company was formed in New Haven, and a large number of mulberry-trees were planted there and elsewhere. In Mansfield, in 1793, three hundred and sixty-two pounds of raw silk were made. In 1832 a bounty of one dollar was offered for every hundred trees three years old, and fifty cents a pound for silk reeled and fit for manufacture. In 1834 the bounty was extended to the Chinese mulberry, and a company was incorporated with a donation of fifteen thousand dollars, thirteen and one third per cent. of which was to be paid to Messrs. Gray and Bolton, the inventors of improvements in silk-machinery, for the use of them in the state. The speculation in mulberry-trees which prevailed in 1839, and the subsequent revulsion, caused much loss in this state.

In 1832 the paper made in Connecticut was valued at $564,000. This is connected with the manufacture of books, which was lately carried on to such an extent, that the number of volumes printed at Hartford was for several years greater than in any other place in the United States, excepting only Boston, New York, and Philadelphia.

New Haven.—This city is celebrated for its beauty, being laid out in squares four hundred feet in size, divided by fine broad and straight avenues, planted with large shady elms and other trees, and well built with edifices in good taste, adorned with gardens, and inhabited by an intelligent and refined population.

This is the largest town in the state, and one of its capitals. It is chiefly distinguished, however, as one of the first colonies, and the site of *Yale College.* The oldest edifice belonging to this venerable and flourishing institution was of wood, and stood near the corner of College and Chapel streets. There are four buildings for students, each containing thirty-two rooms, a chapel, with a philosophical chamber and apparatus, and a lyceum, with recitation-rooms and the library. In the rear are the Trumbull picture-gallery, the common's hall, in a small building with the splendid mineralogical cabinet above, purchased from the late Colonel Gibbs, of New York. A new building has lately been erected for the accommodation of the literary societies of the college. In another building is the chemical laboratory, where Professor Silliman delivers his lectures. The institution has above five hundred scholars.

Next north of the college is the house of the president, and the professors have pleasant residences in the town.

The medical institution is at the north

New Haven Green.

end of College street, and the theological seminary on the green.

The burying-ground is situated opposite the medical institution, and occupies a large extent of land, planted with trees, and containing a great number of beautiful monuments of different designs.

The old burying-ground was in the middle of the green, in the rear of the Centre church; and there are to be seen two ancient stone monuments, of a small size, which are supposed to mark the graves of two of the regicide judges, Whalley and Dixwell.

The *Farmington and Northampton Canal*, commencing near the head of the wharf in this city, is crossed by the traveller, in going up from the steamboat, near the market. The basin is large and commodious; and the canal, passing through a part of the city and bending round along the outskirts on the north side, intersects several streets, by which it is crossed on handsome bridges. It extends to Northampton, Massachusetts.

There are pleasant rides in various directions from New Haven, the roads being numerous, and the face of the country favorable.

The *Judges' Cave* is on the summit of West rock, about a mile north of the bluff. It is formed by the crevices between seven large rocks, apparently thrown together by some convulsion. It is small, and entirely above ground, with a rude rock, like a column, on each hand. That on the right has this inscription:—

"Opposition to tyrants is obedience to God!"

to remind the visiter that the place once afforded shelter to Goffe and Whalley, two of the judges of King Charles the First, who escaped to the colonies and secreted themselves for some time in this solitary place. They were supplied with food by a family which resided near the foot of the mountain, and a little boy was despatched for them every day, who left a basket of provisions on a rock, without knowing what cause he was subserving. The place commands an extensive view upon the country below, with a large tract of Long island and the sound.

The manufactory of muskets is two miles north of New Haven, on the road to Hartford by Meriden, and at the foot of East rock. It was established by Mr. Whitney, the well-known inventor of the cotton-jin.

The *New Haven and Hartford Railroad*, forty miles long, begins at the steamboat wharf, crosses Quinnepiack river, and passes through the townships of North Haven, Wallingford, Meriden, Berlin, and Wethersfield.

It pursues the general course of the "old colonial road," the route taken in early times between New Haven and Hartford, which were independent colonies. It was originally an Indian trail.

Beyond New Haven, in Long Island sound, lies a cluster of islands called the Thimbles, famous in the traditions of the neighboring Connecticut coast, as the ancient resort of Captain Kidd, the notable pirate, whose treasures of solid gold, it is still believed by some, are concealed somewhere hereabouts.

Saybrook.—At this place was the first settlement made by Europeans on Connecticut river. It was undertaken at the earnest solicitation of many of the rightful proprietors of the country on its banks, who had been despoiled of their possessions by their formidable enemies, the Pequods. The River Indians twice made application to the English at Plymouth and at Boston to obtain settlers from their native soil, offering to give them land enough, and to pay two hundred beaverskins annually for the benefit of their society. But the undertaking was considered too hazardous; and it was not until the year 1635, when the Dutch at New York showed a determination to seize upon the country, which they claimed as their own, that a small detachment of men was sent from Boston to prepare for opening a trade with the Indians, and to build a fort at the mouth of the river. Their haste was soon justified by events; for immediately after their landing, a Dutch vessel entered, and, proceeding up to Hartford, landed a body of men, who soon established themselves in a fort they called Good Hope, on a spot they obtained from Pequod usurpers.

The settlement of Saybrook was begun under a grant made to Lord Say and Seal, Lord Brook, and others, by George Fenwick, esquire, who fled to this country with his family. The old fort stood near the present fort hill, upon an eminence which has since been destroyed by the waves; and the ground immediately behind it was afterward occupied by the fields and habitations of the colonists. It was expected from the first that the situation would render the place a great city; and after the fear of the Indians had subsided, the whole peninsula, which bears the name of Saybrook point, was laid out with the greatest regularity into fields of an equal size, except such parts as were reserved for the erection of public buildings.

Many emigrants were once collected in England, and prepared for a voyage to this place. Some persons of high rank and importance were among them; and it is a well-authenticated fact that Oliver Cromwell had determined to embark in the enterprise, and was once on the very eve of quitting England for ever, when some unforeseen occurrence prevented him.

The want of a harbor, and the obstacles presented to a free navigation by a large sandbar at the mouth of the river, have effectually prevented the expectations of the settlers of Saybrook from being realized; and no remains of their works can now be discovered, except in the rectangular forms of the fields, and the cellars of some of their dwellings, just beyond the burying-ground, the foundation-stones of which have since been employed in building the neighboring fences. One of the largest excavations is said to have been the cellar of the old college building. The soldiers were frequently attacked within a short distance of the fort by the Pequods, but they afterward ran a palisade across the isthmus which leads from the mainland. Yale college was placed here for a time.

Connecticut River.—The shores of this principal stream of New England present a continued succession of hilly and picturesque country, with few interruptions of level land, from a little above Saybrook as far as Middletown. The roughness and rocky nature of the soil prevent the cultivation of many mountainous tracts, yet there are farms enough to give a considerable degree of softness to the scenery. The variety of rocky and wooded banks, mingling with little patches of cultivated ground, and the habitations scattered along the river, is very agreeable, and often affords scenes highly picturesque and delightful.

Essex.—This is a small village, situated on the ascent and summit of a handsome elevation, seven miles from Saybrook. During the late war with Great Britain, this place was taken by the enemy, who came up the river in launches, and, taking the inhabitants by surprise, occupied the town for a few hours.

East Haddam.—The landing-place here is rocky, mountainous, and wild, and a good specimen of a large portion of the town to which it belongs. This region is famous for a kind of earthquakes and subterranean sounds, which were formerly common for a short distance round. They gave occasion to many superstitious reports, but have ceased within a few years. They were called *Moodus noises*, after the Indian name of the place. Large beryls and many other rare minerals are found in the neighborhood.

Haddam is built on an eminence fifty or sixty feet high, which appears like the remains of an old bank of the river, descending to a little meadow which is covered with orchards, grazing ground, &c., while a range of commanding hills rise beyond.

The Narrows.—Here the river turns abruptly to the east, and flows between two lofty hills, which it has divided at some long past period, before which, there is every reason to believe, the country for a great distance above was covered by a lake.

Fort Hill is the last elevated part of the southern bank. It was formerly a little fortress belonging to Sowheag, an Indian chief, whose dominion extended over the present towns of Middletown, Chatham, and Wethersfield.

Middletown is beautifully situated on the western bank of the Connecticut river, where the water is spread out to a considerable breadth, and disappears so suddenly at the Narrows, that, from many points of view, it has the appearance of a small lake, with high, sloping, and cultivated shores. This is a most agreeable residence.

The Wesleyan university has a building one hundred and fifty feet long, fifty broad, and four stories high, with rooms for scholars; a chapel, with recitation-rooms above, both of stone; and an eating-hall of brick, one hundred and twenty feet long, with a piazza.

The quarries of freestone on the opposite shore, in Chatham, have furnished a valuable building material for some years, and have been worked to a considerable extent.

The *Lead Mine* is about two miles below the town, on the south shore of the river, where are several old shafts, which were sunk in the revolutionary war, in a slate rock. The ore is sulphuret of lead, in veins of quartz, partly crystallized, and affording a few specimens of fluate of lime, and other minerals.

The *Cobalt Mine* is about five miles east, in Chatham, at the foot of Rattlesnake hill. It is not worth working, at the usual price of the metal. Just south of it is a very pretty waterfall, about thirty feet high.

WETHERSFIELD.—This place is three miles from Hartford, and has a fine light soil, on an extensive level, probably once the bottom of a lake since drained by the deepening of the river's channel. It is peculiarly favorable to the culture of onions, which are exported in great quantities to various parts of the country, the West Indies, &c.

Wethersfield was the second settlement made by white men in Connecticut. In 1635, three or four men came to this place and spent the winter.

The Connecticut Stateprison.—The situation of this institution is healthy, retired, and convenient to the water and the great road. It was completed in 1817. What have heretofore been regarded as the necessary evils of prisons will be found in this prison to be greatly reduced, and in many respects, even with regard to the prisoners, converted into benefits.

Here the Auburn system has been established with some few deviations.

The whole is under the direction of the superintendent—a man of firmness, judgment, and humanity. The men are brought out to their work at signals given by the bell. They lodge in solitary cells, and are not permitted to converse together while at work. They take their food in their cells, and when going to and from work or prayers, are obliged to march with the lock step. No blows are allowed to be given by the officers except in self-defence.

The smiths' fires are supplied with Lehigh (Pennsylvania) coal for fuel, and part of the heat is conducted away in pipes to warm the apartments. The cells are furnished with comfortable beds and bedclothes, and a bible for each. They are ranged in rows, and the keepers can look into them through grated doors; at the same time the prisoners are not able to converse with each other. The effects of evil communication, so much and so banefully cherished in our old prisons, are thus effectually prevented. Neither officers nor convicts are allowed to use ardent spirits.

HARTFORD, one of the capitals of the state, is on Connecticut river, thirty-four miles north of New Haven. It is a place of considerable business. There are the City hotel, coffeehouse and other inns, several fine churches, &c.

The Charter Oak.—In the lower part of the town, in the street which runs east from the south church, is the ancient and respectable seat of the Wyllis family, who were among the early settlers of Hartford, and have made a conspicuous figure in the history of the state, as well as of the town, by holding the secretary's office for a long course of time. The principal object of curiosity here, the fine old oak, stands on the street in front. It is said to have been a forest-tree before the land was cleared, yet it appears as firm and vigorous as ever. In a hole in its trunk was hidden the charter of the colony, when Sir Edmund Andross sent to demand it in 1687; and there it remained for some years. This interesting document is still preserved in the office of the secretary of the state.

The Asylum for the Education of the Deaf and Dumb, is about a mile west of the town, on Tower hill. It was the earliest institution of the kind in America. The principal building is large, ornamented with pilasters, and surrounded by a garden and pleasant grounds. The house of the superintendent is near by, and the whole enjoys a fine situation, with a very commanding prospect and a healthy neighborhood.

The number of scholars is about two hundred. Some of them are supported by a fund belonging to the institution, and others by the states of Massachusetts, New Hampshire, &c. Ten similar institutions now exist in New York, Philadelphia, Kentucky, &c.

The *Retreat for the Insane*, a little south of the city, makes a handsome appearance, being a stone building one hundred and fifty feet long and fifty feet wide, the wings having three stories, and the main building four. It is capable of containing about fifty patients, and is warmed by flues. The grounds connected with the institution include about seventeen acres. A young lady who had been severely afflicted with deep melancholy, but recovered at this institution, wrote the following lines, which were handed to the excellent matron on leaving the place:—

"Farewell, Retreat; I will remember thee,
For thou hast been a hiding place to me:
When, on the waves of sorrow, hither driven,
I found this refuge to the helpless given.
Oh, what an hour of darkness and despair,
When not a ray of hope was shining there,
But one continued storm my sky o'erspread,
And poured its waters on my weary head!
Then did thy gentle form, amid the gloom,
Appear like Mercy smiling o'er the tomb;
With tender accents sooth my fears to rest,
And smooth the anxious billows in my breast:
With generous feeling, still each want supply—
Now seem to sympathize in every sigh.
How dear the hand that wipes the tear away,
And kindness, doubly sweet in such a day!
Here memory, too, shall trace thy love sincere,
And oft, in fancy, hear thy footsteps near.
Deep in my heart shall this remembrance be —
The sorrows I have known, thy love to me.
And, though divided by Time's flying hour,
Yet may we bow before the Mighty Power
Which bids us live and strive to share his love,
That we may meet in brighter worlds above."

NEW LONDON is fifty-four miles east of New Haven, and one hundred and twenty east-northeast of New York. It is situated irregularly, principally at the foot of a hill facing the east, and wears an appearance of decline; but some of the houses are handsome, and there are several fine situations near the top.

The harbor is one of the most accessible, safe, and commodious, in the United States, lying near the ocean and the sound, almost surrounded by high land, and having water enough for ships-of-war quite up to the wharves, with a fine sandy bottom near the shores.

Fort Griswold, opposite New London, was garrisoned by a few continental troops in the year 1781, during the revolution, when Benedict Arnold, after his desertion of the American cause, appeared off the harbor with a British force on the 6th of September; and landing eight hundred men on each point of the harbor, marched up and took Fort Trumbull, and burned the town. Col. Eyre, who commanded the troops on the eastern shore, proceeded toward Fort Griswold, and sending in a flag of truce, demanded a surrender.

But, before this time, Colonel Ledyard had entered the fort and garrisoned it with one hundred and twenty men, chiefly militia volunteers from the neighborhood. The British troops had advanced under cover of a wood, and invested the fort; but the Americans, after defending themselves for some time, and beating off their enemies once, finally surrendered when resistance would have been entirely useless. The enemy had lost forty-one officers and men, who were buried near the spot; with Colonel Eyre, the commander, wounded, and Major Montgomery killed. After the surrender, however, a massacre of the prisoners took place, which cast the deepest disgrace on the expedition; seventy officers and men being the victims, most of whom were heads of families.

Fort Hill is a commanding eminence about four miles east from New London, and derives its name from a Pequod fort which formerly occupied its summit. The road crosses it near the southern limit of the fort, and a small church stands a quarter of a mile above, within the extensive space once enclosed by that palisaded work. It was the great fortress of the terrible Pequod nation, which makes a very conspicuous figure in the early history of the eastern colonies. They had fought their way from the interior, and seated themselves in the present limits of Groton, where the few poor remains of their descendants still are found. On the arrival of the English, they had extended their conquests a considerable distance up Connecticut river, and the eastern and western Nehantics were subject to them.

In consequence of the murders they had committed, and the attack with which they had threatened the infant settlements at Hartford, Windsor, and Wethersfield, the inhabitants formed an expedition in the spring of 1637, led by Captain Mason, and attacked their other fort on the Mystic, burning it, and killing about six hundred persons; after which the natives fled from their country, and having suffered another terrible slaughter in the swamp at Fairfield, were reduced to slavery, and ceased from that time to be an object of terror.

This hill commands an extensive and delightful view, being almost entirely clear of obstructions, and superior in height to the neighboring hills. A considerable extent of Long island and the sound are overlooked from the summit, with various islands, bays, and points, on the Connecticut coast. At the time of the burning of Mystic fort, it was occupied by the chief sachem, Sassacus, who hastened to the relief of his subjects, but arrived too late to render them any assistance. On his return here, he burned the wigwams and palisades, and immediately fled for refuge to the Mohawks, by whom he was beheaded.

Stonington.—This is a small but busy town on the coast, long engaged in whaling and sealing. Steamboats run daily hence to New York.

The *Providence and Stonington Railroad,* forty-seven miles, leaves the shore of Long Island sound, at the steamboat wharf in Stonington; passes through the town; crosses Pawcatuck river into Rhode Island; up Charles River valley to Sherman's pond, South Kingston; north to East Greenwich; and across a bridge to Providence, connecting with the Boston and Providence railroad. It was finished in 1837, and cost two millions of dollars. Summit, three hundred and two feet; maximum grade, thirty-three feet; fourteen miles nearly level; minimum radius, one thousand six hundred and thirty-seven feet, in one spot four hundred and eighty.

On descending the hill which leads into Stonington, Porter's rock, thirty or forty feet high, is seen a little off the road on the right hand. Under the shelter of it, it is said, Captain Mason encamped with his little army on the night of May 26, 1637 (old style), a few hours before his successful attack on the second Pequod fort, which was on the top of a hill about two miles south of this place.

The Mohegan Tribe of Indians.—The Pequods lived near New London, and the Mohegans in and around Norwich.

Uncas, the sachem of Mohegan, was believed to be of Pequod descent, but in a state of successful revolt at the time the English became acquainted with him. His chief residence was near Trading cove, now the centre of the Indian reservation; but the burying-ground of the royal family was near Norwich landing. He had conquered the country as far north as about the present Massachusetts line, but became an early friend of the whites, and rendered them important services, particularly in war, as well as his successors, the later Mohegan chiefs.

Before this part of the state was settled, Uncas was once so closely besieged by his enemies the Pequods, that he suffered extremely from a scarcity of provisions, and was relieved only by the care of a man named Leffingwell, who was despatched from Connecticut with a boat loaded with provisions. In gratitude, Uncas gave him a large part of the present town of Norwich for this important service. There is a rock still pointed out on the shore, called Uncas's chair, where the sachem is said to have sat watching the arrival of his friends.

The poor remains of this tribe reside on the lands secured to them by the state

Bridge at Norwich.

government, and live in all the ignorance, idleness, and thriftlessness, common to the Indians in this part of the country—melancholy testimonies of the degradation to which the most active human minds may sink when every customary impulse to exertion has been stifled, and no new incitement extended.

NORWICH is in New London county, at the head of navigation on the Thames. It is eighty miles southwest of Boston, and has two villages, of which Chelsea landing is the principal. The city is remarkable for its singular situation, which is peculiarly beautiful and romantic—most of the buildings being on the declivity of a hill, and the streets rising one above another, ornamented with handsome churches, a townhall, an academy, and many elegant dwellinghouses. It is equally remarkable for its appearance of business, which is much favored by the numerous manufactories in the neighboring country. In the rear of the hill, about a mile north, is a beautiful plain, on which are laid out several handsome streets, shaded with ancient trees, which render it a very pleasant place.

On the way thither is seen the cove, at the upper end of which are the falls of Yantic, a stream which pours over a ledge of granite about forty feet high, and supplies several manufactories with water. The place is highly picturesque. A rock, seventy or eighty feet in height, overhangs the stream, whence a number of Narraganset Indians, pursued by the Mohegans, precipitated themselves.

The Burying-Ground of the Uncases.—This is on the elevated bank north of the cove. There are stones marking the graves of numerous members of the royal family of the Mohegans, and a few of them bear English inscriptions. The family is now extinct.

Uncas, the old friend of the pilgrims, is buried here. He and his nation were the only steady allies they ever found among the Indians, firm and powerful enough to render them very essential service. He was a man of extraordinary talent, and withal extremely politic; but he refused to join the Indians against the English, and died a friend of the white men.

The Bridge.—The accompanying engraving represents the high bridge across the Thames, just below the falls. The rocks are high and precipitous, and the violence and roaring of the stream, especially at high floods, strike the traveller with awe and fear. The stream here makes a rapid descent down a rough and rocky channel, over which the passenger seems hanging in the air, and about to be borne away by the impetuous and irresistible current. A short distance below, the bed of the river becomes level, and soon the water spreads over a wide surface, forming a broad and beautiful cove, which looks like a small, resplendent lake, with varied and pleasing scenery displayed along its margin.

The *Worcester and Norwich Railroad*, fifty-eight and a half miles long, passes up the valley of the Quinnebaug, near Jewett's city, and many manufactories, through Westfield, Pomfret, Oxford, &c., to Worcester, where it meets the railroads to Boston and to New York. It was opened in 1840; cost one million; the maxium grade, twenty feet.

Sachem's Field, one mile and a half from Norwich, is a small elevated plain, on which a battle was fought, in 1643, between about nine hundred Narragansets, inhabiting Rhode Island, and five or six hundred Mohegans. The sachem of the former, Miantonimo, intending to chastise Uncas for his adherence to the English, secretly advanced into his country with an army. Uncas, aware of his approach, met him on this plain, where both parties halted; he then resorted to this stratagem: stepping forward, he challenged Miantonimo to decide the quarrel single-handed. This, as he expected was refused; and while his enemies were unprepared, he gave a signal by falling down, when his men set up a yell, discharged their arrows, and rushed forward. The Narragansets fled, and many were killed. Uncas himself captured Miantonimo, who was too haughty to ask for quarter or speak a word; he was taken to Hartford, tried, and given to Uncas for execution; he was brought back, and, while marching across the field, tomahawked near the road.

John Winthrop

First Governor of Connecticut.

JOHN WINTHROP, FIRST GOVERNOR OF CONNECTICUT.—This distinguished gentleman, for many years the governor of Connecticut, was the eldest son of John Winthrop, the first governor of Massachusetts, and founder of the city of Boston—that famous pattern of piety and justice, as he is called in the early chronicles of New England—who emigrated to America in 1630, and brought with him the confidence and respect of the government he had left, and the most exalted and upright faculty for the duties he came to assume. Graham, adopting the thought of a classic historian, says of him that he not only performed actions worthy to be written, but produced writings worthy to be read. His son John—the subject of this brief memoir—was scarcely less distinguished. He was the heir of all his father's talent, prudence, and virtues, with a superior share of human learning—much addicted to philosophical study, and especially to physical science. He was one of the early patrons of the London Royal Society. Sir Hans Sloane, and three other members of that society, some fifty years afterward, in commending the grandson of this gentleman to the notice of their associates, bear honorable testimony to the good repute in which the ancestor was held. They speak of the learned John Winthrop as "one of the first members of this society, and who in conjunction with others did greatly contribute to the obtaining of our charter; to whom the

Royal Society in its early days was not only indebted for various ingenious communications, but their museum still contains many testimonies of his generosity, especially of things relating to the natural history of New England."

John Winthrop was elected governor of Connecticut for several years, in which station his many valuable qualities as a gentleman, a philosopher, and a public ruler, procured him the universal respect of the people under his government; and his unwearied attention to the public business and great understanding in the art of government, were of unspeakable advantage to them.

He was twice married, his second wife being the daughter of the celebrated Hugh Peters. By this marriage he had several children, two of whom were sons. The elder, Fitz-John, followed in the footsteps of his father—was elected governor of Connecticut, and held that post for nine years, commencing in 1698, and continuing till the day of his death. Thus father, son, and grandson, died in the highest office to which the affections of the people could exalt them. The younger son was a member of the Massachusetts council, under the new charter granted by William and Mary, and afterward chief justice of the superior court of that state. His name was Wait Still, a compound of two family names—the middle name being derived from the intermarriage of Adam, his great-grandfather, with the family of Still.

Wait Still Winthrop, the chief-justice, appears to have left but two children, of whom John, the only son resembled his grandfather in an ardent devotion to science, and like him became a distinguished member of the Royal Society; his introduction to that body being greatly facilitated by the respect in which the memory of his ancestor was yet held. Attracted by the love of his favorite studies, and his attachment to the society of learned men, he removed to England, and died in 1747. He had seven children, of whom two were sons, John Still and Basil. On the 4th of Sept., 1750, the former married Jane Borland, of Boston, whose daughter Ann married the late DAVID SEARS, Esq.,* of that place.

The name of WINTHROP shall be remembered so long as nations exist. It will rank with Newton, Boyle, and Locke, and those philanthropists of every age, who are an ornament to human nature, and whose lives have been devoted to the cultivation of the moral graces, and the advancement of social and religious happiness; enlarging the circle of the human mind, and adorning the principles of philosophy with the precepts of piety. Their fame is identified with the progress of knowledge and the diffusion of virtue. The history of such men sheds a bright and undying lustre upon their country, and will call forth the grateful recollections of unborn generations, so long as truth shall triumph over error, and the influence of Christianity be felt in removing vice and superstition from the hearts of men.

* Of this gentleman a note will hardly allow us the proper space to speak of his character and virtues. He was born on the 12th of August, 1752. He removed from Chatham to Boston in 1770, and visited England in 1774. He became acquainted with Dr. Franklin in London, and took letters to his friends in France and Holland. He remained on the continent nearly two years, and with difficulty made his way back to Boston. In various modes his services were useful to his country. During the presidency of the elder Adams he was one of a committee of the citizens of Boston for building a frigate (the Boston), towards which he subscribed three thousand dollars, and presenting it to government. He was largely interested in the India and China trade, and added much to his fortune. He was distinguished as an intelligent and able financier—a director in the first "bank of the United States," from its commencement to its termination—often a referee in intricate cases of mercantile equity; and his whole career was marked by the most incorruptible integrity, which never for the sake of a paltry advantage violated that punctilious delicacy which is indispensable to the character of a gentleman.

"An easy mien, engaging in address,
Looks which at once each winning grace express,
A life where love and truth were ever joined,
A nature ever good and ever kind,
A wisdom solid and a judgment clear,
The smile indulgent, and a soul sincere."

Mr. Sears was the proprietor of a large estate in Waldo county, in Maine, the settlers and tenantry of which honored and revered him, and as they became proprietors of the soil testified their gratitude for his patriarchal treatment by naming their towns in his honor. He was generous and charitable—the founder of the widows' fund in Trinity church—and a contributor to numerous charities. He died in front of his house in Beacon-street, struck instantly dead by a stroke of apoplexy, as he was getting into his carriage to make an afternoon visit, on the 19th of October, 1816. "By this affecting event, this town [Boston] has lost an eminent merchant and excellent citizen; an only child, an affectionate parent; this church [Trinity], a distinguished benefactor; society at large, a well-bred and hospitable gentleman.'

The Landing of Roger Williams

RHODE ISLAND.

THIS state, the smallest in the Union, is bounded on the north and east by Massachusetts, south by the Atlantic ocean, and west by Connecticut. It is about forty-nine miles long and twenty-nine wide, and contains one thousand three hundred and sixty square miles, of which one hundred and thirty are embraced in Narraganset bay. The population in 1850 was 147,654.

The northern portion of the state is hilly, and that near the coast is low and level, but healthy, being tempered by the seabreeze. There are several islands in and near Narraganset bay, the principal of which, Rhode Island (called after the isle of Rhodes in the Mediterranean), has given name to the state.

There are several rivers of great value for manufacturing, which is carried on in various branches, but chiefly in cotton, to the great benefit of the state. The principal rivers are as follows: Pawtucket, Providence, Wood, Pawtuxet, and Pawcatuck; and several manufacturing villages, of considerable size, are built on their banks.

The commerce of the state has long been considerable; but of late years it has been transferred from Newport to Providence, where it now centres. Unhappily the slave-trade was formerly carried on extensively from Rhode Island; but that inhuman traffic has ceased.

Rhode Island presents several strong contrasts, when viewed in different aspects. Although the smallest state in the Union, and containing but a small number of inhabitants, yet it has a very large proportion of persons engaged in manufactures, and was the first in which the manfacture of cotton was effected by machinery. Although the first of the colonies in which general religious toleration, or rather equality, was established, contrary to the general impression, that system was allowed to exist but two years; for Roman catholics were then denied the liberty allowed to others.

The history of this state is interesting for important events which occurred within its territory at different epochs. It was the scene of some of the first and the latest events of the eventful war of King Philip, or Metacom, who was a native of its soil, and fell at the foot of Mount Hope. The Narragansets, one of the most powerful Indian tribes in New England, were reduced by a war carried on in this territory.

This tribe is now reduced to three or four hundred, composing about fifty families, who reside on the Indian lands. Individuals of the tribe were lately in possession of three or four thousand acres of land, about one third of which was cultivated. The tribe own twenty or thirty acres of woodland, seventy acres of swamp, and nineteen acres on Short Neck; they have a church, with a regular baptist clergyman (an Indian); and a schoolhouse, in which school is kept in winter by the Indians, and in summer by the missionary society: it consists of forty or fifty scholars.

In the revolution, Newport was taken and occupied by the British forces until relieved by a French fleet, coöperating with the American army.

The following extract is from a letter written by a distinguished historian :—

"Rhode Island was foremost in the following events :—

"*May* 17, 1744. The delegates from the town of Providence were instructed to prevail on the assembly to use their influence with the other colonies to promote the convening of a continental congress—a few days earlier than the action of any other public body on the subject.

"*June* 15, 1774. The assembly chose delegates to the congress two days before Massachusetts, which I believe has hitherto been considered the first to elect delegates.

"*August*, 1775. The assembly recommended to the congress to build and equip a continental navy; the first recommendation of this sort by any public body.

"*May*, 1776. Act of abjuration on independence was passed; the only step of this description, as far as I know, taken by any assembly, or colonial convention, before the declaration of congress. The resolves of Mecklenburg county, in North Carolina, were of the same tenor, but the meeting consisted of delegates from one county only, and these seem not to have been chosen upon the usual principles of representation.

"There are passages in the colonial history of Rhode Island most honorable to the patriotic spirit of the people. The assembly petitioned against the famous 'sugar act' of 1773.

"The petition was rejected by parliament. A curious debate on the subject may be seen in Hassard's Parliamentary History, vol. viii., p. 1261."

NEWPORT.—This place possesses one of the best harbors in the United States. The entrance is protected by Fort Adams, on Brenton's point. It embraces an extent of about 130 acres. A range of guns lines the shore toward the west, and the casemates, &c., are very strong.

Newport extends about a mile along the shore, and its natural beauties pass quite beyond any seaside resort in this country. It has become very popular as a place of summer residence. In the hottest weather, and at all hours of the day, a cool sea-breeze can be enjoyed here. The range of the thermometer, in fact, at all seasons of the year, is less than at almost any other place in the United States. The romantic variety and picturesque elegance of its coast scenery, where the salt spray, foaming against the rocks, momently dashes itself into rainbows, present the most enchanting splendors of impression that land, and sea, and sunshine, in their combinations, can produce. A walk along the cliffs is like a ramble through a select gallery of Birch's marine views. To sit on high upon some "coin of vantage" in the rock, and gaze upon the white waters wrestling in undying wrath

Newport.

with the eternal bases of the earth, while the spirit of beauty, prevailing over both, transmutes the terror into glory, and spreads out before the imagination an exhaustless banquet of visionary delight, is a pleasure that invests that region in a spiritual lustre, and consecrates it to the enthusiasms of the poet as much as to the enjoyments of the gay. The drives in the neighborhood of the town, are varied and beautiful.

The beach behind the town, like the whole circuit of the city on the land side, was defended by a line of troops, batteries, &c., during the possession of it by the English in the revolutionary war; and the opposite high grounds were occupied by the American army, whose headquarters were on Taumony hill, about a mile and a half from the town—an elevation which affords an extensive view on every side. General Prescott was taken here during the war by a bold party of men under Colonel Barton, who landed secretly from a boat in the night, went to the British headquarters, and conveyed their captive away, before the land or naval forces, then in the harbor, could prevent them. The place was blockaded by the British fleet.

During the possession of the place by the enemy, the trees were cut down for fuel; and although the soil is admirably calculated for the growth of fruit-trees, and was before that period quite covered with the finest orchards, it is now so divested of trees of every description, as to appear remarkably naked and monotonous for an American scene. The fertility of the ground, and the excellence of the crops, as well as the neatness and precision with which the fields are cultivated and regularly divided by fine stone walls, present, however, a picture of agricultural beauty rarely paralleled in the United States. The island, fourteen miles long and not three miles wide, contained in 1827 more than thirty thousand sheep.

Mount Hope, famous as the ancient royal residence of the Narraganset Indians, and particularly as the abode of King Philip, and the scene of his death, is seen from a few miles beyond Newport, toward the northwest. It rises in Warren, on the shore of an arm of the bay. Prudence island is about five miles in length, and presents the same fertile soil and gently-swelling surface as that of Rhode Island. The inhabitants are few, as are those of Patience and Hope, islands of a much smaller size. Despair is a cluster of rocks on the left, near the island of Hope, the north end of which is twenty miles from Providence.

Coal Mine.—An extensive mine of anthracite or incombustible coal was opened a few years since near the end of the island, in Portsmouth, about two miles from Bristol ferry; it was not extensively used, and the work was soon abandoned.

PROVIDENCE is the second city in New England. Population in 1851, about 45,000. It is beautifully as well as advantageously situated at the head of navigation, on the river Providence.

The town was settled in the year 1636 by Roger Williams, who left the old colonies in consequence of a disagreement in religious doctrines. He built his house on the shore, near the present episcopal church. Many of the society of quakers, or friends, afterward joined him, whose descendants form a large share of the population of the state.

Brown University, the principal institution of learning in the state, is built on the summit of a high hill, decorated with some of the finest houses in this part of the country, dispersed among spacious gardens, and mingling the delights of the country with the splendor of a city. It was founded in 1764; has about one hundred and fifty students; and its library contains twenty-five thousand volumes.

The academy, near the college, is a large institution, and was established by the friends, or quakers.

A man in boring for water, a few years ago, at the end of a wharf, many yards distant from the original land, bored through a stream of mud; then through a bog meadow, containing good peat; then through a sand and quartz gravel. At this point, water impregnated with copperas and arsenic broke forth; but, determining to proceed further, he next

Brown University.

struck a vineyard and drew up vines, grapes, grape-seeds, leaves, acorns, hazelnuts, pinenuts, and the seeds of unknown fruits, together with pure water. This was thirty-five feet below the bed of the river.

The *Boston and Providence Railroad*, forty-one miles in length, begins at India wharf, in Providence, near the steamboat landing, and, passing through the town, leads through Foxboro', Walpole, Dedham, Roxbury, and other towns. It was opened in 1835, and cost nearly two millions of dollars; the curvatures are gentle; least radius, five thousand seven hundred and thirty feet; highest grade, thirty-seven and a half feet; summit in Sharon, two hundred and fifty-six feet above tide. There is a viaduct of granite in Canton, seven hundred feet long, and above sixty feet high, over Neponset valley. There are many embankments and excavations in rock.

Blackstone Canal.—This canal, which reaches from Providence to Worcester, Massachusetts, runs along the course of the Blackstone river for several miles. It is forty-five miles long, eighteen feet wide at the bottom, and thirty-four feet at the surface. There are forty-eight locks, all built of stone, which overcome a rise and fall of four hundred and fifty feet. The size of the locks is eighty-two feet in length, and ten in breadth; and the cost of the whole work was about half a million of dollars. The water is chiefly derived from Blackstone river, but there are large ponds at different parts of the route which can be drawn upon at any time. The whole work was completed about 1828.

PAWTUCKET is one of the largest manufacturing places in this part of the country. The banks of the river are varied and somewhat romantic; while the fall, which is under the bridge, furnishes a most valuable water-power. Cotton is principally manufactured here, though there is machinery devoted to other purposes. The village is divided by the Blackstone or Pawtucket river. The residents of the left bank call it "Pawtucket, Massachusetts"—those of the right bank, "Pawtucket, Rhode Island." The population is over seven thousand. There is quite a number of handsome edifices for public worship, banks, taverns, &c. There are three distinct falls, on which manufactories have been erected. The upper or Valley falls are about a mile from the main part of the village. Here there are five large mills. About half a mile lower down are the Central falls. Here are four large factories.

Early History of Cotton Manufactures in America.—As Rhode Island was the state into which the manufacture of cotton by machinery was first introduced, the following brief sketch of its history may be appropriately introduced here.

Looking back to the incipient state of our manufactures, we can not but be impressed with absolute astonishment at the rapid strides they have made toward perfection. In 1727, the only spinning-machine in the whole extent of our country was one spinning-jenny, with twenty-eight spindles, worked by hand. At the present time, millions of capital are employed in spinning and weaving, every sloping stream is converted into a mill seat; and by the industry of our own hands, with the aid of labor-saving machinery, we manufacture not only what is necessary for our own consumption, but also for exportation. We copy from a Providence paper the following facts in the early history of cotton-spinning in the state, by Mr. William Anthony, of Coventry; they can not be uninteresting to our readers:

"In 1786, Daniel Anthony, Andrew Dexter, and Lewis Peck, of Providence, formed a copartnership for the manufacturing of what was then emphatically called *homespun cloth.* They commenced spinning by hand, and manufactured *jane* from linen-warp with cotton-filling. About that time machinery was imported from England by Major Orr, of Bridgewater, Massachusetts; and this company sent Mr. Anthony to Bridgewater for the purpose of obtaining a draft of the machinery, if practicable. The machinery was not in operation, nor was that the intention of Major Orr; he kept it merely for the purpose of being inspected by the curious, and others willing to hazard the experiment of establishing a manufactory. From a draft of the machinery a jenny was constructed The spindles (twenty-eight in number) and brasswork were made by Daniel Jackson, of this town, an ingenious coppersmith. This jenny, probably the first ever put in motion in the United States, was placed in the chambers of the markethouse in Providence, and there worked by hand.

"Joshua Lindley, about that period, built a carding-machine from Major Orr's pattern. It was something similar to those used at the present day for carding of wool, the cotton being taken off the machine in rolls and roped by hand. The company caused to be built from Major Orr's pattern a spinning-frame, somewhat similar to our water-frames, but very imperfect. It consisted of eight heads of four spindles each, and was carried by a crank turned by hand. The first head was made by John Baily, a very ingenious clockmaker of Pembroke, Massachusetts; and the other seven, with the brasswork and spindles, by our townsman, Daniel Jackson. The lad who then turned the wheel has ever since devoted his attention to the manufacturing of cotton, and it affords us pleasure at this time to number him among the wealthy and most respectable portion of our community.

"In 1788, Joseph Alexander and Jas. M'Kerris, from Scotland, came to Providence, and understanding the use of the flyshuttle, they undertook to weave *corderoy;* a loom was built, agreeably to the direction of Mr. Alexander, and placed in the chambers of the markethouse; it used the flyshuttle, which was probably the first ever introduced into this country. The corderoy was wove with linen warp and cotton filling; but the manufacture of that description of cloth was abandoned, in consequence of no person being found who could cut the corderoy, and raise the pile which formed the ribs and gave it the finish.

"The spinning-frame, after being used some time at Providence, was sent to Pawtucket, and there attached to a wheel and propelled by water-power. This machine was very imperfect; all the carding and roping was done by hand. It was used a short time and then sold to Moses Brown, esquire.

"Manufacturing was in this infant and imperfect state when Samuel Slater, esquire, arrived from England. He was a manufacturer, and could both build and use machinery. The old machinery was all thrown aside, and that built under the direction of Mr. Slater substituted in its place.

"But few had then sufficient faith in the experiment to hazard their capital in so doubtful an enterprise as the manufacture of cotton. The manufacturers at that season had everything to contend against. By the policy of England, the exportation of machinery was prohibited. Our artisans, like our manufacturers, were in their infancy; our iron, steel, and brass workers were few, and they of course entirely unacquainted with any kind of *millwork,* for we find that the head to the first spinning-frame was made by a *clockmaker.* There also existed a prejudice against manufacturing, both at home and abroad. Every argument which ingenuity could devise was urged against the measure. It was represented as demoralizing to society, as repugnant to republican principles, as ruinous to those engaged in it, and to the very liberties of the country. We were then a commercial people, and the commercial part of our community viewed with no little jealousy the establishment of manufactures. England, and Englishmen in this country, opposed it, knowing that our real advantages were so great, that, if once established, we would become a powerful and successful rival. But arguments, and remonstrances, and opposition of every kind, proved unavailing. The enterprise of a few individuals overcame every obstacle, and within forty years from the establishment of a single hand spinning-frame, with no great assistance from government, we find our manufactures in their present flourishing and enviable situation. We can not dismiss the subject without expressing a feeling of exultation, that our town was the first in the country to establish and patronize this invaluable branch of national industry, and our markethouse the repository of the first spinning-frame ever set in motion in the United States."

Block Island.—This most southern part of the state is a lone and desolate little island, lying far distant from the mainland, with but an irregular and precarious connexion with any other part of the country.

No class of citizens of the United States—says a writer—are less understood in Rhode Island, than the inhabitants of Block island. Shut out from the world by the barrier of the ocean, all communication cut off except when the waters are tranquil enough to permit their boats to float upon their bosom, this island appears to be a little world by itself, apart from everything but the white-crested billow, and the dense blue sea-fog. The island lies high in the water, on an average ten feet higher than Montaug point, which is the nearest land. It is nearly destitute of a harbor, even for its fishing-smacks, as a northwest wind sweeps down Long Island sound on the one hand, and a south wind drives in from the Atlantic on the other, rendering insecure any position that might be taken around her fated land.

Many is the fine ship that has laid her bones upon the rocks that stud the extreme points of this no-man's-land, and many more have but just escaped a similar fate; and scarce a mariner comes in view of it that does not call to mind some shipmate who made his last splice in that neighborhood, and died within view of his destined haven. Block island is a beacon of joy to thousands who come in from the "sheep-pasture," as the Yankees term the Atlantic, and who from a foreign land seek that of their nativity; it is the point whence they take their departure, and the first land they make on their return, and for that reason is greeted by the returning seaman as the first glimpse of his much-loved home. But when they make it a "lee-shore," with a stiff breeze, it is more an object of terror than anything else, for ten to one are the chances of escape from destruction.

But from the island we turn to that singular race who inhabit it. A Block-islander has been the same, without a shadow of change, since his island was first inhabited. One would know him by his look alone—his weather-beaten face, and an eye that, to all appearance, has been bleached while penetrating the fog that hangs above and around the island like a canopy. One would know him by his form: built for strength rather than for beauty, and that natural strength increased by constant hardships and exposure to water and to sun, the frame is spread to a degree that could not fail to be ever known after having been known at all. But, most of all, he would be known by his dress. Having seen the costume of one Block-islander, you have seen them all—it is a curious mixture of the New England farmer and the seaman. There is the homespun pepper-and-salt, or black broadcloth, and upon its surface a huge patch of Russia duck; the tarpaulin hat which marks the seaman, and the cotton bandanna handkerchief that tells of him from the Green mountains; but most of all have we looked at what covers his legs from one extremity to the other, and are denominated boots: these are known wherever they are seen—from one extremity of the continent to the other; they could have been modelled at no other place, and an attempt to imitate them would be as fruitless as unprofitable; water could not penetrate, and fire could hardly consume, this part of their wardrobe, and they will stand for ages, as monuments of the taste of the people who invented them. They are worn by all classes, from young to old.

The females of Block island, too, can face the gale, and defy rains, or snows, or freezing winters. They are almost as hardy as their husbands, and not unfrequently venture so far upon the sea that the sail of their clipper-boats are seen only as specks on the horizon.

Rhode Island, small as it is, has been as fruitful in eminent men as any other state in the Union, however large. As early as 1723, it was the residence of the celebrated divine and philosopher, Dean Berkley, afterward bishop of Cloyne. It is said that he wrote his Minute Philosopher while there.

The first anatomical and surgical lectures ever delivered in America were given at Newport, about the year 1760, by Dr. William Hunter. A year or two after, lectures on electricity, with the Franklinian experiments, were given by Solomon Southwick, the father of the gentleman of the same name in Albany. From about 1756, there was more general literature in Newport, and through the island, than perhaps any other part of America, which was owing to a very well-selected public library given by Abraham Redwood, esquire, a very opulent and generous person belonging to the society of friends. He gave five hundred pounds sterling for the books in London. These were selected with great judgment by the colony agent, and some were added by private donations. President Styles was its librarian between twenty and thirty years. After a British army took possession of the island, this valuable selection of books was despoiled of a great portion of the English classics, histories, voyages, and travels, and whatever came under the head of entertaining books. The library is still respectable.

Among military men, Rhode Island gave to the nation General Greene and Commodore Perry. The once very beautiful scenery which embellished the island, and its character for healthfulness, drew to it every summer numbers of opulent invalids, with not a few men of property, who sought pleasure and agreeable residence. It was the permanent residence of many men of independent fortune, past the meridian of life, from different parts of Europe and the West India islands, and who chose that spot in which to spend their days. This accounts for the large number of tories, or gentlemen who wished for no alteration in government and the habitual order of things.

Besides very handsome country-seats, that island contained three gardens that merited, in some measure, the name of botanical gardens, having greenhouses and hothouses, with curious foreign plants. Those belonging to Malborne, Redwood, and Bowler, were the most distinguished. The most elegant and costly dwellinghouse in the twelve colonies was the country-seat of Colonel Malborne, which was accidentally destroyed by fire previous to the revolutionary war. The beautiful spot now belongs to another family.

Before the revolution, Rhode Island with its capital (Newport) was the most agreeable spot on the Atlantic shores. It enjoyed a very considerable commerce: the most lucrative, although not the most moral, was the trade to Africa. Newport was then, from the causes already mentioned, a lively, genteel, and literary town, and Providence was comparatively small. But after the British took possession of it, the town of Providence rose rapidly on the ruins of the capital. Upward of nine hundred buildings, of all descriptions, were destroyed by the British, principally for fuel; and what was equally, if not more, to be lamented, they also destroyed, through necessity, all the beautiful woods and ornamental trees on that fine island. During these calamities, Providence, Bristol, Warren, and several towns on the Narraganset shore, increased in size and consequence, leaving the island, like an old battered shield, held up against the enemy. If the general government can do anything to recover it to a condition in any respect equal to its former consequence, they ought, in gratitude, so to do; for where is the spot in the United States that has suffered so much as Newport on Rhode Island?

While we are disposed to eulogize Rhode Island, there is one thing we have always regretted, and that is its penal code. In point of health and propriety, her prisons were far behind those of other states; and the severity of their punishments far more rigorous than in most of the other colonies and states. Their whipping at the cart's-tail fell but little short of the Russian knot; and their ear-croppings and brandings long continued after other states had meliorated their punishments for theft and forgery.

The following shows the population of the state at different periods:—

Year	Population	Year	Population
In 1730,	17,935	In 1800,	69,122
1748,	34,128	1810,	76,931
1774,	59,678	1820,	83,059
1783,	51,809	1830,	97,199
1790,	68,825	1840,	108,830

In 1850, 147,654.

THE TOMB OF KOSCIUSKO, WEST POINT.

NEW YORK.

No state in the Union occupies, at the present time, a more prominent position than New York, or, in many points of view, a more interesting. One of the earliest in the history of the colonial settlements, occupying one of the largest territories among the original thirteen states, touching, with its extensive arms, the ocean, and two of the larger lakes, including for a century the most powerful body of Indians within our borders, and some of the principal paths of foreign invasion, her scenes of early enterprises and military operations, often distinguished by the bold and beautiful traits of nature, have been in turn the witnesses of extending civilization, and the triumphs of modern science and art enlisted in her service. Where the Indians, sent out or led on by the French Jesuits in Canada, laid the ambush, or fell upon the defenceless frontier settlement, or where the armies of France and England contended for the possession of American forests. in the course of years the same places witnessed the strife between the colonies and the mother-country; and, since it ceased, have been enlivened by the passage of steamboats or rail-cars, or afforded sites for flourishing towns and cities.

To give more than an imperfect outline of the past and present condition of so large, populous, and important a state, in the few pages allotted to it in a work like this, will be impossible; and, to avoid the necessity of falling into a mere record of dry statistics, we must confine our attention to some of the leading natural features, the most important epochs in history, works of art, and other points of interest.

Hudson River.—This stream, as one of the most important channels of commerce in the Union, merit special attention. Its natural advantages have been immensely surpassed by those added by art: for, since the construction of the canals, especially the Grand or Erie canal, an extent of territory has been opened, surpassing, a thousand times, that which borders the stream and its branches. The railroads already made increase the amount of navigation and valuable freights annually borne upon the bosom of this noble river; and those proposed and partly completed, promise still greater and incalculable results. Of those more recently completed, the New York and Erie railroad, described on another page, is by far the most important, forming, as it does, a second and more rapid communication between the Atlantic sea-board and the lakes.

The Hudson rises in the wild, elevated, and almost uninhabited region west of Lake Champlain, and flows, at first, nearly north, then east, and finally south, till it falls into New York bay, passing through which and the lower bay, its waters mingle with those of the ocean, at Sandy Hook. The latter and principal part of its course is remarkably straight, and almost due south. After receiving several small branches in the upper regions, it is swelled by the Mohawk at Waterford; and soon after reaching Troy, the head of steamboat navigation, passes Albany, where the northern and Erie canals communicate with it, through a spacious basin. From that place to its mouth, the Hudson is navigated by a number of steamboats, sloops, canal-boats, and vessels of larger size, worthy of the principal commercial river of the United States, flowing into the Atlantic. Although it passes through a line of mountains at the Highlands, that are commonly regarded as the Allegany range, it pursues its way with a smooth and unbroken current, causing no interruption to navigation.

It has two large expansions below that point, called Haverstraw and Tappan bays, after which it proceeds, with a breadth but little increased, till it reaches the city of New York. The tide is evident even at Albany; but the water is perceptibly affected by the brine of the Atlantic only as high as Polopel's island, at the northern extremity of the Highlands. The numerous and flourishing towns upon its banks, with the variety of taste displayed in the country-seats occupying the heights, declivities, and shores, intermingling with the beautiful and sometimes wild scenery with which nature has enriched it, and which is widely and so justly celebrated—all these, combined with the evidences of industry and wealth, displayed by the fleets of vessels of different kinds continually ploughing its waters, render the Hudson one of the most agreeable routes for a traveller.

In summer, the number of travellers passing up and down this river is almost incredible: for it lies on the way between the commercial metropolis of the Union and several of the principal points to which travellers for business or pleasure direct their course: Ballston and Saratoga, Lakes George and Champlain, Canada, Niagara, and the West; while by numbers this attractive route is chosen in going to Boston, the White mountains of New Hampshire, and other parts of New England.

One of the remarkable objects on the Hudson is the trap range, on its western bank, extending from Weehawken bluff ar up toward the Highlands, called the Palisades. It often presents a precipitous wall, totally inaccessible from the water, except occasionally; and for some distance it rises about four hundred feet perpendicularly.

Mountains.—The Allegany range enters this state from New Jersey, and crosses the Hudson at the pass of the Highlands, celebrated for its scenery, and for some important events in the Revolutionary war, and passes into New England.

The Catskill mountains rise at some distance above the Highlands, about seven miles west of the river, and present a range of rocks, covered with a thin coat of forest-trees, with several peaks rising a little above the general outline, the loftiest of which, the Crow's-Nest, is about three thousand five hundred feet above the ocean. The poverty of the soil and the roughness and almost inaccessible nature of the surface, render this wild region the retreat of deer and wolves. The abundance of oak-trees is such, that numerous tanneries are found

View of the Palisades, Hudson River.

in that region. The village of Hunter is situated halfway up the mountain, at an elevation considerably higher than any other within the limits of New York. The Mountain house, in the upper parts of this Alpine region, is the resort of numerous travellers of taste in the warm seasons; and, while it affords every comfort, and many of the luxuries of life, it commands one of the most extensive and delightful views to be found within the circuit of the Union, with easy access to the wild valley of the Cauterskill creek, and its remarkable cascades.

Oswego River is a very remarkable stream on account of one singular peculiarity. It is the drain of almost the whole cluster of small lakes in the middle of the state of New York. Having its head in Canandaigua lake, in its easterly course, it receives the outlets of all those which empty northward, and at length, after passing several villages, receives the Oswego canal, and falls into Lake Ontario at the village of Oswego.

Genesee River.—The scenery along the course of this river is wild, where it passes through the high and rocky ridge which bounds the rich "Genesee Flats," on the south. The banks, for a considerable distance, are perpendicular, as if cut through by some irresistible torrent, exposing to view the strata far below the original surface. The extensive valley which succeeds, so celebrated for its fertility, affords the stream a smooth and level channel, by which it gently meanders through a scene of peculiar richness, in summer waving with some of the best wheat in America. The stream, by wearing away the limestone rocks above, annually enriches the soil by its deposites; and this natural manuring process is aided by the action of the wind, which, in blowing down the rocky chasm just mentioned, brings with it particles of dust from the crumbling surface, and spreads them far and wide over the meadows. So important are the effects of this process, that the land is perceptibly richer, on the upper part of the valley, as we approach its rugged boundary.

Moving northward, the Genesee flows toward the great mart and manufactory of those stores of grain which its shores yield in such abundance; and that large and flourishing town owes its existence, or at least its importance, to the abundant water-power afforded by the sudden descent of its waters over the steep falls at that place. Both sides of the stream are there lined, for a great distance, by mills of the largest size, constructed in the most substantial manner, which are celebrated for the excellency, as well as the amount of the flour which they annually produce.

It is remarkable in the history of this part of the state, that the superior fertility of the Genesee Flats long remained unknown, as well as the peculiar fitness of the soil for wheat. Thousands of emigrants from New England, says Darby, settled on other tracts of land further west, where they were satisfied if they could raise thirty bushels of corn on an acre. But the value of this fertile region is now well appreciated; and sixty bushels of corn, or twenty-five of wheat, are annually yielded by thousands of acres. A finer sight can hardly be shown in any part of our country, than this region, when covered with its waving crops.

The Genesee Flats were a favorite district with the Indians; and the last blow received by the Iroquois, in the Revolutionary war, was given here, when a large village was burnt, and they were driven from their richest planting grounds. The remains of ancient mounds and other traces of past generations, prove that the banks of the stream were long the residence of a large population.

Springs.—New York abounds in mineral springs, and of very different qualities. Some of them possess highly sanative properties, and are the most celebrated resorts in America, by invalids and travellers for pleasure. Others are merely curiosities, on account of the peculiar substances held in solution by their waters.

Gas springs are among the latter; and these are found in several places in the western parts of the state, chiefly at

Bristol, Middlesex, and Canandaigua, where they, in some places, rise from small hillocks, and the hydrogen which forms a large constituent of the gaseous exhalations, readily burns on being touched with flame, and sometimes continues to blaze for several hours, even when surrounded with snow. In the geological volumes of the reports of the scientific survey of the state, all the particulars may be found, relating to this and to many other subjects, connected with the rocks and soil of the extensive and diversified territory.

Ballston Springs.—The old chalybeate spring, in the centre of the village of Ballston Spa, near the Kayderoseros brook, was known to the Indians, and highly valued by them. It was visited by Sir William Johnson, before the Revolutionary war, at the recommendation of an Indian, for the improvement of his health; and he was carried for a considerable distance on a litter, there being at that time no road. The vicinity of the spring was marked by the feet of numerous deer, and paths were trodden by them to their favorite drinking-place, from every direction. For several years after the war, there were no better accommodations at the place than a miserable loghouse; but it gradually became a place of considerable resort; and about the year 1814 or1815, was a village, with several houses for lodgers, one of which, the Sans Souci, had accommodations for about one hundred and fifty persons. Several other springs had been discovered, and more were afterward found, all situated in the small alluvial valley of the Kayderoseros. These differed in nature: some being pure water, others chalybeates, sulphurous, and saline. This place, however, for many years, has been superseded by

Saratoga Springs.—This is now by far the most important watering-place in the Union, for the number of visiters. There are five or six hotels of the largest size, and numerous smaller ones, all standing on one street, and within a short distance of the principal spring; and the place, during the warm season, especially in the months of July and August, is generally crowded to overflowing, by thousands of persons, from all parts of this country, and from many foreign lands. The railroad offers every facility for travelling, and several interesting places lie in the vicinity, while through the place lies the grand route to Canada, by Lake Champlain.

The *Congress spring*, at the southern end of the village, affords a plentiful supply of saline water, in which Glauber's salt abounds, accompanied with portions of lime and magnesia, and a slight trace of iron, and abundance of carbonic acid gas, all which together render it one of the most useful of natural mineral waters in the world. It is recommended for many cases of disease, and great quantities are bottled for the supply of cities and towns in all parts of the Union, while much of it is sent abroad. It was discovered soon after the Revolution, in the bed of a small brook, which flows through the narrow, marshy strip of ground, in which all the other springs at this place are situated, including the *Iodine spring*, which is a great rarity.

The *Round Rock spring* was known to the Indians, and is named from a hollow conical mass of rock in which it rises, and over the top of which it formerly flowed. A tree, it is said, fell upon it some years ago, and caused the crack through which the water now escapes, near the level of the ground. The water is a feeble chalybeate, of little value or interest, and holds in solution a portion of lime, whose gradual deposition, on the escape of the carbonic acid, no doubt formed the singular cone, which naturally has made it an object of popular curiosity.

Natural History.—A few years ago the legislature of this state authorized a scientific survey of its territory, appointed some of the most eminent naturalists in different departments and appropriated considerable sums of money to pay the expenses. The state has now been traversed and examined, reports have been made, accepted, and printed, and we have already eleven volumes, elegant quartos, abounding in facts, and illustrated by hundreds of engravings, representing the rocky strata, and other geological features, with the plants, insects, reptiles, fish, birds, and beasts, inhabiting the land and water. The descriptions partake of the popular style, to a considerable extent, in order that the common reader may not be debarred from the perusal, by language too strictly technical. The last volumes are soon to appear. The following general views of the regions, climates, and animals of the state, we abridge from those reports.

New York lies within the temperate zone, in an irregular triangle, with its apex on the Atlantic, and its sides on the western border of New England, the St. Lawrence and Lake Ontario, and the northern boundaries of Pennsylvania and New Jersey. Long island forms a sandy spur, extending from the harbor of New York, eastward, about one hundred and fifty miles. Including Long island, the state extends through eight degrees of longitude, and from forty degrees and three minutes, to forty-five degrees, of north latitude, with more than forty-six thousand square miles. It covers a surface greater than Poland, Scotland, or Naples and Sicily; three times larger than Switzerland, and almost equal to England. It is nearly in the latitude of Italy, the south of France, and the north of Spain; and resembles them in the heats of summer; but yet the winters are as severe as those of the northern countries of Europe. The mean length of the winter in ten years was one hundred and sixty-five days, or about five months; and the mountains, although none of them exceed the height of five thousand feet, have a much colder climate than corresponding elevations in Europe. Within the boundaries, are animals, which are found, in the old world, only at great distances from each other; as the Cervidæ and Mustelidæ of the south of Europe, and the Muridæ and Vespertilionidæ of the north.

There are four districts, distinguished by geographical peculiarities, and not less by zoological.

1. *The Western District*, bounded on the east by the Mohawk valley, and is chiefly elevated on the Allegany table-land, furrowed by valleys lying north and south, once probably outlets of an inland ocean. The descent westward is sudden, to Lake Erie; while ten or twelve small lakes in the middle are drained by the Genesee river, and visited by salmon from Lake Ontario. The great lakes have much influence on the climate. Here are found the northern lynx, with the deer-mouse and porcupine. Streams flow from this district to the Mississippi, and to the Susquehannah and Delaware.

2. *The Northern District* has mountains, some five thousand feet in height. with Lake Champlain, one hundred and forty miles long; and is inhabited by several fur-bearing animals: the sable and beaver, and also by the mouse and the wolverine. It is the southern limit of migration of many of the arctic birds, as the Canada jay, spruce-grouse, swan, raven, and arctic woodpecker.

3. *The Hudson Valley District* lies in the form of an inverted L; and, though small, it is highly interesting, as it contains many of the animals of the adjacent New England states, while on the west it has the Catskill mountains, some of which rise four thousand feet, and are still the habitation of wolves, deer, panthers, and bears. The Erie canal has brought into the Hudson the soft-shelled turtle and the rock bass from the lakes; as the yellow perch and the muskalonge have found their way from Lake Erie to the Mississippi through the Ohio canal. The southern part of this district teems with inhabitants of the ocean. It is remarkable that some species of animals find the Hudson their natural eastern boundary, as the opossum, chain-snakes, brown swift, buzzard, and several other birds, come to its western borders, but never cross it. At the same time, there are some species which abound in the counties on the eastern side, but are never seen on the western.

4. *The Atlantic District*, or Long Island, runs about one hundred and fifty miles northeasterly; with a mean breadth of ten miles, having low sand hills in the northern part, only in one place three hundred feet high. The bear, wolf, and otter, have been exterminated:

but the deer remain; and, although much hunted, are believed to be on the increase, since they have begun to be protected by law during the breeding season. This remarkable tongue of land, stretching nearly at right angles from the coast south of it, is the first resting-place offered to many of the birds, on their migrations from the West Indies and other southern regions, after a long flight over the waters of the ocean. It happens also to lie in such a latitude, that it is at once the northern limit of the tropical birds, and the southern limit of the arctic. In winter the eider-duck is found on Long island, the little white goose, the cormorant, the awk, and many others from the Arctic ocean; while in summer are to be seen the turkey-buzzard, the swallow-tailed kite, the fork-tailed fly-catcher from Guiana, &c., &c. Here is also the natural limit of certain species of fish, some from the north, and others from the south.

"American quadrupeds have attracted but little attention," remarks one of the writers of the scientific reports, Dr. Dekay, "until within a short period; and were then, at first only noticed by foreigners. The few Americans who afterward began to procure specimens, sent most of them abroad, where only they found them appreciated. De Liancourt, De Chastellux, and some other mere travellers, did much; and such scientific explorers as Bosc, Kalm, Micheaux, and Pal de Beauvois, have done much more. The Philadelphia Academy of Natural History, the Lyceum of New York, and other scientific societies in Boston, New Haven, and Salem, have accomplished much since their formation." The American Journal of Science and the Arts, established and conducted by Prof. Silliman, has also powerfully contributed to the cultivation of zoological study and research, as well as of other branches.

Many remains of mammoth and other extinct animals have been found in the state of New York; and the only entire skeleton of the mastodon ever obtained was dug from the earth near Newburgh, in 1845

LAKES.—New York contains more lakes than any other state in the Union: and, if we cast our eyes upon the map, and observe their number and importance, with those larger ones which together form a large proportion of its boundaries, we might be disposed to give it a new but appropriate geographical appellation, and call it "the Lake state."

Lake George.—The most picturesque of the American lakes, lies just within the southern limit of the northern mountain ranges, and combines the wildness and sublimity of Scotch scenery with the richness and beauty of native American forests, intermingled with occasional marks of progressive cultivation. Lake George, the beautiful sheet of water to which we allude, is twenty miles in length, and about one mile in width; and is completely shut in by eminences of considerable elevation, which form a succession of bold scenery, as the traveller passes over the smooth surface in the steamboat which ploughs its crystal water. French mountain, at the southern extremity, looks down upon the ruins of Forts George and William Henry, which were erected to repel the invasions of the people whose name the mountain bears, in the colonial wars; and several other peaks rise conspicuously below, and, at the Narrows, in the middle of the lake, almost close up the passage, which is still more impeded by numerous little islands of various forms, which seem, from a distance, like a fleet of light-boats, becalmed, on a party of pleasure.

The beautiful sheet of water was, in former times, disturbed by scenes of war; and the remains of military works near its southern extremity, with historical associations connected with different points on its shores, redouble the interest of the intelligent traveller who resorts to its delightful borders, and glides over its glassy surface. The ruins of the two forts beforementioned, George and William Henry, and which were the scenes of important events, are seen on its southern shore.

Lake Champlain.—Lake Champlain, interesting from its historical associations, is long and narrow, separates the states of Vermont and New York, and is distinguished for its beauty. Its waters are generally quiet, never being wrought into anything more than gentle billows; and its width, being such that both shores are distinctly visible through its whole length, gives it somewhat the appearance of a broad river. The celebrated fortresses of Ticonderoga and Crown Point are on its southern portion. In its wider parts, picturesque little islands seem to rest on its bosom; three of which, lying near together, of similar size and shape, are called the "Three Brothers."

The "North and South Hero," are two larger islands, which occupy quite a considerable space in the length of the lake. They are inhabited by a numerous population, and have their schools and churches. About three miles from the Vermont shore, is a small island, inhabited by one family, who, like Selkirk, "have none to dispute their right" to their little secluded home.

In a passage up the lake, through which ply the splendid steamboats on the grand route to Canada, you look out upon two states at the same time. On the right is Vermont, with its verdant shore; and in the distance are the "Green mountains." On the left is the north part of New York, looking quite as mountainous, and as much diversified with hills and dales, rich in mines of iron, but still almost covered with forests. On both shores, beautiful villages are frequently seen, stretching down to the water's edge, and adding much life and interest to the landscape. None who pass up this lake, but feel a peculiar interest in that part of it, where the memorable "Battle of Plattsburgh" was fought.

That part of the lake abounds in delightful views, especially where we approach Plattsburgh, and pass over the waters memorable as the scene of the naval victory of Commodore M'Donough over the British fleet under Commodore Downie. War is to be deprecated in all its forms, and its existence exceedingly to be deplored, as a sad relic of barbarism; still, as events of history and reality, all feel an equal interest in scenes that were acted here.

History.—The history of this state naturally itself divides into periods, corresponding in general with those most remarkable in that of the older colonies and states; and under each of these many interesting and instructive events and incidents are recorded, some of which will be alluded to in their appropriate places, with that brevity which is made necessary by the nature of this work. Abundant sources of information are at hand, for any who wish to pursue any branch of New York history in detail; for no state in the Union, perhaps, is better furnished in this respect, especially in works of recent publication. Although fewer men of letters were found among the early inhabitants in colonial times, numerous historians, as well as other writers, have devoted their pens to subjects around them; and within a few years the Historical Society has made great and very successful exertions to collect and preserve records of all kinds, calculated to throw light upon any period of history. The legislature, at their invitation, sent an intelligent agent to Europe, a few years ago, Mr. Brodhead, who brought back an invaluable collection of documents, in different languages, from the archives of Holland, France, and England, respectively illustrating the periods of Dutch settlement and rule, of English extension and French invasion. Future historians will find here a rich addition to previous annals, and the means of correcting former errors and of illustrating numerous points which require elucidation.

Indian antiquities have been studied with zeal, and are now prosecuted with new advantages. Under the authority of the legislature, that well-qualified investigator, Henry R. Schoolcraft, was employed in 1846, to take a census of the Indians in the state; and he collected a mass of the most valuable facts ever obtained, relating to any family of the human race, illustrating the changes occurring in the transition state, from the savage toward the civilized condition. In this survey, as might be

View of Albany, from Greenbush.

expected, the influence of Christianity is strongly exhibited, as the grand civilizing agent, and lessons of an important character are given, well calculated to guide philanthropists in their future undertakings in favor of the much-neglected, abused, and belied race of redmen.

The reader must be referred for information on the history of this state in all its different periods and epochs, to the following authors among many others: Colden, Smith, Clinton, Campbell, Yates, Moulton, &c. Barber's volume is well adapted to the common reader, abounding in local descriptions and anecdotes, illustrated with many engravings. We have here merely room to allude to the chief events in the early history of the colony.

Henry Hudson, an Englishman in the service of the Dutch East India company, discovered the Hudson river in 1609, and ascended it about one hundred and sixty miles. It was in consequence of this discovery, that the Dutch laid claim to the territory on both sides of the river, and called it New Netherlands. The position now known as Albany, was, in 1613, named by the few Dutch who discovered it and built a fort there, Fort Orange; and in the next year, several trading-houses were erected upon Manhattan island (now New York), to which they gave the name of New Amsterdam.

The English were not well pleased by what they considered the intrusions of the Dutch. They claimed that this part of the territory properly belonged to Virginia; and, in the same year, Captain Argal came with a fleet of three ships, and demanded the surrender of the fort. They submitted without resistance, because their numbers were very few. But a new governor arrived from Holland, and the Dutch would allow the authority of the English no longer, and they retained possession until 1664. They built Fort Good Hope on the Connecticut, at Hartford, and another on the Delaware, and then claimed a right to all the extensive regions between these two rivers.

But the Indians did not let the Dutch remain long in peace. In 1646, a battle was fought at a place called Strickland's plain; and the savages were defeated with great slaughter. The colonies of New Haven and Connecticut were at this time disputing with the Dutch; but, in 1650, a treaty was made at Hartford, by which the Dutch gave up their claim to the territory belonging to those colonies, except the part which they then occupied.

Five years after this the Swedes, who had settled on the west side of the Delaware river, were attacked and subdued by the Dutch governor, Stuyvesant, with a fleet of seven ships. But ere long, the Dutch were met again by their old enemies the English. In 1664, in consequence of the grant which Charles II. had given to his brother, the duke of York and Albany, and which secured to him all the lands owned by the Dutch, a squadron appeared in the harbor of New York, which was commanded by Colonel Nichols. A surrender was immediately demanded by the English, who promised to secure the rights of life and property to the inhabitants. The governor wished to make resistance, but the inhabitants prevailed upon him to submit. The English thus took possession, and called it New York, in honor of the duke of York; and not long after Fort Orange was also taken, and named Albany.

Nichols now became governor; and his administration was mild and successful.

We have not room to notice the successive governors of the colony, nor the various events which distinguished the successive periods, through the contests between England and other powers, which had more or less influence on this side of the Atlantic. We can only refer, in their places, to some leading events in the French and the Revolutionary wars, and in that with England of 1812.

ALBANY.—This city presents several superior claims to our attention. In point of history it is the oldest settlement by Europeans on the Hudson for, unusual as it is in founding colonies, the mouth of the stream was not occupied

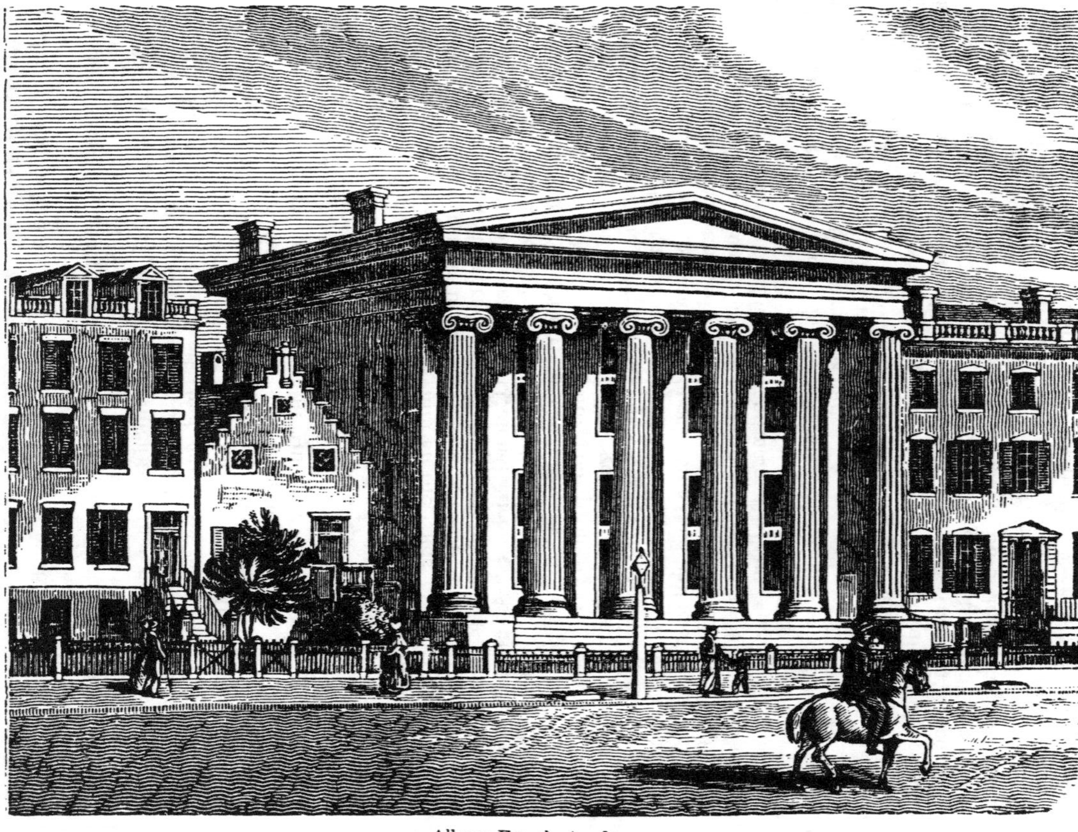

Albany Female Academy.

by the Dutch until they had first established themselves at this place, one hundred and fifty miles and more from the sea. This was the scene of many important councils and treaties with the Indians, especially the Five Nations; and in the grounds of the old capitol were interred numerous savage memorials of peace and amity. During the French wars, Albany was often the grand point of rendezvous for the troops required of New England and New York, in military expeditions against Canada. Burgoyne's expedition, in 1777, had the capture of this city as its first object, after gaining possession of Ticonderoga, and it was saved only by the battles of Saratoga. Albany has been the capital of this state ever since its formation; and here is the point at which concentrate the principal canals and railroads of New York—the uniting link in the chains connecting the commerce of the lakes with that of the great northern ports, Boston and New York.

Albany is well situated to make a striking appearance to a person approaching by the river, or viewing it from the opposite, elevated shores of Greenbush. A crowded mass of houses seems to cover the entire declivity, which rises suddenly from the level of the shore to the summit, which is crowned by the statehouse with its dome. The broadest and perhaps the principal street (State street), well built, with many large edifices, hotels, stores, and private residences, leads from the base of the hill to the gates of the statehouse, starting from the chief avenue of business, Market street, which extends, with several parallel streets, far up and down the city, north and south.

The canal-basin occupies the front of the town for about one half its length, being shut in from the river by the pier, which commences at the north, and terminates opposite the foot of State street. Here are seen mingling the boats of Lake Champlain, Erie, and the Ohio canal, with the steamboats sent from New York to tow them to the mouth of the river, where many of them exchange the abundant products of the interior for the various stores brought from our own and foreign coasts. The railroads come in with their share of valuable freights; and Albany presents, on every hand, abundant and gratifying proofs of the sagacity of those enlightened councils, which opened the grand channels of commerce, for the wide and lasting benefit of the state and the country.

The Albany Female Institute.—This seminary was founded by private subscription, and has been a flourishing and useful institution, conferring a high and solid education on thousands of the youths of this city and other places near and distant. The plan, in some important respects, was new: it being the design to afford, at the cheapest possible rate, a superior education on females of all ranks in society; and so successful has it proved, that several other institutions have been formed in imitation of it, which have in like manner been highly useful, particularly the Rutgers Institute in the city of New York.

The Albany Female Seminary.—This is another institution occupying a commanding situation on the top of Capitol hill, near the statehouse and several other public buildings. It is founded on a plan which does great credit to the state of New York, which has so honorably distinguished itself by its liberal provision for the diffusion of education.

The central *Normal School* is also established in Albany, and is doing important good by preparing teachers for the common schools.

The City-Hall was built in 1832, of white marble from Sing-Sing, quarried and hewn by the prisoners, with a basement, and a façade with six Ionic columns and a dome covered with gilding, the only specimen of the kind in the United States. The circular hall or rotunda contains a statue of Hamilton, copied from one by Greenough, which was destroyed in the New York exchange by the great fire. There are also portraits of Clinton and Walter Scott in relief, surrounded by emblems.

The State-Hall.—This edifice stands near the city-hall, and is one hundred and thirty-eight by eighty-eight feet,

St. Paul's Church, Albany

and sixty-five feet in height. It is of brick and stone, faced with marble, and contains the offices of the comptroller, treasurer, attorney-general, surveyor-general, &c.

The Capitol is constructed of stone, and cost one hundred and twenty thousand dollars. It contains the chambers of the senate and the representatives, in which are found full-length portraits of Washington and the governors of New York.

There are six banks, and twenty-five churches of different denominations.

The Rensselaer Mansion is a venerable edifice a mile north of the city, the residence of the Patroons of that name, proprietors of one of the great entailed estates in this state, which have been retained in several old Dutch families from past generations. The estate embraces vast tracts of land in different counties, large portions of which occupied by tenants, at various rents, usually small, and often trifling. Within a few years great dissatisfaction has been excited among the people, and, in 1845, bands of men, on this and other manors, armed and disguised, set the laws at defiance, and committed some acts of violence, even murder. The militia were called out, arrests made, and trials and imprisonments at length suppressed the "anti-rent riots."

The Indians knew Albany by the name of *Scagh-negh-ta-da*, which is said to express, in their language, "*The End of the Pine Woods;*" and this term has since been applied to Schenectady, the town at the western extremity of the elevated pine-barren tract which was thus alluded to, there fifteen miles across, and still almost uninhabited. The Dutch called the place Beaverwyck, on account of the principal article of the trade which they here carried on with the natives; and afterward Willemstadt. The name Urania, or Fort Orange, was never extended to the town, it is affirmed, but confined to the small fort which was erected by the Dutch on their first occupying this point. The present name was conferred by the English, as has before been remarked. It is supposed that the first white man who ever visited this spot was one of the companions of Hudson, Hardwicke Chrystance, who was sent from his vessel on an exploring party, in September, 1610. Tradition says he landed somewhere near the present North Market street. The trading-house and fort was built that year or the next on the northern extremity of Boyd's island, a little south of the present ferry. It was, however, overthrown and carried away by the flood, in the next season. A higher station was then chosen, on a hill two miles distant, at a place called "*Kidderhooghten*," by the Dutch, and by the Indians, "*Ta-wass-a-gun-shee*," or *Lookout Hill.* Another position was preferred ere long, and there Fort Orange was finally erected. The spot is near South Market street, and near that now occupied by the Fort Orange hotel. Eight large cannon were mounted for defence, of the sort then known to the Hollanders by the name, "*stien gestuckten*," or stone-pieces, because, as is said, they were capable of throwing large stones instead of iron shot.

But, for about twenty years after this occupation of the spot, the Dutch spent only the trading seasons at Fort Orange, returning annually to their own country, with the products of their trade. In 1625, the Dutch West India company offered large tracts of land to any persons who would colonize the country, and great numbers came over between that time and the year 1635, from some of whom many of the principal families of the present day have derived their names.

Wood was used in Albany in all buildings except the fort until 1647. The town was surrounded by a palisade for about a century, and the strict laws respecting trade with the Indians, induced numbers of persons to remove to the Schenectady Flats, where they could trade with the natives with greater freedom. The first church-building erected was at the corner of State, Market, and Court streets, and, after being enlarged several times was taken down in 1806, and the stone used in building the present South Dutch church. The houses of Albany were built in the style of

View of State Street, Albany.

Holland, of small bricks, with the gable ends to the street, and troughs under the eaves projecting far over the streets. The Dutch language has not even yet wholly fallen into disuse, in some families. The city charter was granted in 1686, and extended westward to the distance of a mile from the river, and northwest to the north line of the manor of Rensselaerwyck, being 13½ miles in length. In 1815 the limits were enlarged, by adding the small town of Colonie. Population, 1850, 51,000.

CANALS.—The *Erie Canal* was the first of any considerable extent in the United States, was planned and executed by the influence of Dewitt Clinton and his friends, and must ever be regarded as the result of labors creditable to them and the state, the period being one in which much opposition was excited against it, in consequence of the ignorance of the people of works of that kind. The project of connecting the navigation of the lakes with that of the Hudson, by means of a channel three hundred and sixty-three miles long, almost every foot of which was to be excavated, and which must be taken across streams and over hills and valleys, appeared to many as visionary and ridiculous; but the difficulty of acquiring land and of reconciling conflicting interests in the choice of routes, conspired to increase the discouragement of the undertaking. Had the calculations of the projectors been unfounded, the result would doubtless have discouraged imitators: but the Grand canal of New York has long been, and will ever be, a monument of successful enterprise, transcending in its beneficial effects the most sanguine expectations.

The Erie canal was commenced in 1817, and finished in 1825. It extends from the great basin at Albany northward, along the right bank of the Hudson, to the mouth of the Mohawk, and thence rising, by nine double locks, to the level of the banks, crosses the Mohawk twice by aqueducts and follows the valley of that stream to Rome. Thence it crosses to the Oswego river near Syracuse, whence the Oswego canal leads to Lake Ontario; and up the valley of that stream it proceeds to the Genesee at Rochester, and onward to the Mountain Ridge, at Lockport, where it rises by five double locks to the level of Tonawanda creek, a tributary of Niagara river, and, a part of the way, by the channel of the former, goes on to Lake Erie at Buffalo.

The canal is there about 500 feet higher than the Albany basin; 200 of which are attained at Schenectady, nearly 300 at Canajoharie, and 400 at the Long Level, above Little Falls. Beyond that are the only two descents on the route, and these are but small.

Among the principal constructions on the route, are the grand embankment, near Rochester, 100 feet high and two miles long; the fine stone aqueducts at Little Falls and Rochester, the former 214 feet long, and the latter stretching across the Genesee, 900 feet, on nine beautiful arches. At Buffalo, is a fine harbor, lined with spacious storehouses, crowded, in the season of navigation, with the numerous steamboats and other vessels employed in the navigation of the lakes. The branch from Syracuse extends through the great salt region; and there are several other branches.

The Champlain Canal.—Parting from the Erie canal at the junction, eight miles from Albany, this important work crosses the mouth of the Mohawk, passes through Waterford, and along the west bank of the Hudson, at the foot of the hilly range called Behmis's heights, the scene of the battle of Saratoga, crosses it at Miller's Falls, to Fort Edward (in the French wars known as the First Carrying Place), passes on to Fort Ann, or the Second Carrying Place, where it enters Wood Creek, following it to its mouth at Whatehall (formerly Skeenesborough), at the southern extremity of Lake Champlain. The elevation overcome on this route is 150 feet, from which the descent is about 75 feet toward the north: the lake being about that height above the river's level at Albany. The length of the route is about 60 miles.

The Delaware and Hudson Canal.—This canal commences at Rondout, and extends to the Delaware river, having

Cascade Bridge, on the New York and Erie Railroad.

been formed for the purpose of bringing coal to New York city from some of the Pennsylvania mines.

The Delaware and Hudson canal was begun in 1825, and finished in three years. It is 108 miles long, and extends from Rondout, 90 miles from New York, to Port Jervis, on the Delaware, a distance of 59 miles, then 24 miles up its eastern bank, to Lackawana river, and up that stream 25 miles to Honesdale. In some places great expense has been laid out in blastings. A railroad of 14 miles connects its extremity with Carbondale, Pennsylvania. The canal is from 32 to 36 feet wide, 4 deep, with locks 9 feet by 76, for boats of 25 or 30 tons.

Railroads.—A continuous line of railroads now extends from Albany to Buffalo, with branches, from several points, connecting with the great Massachusetts railroad to Boston, and the Hudson river road to New York city.

The New York and Erie Railroad.—This road extends from the Hudson river at Piermont, twenty-four miles from New York city, through the southern tier of counties of the state (passing twice into Pennsylvania) to Dunkirk on Lake Erie, a distance of five hundred and forty miles, the latter place being forty-five miles southwest of Buffalo.—A charter was obtained for this road in 1832. The company was organized in 1833, and the route was surveyed in 1834. The road was commenced in 1836; but was suspended soon after in consequence of the commercial revulsion of 1836–'37.—But aided by a loan of the credit of the state of three millions it was recommenced in 1841, and successive portions of the road put in operation from time to time till it was finally completed and opened to the public its entire length, in April, 1851.

The cost of the Erie railroad, as stated in the report of the directors, up to April, 1851, was $20,500,000; of which $2,500,000, at least, is chargeable to equipment-account. The amount of capital stock issued is $5,790,000, leaving the remainder of cost, in the form of bonds and other debts against the company, $14,710,000; exclusive of the three millions loaned by the state, and relinquished to the company on conditions which have now been complied with; and $750,000 relinquished by the original stockholders on certain conditions, in 1845, making the total cost of the road and equipments $24,250,000; although the liabilities are only about $20,500,000.

The immense importance of this road can scarcely be estimated. It opens a trade with fertile regions hitherto difficult of access, while it will bring to New York a large part of the increasing products of the lake counties, so disproportioned to the capacities of the Erie canal, even when enlarged under the recent act of the legislature.

CASCADE BRIDGE (a view of which is given overleaf), is situated 188½ miles from New York, and 271½ from Dunkirk. It cost about $70,000 and is the work of John Fowler. This stupendous structure consists of a single arch, 250 feet in width, thrown over a ravine 184 feet in depth. The span of the arch has a rise of fifty feet, and far surpasses in width any other in the world, constructed of timber. This ravine is very narrow, and is approached and crossed so rapidly, that a person in the cars can form no idea of the bridge itself, though he may judge of the depth of the gulf by a glance at the tops of the trees, descending, row by row, to the rocky, thread-like stream at the bottom of its gloomy jaws. Instead of resting upon frail piers erected by the hand of man, each leg of the arch is supported on and in deep shelves hewn in the solid rock, that rises, wall-like, on both sides of the chasm; and while these eternal foundations stand, so will the bridge.

The Hudson River Railroad.—This work forms one of the most important means of transport and travelling within the limits of the state. It passes along the valley of the Hudson river close to its eastern bank. It is one hundred and forty-four miles long.

The New York and New Haven Railroad affords an uninterrupted line of railroad to Boston, through Connecticut.

There are several other roads within the state, which our limits will not permit us to describe.

SEMINARIES OF LEARNING AND RELIGION.—Ere concluding this brief notice of the public affairs of the state, a few facts may be appropriately added respecting this important department.

Universities and Colleges.—Columbia college, in the city of New York, was founded in 1754; Union college at Schenectady, in 1795; Hamilton college at Clinton, Oneida county, in 1812; Geneva college at Geneva, in 1824; and the New York university, in the city of New York, in 1831; Madison university founded at Hamilton, in 1820; and Rochester university at Rochester, in 1850, with an endowment of $150,000.

The universities and colleges are under the inspection of the regents of the university of the state, and have the distribution of the literary fund.

Theological Seminaries.—Lutheran at Hartwick, in 1816; Protestant Episcopal in New York, 1819; Baptist at Hamilton, 1820; Presbyterian at Auburn, 1821; Union at New York, 1834; Roman Catholic at Fordham, 1840.

Medical Colleges.—There are two in the city of New York: viz., the college of physicians and surgeons, and the New York school of medicine; and a third at Fairfield, called the college of physicians and surgeons for the western district, and another at Buffalo.

Academies are numerous, and the principal ones are under the direction of the state, and make annual reports of scientific observations, &c.

Normal Seminary.—At Albany is a central school for the instruction of common-school teachers. Here also is published a journal for the benefit of the schools, extensively diffused among teachers and school officers.

COMMON SCHOOLS.—The first report to the legislature, showing the number and condition of the schools in New York, was made in 1798, when the number of schools in the state was but about 1,500 and the number of scholars about 60,000. The first appropriations for common schools was made in 1795, and was on a scale of liberality which shows a just appreciation of the importance of this fundamental interest in the infancy of the state. The sum appropriated was $50,000 annually for five years. In 1805, a permanent school fund was founded by the appropriation of half a million of acres of the vacant lands of the state. The annual returns from the school districts were incomplete till 1817, when there was 5,000 schools, and over 200,000 scholars, exclusive of the city of New York. In 1821, the number of pupils had increased to over 300,000; and since that period the increase in the number of schools, and of children instructed, has borne a near proportion to the increase of population, till by the last report of the state superintendent of common schools, the number of school districts is shown to be near 12,000, and the children instructed, about 800,000. The annual appropriation from the income of the permanent fund is now $300,000 and from taxes $800,000, of which $55,000 is appropriated to the purchase of school libraries and apparatus, and the remainder is applicable exclusively to the payment of teachers' wages and the support of schools.

Since the foundation in 1835, the district libraries have grown to the amount of 1,500,000 volumes. The benefits of these depositories of intelligence, accessible to every mind in the state, can never be adequately estimated. They will be abundant in the fruits of industry, virtue, and refinement, through all coming generations.

A striking illustration of the progress of education in this state is found in looking at the views of her early statesmen as to the degree of instruction to be provided in the common schools. The regents of the university, in 1793, suggest to the legislature "the numerous advantages which they conceive would accrue to the citizens in general, from the institution of schools in various parts of the state, for the purpose of instructing children in the lower branches of education, such as reading their native language with propriety, and so much of writing and arithmetic, as to enable them, when they come forward into active life, to transact with accuracy and despatch, the business arising from their daily intercourse with each other."

And this, less than sixty years ago, was the highest view of popular education entertained in a state, which now has its noble and munificently-endowed seminaries and colleges, its armies of teachers, and its hundreds of thousands of pupils.

SCHENECTADY.—This is one of the oldest towns in the state, and was for a long time important as a frontier position, nothing but a wilderness being found between it and Canada. For a number of years it has been distinguished as the seat of one of the most flourishing literary institutions in the state, Union college, the edifices of which occupy a pleasant and commanding position, overlooking the extensive meadows of the Mohawk, surrounded by a succession of undulated and hilly country, and enlivened by the Erie canal and the lines of railroads which here meet by various routes from Albany, and proceed on in company, with occasional separations, to Rochester, and finally terminate together at Buffalo.

In the year 1769, Schenectady, while a mere village, fifteen miles west of Albany, garrisoned by a few troops, was the victim of the jealousies and contentions of those sent for its protection; for the soldiers having deserted their posts, one of those secret predatory bands of savages, which were long the scourge of our frontier settlements, led on by Frenchmen from Canada, fell upon it in the dead of night, massacred almost every man, woman, and child, and burnt their dwellings. A few fugitives escaped, and carried the shocking tale to Albany.

The exposed state of the country west of this place was so great, and the number of the people so small compar ed with the extent of unoccupied land, that inducements were not found to extend settlements fast beyond this point; and even down to the period of the Revolutionary war, nearly the whole middle and western parts of New York were included in a single county.

A few scattering villages only were then to be seen, at Cooperstown, Johnstown, &c., &c., usually with block houses, or other slight means of protection, provided against the apprehended dangers of savage parties. The five nations of Indians, viz., the Mohawks, Oneidas, Cayugas, Onondagas, and Senecas, who had been, for the most part, friendly to the English through the French wars, were, many of them, drawn over to the British interest by John Johnson, one of the sons of Sir William Johnson, who had long exercised the most important influence over those savage people. By the aid of the celebrated Brandt, a half-blood of doubtful character and courage, a series of calamities was brought upon those weak and defenceless settlements, which can not be recounted without exciting the mingled feelings of commiseration and horror. But, for those events, as well as for other particulars, relating to the history of that now populous and prosperous portion of the state, we must refer our readers to the works of Mr. Campbell (a descendant of a family of the sufferers), the Life of Colonel Willet by his son, and the Life of Brandt, by Mr. Stone.

Schenectady Lyceum.—This institution (a view of which is given on the opposite page) was erected a few years since, to supply a deficiency, long felt, in a city so long and so honorably distinguished as the seat of a seminary of the highest class. It is designed for the instruction of boys in studies preparatory to college and business; and enjoys an advantageous and convenient situation. The principal building is of an octagonal form, of brick stuccoed, in a fanciful Gothic style, with pointed doors and windows, and surmounted by a steeple. In advance of this, and of the line of the yard-fence, are two small buildings belonging to the institution; and the grounds beyond are shaded with large and fine trees. The upper rooms in the main building are occupied by the Lyceum society, and for scientific purposes.

Cooperstown.—This pleasant village, two hundred miles from New York, by way of Catskill, and sixty-six from Albany, enjoys a beautiful situation on Otsego lake, on a gentle eminence at its south end, backed by a hilly range of considerable elevation, in which the cleared and cultivated land is agreeably mingled with the forests. The streets, broad and straight, are well shaded with trees, and lined with dwelling-houses, many of them of rather an old and venerable appearance. To the Indians it is said to have been a favorite place of resort.

The first white inhabitant was Mr. John Christopher Hardwick, who resided here for a short time, about ten years before the Revolutionary war; but in 1788, the first permanent settlement was made by Mr. William Cooper; and two years later, the county of Otsego was formed, of which this town is the capital. Remains of a road are still to be seen, which was cut through the forest by a brigade of General Sullivan's army, from Fort Plain to the head of Otsego lake; and at the outlet are some traces of a dam constructed by the troops, at the direction of their commander, General Clinton, by which the water was made to rise, and then, the dam being broken down, allowed it to rush down in a torrent, which cleared the channel of the incumbrances of logs that impeded the passage.

Cooperstown is deservedly admired by travellers, and annually the resort of citizens, seeking the pleasures of the country in the summer season. The population however is small, the number of dwelling-houses being only about a hundred and sixty. The people are distinguished for their refinement and courteous manners.

Cooperstown may be taken as a favorable specimen of one of the several classes of New York villages: such as have grown up since the Revolutionary war, and have no associations with the

Schenectady Lyceum.

sufferings and dangers of the earlier settlements, and yet removed from canals and railroads, and every other influence which might have given it a rapid growth or sudden and great prosperity. Left to the steady but slow improvement of an agricultural neighborhood, it presents fewer evidences of increase in wealth or numbers, but is less liable to some of the evils incident to many other places.

There are a few small manufactories along the banks of the outlet of the lake, where about eight thousand spindles are employed in cotton-spinning, and on that of Oak creek, one of the numerous small streams in this county, most of which flow southward into the Susquehannah.

Otsego county is hilly, and in some parts mountainous, being crossed by the Susquehannah and Kaatsberg ranges. There is much good grass land. Limestone is found near Schuyler's lake in Cherry Valley, and iron ore in several places.

Cherry Valley is one of those unfortunate villages which suffered from Indian barbarity in the Revolutionary war; and it may be noticed in this place. It is fourteen miles northeast of Cooperstown, and fifty-three west of Albany, amidst the high and irregular ground which gives rise to Canajoharie creek and several other early tributaries of the Mohawk, with the head stream of that river. Several vales lie between the neighboring hills, which possess a fertile soil; and one of these, with the wild cherry-trees that naturally abounded in the neighborhood, gave to the place its pleasing name.

It happened to lie so exposed and defenceless, in the early years of its history, that it shared in the dangers of the other scattering settlements in the neighboring region, and was finally surprised by a band of Indians, led by the notorious Col. Butler, from Canada, and fell under a general and indiscriminate massacre, in which whole families, men, women, and children, bled under the tomahawk.

The particulars given of this mournful tragedy by Wm. W. Campbell, in his valuable "Annals of Tryon County," are painful in the extreme, but yet valuable to impress future generations with abhorrence of war, and especially that unwarrantable practice, in which several civilized nations have engaged, of hiring savages to exercise their bloodthirsty ferocity upon the innocent and defenceless. The sketch given in that work, of the history of the settlement, and the character of the people, renders their fate the more deeply interesting. We shall here introduce an account abridged from its pages.

The survey was made in 1739, and the ground first occupied by Mr. Lindesay, a Scotch gentleman, of some fortune and distinction. He took with him his wife and his father-in-law, a Mr. Congreve, a lieutenant in the British army. The low ground was then covered with a thick forest of beech and maple, mingled with wild-cherry trees, the highlands with evergreen; and the native wild animals, even the deer, elk, bears, and wolves, undisturbed by civilized man, ranged through the woods, being hunted only occasionally by the Mohawks. The settlers sought the friendship of the wild men, and with success. In the winter of 1745, while the snow lay very deep, and the journey to the nearest neighbors, on the Mohawk river, 15 miles off, was impossible for any of the family, all the provisions were consumed, and nothing but famine and death were in prospect. An Indian, travelling on snowshoes, becoming acquainted with their situation, supplied them with food through the remainder of the season, by bringing, repeatedly, loads upon his back all that distance.

The following year, the settlement was increased, by the addition of several Scotch and Irish families, who removed from Londonderry, in New Hampshire, at the invitation of the Rev. Samuel Dunlop, one of their countrymen, a gentleman of education and travel, who had been induced by the present of a large tract of land, to join Mr. Lindesay. They brought an addition of thirty persons, and the aspect of the place was speedily improved by their industry. A house was built of logs, for religious use, on the declivity of a little hill, near the house of the pastor, whose support was secured by the payment of ten shillings for every hundred acres of land, added to products of his own labor, and the voluntary contributions of his parishioners.

In 1744, Mr. Congreve joined the British army as lieutenant, in place of his father-in-law; and Mr. Dunlop opened the first grammar-school in the state west of Albany, at which were taught a number of boys from the settlements on the Mohawk. Several of these were distinguished men in the Revolutionary war.

In 1778, the apprehensions of an invasion from Canada was general in Tryon county; and, on account of the weakness of this solitary village, numbers of the inhabitants left their homes for places of greater safety. In the autumn, however, the danger being supposed to be past, they returned. But an expedition had been prepared at Montreal, consisting of seven hundred tories and Indians, who proceeded, with Brandt and Butler at their head. Rumors of their approach spread a new alarm; but Colonel Alden, commander of a few soldiers, stationed at Cherry Valley, refused to admit the women and children into the fort, and to quiet their apprehensions, sent out a scouting party, who were surprised asleep, and captured by the more cautious enemy.

The invaders, on the 10th, reached a hill, a mile southwest from the fort, where they remained concealed till the next day; and then, having learned from their prisoners, that the officers lodged in several dwelling-houses in the village, made preparations to surround them all by small parties, while the main body should assail the fort. Mr. Hamble, who was that morning riding into the village, being unable to discover distant objects, in consequence of the hazy weather, and the falling sleet, was fired upon and wounded by some of the Indians, and hastening on his horse, gave the alarm to Colonel Alden, and then turned for the fort. The colonel, who had always discredited the reports of danger, still doubted them; but, on his way to the fort, was pursued and scalped by one of the enemy. The Senecas, who were the most fierce of the Five Nations, were foremost in the attack. They assailed the house of Mr. Robert Wells, and killed the whole family within, consisting of the father and mother, four children, his brother, sister, and three domestics. A little son alone remained, who had been sent to school at Schenectady. He was afterward a distinguished counsellor of New York city, the Hon. John Wells. Miss Jane Wells, the sister of the proprietor of the house, and a young lady of superior character and exalted piety, having escaped by the door, sought safety in the woodpile; but an Indian discovered her, and, after deliberately wiping his scalping-knife on his legging, sheathed it, and seized her by the arm, at the same time, brandishing his tomahawk. The captive remonstrated with him in the Indian language, with which she had some acquaintance; and one of the tories among the invading party, named Peter Smith, who had once lived with the family of Mr. Wells as a servant, interposed and begged the savage to spare her life, pretending that she was his sister. But this availed only to procure a short delay. The next moment the interesting young lady fell dead from a blow of the tomahawk.

The house of the venerable pastor was entered by the enemy, and his aged wife immediately put to death; but one of the Mohawk chiefs, named Little Aaron, led him out of the house, and kept him under his protection. An Indian, running by, pulled off the old gentleman's hat; and the chief pursued him and brought it back. The old man was thus rescued from massacre; but the shock he received was so great, that, although he was set at liberty soon after, he died a few months subsequently. The fort was not taken by the enemy; but, on the first alarm, a gun was fired from it, which gave intimation of the attack.

One of the householders, Mr. Mitchell, discovered the enemy, while at a distance from his house; and finding it impossible to reach it, he escaped to the woods, and remained concealed until the savages had accomplished their work of destruction, and taken their departure. On returning home, a sad spectacle met his view—the bodies of his wife and four children. The house was burning, but he succeeded in extinguishing the fire. On examining the bodies, he found evidences of remaining life in one of them—his little daughter. He immediately raised her, and endeavored to resuscitate her; but just then, observing some of the enemy approaching, he concealed himself, and, when they came up, saw one of them, a tory, named Newbury, strike the innocent little victim with his hatchet, and thus put an end to his last hope. The next day the disconsolate father, wholly unassisted, removed all the corpses, on a sled, to the fort, where the soldiers assisted him to inter them. The same Newbury was executed for his crimes the next year, on the testimony of Mr. Mitchell, having been arr sted when engaged as a spy, in the ar. y of General Clinton, at Canajoharie.

Mr. Campbell's house was attacked, and his family were taken into captivity. He was absent; but, although he hastened homeward on hearing the gun fired in the fort, he arrived too late to render any assistance. The number of inhabitants killed was thirty-two, and of soldiers sixteen. A few persons escaped to the Mohawk, and the remainder were made captive. The buildings were all burned, the settlement was laid waste, and abandoned by the survivors, until more peaceful times.

Little Falls.—This is one of the favorite spots with travellers of taste; and there are but few points at which are assembled, within so narrow a space, such a display of picturesque scenery, with so many works of useful science and art. Here the Mohawk river, having reached the eastern boundary of the rich German Flats, once the bottom of a lake, pours through the descending, rocky channel cut by the current, where the waters, in some long-past age, found an outlet through their ancient barrier. Here, to form an artificial passage for boats arriving at the end of the Long level on the Erie canal, the rocky shore has been excavated, and lofty walls erected, and sufficient breadth gained, to conduct that noble work, by successive locks, down to the level which extends below. The railroad has since found a path for its more rapid vehicles; and now the roar of the river mingles with the sounds of the locomotive and the bugles of the boatmen.

The accompanying engraving gives an accurate and pleasing view of the natural scenery, and some of the works of art, which stand in such striking contrast in this picturesque and remarkable pass. The village in the distance is that of Little Falls, which takes its name from the continued series of cascades, by which the Mohawk here finds its way to the meadows stretching through the eastern valley. The principal fall on this stream, the Cohoes, near its mouth, makes these comparatively second in importance; and hence the term by which they are distinguished. The channel is in several places divided by rocks and islands, of rough and ragged forms, which bear the appearance of having been worn away by the force of a current far more deep and impetuous than any now ever produced by the river, even at its highest floods; and the descent of the channel is so great as to render the passage impossible, even in small boats.

It is, therefore, doubly interesting to the spectator to observe the triumph of art, with the obstacles of nature which have been overcome, in full view. If passing through this dark, wild, and romantic gorge, in a canal-boat, he glides smoothly along upon the glassy surface of the canal, and here and there is gradually raised or let down, by the locks, from one level to another, without injury or inconvenience, by the same element which is seen, in its natural, untamed state, rushing and raving furiously below. Or, if he is a passenger in one of the cars which pursue the railroad track, from the other side of the river he beholds the same scene, from a different but no less striking point of view, and, in a few moments, makes a rapid transition from one to the other of those

Village of Little Falls.

smooth and fertile meadows which extend along the banks of the Mohawk, at different levels, above and below the falls.

One of the high hills on the southern bank of the river, at this place, has a remarkable cave; and the geological features of the region are worthy of attention. Beautiful crystals of quartz are found in the neighborhood, in considerable abundance, and are washed from the micaceous slate by every rain. Passengers in the rail-cars sometimes have an opportunity to purchase a few, of the children who take pains to collect them.

The Marble Aqueduct, two hundred and fourteen feet long, and sixteen feet wide, is one of the best-constructed and beautiful works on the line of the canal, crossing the Mohawk on five large arches, to bring over a supply of water from the old canal on the northern bank. The central arch is seventy feet span.

Few constructions can be found which present to the eye, in so forcible a contrast, the rude obstacles of nature with symmetry and beauty of useful art.

The first settler in this wild spot was a Scotch gentleman, Alexander Ellis, who, by the aid of Sir William Johnson, obtained a patent of the surrounding tract. The river makes a descent of forty-two feet, by two rapids, within the distance of two thirds of a mile, with a broad interval of smooth and deep water. Above these is a dam, divided by an island, over which the water pours in small cascades. The romantic pass which opens through the ridge of mountains, is about two miles in length, and of an average breadth of only five hundred yards, while rough and woody heights, rises on each side nearly four hundred feet. Everything here, and above and below, indicates that a lake once covered the great German Flats; and it is calculated that, if a dam were now built here seventy feet high, that rich and extensive alluvial tract would soon be overflown, and the new lake would find an outlet through Wood creek into Oneida lake and Ontario. The rocks are deeply worn, often by large and deep circular drills, such as are found at many similar spots. One of these is two and a half feet in diameter, beginning at the top of a rock thirty feet above the present level of the river; and, being broken below, allows a visiter to see the sky above, through the whole length of the funnel. The canal descends at this place by five locks, each of eight feet lift.

In 1789, several prisoners were taken by a party of Indians, at a mill; but two men escaped, by retreating under the waterwheel, whence the savages could not dislodge them.

Rome.—This village was named at a time when unfounded expectations were entertained of its rapid and extensive growth. Its population, in 1850, about 8,000 It occupies a place of great importance in the French and Revolutionary wars, as it was one of the carrying-places on the ancient Indian route between Lake Ontario and the Mohawk, by the way of Oneida lake and Wood creek. The *Black-river canal* (an important work) passes the village, as well as the railroad and Erie canal. The ground is the summit-level between Lake Ontario and the ocean, four hundred and thirteen feet above the Hudson at Albany, from which it is distant one hundred and twelve miles. The United States arsenal, and barracks for one thousand men, were built in 1813.

Fort Stanwix (of which only some marks remain in the soil) was erected in 1758, and was at first merely a square fort, with four bastions, a covered way and glacis, surrounded by a palisaded ditch. It cost £266,400, but, through neglect, was in ruins at the beginning of the Revolution. Having been hastily repaired, and named Fort Schuyler, on the 3d of August, 1777, it was invested by Colonel St. Leger, with a large mixed force from Canada, comprising one thousand Indians. Colonel Ganzevoort, however, resolutely refused to surrender; and, although in command of only seven hundred and fifty men, sent out Colonel Willet to make a diversion in favor of General Herkimer, who was advancing to his relief, and with such success that the enemy were driven from their camp, leaving their baggage and even papers.

Utica.

Twenty wagon-loads of spoils were brought into the fort. The invaders, however, returned, and the siege was closely pressed; but Colonel Willet and Major Stockwell succeeded in passing by stealth through the midst of the enemy, and reached General Sullivan's camp at Stillwater, who sent General Arnold with assistance. That sagacious officer (afterward a traitor) so terrified the invaders by exaggerated reports, that they fled in a panic, and failed in their enterprise as utterly as General Burgoyne, to co-operate with whom, they had come from Canada.

Utica.—This city, situated on the southern bank of the Mohawk, occupies one of the important points where the line of the Erie canal and the railroad coincide, and are crossed by several country roads. It has the additional advantage of lying on a tract of fertile land, the river alluvion in that country being broad and rich. It is ninety-six miles west of Albany, and two hundred and forty-one miles from New York. Fort Schuyler, an earth work, thrown up here in the old French war, was the first point ever occupied here by white men; but, as Whitestown, for some years after its settlement, was the principal place of resort in this region, as late as 1793, there were but three dwellings in Utica. Rome was afterward marked out, as the site of a future city; but, although the Western Inland Navigation company, chartered in 1792, opened a canal from the bend of the Hudson here to Oneida lake, and expectations were entertained of a great trade taking that direction, in 1800, the Seneca turnpike was opened through Utica, which gave the latter place the advantage. It has continued to increase ever since. The population in 1830 was 8,323, and in 1850, 17,240. It was made a village in 1798, when it received the name of Utica, and it was incorporated as a city in 1832. It contains fourteen churches, three banks, numerous stores, and a number of handsome private houses, with much refined and intelligent society. The streets of Utica are generally pleasant, many of them being planted with trees and lined with neat yards and gardens; while the hotels are large, and the point where the canal and railroad pass the principal street is one of great activity and bustle. The view in every direction is over an extent of level ground, and bounded by the hills enclosing the valley of the Mohawk.

Clinton.—The pleasant village of Clinton, situated nine miles from Utica, is the seat of Hamilton college. This institution owes its origin to the Rev. Samuel Kirkland, a missionary to the Oneida Indians. He was one of the pupils of the celebrated school of Mr. Wheelock, and graduated at Princeton in 1765. In the following year he removed to this place, and commenced a long, self-denying, and successful course of missionary labors among the Oneidas, over whom he obtained a strong and beneficial influence, of great importance in the Revolutionary war. While the other nations of the savage confederacy joined the English, the Oneidas remained true to our cause. After the peace had been restored, he received a grant of land in this place and neighborhood, called Kirkland's patent, and again took up his residence here in 1792.

The remarkable chief Skenandoa, with many of his people, became intelligent Christians under the instructions of their devoted pastor. In 1793, he obtained a charter for a seminary of learning, designed for Indians as well as whites, under the title of the Hamilton Oneida academy, which has since been raised to the rank of a college.

Trenton Falls.—The West Canada creek, in flowing through a long, deep, and narrow ravine, presents a succession of wild and romantic scenes, so striking and so interesting, that this region has been for some years a favorite point of observation to travellers of taste in the western tour. It is common for parties to stop at Utica, and devote a day to an excursion to Trenton Falls. The stream makes successive falls, four of which are the most considerable, but all varying in form and appearance. The largest is two miles northwest from Trenton village, where, within a short distance, it is precipitated down three perpendicu-

the rocks, rushing over the intermediate spaces by steep and rough channels, in a furious and turbulent manner. The first of the falls is forty-seven feet in height, the second eleven, and the third forty-eight; and such is the variety in the directions of the sheets of water and the surrounding objects in that wild and secluded dell, which is shut in on both sides by perpendicular banks of dark limestone, from one hundred to one hundred and thirty feet in height, that the impressions made on the mind of a spectator are at once awful and pleasing.

SYRACUSE.—This is a large and flourishing village on the Erie canal, one hundred and thirty-three miles west of Albany, at the junction of the Oswego canal. Population, 1850 22,235.

The great *Salt-Spring*, at Salina, is the most valuable in the Union, as it is abundant in water, very highly charged, and the supply is taken to numerous manufactories, where the salt is extracted and purified by the most approved processes.

The spring rises on the marshes of Salina lake, a salt pond, six miles long and two in breadth, whose waters are impregnated to such a degree that its shores are lined with plants usually found only on the borders of the sea. The lake is surrounded by limestone hills, containing petrifactions; and gypsum abounds in the neighborhood. The spot is a portion of that extensive region which reaches from the Atlantic to the Pacific, between the latitudes of thirty-one and forty-five degrees north, whose course is here and there betrayed by brine springs. In this state, such springs exist in the counties of Onondaga, Cayuga, Seneca, Ontario, Niagara, Genesee, Tompkins, Wayne, and Oneida; but that of Salina is by far the most valuable and productive. According to published statements, a bushel of salt may be obtained from forty-five gallons of water; and analysis gives the following results for forty gallons:—

Weight, 355 pounds; saline matter of all kinds, 56 pounds. Of this, muriate of soda is 51 pounds; carbonate of lime, colored by oxyde of iron, 6½ ounces; sulphate of lime, 2 pounds, 4 ounces; muriate of lime, 1 pound, 12½ ounces; and probably some muriate of magnesia and sulphate of soda.

The water is raised from the spring by a forcing-pump; and distributed through pipes and troughs to numerous manufactories, large and small, of different kinds, in the villages of Salina and Syracuse, and a considerable tract of land lying between them. In some places are seen large buildings, in which the water is evaporated by artificial heat; but the greater part is exposed, in shallow wooden vats, to the heat of the sun, being covered by sliding roofs when threatened by rain. A branch of the Erie canal affords the means of easy transportation, and immense quantities of salt are annually transported to all parts of the country.

The vats are about sixteen by seven feet, and four inches deep, and are supplied with water sent from pump-houses through hollow logs. Between the rows of vats, sufficient space is left for carts to pass, in which the salt is removed. The salt made in this manner is coarse; that formed by artificial heat is fine. From fifteen to twenty-five boilers are used, usually placed in rows, which are supplied with salt water much in the same manner as the vats; and heat is applied below, where fires are kindled in furnaces. In some manufactories, steam-pipes are used for heating, and pass through the water. The new spring at Salina yields water more strongly impregnated with salt than the old spring; that is, in the proportion of fifty to seventy. Fresh water being reckoned at 0, and water saturated with salt at 100, a cubic foot of water from the new spring yields fourteen pounds of salt.

Two mills on every bushel here are to be paid to the state for pumping the water, and six cents a bushel on all the salt made. About three millions of bushels are manufactured annually; and the business, in all its branches, occupies about three thousand men, in the four villages of Syracuse, Salina, Geddesburgh, and Liverpool.

A French colony for the Onondaga country was planned in the year 1655, by the Jesuit Dablon, who procured at Quebec fifty soldiers, under the command of Lieutenant Lawson, and set out with them the next year, to undertake one of their missions at this place. Under so powerful a guard, with the approbation of the Jesuit superior-general, Francis Le Mercier, the expedition sailed up the river; but it was attacked by four hundred Mohawks, before they reached Montreal, who were jealous of the Onondagas, by whom the enterprise was encouraged. The Indians being repulsed, the party proceeded; and, after some delays and dangers, arrived at the appointed place of settlement. This is supposed to have been on the borders of Salina lake, as mention is made of a salt-spring. They were for a time very kindly treated by the Onondagas, who inhabited this region. Scarcely two years, however, had elapsed, before strong symptoms of hostility were exhibited; several murders were committed, and a large army of the Six Nations was assembled.

The colonists became alarmed, and resolved on flight. By practising the greatest caution and secresy, they succeeded. Canoes were made with all haste in the house of the Jesuit, and a young Frenchman, who had been adopted by the Indians, and enjoyed their full confidence, persuaded them to make a great feast; at the close of which they betook themselves to sleep; and when they awoke the next day, their intended victims were not to be found. Having launched their canoes in the night, and taken their young countryman with them, the colonists got such a start of their enemies, that they arrived in safety at Montreal.

Auburn.—This beautiful village, situated on Owasco lake, is worthy of the pleasing associations connected with its name, which Goldsmith's favorite poem has celebrated. Population, 9,548.

The stateprison, located here, is quite a handsome building. It stands back about eighty feet from the road, and covers, including the grounds, about twenty-five thousand square feet. The wall that surrounds it is two thousand feet long, thirty feet high, and, at the base, four feet thick. On the southern side there is a small creek, from which, by means of a wheel and shaft, power enough is obtained to work all the machinery inside of the walls. The prison consists of two wings, and the main body of the house, which forms three sides of a square; the wings being two hundred and forty feet long, and twenty-five feet deep, and the house two hundred and eighty feet long. It was begun in the year 1816, and the cost was five hundred thousand dollars. The expenses of the prison, in the year 1839, were $51,671.21, and the money that was earned in the same year was $60,161.46. The prisoners number, in the course of a year, from six to seven hundred. Every sabbath they are instructed in the great truths of the Bible, and the younger portion are taught reading, writing, and arithmetic. When this prison was first built, there were five hundred and fifty cells; but lately a few more have been added. These cells are arranged in four stories, and are seven feet high, seven feet long, and three and a half feet wide. They are very well warmed, lighted, and ventilated, and everything fixed for the comfort of the prisoners. The space between the cells and the outside wall is ten feet wide, and is open from the roof to the ground. The passages to the cells are three feet wide, extending out from the wall in front of each cell. They being constructed in this manner, perfect silence can be preserved through the night, as the slightest noise or whisper is heard by the watchman on guard below. This precaution is taken in order to prevent any conversation during the *night*. The same care is taken in the daytime, for they are made to work without speaking. The prison-bell rings soon after daybreak, which is a signal for the prisoners to rise, and soon after the keeper unlocks the doors. The prisoners then come out of their cells, each one taking his pan that is used for his food, his kettle for water, and his tub. They then put these different things in their respective places, and in lockstep walk to the workshops, where they work until the prison-bell rings

View of Auburn.

again, and then in the same manner go to the eating-room. The tables that are used here are very narrow, to prevent any intercourse. In about half an hour they are ordered, by the ringing of the bell, to return to the workshops, and here work until twelve o'clock, when again they go and take their dinner in the same way. As evening comes on, the prisoners go to the place where they left their tubs in the morning; and when the word of command is given, each takes his own up and proceeds to the mess or dining-room, where each one takes his can of water and his pan of food, and then all walk in the same close step to their cells. As they enter, they pull the door to after them, and are then locked in by the turnkey, who has two keys entirely different from any others in the prison. The prisoners are divided into companies; and each company occupies a separate gallery. The turnkeys go around through the different galleries in stocking-feet, to see if the convicts are in bed.

The stateprison at Auburn is important in an historical point of view, because it is that in which a new system of prison-discipline was commenced, which has since been extensively adopted in the large stateprisons of this country, and, with various modifications, in France and elsewhere. It was invented and first practised by Mr. Lynds, afterward superintendent of the Sing-Sing prison. The grand object of it is to prevent all conversation and interchange of thoughts between the convicts. In all prisons previously in use, where considerable numbers of persons were confined, unless for offences of peculiar kinds, or under oppressive systems of government, numbers of prisoners were, from time immemorial, placed in common halls, often in a very crowded manner; and not only immoral conversation, but the basest crimes, might be indulged in. So great were the evils of that system, that many innocent persons have been ruined by their contact with felons of the worst character, while awaiting trial. The expense of keeping and guarding men in such circumstances was very great; and to Mr. Lynds belongs the honor of the inestimable improvements which have been made, although he was accused of occasional practices of unnecessary severity, in the punishment of offenders or suspected persons among the prisoners under his charge.

Not a word is allowed to be spoken by the convicts while at work; and each small party of laborers is attended by a sentinel, at whatever employment, and every infringement of the rule of strict silence which he can observe is instantly reported and punished. Their cells are solitary, although arranged side by side in long rows, and separated only by single walls; and sentinels are so posted, at night, that no communication can be carried on between any of the prisoners. In the largest prisons, where a thousand or more persons are confined, a dead silence reigns from the hour of retirement till that of breakfast. A few men are sufficient to guard a great number, thus isolated in mind, and yet made to move and act in compact bodies. A plot is impossible: one man can not even form an acquaintance with another. Whenever they move, they are required to march at a regular step, in single file, and close together; a difficult march, which requires strict attention. They often receive their food on returning from work, without stopping; for being marched through the kitchen, each takes his can from a table, and carries it to his cell.

Religious services are often held in chapels connected with the prisons, and chaplains usually find many of the convicts accessible to their private instructions. Each cell has a Bible, and sabbath-schools are often kept by benevolent people of the neighborhood. In some cases, also, as in New York city, societies provide temporary lodgings and work for discharged convicts, and otherwise interest themselves in their welfare.

The Prison-Discipline Society, which was formed in Boston about twenty-five years ago, early recommended the principles on which the Auburn prison was conducted, and greatly contributed to their general adoption in the United States and foreign countries.

Geneva Medical College.

GENEVA.—This place is conspicuous among the lake villages for the beauty of its appearance from the water. It stands at the outlet of the lake of the same name, upon the western bank; and the houses of some of the more wealthy inhabitants occupy the summit of the higher ground, which rises one hundred and twenty feet, just behind the busiest streets, and descends with a hasty but graceful slope to the water, adorned by the gardens, green with useful plants, and gay with blooming flowers. The surrounding country presents that gently-varied surface peculiar to this part of New York, where, for many miles, the ground has the appearance of having been channelled from north to south. The lowest depressions are occupied by several of the small lakes, while the heights of the intermediate ridges command extensive and pleasing views over the gently-undulated country between.

The settlement of Geneva was begun in the year 1794, by Mr. Austin and Mr. Barton; and the act of incorporation was passed in 1812. The number of dwellings is about five hundred; and there are nine churches, a bank, &c.

The Geneva College was one of the earliest institutions which adopted a plan of studies adapted to young men preparing for other professions than those usually termed "learned;" and, like several others since established in different places, affords instruction in practical branches to such students as prefer to pursue them. The buildings occupy a remarkably fine, agreeable, and commanding situation, on the elevated shore of the lake, near the southern extremity of Main street.

This college, incorporated in 1825, has professors of mathematics, natural philosophy, Latin and Greek, statistics and civil engineering, modern languages, history and belles-lettres, chymistry and mineralogy. There is also a medical department, commonly called—

The Medical College of Geneva.—The building belongs to the medical department of the college, which is under the direction of four professors. The inhabitants of this beautiful town have distinguished themselves by their liberality in providing and supporting institutions of the most valuable character; and few places of equal size can be found in the country better provided. This building, with the others connected with the college, is an ornament to the town, while it makes a conspicuous appearance from a distance.

ROCHESTER.—This flourishing and important city in this part of the state, is of such recent growth, that, until the year 1810, there was not even a single dwelling on its site. The whole tract was once a mill-lot, and was purchased, in 1802, by Nathaniel Rochester and two associates, at $15.50 an acre—$1,750 in all. Some of the land on the eastern bank of the Genesee was sold at eighteen pence an acre in 1790, by the great speculators of the day—Phelps and Gorham. In 1816, the population was only three hundred and thirty-one.

The flour business is extensively carried on at Rochester. There is a large number of gristmills, with runs of stones sufficient to grind several thousand barrels of flour daily. The amount made annually amounts to near a million of barrels. There are also several woollen and cotton mills, with many saw and other water mills of different kinds in this busy town.

Few towns in the Union present such evidences of a great and lucrative business, on so small a space of ground, as Rochester, in the immediate vicinity of the river, at and below the aqueduct. The mills above referred to, form a double line of large, massive, stone buildings; and the greatest activity prevails in and around them, where crowds of men are constantly employed in the various kinds of business which are carried on in them, and in the various other mills and manufactories adjacent, as well as at the depôts of the canal and the railroad. Above twenty churches, several of them remarkably handsome, as well as capacious edifices, are among the public buildings, although the first presbyterian church, which is the oldest, was erected in 1815; and so late as in January, 1813, at the celebration of the Indian new-year, the Senecas performed their last heathen ceremonies on the ground, near the site of the present Bethel church. An interesting account of these, as well as of many other particulars relating to Rochester, may be found in the history of the town, published in 1835.

The falls of the Genesee at this place are one of the most remarkable of the cataracts in New York, and rendered by art the most useful. The upper one is small, making an inconsiderable descent over a rocky bed of only a moderate angle of descent; but, as the grand aqueduct is built over it, the effect of the flowing water is increased by the obstruction of the channel by the masses of stonework, and the contraction thus formed of the passage. The middle fall is the principal one; and that is perpendicular, over a rocky precipice, which rises like a wall from the lower to the upper level of the river. In pouring over this, the water plunges ninety-six feet, sometimes in a few small streams, but, in floods, in a general sheet. It was here that the celebrated Sam Patch, after performing many astonishing leaps, unharmed, from fearful heights, lost his life, in the year 1829, by jumping from the rocks into the basin.

Below this spot, the river flows a mile and a half, through a wide and deep channel, passing several rapids, when it reaches the two lower falls. Here the surrounding scenery is rough and wild; and the river first pours over a precipice twenty-five feet high, and immediately afterward over another of eighty-four feet. The banks below are high, rocky, and perpendicular, for a considerable distance, showing numerous stratifications, which have been cut through by the current. Across the awful chasm a wooden bridge was erected, in 1819, of one noble arch, whose chord was three hundred and fifty-two feet, and the versed sine fifty-four feet. The entire length of the bridge was seven hundred and eighteen feet, and the width thirty feet. The top of the arch was not less than one hundred and ninety-six feet above the river. It contained seventy thousand feet of timber, and sixty-four thousand, six hundred and twenty feet, board measure. Just one year and a day after its completion, it fell in ruins by its own weight, the sides of the arch pressing up the top.

Falls of Niagara, viewed from Table Rock.

CARTHAGE, a small town on the eastern bank, is a place of considerable business, as a communication between Rochester and Lake Ontario was established some years since, by an inclined plane from the high bank to the river, where boats received and discharged cargoes. The business has greatly increased; and there are now three railroads from Rochester to the navigable part of the river, six miles from the lake-shore.

BUFFALO.—This city, before referred to, as one of the principal inland towns of the state, and the centre of the lake and canal navigation and railroad communication, is pleasantly situated on the summit, declivity, and base, of the table-land which borders the end of Lake Erie and the head of Niagara river. The streets are broad, clean, and well built, and numerous blocks of stone-houses border the stream which here pours into the lake. A lighthouse, a pier, and an improved harbor, all subserve the extensive commerce of the place.

Niagara Falls, celebrated throughout the world as the most stupendous of cataracts, lies partly in the state of New York and partly in Canada. A more sublime spectacle can not easily be conceived, and none can anywhere be found on earth to compare with it. The river Niagara, a broad, deep, and rapid stream, the outlet of Lake Erie, the deepest of the American inland seas, also discharges the waters flowing toward the ocean from the whole chain of lakes above. Passing, with a hasty but unbroken current, by Grand island, it soon approaches the verge of the mountain ridge; and, after rushing for about half a mile down a declining, rocky bed, forming the rapids, it is precipitated over a precipice one hundred and sixty feet high, into a gulf of unknown depth below, with a roar which is sometimes audible at the distance of twenty miles.

It is remarkable that the sheets of falling water are entire and unbroken, from top to bottom, in their whole extent, without any interruption worthy of being mentioned. Goat island, near the middle, divides the river for some distance above and at the fall. On the New York side, the cataract presents a straight line; but between Goat island and the Canada side, it is curved inward, forming the Horseshoe. Thousands of travellers annually visit the spot, to admire this great natural curiosity; and fine hotels, on both sides of the river, afford them ample accommodations. Staircases have been excavated at different places, by which visiters can get safely down to the best points of view. A walk under the cliff is very interesting; but to pursue the slippery and dangerous path under the sheet of water, beneath the falling torrent and the mighty rock over which it falls, requires both courage and caution. Parties, however, often incur the hazard, and submit to the inconvenience caused by the extreme dampness of the atmosphere, which is constantly surcharged with spray, and, being agitated by conflicting currents of wind, soon wets one to the skin.

Every change of season, weather, and light, imparts some peculiar aspect to this extraordinary scene. The rising sun gilds the edges of the cataract, and illuminates the upper banks, with their wild crests of overhanging trees, while the darkness of the awful gulf below is enhanced by the unintermitted roaring and concussions of the tremendous masses of water dashed together. The lofty column of mist, which for ever stands, like a cloud, over this scene of noise and fury, is sometimes dark as a thunder-storm, but more frequently of a snowy whiteness, and illuminated and painted by rainbows, whose arches vary in their position and direction with the course of the sun. Night casts a tone of majesty over the scene, as difficult to be duly described as to be witnessed without emotion, especially when the moon silvers the rocks, the water, and the spray, or when, in winter, it falls upon the forest-trees, glazed with the frozen spray, and upon the immense icicles, often more than a hundred feet in length.

It is almost impossible for any living thing to survive the descent of this awful cataract. Deer and other animals have sometimes been carried down, while attempting to swim across the river above; and, in several instances,

View of Niagara Falls from the Clifton House.

The Van Kleeck House.

men have been borne down to the awful verge, and plunged to unknown depths in the black gulf beneath.

The vicinity of Niagara has been signalized by several important military events. The French fortress of Frontenac, at the mouth of the river, was captured by the British, after a siege; Fort Erie, at the head of the stream, was taken by the Americans, in the war of 1812; Buffalo was burnt by the enemy; Lewistown was taken, by an American force, by a bold *coup-de-main*, after crossing in boats, and scaling an almost inaccessible height on the shore. The battle of Lundy's Lane and Bridgewater was fought within a short distance of the cataract, and gave the Americans some of their greatest advantages in that unhappy contest.

Grand island, a little above the cataract, is a good agricultural region, and is remarkable as the site of the proposed city of "Ararat," offered as a gathering-place of the Jews, and as a camp occupied by the invaders of Canada, in the late attempt at revolution.

The passage to the islands, over the bridge, affords the visiter a gratifying though an agitating view of the rushing stream, just as it pours furiously by to its stupendous leap down the awful precipice. With astonishing skill and boldness, the slight fabric has been constructed, from rock to rock, across the wild and dangerous channel; and the spectator views its waves with awe and fear, as they glide beneath his feet, and intimate the sudden and fatal consequences of a single misstep.

The Welland canal, on the Canada side, gives a passage to lake-vessels from Erie to Ontario.

A wire-bridge across Niagara river, below the falls, has been built, and is of sufficient strength to allow the passage of great weights.

Without naming numerous other places and objects of great interest, we return to the Hudson river.

Poughkeepsie.—This is one of the pleasantest villages in the valley of the Hudson, but is so situated, at the distance of a mile from its eastern shore, as to be quite out of sight to travellers passing in steamboats. It is one of the most flourishing villages in this part of the state; and its settlement dates back to about the year 1700, when it was first inhabited by a few Dutch families. The soil is favorable to cultivation, while the stream which flows through the town makes a succession of falls, amounting, in all, to a descent of about a hundred and sixty feet, and affords water-power to various mills and manufactories. The place contains three printing-offices, two banks, and eleven churches, with twelve schools. Population, 1850, 11,080.

The Van Kleeck House.—This was the first house ever erected in Poughkeepsie. It was the residence of Myndert

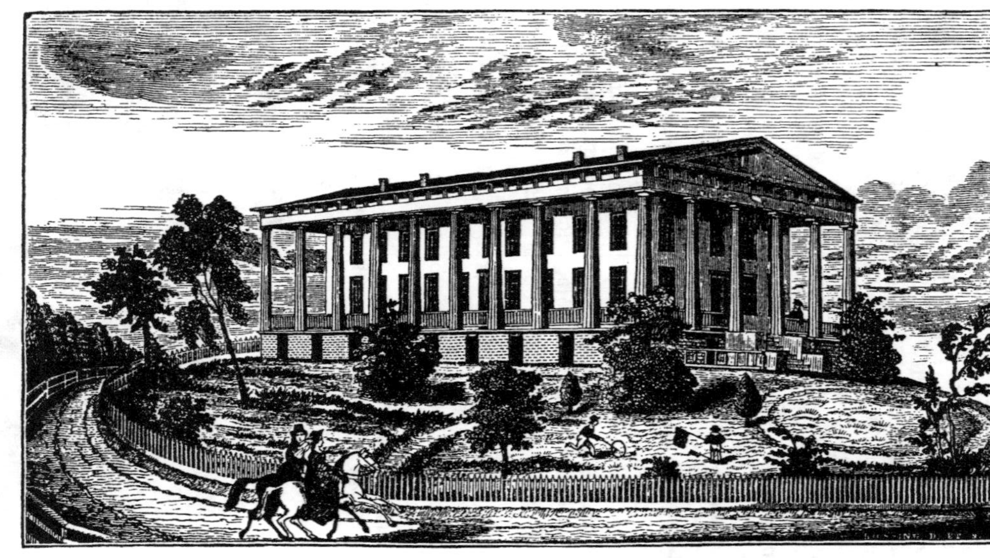

The Collegiate School. Poughkeepsie.

Church of Our Lady at Cold-Spring.

Van Kleeck, one of the first settlers in the county; and the remarkable building, with the surrounding grounds, was in possession of his descendants in the year 1835, when it was taken down. It was built in 1702. It was for many years a public-house; and, in 1787, was occupied by the legislature as a state-house. The session held there was the eleventh, and the governor of the state was then George Clinton.

The Collegiate School is an institution for education, in a large building one hundred and fifteen feet by thirty-five, well proportioned, with a fine colonnade, and surrounded by spacious grounds, tastefully adorned. The building cost forty thousand dollars; and it commands a fine view of forty or fifty miles upon the surrounding country, with the ridge of the Catskill mountains, twenty miles distant toward the south. Poughkeepsie lies below, about a mile in front; and the elevation occupied by the edifice commands a charming view of the Hudson, enlivened by numerous steamboats and other vessels engaged in its varied and active commerce.

Poughkeepsie is one of the largest manufactories of locomotives in the United States. The surprising success of Americans, in the improvement and construction of the most complex and powerful steam machines, and especially of this class, has excited admiration abroad, as well as at home; and multitudes of our locomotives are now performing the labors of some of the principal railroads of Europe, while our furnaces and workshops are resounding with the preparations for many more.

Roman Catholic Church at Cold-Spring.—A few miles below Poughkeepsie, and opposite West Point, on an elevation commanding a view of the river, is this neat little edifice, just above the landing. It is of plain, Grecian style, with four Doric columns. The material is brick, but the whole is covered with stucco, which gives it the appearance of white stone.

The Stone-Church at Dover.—About twenty-four miles east from Poughkeepsie, near the village of Dover, is a remarkable cavern, which, from the peculiar, angular form of its roof, has received the name of the "stone-church." This natural cavity appears to have been

Dover Stone Church.

slowly formed by the flowing of a stream, which, coming down the mountain in which the cavern is found, enters at a narrow fissure in the roof, and, descending from crag to crag, presents a beautiful succession of cascades, till it reaches the level of the floor, where it spreads out in a quiet little pond. The whole cavern is large, being divided into two compartments by an immense rock which has fallen from above. The inner chamber is about seventy feet in length, while the Gothic arch above is twenty feet in width, and the top about two hundred feet high.

"The scene," remarks a visiter, "is well fitted to inspire devotional feelings: the heart acknowledges the power of the Creator, and rises in admiration of his works."

Troy is one of the numerous towns in this state which display striking evidence of rapid, substantial, and permanent improvement, which has been so extensively occasioned by the enlightened internal policy of the government, and accomplished by the intelligence and industry of the people. A view from Mount Ida, an eminence rising abruptly from its eastern border, embraces a scene of life and activity seldom surpassed. A young and flourishing city below, with streets crowded with busy people, the noble Hudson sweeping majestically by, crossed by a fine pier, which serves the double purpose of a bridge and a viaduct to the railroad—the combined trunk of the Champlain and Erie canal, floating the crowded boats from the north and the west—several of the splendid New York steamboats, which penetrate to this highest accessible point: all these are embraced within the immediate range of the eye, with the various signs of bustle to which they give rise. The United States arsenal, at Watervliet, stands opposite; while nearer by, the environs of Troy are beautified by the mansions and gardens of some of the wealthy citizens, and the rumbling of machinery, and the smoking of chimneys, betray the vicinity of some of the largest and best manufactories in the country. Some of these are supplied with moving-power by the

St. Paul's Church, Troy.

small but constant streams flowing down the eminence on which the spectator is supposed to stand; and such is the variety found among the factories, mills, &c., in this immediate vicinity, that we can not pretend to give a full account of them. Population, 1850, 29,000.

Plattsburgh.—This town, the capital of Clinton county, one hundred and twelve miles north of Whitehall, and one hundred and sixty-four miles from Albany, enjoys an advantageous and pleasant situation, on the western side of Lake Champlain. The township is supplied with many fine mill-seats, by the Saranac and Salmon rivers, and several other small streams; and the eastern part of it is generally level, although the western is hilly. The village stands on the lake-shore, at the mouth of the Saranac. In speaking of Lake Champlain, on a preceding page, we alluded to the important naval victory achieved on the Cumberland bay, opposite this place, in the last war with Great Britain, in 1814.

Plattsburgh was twice taken by their troops, but the country below was finally delivered from danger by the event just mentioned. The victorious American squadron, under Commodore McDonough, had 820 men, and 86 guns, and the British 1,050 men, and 96 guns. The following recollections of the battle are from the pen of a friend:—

"*The Battle of Plattsburgh.*—It was a bright sabbath in September, one of those rich, soft, and mellow days that begin to wear the sober tints of autumn, that my childish heart was made sad by the scenes and the sounds of war. Our home was on the eastern border of the lake, just across from Plattsburgh; and, for many long months, the event of battle had been the theme of conversation by the fireside, among men as they met in their daily haunts, and friends by the wayside. Preparations were going forward for defence; and among men there was enlisting, draughting, &c., and all things wore the aspect of some impending evil, which threw a kind of gloom over the feelings, in which all sympathized. We lived within less than a day's march of the enemy's ground, and consequently were often alarmed with conjectures and painful suspense, in regard to their movements. Often were we surprised with rumors of the near approach of the British—that they had crossed the lines—were marching down upon us, &c., which kept the inhabitants in a very uneasy and unsettled condition. But so many false alarms had a tendency, at length, to lull them into a state of indifference, or to allay their apprehensions so much, that people had resumed their avocations in comparative quiet.

"But at last the event burst upon us, with all the dreaded realities of bloodshed and war! The scene was sufficiently distant to prevent immediate danger, yet all knew that their future security hung on the *result*, and every eye was strained, and every heart beat with deep anxiety, for the sequel.

"It was a peaceful sabbath morning; the sun had risen with its accustomed splendor, and nature wore the stillness peculiar to the sacred day. But alas! it was a strange sabbath with man. The booming sounds of guns came across the water, in such quick and rapid succession, that they shock the earth, and sounded like heavy and deep-toned thunder. The engagement lasted two hours and twenty minutes; and we knew the work of death was going on at every new report. Such a sabbath may this land never see again! It was not a 'day of rest,' or of worship, but one to be remembered with feelings of horror and dread. A few gathered in the morning, aged men, women, and children, in a lonely group, for worship; but, as the excitement increased, every man fled from the village, and, in short, almost every one had climbed to some height on the hills, or in the steeple of the church, to read, in the progress of events, our consequent destiny. When the British ships struck their colors, and *victory* was the cry, there was great rejoicing, in the sure and delightful feeling of safety, far more than in that of success.

"Men and boys had nearly all crossed over the lake to witness the scene, from the hills about the village, and were spectators of the bloody affray. One of my brothers went aboard one of the vanquished ships, soon after the action ceased. The deck was strewed with the dead and dying, weltering in gore. The gallant Downie, who had commanded the British forces, lay on a large iron chest, just as he was slain. Victory was the theme and the cry of the conquerors; but grief and dismay were the feelings of the vanquished.

"The officers who fell in these encounters, both by land and water, were buried side by side in the graveyard at Plattsburgh. Monuments have been erected to all. Friends and foes sleep as quietly as if they had never had collision here on earth. Commodore Downie, though slain in the invasion of our country, as the officer of the highest rank, is placed in the centre; and a tablet, erected to his memory, bears the following inscription:—

"'Sacred to the memory of George Downie, Esq., a post-captain in the British navy, who gloriously fell on board his B. M. ship Confiance, while leading the vessels under his command to the attack of the American flotilla, at anchor in Cumberland bay, off Plattsburgh, on the 11th of September, 1814.—To mark the spot where the remains of a gallant officer and sincere friend were honorably interred, this stone has been erected by his affectionate sister-in-law, Mary Downie.'

"The family of Dr. Davidson were residents of Plattsburgh at this time; and Mrs. Davidson, in a work of hers called 'Selections,' has given an interesting sketch of events that occurred in her own family during the scene of those eventful days.

"After some months, the vessels were taken to the head of the lake, at Whitehall. Circumstances of travelling just at that time gave me an opportunity, in the impressible season of childhood, to see from the tall masts the British and American flags floating lazily in the breeze, the conquered 'lion' looking just as fierce and terrible as if he had not been a captive among Americans. We were invited on board, and saw the mutilated ships of war. They were making preparations to sink them in the lake, which was afterward done, for preservation, and the soldiers were rolling cannon-balls into their holds, as weights.

"Commodore M'Donough was present—a man of middle stature; but there was nothing in his looks or manner which indicated aught of the exciting scenes through which he had passed. It is said of him that, after the enemy's fleet hove in sight, the men of his ship were assembled on the quarter-deck, when he kneeled down, and, in humble and fervent prayer, commended himself, his men, and the cause in which they were engaged, to the 'God of battles,' and arose from that posture with a calmness and serenity on his brow which showed that he had received comfort and assurance from above.

"The dead of both armies were taken to the small islands near the scene of action, and there buried. Those waters now look as blue and as beautiful as if never disturbed with war; and those islands are as green and verdant as if never broken with new-made graves."

New York City.—The site of this city, which was first occupied by Europeans in 1614, or 1615, and then only by the erection of a blockhouse near its southern extremity, is now the most populous, as well as the most important, on the western continent, and vies, in commercial rank, with many of the principal ones of the old world. It now occupies the whole of Manhattan island, being conterminous with the county of New York. Its limits, therefore, extend to the narrow channel between the Hudson and East rivers, called Harlem river; a distance of $14\frac{1}{2}$ miles, with a breadth varying up to two miles, and an area of $21\frac{3}{4}$ square miles. The southern portion, forming about one sixth of the whole, is occupied by the main body of the population, amounting, in 1840, to 312,710, and in 1850 to 515,547. The number of buildings, in 1850, in the compact part of the city, was 37,730; the valuation of real estate, $227,000,000, and of personal estate, $93,000,000.

The harbor is very capacious, with good anchorage for the largest ships, almost wholly free from shoals, and with currents strong enough to keep it usually free from ice in the winter, even when more southern ports are obstructed. Governor's and Bedlow's islands are strongly fortified; and the entrance to the lower bay is defended by Fort Hamilton, on Long island, Fort Lafayette, on a rock in the water, and batteries on Staten island, opposite. The Hudson river opens a natural navigable channel of 150 miles to Albany, and with the various canals and railroads heretofore mentioned; while the East river communicates with Long Island sound, which pours much trade into this city. Lines of the most capacious and splendid steamboats lead daily, and almost hourly, in all directions; and new channels of communication are now in preparation, which will still further facilitate and extend the great commercial relations of New York.

The streets in the lower and oldest part of the city are generally narrow and crooked; but in the upper portion, to which many of the inhabitants have changed their residences within a few years, they are straight, broad, well built, and more agreeable.

The number of churches is 245. Of these there are—baptist, 31; congrega-

View of New York City

tional, 9; Dutch reformed, 17; friends, 4; Jewish, 11; Lutheran, 5; methodist episcopal, 31; methodist protestant, 2; presbyterian, 35; associate presbyterian, 4; associate reformed presbyterian, 2; reformed presbyterian, 4; protestant episcopal, 47; Roman catholic, 21; unitarian, 2; universalist, 4; Welsh, 3; miscellaneous, 16.

There are about forty banks, exclusive of eleven for savings. There are asylums for lunatics, at Bloomingdale; colored, indigent, and aged, at 42d street; deaf and dumb, 50th street; blind, 9th avenue; orphans, 117th street, and 71st street, 6th avenue, Prince street, 11th street, and colored orphans, 12th street; lying-in women, Marion street; old ladies, 20th street.

Schools.—Ward schools, 19; primary, 3; schools of the Public School Society, 18, and primary, 59. Both the ward and the public schools are free to children of all classes, and wholly gratuitous, even to the books used by the children. The latter were commenced about thirty years ago, through the exertions of a few benevolent individuals, at a time when public education was neglected; and, under the charge of a very faithful and intelligent board of trustees, and superintended by Mr. Seton, a devoted friend of the poor and ignorant, they rose to a high eminence, under the liberal patronage of the state.

The eighteen schoolhouses of this society, above-mentioned, are fine brick buildings, usually about eighty by forty feet, and two or three stories high, able to contain from five to twelve hundred children each. The monitorial system is practised.

The ward schools have since been established, in which that system is not used. The trustees and other officers are chosen annually by the people, and their schools are multiplying.

The Institution for the Education of the Deaf and Dumb.—This institution is situated near 33d street and 4th avenue. The building is 110 by 60 feet, and contains about two hundred pupils, from all parts of the state, many of whom are supported and instructed at the public expense. The building affords sleeping and dining-rooms, with apartments for recitation, the family of the superintendent, and the eight instructors, the kitchen, &c. The system of instruction resembles that practised in the other deaf and dumb asylums in the United States, being founded on the principles of the Abbé De l'Epée and the Abbé Sicard, introduced into this country by Mr. Gallaudet, at the expense of the American asylum at Hartford, about the year 1815.

The Institution for the Education of the Blind, is erected on land presented by James Boorman, Esq., at the expense of the state, aided by a gift of fifteen thousand dollars from Mr. Burke, and other donations. The building faces the Hudson river, at a short distance from the bank, and contains lodgings for a large number of pupils, most of whom are supported by the state. They are taught the common branches of learning, with vocal and instrumental music, and several useful handicrafts best adapted to their abilities, chiefly the manufacture of baskets, rugs, bandboxes, and carpets.

The Croton Aqueduct.—The city of New York is abundantly supplied with pure and wholesome water, by a work of greater length than any other in the country, and at a greater expense. The supply is derived from the Croton river, in Westchester county, at a point about forty miles from the city. That stream is dammed, and is capable of affording a much greater quantity than can be needed in a long course of years. The aqueduct passes most of the way under ground, through a pipe of masonwork, constructed in the most skilful manner, but crosses several streams, the broadest of which is Harlem river. The bridge thrown across is one of the most important constructions on the line. It is 1,450 feet long, with fifteen arches—eight of them eighty feet span, and seven of fifty feet span, 114 feet above tidewater at the top.

The receiving reservoir is at 86th street, about five and a half miles from the city-hall. It covers thirty-five acres, and contains one hundred and fifty millions of gallons. There the water is received, and allowed to stand long enough

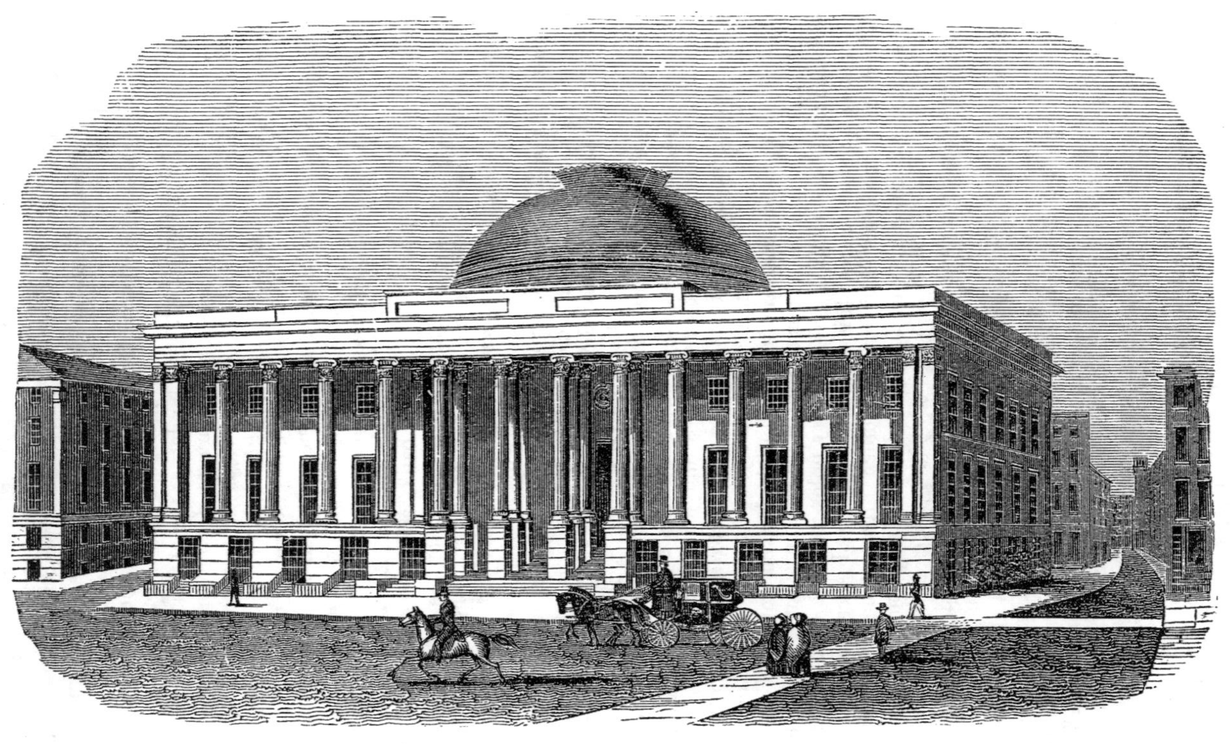

Merchants' Exchange, Wall Street, New York.

to deposite the particles of sand and clay it has brought down, and then it is drawn off into the second or distributing reservoir.

This reservoir is situated at 42d street, on the height of ground about three miles from the city-hall. It is an immense structure of hewn stone, resembling a modern fortress of the first class, covering four acres, and capable of containing twenty millions of gallons. From this iron pipes lead off, gradually branching in different directions, with stops, hydrants, &c.

Many houses are now supplied with this excellent water, not merely for culinary purposes and drinking, but also for bathing, &c. There is also reserved a supply for the extinguishment of fires, of inestimable value to the city, which has heretofore suffered most severely for the want of it.

Several of the public squares are adorned with beautiful fountains, some of which throw the water nearly a hundred feet perpendicularly, not, as at Versailles, after being raised by machinery, but by the force of the natural head.

Public Squares.—The Battery, named from the use made of it in early times, is a fine public walk on the southern extremity of the island, shaded with trees, and commanding a delightful view upon the bay. Being exposed to the sea-breezes, and in full view of the numerous boats and vessels of all descriptions, continually passing, the Battery is a favorite resort in warm weather. Castle-Garden is a place of amusement, formed in an old fort, connected with the Battery by a short bridge, near which floating-baths are moored in the bathing season.

The Bowling-Green, just north of the Battery, is a small circular green, surrounded with an iron railing, shaded with lofty trees, and ornamented with a beautiful fountain, where a stream of Croton water is thrown about ninety feet into the air, and falls upon a beautiful structure of marble, and thence into a basin. The Washington, 1 Broadway, was the headquarters of Lord Howe, in the Revolution, and, after the close of the war, was occupied by General Washington. The Atlantic, and several other hotels, stand opposite or near this favorite square.

The Park.—This is the most central and important of the public squares, at the junction of two grand avenues of the city, Broadway and Chatham street, containing the city-hall, the new city-hall, and the hall of records, and is surrounded by many other important edifices, such as the Astor house, Tammany hall, Stewart's store, museum, &c. It contains, also, a public fountain, within a basin about one hundred feet in diameter, which has a variety of jets, that are occasionally changed. When the water is thrown in a single stream, it ascends to the height of seventy feet, presenting a majestic appearance.

St. John's Park, in the western part of the city, is private, being accessible only to the inhabitants of the surrounding houses. It is closely planted with trees, and has St. John's church fronting it on the east.

Washington Square, between 4th and 6th streets, just west of Broadway, lies in front of the university, and one of the reformed Dutch churches.

Union Place, at the northern termination of Broadway, is in an elliptical form, enclosed with a fine iron fence, having a public fountain in the centre, with ornamental jets, and is a delightful place of resort to the inhabitants.

Further up the city are other public squares, as Madison square, Hamilton square, and others, not yet regulated. On the east are Tompkins square and Bellevue, the latter the seat of the almshouse.

Wall Street, the central point of the banks, insurance offices, &c., contains the exchange and the customhouse. The exchange is of Quincy granite, three stories high, and a basement, covering a block between four streets, and is 197 feet 7 inches on Wall street, 144 on one side, and 170 on the other, with a large dome above, 100 feet high.

The customhouse, at the corner of Nassau street, is of white marble from Sing-Sing, and in the form of a Grecian temple, with a colonnade at each end,

The Old Billop House, at Bentley, west end of Staten Island.

and pilasters on the sides. The interior is almost wholly of hewn stone. The principal hall is in the centre; and all the departments are well arranged, with ample accommodations for the numerous offices and clerks.

The City-Hall.—This fine and spacious edifice occupies the centre of the park, facing the south, and presents a beautiful Grecian front, of 216 feet in length, rising from a broad terrace. A flight of wide steps leads up to arched entrances, above which is a balcony on the second story. The two wings have halls in front, devoted to the common council, the superior court, &c., while other courts and offices are accommodated in other parts of the building. On the top is the great fire-bell, which indicates, by the number of strokes, the districts of the city in which fires are burning, for the direction of the fire-companies. A view from the cupola affords one of the finest prospects of the city.

Trinity Church, on Broadway, opposite the head of Wall street, occupies the site of the first episcopal church erected in the city, in 1696, except the chapel in the front. It is of sandstone, in the Gothic style, 137 feet long, 36 feet wide, and 67 feet high, with a tower 30 feet square, and a steeple whose top is 283 feet from the ground. In the rear is a vestry, 72 feet long. The church contains an organ, which cost $10,000. In the burial-ground surrounding the church, lie interred many distinguished persons, particularly Alexander Hamilton and Captain James Lawrence.

Prisons.—The *Halls of Justice* is the city prison popularly known as the "Tombs," and is situated a little north of the park. It was built, about ten years ago, to obviate the evils of the bridewell, which was constructed on the defective principles of the old system. The building is 200 by 253 feet, of granite, in the Egyptian style, and contains various court-rooms. The cells are solitary, to prevent communication between the prisoners, but provision is made for ventilation and warming the cells, by openings in the wall. Measures are taken for the religious instruction and moral improvement of those confined.

The Penitentiary, on Blackwell's island, in the East river, is an immense stone structure, on the Auburn plan, with a chapel, keepers' rooms, &c., in the centre, the cells for females in the south wing, and for men in the north. Each wing is more than 200 feet long.

BROOKLYN.—This city is on Long Island, opposite New York city, with which it is connected by ferries, upon which steamboats ply, every few minutes, day and night. Its beautiful and elevated situation has made it a favorite residence of many persons doing business in New York. It contains a city-hall, thirty churches, several banks and insurance companies, and over seventy thousand inhabitants. The *Lyceum* is a fine building of granite, with a spacious lecture-room. The *City Library* of 3,000 volumes, has a fine building and reading-room.

The Navy-Yard has extensive grounds enclosed, with an arsenal, stores, ship-houses, docks, the naval lyceum, &c. The naval hospital at a little distance, is a fine, large building.

Greenwood Cemetery is an extensive tract of ground, about three miles below Brooklyn, and situated on the bay. It has an undulated surface, and is laid out in lots, the access to which is by pleasant, winding carriage-roads. The forest-trees are left standing in many places, shading the little lakes, or covering the hills, and, in others, those of various foliage are intermingled by art; while tombs and monuments, usually planned and executed with taste, are already scattered in all parts.

Staten Island, with an elevated and varied surface, offers many fine sites for villages and country-houses, and is the resort of many citizens, access being made frequent and convenient by numerous steamboats. The quarantine hospitals are situated on the northeastern side; and a little below is the "seamen's retreat," a noble institution, supported by the "hospital money" paid by sailors.

Hoboken and Weehawken, on the shore of New Jersey, opposite the city, are pleasant retreats.

History of the Sons of Liberty in the olden time.—The American Revolution, which has produced such extraordinary results both at home and abroad, and which is destined to cause still greater changes in the European world, will elevate the eighteenth century beyond that of any of its predecessors in the annals of history. The success of the great struggle for liberty, which was by the many supposed hopeless, and which present historians deem almost miraculous, was brought about by the courage and perseverance of a few indomitable spirits, whom no labor could weary or danger appal; and it was by their moral courage, perseverance, and intrepidity, that this great Revolution was begun, continued, and ended.

Many of those who figured largely in the history of the times, and some even who swayed the councils of the nation after the struggle was successfully begun, were content with encouraging the revolt of others, without committing themselves, and kept within the pale of safety until they could embark without fear upon the perilous sea. But there were others who were not only the principal agitators, but actors themselves in the most daring exploits; and who threw themselves into the breach in the most dangerous conjunctures. Had it not been for these, who took upon themselves the fearful responsibility of directing and participating in overt acts of rebellion, the studied arguments of others who wished to bring on a crisis, but blenched from its dangerous concomitants would have been unavailing.

In the year 1765 Isaac Sears, afterward better known by the name of King Sears, a man of great personal intrepidity, forward in dangerous enterprises, and ready at all times to carry out the boldest measures, became the originator and leader of a patriotic band, who associated themselves together under the name of the "Sons of Liberty." Their organization soon pervaded every part of the colonies, and was the *germ* of the Revolution. By their intrepidity the spirit of the masses was aroused, and by their persevering industry and zeal the people were excited to oppose all efforts to enslave them. These bold spirits formed the nucleus of the future armies of the Revolution; and it is to the moral courage which they displayed, and the indomitable resolution with which they braved all danger, that the world is indebted for the illustrious example set by the infant colonies to Europe, and the foundation of a great and glorious republic.

The influence of these patriotic men, and the successful issue of the struggle begun by their boldness and sustained by their energies, has scattered abroad the seeds of freedom, which have borne fruit, in encouraging a spirit of inquiry throughout the civilized world, which has reformed despotic governments, and regenerated the fairest empires of the Old World.

If the successful issue of the Revolution has solved the problem of the possible existence of a free yet powerful government, it is, first, to the devoted individuals who, despising the dangers and disgraces to which they were exposed, set at naught the penalties and disqualifications of conspiracy and treason, and entered into the contest with a full knowledge of all its hazards, and a determination to persist to the death to effect their emancipation—secondly, to those brave men who bore arms in the subsequent struggle—that the great meed of applause is due. To all these, however obscure their names or imperfect their efforts, the nation at large owes a deep and lasting debt of gratitude.

The task of perpetuating the fame of many of the great leaders of the Revolution has fallen into the hands of able historians, who have well performed that duty. To rescue from oblivion and to do justice to the founders of our liberties, whose deeds, active or passive, whose personal or moral courage was instrumental in producing great and universal benefits to mankind, is peculiarly the duty of the present age. Now, when the present race, who first opened their eyes to an emancipated country, to enjoy the blessings purchased by the blood of their fathers, are fast verging to the grave, it is incumbent on all who have the means of elucidating past transactions, or the power to do justice to the actors in the scenes which have preceded them, to lend their efforts before they are called to their own exit, lest the deeds of their ancestors be forgotten.

It has often been remarked by historians as a duty every true patriot owes to the public and posterity, to bring to light whatever can be collected from the perishing materials of former days. There are ancient manuscripts in every part of our country, which are thrown aside as waste-paper in families not aware of its value. This kind of knowledge deals much, to be sure, in dry detail; but *facts*, upon which historians can afterward enlarge and philosophize, are what are chiefly important. We deem it a matter of such consequence that, if the exertions of individuals be not sufficient for the purpose of collecting and preserving these materials, public authority should lend its aid to accomplish this object, which is, in a peculiar degree, of public concern and interest. In this way are preserved to posterity the undoubted records of our early history.

The intent of the first association of the "Sons of Liberty" was to put down the stamp-act; and when this was effected the objects of the society appeared to be accomplished. But the acts of parliament, simultaneous with and subsequent to the repeal, gave to the more sagacious a cause for alarm greater than the obnoxious bill which had been rescinded. The billeting act, or mutiny bill, by establishing a standing army in the colonies at their own charge, was intended to strengthen the arm of the royal authority, to overawe the assembly, and to coerce the people to acquiesce in the impositions of the parliament.

History is full of the resistance to the enormous assumptions of the mother-country by New England and at the south; but little is said of the attitude of New York in that dangerous crisis. And yet in that colony, where the power of the sovereign was almost omnipotent, notwithstanding the exertions of the most wealthy inhabitants whose large estates were held by grants from the crown and whose subservience to the royal mandates influenced the assembly, and all those who subsisted by the royal bounty, there was found a chosen few who remained constant to the last; and who, when all seemed lost, kept alive the spirit of resistance, until from a feeble and hopeless minority they were enabled to triumph over the power of the colonial government and prostrate the royal authority for ever.

The association of the "Sons of Liberty" was organized in 1765, soon after the passage of the stamp-act, and extended throughout the colonies, from Massachusetts to South Carolina. It appears that New York was the central post from which communications were despatched to and from the east, and to the south as far as Maryland; which province was the channel of communication to and from its neighbors of Virginia and the Carolinas.

As the postoffices were under the control of the government, and the riders not at all times reliable, the committee of New York (and probably the other provinces adopted the same course), upon extraordinary occasions, despatched intelligence by special messengers; and if need were, a part of their members visited in person the neighboring associations to insure the perfect organization of the patriotic league.

The New York association had a correspondent in London, to whom an account was given of their proceedings, and from whom intelligence was from time to time transmitted of their proceedings and the supposed designs of the ministry, which in its turn was disseminated among the people by the association at home. A record of the names of the most active of their leaders would be a desirable document, but as this would be difficult to be obtained without great labor, and, perhaps, by a single individual impossible, a list of the committees in the different provinces, so far as they can be ascertained, from the remaining papers of the committee of New York, might be the means of initiating inquiry in other quarters toward producing the desired result.

Those from Maryland will appear from the following extract from the proceedings of the "Sons of Liberty," March 1, 1766.

"The Sons of Liberty of Baltimore county, and Anne Arundel county, met at the courthouse of the city of Annapolis, the first day of March, 1766.

"On motion of a Son of Liberty to appoint a moderator and secretary, the Rev. Andrew Londrum was chosen moderator, and William Paca, secretary.

"Joseph Nicholson, of Kent county, presented an address from that county, signed William Ringgold, William Stephenson, Thomas Ringgold, jr., Joseph M'Hard, Gideon M'Cauley, Daniel Fox, Benjamin Binning, William Bordley, Jarvis James, William Stukely, Joseph Nicholson, jr., James Porter, Thomas Ringgold, James Anderson, Thomas Smyth, William Murray, Joseph Nicholson, George Garnet, S. Boardley, jr., Peroy. Frisby, Henry Vandike, and John Bolton."

William Paca, Samuel Chase, and Thomas B. Hands, were the Anne Arundel county committee.

John Hall, Robert Alexander, Corbin Lee, James Heath, John Moale, and William Lux, were the Baltimore county committee.

Thomas Chase, D. Chamier, Robert Adair, Patrick Allison, and W. Smith, were the Baltimore town committee.

Pennsylvania.—William Bradford and Isaac Howell were the correspondents at Philadelphia.

New Jersey.—Daniel Hendrickson, minister, Peter Imlay, jr., Jos. Holmes, jr., Peter Covenhoven, jr., and Elisha Lawrence, jr., were the committee of Upper Freehold—Richard Smith, of Burlington, and Henry Bickers of New Brunswick.

Connecticut.—Jo. Burrowes; Jonathan Sturgis, Fairfield; John Durker, Norwich; Hugh Leollie, Windham.

New York.—Isaac Sears, John Lamb, William Wiley, Edward Laight, Thos. Robinson, Flores Bancker, Chas. Nicoll, Joseph Allicoke, and Gersham Mott.

Jeremiah Van Rensselaer, Mynhard Roseboom, Robert Henry, and Thomas Young, Albany.

John S. Hobart, Gilbert Potter, Thos. Brush, Cornelius Conklin, and Nathaniel Williams, Huntington, Long Island.

George Townsend, Barack Sneething, Benjamin Townsend, George Weeks, Michael Weeks, and Rowland Chambers, Oyster Bay, Long Island.

The first organization of the Sons of Liberty was dissolved at the repeal of the stamp-act; and while the hope was strong that similar associations would no longer be necessary, the committee received a letter from their faithful correspondent in London, of the following import:—

LONDON, *28th July*, 1766.

Gentlemen : I flattered myself to have heard from you by the last ships, but am informed your society is dissolved, which I am glad to hear, as the cause of your complaint is removed. But I think it necessary to assure you that the continual account we had of the Sons of Liberty, through all North America, had its proper weight and effect.

As our gracious sovereign rules over none but free men, and in which he glories, it therefore can not offend him that his numerous and faithful subjects in America claim the appellation of Sons of Liberty. Permit me, therefore, to recommend ten or twenty of the principal of you, to form yourselves into a club, to meet once a week, under the name of Liberty Club; and for ever, on the 18th of March, or first day of May, give notice to the whole body to commemorate your deliverance, spending such day in festivity and joy. I beg pardon for taking the liberty to advise you; but I am firmly of opinion it will have such effect as you wish.

I have the honor to be, gentlemen, your most humble servant,

NICHOLAS RAY.

P. S.—The commercial acts and free ports which we lately sent to all the colonies I believe will give you pleasure.

To the Sons of Liberty, New York.

To this letter the committee returned the following reply :—

NEW YORK, *October* 10*th*, 1766.

SIR: Your esteemed favor of the 28th July last, we have duly received; and observe with the greatest regret your disappointment at not hearing from us, agreeably to your expectations, which, permit us to assure you, was not owing to any remissness on our part, or want of respect; but to the dissolution of our society, which happened immediately upon the repeal of the stamp-act.

Your proposal with regard to a number of us forming ourselves into a club, we have already had under consideration. But as it is imagined that some inconveniences would arise, should such a club be established just at this time, we must postpone the same till it may appear more eligible; at the same time we take the liberty to assure you, and all our good friends on your side of the water, who so nobly exerted themselves in behalf of us, and the expiring liberties of their country, that we still do, and ever shall, retain the most grateful sense of the favors we have received; and that we shall use our utmost endeavors, consistent with loyalty, to keep up that glorious spirit of liberty which was so rapidly and so generally kindled throughout this extensive continent. In order to which, we shall not fail hereafter to celebrate the anniversary of the repeal, with every demonstration of gratitude and joy, on the memorable eighteenth day of March.

We have the honor to be, in behalf of the Sons of Liberty, sir, your most obedient and obliged humble servants,

ISAAC SEARS, EDWARD LAIGHT,
FLORES BANCKER, JOHN LAMB,
CHAS. NICOLL, JOSEPH ALLICOKE.

To Mr. Nicholas Ray, merchant, London.

It was not long before the necessity for reorganization became apparent, and most of the committee, who had acted with so much vigor and zeal, were found equally vigilant on every emergency. Of the persons before named of the New York association, Mr. Allicoke alone is known to the writer to have espoused the cause of the king. But with the exception of Messrs. Nicoll and Bancker, whose names do not appear on any of the subsequent committees, the others were the most determined opposers of the crown and steadfast adherents to the revolutionary party.

BIOGRAPHY OF COLONEL ISAAC SEARS.—Among those who originated the opposition to the stamp-act, and who banded themselves together at the first encroachments of the mother-country, under the designation of associated SONS OF LIBERTY, there existed, of course, a great diversity of intellectual endowments; nor did all render to their country in those perilous days the same important services. Like the luminaries of heaven, each contributed his portion of influence; but, like them, they differed, as star differs from star in glory. In the constellation of great men which adorned that era, whose united boldness and constancy drove the ministeral party to abandon their open attempts, and to mask their resolved purposes under measures less palpable to the general perception, few shone with more brilliancy, or exercised a more powerful influence, than the subject of this brief memoir.

This gentleman was born at Norwalk, Fairfield county, Connecticut, in the year 1729. From the records of his native town, we learn that his parent Joshua Sears came from Harwich, Barnstable county, Massachusetts, and bought lands in South Norwalk in 1720, from his brother-in-law, Josiah Thatcher. By the Harwich records, after careful researches made by Amos Otis, Esq., a distinguished antiquarian, it appears that Joshua was a resident of Harwich, and married Mercy Thatcher, in 1719, and removed to Connecticut. His pilgrim ancestor, Richard Sears, originally of Colchester, England, stands inscribed—one of eighty-nine names—on the first rate-list, in the old colony records. He came from Holland, with sixty persons, and landed at Plymouth on the 8th of May, in 1630, the last, or among the last, of Robinson's congregation at Leyden.

Colonel Sears was engaged for several years in an extensive and profitable business, as a dealer in European and India goods, at New York, New Haven, and Boston. But in 1763, when it was announced that the British ministry had in view to tax the colonies for the purpose of raising a revenue, which was to be placed at the disposal of the crown, his mind was turned to politics. and became in a great measure detached from mercantile pursuits. The cause of freedom at once became an all-engrossing subject with him. He felt its inspiration. It occupied his warmest thoughts, enlivened his conversation, and employed his pen. In respect to his private affairs, this was an unfortunate trait of character; but most fortunate for his country, since he thus acquired an extensive knowledge of those principles of rational liberty which he afterward asserted and maintained with so much energy.

At a public meeting held on the 6th of November, 1765, Sears and four others were appointed the committee of correspondence with the other colonies. Botta, in his history of the United States, says that it was difficult to fill the committee; but that Sears first volunteered, and was joined by four others, whose names, he regrets, are not known.*

On the 26th of December, 1765, this committee notified the public that they would soon be called upon. Information had been received that a further importation of stamps was expected. On the 7th of January, 1766, they arrived, were seized and destroyed, and notice sent to Philadelphia. The answer to that despatch is directed to Messrs. Sears, Lamb, Robinson, Wily, and Mott. No other committee is known to have existed at that time, and that committee managed the correspondence with the different colonies, and with the interior of the state. They framed articles of union for the different colonies, which were sent to the eastward for concurrence, and after it was obtained, despatched them to Baltimore to be approved, and sent further south for adoption. Of this, proof is to be found in the original draughts of letters (or copies) and replies that were addressed to those gentlemen.

It is believed that the principal letters, instructions, &c., forwarded to the sister-colonies, were prepared by Mr. Sears, as the chairman of the association. In various ways his appeals made the most powerful remonstrances against the injustice of England, in debasing Americans from the character of free subjects to the state of tributary slaves. The "Sons of Liberty" were among the first who urged the necessity of that mutual understanding and correspondence among them, which laid the foundation of their future confederacy; led to the first continental congress at New York, in 1766; prepared the way for the continental congress which assembled in Philadelphia on the 5th of September, 1774; and eventually resulted in the public and explicit declaration of independence on the ever-memorable 4th of July, 1776.

Apart from the higher, the epochal incidents in the life of humanity, the epitomes of years, deeds, and nations, there are events which do not claim to be inscribed upon the page of general history; and yet, from the deep local influence they once exercised, still preserve a commemorative interest, and convey an impressive lesson. The great war of our independence is rife with such illustrations. Its memories and heroes crowd so thickly upon us, that its history can not yet be written. But as each day adds to the legendary store, and we draw nigh the hour when it *may* be traced, time silently distils the mass of events, and the mingled vapors which ascend from the alembic, will be condensed by impartiality into truth.

The events we are about to recall, occurred in New York and its vicinity, between the months of September, 1775, and September, 1776.

The revolution was hardly three months old. But already from the cradle of liberty it had strangled its serpents at Lexington and Bunker's hill. The American army, encamped around Boston, owned WASHINGTON'S command, and held at bay the beleagured British. In the oppressed colonies, a spirit of resistance had organized the resolute yeomanry; and with the victories inscribed upon the national escutcheon, the patri-

* They were John Lamb, Gershom Mott, William Wily, and Thomas Robinson.

otic chord was vibrating in every heart. War had not yet disturbed our goodly city, which lay in unconscious repose, on the mellow night of the 23d of August, 1775. One or two riots, the result of political faction, rather than of unadulterated rebellion, alone gave tokens of a turbulent spirit. The English governor, Tryon, still dwelt here, an object of courtesy, though of mistrust. In the North river, off the fort, lay the Asia, a British man-of-war, with whose presence people had become familiar. The public mind was in a state of vague apprehension. It remained for its hopes and fears to assume a definite shape.

Toward midnight, our forefathers were aroused from their first slumbers by the thunder of artillery. At that silent hour, the ominous sounds were unwelcome visitants. The cannon peals were relieved by the sharp discharge of musketry; and the stillness that ensued was occasionally broken by the hasty footsteps of one summoned to his duty, with unbuckled sabre trailing on the ground, or by the agitated cry of a helpless woman, fleeing from the audible danger. Drums beat to arms; volley after volley announced the continuation of the strife; and the half-waked dreamer no longer mistook these cries of war for the echoes of eastern battles. As the night advanced, one body of men succeeding another was revealed by the blaze of torches, and the cumbrous wheels of the field-piece they were dragging, seemed to leave reluctantly the scene of conflict. By-and-by, troops of dwellers in the lower part of the town escaped through the streets, from their menaced or shattered abodes, in confusion and fear. Was the enemy in the city? the Battery taken? Were the troops forced to retreat before a victorious foe? These interrogatories were breathed rather than spoken, or if put, were not answered. It was a memorable night, and something seemed to have delayed the approach of morning.

The town was early astir. At break of day, many inhabitants were seen issuing from their dwellings, and wending their way to the Battery. To those already assembled there, when night uprolled her curtain of clouds, the glowing dawn that shot over our noble bay, disclosed traces of disorder, and ravages of the cannon-ball, on the one hand and on the other, the smoke still ascending from the angry artillery to the powder-stained rigging of the Asia. Moreover, the field-pieces, which but yesterday guarded the Battery, were gone. These the timid received as tokens of danger, and prepared to depart; the intrepid hailed them as auspicious omens of future victories.

The twenty-one pieces of ordnance had been removed by order of the provincial congress. Col. John Lamb's artillery corps, and the "Sons of Liberty," headed by Colonel Sears, were the heroes of the adventure. The efforts of the enemy to protect these royal stores, had proved unavailing. Warned of the intended movement, Captain Vandeput, of the Asia, detached an armed barge to watch, and if needful, interfere with, its execution. A musket fired from this boat, drew Colonel Lamb's volley, and a man on board was killed. The Asia fired three cannon. The drum beat to arms in the city. The man-of-war sustained the cannonade. Three citizens were wounded, and the upper parts of various houses near Whitehall and the fort, received much injury. A son of Colonel Lamb, whose regiment covered the cannons' retreat, is now living in this city, and in the rooms of the "Historical Society" may be seen one of the very balls fired into New York that night.

James Rivington was, then, the editorial and proprietary publisher of the "New York Gazette,"* and as the oppo-

* This Gazette attained the greatest notoriety during the revolutionary war, and was at first entitled, *Rivington's New York Gazetteer; or, The Connecticut, New Jersey, Hudson's River, and Quebec Weekly Advertiser.*

This Gazette commenced its career April 22, 1773, on a large medium sheet folio. It was printed, weekly, on Thursday; and when it had been established one year, this imprint followed the title, "Printed at his EVER OPEN and uninfluenced press, fronting Hanover square." A large cut of a ship under sail was at first introduced into the title, under which were the words "New York Packet." This cut soon gave place to one of a smaller size. In November, 1774, the ship was removed, and the king's arms took the place of it. In August, 1775, the

site party subsided in the expression of its political sentiments, and loyalism was no longer in terror of a Sears, he not only gave free vent to his own views, but so far forgot himself, as sadly to abuse those of his radical neighbors. Emboldened by their quiet reception of his denunciations, he expressed these in still more forcible tones, and doubtless exulted in this victory over whig opinions.

It was high noon, on Thursday, the twenty-third of November. The Gazette had been issued that morning, and the worthy editor was seated in his cabinet, examining the new-born sheet, just like any gentleman of the press in our day, when the sound of hoofs on the pavement beneath, drew his attention to the window. Looking out into the street, he beheld, with dismay, his old enemy, Col. Sears, at the head of an armed troop of horsemen, drawn up before his door. The men and their leader dismounted with the utmost deliberation, and a part of them entered the printer's abode. A few moments after, he saw his beloved printing-press cast into the street, and heard the tumult raised in the compositors' room above him, by those engaged in the work of demolition. To his despair, the materials thrown upon the pavement were speedily transferred to the dock, and the invaders sallied forth with many a pound of precious types in their pockets and handkerchiefs. A large crowd, collected by so unusual an event, stood aloof, quiet spectators of the scene. The cavaliers remounted their steeds, and rode off toward Connecticut, whence they came, and where, as was subsequently ascertained, the offending types were melted down to bullets. Thus liberty assailed the freedom of the press, and the balls whilom cast with joy into types, reassumed their pristine shape and destination; the ploughshare was reconverted to the sword.

Although no opposition was offered to these proceedings, by the body of citizens assembled near Rivington's door, there stood upon a neighboring stoop a lad of eighteen years of age, with an eye of fire, and an angry arm, haranguing the multitude in a tone of earnest eloquence. He urged that order should be preserved; appealing warmly to the dignity of citizenship, "which," said he, "should not brook an encroachment of unlicensed troops from another colony," and offering to join in checking the intruders' progress. The sins of Rivington could not be forgiven; but the youthful orator was listened to with respectful deference by that crowd which already recognised the genius and fervor of ALEXANDER HAMILTON.

A detailed account of all the important exploits in which Sears was either the leader, or bore a distinguished part, would far exceed our prescribed limits. He was elected to the New York provincial congress, which met in October, 1765; and was the first person who made a motion to erect fortifications on the island. They were projected on a comprehensive scale. With an intelligent eye, he embraced the extensive localities to be defended, and detected their vulnerable points. He also acted a conspicuous part in the excitement occasioned by the Boston port bill; and was warmly recommended by General Washington to Major General Lee, for his zeal and fidelity.*

words "*Ever open and uninfluenced*" were omitted in the imprint.

The Gazetteer was patronized in all the principal towns by the advocates of the British administration who approved the measures adopted toward the colonies; and it undoubtedly had some support from "his majesty's government." The paper obtained an extensive circulation, but eventually paid very little respect to "the majesty of the people;" and, in consequence, the paper and its publisher soon became obnoxious to the whigs.

While in England, Rivington supplied himself with a new printing apparatus, and was appointed king's printer for New York. After the British gained possession of the city, he returned; and, on October 4, 1777, recommenced the publication of his Gazette under the original title, but in two weeks he exchanged that title for the following: "Rivington's New York Loyal Gazette;" and on the 13th of December following, he called his paper, "The Royal Gazette." Imprint: "Published by James Rivington, Printer to the King's Most Excellent Majesty." The Royal Gazette was numbered as a continuation of the Gazetteer, and Loyal Gazette, and was published on Wednesdays and Saturdays; printed on a sheet of *royal* size, with the *royal* arms in the title.

* The following letter from General Washington, dated Cambridge, February 26, 1776, to his aid-de-camp and secretary, General Joseph Reed, will be read with interest:--

"You must know, my dear sir, that Colonel Sears

Owing, probably, to his exclusive attention to politics, he lost his entire capital, a few years after the close of the war. He had freely expended his wealth, and the best portion of his life, in the service of his country, from 1765 to the successful termination of the revolutionary struggle. The knowledge of facts like these diminishes the wonder which has sometimes been expressed, that America should have successfully contended with Great Britain. Her physical strength was comparatively weak; but the moral courage of her early patriots was to her instead of numbers, of wealth, or of fortifications.

We close this imperfect sketch with a short extract from the journals of MAJOR SAMUEL SHAW, of Boston, the first American consul at Canton,* being the only authentic account we have of the last days of this brave man:—

"Toward the close of November, 1785, proposals were made to me by Colonel Isaac Sears, and other gentlemen in New York, to take a concern with them in a voyage to Canton, with Mr. Sears to superintend the business. A suitable cargo having been provided, we sailed from New York, on the 4th of February, 1786, bound to Batavia and Canton. * * * On the 4th of July we anchored in the road of Batavia. Having transacted our business there, we left for Canton on the 23d of the same month,—Mr. Sears and the captain being confined to their beds with a fever, which had attacked them two days before. * * * We arrived at Canton on the 10th of August, Mr. Sears still remaining very sick. After remaining there three days, he began to recover slowly; and at one period he had so far got the better of his disorder as to leave the vessel, and pass two days with us at the factory; when, finding the air did not agree with him, he returned on board ship. There, at first, he continued to gain strength daily; but in a short time after he relapsed, and a flux setting in with his fever, the disease baffled the efforts of medicine, and carried him off on the 28th of October, in the fifty-seventh year of his age. His remains were interred the next day, on French island, with the usual solemnities; and previous to our ship leaving Whampoa, a tomb was erected over him, and a suitable inscription placed upon it. To give his character in a few words: he was an honest man, an agreeable acquaintance, and a warm friend." pp. 219 and 227.

DUNLAP, in his useful history, has done much to perpetuate the names of many of the Sons of Liberty. He speaks of Sears, M'Dougall, and Willett, as composing the most efficient and determined committees, from 1765 to the breaking out of the war, and who were in active correspondence with the patriots of the other colonies, and aided by their labors to keep up the ardor of opposition to the encroachments of the ministry. It is matter of much regret, that more ample materials do not remain to do justice to these and others of the fraternity.

It may safely be said, that wherever danger was to be encountered, or responsibility to be incurred, ISAAC SEARS was to be found; and with him was indissolubly associated his efficient coadjutor, JOHN LAMB. These were emphatically the tribunes of the people.

was here, with some other gentlemen from Connecticut, when the intelligence of Clinton's embarkation came to hand. * * * What, then, was to be done? Why, Col. Sears and the other gentlemen assured me, that if the necessity of the case was signified by me, and that Gen. Lee should be sent, one thousand volunteers (requiring no pay, but supplied with provisions only) would march immediately to New York, and defend the place until congress should determine what should be done; and that a line from me to Governor Trumbull would facilitate the measure."

* Boston: published by Crosby and Nichols, 1847, a valuable contribution to our revolutionary history.

Fac-simile of the Signature of Isaac Sears.

NEW JERSEY.

The situation of this state is in some respects quite peculiar. It is long and narrow, and lies between two of the largest and most important states in the Union. While, on the one hand, its territory is thus rendered highly important, as the only direct thoroughfare between them, on the other, strong influences oppose the existence of a single, united spirit among the people. The Hudson and New York city attract the business of East Jersey, as the Delaware and Philadelphia do that of West Jersey.

In several respects, however, this state has points of interest equal to any of her sisters of the Union, which will be in some measure exhibited, even in the few pages which we have to devote to the following description.

New Jersey possesses a considerable variety of climate, for a country of so small a surface, as its length is two or three times greater than its breadth, and it stretches directly north and south, while there is a considerable difference of elevation between the low, sandy regions in the southern parts, and the hilly and almost mountainous northern counties. Much of the former district also lies near the sea, while the latter is removed to a distance from it.

The Allegany range, crossing the northwestern parts, gives them the character just alluded to; and, while it affects the soil and vegetable productions, yields rich mineral products, several mines of copper and iron being wrought—the latter to much advantage. The proportion of good land is not large, as the "piny woods" in the south too nearly resemble the "pine barrens" of the southern Atlantic border, of which they appear to be the beginning; while through the elevated districts are considerable tracts inconvenient of access, or incapable of cultivation. The railroads and canals, however, which cross the state in several places, afford important facilities for transportation as well as for travelling.

HISTORY.—Henry Hudson entered Delaware bay on the 28th of August, 1609, and made an attempt to penetrate by it into the continent, a short time before he discovered the harbor of New York (namely, September 3), and the river which bears his name. The first settlements made by Europeans on the soil of this state were but a little subsequent to the first occupation of Manhattan island. The first Dutch vessel came out to trade in the Hudson in 1610, and the fort was erected at the Battery in 1614. In the latter year a redoubt appears to have been thrown up on the Jersey shore. About the year 1618, a colony of Danes or Norwegians, who had come out with the Dutch, made a settlement at Bergen, opposite New York. The first settlement in West Jersey is believed to have been made in 1623, by Cornelius Jacobse Mey, whose name is commemorated in Cape May. He proceeded up Delaware bay to Timber creek, a little above Camden, where he built Fort Nassau. He sailed in the employment of the Dutch West India company, which had been formed in 1621. Individuals obtained charters from that association, to large tracts of land, subject only to the Indian claim, one of which, opposite New York, extended thirty-two miles by two. One man thus obtained a tract sixteen miles square, at Cape May, bought of nine Indian chiefs. Some of these great landholders associated, and sent out David Petersen de Vries in a ship, to make a settlement on the Delaware, in 1630. He found Fort Nassau in the possession of the Indians, and no traces of its former occupants. He built another fort, and left it to return to Holland; but the garrison were soon massacred to a man. After another unsuccessful attempt to plant a colony, the treachery of the natives discouraged the company, and the enterprise was abandoned.

In 1637, two Swedish vessels arrived in the Delaware, and settlements were commenced on the western side, but lands were occupied only on the eastern. In 1642, Printz Hall came over as governor, under the appointment of the queen of Sweden, and established his residence on Tinnicum island, building a fort, laying out a garden, and erecting a church and several houses. Among his companions were John Campanius Holm, afterward the historian of the colony, and an engineer named Lindstrom, who published a map of the Delaware and its borders. There has been much doubt respecting the grounds on which the Swedes rested their claim to this part of the country; and they soon found it contested by the Dutch, who, having reoccupied Fort Nassau and several other points, were called upon to surrender them, and, on their refusal, compelled to submit by force. Governor Stuyvesant, of New York, soon interfered, and regained the Dutch positions, and easily reduced the Swedish posts, finally capturing the seat of government at Tinnicum island. This blow terminated the Swedish power on the Delaware, called by them New Sweden.

In 1640, a number of English colonists arrived from New Haven, claiming a right to occupy the soil under British authority; and thus the foundation was laid of disputes, which from time to time caused considerable difficulty. The tradinghouse which they erected was destroyed in one case; and in others their goods were confiscated, and some of the men imprisoned. The British and the Dutch governments had some warm altercations on the question of right to this part of the country. It is reported that some of the descendants of the early New Haven colonists still remain in Salem, Cumberland, and Cape May.

The year 1664 was the epoch of the reduction of the New Netherlands (now New York), by Colonel Nichols, at the command of Charles II. Sir Robert Carr soon after obtained possession of the posts and colonies on the Delaware, having entered the bay with two frigates, and expended "two barrels of gunpowder and twenty shot." The same year, Charles, by a royal patent, conferred it upon the Duke of York; and he conveyed a large tract, named "Nova Cæsarea" (New Jersey), to Lord Berkeley and Sir George Carteret. The name then bestowed, and which is still retained, is said to have been chosen in compliment to Carteret, because he had defended the island of Jersey against the "long parliament" in the civil wars.

Berkeley and Carteret conferred a constitution on the colony, securing to all equal rights and privileges, including liberty of conscience; and the latter was appointed governor, and took up his residence at Elizabethtown, in 1665. Having purchased land from the Indians, he sent an invitation to Connecticut for settlers, on such favorable terms that many accepted it, and the population of the colony rapidly increased.

But in 1672, difficulties, which had arisen between some of the older settlers and the proprietors, proceeded so far that an insurrection broke out, in consequence of the demand of the latter of rents for lands purchased by the former before the date of the charter of King Charles. The result was, that the governor was driven from the colony; and he repaired to England for redress, while his officers were resisted, deposed, and imprisoned by the people.

The New Netherlands being recovered, in 1673, by the Dutch, New Jersey passed with her again under her former proprietor. But this change was followed, the next spring, by a more permanent arrangement by treaty, in consequence of which the English were restored to the possession. The duke of York, to prevent any exposure of his title to question, on account of the intervention of the late Dutch conquest, procured a new patent; and, in 1664, Sir Edmund Andross arrived, with the authority of governor of the province of New York, claiming jurisdiction over New Jersey also, under pretence that the proprietors had lost their property by the Dutch conquest. This arbitrary man, whose injustice and oppression caused so much evil in New England, gave place to Philip Carteret, in 1675, who resumed the government of East Jersey, and so conciliated the colonists that order was restored. He postponed the demand of the payment of quitrents, but, on the other hand, in a list of "concessions" which he published, he laid some restrictions on political freedom. He attempted to open a trade with New England; but Andross, still governor of New York, opposed him, pretending that it would injure his colony. At length Andross sent to Elizabethtown, to seize Carteret and take him to New York.

Lord Berkeley about this time offered his share of the province for sale, as its prospects were not flattering; and it was conveyed to John Fenwick, in trust for Edward Byllinge, members of the society of friends, for one thousand pounds. The part sold was afterward called West Jersey, a designation often used at the present day. In 1675, the first English vessel arrived in the Delaware which ever visited West Jersey, and it brought over Fenwick and his two daughters, with a number of servants, and a company of settlers. He selected a pleasant and fertile spot, which he named Salem, and there planted his colony. The following are the names of some of the colonists: Edward Champness, Edward Wade, Samuel Wade, John Smith and his wife, Samuel Nichols, Richard Guy, Richard Noble, Richard Hancock, John Pledger, Hippolite Lefevre, and John Matlock. These men, and others whose names are not given, were heads of families. It was two years, however, before another ship arrived, probably in consequence of a difference which arose between Fenwick and Byllinge. Byllinge was sharer to much the greater amount, having ninety out of a hundred shares, while Fenwick had but ten. Byllinge, however, failed in his business, which was that of a merchant; and the management of his property here was intrusted to William Penn, and his quaker friends, Gowen and Lucas, by whom much of it was sold to different purchasers. These proprietors published a plan of government, under the name of "concessions," by which "the proprietors, freeholders, and inhabitants of each of the ten proprieties, were authorized to meet annually, and choose by ballot one man each, to act as commissioners." A deed was then made between Sir George Carteret and the trustees of Byllinge, dated July 1, 1676, fixing the boundary-lines as follows: "We have all that side on the Delaware river, from one end to the other: the line of partition is on the east side of Little Egg harbor, straight north, through the country, to the utmost branch of Delaware river, with all powers, privileges, and immunities, whatsoever. Ours is called *New West Jersey;* yours is called *New East Jersey.*"

Two companies of London and Yorkshire friends were among the purchasers of lands in New West Jersey; and, in 1677, commissioners came out to purchase land of the Indians, &c. The ship in which they came out arrived at New Castle on the 16th day of the 6th month, old style, bringing also two hundred and thirty passengers as colonists. They were glad, for a time, to land at Rackoon creek, and take up with such poor accommodations as they could find in the houses and cowsheds of the few Swedes whom they found occupying the spot, and found snakes numerous, creeping about the buildings. After making purchases of the Indians, who were numerous, the settlement of Burlington was commenced, and first called New Beverley, and afterward Bridlington; soon after which it received its present name. The following are some of the masters of families who formed this settlement: Thomas Olive, Daniel Wills, William Peachy, William Clayton, John Crips, Thomas Eves, Thomas Harding, Thomas Nositer, Thomas Fairnsworth, Morgan Drewit, William Renton, Henry Jenings, William Hibes, Samuel Lovett, John Woolston, William Woodmancy, and Christopher Saunders; Robert Powell, William Wilkinson, and William Perkins, died on the passage, but left families.

In 1679, George Carteret died, and, according to his will, East Jersey was sold, to pay his debts. The indenture of lease and release is dated February 1 and 2, 1681–'82, and conveys the property to William Penn and eleven others, who, in the following year, published a description of the country, with a plan of a town. These men were called the "twelve proprietors." Each of these took a partner; and to these "twenty-four proprietors" the duke of York made a new grant of East New Jersey, on the 14th of March, 1682; at which time about seven hundred families were supposed to be residing in that part of the country.

A brief notice of important epochs is all we have room to give after this period. In 1702, in consequence of prolonged disputes and difficulties, the proprietors resigned the government of the colonies to Queen Anne, who, on the 17th of April, 1702, accepted the offer, and reunited the East and West into one province, appointing her kinsman, Edward Hyde (Lord Cornbury), the governor. He was grandson of the chancellor, Earl of Clarendon. The commission and instructions then given him remained as the constitution of New Jersey until the Revolution. The governor and twelve councillors were appointed by the crown; and twenty-four members of assembly, elected by the people for an indefinite term, met at Burlington and Perth Amboy alternately. Among these instructions was one allowing liberty of conscience to all, except papists, and one prohibiting printing in the colony.

In 1702, the period when New Jersey became a colony of the crown, the population was estimated at twenty thousand; of which twelve thousand were set down for East, and eight thousand for West Jersey. Lord Cornbury was kept in prison, for debt, from 1703 till the death of his father, when he was raised to the peerage, and was released by law. He is said to have been more detested by the people than any other governor the province had ever had. Governor Lovelace, Lieut. Governor Ingoldsby, and Governor Hunter, were in turn at the head of the colony; under the second of whom paper-currency was first introduced into New Jersey, with its long train of evils. One of the pretexts for it was to raise funds for an expedition against Canada. William Burnet, son of the celebrated Bishop Burnet, was appointed governor in 1710, and held the office ten years, and afterward was governor of New York and New Jersey until 1727. The last of the royal governors was William Franklin, son of the celebrated Benjamin. He entered upon his office in 1763, the epoch signalized by the treaty by which France ceded Canada to Great Britain, and thus terminated the harassing wars which for half a century had caused great evil to the colonies. New Jersey contributed liberally to the expeditions marched against Canada in 1758, 1759, and 1760; for, although her quota was but five hundred men, she raised and supported a thousand, and, in 1761, and 1762, six hundred men, and incurred a debt of forty thousand pounds.

As the Revolution approached, New Jersey was among the foremost opposers of British oppression. In July, 1774, the people of the different counties held meetings to express their condemnation of the closing of the port of Boston, &c., &c. Delegates went to the congress in Philadelphia, who reported to the assembly, on the 11th of January, 1775.

The governor, however, who was opposed to resistance, endeavored to defeat the wishes of the people and legislature, particularly by refusing to convoke the latter. The delegates were, therefore, appointed by a convention. On the 23d of May, 1775, the second convention assembled at Trenton, and laid a tax of ten thousand pounds, to support a company or more, which it ordered to be raised in each of the townships and corporations. This was confirmed by the provincial congress, which met in August following, and directed the organization of fifty-four companies, of sixty-four minute-men each. Ten battalions were accordingly formed: one in each of the counties of Bergen, Essex, Middlesex, Monmouth, Somerset, Morris, Sussex, Hunterdon, and Burlington, and one in Gloucester and Salem together. Independent light-infantry and rangers were raised in Cumberland and Cape May.

At the same meeting, a resolution was adopted which rendered the people and their representatives less dependent on the will of the governor. It provided that, during the controversy with the mother-country, the voters should annually meet and choose deputies to the provincial congress; and this body was invested with the powers of government. In vain the governor made another effort at resistance. He held one more meeting of the legislature; but it was the last. They would not consent to declare that they had no intentions to proclaim independence. The body was prorogued till January, 3, 1776; but it never met again.

The provincial congress assembled again on the 10th of June; and, on the 18th of July, a few days after the declaration of independence at Philadelphia, New Jersey assumed the title of a state. The seal which was then adopted and made is still in use, though much worn. A copy of parts of it is under the vignette at the head of this description. The head of a horse over a globe is supported by figures of Liberty and Ceres, while three ploughs are placed between them, and the following legend surrounds the whole: "The great seal of the state of New Jersey: MDCCLXXVI." It is made of silver, two and a half inches long, and three eighths in thickness.

On the 25th of June, Governor Franklin was made prisoner, by the command of the provincial congress, as an enemy to the liberties of the country, and sent to Connecticut, under a guard, to be kept under the charge of Governor Trumbull, who placed him, with several other advocates of British authority, in Middletown. When released, after a considerable time, he went to England, where he enjoyed a pension.

William Livingston was appointed governor of New Jersey, by the new legislature, on the 31st of August; and he was annually re-elected for fourteen years. And now commenced the long course of trials which the Revolution brought in its train, and in which this state suffered most severely. Her peculiar situation, which renders it, during peace, the thoroughfare of important commerce and travel, exposed her, in the war, to the passage and the occupation of armies, and as the theatre of incursions. The navigable waters on her boundaries, so convenient and safe to the hundreds of merchant-ships and steamboats, by which they are crowded in our day, then gave too easy access to the enemy's fleets and squadrons. Her plains, now covered with fields and villages, churches, schoolhouses, and country-seats, and crossed by canals and railroads, which science has marked out, and which industry employs, were then traversed by armed troops, and often stained with blood. On the heights where the husbandman or the citizen comes to erect his rural residence, are often found traces of entrenchments, thrown up at the command of Lord Howe or of General Washington. In the following pages will be found brief notices of some of the principal military movements and events which took place in the course of the war.

New Jersey has the honor of being a very early and decided advocate of temperance; the value of which our country has been solemnly taught by a long course of bitter experience. The modern practice of opposing intemperance by association is extensively adopted in this state.

The first laws of the colony imposed fines of a shilling and two shillings and sixpence for what they denominate "the beastly vice, drunkenness;" and, in 1682, the sum was raised to five shillings, and sitting in the stocks for six hours was substituted when that was not paid. Liquors, however, were then allowed to be sold in small quantities, though at first they were not. In 1688, an "ordinary," or tavern, was required by law to be kept in each town; but the keepers were restricted in the sale of liquors to quantities not less than two gallons. In 1677, they were allowed to sell by the gallon, and, in 1683, by the quart.

The decent observance of the Lord's day was required by law. Swearing was fined one shilling in 1668, and, in 1682, two shillings and sixpence for each oath. If the fine was not paid, the culprit was put into the stocks, if under twelve years of age, or whipped, if above that age. "All prizes, stage-plays, revels, games, masques, bull-baitings, and cock-fightings, which excite the people to wickedness, cruelty, looseness, and irreligion," were to be discouraged and punished by courts of justice; and nightwalkers and revellers were to be imprisoned till morning, examined, and, if necessary, bound over to appear in court. From 1675 to 1682, "the resistance of lawful authority by word or action, or the expression of disrespectful language referring to those in office," was punishable. In 1676, all liars were added to the list, with a fine of twenty shillings for the second offence.

The first day of public thanksgiving was appointed by the general assembly on Wednesday, November 2, 1676; the second, on account of the discovery of the gunpowder plot, November 26, 1679; the third, June 11, 1696, for the defeat of the plot against King William.

Slavery was introduced in the earliest days. The "concessions," in the time of Carteret, offered to every colonist one hundred and fifty acres of land; and, "for each weaker servant or slave," seventy-five acres. But few, if any, slaves were then brought into the colony. At a subsequent period, however, they were imported in great numbers; and barracks were erected, as tradition relates, at Perth Amboy, to receive negroes from slave-ships. In 1734, an alarming negro-rising occurred on the Raritan, the object of which was to obtain liberty by massacring the whites, and joining the Indians and French. From allusions made in some of the old newspapers, it appears that negroes were sometimes burnt alive for certain offences. In 1750, two negroes were punished in this manner, for the murder of their mistress, and all the blacks in the neighborhood were required to be present. The law under which this horrible punishment was inflicted was passed in 1714, and provided for capital punishment for murder, &c., "in such manner as the aggravation or enormity of their crimes shall merit and require." The mode of trial was changed in 1768, but the manner of death was not fixed. In 1778, an insurrection was apprehended.

Early attempts were made at the whale-fishery on the coast; but De Vries said it was unprofitable in 1633.

Roads and other channels of communication, for which New Jersey is now so remarkable, were commenced under the direction of the colonial legislature, in 1676. The first roads were those used by the Dutch, in going from New York to their settlements on the Delaware, and were horse-tracks. The upper road extended from Elizabethtown point, or near it, to New Brunswick, probably the route now called "the old road," crossing the Delaware, by fording, a little above Trenton. The lower left the upper five or six miles from the Raritan, and extended to Burlington. In 1695, the innkeepers at Elizabethtown, Piscataway, and Woodbridge, were taxed to keep this road in repair; but only ten pounds were expended upon it annually. In 1744, stage-wagons ran twice a week between New Brunswick and Trenton. In 1750, a stage-boat began to sail from New York, once a week, for Amboy, and a wagon left the latter place the next day for Philadelphia. The next year an opposition boat was advertised, with "a fine, commodious cabin, fitted up with a tea-table," &c., to run twice a week. In 1756, a stage-line began to run between Philadelphia and New York, in three days, through Trenton and Amboy.

The first newspaper in the colony was the "New Jersey Gazette," begun December 5, 1777, at Burlington, by Isaac Collins, which cost twenty-six shillings a-year. The sheet was only twelve by eight inches; and the paper ceased to appear in 1786. The second monthly magazine in the whole country was "The American Magazine," published at Burlington, which began in 1758, and expired at the end of two years. Each number contained about forty pages octavo, and the matter was very respectable. The printer of this work was James Parker, son of Samuel Parker, of Woodbridge. He was apprenticed to William Bradford, the first printer in New York, in 1725, and was advertised by him as a runaway in 1733. But nine years after he was at the head of a respectable establishment: and he must have become reconciled to his old master, for he noticed his death, in 1752, in a very respectful printed article. He brought the first printing-press into New Jersey, in 1751, and printed public documents.

Trenton, the capital of the state, is pleasantly situated at the falls or rapids of the Delaware, and the mouth of Assunpink creek, in forty degrees and thirteen minutes north latitude, and two degrees and sixteen minutes east longitude from Washington. It is fifty-five miles southwest from New York, thirty miles northeast from Philadelphia, and ten miles southwest from Princeton. The population, in 1850, was 6,766, or, including the borough of South Trenton, more than 9,000.

The Statehouse stands on the elevated bank of the Delaware, in the north part of the city, commanding a pleasing view down a green slope to the level borders of the stream, which here is shallow. The building is of stone, plastered, and is one hundred feet long, sixty wide, and contains halls for the two houses of the legislature, offices, committee-rooms, &c. There is a spacious yard around it, which sets off the building to advantage.

The city contains, also, the lyceum, the city-hall, and seven churches; and the stateprison is at a short distance.

The bridge is of wood, eleven hundred feet long, with five arches resting on four piers and two abutments. It was commenced in 1804, and constructed by Mr. Burr, on whose skill it reflects much honor, as it has lasted nearly half a century, and was passed uninjured by the flood of 1841, which destroyed others built long after it. It serves not only for the purposes of ordinary vehicles, horses, and footmen, but sustains the tracks of the Philadelphia and Trenton railroad.

The County Buildings.—These are situated in South Trenton. The courthouse is a neat edifice, with six Ionic columns and a cupola. The basement is of sandstone, and the steps of granite. The offices of the clerk and surrogate stand a little in the rear. All are neatly stuccoed.

The Stateprison is constructed on a singular plan. The front building contains the residence of the keeper and his assistants; and in the rear are two long wings, running back from it, diverging from each other at a right-angle, with a passage leading through each, between two rows of cells. The whole is surrounded by a stone-wall, three feet thick, and twenty feet high, enclosing a square of four acres. Tubes pass through the cells to warm them in winter, and flues are made in the walls for ventilation.

The prisoners are kept at work, making chairs and shoes, and weaving. By judicious management, with cash sales, the income has been made to defray the expenses, and even to leave a surplus. All communication is prevented, and attention is paid to the moral improvement of the inmates. The prison contains a library for their use, of three hundred volumes.

The Battle of Trenton.—This place was the scene of one of the most celebrated of Washington's master-strokes. He excelled most commanders in striking an unexpected and successful blow, just at the time when it would produce the most important effects, by intimidating his enemies, and encouraging the country.

In December, 1776, the American army had long been on the defensive, or rather had retired, for fear of the enemy, beyond their reach. After the capture of New York, in August, Washington, with the remains of his army, after unsuccessful attempts to make a stand at different points, had been driven across New Jersey, and, barely escaping capture, retreated into Pennsylvania. To many the war seemed already at an end. The British troops proceeded to occupy the principal points on the great road through the state, and three regiments of Hessians, under General Rahl, and a troop of light-horse, were quartered at Trenton. On the evening before Christmas, December 25th, there was not an American soldier on the east side of the Delaware, and the stream was loaded with floating ice, so that it seemed impassable. The Hessians, in security, engaged in their accustomed celebration of the night with immoderate drinking; and about midnight the camp was in such a state as Washington had calculated on, at the hour of his premeditated assault. A large number of boats, which he had collected with all possible secresy, came silently across the river, in three divisions, nine miles above, by pushing their way, in the best manner they could, through the ice. It was morning before they reached the town, when two bodies of troops fell upon the enemy at once, from different quarters, pressing immediately toward the middle of the town, to prevent the enemy from forming. They made no regular stand, and some of them attempted to escape to Princeton, but were prevented; when the whole body surrendered, amounting to twenty-three officers and eighty-six men. Only twenty or thirty were killed, and eight wounded, including the commander. On the American side were none killed, and only two officers and one or two privates wounded. A few of the enemy escaped by the Bordentown road, which General Ewing was to have provided against; but he was unable to cross the river. General Cadwallader, with the Pennsylvania militia, was likewise unable to take part in the affair, as only a small part of his troops could be got over. Washington had intended to capture the other posts on the Delaware; but he thought it prudent to recross the river the same evening, and thus retired to Pennsylvania.

The Battle of Assunpink was fought a short time after that of Trenton. Washington, finding the enemy did not advance, again crossed the Delaware, and took post on the south bank of Assunpink creek. On the 2d of January, four or five thousand British troops marched from Princeton to attack him. The enemy made three charges upon the bridge, but were repulsed by his cannon, with about 150 killed. When night came on, Washington, knowing his force quite insufficient, ordered the camp-fires to be well fed, and drew off his forces with so little noise that the enemy did not know of their disappearance. Washington reached Princeton in the morning, which was occupied by a large British force.

Princeton.—This pleasant town is distinguished as the seat of the principal literary institution in the state, and one of the oldest and most respectable in the country—the college of New Jersey.

A. Anderson Sc.

Dr. Alexander's Chapel. Dr. Hodge's.

THEOLOGICAL SEMINARY OF THE PRESBYTERIAN CHURCH. PRINCETON, N J

Here is also the presbyterian seminary. The country in the neighborhood is agreeably diversified, with a good soil, peculiarly favorable to apples. It contains several churches, academies, and schools. There are several handsome houses, with gardens and yards arranged with taste; but the college-green, with its several buildings, is the principal ornament. In the rear of it, but fronting on the street, is Nassau hall, the oldest college-building, which has a venerable appearance. It has four low stories, chiefly appropriated to the students. Before the battle of Princeton, it was used for barracks, and the lower story for stables, and was defended by a party of the British troops, and stood a sharp fire from Washington's soldiers. A cannon-ball entered the chapel, and tore away the head of a picture of King George II. The library is a building a little west; and on the east is a building devoted to recitation-rooms, the chymical laboratory, &c. A little in its rear is a new college-building; and in front, near the street, and near both extremities of the grounds, are the houses of the president and the professors.

The college was founded in 1742, and owed its origin to a division introduced into the presbyterian church in the days of Whitefield; from which two synods arose—that of New York and that of Philadelphia.

Nassau hall, the principal edifice, was built in 1757, and was thus named in honor of King William III., on request of Governor Belcher, who had presented his valuable library, of 474 volumes, to the institution, and after whom the trustees proposed to call it. The building was one hundred and seventy-six feet long, fifty wide, and four stories high. The governor's library suffered much from the British and American soldiers, who in turn occupied the building; and almost all the remaining volumes were destroyed by fire, which, March 6, 1802, burnt all the edifice except the walls, which still remain.

ELIZABETHTOWN, on a small stream which flows into Staten island sound, four miles from Newark, was named after Lady Elizabeth, wife and executrix of Lord Carteret. It contains four churches, a bank, a courthouse, a jail, several public and private schools, and about 3,000 inhabitants. It is situated on low, level ground, with a good soil. By steamboat, it has a communication with New York several times a day, as well as by the New Jersey railroad, which forms an important link in the great line of railroads that now extends along almost the whole Atlantic border of the United States. Elizabethport, two miles from the principal village, is the landing-place of the steamboats.

NEW BRUNSWICK.—This city, the capital of Middlesex county, stands on the west side of Raritan river, fourteen miles from its mouth, twenty-six miles northeast from Trenton, and twenty-nine from New York. It lies partly in Franklin, and partly in North Brunswick, Albany street being the dividing line. Near the river the streets are narrow, and the ground low; but on the hill, which rises behind, everything is changed for the better. Here are a courthouse, jail, and eight churches, with near eight thousand inhabitants. Steamboats ply daily to New York. The New Jersey railroad passes through the town; and the Delaware and Raritan canal commences here, which extends to Bordentown, forty-two miles. It is seventy-five feet wide, and seven feet deep, allowing sloops to pass of from 75 to 100 tons. It is supplied by a feeder from the Delaware, twenty-three miles long; including which, the cost was $2,500,000. An old bridge, now useless, was built across the Raritan at New Brunswick, in 1811, at an expense of $86,687. There is another for the railroad.

Rutgers College stands on the high ground in the northwestern quarter of the town. It was founded in 1770, with the name of Queen's college; but being unendowed, it did not go into operation until 1781. In 1810, it was connected with the general synod of the reformed Dutch church, and, in 1825, the building was purchased by the synod, and the present name was given to the institution, in honor of Colonel Rutgers, of New York, a liberal benefactor; since which time it has flourished.

Washington's Headquarters at Morristown,

Newark, the most populous town in the state, is situated on a fine, level tract of ground, on the west side of Passaic river, nine miles west from New York, and forty-nine northeast from Trenton. Vessels of one hundred tons come up to the wharves; the New Jersey railroad passes through the town, on the way from New York to Philadelphia; and here is the commencement of the Morris and Essex railroad. The Morris canal passes through the place, which opens a channel of transportation between New York and the Delaware river.

The principal streets are wide, well built, and shaded with trees. Two large squares, in the middle of the town, add much to its beauty. It contains three banks, a courthouse, twenty-five churches, an apprentices' and a circulating library, a mechanics' association, and, in 1850, 38,885 inhabitants. The coasting-trade is considerable, and a whaling and sealing company was incorporated in 1833. Manufactures of several kinds are carried on to a great extent, especially in leather, carriages, &c.

Newark was first settled by a colony from Connecticut, in May, 1666, in compliance with the "concessions" sent to New England by Lord Carteret. Captain Robert Treat, John Curtis, Jasper Crane, and John Treat, having been sent from Guilford, Branford, and Milton, in that state, and made a favorable report, especially in favor of this place, they were sent again, and laid out the town, with the main streets and squares. Thirty families, from those towns and New Haven, at length arrived; but the Hackensack Indians refused to let them land, until they had satisfied their demands. They soon made a purchase, to the satisfaction of the wild men, giving them one hundred and thirty pounds New England currency, twelve Indian blankets, and twelve guns, for a tract of land now including the townships of Springfield, Livingston, Orange, Caldwell, and Bloomfield.

Paterson.—This town, thirteen miles north of Newark, and seventeen northwest of New York, is situated at the falls of the Passaic, at a spot abounding in romantic scenes, and peculiarly favorable for manufacturing by water-power. The stream makes a perpendicular descent of seventy feet over a precipice, in a sheet of foam, which is partly concealed by a projecting rock. A deep sluice, cut through the hard bank, draws off the water for the numerous manufactories below, so that the river is left almost dry in the summer-season.

The town contains two banks, a philosophical society, with a library, an academy, fourteen churches, and twenty two thousand inhabitants. It was chosen for the site of a great cotton manufacturing place by Alexander Hamilton, who, with his associates, were incorporated, in 1791, with a capital of a million of dollars. The early period at which their design was formed testifies to their intelligence and foresight, as the inventions of Arkwright were almost unknown in the United States. A board of directors was appointed, consisting of William Duer, John Dewhurst, Benjamin Walker, Nicholas Low, Royal Flint, Elisha Boudinot, John Bayard, John Neilson, Archibald Mercer, Thomas Lowring, George Lewis, More Furman, and Archibald M'Comb; and William Duer was made the principal officer. In 1792, when this spot was selected, there were not more than ten houses in the place, which was named in honor of Governor William Paterson. Major L'Enfan was appointed engineer, and began to cut the race on a scale unnecessary large and expensive, and resigned in a short time. He was succeeded by Mr. Colt, who adopted a more economical plan; and the first factory was completed in 1794. It was ninety by forty feet, and four stories high; and yarn was spun in it that year by water The year preceding, the operation had been performed by ox-power. In 1794, calico-printing was done, on unbleached muslins purchased in New York. The society at the same time directed the superintendent to plant mulberry-trees; and, at the proposal of Mr. Colt, a teacher was employed to instruct the work-children gratuitously on the sabbath. This was, no doubt, the first sabbath-school in the state, if not in the Union. It differed, however, from our common

Source of the Passaic River.

sabbath-schools, in being taught by a hired teacher. In 1796, in consequence of losses of money sent to England for machinery, the misconduct and ignorance of foreign workmen, and the novelty of the undertaking, the company failed; and the building was leased, and used for spinning candlewick and yarn, until it was burnt, in 1807. In 1814, Mr. Roswell L. Colt, son of the gentleman above-named, purchased the shares and revived the company; and the place has long been one of the most flourishing manufacturing towns in this country, though it suffered a great and unavoidable interruption after the war of 1812. The supply of water is very valuable, and has been enlarged by a dam, four and a half feet high, erected on the top of the fall; and the water is distributed by three short canals, at different elevations. The Passaic is navigable for sloops; and it not only has good common roads, but the Morris canal, and a railroad to Jersey city.

MORRISTOWN.—This is the capital of Morris county, and stands on a fine, elevated plain, in the midst of a varied and picturesque region. It is distant fifty miles from Trenton, nineteen from Newark, and twenty-six from New York. The streets are wide, straight, and laid out at right-angles; and in the centre of the town is a large square, surrounded by neat dwellings, and several churches and other public buildings. A large and splendid hotel here, erected by Mr. Givens, was accidentally burnt in 1846. An aqueduct, about a mile in length, supplies the village with water; and there are several manufactories at Speedwell, on a small stream. The Morris and Essex railroad, extending hence to Newark, was finished in 1838, and affords important advantages to the town.

Washington retreated to this spot, in 1777, after the battle of Princeton. His headquarters are still pointed out, as well as different points connected with interesting associations of that important period. Several important events, and many interesting incidents, occurred in the two seasons when Morristown was the residence of Washington. Hosack, in his "Life of Clinton," mentions that Washington once visited the Rev. Dr. Jones, pastor of the presbyterian church in that place, to inquire whether Christians of other denominations might be admitted to partake of the communion at the semi-annual celebration of it by his people, which he had understood was approaching. The reply was: "Most certainly; ours is not the presbyterian's table, general, but the Lord's." The general replied: "I am glad of it; that is as it ought to be. I propose to join with you on that occasion, though a member of the church of England."

The Source of the Passaic.—The picturesque scene represented in the accompanying engraving, is at the head of the principal stream of New Jersey, on whose banks are situated some of the most important towns mentioned in the preceding pages, and whose waters form the picturesque cascade, and turn the busy wheels of Paterson.

The Passaic rises in Somerset and Morris counties, and makes a remarkable bend round the county of Essex, so as to form almost its entire western, northern, and eastern boundaries. It has several tributaries, the principal of which are the Pompton and the Rockaway. The former is formed by the confluence of the Pequannock and the Ramapo, which rise in New York. Most of the regions watered by the Passaic and its branches are rough and wild, abounding in mines, and in forests, which supply fuel for reducing them. The failure of the latter, however, has been the chief cause of the abandonment of some of the mines.

Standing at the source of the Passaic, amid the romantic and solitary scenery which surrounds him, a spectator may reflect with interest on the peculiarities of the country through which it flows, and the various useful ends to which its waters are applied, during its short but varied course. It is not in vain that it has its head at so considerable an elevation above the ocean. In its short, but busy career, it performs an immense amount of labor, in turning wheels which move a variety of machinery, whose products are so valuable as to add materially to the wealth of the state.

Head-Waters of the Juniata and the Allegany Mountains.

PENNSYLVANIA.

This state, one of the largest of the original thirteen, lies between New York and Virginia, two of the other most extensive of that number, with Ohio on the west, the most populous and flourishing of the younger members of the Union; while its eastern boundary divides it from New Jersey, and it adjoins Maryland for a short distance on the southeast. Lake Erie touches it on the northwest. The Allegany ranges divide it into two parts: forming three distinct, though unequal sections, counting the mountainous part as the central one. These mountains deviate considerably from their general line in the interior of Pennsylvania. They cross the boundary of Virginia with a course nearly northeast, soon incline northeasterly, and at length run for some distance eastwardly; then stretching again more northwardly, cross the New York line in the usual course, northeast. The most easterly ridge enters the state in York county, and is cut through by the Susquehannah, a river which, instead of conforming its direction to that of the mountains, crosses the entire range nearly at right-angles.

The Delaware river, which forms the whole eastern boundary, rises in the state of New York. A system of canals forms an important line of navigation for boats and arks from the Lehigh river to Philadelphia, by which the productive coal-mines at Mauch-Chunk send thousands of tons to that city. The Delaware communicates, also, at different points, with the Delaware and Hudson canal, the Morris canal, and the Delaware and Chesapeake canal, and, through the Schuylkill, by the improved navigation of that river, and the great Western canal line, to the Ohio. At the same time, the numerous and long lines of railroads, crossing the country in different directions, meet the Delaware at Philadelphia; while the navigation of that noble stream by steamboats, coasting and foreign vessels, adds another very important branch to the extensive commerce of the state.

The Susquehannah, though flowing through regions abounding in various products, is naturally so much broken by the irregularity of the surface, that it was navigable only for boats, and at great risk; and, at the same time, the more important agricultural portion of the state, west of the mountains, offered strong inducements to the opening of a channel of communication between it and the commercial capital. The example of New York encouraged the undertaking; and Pennsylvania embarked more extensively than any other state in the construction of canals. Immense labors were performed. Railroads were in some places connected with them. But the first results proved unfavorable, and a general depression for a time succeeded, so great that the legislature at length resorted to a temporary suspension of payment; but arrears are now paid, and prospects improving.

The History of the settlement of Pennsylvania, and the early years of its colonial existence, have ever been regarded with peculiar interest, on account of the professions and character of the people, and especially their founder. The earliest European colony was planted in this state by Swedes, in 1627, or 1628, and conquered by the Dutch, from New York, in 1655. But the English having taken possession, in 1681, William Penn obtained a grant of land on the Delaware, landed at New Castle, and entered upon the government of about 3,000 inhabitants—Swedes, English, Dutch, and Finlanders.

A place called by the Indians Coaquanock, was chosen for the site of a city, and named Philadelphia, a name corresponding with the pacific principles of the society of Friends, of which Penn was so distinguished a member. By his mild, just, and humane treatment of the Indians, he set an example worthy of imitation, and gave the poor savages, so often misunderstood, abused, and misrepresented, opportunities to display some of the virtues of which they have too often been declared to be destitute. A characteristic anecdote is told, by tradition, of the sagacity and Christian liberality of William Penn, which forcibly illustrates the truth, that the way which is right is usually that which is most profitable in the end. The Indians once came to him with a complaint that they had been under some misapprehension in the terms of a bargain they had made with the white men, who had purchased of them a large tract of land. The colonists at the same time represented that the bargain, though hard for the Indians, was a fair one, and that they were ready to fight for it. Penn, however, in consistency with the principles of the gospel, which he professed, inquired of the Indians how much more they considered the land worth than they were to receive; and, on being informed, made such an addition of the articles used in trade as fully satisfied them, though really of trifling value, and thus not only prevented immediate bloodshed, and other evils attendant on war, but confirmed the grateful wildmen in their pacific spirit and friendly attachment to the colonists, most favorable to the permanency of a good understanding and free trade for the future.

The relations between Pennsylvania and Connecticut were disturbed for a number of years, after the settlement of a colony from the latter in the valley of Wyoming, which was claimed under the patent of King Charles, as it lay in her territory, as marked out by the two parallels extending to the South sea. The encroachments of the French in the west, on the Ohio river, threatened Pennsylvania, as well as Virginia; but, until the Revolutionary war, her inland position, and the obstacles presented by her mountains, contributed to secure her from most of the trials through which many of the other colonies had to pass, in the early stages of their history. Having no internal enemies, in consequence of the just and pacific policy pursued by Penn, she had little to disturb the peaceful lives of her inhabitants, until the Revolutionary war involved her in a full share of the public sufferings and losses. Her capital, after

Treaty of William Penn with the Indians.

serving as the seat of government, subsequently to the capture of New York, was threatened by the enemy, in 1778. A strong expedition having been sent from New York to the Delaware, succeeded in maintaining itself in Pennsylvania for a time: after several battles, Washington retreating to Valley Forge. The enemy were, however, ere long, compelled to retreat, and evacuate the country on the west of the bay and river.

The "whiskey rebellion," which broke out in a part of the state, soon after the restoration of peace, kept the country for a time in a state of alarm; but, after its suppression, Pennsylvania soon began to share with other members of the Union, in the career of prosperity which has so greatly distinguished our country, and has been one of the most remarkable of the states for the extent and success of its manufactures. Her iron-mines and manufactories, with her coal-mines, are the grand sources of her wealth, although her commerce is considerable.

Coal-Mines.—Among the natural productions of the state of Pennsylvania, those of the coal-mines take the most important place. On both sides of the Alleganies lie extensive and apparently inexhaustible beds of excellent coal, many of which are on the immediate banks, or near to the sources of streams, which have been rendered navigable where the aid of art and science have been required; and the immense and increasing supplies, annually transported, subserve the convenience and comfort of millions of people, not in this territory alone, but in half the states of the Union. Numerous steamboats and railroad-cars, as well as manufactories of different kinds, borrow their motive-power from these mines; while almost entire towns and cities derive from them their vast supplies of fuel.

The coals of Pennsylvania are of two kinds; and it is remarkable that, while that on the eastern side of the Alleganies is anthracite, that on the west is bituminous. The latter has rendered Pittsburgh the Birmingham of America.

Literary Institutions, &c.—Literary publications and scientific institutions were established in Philadelphia in her colonial days, chiefly by the labors and example of Dr. Franklin, who for a long time exercised a great influence on the country, and whose fame is universal. Massachusetts, however, lays a claim to a considerable share of the honor of his character and life, as he was a native of Boston, and there received his apprenticeship in the art which had so strong an influence in directing his practical course in life.

Printing was introduced into the bounds of the present state of Pennsylvania, in 1687, when the first sheet, an almanac, was published by William Bradford. The first newspaper issued, was "The American Weekly Mercury," a half-sheet of "post-paper," by Andrew Bradford, dated Dec. 22, 1719. There was at that time only one other in the colonies, viz., at Boston. The second was commenced in 1728, and passed, in a few months, into the hands of Benjamin Franklin. It existed more than a century. Several others were published in the middle and latter part of the last century; and the first German paper appeared at Germantown, in 1739. There were not fewer than six magazines before the Revolution. "The American Daily Advertiser" was the first daily paper in America, and commenced its daily appearance in 1784. "The Pittsburgh Gazette," the first newspaper in the western part of the state, began about 1786. "An imperfect list of the periodical journals" published in the state, between the close of the Revolutionary war and 1828, given in the American Almanac for 1835, names thirty-six. The number has since greatly increased, in every department.

State-Government.—The governor is chosen by the people for three years, but cannot hold the office over six years in nine. He must be thirty years of age, and have resided in the state for seven years. The senate consists of thirty-three members, elected by the people for three years, one third being chosen annually. A member must be twenty-five years of age, and have resided four years in the state, and the last year in the district in which he is chosen. The

View of Philadelphia, and the Navy-yard.

house of representatives consists of one hundred members, elected annually by the people. A member must be twenty-one years of age, have resided in the state three years next preceding his election, and the last year in the district for which he is chosen.

All judicial officers are elected by the people at the regular state election. The judges of the supreme court hold their offices for fifteen years; those of the court of common pleas hold theirs for ten years; and the associate judges of the court of common pleas hold theirs for five years. The secretary of state is appointed by the governor, and holds office during his pleasure. The treasurer is elected annually by the joint-ballot of both houses of the legislature. The legislature meets annually at Harrisburgh on the first Tuesday in January.

The Merchants' Magazine, just quoted, well describes Pennsylvania in the following figurative language :—

"She is, indeed, the keystone state. While one arm rests on the Atlantic, she lays the other on the Ohio, and her hand plays with the waters of the lake. Within her hills is stowed the fuel of ages; and iron, the world's civilizer, to bind the continent, and insure the stability of this great government; Erie, her outlet on the lake, Pittsburgh, the head of the eastern branch of the mighty valley, and Philadelphia, not only the beautiful city of the plain, but destined to be the leading city of the north, a city worthy so great a state. In her present competition, her rivals are cast. The mass of productions of the forest, agriculture, and the mines, are derived from Ohio, Indiana, Illinois, Michigan, and the ascending trade of the Mississippi valley."

The coal-mines of England, it has been remarked by the president of the British Statistical society, have yielded more profits than were ever derived from the gold-mines of Peru; but, without the aid of steam, they would have been comparatively worthless. The products of the Pennsylvania coal-mines are already so great that it would be difficult to estimate them; and such are the annual increase of the demand, and the abilities of the machinery employed in mining and transporting, that the prospects of the business are almost too great to be mentioned. Professor Bakewell remarks, that the proximity of coal-mines and beds of iron ore afford strong evidence of the provision made by the Almighty for the benefit of man. Pennsylvania, says the Merchants' Magazine, is the only state which has direct access, by water, at once to the ocean, the lakes, and the Mississippi: we perceive that her position justifies high anticipations of her future wealth and prosperity. The real estate of Pennsylvania, according to the same work, was estimated, in 1846, on the best data, at one thousand four hundred millions of dollars, and the personal property at seven hundred millions; making an aggregate of two thousand one hundred millions, or more than three times that of New York. Such an estimate must surprise almost every one; but, to sustain it, the writer gives the following statements: "Each of the three vast beds of anthracite coal, in this state, are about five miles in breadth, and sixty-five in length, with an area of 325 square miles, or 208,000 acres; that is, in all, 975 square miles, or 624,000 acres. If the supply of coal from anthracite mines, for 1847, is estimated at 2,800,000 tons, at four dollars per ton, which is the average price at tide-water, we have an amount of eleven millions two hundred thousand dollars. Most of the mines are owned by citizens; and the balance of trade with other cities is constantly in favor of Philadelphia."

It is amusing to record some of the anecdotes related of the coal-trade in its early days. Mr. Charles Miner, of Wilkesbarre, and Mr. Cist, sent off the first ark-load of coal from Mauch Chunk, on the 9th of August, 1814. The boat soon ran against a rock, which broke a hole in it. The men prevented the leak from sinking it, by taking off their coats and stuffing them into the hole. When at length the cargo reached Philadelphia, the expenses amounted to fourteen dollars a ton. The owners then found it necessary to call at houses, blacksmith-shops, &c., and urge the people

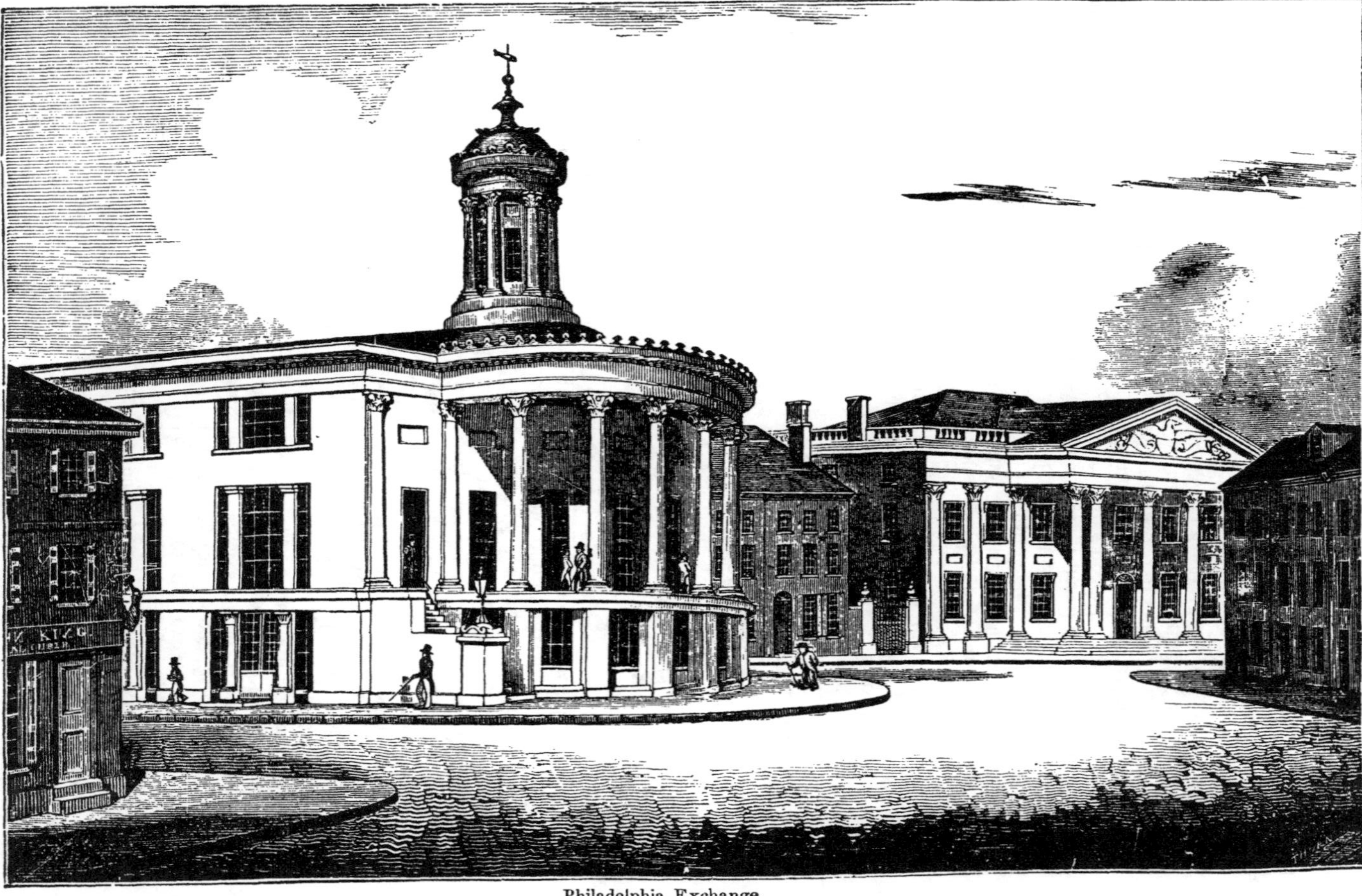

Philadelphia Exchange.

to try the coal in their grates and furnaces, and even to hire journeymen to give it a fair trial, after publishing handbills, in English and German, with a minute description of the manner of kindling and treating it. In 1812, Col. George Shockmaker took nine wagons, loaded with coal, from the Schuylkill mines to Philadelphia, and succeeded in selling two of them. It was with difficulty that he could persuade any persons to try the remainder, which he left without selling.

The amount of foreign coal imported into the United States, in 1846, was 156,853 tons, worth $378,597; which is very small, compared with the above estimate for the supply of anthracite from the mines of Pennsylvania.

Philadelphia.—This city was originally confined to a point on the western bank of the Delaware, five miles above its confluence with the Schuylkill, and about one hundred from the ocean. The river is of sufficient depth for the free admission of vessels of the largest size; but the navigation is subject to a long interruption, by ice, during the winter months. The city now extends quite across the broad, level space to the Schuylkill, a distance of about two miles, while the northern and southern districts, and several adjacent villages, having received portions of the increasing population, now contain, together, a large, compact mass of houses, with a population inferior to no city in the United States, except New York.

Almost without a single exception, Philadelphia is laid out on a plan of perfect regularity. The streets are perfectly straight, and those running north and south are crossed at right-angles by those running east and west, at equal intervals. The former are distinguished by the cardinal numbers—First, Second, Third, &c., beginning near the Delaware, as far as Independence square, in the centre of the city; and between the western limits and that point, by the designation of Schuylkill—First, Second, Third, &c. The principal cross-streets are named after trees, as Walnut, Chestnut, &c., except the central, which is Market street, and one or two others. These principal streets so far alluded to, form fine, large squares, which are subdivided by streets of a second class, and inferior breadth, of which those running east and west bear the names of shrubs and inferior plants.

Philadelphia is distinguished by its neatness, as well as uniformity, and contains many institutions of science, learning, and beneficence, as useful as they are honorable to the inhabitants.

Philadelphia is remarkable for a neat and pleasing style of building. Hundreds of houses, of the first class, have basements and steps of white marble; and the pavements, which are generally wide, are carefully washed and swept. Great cleanliness prevails through a large part of the city, although the surface of the ground is so flat as to be rather unfavorable. Sewers have been constructed to a considerable extent, and the good habits of the people are the chief cause of this important feature in their city, which is favored by the absence of great thoroughfares, the passage of carriages being confined to no particular streets.

Markets.—The principal markets are concentrated in Market street, in which a long line of buildings, well planned, and built for the purpose, extends about a mile, and is proverbial for convenience and neatness. Abundant supplies of the best articles of food are displayed, with neatness and in good order, while sufficient room is allowed to buyers and sellers. For good meat, butter, and some other products of the fine agricultural districts in the neighborhood, Philadelphia has long been celebrated. South of the city lies an extensive tract of fertile meadow-land, where rich pastures and fine gardens abound; the benefits of which are enjoyed by the inhabitants.

The large draught-horses, reared with great care by the Dutch farmers, for use in their heavy wagons, are seen in great numbers.

The Philadelphia Library is one of the earliest, most extensive, and valuable, in the country, and was founded by the exertions of Benjamin Franklin, about the year 1727, when a little

The Custom-House, formerly the United States Bank, Philadelphia.

club of young men was formed by Franklin, and used to meet in Pewter-Platter alley, for reading and debate, and commenced the collection by giving their own books. Several of the members afterward became distinguished men, particularly Thomas Godfrey, the inventor of the mariners' quadrant. Fifty new members were added in 1730, and, in 1742, Thomas Penn incorporated it. The colonial legislature, in 1769, comprehended several other libraries with it, under an act conferring upon it its present name. "This," says Franklin, "was the mother of all the North American subscription libraries, now so common."

The American Philosophical Society, opposite the Philadelphia Library, is another of the principal institutions of the city, which claims Franklin as its founder. In 1743, he formed a small society for the purpose of pursuing curious experiments and inquiries; and, after its decline, and that of a second, commenced in 1750, the American Philosophical Society, and the American Society for the Diffusion of Useful Knowledge. These two societies were combined, in 1769, under a common title, and Franklin was elected president. Provision was made, by David Rittenhouse, to observe the transit of Venus. Several subjects of great public importance were early considered by this society, which show the science and benevolence of the members.

The American Historical Society, which has distinguished itself by the publication of the writings of their late president, Mr. Duponceau, was formerly only a department of the Philosophical society.

The Exchange is situated at the corner of South, Third, and Walnut streets, and on the angle formed by the intersection of Dock with Walnut and Third streets. It was built in 1833, by the merchants and citizens of Philadelphia. It is constructed entirely of marble—is a rectangular parallelogram in form, ninety-five feet front on Third street, by one hundred and fifty on Walnut street. On Dock street, however, is a semicircular projection, ornamented from the top of the basement story with six beautiful Corinthian columns; the capitals worked by the best Italian artists. This portico is of the height of two stories, and communicates with the "exchange-room," by means of nine separate windows, which may be used as doorways. A hall passes through the centre of the building, from Dock to Third streets, and another likewise communicates with this from the north side. The basement story is fifteen feet in height, is arched throughout, and has twelve doorways on the Third-street front and flanks. On the right or north side of the hall, is the postoffice, seventy-four by thirty-six feet, and on the left are several insurance offices and banks, and the session-room of the chamber of commerce. Two flights of stairs, one on each side of the hall, ascend to the second floor; at the head of these is the entrance to the exchange-room, which is on the east front, extending across the whole building, and occupying an area of 3,300 superficial feet. The ceiling, extending to the roof, is of the form of a dome, and supported by several marble columns. Its pannels are ornamented with splendid fresco paintings, representing Commerce, Wealth, Liberty, &c., beautifully executed, appearing to have as striking a relief as sculptured work. The roof of the building is oval, and surmounted by a circular lantern that rises forty feet.

The Customhouse, located in Chestnut street, is a splendid edifice of white marble, on the plan of the Parthenon of Athens, except that the side colonnades are wanting.

The Girard Bank is a marble building, with six beautiful Corinthian columns. A portion of it is represented in our engraving of the exchange.

The Bank of Pennsylvania, opposite the Girard bank, has two fronts, on Second and Dock streets, each with six Ionic columns.

The Statehouse, containing the halls of the old Congress, is interesting from its associations with the important period of the Revolution, and especially with its commencement. Independence hall, the apartment east of the entrance,

Old State House. or Independence Hall, Philadelphia.

is that in which the Declaration of Independence was adopted and signed, and in which Washington was appointed commander-in-chief of the army.

The large square, in the rear of that edifice, is shaded by many fine old trees; and Washington square, just beyond it, which was enclosed but a few years ago, has several elegant churches around it, and many fine houses. But the most conspicuous public place is Independence square, before named, situated between Chestnut and Walnut streets.

Girard College.—This splendid edifice strikes the eye with admiration from a distance, presenting a noble colonnade, of white marble, of great size, and the elegant proportions of the most celebrated Grecian models. It has been erected with immense sums of money bequeathed by the late Stephen Girard, long an eminent merchant of Philadelphia, for the education of orphans. The peculiar restrictions laid on the execution of the will, in several particulars, threw embarrassments in the way of the speedy execution of the enterprise, and the institution has never gone into operation.

Schools.—Philadelphia has long been supplied with schools, in much greater proportion than the state at large, in which they were neglected, until 1809, and were but little extended or improved by the act of the legislature of that year. Within a few years past, exertions have been made to establish a universal system of common education, and great advances have been made in some parts of the state; but a large proportion of the inhabitants being indifferent to the claims of education, has presented great obstacles to the rapid change so desirable. The German population, distinguished as they generally are for industry and frugality, are too much opposed to the improvements desired by many of their fellow-citizens; and all attempts made to rival the noble example of New York and some other states, have been disappointed. In Philadelphia, however, the public schools have been placed upon a very high footing within a few years; and not only the city, but the state and the country at large, are likely to participate in the advantages of so enlightened a measure.

The practice of humanity and Christian philanthropy, which is made so prominent a feature in the system of the friends, or quakers, has shown its influence in various important departments. The improvements in prison-discipline, which we have noticed at some length in the description of New York, in which state the plan which now prevails in this country, and, to a considerable extent, in Europe, was first brought into operation at Auburn, have been partially adopted in this city. Dr. Rush, of Philadelphia, however, first recommended radical improvements, founded on somewhat similar grounds, in 1787, at a time when public opinion was so unprepared to put them into operation, and even to appreciate them, that they were regarded as visionary. A prison was erected, in 1790, on a plan corresponding with his views, which was the first step in the way of improvement. The prisoners were treated with more humanity, kept clean, and subjected to regular hours, labor, and silence, being watched day and night. They were credited for the products of their labor; and half the excess of the amount, after fines and expenses, was paid on the expiration of the sentence. But several grand defects of the old system were retained in that prison, which further experience condemned. One of the principal of these was the common rooms, in which numbers of convicts spent their time together, by day and by night. No vigilance was sufficient to prevent demoralizing intercourse; and reformation—the great object in view—was not satisfactorily secured. The prison has since been demolished, and others have been erected, on different plans, on the northeastern borders of the city.

The Penitentiary, near Fairmount, is an immense edifice of granite, with a large yard, 650 feet square, surrounded by a wall forty feet high. The plan of this building is wholly different from any before erected. It is designed for solitary confinement, in the strictest

Eastern State Penitentiary, near Fairmount.

sense of the term. Rows of cells, on one level, are arranged in seven long lines, radiating from an octagonal building in the centre, where a single sentinel is placed to watch and listen, guarding several hundred convicts. Objections have been made to this system, on the ground of expense, and the difficulty of finding occupation for the prisoners, useful to them, or profitable to the institution, as well as to the evil effects, physical, mental, and moral, sometimes resulting from uninterrupted solitude. General Lafayette remarked, facetiously, while on a visit to this prison during its construction, that solitary confinement had been tried on him at Olmutz, without changing his character or habits.

The House of Refuge, for juvenile delinquents, in the same vicinity, is conducted on the same general plan as other similar institutions at New York and elsewhere, and with similar beneficial results. Vagrant and convicted boys and girls are placed there, under the charge of keepers and instructors, and are trained in good schools and various kinds of useful business, and then apprenticed, chiefly to humane persons in distant and retired country situations. Some of the boys have been sent to sea; and many unfortunate children have been rescued from ruin by such humane treatment.

The Pennsylvania Hospital.—This noble institution was founded by Dr. Thomas Bond, in 1751, aided by Franklin and others. The grounds are fine, and it contains a statue of William Penn, with West's celebrated picture of Christ healing the sick, presented by its author, a native of this state.

The University of Pennsylvania, on Ninth street, has two fine edifices, one of which is for the medical department. The origin of this institution is traced back to 1764, when a subscription was opened for an academy and charity-school, in which English, mathematics, and Latin, were to be taught. It was incorporated and endowed in 1753; and among its pupils was Lindley Murray, author of the English grammar. It was incorporated as a college in 1755.

Medical instruction was first given by Dr. William Shippen, in 1764, in a course of anatomical lectures, to ten pupils. Dr. John Morgan was his associate the next year—both being graduates of Edinburgh. Dr. Kahn was made professor of botany in 1768, and in 1769 Dr. Bush of chymistry, while Dr. Bond was clinical lecturer in the Pennsylvania hospital. This medical college has now about four hundred students.

The United States Mint was erected in 1830, after one of Mr. Strickland's designs. It is entirely of white marble, has a front on Chestnut street of 122 feet, and one on Centre square. The whole process of making money, assaying, refining, and coining the metal, is carried on in this building. The mint was established in 1790; and in 1793, they commenced coining in the building now occupied by the Apprentices' Library company, in Seventh street. Mr. R. M. Patterson has been at the head of this establishment for several years. Since the discoveries of gold in California, the amount of coinage has been largely increased.

The Naval Hospital is situated about two miles southwest from the centre of the city. The expense is defrayed by funds contributed by the officers and seamen of the United States navy, out of their pay. The building is on an eminence, commands an extensive view, and makes a fine appearance from a distance. The front is 386 feet in length, three stories high, and it is large enough to lodge three or four hundred persons. The first story is of granite, and the second and third of marble, both of which kinds of stone are found in abundance in the vicinity of Philadelphia.

The western side of Philadelphia is a scene of much bustle and business. Several fine bridges cross the Schuylkill, and the wharves below are landing-places for vessels coming from Delaware bay and the ocean, for the canal-boats of the Schuylkill navigation, and the Union canal, which leaves that line at Reading for the Susquehannah. Above, a fine stone dam crosses from bank to bank, and shows the first of the long and expensive series of works which form an uninterrupted channel of communication between the Schuylkill coal-mines and the city. Fairmount, a high, steep eminence, rises near the same spot, on the top of which are the immense reservoirs for the supply of Philadelphia with water, which is raised from above the milldam, by five large waterwheels, and allowed to stand for a time in two reservoirs, of the capacity of eleven millions of gallons, until it deposites the earthy particles. It is then distributed throughout the city, through pipes more than a hundred miles in extent.

The Wire Suspension-Bridge.—This wonderful and beautiful specimen of art was erected in 1842, at the expense of fifty thousand dollars, by Mr. Charles Elliot, for the city and county of Philadelphia. It occupies the site of the celebrated Wernwag's wooden-arched bridge, the longest in the world (with an arch of three hundred and forty feet span), burnt down a short time previously, and connects the two sides of the Schuylkill at a very important point.

The length, from one abutment to the other, is 343 feet, and from one of the supporting rollers to the other, at the apex of the columns, 357 feet, while the breadth, including the floor and the footways, is 27 feet. The wire, of which an immense quantity was used in the fabric, is one eighth of an inch in diameter. This is formed into five cables for each side; each is constituted of 260 strands, two inches and five eighths in diameter, weighing four tons, and able to support eight hundred tons. Seventeen short and smaller cables, hanging from each of these, to support the floor-beams, are made of smaller wires, and able to support two tons each.

The large cables pass over iron rollers on the pillars, by which the tension is equalized, and are fastened around many strong iron bars, transversely imbedded in rocks or masonry. The towers are enormous columns of granite, from the state of Maine. The iron was quarried at Juniata, and manufactured at Easton—all in this state.

The arched bridge spoken of above, the predecessor of the wire-bridge, was finished in 1813, at an expense of one hundred and twenty thousand dollars, and exceeded the largest of all others by ninety-six feet in the span. It was fifty feet wide at the abutments, and thirty-five in the centre, being by this form braced against lateral pressure.

The Permanent Bridge was erected, at the foot of Market street, by a company incorporated in 1798, and cost $300,000, including the land. The work was a great one, at that early day, when no such structure had been undertaken in the country; but it was successful. Indeed, it might be regarded as an enterprise of magnitude at any period, as the depth of the river presented formidable obstacles to the sinking of piers. The western one was founded at a depth of forty-one feet below high-water level.

Fountain Park.—This is not only one of the most remarkable situations in the country, in point of picturesque beauty, but also endeared to us by historical associations of the most romantic character. Here, by the shore of the Schuylkill (or Manayone, as it was called by the aborigines), occurred some of the most desperate fights recorded in the annals of Indian warfare. Here, the axe of the first settler under Penn awoke the echoes of the woods. At the hour that the battle of Germantown was raging around Chew's house, here, at least three miles from that celebrated spot, the Hessians were endeavoring to crush a band of continentals, inferior in arms and discipline, but not in iron courage. After twelve bloody onsets, that poured from the hill into the valley, the continentals drove their enemies across the river, at the ford, whose traces are now obliterated by the rising of the waters, from Fairmount dam. This ford is situated on the southern verge of Laurel hill, one of the most beautiful spots on the globe, whose spires and monuments are now visible from the mansion.

It was here that William Penn loved to wander, contemplating, either in his walks on shore, or in his excursions on the river, the rise and progress of his much-beloved colony. In those wanderings, perchance, he already saw—for he was a deep thinker—his colony rise

New Suspension bridge at Fairmount.

into a state: that state one of the great nations among thirty independent commonwealths.

The time is not distinctly marked when the original fabric, reared sometime in the commencement of the 18th century, was succeeded by the present beautiful mansion—the production of the princely taste and spirit of Pennsylvania's first governor, Thomas Mifflin. Yet it is a fact distinctly established, that some of the most important councils held by Washington during the Revolution, took place on this spot. The grass, spreading greenly before the porch, has been pressed by the feet of a Franklin, a Volney, a Priestley, a Jefferson, an Adams, engaged in careless converse, or philosophical discussions.

The ambassadors of kings have here met the republican fathers of America. The mind wanders back, through the arcades of time, and beholds the rich display of contrasts which were exhibited in the olden time—the handsome apparel of counts, dukes, nay, princes, contrasted with the plain uniform of Morgan, the rifleman, or the modest costume of Jefferson, the author of the Declaration of Independence.

When Washington was president, he was wont to leave his country residence, in Germantown, and stroll by the lake northward of the mansion, his imposing form reflected in its waves; or, seated on the porch, he would gaze on the Schuylkill, thinking over again the trials and battles of his life, from Braddock's defeat to the fall of Yorktown.

These are remarkable associations. Among other memories, we must not forget that the singular round, or sexagonal tower, that rises a hundred yards to the east of the mansion, was once the hermitage of religion and the closet of eloquence. The celebrated clergyman, Dr. Smith, who preached those stirring and remarkable sermons during the war, built this tower, filled it with his books, and here elaborated his most finished productions. The doctor was a Scot by birth, but an American in feeling. His grandson, Richard Penn Smith, now resides on the ground, and inherits in a great degree the genius of his ancestor.

Perhaps not the least interesting reflection of all is presented in the fact that the old mansion, once hallowed by the presence of Washington, Lafayette, and Wayne—enlivened by the visits of noblemen of royal blood, is now the domain of a gentleman whose only heraldry is recorded in his honest rise to fortune and fame, from the walks of toiling life into one of the first publishers and literateurs of the country. We need not refer to Andrew M'Makin, Esq., proprietor of the "Courier," whose delightful family are always ready to extend the old-fashioned rites of hospitality to the stranger, and render a visit to Fountain Park (or Aromana, as the Indians called it and its lakes) a journey of homeborn pleasure. It is rarely that literary labor meets with a repose like this—much more rarely are its honors worn so well, or with such unpretending grace.

Reading, fifty-four miles from Philadelphia, is a place of considerable importance, and contains some handsome public buildings. The Union canal begins two miles below Reading, passes up the western shore of the river to the valley of the Tulpehocken, and then follows that valley till within five miles of Lebanon, where begins the summit-level. In all this distance, it rises 311 feet, by numerous locks of four and eight feet lift. The canal is twenty-four feet wide at bottom, four deep, and thirty-six on the surface. On this part of the canal is the tunnel, an excavation bored through a hill for a distance of 729 feet, 25 feet being first cut away. This dark and gloomy passage is eighteen feet in width, and fourteen feet high.

Schuylkill Water-Gap.—This is a narrow gorge, through which the river runs over a steep and rocky channel, for four or five miles, leaving no room upon its banks, which rise abruptly on each side to the height of several hundred feet. The road has been cut out along the face of one of these ranges, at a great elevation, where the surface is in many places of such a declivity as to require it to be supported by walls of stone. The views which are here afforded to the traveller, are romantic and varied in

Fountain Park, the Residence of Andrew M'Makin. Esq., Proprietor of the **Philadelphia American Courier.**

a high degree. This interesting scene somewhat resembles that on the Delaware represented in the vignette.

The Little Schuylkill River, a branch of the principal stream, runs through a valley of the same general description; and here lies the road to Mount Carbon.

The Tunnel.—This a place where a hill has been bored through 375 yards for a canal, about three miles from Orwigsburgh.

MOUNT CARBON is near several coal-mines. The coal-country in this region begins in Luzerne, on the upper part of the Lackawana river, following its course to the Susquehannah, and along that stream, principally on the eastern bank, to eighteen miles beyond Wilkesbarre. It runs south to the Lehigh river, and thence southwest, through Schuylkill county. It extends about one hundred miles, and at the middle of the range is eight or nine miles wide, but narrower toward each end.

At Mount Carbon the coal occurs in beds of four or five feet in thickness, running east and west, and dipping to the south at forty-five degrees, with a slate-rock immediately over it, and strata of sandstone and earth above. The slate presents the impressions of organized substances imbedded in it, as the leaves of laurel, fern, &c.

In consequence of the inclination of the coal-veins into the earth, the miners have, in some places, sunk shafts to the depth of one hundred and fifty feet, with lateral excavations, east and west, of various lengths to three hundred feet. Two small carriages, called "trams," are used in a sloping shaft to bring the coal out, being made to descend by turns; but in the horizontal one, which has been carried in several hundred feet, they use wheelbarrows.

POTTSVILLE.—This is the capital of Schuylkill county, and the centre of the coal-business, on the western part of the great anthracite region, extending eastward to Mauch Chunk. It contains nearly eight thousand inhabitants, and enjoys a romantic situation in the midst of the mountains, whose mineral treasures, so recently brought to light, employ a large population, and create a scene of bustle and profitable industry all along the course of the stream below, and powerfully contribute to the prosperity of many distant manufactories, and to the movements of commerce.

Lehigh Coal-Mines.—The first discovery of coal at Mauch Chunk is said to have been made by a hunter, as late as 1791. The first indications he noticed were bits of anthracite adhering to the roots of a fallen tree. A company was formed for the purpose of mining it the following year, called the Lehigh Coal-Mine company, who secured a tract of land embracing the present mine, made a rough road to it from the river, and began to dig the coal, and transport it to the stream. But the navigation was so difficult that the enterprise failed.

The improvement of the navigation of the Lehigh was commenced by the legislature of the colony, as early as the year 1771. Laws for the same object are found in the statute-book of the state, under the dates of 1791, 1794, &c. A company undertook to clear the channel, and, after spending thirty thousand dollars, gave up the attempt. Different persons, in the meantime, who had taken leases from the coal-mine company, made unsuccessful exertions to transport the coal to Philadelphia; the last of whom, Messrs. Cist, Miner, and Robinson, have been before mentioned. They abandoned their attempts in 1815.

Wonderful as it now appears, the difficulty of igniting anthracite coal was sufficient to prevent its introduction for many years; and the incredulity of the public continued to be too great to be overcome by the exertions made, until the year 1818, when two mining companies were formed; and, in 1820, three hundred and sixty-five tons were brought down, and sold in Philadelphia at eight and a half dollars a ton, delivered, which fully satisfied the demand. Both companies were soon formed into one; since which its operations, much facilitated by great improvements in the navigation, have been vast and beneficial. By means of dams, the water of the Lehigh, which is insufficient for continual use, is stopped, and occasionally allowed to flow for a short time, floating down at once numerous rude boats or boxes, called arks, laden with coal, from sixteen to eighteen feet wide, and twenty to twenty-five in length. It was soon found convenient to connect two of these, and afterward, three, four, and more, so that the temporary flood might carry them down together, without separating them or striking them against each other, while at the same time they would conform to the rough surface of the water, as no single vessel of great length could possibly do, and might be navigated and managed separately at pleasure. Ingenuity devised improvements of other kinds also; for machinery was soon brought into use, by which planks were joined for an ark, put together, and launched, in forty-five minutes, by five men.

A branch of the Pennsylvania canal was finished not long after, along the western bank of the Delaware; and thus the only remaining work, necessary to a convenient and uninterrupted communication between the mines and the city, was completed.

The Delaware and Hudson Canal commences at Kingston, on the Hudson river, and runs over to the Delaware river, through the valley of the Neversink creek, thence up the valley of the Delaware to the Lackawaxen creek, and up that creek to the foot of the railway. This is a continuous canal of 117 miles in length. The railway commences at the termination of the canal, and runs over Moosick mountain to the coal-mines at Carbondale, on the Lackawana creek, sixteen and a half miles, overcoming an elevation of 858 feet.

At Easton is the dam over the Delaware, at the termination of the works for improving the navigation of Lehigh river, from Mauch Chunk to this place.

Bethlehem is a neatly-built place, in a romantic and delightful situation, along the course of a swift-running brook. It is inhabited by Germans, and is the seat of an old Moravian school.

The works on the Lehigh river are on a large scale. The river descends 365 feet, and requires fifty-two locks and twenty-one dams. The locks are intended for steamboats capable of carrying 150 tons of coal, one hundred feet long and thirty feet wide.

The Lehigh water-gap is twenty-five miles from Easton, and eleven from Lehighton, six miles from Mauch Chunk. The first objects that attract attention, near the village of Mauch Chunk, are the lock in the river, and the chute, or inclined plane, at the end of the railway, down which the loaded coal-cars slide to the wharf on the river, where they load the boats and arks. The latter carry about ten tons. The trains of cars coming down the railway will often be heard rumbling as the traveller approaches the village.

Mauch Chunk, ninety miles from New York, and seventy from Philadelphia, is shut in by rude mountains, of such height that the sun is invisible to many of the inhabitants during the short days.

The railway leads from near the coal-mines to the Lehigh river. This was the second ever constructed in the United States—the Quincy railway, in Massachusetts, being the first. It extends a distance of nine miles, along the side of a mountain.

The coal-mine lies a little on the opposite side of the mountain; and the coal-cars are first made to ascend to the summit of the railway up an acclivity of five eighths of a mile. The summit is 982 feet above the river. The average rise of the way is eighteen inches per one hundred feet, which is scarcely perceptible to the eye, and enables a single horse-power to draw up three empty cars.

The cars are made of strong oak timbers, and planked up on three sides, with a swinging door in the rear. They are six feet four inches long, three feet wide at top and two feet at bottom, and about three feet in depth, resting on wheels with cast-iron rims or felloes two feet in diameter, one inch thick, and about four inches in breadth, with a strong edge or flanch, one inch in thickness, and about two inches wide, which prevents them from slipping off the rails.

The cars may be stopped immediately, by a long lever, which brings strong bearers against two of the wheels, and causes great friction. The guide to every brigade of eleven cars holds a rope attached to all the levers. Several hundreds of such cars are in use. They carry the coal to the chute above the river, down which they are sent.

At the end of the railroad is a platform, on the bank of the Lehigh river, down which the coal is let over one of the rails, on an inclined plane of 750 feet (200 feet perpendicular height), to the stone-houses, the wharf, and the boats. Each loaded car is connected to an empty one, which it draws up, by a rope that passes round a large cylinder or drum. A car goes down in about one minute and twenty seconds.

The mine opens upon the road by passages cut in the earth. These conduct into an area formed by the removal of coal, where carts drive in, load, and then pass out at the other passage.

PITTSBURGH.—This is the greatest manufacturing town of the west, and has furnished a large proportion of the steamboats which navigate the Mississippi and its branches. It occupies a low point of land, at the junction of the Allegany and Monongahela rivers, whose united stream is named the Ohio. It is three hundred miles west from Philadelphia, eleven hundred from New Orleans, by land, and over two thousand by water, yet has almost daily communication with it by steamboats. A part of the city now covers Ayres' hill, and part of the sides of two other eminences; while four small towns, Allegany, Sligo, Manchester, and Birmingham, at short distances, occupy points on the banks.

A bridge of eight arches, and fifteen hundred feet long, crosses the Monongahela, erected in 1818, at an expense of one hundred thousand dollars; while four bridges cross the Allegany, as well as the noble aqueduct of the Pennsylvania canal. The city contains about seventy churches, and the population, in 1850, was 80,000.

It is rare, indeed, to find so many advantages concentrated in one spot, as those which combine to give to Pittsburgh its great manufacturing and commercial importance. It not only occupies the head of the navigation of the Ohio, but it is the radiating point of the great western system of canals and railroads; while its relation to extensive and fertile regions of Virginia and New York, as well as of the state to which it belongs, and the abundant supplies of coal and iron at its command, brought into use by its enterprising inhabitants, have given it the highest rank among the cities of the west.

The fine engraving accompanying this description is copied from one of Mr. Bartlett's correct and elegant prints, and gives a just picture of this large and flourishing town; but nothing except a visit to the place can convey an adequate idea of the amount of business carried on in various branches of manufacture.

The principal manufactures of Pittsburgh are all things that pertain to the construction and furnishing of steamboats, especially the engines for their use, and such as are employed in various mills, &c., with a great variety of machines, implements, and tools, of wood as well as of iron, including ploughs, &c., &c. Bar and rolled iron are made in large quantities, as well as nails, glass, cotton cloths, leather, and boards. The steam-power in use in these and various other branches of manufacture, amounts to several thousand horse-power. Several steamboats arrive and depart every day, with many more canal-boats.

There are several banks and insurance companies, a board of trade, with an exchange-room and a reading-room, and about a dozen companies managing freight and the transport of passengers on the canal.

The Courthouse occupies the summit of Grant's hill, where it makes a conspicuous appearance, and commands an extensive and interesting view over the city, the river, the neighboring villages, and the surrounding country. It is one hundred and sixty-five feet in length, one hundred in breadth, and has the jail in its rear. The rotunda, a fine hall, sixty feet in diameter, is in the second story, surrounded by court and jury-rooms. The structure is large, substantial, elegant, and costly. It was five years in building, cost two hundred thousand dollars, and is creditable to the state, both on account of its style, plan, and execution. Its material is the fine, gray sandstone, which abounds in some parts of the neighboring hills.

The Western University of Pennsylvania is situated at Pittsburgh. The institution commenced operations in 1822, and the buildings were erected on Third street, in 1830. The edifice has a high basement of hewn stone, with arched entrances, and two stories above, with a portico projecting in the middle, having four Ionic columns. It is surmounted by a cupola, with windows on all sides.

The Water-Works.—Pittsburgh is supplied with water from the Allegany river, which is raised, by steam-power, to a reservoir on Grant's hill, one hundred and sixteen feet high. The reservoir is eleven feet in depth, and capable of containing a million of gallons.

The Western Theological Seminary is situated at Allegany city. It is under the direction of the general assembly of the presbyterian church, by whom it was founded in 1825. The building occupies a fine, airy position, on the summit of an elevated ridge, rising one hundred feet from the bank of the river, and contains six thousand volumes in its library. A workshop was connected with it, with the intention of employing the students in manual labor.

The theological seminary of the associate reformed church, which was founded in 1826, is also situated in this town.

The Western Penitentiary of Pennsylvania.—This extensive prison stands on the shore of the Allegany, at the western extremity of Allegany city. It was completed in 1827, and cost $183,-092, including all the furniture, &c. The system of solitary confinement is here in practice; and the prisoners are employed, at solitary labor, in the weaving of carpets, making shoes, and picking oakum.

The United States Arsenal is at Lawrenceville, two and a half miles above Pittsburgh, on the left bank of the Allegany, opposite Wainwright's island. That insular spot is celebrated as the scene where Washington was driven on shore on his raft, in his first attempt to cross the stream, on his return from his mission to Venango. Considerable numbers of arms are manufactured in the arsenal, including ordnance; and here a large supply is constantly in store. Here, also, equipments are made and kept, for the southern and western military posts, the place being at once central, and conveniently situated for communication with different parts of the country.

History.—The history of Pittsburgh is highly important, as it was the first point occupied, in all this western region, by the English, and was the scene of contest between that nation and the French. Under the belief that "the forks of the Monongahela" were within the bounds of Virginia, George Washington was sent, in 1753, to select a site for a fort, who chose this spot; and troops were soon sent to occupy it, while Pennsylvania despatched a force for the same purpose, considering the place a spot within her own territory. But, on the 7th of April, 1754, while Ensign Ward, with forty men, was engaged in building a fort, during the absence of the superior officers, sixty batteaux and three hundred canoes appeared, loaded with one thousand of the enemy's troops and Indians, descending the Allegany. They landed and demanded a surrender; which was complied with, on condition that the English should be allowed to depart unmolested, with their working-tools.

The capture of this fort was the first act of hostility in the last French war, as it is commonly called in this country, which continued for seven years. The French commander, Gen. Contrecœur, immediately commenced the erection of Fort Duquesne on the same spot.

In 1755, General Braddock, at the head of an army, consisting of British troops and American militia, after many delays, approached this place, and the army threw the French into a state of great alarm. Their fort was a mere stockade, quite unfit to resist artillery; and Captain Beaujeu, with great difficulty, persuaded some of the Indians to accompany a portion of the French sol-

View of Pittsburgh, from the northwest.

diers to march out and await the approach of their enemies in an ambush. The plan, however, proved successful, in consequence of the self-confidence of the British general; for, in spite of the most earnest expostulations of Washington, he persisted in proceeding without precaution, and would not allow an advance guard or scouts to explore the trackless forest before and around them. The consequence was, that, after crossing the river and reaching a piece of smooth ground, up an acclivity, where they were among the trees, they received a sudden and destructive fire, on both sides, from large bodies of the enemy concealed in two ravines parallel to the line of march, and, after three hours' fighting, were totally defeated. The British commander, and many officers and men of the two regiments of regular troops, with a large part of the colonial militia, were killed. Those who were finally saved, owed their lives to the skill and boldness of Washington, who here first displayed some of those peculiar qualities which afterward proved as useful to the country as honorable to himself.

Strange as it may seem, there is good reason to believe that the force by which that powerful expedition was defeated, was quite insignificant. Washington wrote to his mother, nine days after the battle, that he was persuaded they "did not amount to three hundred men, while ours consisted of about thirteen hundred well-armed troops, chiefly regular soldiers, who were struck with such a panic that they behaved with more cowardice than it is possible to conceive. The officers behaved gallantly, in order to encourage their men, for which they suffered greatly."

Easton.—This is an important town, situated at the mouth of Lehigh river. The canal-basin and locks, with the bridges over that stream and the Delaware, are expensive works. The coal-trade, the slate quarries, the surrounding grain-country, and the manufactories of the place, many of which are moved by water-power, combine to render the town one of much business and prosperity. There are at least twenty saw-mills, several oil-mills, &c., within a short distance. The Delaware bridge cost sixty-five thousand dollars. The Lehigh bridge is of wood, in the place of one of chains, which was destroyed by a flood in 1841.

Lafayette College.—This institution, established in 1826, for a military academy, was changed to one of a collegiate character in 1832; and, two years afterward, the building was erected, which is one hundred and twelve feet by forty-four, and contains sixty rooms. It is named "Brainard hall."

Easton was an important place in the middle of the last century, as it was a favorite council-town of the Delaware Indians. During the French wars, great exertions were made by the Jesuits in Canada, to detach this powerful nation from the English interest Important councils were held here in 1756, 1757, and 1758, at which all differences were adjusted between the Delawares of several tribes and the Six Nations of New York, by Teedyuscung, chief of the Delawares, assisted by the quakers, in opposition to a strong combination of men less friendly to the claims of the red men.

The Valley of Wyoming.—This narrow tract of country has attained melancholy celebrity, from the tragical fate of its early colonies, which has been recorded, in an appropriate style, by one of the most chaste and popular modern British poets. This beautiful and secluded region is shut in by the ranges of the Shawnee and Lackawannock mountains on one side, and the Wyoming and the Moosic, about six miles distant, on the other. It is watered by the Susquehannah river, which, as has been before remarked, runs in a direction across the rude barriers of nature. On reaching this valley, however, it deviates awhile from its general course in this part of the state, and meanders, with a gentle current, for about eighteen miles, nearly parallel with the ridges of the mountains. It then bursts its way though Wyoming mountain, and pursues its course through Columbia county.

The first settlers here were from Connecticut, as has been before mentioned,

The Wyoming Valley, from Prospect Rock.

and several towns were for some time represented in the legislature of that colony, by deputies elected here, who annually performed the then long and toilsome journey to Hartford. The manners and habits of the present day bear strong traces of their origin, although considerable additions have been received to the population from the Germans and Scotch-Irish of the surrounding country, with many miners and laborers, from Wales and Ireland, in the mining regions.

"Few landscapes," says Professor Silliman, "can vie with the valley of Wyoming. Excepting some rocky precipices and cliffs, the mountains are wooded from the summit to their base; natural sections furnish avenues for roads, and the rapid Susquehannah rolls its powerful current through a mountain-gap on the northeast, and immediately receives the Lackawanna, which flows down the narrower valley of the same name. A similar pass between the mountains on the south gives the Susquehannah an exit; and, at both places, a slight obliquity in the position of the observer presents to the eye a seeming lake in the windings of the river, and a barrier of mountains apparently impassable. From the foot of the steep mountain ridges, particularly on the eastern side, the valley slopes away, with broad, sweeping undulations in the surface, forming numerous swelling hills of arable and grazing land; and, as we recede from the hills, the fine flats and meadows, covered with the richest grass and wheat, complete the picture, by features of the gentlest and most luxuriant beauty."

The lower part of Wyoming valley was occupied by some of the Shawnees, soon after the arrival of William Penn at Philadelphia, those Indians having received permission to settle there from the Six Nations, who claimed the country. When some of the Delawares, not long subsequently, were driven, by the encroaching whites, from their lands above the forks of the Delaware and Lehigh, the Six Nations allowed them to occupy the eastern side of Wyoming valley, where they built a town called Maughwaurame, just below the site of Wilkesbarre. This was done in 1742; and that same year arrived among them the celebrated Moravian missionary, Count Zinzendorf, accompanied by his friend Mack, with his wife. The Delawares, jealous of white men (in consequence of having been overreached by an artifice in a contract for the sale of a portion of their lands on the Lehigh, by which they had been deprived of the whole), meditated the butchery of the man who had forsaken country and possessions for the disinterested love of mankind, and devoted himself, with the evangelical spirit of primitive Christianity, to the trials of a missionary among the heathen. His life, however, was spared; and he, with his companions and followers, lived to introduce the gospel among that nation of our aboriginal red men. The mission was removed, a few years after, to Wyalusing, after the commencement of the Connecticut colony. The Shawnees, in the lower part of the valley, had been invited by the French on the Ohio to join a part of their nation who resided among them, but had been prevented from a compliance by the influence of the Moravian missionaries. An accident, however, induced them to change their minds. One day, during the absence of the Delaware warriors, two children, from the different tribes, while at play on the banks of the Wyoming, fell into a dispute about a grasshopper which one of them had caught. This at length drew in their parents and friends, until, to settle a question of rights and boundaries which was raised, it led to a battle, and the defeat and expulsion of the Shawnees. Thus enmity was created on both sides, which, with other causes, laid the way for the scenes of blood which ere long ensued.

The charter of Pennsylvania was unhappily drawn up so as to interfere with that of Connecticut, both embracing this region, the right to which was vested by the former in William Penn, and by the latter, at a time long anterior, in the people of Connecticut. Under these circumstances, the first settlers from that colony arrived in 1762, to the number of two hundred; and a long course of remonstrances, rivalry, military preparations, and even military operations, commenced between them and the Pennsylvanians.

In 1777, at a time when almost all the able-bodied men of the Connecticut settlements were absent with the Revolutionary army, a large body of Indians came down the Susquehannah, led by the inhuman Colonel John Butler, whose savage conduct at Cherry valley has been noticed in the description of New York. His force consisted of his own tory rangers, a detachment from Sir John Johnson's Royal Greens, in all about four hundred, and seven hundred Seneca Indians. To meet them, only four hundred could be mustered, consisting chiefly of old men and boys, and these undrilled, ill provided with arms, and many of them unaccustomed to war, and ill-fitted for the field by their youth or age. Choosing for their leader Colonel Zebulun Butler, who happened to be at the place, they took post on the side of the Susquehannah, with the steep bank on their right, and a swamp on their left, and there withstood the enemy, until, after a desperate fight, and the loss of two thirds of their number, the invaders triumphed. Many of the prisoners were butchered in cold blood after the surrender; and numbers of those who escaped, were barely able to reach their women and children, left in the stockaded forts below, in time to induce them to desert the valley and seek safety in flight. Hundreds of weak and defenceless widows and orphans were soon wandering over the mountains, and pursuing their melancholy way to distant settlements, and even back to Connecticut. Some parties lived for several days on whortleberries; and one, consisting of a hundred persons, had but a single man. One of the stockades, called Fort Forty, having received a few of the fugitive soldiers, made a show of defence on the approach of the victorious enemy, and obtained an honorable capitulation, drawn up in the handwriting of their clergyman, and signed by Colonel Butler; but, no sooner had the tories entered at one gate, and the Indians at the other, than they began to threaten and rob the inmates, whose weakness they had now discovered. They, however, did not proceed to bloodshed; but as it was perceptible that no security could be enjoyed, the people in a few days followed the example of their predecessors, and set out on foot to find some place of safety. For several days and nights the houses and barns were burning in all parts of the valley, while hundreds of corpses lay bleeding, from the weapons of the white and the red men, who seemed to rival each other in wanton barbarity, thus adding another to the awful lessons which history has so often recorded, on the diabolical spirit that war can enkindle in the human heart.

In 1779, Gen. Sullivan passed through the valley with his army, on his expedition against the Six Nations, and, in October, returned to Easton, whence he had marched, having devastated some of the richest of their country.

In March, 1784, after the valley had again become populous, on the breaking up of the ice in the river, a dam was formed, by its stopping, at the narrow gorge through which it leaves this beautiful region. The water rapidly rose over the land, driving the inhabitants to the hills, and leaving, after subsiding, many lands injured, and much property destroyed.

After the close of the Revolutionary war, violent animosities were raised between the "Pennamites" and the "Connecticut boys," as the two old parties were called, and were carried to great lengths; but a permanent adjustment of the long dispute was finally made by the legislatures of the two states interested.

Montgomery County is a part of the state most abounding in iron-mines. It is situated in the heart of the central range of mountains, and is exceedingly wild and rough, with small valleys interposed between numerous tall and romantic eminences, such as Tuscarora mountain, Black Log, Sideling hill, the Terrace, Allegripus, Tussey's, Black Eagle, &c. Near the southwestern extremity of the county rises a very conspicuous and remarkable eminence, called Broadtop mountain, which contains a singular coal-basin, with thin seams of bituminous coal, from one to four feet in thickness. The Juniata river, with several of its branches, waters different parts of this wild, Alpine region.

Montgomery county lies along the Schuylkill river, and formerly belonged to Philadelphia county. It comprehends some of the earliest settlements, with remains of the first colonists, and evidences of their substantial habits, as well as some of the more modern works of internal improvement. The surface is agreeably varied, with much picturesque scenery, whose beauties are enhanced by the hand of persevering and successful culture, as well as by the works of science, enlisted in the service of an enlightened public spirit.

The southeastern extremity of the county is traversed by a belt of primitive rocks. The primitive limestone of the Great valley crosses the Schuylkill at Swedesford and Conshohocken, affording valuable quarries for the supply of white marble to Philadelphia; and red shale constitutes the rocks of other parts, whose debris forms a productive soil, while sandstones prevail in some places. Stone turnpikes, and other good roads, are numerous. The Reading railroad and the Norristown and Philadelphia railroad pursue the course of the Schuylkill for some distance, while the works of the Navigation company, before mentioned, afford another important channel of transportation. On these are several bridges, and other works, worthy of particular attention. Copper-mines are believed to have been formerly opened in different parts of this county, and there are reports of silver and lead-mines having been known. Numerous mills and manufactories are kept in operation by the water-power provided at the various dams on the river.

The first settlements were made in the southeastern part of Montgomery county by Swedes and Welsh, and in the north by Germans, all of whom long retained their appropriate languages. But of these, only the German remains at the present day. Religious services were first held by the friends, or quakers, in Oxford, in 1683, and in Horsham in 1716. The first meetinghouse of the Welsh friends was built in North Wales in 1700, and the second in 1712. In lower Merion township, a friends' meetinghouse was erected as early as 1695, which is still standing and in use, having been lately repaired.

The first Swedish church was erected at Swedesford in 1763, the Swedes having come into the county, as it appears, some time after the Welsh. The Swedish churches, in different towns in this county, were incorporated together, by John Penn, in 1765, and this charter was renewed in 1787, by the state legislature. Remains of old Swedish customs, as well as families, are still found, especially about Norristown.

A few Germans, having early come over from Europe to join the colonists of William Penn, and settled Germantown, near Philadelphia, sent back to their countrymen such favorable accounts that they had numerous followers, especially from the Palatinate, between 1700 and 1730. They occupied the territory about the head-waters of Perkiomen creek, and Lutheran and German reformed churches were afterward founded. In 1741, however, although there were about a hundred Lutheran communicants at New Hanover, or the Swamp, the only place of worship was a log-hut, and it was not until 1767 that a church was built of stône, which is still in use by a congregation of five hundred members. The German reformed congregation was formed about the year 1747, and their present brick edifice was erected in 1790. Numerous Lutheran congregations are now concentrated about Latrappe, extending among the neighboring towns in Bucks county, where the German language is still generally spoken. The old church standing in the village of Trappe, was erected in 1743, by Rev. Henry Melchior Muhlenberg, who is called the father of the Lutheran church in the United States. Every pew in the building, and every seat in each, has its number branded into the wood with a hot iron; and a tablet over the door bears a Latin in scription, now almost illegible, bearing the above date and the name of its founder, whose remains lie interred in the churchyard.

Several congregations of German baptists, or Mennonists, are also found in this neighborhood, whose ancestors came to this country about the period included between the years 1706 and 1717. In the northeastern part of the county, near Goschenhoppen, is a small body of Schwenckfelders, named after Gaspar de Schwenckfeldt, a Silesian nobleman, born in 1490, who taught doctrines condemned by Rome, and incurred persecution for them, yet differed essentially from Luther. His followers were protected by Count Zinzendorf for eight years, when they came to Pennsylvania, where they arrived some time before 1740.

Valley Forge, a wild and secluded valley in the mountainous region of this county, is associated with one of the most gloomy and desperate periods of the American revolution. The British army, after landing on the Delaware, gained the battle of Brandywine, September 11, 1777, and Washington retreated, with his feeble army, to Germantown, and, after one day's rest, crossed the Schuylkill, and advanced on the Lancaster road, to endeavor to stop the progress of the enemy, but was prevented by the injury of his ammunition, caused by a severe rain. The enemy then taking the road toward Swedesford, induced Washington to leave that to Philadelphia open, and, taking advantage of the opportunity, entered that city; to guard which, he occupied Germantown with the largest body of troops. This was one of the great epochs in the history of the Revolution, when to most, even of the friends of American independence, the cause was regarded as hopeless. But not so with Washington. He drew off the remains of his army to this wild, inhospitable spot, and here struggled through a severe winter, under the most trying privations, awaiting an opportunity, which at length arrived, for the striking of an unexpected blow. He once wrote to congress: "For some days there has been little less than a famine in the camp. A part of the army have been a week without any kind of flesh, and the rest three or four days." Strong exertions were at this time made to supersede him in command, but without success.

Mrs. Washington visited him in this dreary retreat; and the house is still remaining which served as his headquarters. It is the substantial stone-mansion of Mr. Isaac Potts, owner of the forge, from which the place has derived its name.

The Mount Carbon railroad was commenced in 1829. It is supported, for some distance along several landings, on thirty-one piers of masonry, and passes through the gap of Sharp mountain, down the Schuylkill valley to Morrisville, where are coal-mines on both sides of the river. At that place it leaves the bank of the stream, and follows the valley of Norwegian creek to Pottsville, a distance of 6,208 feet from its commencement. A branch, 14,200 feet in length, leads to the Centreville mines, which belong to the North American coal company, and affords access to the celebrated Peach mountain and other mines. The west branch is 16,400 feet long, and reaches to Marysville, with the Diamond and Oak-hill coal-mines and others.

Several other local railroads are now in use; and the long one to Reading and Philadelphia has greatly increased the facility of transportation. The Danville road, an immense work, from the great natural obstructions to be overcome, was proposed in 1826, and in 1834 was completed as far as Girardsville, ten miles, with a tunnel seven hundred feet long, and four inclined planes. But another tunnel, of twenty-five hundred feet, necessary to open a passage into the Girard mines, has not been completed.

As the beds of coal near the surface of the earth become exhausted, the miners dig deeper, or abandon the old mines for new ones. In the former case, wide passages are cut into the earth, at a declining angle of about forty degrees, which serve for the entrance of empty cars on one rail-track, and the exit of the loaded ones on another. Steam-engines are employed to pump out the water, as well as to draw up the coal. Some of these mines are worked under the very town of Pottsville, and extend several hundred feet. The deeper the mines are sunk, the more pure and valuable is the coal usually found.

PORT CARBON is the village at the landing, at the head of navigation, on the main branch of the Schuylkill, two miles northeast from Pottsville. At the bottom of a deep and wild valley are seen long ranges of building, with several short railroad lines concentrating from the valley of Mill creek, and the mines wrought along its romantic borders, and the villages of Patterson, Middleport, New Philadelphia, and Tuscarora, whose existence dates back only to the year 1828.

MINERSVILLE, the principal mining village on the western branch of the Schuylkill, has a railroad, several mills and manufactories, and two churches; and numerous other villages are found in this region. Population, 1850, 2,984.

The position of the coal-beds in the Schuylkill valley being beneath the surface of the ground, requires mining in the usual way, while at Mauch Chunk the anthracite is dug and removed, like stone from a surface-quarry. A sudden, terrific, and fatal accident occurred at one of the great mines in 1845, in consequence of the insufficient supports left by the workmen in digging away the coal, when the immense weight of the mountain above sank down and filled up a considerable part of the excavations. A very remarkable phenomenon attended this fall. The descent of the mass was so sudden, that the air was driven violently from the halls and galleries of the mine, through the external openings, as from an immense bellows, and with such force that carts were blown along to some distance and broken. Several lives were lost; and one man, who was shut in by having the passages around him closed, after feeling about him in the darkness, and working a long time among the loose rocks, succeeded in digging out, after a confinement of about forty-eight hours.

YORK is eighty-three miles from Philadelphia. This town stands on Codorus creek, eleven miles from the Susquehannah, to which is a line of improved navigation. A railroad leads to Baltimore. York is a place of five thousand inhabitants, and is remarkable as the seat of government of the United States for a time in the year 1777, during the occupation of Philadelphia by the British. Some manufacturing is carried on here; and it contains ten churches, a courthouse, academy, bank, and a lyceum, which is in possession of a cabinet of minerals. The railroad affords frequent and easy communication with Baltimore, as well as Philadelphia, while stagecoaches depart daily for Harrisburg, and twice a week for Chambersburg.

The York Sulphur-Springs are situated twenty-one miles south of Harrisburg, and the scenery which surrounds them is striking and pleasing. The place is one of fashionable resort.

HARRISBURG, one hundred and seven miles from Philadelphia, is the capital of Pennsylvania. The statehouse occupies a lofty and commanding situation, on Mount Airy. It is an edifice of considerable size, being one hundred and eighty by eighty feet; and the senate and representatives' chambers are spacious apartments. The library of the state, contained in this building, amounts to above six thousand volumes.

The scenery around this town is remarkably picturesque and varied. It occupies a point on the Susquehannah, where it breaks through the range of the Kittatiny mountains, and is crossed by two fine bridges. The population, in 1850, amounted to 8,173; and among the public buildings are ten churches, the courthouse, two banks, and academy, the prison, and the arsenal.

Stage-coaches run from Harrisburg to Pottsville, Northumberland, and Baltimore, through York; while railcars depart daily for Chambersburg, and three times every day for Philadelphia.

CARLISLE, in the Cumberland valley, eighteen miles from Harrisburg, is one of the oldest settlements, and the seat of Dickinson college, a methodist institution, founded in 1783. The number of students is nearly two hundred, under the care of seven professors. The libraries contain twelve thousand volumes, and the chymical, philosophical, and mineralogical collections and departments are well supplied.

The United States barracks were erected in 1777, chiefly by the labor of the Hessian prisoners captured at Trenton.

The Sulphur-Springs, four miles from the village, are celebrated for their efficacy in cutaneous and other diseases, and are the annual resort of many visiters. They are situated in the midst of the Blue ridge; and the picturesque scenery, with the embellishments of art displayed in the walks and gardens, offer many attractions.

Chambersburg.—This town, situated at the junction of the Falling-Spring creek with the Conecocheague, enjoys the advantages of a railroad connexion with Harrisburg and several considerable manufactories, though a small place, with between three and four thousand inhabitants. Population, 1850, 4,300.

Bedford is two hundred and six miles west from Philadelphia, and stands on a branch of Juniata river. It contains five churches, a courthouse, and an academy, with eleven hundred inhabitants. It derives its principal interest, in the eyes of most strangers, from the springs in its immediate vicinity.

The Bedford Springs are five in number, situated in a narrow valley a mile and a half south of the town, from which they derive their name. They are distinguished from each other, as the Sweet spring, Sulphur, Fletcher's, Anderson's, the Limestone, and the Chalybeate, possessing a variety of properties. Several houses are kept for the accommodation of visiters, with baths of different kinds supplied from the springs. A little lake has been formed, on which pleasure-boats are kept for the amusement of visiters; and the place is annually resorted to by considerable numbers. As Philadelphia stage-coaches arrive and depart daily, the access is convenient.

Cannonsburgh is a town of about one thousand inhabitants, situated eighteen miles southwest from Pittsburgh, and is the seat of Jefferson college. That institution was founded in 1802, and contains about a hundred and fifty students, with 4,500 volumes in its libraries. The last Thursday of September is the time for holding the annual commencement. The medical department of this college is situated in Philadelphia.

The theological seminary of the associate church is also established in this place.

Washington.—This town is twenty-five miles north of Pittsburgh, and occupies a lofty situation, containing above two thousand inhabitants, with nine churches, two academies, and a courthouse. Stage-coaches depart daily for Pittsburgh, Wheeling, and Baltimore.

Washington College was founded in 1806, and now contains about one hundred students. It possesses a mineralogical cabinet, philosophical apparatus, with libraries embracing from two to three thousand volumes.

Meadville, on French creek, is the seat of Allegany college. That institution was founded in the year 1815, and contains about one hundred and fifty students. The volumes in the libraries amount to about eight thousand.

Erie.—This town, situated on the summit of a lofty bluff, which rises from the shore of the noble lake from which it has derived its name, has one of the best harbors on that inland sea. It contains a number of handsome public and private buildings, with seven churches, a bank, and an academy, with 6,000 inhabitants.

This place is remarkable for the rapidity and success with which the fleet of Commodore Perry was built, in the war of 1812, to meet the British forces on the lake. The ships were ready for sea in seventy days after the felling of the timber; and in a short time they returned to this port, bringing with them the enemy's captured squadron. The flag-ship Lawrence still shows its remains in the harbor, the state of the country in this region happily creating no demand for warlike operations. The old French fort Presque-Isle was situated at this place, and some traces of it are yet distinguishable.

Birmingham, in Chester county, is a

small town situated on Brandywine creek, near the scene of one of the most important battles ever fought within the limits of this state, as it caused the rout of the American army sent to oppose the British forces on their way to Philadelphia, and opened the way for the occupation of that city for a considerable time. A commanding hill, near the village, affords a view of the field of battle, which had some unfortunate features, as the following brief description of the action will show. Had the Brandywine river been fordable in but a few places, the American troops would not have had to guard the whole line. The ability of the enemy to assail it at any point at any moment, kept our commander-in-chief in a continual state of anxiety, and the enemy availed himself too successfully of the advantages in his possession.

The Battle of the Brandywine.—This important action was fought on the shore of the stream whose name it bears, on the 11th of September, 1777, between the British forces under General Howe, and the American army commanded by General Washington. The enemy had arrived from New York, in their fleet, in the Chesapeake, late in the month of August, and Washington was thus relieved from uncertainty respecting their designs. Presuming that they were now resolved to seize upon Philadelphia, he immediately called upon all the corps of the regular army which could be spared, to join him by forced marches, and sent requisitions to the governors of the neighboring states for their militia. The British landed on the 25th, near the head of Elk river, 18,000 strong, and well provided in all respects, except horses, in which they were quite deficient, having lost many the preceding season, from the scarcity of forage. It is presumed that they might have acted with greater efficiency on the plains of Pennsylvania, if they had been stronger in cavalry.

Gen. Knyphausen, having remained at the landing with the rear-guard, to cover the debarkation, followed the van in a short time, and the whole army took post along Christina creek, from Newark to Atkins, after the column of Cornwallis had routed Maxwell's riflemen, who ventured to harass them on their march. On the enemy's approach, the American army proceeded to encamp behind White Clay creek; but Washington, finding the ground disadvantageous, retired to the Brandywine, and occupied the heights from Chadsford toward the southeast, while Maxwell, with his riflemen, hung upon the enemy's flank. General Armstrong, with the militia, guarded a passage below the camp, and the main body took a position to prevent the easiest passage of the river, it being fordable, however, in all parts.

General Howe gave the right of his army to General Knyphausen, and the left to Cornwallis; the former to engage the attention of the Americans by a feint to cross the stream, while the latter should push to a place above, where the crossing might be more easily effected. Maxwell for a while maintained a spirited skirmish with the British marksmen, but finally fell back before Kniphausen, who made so many demonstrations of a resolution to force the passage at Chadsford, that his feint proved successful, the Americans becoming so much engrossed by him as to allow Cornwallis to accomplish his object with but little difficulty. Having crossed the forks of the Brandywine, at Trimble's and Jeffrey's fords, he marched down the bank toward Dilworth, to fall upon the American right flank.

The first intelligence which Washington received of this was an exaggerated account, that a large part of the British was approaching, under the command of Howe; and he instantly gave orders to Sullivan to cross the river above, and fall upon Knyphausen's left, intending himself to pass below and attack his right. At that moment, however, another messenger brought him the false report that the enemy had not yet crossed the stream. His former command was then countermanded; and the next intelligence assured him of the truth. No time was to be lost; for the enemy were now fast approaching his right wing, on the advance of which was General Stevens, with Stirling and Sullivan next in order, with their respective brigades. Sullivan took command of the whole wing, as the senior officer, while Washington, with Greene, took post between it and the left wing at Chadsford, ready to reinforce either which might require his aid.

The ground occupied by Sullivan was well chosen, and very advantageous; but the enemy did not allow him to collect all his troops, and he was forced to give way, after a manly resistance, and fled to the woods in their rear, and along the road by which Greene was now approaching to their aid. To prevent the confusion of the fugitives from being communicated to his own troops, Greene opened his lines to the right and left, and, after giving them passage, closed again, and, facing about, retired in good order, keeping the enemy in check by a steady fire of artillery. The Pennsylvania and Virginia militia, who composed his brigade, made a vigorous stand in a defile on the road, where they for some time brought the enemy to a halt.

General Knyphausen now advanced to the ford in earnest; and the Americans left in defence of the intrenchments and battery on the opposite side, seeing some of the British troops approaching on their right, in pursuit of their retreating countrymen, abandoned the ground and retired. General Greene was the last officer on the ground, and left it only when darkness had come on. The Americans, routed, reached Chester that night, and Philadelphia the next day; their entire loss being stated at about three hundred killed, six hundred wounded, and four hundred prisoners. Ten field-pieces and a howitzer also fell into the hands of the enemy. The enemy lost, in all, about five hundred men.

In this action, the foreign volunteers, so recently enlisted under the American standard, performed good service. The Marquis Lafayette, while rallying his troops, received the wound in his leg which rendered him a cripple for the rest of his life; but it did not prevent him from continuing his labors through the fight. Captain De Fleury had a horse killed under him, and the Baron St. Ovary was made captive.

On the day following the battle, a body of the enemy's light troops marched to Wilmington, in Delaware, and made prisoner of the governor, and seized a quantity of money and other property, public and private, with some papers of importance. There being no longer any force sufficient to resist him, Lord Cornwallis entered Philadelphia, on the 26th of September, with a body of British and Hessian grenadiers, leaving his army encamped at Germantown: the number of royalists in that city at the time being so great as to leave him little room for apprehension. General Washington, in the meantime, retired, with the few troops he could command, to Skippack creek, on the banks of the Schuylkill; a wild region, difficult of access, and a favorable retreat in his circumstances, which rendered the protection of nature necessary to his safety.

Interesting Facts in the History of Pennsylvania.—It was designed by Penn that Philadelphia should never be closely built. He named it thus, as he remarked, "before it was born," in order to express the principles of benevolence on which he intended to have its concerns conducted, and intended that it should always be "a greene towne," with ample room for the convenience and comfort of all the inhabitants. It still presents a general aspect quite different from that of the most crowded cities of the Old World, with respect to the streets, which, instead of being narrow, crooked, and dirty, are straight, wide, and clean. His plan, however, has been in some points encroached upon. He insisted that the bank of the Delaware should be kept open and unoccupied by buildings and enclosures, and resisted every proposal to abridge the freedom which the public enjoyed, in approaching the water. An unhappy change has since taken place; and there are now few cities in our country where the wharves are more crowded and inconvenient.

The plan of his new city appears, from Penn's original instructions to his three commissioners, to have been very large. These men, William Crispin, John Bezar, and Nathaniel Allen, were sent out in the autumn of 1681, to select a site and lay out the great city. The Pennsylvania Historical society have published at length the written instructions with which they were furnished.

He directed that "the creeks should be sounded on every side of Delaware river, especially upland, in order to settle a great towne." His object was to find a place "where most ships may ride, of deepest draught of water, if possible, to load and unload at ye bank or key side, without boating and lightering it." He directed that the earth should be dug, to ascertain that the soil was dry and healthy, and that ten thousand acres should be laid out for the liberties of the town.

Twelve square miles would have been required, by the plan, for all the purchasers; and this, with other requisitions, induced the commissioners to defer the selection of any site, and to await the arrival of Penn. They examined and described the site of Chester, a place on the elevated bank at the mouth of Poquessin creek and Pennsbury manor, as well as the place where Philadelphia stands, which proved most agreeable to the governor. It is said, by tradition, that he took an open boat, at Chester, and proceeded to Wicacoa, with a few friends, toward the end of November, 1682, and found the site of the present city occupied by three Swedes, brothers, named Swenson, a name since altered to Swanson. The river's bank was then high, and covered with a thick growth of tall pines, a place which the Indians called Coaquannock. It seems that the spot had something, even in its wild state, which recommended it for a settlement: as Proud says that some of the passengers in the first ship which ever sailed so far up the Delaware (namely, the Shield, Captain Towes, from Hull, December, 1678), exclaimed, "It is a fine place for a town." He mentions, also, that the shore was bold and high, so that, in turning, some of the tackling struck the trees.

This was a vessel bringing out colonists for New Jersey. Penn arrived four years later; and, having purchased the ground of the three Swedes above-mentioned, he began to lay out his new city, and to prepare for its construction. It is remarkable that numbers of the people who had preceded him, for some time after their arrival, had taken up their dwelling in caves under the steep bank. The first house erected was that of George Guest, which was not completed when Penn arrived. It stood near Powell's dock, in Budd's row, and long served as a tavern, under the name of the Blue Anchor.

The first person born in Philadelphia was said to be John Key, and his birthplace was one of the caves just mentioned, near Sassafras street, which was long known as the "Pennypot." He lived to the age of eighty-four, and died at Kennet, on the 5th of July, 1765. William Penn, it is said, gave him a lot of ground. He used to walk into the city until within six years of his death, and was generally known, in the latter part of his life, by the name of "the first-born."

Between twenty and thirty vessels arrived in the course of the first year, bringing out great numbers of quakers, who had left their homes to avoid the persecutions to which they were exposed. They were so numerous, that not only Philadelphia became at once a considerable town, but the country was well supplied with inhabitants along the river's borders for a distance of fifty miles, from Chester up to the falls at Trenton.

The house of Thomas Fairbank, at Shackamaxon, near Kensington, was occupied, in 1681, as a quaker meeting-house; and the following year a boarded building was erected for this purpose, in the city. Another was erected near the centre of Philadelphia, in 1684; one in Front street, in 1685; the great meetinghouse in High street, in 1695; one on the hill, in Pine street, in 1753; and the present one in High street, in 1755.

Between 1682 and 1714, no less than three hundred and fourteen marriages were performed among the quakers; and in the years 1681, 1682, and 1683, about fifty vessels arrived with passengers. Among these were a number of German converts to the quaker principles, the disciples of William Ames, an Englishman. Having "borne public testimony" in their native place, Krisheim, near Worms, in the Palatinate, they seized the opportunity offered by Penn, to take up their habitation in America, in a state founded by one of their own faith, and settled at Germantown, which derived its name from them. Among them were persons of all ages, and some who had been brought up in ease and plenty. To them the common trials of the colonists must have been severe, as some of the new-comers were obliged to occupy hollow trees, as well as caverns, while preparations were making for the erection of houses or huts; and most of these afforded poor accommodations, and even but little protection from the cold and storms of the winter.

The celebrated treaty made by Penn with the Indians has always been a compact of peculiar interest, on account of the principles of justice and humanity on which it was founded, the sacredness with which it was observed, and the extensive, lasting, and beneficial effects which it produced. Yet it is remarkable that no written memorial of it remains, beyond a few allusions to it made in contemporaneous documents, and that everything else relating to it depends upon the authority of tradition. The spot is pointed out, on the bank of the Delaware, where the council assembled in 1682, under an elm-tree, at Kensington, where a plain obelisk now stands, erected by the Penn society, in 1827, bearing the following brief but appropriate inscriptions:—

On the north side: "Treaty-ground of William Penn and the Indian natives, 1682."

On the south: "William Penn: born 1644; died 1718."

On the west: "Placed by the Penn society, A. D. 1827: To mark the site of the great elm-tree."

On the east: "Pennsylvania founded, 1681, by deeds of peace."

A long memoir was presented to the Pennsylvania Historical society, in 1836, by Messrs. Duponceau and Fisher, on the subject of Penn's first treaty, in which the opinion was expressed, that it was one of friendship, and had no relation to the purchase of land.

Letitia House.—This celebrated building, still standing in a street of Philadelphia of the smaller size, has excited much attention within a few years, since the spirit of antiquarian research has arisen, as it is believed to have been erected for William Penn's own use, by William Markham, in the year 1682, the year before his arrival. It is of brick, of small size, two stories high, with a single window on each side of the door, a steep roof, a stack of chimneys, and a single dormer-window in front. A rustic roof projects over the door, which is entered by rising a single step from the street; and an old-fashioned, wooden cellar-door, nearly flat, opens under each of the windows. The little street in which it stands is named Letitia court, and opens on Market street, between Front and Second streets.

A letter of Penn is preserved, in which he allows his "cousin Markham to live in his house in Philadelphia, and that Thomas Lloyd, the deputy-governor, should have the use of his periwigs, and any wines and beer he may have there left for the use of strangers." It appears that Penn, having been accustomed to the luxurious style of King Charles II., and to the upper classes of society during his travels on the continent, never renounced all traces of his early habits, even after he had placed himself at the head of the friends in their great colony in America. He paid much regard to dress and forms in public; and was, according to descriptions and pictures remaining of him, before he came to America, "quite a finished gentleman, eminently handsome, the appearance of his countenance remarkably pleasing and sweet, his eye dark and lively, and his hair flowing gracefully over his shoulders, according to the fashion set by the worthless but fascinating Charles II." His portrait, presented to the Historical society by his grandson, bears witness to the accuracy of this description; and it would seem, from writings extant, that he maintained, in his colony, habits in several respects corresponding with his earlier life.

In his cash-book are proofs that he had four periwigs, silk hose, leathern gambadoes, or overalls, and many fine beaver hats, furbished up at the hatter's, while a greater number still he presented to his friends, one of which he commends for having "a true mayoral brim." It is handed down by tradition, that he wore, also, silver shoebuckles.

He had an elegant house at Pennsburg, which has been compared to a kind of palace, abounding in rich furniture, and supplied with liquors, though he was not fond of spirits, and had an aversion to tobacco, so often their concomitant. There is but a single charge of tenpence worth of this in the cash-book. He was very hospitable, and made provision for the entertainment of strangers during his absence.

His benevolent regard for the Indians carried him so far that he often visited them, was present at their feasts and merry-makings, and sat with them upon the ground, to partake of their hommony and roasted acorns; by which exhibitions of kindness he greatly attached them to him. A remark of his is recorded, which reflects the highest credit on his character. "The saying is," said he, "that he who gives to the poor lends to the Lord: but it may be said, not improperly, the Lord lends to us to give to the poor. They are, at least, partners by Providence with you, and have a right you must not defraud them of."

The following passage, in his parting instructions to his wife, deserves to be written in gold; and its observance in this country would have given a better aspect to American society than we witness at the present day:—

"Let my children be husbandmen and housewives: it is industrious, healthy, honest, and of good report. This leads to consider the works of God, and diverts the mind from being taken up with the vain arts and inventions of a luxurious world. Of cities and towns of concourse beware. The world is apt to stick close to those who have got wealth there. A country life and estate I love best for my children."

Sir William Penn, father of the founder of Pennsylvania, was born at Bristol, and was a distinguished admiral in the British navy, and commanded the fleet at the capture of Jamaica, in 1655. The protector confined him awhile in the Tower, for absenting himself without leave from the American station. He was member of parliament; and, under Charles II., had a high command under the Duke of York, and participated in the capture of the Dutch in 1664. He was knighted by that king, and died at his house in Wanstead, Essex, in 1670, at the age of forty-nine.

His son William was born in London, in 1644; and having warmly adopted the quaker principles, while in college at Oxford, from the preaching of Loe, he was expelled for nonconformity; and his father, in 1662, after having "whipped and beaten" him, turned him out of doors for the same offence. The admiral, however, afterward relented so far as to send him to France, and then to enter him at Lincoln's Inn as a law-student. While settling an estate in Ireland, he again met Loe, and resumed the strict quaker practices; so that, on his return home, he refused to take off his hat in the presence of his father, and even before the king; for which he was again turned upon the world. He began to preach and write in 1668. He was imprisoned in the Tower and Newgate, but soon was left, by his father's will, in possession of an estate worth £1,500 a-year.

In 1667, he married, and devoted himself to the defence and promotion of his favorite doctrines. Ten years after, he visited the continent with Fox and Barclay, and soon after received from the king a grant of the country whose interesting history and condition we have been contemplating.

The following minute account of the burial-place of William Penn, &c., is taken from the English "Historical Register:"—

The Grave of the Founder of Pennsylvania.—The traveller, in passing from Beaconsfield to the neighboring village of Chalfont St. Giles, in Bucks, passes a small enclosure on the right-hand side of the road, known as the friends' or Jourdan's burial-ground. But though no monumental stone attracts attention, and the sunken graves, hidden in the tall grass, escape the passing glance of a stranger, it well deserves to be recorded as the resting-place of William Penn, the founder of Pennsylvania.

A fragment, supposed to have been written by one of the vicars of Penn, a village not far from Chalfont, deriving its name from the ancestors of William Penn, who possessed the manor at a very remote period, is still preserved in the register of that place, and presents a curious record of the occupiers of the principal graves.

The Road.						The Meetinghouse.
		1	2	3	4	
	5	6	7	8	9	
	10	11	12	13	14	

No. 1. Letitia, daughter of Wm. Penn.
2. Springett, son of William Penn.
3. Margarette Frame and her son Thomas, in the same grave, daughter of William Penn.
4. John Penn, son of William, governor of Pennsylvania.
5. The great William Penn, with his second wife upon his leaden coffin. Prince Butterfield remembers his second wife being buried, and seeing the leaden coffin of William, whose head lies contrary to the rest, with his feet to the north.
6. Giulielma, daughter of Sir William Springett, first wife of William Penn.
7. Isaac Pennington's wife, the widow of Sir William Springett, of Darling, in Sussex.
8. Isaac Pennington, an able lawyer, who married the widow of Sir William Springett, mother to William Penn's first wife.
9. Joseph Rule, a man that used to go about London preaching, in a white coat and a long white beard.

Nos. 10, 11, 12, 13, 14. William Penn's younger children.

Seven graves from the hedge, in a line above William Penn, lies Thomas Elwood, who used to read to Milton, and lived on Hanger hill. On his left hand, nearer the hedges, lies his wife.

Extract from the Register, Sept. 12, called by the friends "eighth month:"—"Our friend William Penn, of Walthamstow, in the county of Essex, and Giulielma Maria Springett, of Tilerend green, in the parish of Penn, in the county of Bucks, proposed their intentions of marriage at the monthly-meeting at Hanger hill."

Prince Butterfield, the person already mentioned as having seen Penn's leaden coffin at the burial of his second wife, was the man who had the care of the burial-ground, and who died between thirty and forty years ago. Many "friends" have been interred within the enclosure, besides those here mentioned; but about fifteen years since it was found too full to admit any others, and the ground has remained undisturbed. In J. Whyth's supplement to the "History of the Life of Thomas Elwood," published in 1714, is an account of his great services to the society of friends. It is added, that "he departed this life on the 1st of the third month, 1713, and was honorably buried in the friends' burying-place at New Jourdan." This Elwood was the great friend of the poet Milton, and suggested to him the idea of writing "Paradise Regained."

In concluding this brief description of Pennsylvania, we may appropriately introduce the following summary of some of the improvements and inventions which have distinguished this state and people. It is abridged from the North American newspaper:—

The quadrant was here invented by Godfrey; here Franklin taught men how to control the lightnings of heaven; on the Delaware, at Philadelphia, John Fitch first proved the power of his rude steamboat; Fulton, a native of Pennsylvania, immortalized his name by maturing that wonderful invention; the first locomotive was set in motion near the corner of Ninth and Market streets, by its inventor, Oliver Evans, who, with the foresight so often noticed as a characteristic of great discoverers, declared that the time would come when one would "breakfast in New York, dine at Philadelphia, and sup at Baltimore;" here was the first bank established in the country, and the first insurance office; here was organized the first sabbath-school, an honor, surely, to be appreciated throughout the Union; Philadelphia first showed us what might be done in supplying cities with water, by her astonishing Fairmount water-works; in her eastern penitentiary, she furnished a model for institutions of that class, which has been extensively approved and imitated, both in this country and in Europe. The first public hospital in the United States was the Pennsylvania hospital; the first institution for the blind was that established in this city. Here, too, before the Revolution, the great discovery which has given us the magnetic telegraph, led Franklin to give signals by electricity across the Schuylkill.

The merchants of Philadelphia, at an early period, built a frigate and presented it to the United States government, the only instance of the kind on record; and the state of Pennsylvania erected a house in Philadelphia, and offered it as a present to Washington. Here, also, a stand was taken against the exactions of Great Britain, in advance of Boston herself; and the first opposition to the landing of tea was made at a public meeting held in Philadelphia, some weeks before the celebrated tea-party executed its work at Boston; and from Philadelphia came forth the Declaration of Independence.

But the part which Pennsylvania has taken in the great works of internal improvements needs to be better understood. The turnpike from Philadelphia to Lancaster was the first undertaken in the Union, and was completed in 1794, at a cost of $465,000. Subsequently, the whole surface of the state was traversed by these roads.

The Schuylkill "permanent bridge," erected in 1798, at an expense of three hundred thousand dollars, was the first great work of the kind attempted in this country. The first Fairmount bridge, with its span of 348½ feet, outrivalling the famous bridge of Shauffhausen, and the wire-bridge, erected in 1817, at the falls of the Schuylkill, which served to suggest the idea to European builders, were an honor to Philadelphia. The bridges in the interior, by their substantial, and even bold character, have done honor to the state.

For the introduction of canals, as well as turnpikes, the country is indebted to Pennsylvania. Even William Penn appears to have meditated on the project of connecting the Susquehannah with the Schuylkill; and, in 1762, David Rittenhouse and Dr. William Smith surveyed a canal-route for the purpose. At that early day, these gentlemen had in view the connecting of the lakes and the Ohio river with the Delaware, by a route of nearly six hundred miles. The survey, under the authority of the legislature of Pennsylvania, was accomplished in 1769. In 1791, a company was incorporated for connecting the Susquehannah and Schuylkill; and in 1792, another was incorporated for connecting the Schuylkill with the Delaware, by the way of Norristown. At the head of the latter was Robert Morris, the celebrated financier. These two companies undertook the work, and proceeded far with it, when, having expended $440,000, they were embarrassed, and suspended operations. These beginnings, however, resulted at length in the completion of the Union canal. The first tunnels excavated in the Union were in Pennsylvania. The first survey for the Chesapeake and Delaware canal was made in 1769, by order of the American Philosophical society, and as early as 1804, one hundred thousand dollars were expended in the execution of the work.

When the period of railroads arrived, Pennsylvania was again the pioneer. The railroad at Mauch Chunk was the first in the Union, excepting only a short tram-road in Massachusetts. From that period to the present, Pennsylvania has been second to no state in the Union, in expenditures for constructing these wonderful annihilators of time and space.

Chesapeake and Delaware Canal.

DELAWARE.

THIS state is bounded on the north by Chester and Delaware counties in Pennsylvania, on the northeast by Delaware bay, on the southeast by the Atlantic ocean, on the south by Worcester and Somerset counties in Maryland, and on the west by part of the same state, viz.: Dorchester, Caroline, Queen Ann, Kent, and Cecil counties. It lies along the Atlantic coast twenty miles, from Cape Henlopen to Fenwick island. The entire outline is two hundred and fifty-nine miles; length, one hundred miles; mean breadth, twenty-one miles; area, two thousand one hundred square miles. It lies between 38° 27′ and 39° 50′ north latitude, and 1° 17′ and 20° 0′ east longitude from the city of Washington.

The state occupies a long and narrow plane, with a gentle eastern slope to the Atlantic and the bay, with a higher and more uneven region in the north. The upper portion has a waving rather than a hilly surface, and the southern is nearly a dead level. The eastern slope is drained by several small rivers, viz.: Indian, Broadkill, Cedar, Mispohan, Motherkill, Jones, Duck, Apoquinimink, Brandywine, &c.

Delaware contains only three counties—Newcastle in the north, Sussex in the south, and Kent between them. The population in 1790 was 59,094; in 1800, 64,273; in 1810, 72,674; in 1820, 72,749; in 1830, 76,748; in 1840, 78,085; in 1850, 90,407. Settlements were commenced at an early date within the territory of this state. Under the patronage of Gustavus Adolphus, king of Sweden, a few feeble colonies were founded here in 1627, before any other Europeans had attempted to occupy the soil. The country received the name of New Sweden, and the settlers were Swedes and Finlanders. They settled along the shores of Delaware bay, but were reduced in 1655 by the Dutch, and again in 1664 by the English. Charles II. included the territory in the grant which he made to the duke of York, by whom it was conveyed to William Penn, in 1682. For several particulars in respect to this part of the history of Delaware, the reader is referred to the description of Pennsylvania.

Delaware had a colonial assembly in 1704, which met at Newcastle, although the territory nominally belonged to Pennsylvania until 1775. The people took an early and active part in the revolution; and many of their militia fell in the unfortunate battle of Long Island, in 1776, when the British army obtained possession of New York. She adopted a constitution as a state in that year; and the constitution of the United States was adopted by a convention on the 12th of June, 1792. Although the smallest state in the Union, it has been honorably distinguished by men of ability and high character in the national government. The present constitution was adopted in 1831.

The governor is elected for four years, but can not be reëlected. The senate consists of three members from each county, chosen for four years. The house of representatives consists of seven members from each county, elected for two years. The sessions of the legislature are biennial, commencing on the first Tuesday in January.

Every male citizen who is twenty-one years of age, and has been a resident in the state one year, and in the county one month, next preceding the day of election, and has paid a tax, is a voter. If he is between twenty-one and twenty-two years of age, the payment of the tax is not necessary.

The courts of Delaware are a court of error and appeals, a superior court, a court of chancery, an orphans' court, a court of oyer and terminer, a court of general sessions of the peace, and such courts as the general assembly may from time to time establish. There are five judges to compose these several courts, whom the governor appoints. They hold office during good behavior. The superior court consists of the chief-justice and the two associate-justices, who do not reside in the county where the court is held; and the court of sessions is composed in the same manner. The court of oyer and terminer consists of all the judges except the chancellor; and the orphans' court, of the chancellor and the resident judge of the county.

Delaware College, situated at Newark, Newcastle county, is the only higher institution of learning in the state. Commencement is held on the 4th Wednesday in September.

There are twenty academies and about one hundred and fifty common schools, with a school-fund of $170,000.

The *Chesapeake and Delaware Canal* was constructed at great expense, and in spite of many discouragements, over one of the most unfavorable tracts of ground ever crossed by a work of that kind. It was intended to open a channel of sloop-navigation between Delaware city, on Delaware river, and the Chesapeake; and the work was successfully accomplished in a few years. It is thirteen miles in length, and lies chiefly in Delaware, but partly in Maryland. It is sixty-six feet wide on the surface of the water, and ten feet deep.

Printing was first introduced into this state in 1761, by James Adams, who then commenced the publication of a newspaper, called "the Wilmington Courant," which ceased in six months. No other newspaper was published in the colony before the revolutionary war.

The Delaware Breakwater.—About twenty years ago, the construction of a breakwater was commenced, by the United States government at the mouth of Delaware bay, at Cape Henlopen, designed to afford protection to vessels passing that exposed part of the coast in stormy weather. The mouth of the bay is twelve or thirteen miles wide, and exposed to the full force of the waves of the ocean, which, in an easterly storm, are extremely violent, being unchecked by the neighboring land, which is too low to offer any resistance to the wind, or any protection from the surges, as they sweep in from the open sea. The ice which floats down the river is sometimes not less dangerous to vessels. The breakwater is formed according to the principles of science, and is an immense work, of stone brought from a great distance, and composing a solid wall with sides standing at an angle, best calculated to withstand and destroy the force of the waves on the one hand, and the fields of ice on the other. As the number of vessels employed in the navigation of the bay is very great and annually increasing, and the coasters and foreign ships occasionally exposed to risk of loss on this part of the coast, in easterly storms, are also very numerous, the value of such a work may be appreciated, when it is borne in mind that there is no other place of refuge within a great distance.

Even in moderate weather the breakwater often affords to many vessels the conveniences of a good harbor, when the state of the wind or of the ice forbids the passage from the bay to the ocean, or from the ocean up the bay.

Cape Henlopen, which forms the southern point of Delaware bay, is in latitude 38° 45′ and longitude 10° 53′ east from Washington.

WILMINGTON.—This town is situated one mile above the junction of Brandywine and Christiana creeks, twenty-eight miles southwest from Philadelphia, forty-seven north from Dover, and one hundred and eight northeast from Washington city. It is built on the dividing line between the primitive region and the alluvion, which lie in juxtaposition through most of the middle and southern Atlantic states. Wilmington, in this respect, resembles Philadelphia, Baltimore, Georgetown, Richmond, and several smaller towns; but owing to the greater depression of the western rocky range in Delaware, Wilmington has less variety of scenery in its neighborhood than most of them.

Brandywine river, however, at a short distance from the town, is precipitated over a precipice, of such height that it affords many mill sites of great value, which have long been employed to great advantage. Numerous manufactories of large size crowd the banks of the stream, most of which are flourmills; the grinding of wheat is also carried on to a great extent, and with such skill that they have long been among the best in the Union, and have done much to render the flour manufactured there highly celebrated.

Sawmills, papermills, cotton and woollen factories, &c., stand also upon the same stream.

Wilmington is governed by two burgesses and six assistants. It stands upon a long and gentle elevation, upon the ridge of which lies the principal street, which is wide and straight.

The principal public buildings are the cityhall, the almshouse, the arsenal, two markethouses, three banks, the public library, sixteen churches, nine academies, and the friends' female boarding-school. The population is at present fourteen thousand.

The Philadelphia and Baltimore railroad lies through this town, and affords communication with both those cities twice a day.

The Brandywine Springs.—This place is much resorted to by visiters, for health and pleasure, in the summer months. It is five miles from Wilmington.

DOVER.—This town, the capital of the state, and county-town of Kent county, is situated on the right bank of Jones's creek, ten miles from its mouth in Delaware bay. The streets are straight, broad, and laid out regularly, and a large public square is in the middle of the town, where the statehouse and several other public buildings are placed to great advantage. There are three churches, one bank, and an academy. A monument has been erected to the memory of Col. John Haslett, who fell at the battle of Princeton, in the revolutionary war.

There is a communication with Wilmington daily by stagecoaches, and with Snowhill (Maryland) three times a week. It is in latitude 39° 09′ and longitude 1° 28′ east of Washington.

NEWARK stands on Christiana creek, and is twelve miles southwest-by-west from Wilmington, fifty-two north-northwest from Dover, and one hundred and thirteen north-northeast from Washington. It contains three churches, the college, an academy, and about eight hundred inhabitants.

Delaware College is situated in this town. It was founded in the year 1833, and received an endowment of $100,000 from the state. It has a president, four professors, one tutor, and about fifty students. The first building of the college was erected in 1833, for eighty students, since which time it has been doubled in size. The centre is three stories high, with a basement, and the wings three stories; whole front, one hundred and eighty feet.

Newcastle.—This town, the former capital of the state, is situated on the west side of Delaware river, and is the site of the old Dutch fort Casimir, and of the village of Nieu Amstel, or New-Amsterdam, founded by the Hollanders. The public buildings are the courthouse, townhouse, arsenal, five churches, the academy, and the public library containing four thousand volumes. The population is about three thousand two hundred.

Lewes, on Delaware bay, is a post-town in Sussex county, one hundred miles northeast-by-east from Washington. It is one of the early settlements, and its appearance is that of antiquity, the houses being old and shingled with cedar.

The *Ocean House*, in this town, is a respectable hotel, for the accommodation of pleasure-parties, often visiting the place.

Delaware City.—The town is situated on Delaware river, at the beginning of the Chesapeake and Delaware canal. It is thirty-two miles north from Dover, and opposite Peapatch island, on which is situated Fort Delaware.

Milford, sixty-eight miles from Wilmington, stands on Mispillion creek. It has three academies and two churches, and contains about nine hundred inhabitants.

Georgetown is eighty-eight miles from Wilmington, and near the head-streams of Indian river. It contains about four hundred inhabitants, a court-house, an academy, a bank, &c. There is a communication three times a week with Wilmington by stagecoaches.

Delaware, in several respects, bears a resemblance to the other two of the smallest states, Rhode Island and New Jersey: lying on the main route of travel and transportation near the Atlantic border, and deriving only a secondary advantage from the vast quantities of merchandise which annually pass through it on the way from larger states adjoining: yet, availing herself of the facilities which nature has afforded her in her narrow territory, she provides employment for the streams as they pour over her rocks, and use for her navigable waters. The chief of the latter is Delaware bay, which is the scene of an immense amount of trade, chiefly with Philadelphia, and much of it in coal. The channels are unfortunately winding and difficult.

The *County of Newcastle*, which embraces the northern part of the state, is bounded north by Delaware county in Pennsylvania, east by Delaware river which separates it from Salem county (N. J.), south by Kent county in Delaware, southwest by Kent county in Maryland, west by Cecil county in Maryland, northwest by Chester county in Pennsylvania. It is thirty-eight miles long from north to south, and twelve miles mean breadth, with an area of four hundred and fifty-six square miles. The county lies between latitude 29° 18′ and 30° 50′, and between longitude 1° 17′ and 1° 38′ east from Washington. The boundary between Delaware and Maryland lies along the ridge of land which divides the waters of the Chesapeake from those of the Delaware; and hence, as might be presumed, Newcastle county has a gentle slope from west to east.

Brandywine creek, with its various branches, drains the northern part of the county, and, flowing almost to Wilmington, falls into the Delaware. Below this stream are the Apoquinimink, Blackbird, and Duck creeks, the last of which forms the boundary of Kent county. In this county is that part of the Chesapeake and Delaware canal which we have noticed elsewhere. It extends to Elk river, a tributary of the Chesapeake. The principal excavation on the route is three and a half miles in length, and at the deepest part seventy-six and a half feet.

Some of the lower parts of Newcastle county, near the Delaware, are low and marshy; but at some distance the surface becomes irregular and even hilly in the north. The soil is generally fertile and produces grain, grass, and fruit. The tributaries of the Brandywine have so much descent as to afford many good mill-seats; and various manufactories are carried on in the interior of the county.

Kent County is bounded on the north by Newcastle county, on the east by Delaware river, on the south by Sussex county, and on the west by three counties of Maryland, viz.: Caroline, Queen Ann, and Sussex. It lies between latitude 38° 50′ and 39° 20′, and between longitude 1° 18′ and 1° 50′ east from Washington. Nearly the whole surface of this county has a slope east toward Delaware bay, and here are the following creeks, viz.: Mispillion, Motherkill, Jones's, and the two Duck creeks. A small part of the western border slopes westward, and is watered by the head-springs of the Choptank and Nanticoke rivers. The surface is but slightly varied, and the soil of middling quality. The length of the county is thirty-two miles, the mean breadth twenty, and the area six hundred and forty square miles.

Sussex County is bounded north by Kent county, northeast by Delaware bay, east by the Atlantic ocean, south by Worcester county (Md.), southwest by Somerset county (Md.), west by Dorchester county (Md.), and northwest by Caroline county (Md.) It is thirty-five miles long from east to west, the mean breadth twenty-five, and the area eight hundred and seventy-five square miles. It lies between latitude 38° 27′ and 38° 58′, and longitude 1° 14′ and 1° 58′ east. Most of the county is table-land, with some parts marshy; and streams flow from it toward all the points of the compass. From the northeast flow several creeks into Delaware bay, east the tributaries of Rehoboth bay, south those of Pocomoke, and southwest those of Nanticoke.

Among the men distinguished in the revolutionary periods of the history of this state was Cæsar Rodney; and some of the most interesting events connected with the important circumstances of those times may be here appropriately introduced, in an outline of his biography.

His grandfather came to this country from England in the days of Penn, and, after a short residence in Pennsylvania, settled in Kent county (Delaware). His youngest son, Cæsar, inherited his estate, which was large, and married the daughter of the Rev. Thomas Crawford, who is said to have been the first clergyman in that part of the country. Cæsar Rodney, the subject of the present sketch—a distinguished statesman of Delaware, and one of the signers of the Declaration of Independence—was born about the year 1730, and, according to the law of entailment then existing in that state, became heir of the family estate. At the age of twenty-eight, he was appointed high sheriff of the county of Kent, after which he was a justice of the peace and judge of the inferior courts.

There are no records of the legislature of Delaware in existence, of an earlier date than 1762, and therefore it has been found impossible to ascertain when Mr. Rodney commenced his career as a legislator. He was a representative for his native county at that time, and was one of the most prominent members, being appointed as a colleague with Mr. M'Kean, to transact some business of importance with the government.

In the time of the stamp-act, much excitement was caused in Delaware; and in 1763 the members of the assembly held a meeting, during the recess of the chamber, and appointed delegates to attend a congress at New York, for consultation on measures to be taken for the general good of the colonies. They unanimously appointed Messrs. Rodney, M'Kean, and Kollock, and the speaker gave them explicit instructions.

The delegates attended, and, after their return, received a unanimous expression of thanks for their services. From that period until the close of the war, Mr. Rodney, with his two associates first named, continued to be the most conspicuous and influential men in Delaware, in opposing the policy of Great Britain, and in sustaining the cause of America. Several circumstances rendered their situation very difficult and dangerous. The country was exposed to invasion, especially by the ships of the enemy, and a large proportion of the people were either favorable to the British government or undecided in their preference for the American. Among other creditable exertions made by him in the legislature of Delaware, he introduced an amendment into a bill, designed to prohibit the slave-trade, which was lost by only two votes.

An attack of cancer in the cheek compelled him to seek medical aid by a residence in Philadelphia, after he had abandoned a previous design of going to Europe. He was made speaker of the house of assembly in 1769, and held that office several years; and he also performed the duties of chairman of the committee of correspondence, formed to promote harmony of views and action throughout the country.

On the 1st of August, 1774, an assembly of delegates met at Newcastle, in compliance with an invitation sent by him, as speaker of the house of delegates, to determine what measures to adopt in the existing crisis; he was chosen chairman of the meeting; and then, in company with Messrs. M'Kean and Read, was appointed to constitute the Delaware delegation to the American congress at Philadelphia. He took his seat in that body on the fifth of September, and the next day was made a member of the grand committee, whose business it was to state what were the rights of the colonies, and when and how they had been violated. The conduct of the Delaware delegation received the unanimous approval of their legislature on their return, and Mr. Rodney was appointed a delegate to the succeeding congress. He soon after received the appointment of brigadier-general of Delaware, and not long afterward appeared in the field, at the time of an invasion of the territory.

Though the presence of Mr. Rodney was deemed highly necessary at home, in the midst of the important and trying scenes of the day, he was present in congress at the time when the question of independence was decided, and was one of its most ardent advocates. On his return, his conduct again received the approbation of the legislature. In the autumn of that year (1776), however, by the exertions of his opponents, his reëlection to congress was defeated, as well as that of Mr. M'Kean; and he spent the succeeding year at home, attending to his private affairs and to the duties of the committees of inspection and of safety, to which he belonged.

Colonel Haslet, who belonged to his brigade, having fallen at the battle of Princeton, General Rodney set out to join the Delaware troops in New Jersey, but on his way was ordered by Lord Stirling to remain at Princeton to forward troops to the army; after the performance of which duties he was permitted to return home, by a highly complimentary letter from General Washington.

He was then appointed a judge of the supreme court, under the constitution of Delaware, which he declined; and was soon after called into the field to quell an insurrection in the county of Sussex.

The invasion by the British army a little later again occupied him, and he marched with the militia of his county, and stationed himself south of the American line, at the command of Washington, to intercept the way between the enemy and their fleet. But his raw troops, in a few hours, returned to their homes in spite of his efforts.

After this he was elected governor of the state, and held the office four years, although the fluctuations of parties were frequent and strong. After that period he declined public offices, as his health had become greatly impaired; and he fell a victim of the cancer early in the year 1783.

The following extract from the preamble to the constitution of the Medical society of Delaware, published in 1789, is interesting on account of its early date:—

"The physicians of the Delaware state had long regretted their unconnected situation. Despairing to obtain some of the most important objects of their profession while thus detached from one another, and convinced that experience has uniformly attested the advantages of literary association, they lately presented a memorial to the honorable legislature on that subject. After duly considering the application, the general assembly, for the liberal purpose of fostering the interest of science, granted a charter of incorporation to a number of the said physicians and their successors for ever, and the name and style of 'the president and fellows of the medical society of the Delaware state.'

"The object of this society is to animate and unite its respective members in the arduous work of cultivating the science of medicine, and its auxiliary branches; with an especial view to its practical use, the alleviating of human misery, the diminution of mortality, and the cure of diseases. To accomplish this interesting purpose, they will direct their endeavors—to investigate the endemical diseases of our country; to trace their effects on its aboriginal inhabitants, and the successive changes they have undergone, in the progress of society from rudeness to refinement; to remark the general operations of political, moral, and natural causes on the human body and its diseases; and, particularly, observe and record the effects of different seasons, climates, and situations, and the changes produced in diseases by the progress of science, commerce, agriculture, arts, population, and manners; to explore the animal, vegetable, and mineral kingdoms, and every accessible department of nature, in search of the means of enriching and simplifying our *materia medica;* to extend the substitution of our indigenous for exotic remedies; to rescue from oblivion, and collect for public view, the fugitive observations of intelligent physicians; to confer honorary rewards on the efforts of genius and industry; to superintend the education of medical students, and connect with the elements of medicine an adequate knowledge of all the kindred and subservient sciences; to enlarge our sources of knowledge, by imparting and disseminating the discoveries and publications of foreign countries; to correspond with learned societies and individuals; to appoint stated times for literary intercourse and communications; to cultivate harmony and liberality among the practitioners of medicine; and, finally, to promote regularity and uniformity in the practice of physic."

A quorum of the fellows of the society having assembled at Dover on Tuesday, May 12, 1789, the constitution was adopted, and the following officers were appointed:—

James Tilton, M.D., president.
Jonas Preston, M.D., vice-president.
Nicholas Way, M.D., Matthew Wilson, D.D., Dr. Joshua Clayton, Dr. Nathaniel Luff, } censors.
Edward Miller, M.D., secretary.
Dr. James Sykes, treasurer.

The following brief but honorable remarks on the condition and prospects of Delaware, were published in the American Museum, in 1789, under the head of an "Epitome of the present state of the Union:—

"Delaware, ninety-two miles in length and twenty three broad by a census in 1790, contained fifty nine thousand inhabitants. This state, though circumscribed in its limits, derives great importance from its rank in the Union. Attached to the new constitution, and having the honor to take the lead in its adoption, there is no doubt of its giving efficacy to its righteous administration."

This state is, as we have before remarked, the smallest in the Union with respect to population; and also in territory excepting Rhode Island.

According to the last census, the population of Delaware was 91,407; that of Rhode Island 147,543. The area of Delaware is 2,120 square miles; that of Rhode Island, 1,360 square miles.

"Battle Monument," Baltimore.

MARYLAND.

This state is bounded west and northwest by Pennsylvania, east by Delaware, southeast by the eastern shore of Virginia and the Atlantic ocean, south by Chesapeake bay, southwest by Potomac river (which separates it from Virginia), west by Virginia, and northwest by Pennsylvania. The outline is remarkably crooked, and, in the western part of the state, the Potomac, which forms the southern boundary, approaches so near to the Pennsylvania line (the northern boundary) that it leaves but a narrow belt, giving the map a peculiar appearance.

It lies between latitude 38° and 39° 43′, and longitude 1° 56′ and 2° 24′ west from Washington. The whole area of the state, notwithstanding the length of its tortuous outline, is only 9,356 square miles, of which the eastern shore contains 3,084. The chief part of the population—with the cities, commerce, and improvement—is west of the Chesapeake. The state, in 1850, contained 582,922 inhabitants. The eastern shore, by its situation, is cut off from intercourse and connexion with the neighboring regions, almost as effectually as if it were an island. The surface is sandy and but little elevated above the ocean, and destitute of hills and of most other advantages.

Those portions of the territory near the ocean and the bay are generally level and low; but the surface rises in the interior, and the middle and western parts are crossed by the Allegany ridges. Of these the Blue ridge is most easterly, and forms a long, uniform, and gentle, but elevated, swell across the state. Grain and grass grow well in the western counties. Valuable mines of iron and coal are wrought in several places; manufactures are carried on with success along some of the streams; the fisheries in the bay and its tributaries are valuable; and commerce is rendered very active by the aid of railroads, steamboats, and vessels of all descriptions. The building of swift-sailing vessels has been carried to the highest degree of perfection, especially in Baltimore.

The Potomac river, which forms so large a part of the southern boundary of this state, is five hundred and fifty miles in length, and navigable for ships of the largest size to Washington. The canal, which extends from the falls at Georgetown almost to its head, makes it navigable for boats through a great part of its length, and approaches near the western states. The Susquehanna empties in Maryland, and is connected with Baltimore by artificial means.

The Patapsco is a small river, but of great importance, being navigable fourteen miles, and having the city of Baltimore at the head of navigation, where its waters form a fine harbor, with shores on one side sloping conveniently for streets and wharves, and on the other high and precipitous, and well adapted for defence.

The Patuxent is one hundred and ten miles long, and navigable fifty miles for vessels of two hundred and fifty tons. Beside these are the Elk river, the Sassafras, Chester, Choptank, Nanticoke, and Pocomoke.

Chesapeake bay is two hundred and seventy miles in length, and differs in breadth from seven to twenty miles, suddenly expanding from one to the other. It contains numerous islands, and is remarkable for the number of coves, inlets, and sinuosities of its borders, which afford access to the water in a thousand places. There is abundance of fish and wild-fowl; and among the latter canvass-back duck is most celebrated, being justly esteemed and preferred above all other water-birds for its rich and delicate flavor. These birds are shot in great numbers in the autumn, and are in great demand, even in the markets of Philadelphia and New York.

Pocomoke bay is a cove of the Chesapeake, lying below the mouth of Nanticoke river. Northwest from it lie Tangier island and Tangier sound, leading into Fishing bay. Above the mouth of Nanticoke river a peninsula projects far into the Chesapeake, forming the county of Dorchester; and on the opposite side this is bounded by Choptank bay, which, in its turns, separates it from Talbot county. This county is much cut up by several coves, inlets, &c., as Treadhaven bay, Broad bay, and St. Michael's bay. Beyond lies another of these remarkable arms of the Chesapeake, viz., Chester bay, which separates the county of Queen Ann from that of Kent. Long as is this line of bay-coast, which we have thus described following its sinuosities, the whole of it is comprehended in a single degree of latitude, lying between thirty-eight and thirty-nine degrees.

Proceeding north from this latter point, Kent county is a peninsula of a semicircular form, lying between the rivers Chester and Sassafras; and next Sassafras bay lie the two rivers North and Elk, beyond which we find the mouth of the Susquehanna, and the northern boundary of the state.

All this part of this state, known as the eastern shore, may now be called an island, since the Delaware and Chesapeake canal opens a complete, although an artificial, water-channel across the neck of the peninsula. It is remarkable that a much greater difference of climate exists on the eastern shore than the mere difference of latitude is sufficient to account for. The lower part is so warm, that even cotton may be cultivated.

The western part of the state is quite cold for so southern a parallel; but this is very easily accounted for, as its elevation is sufficient to render the temperature in winter equal to that of the Atlantic coast as high up as latitude forty-four degrees forty-three minutes. The elevated valleys in Allegany county, although very fertile, have a climate too cold for wheat.

The want of intimate communication between these two parts of Maryland, and the semi-isolated situation of the counties and many of the towns of the former with respect to each other, are unfavorable to improvements of almost every kind. The productions of every neighborhood are brought to the shore of one of the innumerable little streams, inlets, or coves, which scollop the winding coast of the Chesapeake, and shipped in small vessels running to different places; while the habits of the people, as well as the nature of the country, thus interrupted by water every few miles, render roads few and short. Intercourse among the inhabitants is limited; there are no large towns; and intelligence languishes, with public spirit and enterprise, under the absence of the ordinary motives. Manufactures are not encouraged by any natural facilities; and all these causes combined give the eastern shore of Maryland its marked characteristics.

Of the three geographical sections into which Maryland is naturally divided, the eastern shore forms the first; and this, as before remarked, has some peculiar features. The Chesapeake peninsula, of which it forms the western slope, from Pocomoke bay to the mouth of the Susquehanna, is a remarkable piece of land, lying between the Chesapeake and Delaware bays, with a portion of its south-eastern border washed by the ocean. The narrow isthmus which naturally connects it with the continent has been artificially cut through by the Chesapeake and Delaware canal, and thus the whole of this singular cape, or rather peninsula, may be said to have become an island. Measured from that point to its southern extremity—Cape Charles—it is one hundred and eighty-two miles in length; and the general form is that of an oval, acuminate leaf, with numerous and irregular lobes and indentations on its margins. The south part, seventy miles long by eight or ten wide, belongs to Virginia; the middle section belongs wholly to Maryland; and the upper is divided between this state and Delaware. The widest part, near the middle, is seventy miles across, the mean breadth of the whole about twenty miles, and the area 4,900 square miles. The surface is generally flat or gently undulated. The eastern border has a succession of low, sandy islands and beaches, with shallow sounds, opening by narrow channels, and is destitute of considerable streams.

The west side of the peninsula, on the contrary, has a number of rivers, of some size and depth, navigable for greater or less distances, and adding to the facilities afforded by the coves and inlets.

The surface of western Maryland has a general and gradual rise from the shores of Chesapeake bay to the sources of the Potomac, about two thousand feet; but the intermediate regions are in several places diversified by hills and mountainous elevations, chiefly the ridges of the Alleganies. The Blue ridge, however, like some of the others, presents a uniform swell, generally so gradual as to leave the ground unbroken and covered with soil. In some other western parts of the state the rocks protrude, and considerable tracts are unfit for cultivation. There, however, the mineral treasures of iron and coal abound, to such a degree as to make great amends for the want of arable soil.

The following results of observations made at the White cottage, near Sandy spring, in 1829 and 1830, will show the mean temperature: From the winter solstice to the vernal equinox, 28.39; vernal equinox to summer solstice, 58.22; summer solstice to autumnal equinox, 69.21; autumnal equinox to winter solstice, 46.96. The following year the mean temperature at the corresponding periods was as follows: 35.63; 58.14; 71.46; 49.23.

History.—The first permanent settlement was made in the territory of this state at St. Mary's, in the year 1631, under William Claibourn, on Kent island The charter granted to Lord Baltimore (Cecilius Calvert) was dated June 20, 1632. He was a convert to the church of Rome, and early proclaimed religious toleration, although in direct opposition to the doctrine and practice of the popes and governments under their influence down to the present day.

Maryland was named in honor of the queen, Henrietta Maria, daughter of Henry IV. of France; and through the Roman catholic influence, which in some points was strong during her day, Lord Baltimore received an amount of power not conferred on the governors of New England or most of the other colonies. He was created sole proprietor of Maryland, restricted by nothing save allegiance to the crown. With the consent of the freemen, he could make laws and raise taxes; and he was to execute the laws of the assembly. The crown covenanted to impose no taxes on the colonies, their goods or commodities; and this exemption was to last forever, though in other colonies it was limited to a term of years. Maryland, as constituted under Lord Baltimore, was therefore a palatinate, the proprietary being invested with all the royal rights of the palace, while the king held him and his domain only as a feudal sovereign. Colonists were promised all the liberties of Englishmen-born.

In November, 1633, the first body of emigrants sailed with Leonard Calvert, the first governor of the province. They consisted of about two hundred English gentlemen and many of their adherents. They went by the way of the West Indies, and spent some time in Barbadoes and St. Christopher's, and did not reach the Chesapeake till the spring following, when, on the 27th of March, they landed on St. Mary's river. According to the custom of Rome, Calvert erected a cross and took formal possession of the country, "for our Savior, and for our sovereign lord the king of England."

He made proposals to the chief of the Indians, whom he found in the vicinity, to commence a settlement on amicable terms, with his consent. But he received for answer: "I will not bid you go, neither will I bid you stay; but you may use your own discretion." The confidence and friendship of the chief, however, were at length gained; and he exerted a pacific influence on some of the neighboring tribes, by which the feeble colony was secured from molestation. A neighboring tract of land was purchased, in the native town of Yocomoco, and the building of the capital commenced, which was named St. Mary's. Among the first buildings were a guard-house and a storehouse, and corn was planted, to secure provisions for the colonists. Not much time had elapsed after the landing, before they received a visit from the governor of Virginia, Sir John Harvey, who, like his people, regarded the new colony with jealousy. While he was there, several Indian chiefs arrived from the interior to pay their respects to Governor Calvert. They were received on board a ship which lay at anchor in the river, and sumptuously entertained. The king of Patuxent had his seat at table between the two English governors.

To make an impression upon the minds of the ignorant and simple savages, when the stores were landed from the vessel, a great display was made. The flags were raised on shore, the men were drawn up under arms, volleys of musketry and discharges of cannon from the ships were given, when the provisions, &c., were deposited in the storehouse. The king of Werowances took this opportunity to enjoin upon the kings of Patuxent and Yocomoco, who were present, to be faithful in their observance of the treaty they had made with the governor of Maryland. He spent several days at the place, and is reported to have said to the governor, in a speech addressed to him before his departure: "I love the English so well, that if they should go about to kill me, I would command the people not to revenge my death; for I know they would not do such a thing except it were through my own fault."

According to the treaty, the English occupied one half of the town, and the Indians the other; and the greatest harmony prevailed, without interruption, through the remainder of the year. The savages performed the most kind and important services to the colonists: they accompanied them into the forest, showed them the best kinds of game, joined them in the chase, and brought home what was taken or killed, feeling well rewarded by the presents they received of knives, tools, and toys. They also afforded them assistance in obtaining fish, while the squaws instructed the strangers in the culture of corn. The females and children became so friendly and confiding, that numbers of them were partly domesticated with the colonists.

Fifty acres of land were given to each settler, and, as their numbers soon considerably increased, the colony assumed a very flourishing appearance. But difficulties soon arose from the conflicting claims of a prior settler. Clayborne, about a year anterior to the date of Baltimore's charter, had received from the king license to trade in parts of America not covered by any patent of exclusive trade, and had formed a settlement at Kent island, for the advantages of the trade of the Chesapeake, which he wished to engross. That island was now in the centre of Maryland, and of course Clayborne looked upon the new colony with no friendly eye. An appeal was made to the courts: but, although he failed in that resort, he troubled the colony in various ways.

The first assembly met in Maryland in 1635, and passed criminal laws, which were chiefly designed to be executed upon Clayborne, and he was soon indicted for murders, piracy, and sedition. To escape punishment he fled to England, when his estates were confiscated, and, in spite of all his influence at court, the lords-commissioners of the colonies pronounced sentence against him.

The second assembly was held in 1637, to consider a code of laws proposed by the governor, which they wholly rejected, substituting one of their own. The province was divided into baronies and manors, with privileges all clearly defined, and laws made to secure private property, to regulate intestate succession, &c. At the third assembly, in 1639, a representative form of government was established.

Slaves are alluded to in an early act of the assembly, in defining "the people," who are said to consist of all Christian inhabitants, "slaves only excepted."

An Indian war broke out in 1642, which was attributed by the Marylanders to the intrigues of Clayborne. After a few years it was terminated by a lasting peace, which was due, in a great measure, to laws passed by the assembly, regulating intercourse with the Indians. Land-purchases were required to receive the sanction of the governor, and the sale of firearms and liquor to the Indians was prohibited.

But in 1645 a rebellion broke out in Kent island, which extended to St. Mary's, and compelled Calvert to make his escape to Virginia. The revolt was suppressed in August following, and the colony again enjoyed tranquillity. An act of oblivion was passed in 1649, which included all except a few chief offenders; and during the same session religious toleration was established by an act of the assembly. Some of its provisions were these: that no person professing to believe in the Lord Jesus Christ should be molested in respect of his religion, nor in the free exercise thereof, or be compelled to the belief or exercise of any other, against his own consent; that persons molesting any other in respect of their religious tenets should pay triple damages to the party aggrieved, and twenty shillings to the proprietary; that those who should apply opprobrious names of religious distinction to others, should forfeit ten shillings to the persons so insulted; that any speaking reproachfully against the Blessed Virgin, or the apostles, should forfeit five pounds: but that blasphemy against God should be punished with death.

In 1650, the constitution of the colony was drawn up in a form which it preserved for a century. The assembly was now divided, those who were called to it by special writ forming the upper house, and the burgesses the lower.

At the same time, Lord Baltimore was recognised proprietary of the province, and received public honors as such. But the assembly passed an act requiring the assent of the freemen to any tax that might be imposed. New difficulties, however, soon arose. Commissioners were appointed in England to place the colony under the control and government of the mother-country; and, Clayborne being one of them, a revolution was soon effected in the constitution, after a short period of opposition, and even civil war. The Roman catholics were defeated, the governor deposed, and the unprecedented and intolerable feudal power and rank of Calvert overthrown. The next assembly acknowledged the authority of Cromwell, who was then protector, and reduced the colony to a state of dependence on England, but abridged religious liberty to such a degree that Roman catholics, quakers, and episcopalians, suffered persecution.

In the meantime, Lord Baltimore had appointed Fendal his representative; and, at the end of two years, the commissioners surrendered the government to him. His first acts were to procure the dissolution of the upper house, and assume the whole legislative power, to lay heavy taxes, to oppress the quakers, and thus to increase the public difficulties. The restoration of Charles II., which soon followed, restored Lord Baltimore to his place, powers, emoluments, and honors; and Fendal, after being convicted of high treason, was pardoned on the ground of incapacity.

During the dissensions which had now been passed through, the colony had much increased. It contained twelve thousand inhabitants. Five years afterward it had one hundred ships and sixteen thousand inhabitants. Every young person was trained to useful labor, and poverty was unknown.

In 1661 a mint was established, which, in 1676, was declared perpetual, by the assembly.

The Dutch settlers at Henlopen, for a time, threatened great troubles to Maryland; but Calvert was successful in negotiating with them, by which some were persuaded to leave that part of the country, and others to come under his government. A tribe of Indians, on the west side of the Delaware, once assumed a hostile attitude; but, by the assistance of some neighboring tribes, they were induced to lay aside all unfriendly intentions, and gave the colony no further trouble. The statute-book of the colony, under the date of 1666, contains a law for the naturalization of the Dutch colonists who remained in Maryland; which is the oldest act of the kind in all the colonies.

In 1671 a tax of two shillings was laid on every hogshead of tobacco exported, half to be expended for the public defence, in a magazine and arms, and half to be given to the proprietary as a mark of gratitude.

Lord Baltimore died in 1676, and was succeeded by his son, Charles Calvert. England had long practised the sending of felons to Maryland, as a place of banishment; and this year the assembly made an ineffectual attempt to put a stop to a system so injurious to the colony. Not fewer than three hundred and fifty were annually landed in the province for several years before the revolution.

As early as 1681, exertions were made to introduce manufacturing; but they were not attended by any important results. The following year, William Penn had an interview with the proprietary, soon after his arrival from England, to effect an amicable settlement of the boundary line between the two territories. They were unable to agree; and, the question being afterward decided in England, the disputed territory was equally divided, and that portion now forming the state of Delaware was taken from the lands claimed by Lord Baltimore.

Discontent had now become great with the proprietary of Maryland, even in England. He was threatened by King Charles with a writ of *quo warranto*, on account of his resisting his majesty's officers in the collection of the parliamentary duties. But on another charge he suffered more seriously; for such was the clamor raised in consequence of the pardon granted to Fendal, that all but protestants were declared to be incapable in future of holding any office under the government of Maryland.

The accession of James II. led to new difficulties in Maryland; and not long after, on a rumor that the Roman catholics and Indians had formed a league for the destruction of the protestants, a protestant league was formed, headed by John Coode, who was authorized by King William to exercise the government for three years. Calvert was tried on sundry charges, but was only deprived of the government—Sir Edward Andross being apointed governor in his place. He was, however, permitted to enjoy his proprietary estate. In 1716 the representative of the Calvert family renounced the Roman catholic religion, and was restored to such rights as he claimed.

The revolutionary period of the history of Maryland contains too many interesting events to be given in a limited space. Several leading men early took a decided part in favor of American resistance, and prosecuted with zeal and faithfulness the great measures which finally established independence. The state adopted the constitution August 14, 1776, and the federal constitution in 1788. In 1790 the territory now forming the federal district, or district of Columbia, was ceded by Maryland to the general government.

Government.—The senate consists of twenty-two members, one being chosen from each county and one from the city of Baltimore, for a term of four years, one half of them biennially. The house of delegates are elected once in two years; and, till the apportionment under the census of 1860, are seventy-two in number. The executive power is vested in a governor who is chosen for four years. The state is divided into three districts, and the governor is taken from each of the three districts alternately. The judicial power is vested in a court of appeals, circuit courts, courts for the city of Baltimore, and in justices of the peace.

The right of suffrage is allowed to each free white male citizen, twenty-one years old who has been one year a resident in the state, and six months in the county.

Education.—The colonial legislature in 1696 appropriated money for education in a college and free-schools, which was absorbed by the college. Washington college was founded in 1782 in Chestertown, Kent county, on the eastern shore; St. John's college in 1784, in Annapolis, on the western shore; and these two were afterward connected and formed the university.

An act was passed by the legislature of this state during the session of December, 1825, to "provide for the public instruction of youth in primary schools throughout the state." This act defines the duties of the superintendent of schools, namely, to digest and prepare plans of instruction; to improve such system as may be adopted, and such revenues as may from time to time be assigned to this object; to prepare and report estimates and expenditures; and to superintend the collection of the revenues appropriated to education. It requires of the justices of the levy court in each of the counties to appoint nine commissioners of primary schools for the county, and a number of other suitable men, not exceeding eighteen, who, together with the commissioners, shall be inspectors of said schools. The act also defines the duties of the commissioners as to dividing the county into school districts; provides for the election of trustees in each district, the erection of schoolhouses, and a semi-annual report of the trustees to the commissioners, &c.

The Roman catholic college at Georgetown was founded in 1784. The medical college in Baltimore was founded in 1807, and in 1812 connected with the faculties of law, divinity, and general science, and formed a body corporate, under the title of the "University of Maryland." Two other institutions—Baltimore and St. Mary's colleges—have funds of their own, by which, with students' fees, they are supported.

Academies, which afford many advantages of education to both sexes, exist in most of the principal towns.

Manufactures.—The manufactures of this state are numerous, various, and valuable. Woollen, cotton, iron, copper, and flour, are among the principal; and most of these are seated on the banks of the streams where the descent of the land affords water-power applicable to machinery. In Baltimore and its vicinity a large amount of manufacturing is done.

Productions.—Flour and tobacco are the staple productions of Maryland; but the former more valuable article vastly exceeds the latter in quantity. Iron is abundant in many of the counties of the western shore, and is manufactured in many places. Bituminous coal exists in Allegany county in inexhaustible mines, and is one of the most valuable natural productions of the state.

THE BALTIMORE AND OHIO RAILROAD. This great work was designed to extend from the city of Baltimore to Wheeling (Virginia), but was delayed in its completion. It was chartered in 1827, and the work commenced in 1828. The state has subscribed three millions and Baltimore three millions. The first portion, to the Point of Rocks, sixty-nine miles in length, has been in operation several years. It has since been finished to Cumberland, a distance of one hundred and seventy-eight miles. It winds along streams, hill-sides, &c., in various places, often among wild scenery. The bridges and viaducts are many, and very expensive. It is proposed to extend it to Pittsburgh, to compete with Philadelphia in measures to secure the trade of the Ohio valley. We select the following statement, in relation to this enterprise, from recent publications:—

"There seems now to be a prospect that this great work of improvement will be pushed forward to completion within a reasonable time. For a long period it has been at a stand—looking, as it were, from the summit of the Alleganies for the most advantageous point to intersect the Ohio river, which was the limit originally prescribed for the stupendous undertaking. But, should the work take the course indicated, a short time only will elapse before the road will penetrate the interior of Ohio, connecting itself with the richest agricultural region between the river and the lakes, and drawing from both a large amount of their transit business. It will soon connect itself with the river again at Cincinnati, thus securing to itself all the advantages and benefits of a junction at a point advantageous for its interests in seasons of low water; while at the same time it will be reaching its long arm through the fertile valleys and broad prairies of our western neighbors, toward the Mississippi. The word will then be—not 'Baltimore and Wheeling,' but '*Baltimore and St. Louis,*'—which will comprehend all the intermediate points."

BALTIMORE.—This is the principal city and port of Maryland, and also one of the largest and finest in the United States. It is advantageously situated near the head of Chesapeake bay, fourteen miles distant, on the river Patapsco, which affords it a commodious harbor, well protected by high land. It occupies a position commanding, by natural and artificial channels of communication, extensive and fertile regions in Maryland and adjacent states, and even with the valley of the Mississippi. It is in latitude 39° 17′ 23″, and longitude 76° 37′ 30″ west from Greenwich, being forty miles from Washington, ninety-seven from Philadelphia, one hundred and eighty-six from New York, and two hundred and ninety from Pittsburg. The population in 1850 was 169,000.

The entrance to the harbor of Baltimore is between Fort M'Henry and the Lazaretto, six hundred yards wide, with twenty-two feet in depth; the second harbor, which is above Fell's point, has fifteen feet water, and the third, or inner, opposite the city, ten or twelve.

The city is about two miles in extent from east to west, and one and a half from north to south, and most of the streets are straight and at right angles. The favorite promenade is in Baltimore street, the principal avenue, which is two miles long; and the west part is the favorite residence of the wealthier citizens. The principal public buildings are the city-hall in Holliday street, the courthouse at the corner of Washington and Monument streets, the state penitentiary, above one hundred churches, eleven banks, seven markets, eight insurance offices, two theatres, the circus, the museum, and the savings bank.

The Merchants' Exchange.—The erection of this building was commenced in the year 1815. It is two hundred and twenty-five feet in length and one hundred and forty-four in depth, the ground plan being in the form of the letter H. It is four stories, including the basement, which is vaulted. The grand hall is eighty-six feet long, and lighted by a dome, ninety feet from the floor.

There are two colonnades at the eastern and western extremities, each of six Ionic columns, in pure style, and each consisting of a single block of Italian marble.

The *Cathedral* (Roman catholic) is one hundred and ninety by one hundred and seventy-seven feet in extent, and in the Ionic style, surmounted by a dome and a cross, the top of which is one hundred and twenty-seven feet high. The building itself is in the form of a cross, built of granite. It has two steeples, in one of which is a bell weighing three thousand five hundred lbs., the tone of which is exceedingly mournful, and can be heard forty miles down the bay on a calm evening. The organ contains six thousand pipes and thirty-six stops.

The convent of the Ladies of Visitation is a large structure, with cupola and cross. Attached is an extensive academy for young girls.

The *Baltimore Museum and Gallery of Fine Arts* is a fine spacious building, on the northwest corner of Baltimore and Calvert streets, remarkable for its two steeples and fine appearance. The interior arrangement and attractions are on a most costly and extensive scale.

The appellation of the "Monumental city" has been conferred upon Baltimore, on account of its containing several splendid national monuments. In some of the burying-grounds, also, there are a great number of superb monuments, many of them erected by the city authorities.

Washington Monument.—This superb and famous national structure, in honor of the Father of his country, was erected by the state.

It is built on an eminence of one hundred feet, at the head of Charles street, and consists of a square base of fifty feet by twenty-four in height, surmounted by a granite column, including the statue of Washington, one hundred and eighty feet in height.

The statue represents Washington in the act of resigning his commission, is sixteen feet high, weighs sixteen tons, and cost nine thousand dollars. The corner stone of the monument was laid July 4, 1815. There are four gates and twelve steps to the main entrance. The inscription over each of the four doors is as follows:—

"To George Washington, by the State of Maryland."

On each side of the base is an inscription:—

"Born February 22d, 1732. Died 14th December, 1799.
Commander-in-chief of the American Army, 15th June, 1775. Commission resigned at Annapolis, 23d December, 1783.
Trenton, 25th December, 1776. Yorktown, 19th October, 1781.
President of the United States, March 4, 1789.
Retired to Mount Vernon, 4th March, 1797."

The exchange, customhouse, courthouse, Barnum's City hotel, and the jail, are distinctly seen from the summit, and a fine view of the city and surrounding country for several miles is enjoyed.

Several women have, within the past few years, precipitated themselves from this giddy height.

Battle Monument.—This is situated on Monument square; it consists of a square base, on which rests a pedestal, ornamented on each corner with a beautifully-carved griffon. From the centre arises a column, on the bands encircling which are inscribed the names of those who fell in the defence of Baltimore in 1814, and in whose honor it was erected. This column is surmounted by a superb statue, representing the Genius of Baltimore, holding a laurel or triumphal crown in her right hand, and an antique helm in her left, emblematic of commerce, having an eagle, bombshell, &c., at her side.

This monument is of white marble, over fifty feet in height, and surrounded by a railing. The statuary is from the chisel of Cuppelleano, an Italian artist.

Armistead Monument in the rear of the city fountain, was erected by the corporation to the memory of Colonel Armistead, in honor of his gallant defence of Fort M'Henry.

The surface of the ground on which Baltimore stands is uneven, and in some parts elevated, so that a great variety of situations is offered, for the wharves, stores, and streets of business, for public monuments and the habitations of the rich. The upper parts of the town are on a ridge of primitive ground, through

Baltimore.

which a small stream, crossing the city, has cut a deep channel through the rocks. That part of the town in the vicinity of the bridge which crosses the stream, has sometimes suffered from sudden inundations in violent storms. Several of the upper streets, lying along the high ground, and being broad, straight, and well built, and in some places adorned with trees and gardens, make a very handsome appearance, and are among the most attractive residences in the United States.

The north parts of the city are the most elevated, and occupy several roundish hills, eighty or a hundred feet above the level of the harbor. The natural surface has here been modified to suit the convenience of the inhabitants, and to render the streets more uniform, so that the ascent from the water, although in some places steep, is nowhere difficult. The lower parts of the city are on the alluvion which borders the bay or basin, and there the streets are more closely built and crowded: still their straightness and regularity render them more convenient and clean than the business parts of many other commercial towns of equal size.

On the south side of the city, at the entrance of the outer or first harbor—on a point of land which rises by a gradual ascent to an eminence—is situated Fort M'Henry, the principal defence of the city by water. This fort endured a bombardment by a British squadron in the war of 1812, through an entire night, and held out successfully. The point is connected with the mainland by a long, low, and sandy neck, over which, as well as the neighboring water, the guns of the fort have an advantageous command.

The country around Baltimore is marked by some peculiar features. Baltimore county extends to Chesapeake bay on the southeast, to Patapsco river on the southwest, to Frederick county on the west, to York county (Pa.) on the north, and to Hartford county on the northeast; having an extreme length, from southeast to northwest, of thirty-six miles, a mean breadth of twenty-five miles, and an area of nine hundred square miles. It may be divided into two sections—the valley of Gunpowder creek, which is hilly, and that of the Patapsco. The great primitive ledge, which extends all along the Atlantic border from the southern to the eastern states, crosses this county, and the sea-sand alluvion, between the bays of the Patapsco and the Gunpowder, lie at its base. All the county is uneven; but above the head of tidewater it becomes more rough and more elevated; and at Reigerstown, seventeen miles northwest from Baltimore, the surface is five hundred feet above the level of tidewater. The elevation is still greater at the southeast foot of the dividing ridge between Baltimore and Frederick counties—the farms are eight hundred feet above the harbor: so that there is a difference of a week or ten days in the seasons. This variety of surface and climate renders the variety of vegetation very great.

The great western railroad from Baltimore, to be extended to the Ohio, skirts along the southwest border of this county; while the Susquehanna and the Washington railroads bring their numerous trains across it to the city, though the latter is connected, as a branch, with the western railroad.

Early History of Baltimore.—The first settlement of Maryland, under the patent of Lord Baltimore, was made on the north bank of the Potomac, at St. Mary's, which was intended to become the capital of the new colony, but is a place of no distinction.

The first settler within the limits of Baltimore was a man named Gorsuch, who took a patent of lands, twenty-eight years later, on Whetstone point. This is now included in the review-ground of the Baltimore militia. Among those who settled soon after him in this vicinity was Charles Carroll, whose estate, on the high ground behind Baltimore, still bears his name. A descendant of his—Charles Carroll, of Carrollton—was one of the signers of the Declaration of Independence. The original purchase of Carroll included some of the most eligible parts of the present city of Baltimore, which, at an early day, were sold by Charles and Daniel

Washington Monument, Baltimore.

Carroll, at prices now surprisingly low, viz., sixty acres, at forty shillings an acre, payment being made in tobacco at one penny per pound.

At that time, Baltimore appears to have been surrounded with a board fence, with two gates for carriages and one for foot-passengers.

The Battle of Baltimore.—Maryland was invaded by a powerful British army in 1814, and Baltimore was saved from capture by the energy of the officers and soldiers hastily assembled for the defence.

A British squadron was blockading the coast, and Commodore Barney sailed from Baltimore to protect the harbors, &c., in the bay, with a flotilla, consisting of a cutter, two gunboats, a galley, and nine large barges. At the mouth of the Patuxent river he discovered two schooners and pursued them. One carried eighteen guns; and as both were soon joined by the barges of a seventy-four, which was soon discovered, he fled into the mouth of the river. They followed, but were driven back, and the commodore returning anchored about three miles distant from the ship. A few days after, a rasée of the enemy arrived, with a sloop-of-war; and the commodore was compelled to retire to St. Leonard's creek, pursued by the smaller vessels and the barges of the larger. There he extended his line of boats across the stream, in order of battle. The enemy twice advanced and were twice driven back, and the eighteen-gun schooner was so much injured by the American shot that she was run on shore and abandoned.

A body of artillery from Washington arrived on the 26th, when a combined attack was made on the enemy from the land and the water, and with success. The British retreated after an action of two hours, and immediately sailed down the river.

A short time after, however, having received large reinforcements from Europe in consequence of the cessation of hostilities with France, the enemy formed the plan of a large expedition, and soon entered the Chesapeake, accompanied by thirty ships-of-war, under Lieutent-General Ross, intending to capture Washington and Baltimore.

After the capture of Washington and Georgetown, the enemy directed his attention to Baltimore. Forty smaller vessels, under Admiral Cochrane, sailed for the Patapsco, and arrived at North point, twelve miles from the city. They were drawn up and anchored in a line across the river, and the debarkation of the troops soon commenced. The landing was completed on the morning of September 12, and the forces prepared to march against the city, amounting to eight thousand, including soldiers, sailors, and marines. At the same time, sixteen vessels, including frigates and bomb-vessels, moved up the river to make an attack by water, in coöperation with the army. The latter anchored at the distance of two and a half miles from Fort M'Henry, which had been timely garrisoned by a strong force of five thousand men.

The British army proceeded, while a body of three thousand Americans moved out to meet them. On intelligence being received by the latter of the enemy's approach, two companies of artillery, a few riflemen, and ten artillerymen with a four-pounder, hastened on to meet their advance, which was reported to be a light corps. But, as the ground was unfavorable to the use of the enemy's cavalry and artillery, the action was sustained by the infantry of the detachments.

General Ross, pressing forward with several of his staff, exposed himself, on an open field, to the fire of a few American sharpshooters posted in an advantageous position, and he instantly received a mortal wound, and fell, with several of his officers. The enemy then pushed on and attacked the American left.

The action now became general, and a sharp contest continued from two to four o'clock, P. M., when the Americans, being in far inferior force, fell back upon the reserve. The next day was spent without renewing the action, the enemy taking position in the afternoon in front of the Americans, driving in their outposts, and preparing for an attack at night. The weather was stormy, however, and in the morning the British reëmbarked, and a bombardment commenced, which lasted till the following morning. An attempt was made to storm Fort Covington, but failed, with loss, and the expedition retreated down the river."

Nature has made generous provision for extensive and various manufactures in Maryland. Baltimore and its vicinity has been said, by a well-qualified writer, to possess "unrivalled advantages" for manufacturing, there not being "on the continent a location more favorable. Everything is cheap; and ready access can be had to all the markets of the Union. Nothing is wanting but enterprise and industry to make the whole nation tributary" to this city.

The Flour Trade.—A most extensive business is transacted in flour in this city. The quantity of wheat-flour and cornmeal inspected during the miller's year, from July 1, to June 30, is about a million of barrels.

The chief wealth of Maryland, we will incidentally remark, is drawn from its agriculture and mines. Mining is now being carried on with great spirit, and since the completion of the canal and railroad from Baltimore to Cumberland, operations have been greatly extended. It is a fact worthy of observation that many of our ocean steamships are using the semi-bituminous coal of this region, and large quantities are used at Pittsburgh and for steamboats on the Ohio rivers. Furnaces, bloomeries, and rolling-mills, for the manufacture of iron, have increased wonderfully in number during the past five years, and turn out vast quantities of cast and bar iron. The principal agricultural produce is wool and pork; wheat, Indian corn, and oats; and tobacco. Maryland stands fourth on the list of tobacco-growing states, and is highly celebrated for the excellency of this staple. Ship-building, chiefly carried on at Baltimore, is also an extensive branch of industry. The coast fisheries employ many hundreds of families, and supply not only sufficient fish for the market of Baltimore, but also no small amount for export.

Annapolis.—This town is distinguished as the state capital, and stands at the mouth of the river Severn, on its right bank, and three miles from Chesapeake bay. It is also the capital of Anne Arundel county. The statehouse, St. John's college, and St. Anne's church, are placed at three points of the city equally distant from each other, forming centres, at which meet, from different directions, the principal streets. The other public buildings are the government-house, methodist church, Roman catholic chapel, the bank, and the seminary. There are about four thousand three hundred inhabitants in Annapolis. It is thirty-seven miles north and seventy-six east from Washington, and thirty miles east of south from Baltimore.

The *Statehouse* is an old building, and has long served for public purposes. The American congress assembled here during some of the most interesting periods of the revolution. The senate-chamber, in which they held their sessions, remains unaltered to the present day. It was there that the solemn scene was exhibited of the resignation of his commission by Washington, after the close of the war.

St. John's College has five professors, one thousand two hundred and forty alumni, and about seventy-five students, with a library of about four thousand volumes. The commencement is held on the 22d of February.

Havre de Grace is a small town at the mouth of Susquehanna river, thirty-six miles northeast from Baltimore and sixty miles from Philadelphia, and contains about fifteen hundred inhabitants. Here commences the Susquehanna canal, which extends from the Chesapeake to the Pennsylvania canals. This town was burnt by the British troops under Admiral Cockburn, in the late war, in 1813.

Steam-ferryboats cross the river here, and the railroad from Philadelphia to Baltimore passes through this place.

Elkton, forty-five miles from Philadelphia and about the same distance from Baltimore, stands at the junction of the two principal branches of Elk river at the head of tidewater. It is a place of some trade, and a neat and pleasant village.

Chestertown is thirty miles southeast from Baltimore, thirty from Chesapeake bay, and eighty-two northeast from Washington. It stands on Chester river, and contains over one thousand inhabitants. This is the seat of justice of Kent county. A branch of the university of Maryland is established here.

Easton.—This town is on Treadhaven bay, thirteen miles from Elkton and Chesapeake bay. It contains three churches, a courthouse, and an academy. The inhabitants are over one thousand. It is a seaport and the seat of justice of Talbot county.

Cambridge, twelve miles distant from Chesapeake bay, is on the Choptank, and contains a courthouse, an academy, and two churches, with about eight hundred inhabitants. Stagecoaches run to Snowhill and to Elkton. It is the seat of justice of Dorchester county, and is thirty-six miles southeast of Annapolis in a direct line, but fifty-three by post-route.

Snowhill is situated on the east side of Pocomoke river, one hundred and sixty-three miles southeast of Washington. It contains a courthouse, an academy, five churches, and about eight hundred inhabitants, and is the seat of justice of Worcester county.

Barren Creek Mineral Springs are twenty-three miles from Cambridge; they are resorted to by numbers of visiters every seasons. The water contains oxyde of iron, soda, and magnesia, with muriatic acid.

Westminster.—This town stands near the head of Patapsco river. It has a courthouse, an academy, three churches, and about five hundred inhabitants. It lies on the border of Frederick county, twenty-three miles northwest of Baltimore.

Emmettsburg is twenty-two miles north of Frederick. It stands on the Monocasy, in the north part of Frederick county, and contains four churches, an academy, and eight hundred inhabitants, and near it is one of the principal Roman catholic seminaries, called St. Mary's college.

St. Mary's College was founded in 1830, and has a president, eleven tutors, and about one hundred and fifty students. Its libraries contain four thousand volumes. The commencement is held in the last week in June. Stagecoaches go to Frederick three times a week.

Frederick.—This is one of the principal towns in the state, being second in importance to Baltimore, from which it is distant sixty-one miles west. It stands on a branch of the Monocasy, in the midst of a pleasant country, with a fertile soil. It is laid out with regularity, and contains some fine private houses, and several conspicuous public buildings—a courthouse, county buildings, a market, twelve churches, two academies, a Roman catholic seminary and charity school, and above six thousand inhabitants. A branch railroad connects this town with the Baltimore and Ohio railroad.

Frederick County next south of Adams county, and southwest of York county (Pa.), lies along the western boundary of Baltimore, Anne Arundel, and Montgomery counties, from which it is, for a considerable part of the distance, divided by the ridge of the Southeast mountain. It extends south to the Potomac and west to the Blue ridge. It is forty-two miles long and eighteen miles in mean breadth, and has an area of seven hundred and seventy-six square miles. It is traversed by the Monocasy, which lies wholly within it, excepting the headwaters. The Cotoctin mountain, a minor branch of the Blue ridge, extends south, from the northwest part of the county, nearly to the Potomac, dividing the valleys of the Monocasy and the Cotoctin. The surface is not generally hilly, and in some parts level; while the soil is favorable to grain, grass, and fruit; and it is one of the best cultivated parts of the state.

Hagerstown.—This town stands on Antietam creek, and is seventy miles west fom Baltimore, with daily stagecoaches to Frederick. It contains nine churches, a townhall, two banks, two academies, and nearly five thousand inhabitants. It is the seat of justice of

Viaduct over the Patuxent on the Baltimore and Washington Railroad.

Washington county, and a place of considerable importance, lying in the centre of a rich limestone valley.

HANCOCK, on the bank of Potomac river, contains two churches, an academy, and about five hundred inhabitants.

CUMBERLAND, one hundred and seventy-eight miles west of Baltimore, is on the Potomac, at the mouth of Wills creek. It contains a bank, a market, five churches, a courthouse, and about two thousand inhabitants. The situation is in a varied and wild region, among the mountains, where coalmines abound. The railroad to Baltimore affords daily communication with that city and the intermediate places. It is the seat of justice of Allegany county, and the eastern termination of the great western road of the United States called the Cumberland road.

ELLICOTT'S MILLS, ten miles southwest from Baltimore, is situated in a wild and picturesque region, and owes its existence as a village to the water-power, which is employed in numerous manufactures, and to the railroad which here crosses the Patapsco, on a fine aqueduct of stone. It stands on the boundary line of Baltimore and Anne Arundel counties.

The Viaduct of the Baltimore and Washington Railroad.—One of the most striking objects in the state is the great viaduct on which the Baltimore and Washington railroad crosses the valley of the Patuxent. A passenger travelling over it in a car has little opportunity to judge of the nature, extent, difficulty, and cost of the construction. The view from the summit is so extensive, and the valley below is seen so nearly under his feet, that the most careless observer must be aware that he is moving at an unusual height above the surface, and that the road is sustained by a long and narrow, though lofty fabric. To an observer, however, from below, or from a point on either side, the scene is of a more impressive description. A lofty and elegant arched bridge extends across a deep and wild chasm, forming a narrow but solid and level path, for the long and heavy trains of cars which pass over it, between the natural banks that bound it on either side. The stream which winds below, and sometimes rises to overflow a great part of the valley, threatens to undermine and tear away this light and elegant structure.

Ample space, however, is left between the piers for the passage of the water, even at the highest floods; and the work has suffered but occasional and partial injuries, from the severest weather and floods. The road is thirty-three miles in length, and one of the most important portions of the great line of travelling from north to south, especially during the time when congress is in session.

The commerce of Maryland is so dependent on the harbor of Baltimore, that it is well for the state that it possesses the important quality of being accessible at all seasons of the year. Even when impeded by ice, it never freezes so thick that it may not easily be opened by strong steam icebreakers and towboats, which are kept in readiness for the purpose. Ships of the largest class can come up to the wharves in the lower harbor; and at Canton they have twenty-six feet water.

"The soil of the state," says Hunt's Magazine, "except in a few portions of it, is well adapted to agriculture. It has numerous never-failing streams, with gradual falls at suitable distances, particularly in the vicinity of Baltimore. For manufacturing purposes, and commercial pursuits, Maryland is not excelled by any other state in the Union. The great American Mediterranean sea, whose borders she skirts, will be a wall of defence about her in time of war, as an invading foe would scarcely withdraw himself from the ocean-field, in this improved age of invention, lest his retreat might be intercepted when he found it necessary to retreat; and the bosom of that sea will in early aftertime waft treasures upon it, that, whether in the character of imports or exports, will add to her riches. Nature has incontestably provided for this result; and the founders of Baltimore (not that anything like prescience is to be ascribed to them, even as regards the state of improvements as they exist at present) so located it, that it becomes a point of concentration, whence again all the travel diverges, if economy as to distance be considered, whether the direction be from north to south, or east to west, and *vice versa*. The near proximity of the seat of national government is no drawback upon, but adds to, her value; and should congress in its wisdom authorize the establishment of a national bank, where is there a city, all matters in reference to other banks and places considered, more eligible and safe, for the present, than Baltimore?

"Nearly all the great prominent agricultural productions of the United States are grown in Maryland, except cotton, sugar, and rice; and each year further developments are made in reference to some exotics. If there were agricultural societies, and fairs held, as in some of the eastern states, where the choice productions of the earth could be exhibited, and competent persons appointed to pronounce upon them and award premiums, it would act as a great stimulant to enterprise, aside from the profits immediately resulting to the grower. So with live stock, of all descriptions; but these subjects are somewhat neglected by the present tillers of the soil, and those of politics have, to too great an extent, usurped their places. Some fifteen or twenty years since, when Maryland was luxuriating in a more palmy sunshine of favors than at present, such exhibitions were not unfrequent, and politics slept: there may be a recurrence of a similar prosperous period.

"Corn, wheat, and oats, thrive kindly in every county. Rye is not so generally cultivated; the western counties appear more congenial to its growth. Buckwheat, barley, and pulse, are not so specially attended to. The yield of flaxseed is only middling, compared with that of other grains."

Potatoes are of excellent flavor, and the crops fair, but not equal to the demand. Small parcels of sweet-potatoes come to Baltimore, chiefly from the southern and eastern counties. Hay is the growth of the western shore, and is chiefly timothy, with some clover. It never exceeds home-consumption. Fruit is better adapted to the same counties, especially apples and peaches, some of which are very superior in quality. Melons, of every variety, are abundant everywhere. Tobacco is cultivated in eleven of the counties, but principally in Prince George, Culvert, Charles, St. Mary's, Anne Arundel, and Montgomery. More than nine millions of pounds were raised in Prince George, and twelve millions in all the counties afterward named, in the year 1839.

Good horses, mules, neat-cattle, sheep, and swine, are raised in every county, but Frederick excels in this branch: in this county, according to the census of 1840, there were then 11,259 horses and mules, 24,933 neat-cattle, 26,309 sheep, and 54,049 swine. The bacon of this county is preferred to any other, bringing at Baltimore from one quarter to one half cent. more per pound.

All the counties produce wool; but the yield is not large—not above three hundred thousand pounds per annum, which was the amount in 1840 for the whole state. Frederick county gave of this fifty-nine thousand pounds. In butter and cheese, also, this county exceeds the others.

The forest-trees of the middle states abound in all the counties of this state. The best woods for fuel are the oaks, hickory, beech, and dogwood. Oak commonly sells in Baltimore at from four to five and a half dollars per cord, and the others at from five to seven dollars. Pine is abundant, but neither the white nor the pitch-pine. The hemlock has its southern boundary in the west parts of Maryland, excepting a small district in the Allegany mountains in Virginia. In New England the bark of this tree, there so common, is much used in tanning. The oak of this state is excellent for shipbuilding, being inferior only to the live-oak. The celebrated dam across the Kennebeck river, in Maine, is built of oak from Maryland. It was cut in Baltimore county near a stream flowing into the Chesapeake. Among the plans for internal improvement is one for a canal through that stream to Havre de Grace. Cedar and locust are abundant in some parts of the lower counties, and are exported in great quantities to the eastern states for shipbuilding, with oak timber. The cedar and locust of Maryland are also in demand for railroads.

The amount of exports annually made from the numerous navigable branches of the bay, it is impossible to ascertain, and difficult to estimate.

Coal abounds, principally in Allegany county, and it is mostly of the bituminous kind. The Chesapeake and Ohio canal, from the falls at Georgetown, along the Potomac, was made chiefly for the purpose of bringing this coal to market. The cost of this work has been very great, and unexpected difficulties were found in the way of the western terminus, along the mountainous region where the coal-beds are situated. The Frostburg coal-basin, according to the report of the state geologist, Professor Ducatel, is forty miles long and five miles wide, containing 86,847 acres. The coal, being fifteen yards in depth, must be in amount more than six thousand millions of cubic yards. Each cubic yard weighs a ton.

The Lonaconing iron region is in the same county, and is estimated to contain three thousand millions of tons of ore, or one thousand millions of tons of crude iron.

Many companies have been formed and incorporated for several years, for the working of the coal and iron mines. Some of them have commenced operations with success. The mines at Elkridge Hone yield iron of superior quality, adapted to fine castings. This and other varieties of ore from the vicinity of Baltimore, yield from about thirty-five to fifty per cent. of iron. Bog-ore is found in Worcester county, and has been wrought to some extent. It yields twenty-nine per cent.

Several copper-mines exist in Frederick county, chiefly near the village of New London. The ore yields about thirty per cent.

The following minerals are also found in Maryland, which will prove valuable, viz.: anthracite, granite, marble, soapstone, limestone, flint, sandstone, slate, potters'-clay, fire-clay, pipe-clay, various ochres, chrome, aluminous earths, &c.

Mineral-springs are common in the west, and the waters of some, which have been analyzed, are found to contain sulphate of magnesia, sulphate of lime, muriate of soda, muriate of lime, carbonate of lime, &c.

STATISTICS.—The population of the state of Maryland, according to the census of several successive dates, has been as follows:—

Years.	Whites.	Free Col'd Persons.	Slaves.	Total.
1790	208,647	8,043	103,036	319,728
1800	221,998	19,987	107,707	349,654
1810	235,117	33,927	111,502	380,546
1820	260,222	39,730	107,398	407,350
1830	291,093	52,912	102,873	446,913
1840	318,204	62,078	89,737	470,019
1850	418,763	73,943	89,800	582,506

AGRICULTURAL PRODUCTIONS.

Wheat	3,541,433 bush.	value	$2,655,075
Corn	8,356,565 "	"	3,133,613
Oats	3,579,950 "	"	919,988
Rye	784,303 "	"	392,151
Buckwheat	47,858 "	"	1,450
Potatoes	1,058,901 "	"	211,780
Tobacco	21,916,012 lbs.	"	1,095,800
Hay	110,816 tons	"	1,100,000
Hemp	117 "	"	14,140
Cotton	7,108 lbs.	"	700
Wool	502,499 "	"	100,500
Hops	2,368 bush.	"	473

The following is the number of live stock, with their value:—

Horses and mules	94,054	$4,000,000
Neat-cattle	238,827	2,000,000
Swine	419,520	1,252,000
Sheep	262,807	394,210

MANUFACTURES.

Number of—

			Value.
Mills—Flour	212	(1,000,000 bbls. before estim. as wheat)	
" Grist	433		$61,000
" Saw	423		
" Oil	9		
" Powder	5	(669,000 lbs.)	
" Paper	16		195,100
Factories—Cotton	15		2,348,580
" Woollen	29		235,900
Potteries	22		61,240
Distilleries	73	(342,813 gals.)	68,562
Breweries	11	(529,640 do.)	105,928
Furnaces, forges, and rolling-mills	30		
Tanneries	159		
Ropewalks	13		61,240
Shipbuilding		(7,890 tons)	227,771

The number of primary and common schools at the present time does not fall much, if any, short of 1,000; scholars about 25,000.

THE DISTRICT OF COLUMBIA.

The District of Columbia was ceded to the United States in 1790, and made the seat of government in 1800. It has ever since been the capital of the Union, and under the government of congress. A spot was selected on the Potomac river, at the head of navigation for ships-of-war (where the navy-yard has since been established), and with a surface deemed favorable for the foundation of a city.

The extent of territory was ten miles square, with the Potomac river flowing through it, and including the mouth of the eastern branch of that river, where the water is deep, and the shores favorable to the site of a navyyard. The land on the east side of the Potomac was ceded to the United States government by Maryland, and that on the west side by Virginia; but the latter has been recently ceded back to Virginia, after long experience of the inconveniences arising from being under the jurisdiction of congress, who have so many, and more extensive interests in their care. The city of Alexandria, lately included in the federal district, is expected to derive special benefits from her restoration to Virginia. Washington and Georgetown are the only towns now belonging to it; and these lie so contiguous to each other, that they have almost the appearance of one continued city.

The district of Columbia is bounded north and east by Maryland, and south and west by Potomac river. It is eight miles long, and about one and a half broad. The capitol stands in latitude 76° 55′ 30″ west from Greenwich. The surface is undulated, and the soil poor. The navyyard is in the eastern part of the district, about one mile from Capitol hill; and from the latter, nearly to the falls of the Potomac, extend Washington and Georgetown, making a striking display when seen from the river below. Railroad cars have communication with Baltimore several times a day, and steamboats ply on the Potomac and down the bay. Some portions of the following description are compiled from several authentic works.

A more beautiful site for a city could hardly be obtained. From a point where the Potomac, at a distance of two hundred and ninety-five miles from the ocean, and flowing from northwest to southeast, expands to the width of a mile, extended back an almost level plain, hemmed in by a series of gradually-sloping hills, terminating with the heights of Georgetown; the plain being nearly three miles in length from east to west, and varying from a quarter of a mile to two miles in breadth; bounded on the east by the eastern branch of the Potomac, where are now the navyyard and the congressional cemetery, and on the west by the Rock creek, which separates it from Georgetown. The small stream from the north, over which the railroad bridge now passes on entering the city, emptied into a bay or inlet of the Potomac about four hundred feet wide, which jutted in from the west to within a quarter of a mile of the Capitol hill, and nearly divided the plain. Not far from the head of this, and south of the Capitol hill, a small stream took its rise in a large number of springs, and emptied into the river at a place now called Greenleaf's point, formed by the intersection of the eastern branch with the Potomac, and was known as Jones's creek. There is a stream above Georgetown, which has always been called Goose creek; but from a certificate of a survey now preserved in the mayor's office at Washington, dated 1663, it appears that the inlet from the Potomac was then known by the name of Tiber, and probably the stream from the north emptying into it bore the same name; so that Moore did injustice to the history of the place, and confounded streams, when he wrote the well-known line—

"And what was Goose creek once is Tiber now."

By the same survey it appears that the land comprising the Capitol hill was called "Rome," or "Room," two names which seem to have foreshadowed the

Washington.

destiny of the place. It is thought that they probably originated in the fact that the name of the owner of the estate was *Pope*, and in selecting a name for his plantation, he formed the title of "Pope of Rome."

It is said that Washington's attention had been called to the advantages which this place presented for a city, as long previous as when he had been a youthful surveyor of the country round. His judgment was confirmed by the fact that two towns were afterward planned on the spot, and the first maps of the city represent it as laid out over the plains of Hamburgh and Carrollsville.

The canoe, or pirogue, in which General Washington and a party of friends first made the survey of the Potomac, was hollowed out of a large poplar-tree on the estate of Col. Johnson, of Frederick county, Maryland. This humble bark was placed upon a wagon, hauled to the margin of the Monocasy river, launched into the stream, and there received its honored freight. The general was accompanied by Governor Johnson, one of the first commissioners for the location of the city of Washington, and several other gentlemen. At nightfall, it was usual for the party to land and seek quarters of some of the planters, or farmers, who lived near the banks of the river, in all the pride and comfort of old-fashioned kindliness and hospitality. Putting up for a night at a respectable farmer's, the general and the two Johnsons were shown into a room having but two beds. "Come, gentlemen!" said Washington, "who will be my bedfellow?" Both declined. Col. Johnson often afterward declared, that, greatly as he should have felt honored by such intimacy, the awe and reverence with which the chief had inspired him, even in their daily and unreserved intercourse, would have made the liberty seem little short of profanation.

While the party were exploring in the vicinity of Harper's ferry, news arrived of the burning at the stake of Colonel Crawford, by the Indians, at Sandusky. Washington became excited to tears at hearing the recital, for Crawford had been one of the companions of his early life, and had often been his rival in athletic exercises. The unfortunate man was brave as a lion, and had served with great distinction in the war of the revolution. Tears soon gave way to indignation, and Washington, pointing to a lofty rock which juts over the stream at its remarkable passage through the mountain, exclaimed, with a voice tremulous from feeling: "By Heaven, were I the sole judge of these Indians, it would be slight retaliation to hurl every spectator of his death from that height into the abyss."

The first corner-stone in the district of Columbia was laid at Jones's point, near Alexandria, April 15, 1791, with the imposing masonic ceremonies of the time, and a quaint address by the Rev. James Muir. By the retrocession of Alexandria, the stone is no longer within the limits of the district.

The first public communication on record in relation to arrangements for laying out this city is from the pen of General Washington, and bears date the 11th March, 1791; in a subsequent letter of the 30th April, he calls it the Federal city. Four months later, in a letter by the original commissioners—Messrs Johnson, Stuart, and Carroll—dated Georgetown, 9th September, 1791, addressed to the architect, Major L'Enfant, he is instructed to entitle the district on his maps the "Territory of Columbia," and the city, the "City of Washington."

On the 18th September, 1793, the southeast corner-stone of the north wing of the capitol was laid by General Washington. The Philadelphia papers of the day were at that time discontinued from the panic of the yellow-fever, so we have no account of the celebration. A speech was delivered, however, by Washington.

The architect, Major L'Enfant, went on to lay out the streets, in the first place, by setting out right angles, after the fashion of Philadelphia, and then intersecting them by those enormous avenues which were contrived to show the public buildings, the president's house, and the capitol, from all quarters; and hence the perplexing dust and triangles of Washington.

It was generally remarked of *L'Enfant* that he was not only a child in *name*, but in education; as, from the names he gave the streets, he appeared to know little else than A, B, C, and one, two, three. It appears, however, by a letter of the commissioners, that they gave these names to the streets at the same time with that to the city; for convenience a good arrangement, since the streets could more easily be found by a stranger under such designations.

The mall upon which the Smithsonian institute and its gardens have been located, was originally designed as the leading avenue from the capitol to the president's house, terminating by a bridge across the river, and meeting a monument which was to have been erected to Washington—an equestrian statue, with a baton in the right hand of the hero pointing to heaven.

Washington—who took so strong an interest in the construction of the capitol as to solicit a loan himself, in a letter to the governor of Maryland—did not live to witness its completion. He died 14th February, 1799. In November, 1800, congress met there for the first time.

At present the attractions of the capital are on the increase. The private architecture is improving; the growth of the city is advancing with the enlargement of the nation; the museums, containing the collections of the exploring expedition, are open; the patent office, with its models of inventions, inviting the attention, every year adding to the associations of the capital; and the bright schemes of scholars and men of science hanging upon the prospects of the Smithsonian institute, its library and its gardens—these confirm the hopes of Washington, and justify the name borrowed from that illustrious founder of the city.

The *Capitol* presents specimens of various styles of architecture. On entering the south wing, several columns are seen, where carvings of Indian-cornstalks are substituted for flutings and filletings; while the capitals are made of the ears of corn half stripped, and disposed so as in some degree to resemble the Corinthian or composite order.

The representatives' chamber is a fine semicircular apartment, with columns of a dark-bluish siliceous pudding-stone, hard and highly polished. It is lighted from above. The gallery is open during the debates, as well as the senate-chamber, which is a much smaller apartment.

The library of congress is in another part of the building; and the great hall contains seven national pictures (each of them twelve feet by eighteen): the Declaration of Independence, Surrender of Burgoyne at Saratoga, Surrender of Cornwallis at Yorktown, and Washington resigning his Commission, painted for government by Colonel Trumbull; Baptism of Pocahontas, by Chapman; Embarkation of the Pilgrims, by Weir; and the Landing of Columbus, by Vanderlyn.

A fine view is enjoyed from the top of the capitol. You look along Pennsylvania avenue westward to the president's house, with Georgetown and the Potomac beyond; the general postoffice, &c., on the right; the navyyard toward the southeast; Greenleaf's point nearly south; and southwest the bridge over the Potomac, with the road to Alexandria and Mount Vernon. The canal begins south of the president's house, and terminates at the east branch.

The capitol presents a noble appearance; its height, the ascending terraces, the monument and its fountain, the grand balustrade of freestone which protects the offices below, and the distinct object which it forms, standing alone on its lofty site, combine to make up the impression of grandeur, in which its architectural defects are lost or forgotten.

The waste lands which lie at the foot of Capitol hill are appropriated for a future botanical garden.

There are many very favorable points of view for the capitol, standing, as it does, higher than the general level of the country. There are views from the distant eminences, which are particularly fine, in which the broad bosom of the Potomac forms the background. The effect of the building is also remarkably imposing when the snow is on the ground, and the whole structure, rising from a field of snow, with its dazzling whiteness, looks like some admirable

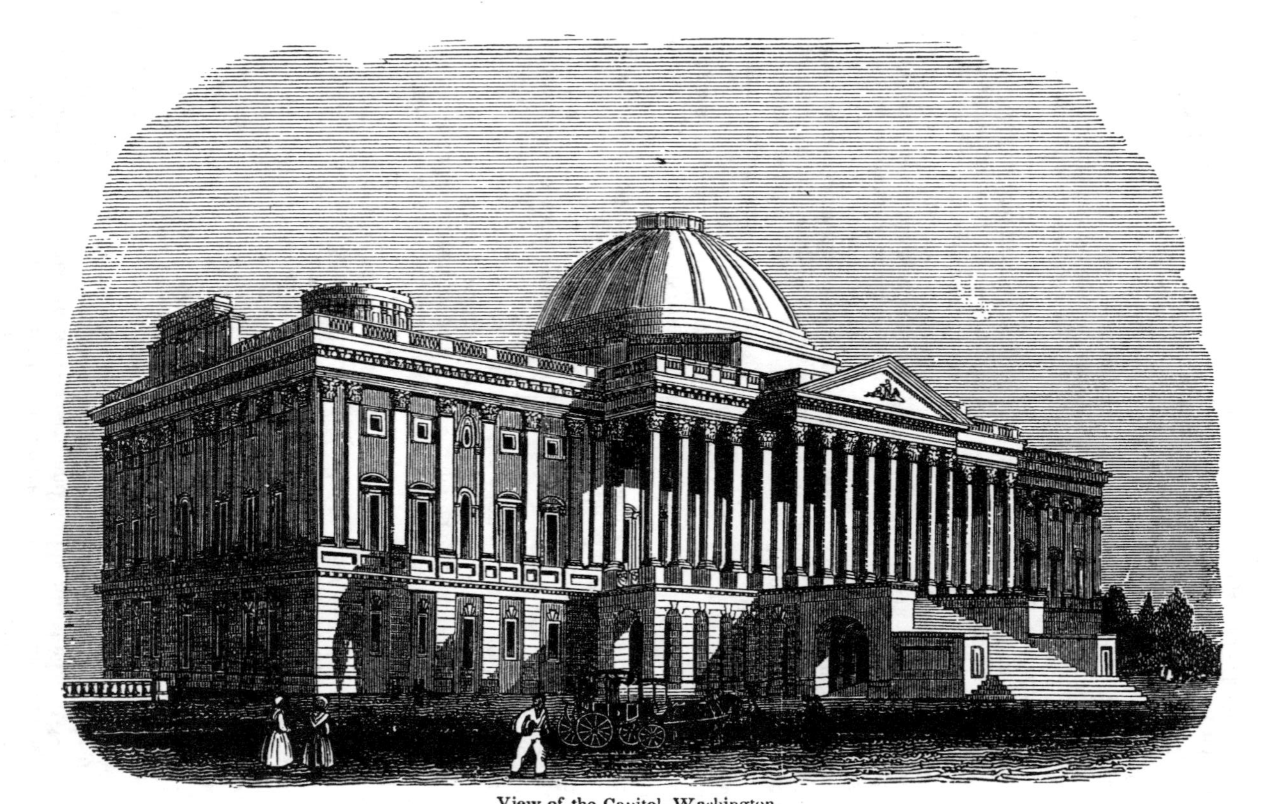

View of the Capitol, Washington.

creation of the frost. All architecture, however, is very much improved by the presence of a multitude of people, and the capitol looks its best on the day of inauguration. The following description was written after viewing that ceremony:—

"The sun shone out of heaven without a cloud on the inaugural morning. The air was cold but clear, and the broad avenues of Washington, for once, seemed not too large for the thronging population—the crowds who had been pouring in from every direction for several days before, and ransacking the town for but a shelter from the night... The sun shone alike on the friends and opponents of the new administration; and, as far as one might observe in a walk to the capitol, all were made cheerful alike by its brightness... In a whole day, passed in a crowd composed of all classes and parties, I heard no remark that the president would have been unwilling to hear.

"I was at the capitol a half-hour before the procession arrived, and had leisure to study a scene for which I was unprepared. The noble staircase of the east front of the building leaps over three arches, under one of which carriages pass to the basement door; and as you approach from the gate, the eye cuts the ascent at right angles, and the sky, broken by a small spire at a short distance, is visible beneath. Broad stairs occur at equal distances, with corresponding projections, and from the upper platform rise the outer columns of the portico, with ranges of columns three deep extending back to the pilasters. I had often admired this front, with its many graceful columns and its superb flight of stairs, as one of the finest things I had seen in the world. The assembled crowd on the steps and at the base of the capitol, heightened inconceivably the grandeur of the design. They were piled up like the people on the temples of Babylon, in one of Martin's sublime pictures. Boys climbed about the bases of the columns; single figures stood on the posts of the surrounding railings in the boldest relief against the sky; and the whole scene was exactly what Paul Veronese would have delighted to draw.

"I was in the crowd thronging the opposite side of the court, and lost sight of the principal actors in this imposing drama till they returned from the senate-chamber. A temporary platform had been laid and railed in on the broad stair which supports the portico, and all preparation made for one of the most important and most meaning and solemn ceremonies on earth. . . . In comparing the impressive simplicity of this consummation of the wishes of a mighty people, with the ceremonial and hollow show which embarrasses a corresponding event in other lands, it was impossible not to feel that the moral sublime was here—that a transaction so important, and of such extended and weighty import, could borrow nothing from drapery or decoration.

"The crowd of diplomatists and senators in the rear of the columns made way; and the ex-president, with the new president, advanced with their heads uncovered; the former bowed to the people, and, still uncovered in the cold air, took his seat beneath the portico. The new president then read his address to the people.

"When the address was closed, the chief-justice advanced and administered the oath. As the book touched the lips of the new president, there arose a general shout, an expression of feeling common enough in other countries, but drawn with difficulty from an American assemblage. The friends of the president then closed around him, the ex-president and others gave him the hand of congratulation, and the ceremony was over."

The President's House.—The residence of the chief-magistrate of the United States resembles the country-seat of an English nobleman, in its architecture and size; but it is to be regretted that the parallel ceases when we come to the grounds. By itself it is a commodious and creditable building, serving its purpose without too much state for a republican country, yet likely, as long as the country exists without primogeniture and rank, to be sufficiently su-

President's House, Washington.

perior to all other dwelling-houses to mark it as the residence of the nation's ruler.

The president's house stands near the centre of an area of some twenty acres, occupying a very advantageous elevation, open to the view of the Potomac, and about forty-four feet above high water, and possessing from its balcony one of the loveliest prospects in our country—the junction of the two branches of the Potomac which border the district, and the swelling and varied shores beyond of the states of Maryland and Virginia. The building is one hundred and seventy feet front and eighty-six deep, and is built of white freestone, with Ionic pilasters, comprehending two lofty stories, with a stone balustrade. The north front is ornamented with a portico, sustained by four Ionic columns, with three columns of projection—the outer intercolumniation affording a shelter for carriages to drive under. The garden-front on the river is varied by what is called a rusticated basement-story, in the Ionic style, and by a semicircular projecting colonnade of six columns, with two spacious and airy flights of steps leading to a balustrade on the level of the principal story.

The interior of the president's house is well disposed, and possesses one superb reception-room, and two oval drawing-rooms (one in each story), of very beautiful proportions. The other rooms are not remarkable; and there is an inequality in the furniture of the whole house (owing to the unwillingness and piecemeal manner with which congress votes any moneys for its decoration), which destroys its effect as a comfortable dwelling. The oval rooms are carpeted with Gobelin tapestry, worked with the national emblems, and are altogether in a more consistent style than the other parts of the house.

The Patent-Office.—This building is a depository for the models of such inventions as are patented in the United States. The old patent-office was a few years ago burned down. The present is a handsome and extensive edifice, and well adapted to the purpose for which it is designed. The contents display in an eminent degree the inventive and ingenious character of our countrymen. There are machines here for almost every purpose—ploughs, harrows, rakes, saws, water-wheels, coffee-mills, corn-snellers, stump-removers, and a multitude of other things, all arranged according to their kinds. In one part are agricultural implements; in another are machines for the manufacture of cotton; in another, those for the manufacture of wool, &c. The number of these inventions amounts to many hundreds, and some of them display admirable skill and contrivance on the part of the inventors.

We make the following extracts from the report of the commissioner of patents:—

The amount received for patents, caveats, reissues, and additional improvements, recording assignments, &c., and for copies, during the year 1850, was $86,927.05. The expenditures for the year 1850, were as follows:—

For salaries - - - - -	$29,260.94
For contingent expenses -	13,430.19
For books for library - -	767.47
For temporary clerks - -	13,361.67
For agricul ural statistics -	3,859.35
For refunding money - -	258.00
For withdrawals - - -	18,013.33
For compensation of librarian	500.00
For pay of district judge -	100.00
For analysis of breadstuffs -	500.00
For restoring models - -	50.00
	$80,100.95

Leaving $6,826.10 to be carried to the credit of the patent fund. The amount remaining in the treasury to the credit of the patent fund on the first day of January, 1851, was $15,331.27. The patent fund, at the commencement of 1850, amounted to about $170,000. But during the year about $160,000 was appropriated by Congress for the purpose of additional wing to the patent office.

During the year 1850, the whole number of applications presented to the patent office was 2,193. Every application which is not finally disposed of upon the first examination, may be the subject of re-examination at any time thereafter; and a large proportion of the time of the examiners is taken up in such reëxaminations. The actual number of applications rejected is less than the number patented, as many of those patented were rejected upon their first examination, in consequence of the applicant failing to specify what was really his invention, and laying claim to what was neither new nor patentable. Such cases are not of unfrequent occurrence. It often happens that two or three rejections are recorded upon one application, each re-examination requiring new investigations and elaborate reasoning to meet the new claims and views of the applicant, and to sustain the decision of the office.

The subjects of applications for patents are comprised under twenty-two general classes, each of them embracing many subdivisions—in some cases more than twenty.

The inquiry is frequently made, How is it that applications for patents multiply so fast? Is there so much room left for improvement in this or that branch of art? Superficial observers are apt to be looking for consummation not only in individual branches of art, but in the whole range of human productions. They regard the wants of man as limitable, his mind as exhaustible, and, with an air of sagacity, will point to a time when the overgrown wings of genius will retard and finally check his career. A look at the past would mirror in its true light this distorted view of things; but even this is not necessary. A liberal survey of the present, a glance at the depths of mind, see "increase and multiply," stamped upon his intellectual as well as his physical nature. The multiplying products of intelligence are no hinderance to his onward movement; and those seemingly formidable accumulations of innovations offer no effective resistance to the wheels of invention. They are rather so many stepping-stones, over which genius is striding up the hill of perfection, whose summit is beyond the confines of time.

It appears that during the year 1844, the number of applications for patents suddenly increased nearly twenty-five per cent. above that of any former year, which, of course, required and produced a corresponding increase of exertion on the part of the examining corps.

It appears that the number of patents does not increase in proportion to the number of applications, but that the number of rejections increases in a much greater ratio; and that in 1844 there were more patents granted than in 1845; and this occurred under the same commissioner, and with the same examining corps. The causes which have produced this result still exist, and will probably continue to exert a steadily-increasing influence throughout the future operations of this office.

In every section of the country may be found worthy and ingenious men, whose energies are directed toward inventions and discoveries in the arts. Some of these are sufficiently informed of what has already been done, in the particular department to which their attention is directed, to avoid, in some good degree, the beaten track; but the number and variety of inventions already made are so great, that few can enter upon a career of invention with sufficient knowledge to avoid a succession of reinventions, which add nothing to the arts, and which it is the duty of this office to reject. Of course, the attention of the uniformed inventor is directed to discoveries of an elementary character. These are necessarily limited in their number, and the field has everywhere been preoccupied by thousands of every variety of mind; and whatever he may fix upon is already public property, or has been appropriated by some one who has preceded him. As invention is rapidly progressing in every part of the civilized world, each year will trench still further upon the only department open to uniformed inventors; and as their number is likely to increase rather than diminish, rejections must inevitably be multiplied; and the consequences, unfortunately, have often fallen, and must continue to fall, upon men whose industry, talents, and perseverance, deserve, and, if well directed, would be rewarded by distinguished success.

While the threshold is thus thronged

by the multitudes who are treading upon each other, the field beyond, to the eye of those who can explore it, is almost limitless. Every discovery which is made appears to shed light upon others hitherto enveloped in obscurity; each furnishes the key to a group, and the things to be discovered seem to multiply in proportion to those already discovered.

The first examination of an application is intended to be as thorough as the condition of the papers and models will admit. If the claim can not be allowed, the machine is carefully examined, to discover whether it comprehends any other feature or combination which would justify the grant of letters-patent. If anything patentable is discovered, the papers are returned to the applicant, with such suggestions as will assist him in mending them and properly modifying his claim; but if nothing patentable is discovered, the application is at once rejected, and the necessary references given; as it is deemed worse than useless to put the applicant to the trouble and expense of amending and perfecting his papers, when it is believed that no amendment could avoid a final rejection. But this office, from its reorganization, has been liberal in reconsidering rejected applications. The applicant is always permitted to amend his papers, and to present new or amended claims, which render it necessary again to examine the application as if it were new. If it is again rejected, this additional rejection is entered upon the record kept by the examiner, and is counted as a rejection. There are instances in every year's experience of cases being represented with different claims two or three times, each change raising questions entirely new, and requiring the same examinations and consideration as would be required by so many distinct applications. All experience of the examining corps has shown the importance of making these re-examinations, as it sometimes occurs that, owing to the imperfect manner in which the papers have been prepared, a patentable feature of the machine has escaped the notice of the examiner.

A part of the applications of every year since 1839 are still pending, and liable to be called up at any moment, though they are in such condition that this office is compelled to await the action of the applicant.

The history of this office for several years, in addition to a great and steady increase of inventions, presents also the fact, always observable in the progress of the arts, that while some classes are receiving numerous and important additions, others appear to receive little or no attention; or, if efforts are made toward their improvement, they fail of success. But succeeding years produce an entire revolution; and those branches whose rapidity of progress had astonished the world, in their turn become torpid, and improvements burst forth with unlooked-for brilliancy from the dust and ashes which have accumulated upon a long-neglected department of the arts. The main current, however, is always onward, although, at some points, it appears to stagnate or retrograde. But let not the inventor be deceived or discouraged; these are but the eddies. Let him persevere; the eddy of to-day may be the torrent of to-morrow.

The commissioner, in his report for 1845, speaks of the existing law by which a subject of Great Britain is compelled to pay into the treasury the sum of five hundred dollars before his application can be examined, and the citizens and subjects of all foreign countries to pay three hundred dollars on their respective applications. He says:—

"These duties were designed to bear some proportion to the duties required of American citizens making applications for patents in other countries, and on that ground may, perhaps, be justified and defended.

"The effect of this provision is unquestionably to prevent the introduction into this country of many useful and valuable discoveries, which would otherwise be patented and introduced. Similar high duties have the effect to exclude American inventions from other countries. Thus all countries are injured by this system of taxing genius for the exertion of its powers, in order to obtain comparatively a very small and trifling amount of revenue.

"It affords no protection to the American inventor to keep out the discoveries of his foreign emulator (not rival) in the arts, by taxing the emanations of his genius with high duties, while the country would derive much benefit from their introduction."

History.—Washington is the only spot where it is practically seen, that, for national purposes, we are one people. The United States forts, arsenals, and navyyards are limited in their associations. At Washington we see a district set apart as the national centre; its inhabitants, in a spirit of patriotism, relinquishing the right of suffrage, to be free from the taint of party spirit, and its very vastness and unoccupied distances pointing to the future, and filling the mind with admiration of the hopes of its founders.

Before the establishment of the district of Columbia, congress occasionally met, according to the exigencies of the case, or the convenience of members, at Philadelphia, Baltimore, Lancaster, Yorktown, Princeton, Annapolis, Trenton, and New York. The different states, in the meantime, coveted the honor of the national city. New York offered the town of Kingston; Rhode Island, Newport; Maryland, Annapolis; and Virginia, Williamsburg.

On the 21st October, 1783, congress, insulted at Philadelphia by a band of mutineers, whom the state authorities were unable to quell, adjourned to the halls of the college at Princeton—a circumstance which doubtless led to the agitation of the question of a permanent seat of government, which was taken up at this time, and continued to be discussed till the formation of the constitution. A resolution of Mr. Gerry, 7th October, 1783, was adopted, that a district be chosen on the banks of the Delaware or the Potomac, near Georgetown, which underwent various modifications (one of which was that both sites be selected), till it was repealed in the following year. On the 30th of October, 1784, the subject was again taken up at Trenton, and commissioners appointed with powers to lay out a district on the Delaware within eight miles above or below the falls, make the necessary purchases, erect public buildings, reserve exclusive jurisdiction, &c. The question as to place was revived in congress in 1789–'90, with the view of securing a central position. A site on the Susquehanna was talked of, and finally the present district determined on, which then went by the name of Connogocheague. New York was not central enough; Philadelphia and Germantown had their supporters, as well as Havre de Grace, a place called Wright's Ferry on the Susquehanna, and Baltimore. The South Carolinians objected to Philadelphia, that the quakers would be for ever dogging the members with schemes of emancipation. Others laughed at the idea of palaces in the wood.

The friends of the new site numbered the names of Washington, Madison, Lee, and Carroll, and their choice was governed by these considerations. It was not desirable that the political capital should be in a commercial metropolis. It was necessary, for the independence of the government and its proper security, that its jurisdiction should be exclusive—that its officers should not be under the influence of the citizens: hence the elective franchise was to be given up, which no large city would yield. Party feeling, which then ran high, was to be avoided; the natural influence of wealth on the spot was feared, and the examples of London and Westminster in the importance of their six members in parliament was quoted. It was desirable that the simplicity of the members of government, in their style of living, should not be contrasted with the luxury of a great city, or be compelled to submit to its costlier charges. Moreover, large quantities of land were wanted, which must be purchased at great expense where land was already dear. Looking to the future, it was thought expedient to provide for all possible wants more amply than could, under any circumstances, be effected in a city already built.

For a central situation, it was seen

that the centres of territory, wealth, and population, could not be united. In determining upon the centre of the line of seacoast, the occupants of the western territory only asked that it should be as far west as the convenience of maritime commerce would allow. The spot chosen admitted of a navyyard, and could be connected by canal with waters which finally rose to the sources of the Ohio. The act finally passed on the 16th of July, 1790.

Among the most important public buildings in Washington are the "Departments," as they are commonly called, or edifices containing the offices of the several secretaries of state, war, the navy, and the treasury. These are large and spacious, and contain apartments devoted to the officers, the numerous clerks, the records, &c. They stand at the distance of two hundred yards from the president's house—two on the east, and two on the west.

The *Treasury Building* has been recently re-erected, the former one having been accidentally burned a few years ago. It makes a very striking appearance, presenting a Grecian front, with a splendid portico four hundred and fifty-seven feet in length.

The other three buildings are of brick, and each one hundred and sixty feet in length, fifty-five in breadth, and two stories high. A broad passage runs through the middle, with numerous apartments on each side; and in the centre is the staircase, which is of large dimensions. The porticoes are ornamented with six Ionic columns. The grounds surrounding the buildings are planted with trees and shrubbery.

Every part of these edifices bears indications of the laborious business which is carried on. The clerks are generally men of intelligence, and many of them of education, as most of the offices require ability, system, and industry. Such is the importance of that acquaintance with many of the offices, which is to be acquired only by experience, that many of them have long been retained by individuals, amid the frequent changes made by the fluctuations of opinions in the country.

The foresight of the congress which selected Washington for the seat of government, has been in many points justified by the results. If there is much to lament in the looseness of manners which, to a considerable extent, prevails in the city during the crowded season of the session, it is easy to see, that were the members and other attendants at the capital exposed to the influences of a large city, like New York or Philadelphia, there would be far more evil to regret in the deterioration of the characters of individuals; and if room is now found for injurious intrigues, hurtful to the public interest, such evils would be multiplied amid a larger population. The means of dissipation and the temptations of luxury and vice are now only such as are prepared or imported for the occasion, and are necessarily fewer and more feeble than those permanently established on a far broader scale in a metropolis. The small size of the city, and the sparseness of the neighboring population, still are, and long must be, too insignificant to overawe congress in their deliberations; and there is at present no local interest strong enough to exercise any powerful influence on their decisions.

The Congressional Burying-Ground.—The cemetery appropriated to the interment of deceased members of congress, situated a mile east of the capitol, is laid out with taste, adorned with trees and shrubbery, and contains a number of appropriate monuments. The design of a new city cemetery has been formed. It is anticipated that the price of the lots will be so low as to permit every family to own one, and the distance not being so far as to prevent those visiting it that do not own carriages. Indeed, it was intended to be so located as to serve the interests of *all*—so that he who walks through necessity, as well as he who rides, may find it an agreeable and convenient place of resort—not too far for the poor, nor too near for the rich. In what direction the city will enlarge itself, it is now impossible to say. If the most remote dell was taken for the purpose, no one can tell how public it might become in a few years.

The State Department, Washington.

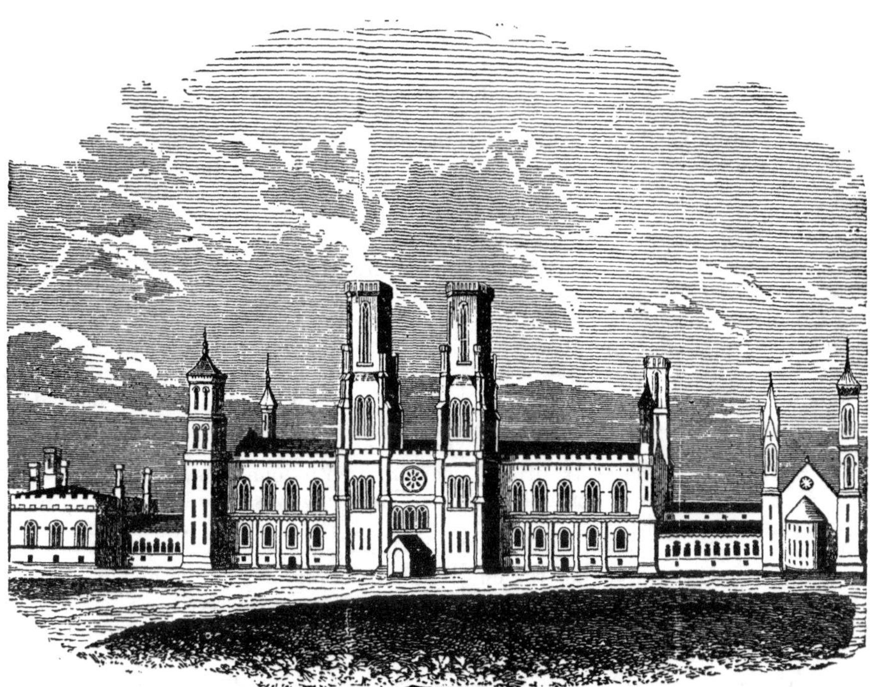

The Smithsonian Institution, at Washington.

The *Smithsonian Institution* has a noble endowment, and is devoted to the promotion of science in its various branches. The funds bequeathed for its foundation having lain for a number of years, accumulating in value, and congress having organized it in 1846, it has commenced operations with flattering prospects. A large edifice has been erected, valuable collections have been begun, and the services of active officers engaged; so that under the supervision of the government, and with abundant pecuniary means at its disposal, it will doubtless afford important aid to the sciences in time to come.

Columbian College was incorporated in the year 1821. The buildings occupy an elevation north of the president's house, and a medical department is attached to the institution. The libraries contain upward of four thousand volumes.

The *Navyyard* contains twenty-seven acres of ground, three quarters of a mile southeast of the capitol, with ranges of stores, shops, dwellings for officers, barracks, the armory, and two large ship-houses, in which ships-of-war of different classes are constructed.

Capture of Washington by the British in 1814.—The better to provide for the defence of Washington and the neighboring country, so much threatened by the enemy's fleet, a new military district was formed in the summer of 1814, making the tenth district in number, and embracing Maryland, the district of Columbia, and a part of Virginia. The president, on the 4th of July, 1814, made a requisition on the governors of those states for ninety-three thousand militia, fifteen thousand of whom were to be raised within the limits of the new military district. One thousand regular troops were added, and the whole force placed under the command of General Winder.

But the news was received, about a fortnight after the requisition had been made, that the British had landed at Benedict. At that time only three thousand men had been collected, and these were, of course, of the most raw and undisciplined description of troops. The enemy's fleet proceeded to invade the shores of the Chesapeake in three divisions. Admiral Cochrane proceeded up the Patuxent; General Gordon sailed up the Potomac against Alexandria; and General Ross, landing at Benedict, marched for Washington, along the right bank of the Patuxent, a distance of twenty-seven miles, intending to assist Admiral Cochrane, on his way, in destroying Commodore Barney's flotilla.

On the 22d of August they appeared in sight of Barney, who immediately destroyed his vessels, and fell back to join General Winder. The president of the United States, General Armstrong, secretary of war, and several other heads of departments, visited the camp at Marlborough, and decided on retreating toward the capital. Expecting the enemy to advance to the east branch of the Potomac, preparations were made for its defence; but it was discovered on the 24th that they were approaching Bladensburg. General Stansbury with two thousand two hundred Baltimore militia, who was on his way to the camp, was ordered back to that point, and was soon joined by General Winder and the main body. The president and heads of departments were present when the battle commenced, but they soon left the field, to secure the important documents in their offices, and hastened to Washington.

The enemy met a spirited resistance, and had indeed a sharp contest to maintain, while crossing the bridge, where their column was swept by the cannon of Commodore Barney from the redoubts, and while pressing up the successive swells crossed by the road. The thick forest on both sides was penetrated with difficulty, even in face of the small force opposed to them. Before long, however, the militia broke and fled in disorder; Com. Barney was wounded and made prisoner, and the day was decided.

The British army lost no time in advancing to Washington, where they met with no serious opposition; and there they set fire to the capitol and other public buildings, mutilated some of the ornaments of the city, and after a short stay, took up their march back to their ships.

The enemy evacuated Washington on the evening of August 25th, and retired to their fleet, having lost two hundred and forty-nine, killed, at Bladensburg, and suffered a total loss, as is said, of four hundred killed and wounded, and about five hundred prisoners and deserters.

Anecdotes of General Washington.—The following may be here introduced. First, an account of the appointment of Washington to the supreme command of the continental army, June 18, 1775—from a private journal, narrating a conversation with John Adams, senior:—

"The army was assembled at Cambridge, Massachusetts, under General Ward, and congress was sitting at Philadelphia. Every day new applications in behalf of the army arrived. The country were urgent that congress should legalize the raising of the army; as they had what must be considered, and was in law considered, only a mob—a band of armed rebels. The country was placed in circumstances of peculiar difficulty and danger. The struggle had begun, and yet everything was without order. The great trial now seemed to be in this question, Who shall be the commander-in-chief? It was exceedingly important, and was felt to be the hinge on which the contest might turn for or against us. The southern and the middle states, warm and rapid in their zeal, were for the most part jealous of New England, because they felt that the real physical force was there. What then was to be done? All New England adored General Ward: he had been in the French war, and went out laden with laurels. He was a scholar and a statesman. Every qualification seemed to cluster in him; and it was confidently believed that the army could not receive any appointment over him. What then was to be done? Difficulties thickened at every step. The struggle was to be long and bloody. Without union, all was lost. The country, and the whole country, must come in. One pulsation must beat through all hearts. The cause was one, and the army must be one. The members had talked, debated, considered, and guessed, and yet the decisive step had not been taken. At length Mr. Adams came to his conclusion. The means of resolving it were somewhat singular, and nearly as follows: he was walking one morning before Congress hall, apparently in deep thought, when his cousin Samuel Adams came up to him and said:—

"'What is the topic with you this morning?'

"'Oh, the army, the army,' he replied. 'I'm determined to go into the hall, this morning, and enter on a full detail of the state of the colonies, in order to show an absolute need of taking some decisive steps. My whole aim will be, to induce congress to appoint a day for adopting the army as the legal army of these united colonies of North America, and then to hint at my election of a commander-in-chief.'

"'Well,' said Samuel Adams, 'I like that, cousin John; but on whom have you fixed as that commander?'

"'I will tell you—George Washington, of Virginia, a member of this house.'

"'Oh,' replied Samuel Adams, quickly, 'that will never do—never.'

"'It must do—it *shall* do,' said John, 'and for these reasons: the southern and middle states are both to enter heartily in the cause, and their arguments are potent: they say that New England holds the physical power in her hands, and they fear the result. A New England army, a New England commander, with New England perseverance, all united, appal them. For this cause they hang back. Now, the only course is to allay their fears, and give them nothing to complain of; and this can be done in no other way but by appointing a southern chief over this force, and then all rush to the standard. The policy will blend us in one mass, and that mass will be resistless.'

"At this Samuel Adams seemed to be greatly moved. They talked over the preliminary circumstances, and John asked his cousin to second the motion. Mr. Adams went in, took the floor, and put forth all his strength in the delineations he had prepared, all aiming at the adoption of the army. He was ready to own the army, appoint a commander, vote supplies, and proceed to business. After his speech had been finished, some objected, and some feared. His warmth increased with the occasion, and to all these doubts and hesitations he replied thus:—

"'Gentlemen, if this Congress will not adopt this army before ten moons have set, New England will adopt it, and she will undertake the struggle alone—yes, with a strong arm and a clean conscience, she will front the foe single-handed.'

"This had the desired effect. They saw New England was neither playing nor to be played with, and they agreed to appoint a day. A day was fixed: it came: Mr. Adams went in, took the floor, urged the measure, and after some debate it passed.

"The next thing was to get a commander for this army, with supplies, &c. All looked to Mr. Adams on the occasion, and he was ready. He then took the floor, and went into a minute delineation of the character of General Ward, bestowing on him the encomiums which then belonged to no one else. At the end of the eulogy, he said: 'But this is not the man I have chosen.' He then went into the delineation of the character of a commander-in-chief, such as was required by the peculiar situation of the colonies at that juncture. And after he had presented the qualifications in his strongest language, and given the reasons for the nomination he was about to make, he said:—

"'Gentlemen, I know these qualifications are high, but we all know they are needful, at this crisis, in this chief. Does any one say they are not to be obtained in this country? In reply, I have to say they are; they reside in one of our own body, and he is the person whom I now nominate—GEORGE WASHINGTON, OF VIRGINIA.'

"Washington, who sat on Mr. Adams' right hand, was looking him intently in the face, to watch the name he was about to announce, and, not expecting it would be his, sprang from his seat the minute he heard it, and rushed into an adjoining room. Mr. Adams had asked his cousin Samuel to ask for an adjournment as soon as the nomination was made, in order to give the members time to deliberate—and the result is before the world.

"I asked Mr. Adams, among other questions, the following:—

"'Did you ever doubt of the success of the conflict?'

"'No, no,' said he, 'not for a moment. I expected to be hung and quartered, if I was caught; but no matter for that—my country would be free; I knew George the Third could not forge chains long enough and strong enough to reach around these United States.'"

In the early days of the republic, it was customary for the president to meet the two houses of congress, on their assembling, and make them a speech, instead of sending in a formal, carefully-written message as now. Various reasons conspired to bring about the change—reasons of convenience which will occur on reflection to every mind, and which it is needless now to specify. We allude to the matter as necessary to a better understanding of the extract below. This extract is taken from a long and very interesting communication in the National Intelligencer, the anniversary of Washington's birthday. The writer describes Washington as he saw him at the opening of congress in Philadelphia.

"I stood on a stone platform, before the door of the hall, elevated by a few steps from the pavement, when the carriage of the president drew up. It was white, or rather of a light cream-color, painted on the panels with beautiful groups, by Cipriani, representing the four seasons. The horses, according to my recollection, were white, in unison with the carriage. As he alighted, and, ascending the steps, paused upon the platform, looking over his shoulder, in an attitude that would have furnished an admirable subject for the pencil, he was preceded by two gentlemen bearing long white wands, who kept back the crowd that pressed on every side to get a nearer view. At that moment I stood so near I might have touched his clothes; but I should as soon have thought of touching an electric battery. I was penetrated with a veneration, amounting to the deepest awe. Nor was this the feeling of a schoolboy only; it pervaded, I believe, every human being that approached Washington; and I have been told, that, even in his social and convivial hours, this feeling in those who were honored to share them, never suffered intermission. I saw him a hundred times afterward, but never with any other than that same feeling.

"The Almighty, who raised up for our hour of need a man so peculiarly prepared for its whole dread responsibility, seems to have put an impress of sacredness upon his own instrument. The first sight of the man struck the heart with involuntary homage, and prepared everything around him to obey. When he 'addressed himself to speak,' there was an unconscious suspension of the breath, while every eye was raised in expectation. At the time I speak of, he stood in profound silence, and had that statue-like air which mental greatness alone can bestow. As he turned to enter the building, and was ascending the staircase leading to the congressional hall, I glided in, unperceived, almost under cover of the skirts of his dress, and entered instantly after him into the lobby of the house, which was of course in session to receive him. On either hand, from the entrance, stood a large cast-iron stove; and, resolved to secure the unhoped-for privilege I had so unexpectedly obtained, I clambered, boy-like, on this stove—fortunately then not much heated—and, from that favorable elevation, enjoyed for the first time (what I have since so many thousands of times witnessed with comparative indifference) an uninterrupted view of the American congress in full session, every member in his place. Shall I be pardoned for saying its aspect was very different from what we now witness? There was an air of decorum, of composure, of reflection, of gentlemanly and polished dignity, which has fled, or lingers with here and there a 'relic of the olden time.'

"The house seemed then as composed as the senate now is, when an impressive speech is in the act of delivery. On Washington's entrance the most profound and death-like stillness prevailed. House, lobbies, gallery, all were wrapped in the deepest attention; and the souls of that entire assemblage seemed pouring from their eyes on the noble figure which deliberately, and with an unaffected but surpassing majesty, advanced upon the broad aisle of the hall between ranks of standing senators and members, and slowly ascended the steps leading to the speaker's chair. I well remember, standing at the head of the senate, the tall, square, somewhat gaunt form of Mr. Jefferson—conspicuous from his scarlet waistcoat, bright blue coat, with broad bright buttons, as well as by his quick and penetrating air, and high-boned Scottish cast of features. There, too, stood General Knox—then secretary of war—in all the sleek rotundity of his low stature, with a bold and florid face, open, firm, and manly in its expression. But I recollect that my boyish eye was caught by the appearance of De Yrujo, the Spanish ambassador. He stood in the rear of the chair, a little on one side, covered with a splendid diplomatic dress, decorated with orders, and carrying under his arm an immense *chapeau bras*, edged with white ostrich feathers. He was a man totally different in his air and manner from all around him, and the very antipode especially of the MAN on whom all eyes but his seemed fixed as by a spell. I saw many other very striking figures grouped about and behind the speaker's chair, but I did not know their names, and had no one to ask; besides, I dared not open my lips.

"The president, having seated himself, remained in silence, serenely contemplating the legislature before him, whose members now resumed their seats, waiting for the speech. No house of worship, in the most solemn pauses of devotion, was ever more profoundly still than was that large and crowded chamber.

"Washington was dressed precisely as Stuart has painted him in Lord Lansdown's full-length portrait—in a full suit of the richest black velvet, with diamond knee-buckles, and square silver buckles set upon shoes japanned with the most scrupulous neatness, black silk stockings, his shirt ruffled at the breast and wrist, a light dress sword, his hair profusely powdered, fully dressed, so as to project at the sides, and gathered behind in a silk bag ornamented with a large rose of black riband. He held his cocked hat, which had a large black cockade on one side of it, in his hand, as he advanced toward the chair, and, when seated, laid it on the table.

"At length, thrusting his hand within the side of his coat, he drew forth a roll of manuscript, which he opened, and, rising, held it in his hand, while, in a rich, deep, full, sonorous voice, he read his opening address to congress. His enunciation was deliberate, justly emphasized, very distinct, and accompanied with an air of deep solemnity, as being the utterance of a mind profoundly impressed with the dignity of the act in which it was occupied, conscious of the whole responsibility of its position and action, but not oppressed by it. There was ever about the man something which impressed the observer with a conviction, that he was exactly and fully equal with what he had to do. He was never hurried, never negligent; but seemed ever prepared for the occasion, be it what it might. If I could express his character in one word, it would be appropriateness. In his study, in his parlor, at a levée, before congress, at the head of the army, he seemed to be just what the situation required him to be. He possessed, in a degree never equalled by any human being I ever saw, the strongest and most ever-present sense of propriety. It never forsook him, and deeply and involuntarily impressed itself upon every beholder.

"His address was of moderate length; the topics I have, of course, forgotten; indeed, I was not of an age to appreciate them; but the air, the manner, the tone, have never left my mental vision, and even now seem to vibrate on my ear.

"A scene like this, once beheld, though in earliest youth, is never to be forgotten. It must be now fifty years ago;

but I could this moment sit down and sketch the chamber, the assembly, and *the* Man.

"Having closed the reading, he laid down the scroll, and, after a brief pause, retired as he had entered; when the manuscript was handed, for a second reading, to Mr. Beckley, then clerk of the house, whose gentlemanly manner, clear and silver voice, and sharp articulation, I shall ever associate with the scene.

"When shall we again behold such a congress and such a president?"

The following beautiful eulogy on Washington, by Lord Brougham, may with propriety be introduced in this place:—

"With none of that brilliant genius which dazzles ordinary minds; with not even any remarkable quickness of apprehension; with knowledge less than almost all persons in the middle ranks, and many well educated of the humbler classes, possess—this eminent person is presented to our observation clothed in attributes as modest, as unpretending, as little calculated to strike or to astonish, as if he had passed unknown through some secluded region of private life. But he had a judgment sure and sound; a steadiness of mind which never suffered any passion, or even any feeling to ruffle its calm; a strength of understanding which worked rather than forced its way through obstacles, removing or avoiding rather than overleaping them. His courage, whether in battle or in council, was as perfect as might be expected from this pure and steady temper of soul. A perfectly just man, with a thoroughly firm resolution never to be misled by others, any more than by others overawed; never to be seduced or betrayed, or hurried away by his own weakness or self-delusions, any more than by other men's arts; nor even to be disheartened by the most complicated difficulties, any more than spoiled on the giddy heights of fortune—such was this great man: whether we regard him sustaining alone the whole weight of campaigns, all but desperate, or gloriously terminating a just warfare by his resources and his courage; presiding over the jarring elements of his political council, alike deaf to the storms of all extremes; or directing the formation of a new government for a great people, the first time that so vast an experiment had ever been tried by man; or finally retiring from the supreme power to which his virtues had raised him over the nation he had created, and whose destinies he had guided as long as his aid was required—retiring with the veneration of all parties, of all nations, of all mankind, in order that the rights of man might be conserved, and that his example never might be appealed to by vulgar tyrants. This is the consummate glory of the great American—a triumphant warrior where the most successful had a right to despair; a successful ruler in all the difficulties of a course wholly untried; but a warrior whose sword only left its sheath when the first law of our nature commanded it to be drawn; and a ruler who, having tasted of supreme power, gently and unostentatiously desired that the cup might pass from him, nor would suffer more to wet his lips than the most solemn and sacred duty to his country and his God required!

"To his latest breath did this great patriot maintain the noble character of a captain the patron of peace, and a statesman the friend of justice. Dying, he bequeathed to his heirs the sword which he had worn in the war of liberty, charging them 'never to take it from the scabbard but in self defence, or in defence of their country and her freedom; and commanding them, that when it should thus be drawn, they should never sheath it nor ever give it up, but prefer falling with it in their hands to the relinquishment thereof'—words, the simple eloquence and majesty of which are not surpassed in the oratory of Athens and Rome.

"It will be the duty of the historian and sage in all ages to omit no occasion of commemorating this illustrious man; and until time shall be no more, will a test of the progress which our race has made in wisdom and in virtue, be derived from the veneration paid to the immortal name of Washington!"

Character of Debates in Congress.—The following is from a letter by a late English traveller:—

"I have frequently visited the halls of the national legislature, since my arrival here, for the purpose of becoming acquainted with the operations of the government, and of listening to the eloquence which is sometimes to be heard within them. It strikes me that there is a considerable difference between the eloquence of the British parliament and that of the American congress. In the latter, they only are distinguished and have influence who handle the subject under discussion with ability—grasp it comprehensively—are familiar with all its bearings—bring to it a mind conversant with all its details, and cast upon it a concentrated blaze of light. In parliament, such a speaker would not be regarded as the most effective, or carry his point so easily, as one who avoids the real merits of the question, plays upon the outskirts of the subject, retorts with brilliancy, and detects and exposes the inconsistencies of his opponent. In congress, however, on all questions in which party considerations are involved, no speaker, whatever may be the power of his intellect, the extent of his knowledge, the flow of his diction, or the beauty of his elocution, will carry a single vote beyond the limit of the party to which he belongs, or the principles or doctrines supported by those who elect him. Almost every member of both branches of the legislature either speaks, or is expected to speak; but wo him who shall have the hardy independence to yield to the influence of truth, or be swayed by the power of eloquence, and shall dare to throw aside the reins of party, and think and act for himself. He knows that his fate would be at once sealed, and his political career closed, perhaps for ever. If a member of the senate, the legislature of the state which elects him would, in all probability, recommend him to resign; and if a representative, his constituents would send another in his place. The eloquence which is employed, therefore, is not intended so much for this arena as for the people among whom proselytes are to be made, and who are either to be brought over to the principles which the orator maintains, or retained in the errors which he supports. An angel's tongue could not move the political partizan from the course his constituents expect him to pursue, and the contest between the orators on both sides in congress is a mere intellectual gladiatorial combat, without any other purpose there than to exhibit their respective powers of eloquence, and call together a numerous audience to listen to them. Members of the legal profession are very numerous in both houses of congress. Few of any other profession obtain the honor of a seat in that assembly, and of course most of them are speakers, if not what may be called orators. In congress, as well as in parliament, there are many very common men both as to education and talents—in so large an assembly, and chosen as they are, that must be expected. Even among the educated and talented, there will often be some decidedly superior to the rest. In the senate of the United States this is strikingly exemplified. I do not hazard much in saying, that there is not to be found at this time an equal body of men of higher intellectual powers, or greater general intelligence. I have become personally acquainted with most of them—witnessed their battles of mind, and listened to their eloquence; and I am satisfied that it would be impossible to surpass them."

The Prospects of Washington.—On the completion of the Chesapeake and Ohio canal, the cities of this district are destined to a rapid augmentation in population and wealth. Few persons but those who have resided here, know of the immense resources of this locality. The water-power of the Potomac and its branches is immense, sufficient to turn hundreds of mills, and the agricultural advantages in the immediate vicinity are superior, or at least equal to, those of any other section of the country. From the coal-mines in Cumberland and its vicinity alone, large fortunes can easily be realized. The supply of that useful, that necessary article to comfort and enterprise, in its quantity, has exceeded alike belief and calculation. The Union can be for a long time furnished with the sole products of these mines.

An investment of capital here by the enterprising citizens of the north, would be sure of rapid and abundant returns. It is incredible that the attention of the sagacious capitalists of New England and New York should not, ere this, have been directed to this quarter.

The anticipations of General Washington may yet be realized. It is said, that in the papers of that illustrious man has been found a calculation of what would be the value of the Mount Vernon estate, when Alexandria should assume that importance in the rank of commercial cities which her happy position intended.

The completion of the canal will be consummated in little more than a year. Its resumed continuation will, of itself, give a great impetus to all kinds of enterprise, and additional value to real estate, in the cities and country at and near its terminus; and it is confidently anticipated that the metropolis will yet attain to eminence among wealthy and populous cities.

The Cumberland Road.—This grand work, which long engaged the solicitude of congress, and was constructed and kept in repairs at great expense from the national treasury, has its commencement at Washington, and extends thence through Fredericksburg (Maryland), and through a considerable portion of Virginia. It is broad, ascends and descends the hills and mountains by easy grades, and, whenever the soil and circumstances are favorable, offers a smooth and hard surface. It has proved of great value to the regions through which it passes, and is a monument to the skill of American road-makers, as well as to the liberality of congress toward a portion of the country, although a later construction of the constitution has put an end to the appropriation of money to works of such a nature.

One of the finest views of Washington, Georgetown, and the surrounding land and water, is found at an elevated point of the Cumberland road, three or four miles west. From that spot the eye embraces a wide and beautiful scene: the broad, shining surface of the Potomac, from where it emerges from between the high and rocky banks which confine its channel above Georgetown, to where it begins to spread out in front of that city, and where, divided by the gently-sloping lawns of Mason's island, it extends on one side along the Virginia shore, and widening on the other, appears to wash the foundations of the president's house as it skirts along Washington, and, passing by the point where was erected the longest, if not the last, bridge that can ever be thrown across it, passes on to Greenleaf's point, where it receives the waters of its western branch. These together form a spacious bay, the northeastern extremity of which is occupied by the United States navyyard, while a canal crosses the low cape which separates them. Further down the Potomac is seen a part of its broad course, almost to the spot where it receives a sad and noble gloom from the overhanging precipices of Mount Vernon.

"Roll softly, Potomac! thou wearest away
The shore that he trod, and the dust where he lay."

At a spot on the shore of this stream, at the foot of the falls, a little above Georgetown, at a convenient landing-place for boats, tradition reports that General Braddock debarked with his troops, when proceeding on his fatal expedition against Fort Du Quesne, in the French war. The place formerly bore the name of "Braddock's landing," and is interesting from its association with the history of the country at that melancholy period, and with the early life of General Washington, who so highly distinguished himself in the unfortunate catastrophe which terminated the expedition.

The wild, picturesque scenery which marks this part of the course of the Potomac, and to which we have before referred, bears marks of the violence with which the current pours by in the season of floods. Evidence of its ravages may often be noticed by the passenger, who will not be surprised that even the chain bridge, constructed with so much caution, solidity, and skill, proved insufficient to avoid or to resist its impetuosity. During a high flood, about five years ago, it was swept away, the piers receiving so much injury as to discourage its restoration.

Among the numerous objects in Washington worthy of particular attention, most of which have been alluded to in a passing manner, are several of the paintings and sculptures which adorn the rotunda of the capitol.

The "*Declaration of Independence*" presents a grave, deliberative assembly (the old congress), at an instant when a scene of the highest importance and the greatest results was performing. The select committee, appointed to draw up a statement of rights and injuries, are in the act of presenting their report, which was the original of the document since so celebrated throughout the world as the "Declaration of Independence." John Hancock is seated in the chair of the speaker, and the members are ranged at their desks; while Thomas Jefferson, John Adams, and Benjamin Franklin (the committee), in the foreground, are presenting the report to Hancock. All the personages present are represented by portraits for which they sat—many of them to the artist himself. A few exceptions, however, are to be made—those who were dead before he began his task, and who left no portraits behind them. The hall, which is still preserved in its original condition (in the old statehouse in Philadelphia), is accurately given in the picture.

The "*Surrender of Burgoyne:*" here the British forces, who surrender after the battles of Saratoga, are seen marching out of camp, after stacking their arms, on a small plain on the Hudson, to which they had retreated. The American staff occupy a conspicuous position; and the whole effect, increased by the picturesque scenery of the spot, is striking and highly agreeable. Some of the American troops, occupying neighboring eminences, had convinced the defeated invaders that further retreat was impossible; and the event thus recorded marks one of the most important periods of the revolutionary war.

The "*Surrender at Yorktown:*" in this picture, the American army, with the French allies, is presented drawn up in two parallel lines—seen in perspective in the fields of Yorktown—and the head of the British column is marching between them toward the spectator: presenting accurate and spirited portraits of many of the distinguished men of the day belonging to the three great nations represented. The splendor of military costume is beautifully harmonized with the pacific aspect of the scene, and the pleasing anticipations which it was well calculated to excite.

"*General Washington resigning his Commission*," the closing picture of this invaluable series, gives a view of the old hall occupied by congress at that period (in Annapolis, Maryland); and the illustrious hero of the piece is placed in a dignified attitude, well corresponding with his character and the nature of the scene. One of the most interesting individuals introduced among the spectators is Lady Washington, accompanied by several members of the family and friends.

Four other scenes connected with the revolution were painted by Colonel Trumbull, which were not chosen by congress, although not on account of their want of interest or value.

The "*Battle of Bunker's Hill*," the first in the series of historical pictures, represents the instant when the British troops, with some of their officers at their head, were making their last and successful assault upon the height whose name was rendered so famous by the events of that day. General Warren has just fallen, and Putnam is seen pressing from behind toward the front, sword in hand; while the mingling of Americans, some of them in their simple working-dresses, with the splendid uniforms of their enemies—the combinations and contrasts of figures and groups, many of them in costumes and with forms and features copied from life, by an artist who was a contemporary and a fellow-soldier—together with the importance and the animated action of the scene, give this fine picture an interest of a superior kind, and impress the feelings of the spectator in a degree which it would be difficult to express.

The "*Battle of Princeton,*" a scene of a like character, and painted in a similar spirit by the same accomplished and faithful hand, exhibits the fall of General Mercer, in full view of the venerable institution of learning, Nassau hall, around and even within which lay the scene of that day's sanguinary struggle. A British grenadier, in the brilliant dress of his corps, is in the act of thrusting his bayonet into the body of the gallant officer, but is restrained by a timely hand. Here, also, the mingling of soldiers of the two armies, in various attitudes and all in energetic action, produces a similar excitement of the mind; while the consciousness that most of the principal personages are represented by true portraits, adds inestimable value to this, no less than to the other pictures of the Trumbull series.

GEORGETOWN.—This is a town and port of entry of considerable trade, situated west of Washington, from which it is separated by Rock creek, over which are two bridges, affording a convenient connexion between the two cities, the centres of which are about two miles apart.

The ground on which the town stands is irregular, and rises to a considerable height above the Potomac, on which the city fronts. The scenery around is varied and pleasant, and on the west stand the picturesque and rocky hills, which here begin to change the aspect of the river's banks. The falls are soon discovered, by following up the narrow gorge through which the stream winds, and through which proceeds the Potomac canal, the largest work of the kind in Virginia, or in any of the southern states.

The *Cannon Foundry* is situated in a secluded valley of these hills, and on the summit of them stands

The Roman Catholic College.—There are two large buildings belonging to it, and it has a president, fourteen professors, about one hundred and forty students, and twenty-five thousand volumes in its library. The commencement is held in July.

The *Nunnery,* or convent of the Visitation, is at a short distance from the college. It was founded in 1798, and contains sixty or seventy nuns, some of whom are employed in the female school attached to the institution.

Chain-Bridge across the Potomac.—Two miles above Georgetown, in the midst of the wild and romantic scenery which there marks the borders of the stream, a light bridge, constructed of wire, was thrown across the channel, a few years ago. Two heavy abutments of stone were built on the banks, narrowing the bed of the stream as far as seemed judicious, and at their extremities were raised columns strong enough to sustain the iron supporters. Depending from the latter, strong wires were extended down to the horizontal mass of woven wire, which formed the main part of the bridge, and on which the floor was laid; and the whole fabric, when completed, presented the neat and light appearance of the drawing.

This spot is ten miles below the Great falls of the Potomac, where the stream is pressed through a passage only one hundred yards in width, and falls thirty or forty feet into a rocky basin. Passing on nearly four miles, it reaches the head of the Little falls, or rapids, the descent of which is much more gradual, over broken rocks and a channel rather rapidly descending all the way to tide-water: about thirty-five feet in all.

Several wooden bridges had been erected across the Potomac, in this part of its course, which had been torn away by the ice or the current in the violent annual floods; and the wire bridge was adopted with the expectation that it would prove more durable. The nature of the valley through which the Potomac flows, renders the rising of the water, at certain seasons, remarkably great and sudden; and the force of the current at this place, especially when loaded with floating ice, is quite irresistible. Piers can not be expected to stand long in the bed of the river, however solid and firm; and the only safe alternative was to extend a light bridge from shore to shore, without venturing to seek support in the middle.

Shannondale Springs.

VIRGINIA.

This state is bounded north by Ohio, Pennsylvania, and Maryland; east by Maryland and the Atlantic; south by North Carolina and a small part of Tennessee; and west by Kentucky and Ohio. The southern boundary alone is a straight line, running on a parallel of north latitude, nearly coinciding with the boundary between Kentucky and Tennessee almost to its western termination—that is, to the Tennessee river. The northwestern boundary is formed by Ohio river, which is followed up to where it crosses the western line of Pennsylvania, giving to Virginia a long and narrow gore of land, which separates Ohio and Pennsylvania, for a considerable distance, in a singular manner. The northeastern boundary is formed by the Potomac, whose tortuous course gives it an irregular outline.

The state is crossed by the ridges of the Allegany mountains, from southwest to northeast, which give it a considerable diversity of climate, soil, and productions, and in which the principal rivers have their sources.

Virginia embraces a larger territory than any other of the old states, and is remarkable for the varieties of surface and climate which it contains. The Allegany mountains mark out one of the four natural divisions of the territory. Next east of this lies the hilly region, beyond which is sea-alluvion. The fourth section is a peculiar feature by which this state is distinguished from Maryland and North Carolina, which lie adjacent on the north and south. It is a broad tract, which slopes west, and is drained into the Mississippi through the Ohio, partly by the Kenhawa and other tributaries of that river itself, and partly, in the more southern parts, by the Tennessee river.

There is a remarkable spot some distance southwest of the centre of the state, where some of the highest sources of several of the principal rivers of the state rise within a short distance, though flowing in different directions: James river, which empties near the southern extremity of Chesapeake bay; Tennessee river, which flows southwest and then west through the state of Tennessee; and the Kenhawa, running into the Ohio.

Though the zones of Virginia are not very distinctly marked, each part has its appropriate character. The oceanic section of Virginia is its tropical climate. Latitude, exposure, and depressed level, all combine to give the Chesapeake counties a more elevated temperature than is found in the interior. This difference is seen on vegetation. In the lower counties cotton may be cultivated successfully, while the uncertainty of grain and meadow-grasses evinces a southern summer. The middle, in all the Atlantic states south from Pennsylvania, we find to be the Arcadia of the state. Middle Virginia is, however, blended with the mountainous, the former containing the whole or great part of the valley counties, Berkley, Jefferson, Frederick, Shenandoah, Rockingham, Augusta, Rockbridge, Botetourt, Montgomery, Wythe, and Washington. The real mountain section lies northwest from the middle, and extends to the Ohio. The extreme western part is, indeed, composed of a congeries of hills with alluvial bottoms, but the actual mountain ridges approach so near Ohio river, and the hills are in themselves so generally abrupt and lofty, as to give an alpine appearance to the country. Taken as a whole, central Virginia has the best soil, though in the mountainous part there is much that is excellent. With the exception of the southeastern counties, grain and orchard fruits are highly congenial to Virginia, and their various products are the natural, actual, and we may safely say the permanent, staples of the state. Of metals, iron ore is abundant in the central and western sections. Brine has been procured on the Great Kenhawa, and salt extensively manufactured.

The *Natural Bridge* over Cedar creek, twelve miles southwest of Lexington, is esteemed one of the most extraordinary natural curiosities in the world. The following is Mr. Jefferson's description, in his Notes on Virginia:—

"It is on the ascent of a hill which seems to have been cloven through its length by some great convulsion. The fissure, just by the bridge, is by some admeasurements two hundred and seventy feet deep, by others only two hundred and five. It is about forty-five feet wide at the bottom, and ninety feet at the top: this, of course, determines the length of the bridge, and its height from the water; its breadth in the middle is about sixty feet, but more at the ends; and the thickness of the mass, at the summit of the arch, is about forty feet. A part of this thickness is constituted by a coat of earth, which gives growth to many large trees; the residue, with the hill on both sides, is one solid rock of limestone. The arch approaches the semi-elliptical form; but the larger axis of the ellipse, which would be the chord of the arch, is many times longer than the transverse. Though the sides of this bridge are provided in some parts with a parapet of fixed rocks, yet few men have resolution to walk to them and look over into the abyss: you involuntarily fall on your hands and feet, creep to the parapet, and peep over it. Looking down from this height about a minute gave me a violent head-ache. If the view from the top be painful and intolerable, that from below is delightful in an equal extreme; it is impossible for the emotions arising from the sublime to be felt beyond what they are here: so beautiful an arch, so elevated, so light, and springing, as it were, up to heaven! the rapture of the spectator is really indescribable! The fissure continuing narrow, deep, and straight, for a considerable distance above and below the bridge, opens a short but very pleasing view of the North mountain on one side, and Blue ridge on the other, at the distance, each of them, of about five miles. This bridge is in the county

Natural Bridge over Cedar Creek.

of Rockbridge, to which it has given name, and affords a public and commodious passage over a valley which can not be crossed elsewhere for a considerable distance. The stream passing under it is called Cedar creek; it is a water of James river, and sufficient in the driest seasons to turn a gristmill, though its fountain is not more than two miles above."

The description of Jefferson first attracted the attention of travellers to this remarkable spot. Of recent descriptions, the best is that by Miss Martineau, which is truly characteristic and interesting, and is as follows:—

"At a mile from the bridge, the road turns off through a wood. While the stage rolled and jolted along the extremely bad road, Mr. L. and I went prying about the whole area of the wood, poking our horses' noses into every thicket, and between any two pieces of rock, that we might be sure not to miss our object; the driver smiling after us, whenever he could spare attention from his own not very easy task, of getting his charge along. With all my attention, I could see no precipice, and was concluding to follow the road without any more vagaries, when Mr. L., who was a little in advance, waved his whip as he stood beside his horse, and said: 'Here is the bridge!' I then perceived that we were nearly over it, the piled rocks on either hand forming a barrier, which prevents a careless eye from perceiving the ravine which it spans. I turned to the side of the road, and rose in my stirrup to look over, but I found it would not do. I went on to the inn, deposited my horse, and returned on foot to the bridge.

"With all my efforts, I could not look down steadily into what seemed the bottomless abyss of foliage and shadow. From every point of the bridge I tried, and all in vain. I was heated and extremely hungry, and much vexed at my own weakness. The only way was to go down and look up; though where the bottom could be was past my imagining, the view from the top seeming to be of foliage below foliage for ever.

"The way to the glen is through a field opposite the inn, and down a steep, rough, rocky path, which leads under the bridge, and a few yards beyond it. I think the finest view of all is from this path, just before reaching the bridge. The irregular rock, spanning a chasm of one hundred and sixty feet in height, and from sixty to ninety in width, is exquisitely tinted with every shade of gray and brown; while trees encroach from the sides, and overhang from the top, between which and the arch there is an additional depth of fifty-six feet. It was now early in July; the trees were in their brightest and thickest foliage; and the tall beeches under the arch contrasted their verdure with the gray rock. and received the gilding of the sunshine, as it slanted into the ravine, glittering in the drip from the arch, and in the splashing and tumbling waters of Cedar creek, which ran by our feet. Swallows were flying about under the arch. What others of their tribe can boast of such a home?

"We crossed and recrossed the creek on stepping-stones, searching out every spot to which any tradition belonged. Under the arch, thirty feet from the water, the lower part of the letters G. W. may be seen, carved in the rock. When Washington was a young man he climbed up hither, to leave this record of his visit. There are other inscriptions of the same kind; and above them a board, on which are painted the names of two persons, who have thought it worth while thus to immortalize their feat of climbing highest. But their glory was but transient, after all. They have been outstripped by a traveller, whose achievement will probably never be rivalled; for he would not have accomplished it if he could, by any means, have declined the task. Never was a wonderful deed more involuntarily performed. There is no disparagement to the gentleman in saying this: it is only absolving him from the charge of foolhardiness.

"This young man, named Blacklock, accompanied by two friends, visited the natural bridge; and, being seized with the ambition appropriate to the place, of writing his name highest, climbed the rock opposite to the part selected by Washington, and carved his initials. Others have perhaps seen what Mr. Blacklock had overlooked—that it was a place easy to ascend, but from which it is impossible to come down. He was forty feet or more from the path; his footing was precarions; he was weary with holding on while carving his name; and his head began to swim when he saw the impossibility of getting down again. He called to his companions that his only chance was to climb up upon the bridge, without hesitation or delay. They saw this, and with anguish agreed between themselves that the chance was a very bare one. They cheered him, and advised him to look neither up nor down. On he went, slanting upward from under the arch, creeping round a projection, on which no foothold is visible from below, and then disappearing in a recess filled up with foliage. Long and long they waited, watching for motion, and listening for crashing among the trees. He must have been now one hundred and fifty feet above them. At length their eyes were so strained that they could see no more, and they had almost lost all hope. There was little doubt that he had fallen while behind the trees, where his body would never be found. They went up to try the chance of looking for him from above. They found him lying insensible on the bridge. He could just remember reaching the top, when he immediately fainted."

Passage through the Blue Ridge.—The following interesting description is in Jefferson's Notes on Virginia:—

"The passage of the Potomac through the Blue ridge is one of the most stupendous scenes. You stand on a very high point of land; on your right comes up the Shenandoah, having ranged along the foot of the mountain a hundred miles to seek a vent; on your left approaches the Potomac, in quest of a passage also; in the moment of their junction, they rush together against the mountain, rend it asunder, and pass off to the sea. The first glance of this scene hurries our senses into the opinion that this earth has been created in time; that the mountains were formed first; that the rivers began to flow afterward; that in this place particularly they have been dammed up by the Blue ridge of mountains, and have formed an ocean which filled the whole valley; that, continuing to rise, they have at length broken over at this spot, and have torn the mountain down from its summit to its base. The piles of rock on each hand, but particularly on the Shenandoah, the evident marks of their disrupture and evulsion from their beds by the most powerful agents of nature, corroborate the impression. But the distant finishing which nature has given to the picture, is of a very different character; it is a true contrast to the foreground; it is as placid and delightful as that is wild and tremendous; for the mountain being cloven asunder, she presents to your eye, through the cleft, a small catch of smooth blue horizon, at an infinite distance in the plain country, inviting you, as it were, from the riot and tumult roaring around, to pass through the breach and participate of the calm below. Here the eye ultimately composes itself; and that way, too, the road happens actually to lead. You cross the Potomac above the junction, pass along its side through the base of the mountain for three miles, its terrible precipices hanging in fragments over you, and, within about twenty miles, reach Fredericktown, and the fine country round that. This scene is worth a voyage across the Atlantic; yet here, as in the neighborhood of the natural bridge, are people who have passed their lives within half a dozen miles, and have never been to survey these monuments of a war between rivers and mountains, which must have shaken the earth itself to its centre."

Wier's Cave, on the northwest side of the Blue ridge, is between two and three thousand feet in length, and comprises various apartments, containing beautiful stalactites and incrustations, which display the most sparkling brilliancy when surveyed by the light of a torch. Near this there is another singular cavern, called Madison's cave; and in one of the ridges of the Allegany mountains is Blowing cave, from which a current of air continually issues, strong enough to prostrate the weeds at the distance of sixty feet. One of the largest mounds in the valley of the Ohio is in Virginia, near the Ohio, fourteen miles below Wheeling. It is about three hundred feet in diameter at the base, sixty at the top, and the perpendicular height is seventy feet. It contains thousands of human skeletons.

Valley of Virginia.—After leaving Winchester, distant from Woodstock about thirty miles east or northeast, we bid farewell to everything like a railroad, and plunge into the midst of the valley of Virginia. The country is undulating in its surface, of limestone formation, and distinguished for its romantic and beautiful scenery. Through this valley flows the majestic Shenandoah, one of those rivers still bearing its ancient Indian name, too melodious and expressive to be changed for a better.

The Shenandoah flows on, a limpid stream, shelving rocks, lying in strata, being often visible on its bottom. Thus the river pursues its course to Harper's Ferry, where, joining its forces to the Potomac, it yields its name to that river, and having saluted the president's mansion familiarly, and the United States capitol at a more respectful distance, proceeds to bury itself in the ocean. Here are some fine views of the Blue ridge, that famous cordon of mountains, stretching itself like a giant rampart across the state, ascending majestically toward the sky in ambitious and impressive forms, catching and deepening its serene cerulean blue, and spreading its own ample shadows over the far-reaching vale below. Here a painter's brush would find strong and striking originals; the poet's lyre would waken the sweetest music among the mountain solitudes above, or the green sequestered shades below. This, too, is the region of thriving farmers, of fat cattle, and fertile lands. In this valley there are many Germans and descendants of Germans.

Twenty-five miles west of Winchester is a section or an adjunct of the Blue ridge, sometimes called the Ice moun tain, from a very peculiar formation of a subterrene, or rather a subsaxumous coat of ice, which, on turning up a stone on the warmest day of summer, discovers itself with a refreshing coolness. It is, in fact, a natural and magnificent refrigerator. No night can be passed here without feeling the necessity of a blanket. The usual place of resort in the vicinity goes by the name of "Capon springs."

Taking the summit of the Alleganies as a central point of view to overlook the state, we find first a wide tract of adjacent country, diversified with all the irregularity of a mountainous region, varying from rough and rocky heights, to picturesque and shady valleys, many of which are rich in mines and mineral springs, where the crowds of gay visiters, mingling with invalids, enliven the picturesque scenes with groups strongly contrasting with the wildness and solitude of nature.

Next eastward of this lies a section, extending to tidewater in the rivers, which amounts to 15,386 square miles; and between that and the eastern boundary is another, with its lower level and navigable waters, and also the sites of the old settlements, having an area of 11,805 square miles.

But the western section, lying beyond the Alleganies, is the most extensive and flourishing. It contains 28,387 square miles. Climate, soil, situation, and the origin of the people, have great influence in stamping a variety of characteristics on these different districts; for while the low eastern regions are warm, and the soil cultivated by slaves, facilities for navigation have raised large towns amid extensive plantations; in the higher districts, other objects and modes of culture have been adopted, while slaves are less numerous, and they often work side by side with their masters. The relations established by the natural features of the western district cement the people more intimately with the Mississippi valley than with those of the Atlantic borders. So great is the difference of seasons found in different parts of Virginia, that vegetation is often far advanced in the spring at Wheeling when it is hardly perceptible along the ridge which divides the waters of the Monongahela from those of the Ohio, in that remarkable, narrow, northwest gore of land before mentioned. The mean elevation of central Virginia is eighteen hundred or two thousand feet above the Ohio, the descent to which is by several plains or natural terraces—gradually descending to the west. The climate of the mountainous regions resembles that of the Atlantic coast, as high up as latitude forty three degrees.

There is a remarkable mountain-ridge from fifteen to twenty miles distant from the Blue ridge, to which it is related as the Blue ridge is to the Alleganies proper. It may be traced through Maryland in the Parr-spring ridge, Pennsylvania (where, as in Virginia, it has no distinctive name), and through New Jersey in the Schooley's mountain ridge.

The counties through which the ridge passes in Virginia are Loudoun, Fauquier, Culpepper, Orange, Albemarle, Nelson, Amherst, Bedford, Franklin, and Henry.

On most maps the mountains present a confused mass; but they are, in fact, divided into five or six distinct ridges. Indeed, says Darby, "the whole state, from the head of tidewater to Ohio river, is formed of a series of mountain-chains and intervening valleys." But the Blue ridge is the most prominent, stands very detached, has the highest points in the Appalachian chain southwest of Delaware river, and everywhere marks the lines between counties.

The interior of Virginia was almost uninhabited, even by savages, when the country was first known to Europeans. A few tribes only occupied any part of its surface, and these dwelt chiefly along the tidewaters. It is capable of supporting a population of three millions, even if the arable parts were as thickly inhabited as some of the most populous districts; but a combination of causes has prevented the increase for some years past.*

* We improve this allusion to the agricultural resources of this state, to introduce in a note the following interesting letter from a son of Virginia, the Hon. William C. Rives, our minister to France. It has reference to his visit to the World's Fair at London; and some valua-

Potomac River.—This noble river abounds with fish, the principal being the white shad, the herring, and the sturgeon. The latter is taken in a manner said to be peculiar to this section of the country. The sturgeon is a noble denizen of the waters, weighing from seventy-five to one hundred and fifty pounds. Every passenger up the Potomac has probably seen the prodigious leaps of this fish, sometimes to the height of ten feet, and his alacrity at mounting a cascade.

ble practical remarks will be found in it respecting the application of science to the development of the natural resources of the state. It also records the success, in England, of M'Cormick's reaping-machine, the invention of a citizen of this ancient commonwealth:—

"PARIS, *Tuesday, September* 30, 1851.

"MY DEAR C——: Having a week or two at my disposal during the last days of the summer, I determined to go over the channel and see for myself that of which the description had filled so many mouths and newspapers for the last four or five months—the GREAT EXHIBITION, or what the French more appropriately call it, the *Exposition Universelle*. I am not prepared to say with the queen of Sheba, after her inspection of the riches of Solomon, 'The half was not told me;' but, on the contrary, making some deduction from the oriental extravagance with which this *wonder of the age* has been celebrated by both pen and tongue, I am yet free to say enough remained to make it an object of just and rational curiosity to all who were in circumstances to visit it.

"A visit to the Crystal Palace is, in truth, a sort of figurative voyage of circumnavigation, by which, within the limits of a comparatively small space, and by a few days' industrious observation, you traverse successively the various quarters of the globe, and see before you the productions, the arts, the riches, and in some degree the respective national manners and customs of them all. And yet this is so contrived as to leave upon the mind of the beholder a strong impression of the material superiority, if not supremacy, of one of these nations over all the rest. ENGLAND has the vast advantage in the Exhibition of being *at home*. One full half of the fairy building is allotted to the display of her riches and resources, her industry and power—in which her vast tributary possessions in the East and the West (India, Canada, and the isles of the ocean), all glittering with barbaric pomp, are made to revolve in due order around the central orb, dazzling by the splendor of her own accumulated and gorgeous wealth. The mind is so acted upon by this studious display of boundless dominion, and riches, and power, in the hands of a single nation, that it hardly recovers from the impression in passing through the successive departments allotted to other nations; for however well filled many of them are with the choicest productions of exquisite taste and superior skill, they all seem dwarfed in comparison with the gigantic development of *England at home*. In this state of *exhibited* inferiority, these nations may legitimately take to themselves the consolation of the lion prostrate beneath the man in the painting—that the man, and not the lion, was the painter!

"If FRANCE, which originated the idea of an exhibition of the products of the arts and industry of all nations, had been permitted by her internal condition to carry it into execution, and Paris instead of London had been the scene of its presentation, a very great difference would, doubtless, have been made in the relative position and appearance of the competing nations. In that case, the advantage of being *chez soi*, concurring with her unrivalled taste and artistic science, and the wonderful resources of her national genius and industry, would have assigned to her the rank of *primacy* which is now held by England in the London Exhibition. Nor would the other nations have had reason to complain of the change of *venue*. The bright climate of France, and the cordial and genial temper of the people, so readily fraternizing with the other families of mankind, would have made of what has been a stern and somewhat jealous encounter of rival pretensions, a real *jubilee* of the heart and senses, marking an era in the social intercourse and happiness of nations, as well as in their industrial progress. As it is, the Exhibition has mainly the character of a highly successful speculation, very sagaciously managed, on British account.

"You will wish to know what sort of figure we of the UNITED STATES have made in this great international congress of industry and the arts. The objects which occupy much the largest space in the Exhibition, and which have been the chief points, indeed, of popular attraction, are objects of luxury and ornament, exceedingly costly in both their material and workmanship, and intended to minister to the factitious wants of overgrown wealth. In the British department alone I counted not less than twenty large rooms, with the inscription in glaring capitals above them of the adored 'precious metals.' The same general character of costly magnificence, varying only in the details, predominated in all the rest of the European departments, from the exquisite mosaics of Italy, and the rich silks, and porcelains, and jewelry, of France, to the beautiful and elaborate malachites of Russia, and was conspicuous even in the 'barbaric pearl and gold' of the Asiatic and African contributions.

"In entering into a competition of so much gorgeousness as this, it was hardly to be expected that so young, and simple, and republican a people as that of the United States, would make a very brilliant *debut*. I always regretted, therefore, that we entered the lists as general competitors. If we had gone in simply and avowedly to show the nations of the Old World some of the most valuable improvements we had made in those manly and useful arts adapted to our circumstances and vigorous youth, and had contented ourselves with an allotment of space proportioned to that object, we should have avoided some mortification, at first, to our national pride. A large space, however, was demanded in the outset for the display of American contributions, which, after successive retrenchments, remained imperfectly filled, and the effigy of the American eagle, in very exaggerated and colossal proportions, was conspicuously placed above the whole. 'The Times,' the Coryphæus of the English press, immediately seized upon these circumstances with its accustomed benevolence toward the United States, taunting us with 'the solitude in the Crystal Palace over which the American eagle stretched its mighty wings,' and representing 'the space we had *grasped* in the Exhibition' as being as 'imperfectly occupied as our vast continent.'

"In spite of these mistakes of our own, and the ill-natured use made of them to our disadvantage by the critics, the solid and intrinsic merit of the American part of the Exhibition finally made itself felt and appreciated by all, and it is now, I think, universally admitted, even in England, where so many jealousies and prejudices are to be overcome, that, in an industrial and useful point of view, no nation contributed more to the Exhibition than the United States. I am most happy to be able to say to you that nothing has had so powerful an agency in working out this honorable result for our national reputation as a *Virginian* invention, of which you were one of the earliest patrons, and which has received the highest honors at the Exhibition, and is now making a sort of triumphal progress through England—I mean M'Cormick's reaping-machine. It was the successful trial of this machine on the farm of Mr. Mechi, at Tip Tree, on the 29th of July last—eliciting as it did the wonder and admiration of all who witnessed it—that commenced the reaction in favor of the American contributions to the Exhibition. The English people began then to think that some 'good thing might come out of our transatlantic Nazareth,' and from time to time they bestowed something more than a passing, supercilious glance at the American department of the Crystal Palace, and found in it other products of American genius and skill, which convinced them that, in this age of progress and invention, stimulated to extraordinary fecundity in the New World, there are not a few things they may learn with advantage of younger nations than themselves.

"Of these other achievements of American ingenuity I have not the time to speak. You have seen them all noticed in the newspaper reports of the Exhibition: they have, the greater part of them undoubtedly, a very high order of merit; but I think I am not misled by a natural partiality for an invention of my own state when I say that the reaping-machine has done most of all to redeem

It is recorded that during the revolutionary war, one of these enormous fish descended from an aerial leap into a ferry-boat, and falling into the lap of an officer seated on the gunwale, broke his thigh! It is caught in the Potomac by a naked hook attached to a line, and drawn with skill under the belly. It is remarkable that this fish is good only in certain rivers: those of the Delaware being thought unfit to eat, while those of the Hudson and Potomac are considered a delicacy.

the honor of our country in the trying, and, to us for a time, apparently hopeless contests of the Exhibition. In proof of this, it is sufficient to mention the fact that it is invariably placed at the head of all the American triumphs in the various notices of the exhibition which have been from time to time published by the European press. I have now before me the leading article of 'The Times' of the 2d instant—the first number of that journal which acknowledged the substantial success of the American part of the Exhibition—in which that success and the reaping-machine, which so much contributed to it, are thus noticed:—

"'On the other hand, it is beyond all denial that every practical success of the season belongs to the Americans. Their consignments showed poorly at first, but came out well upon trial. Their reaping-machine has carried conviction to the heart of the British agriculturist. Their revolvers threaten to revolutionize military tactics as completely as the original discovery of gunpowder. Their yacht takes a class to itself.'

"And again, in an article of the same journal of the 27th instant, reviewing the general result of the Exhibition, are the following remarks:—

"'One point that strikes us forcibly on a survey of the last few months is, the extraordiary contrast which the attractive and the useful features of the display present. It will be remembered that the American department was, at first, regarded as the poorest and least interesting of all foreign countries. Of late it has justly assumed a position of the first importance, as having brought to the aid of our distressed agriculturists a machine which, if it realizes the anticipations of competent judges, will amply remunerate England for all her outlay connected with the Great Exhibition. The reaping-machine from the United States is the most valuable contribution from abroad to the stock of our previous knowledge that we have yet discovered, and several facts in connection with it are not a little remarkable.'

"It has been a source of patriotic and I trust legitimate pride to me, as a Virginian, that an invention emanating from my own state, and I may say from my own neighborhood indeed, has done so much to procure honor to the American name abroad, and to vindicate the claims of American genius and enterprise to the respect and gratitude of other nations. In these feelings you and your friends around you, who know so well both the invention and the inventor, will, I am sure, largely share. I can not describe to you the feelings of home delight, not unmixed with triumph, with which, on one of the days that I attended the Exhibition, I saw the '*Virginia* Grain-Reaper' (for by that name M'Cormick himself entered his machine on the official catalogue of the Exhibition) as much surrounded by curious and interested spectators as the priceless Indian diamond—the Koh-i-noor, or Mountain of Light—which usually attracts the largest and most eager crowds. It is in the country, however, when it is at work, sweeping with ease over its fifteen or twenty acres of thick-standing wheat a day, that it excites the strongest enthusiasm, as it achieves its greatest triumphs. On some of these occasions as many as fifteen hundred or two thousand persons have been assembled to witness its performance; and they have *cheered* it with loud and hearty plaudits, when it has finished a row or turned a corner of the field, as if it were some great living hero or conqueror. M'Cormick himself has been *fêted;* and when in acknowledging a toast, with true Washingtonian modesty and Spartan brevity, he said he was 'more accustomed to working than speaking, and preferred always that his machine should *speak* for itself,' he brought down as thundering applause as ever greeted an orator in the house of commons.

"Everybody in England now wonders that a machine at once so simple and so effective, and so precisely adapted to the wants of British agriculture, should never have been invented and brought to perfection by some of their own people, and that it should have been reserved for a modest inhabitant of the mountains of Virginia, more than three thousand miles distant, to conceive, and execute, and bring to them, what so exactly suited them, without their having been able previously to form a distinct conception either of its nature or its practicability. What renders this the more extraordinary (and it is a circumstance which greatly enhances both the merit and the glory of the American invention) is, that the minds of the most ingenious mechanicians in Great Britain had been earnestly directed to the same object, for the catalogue of the Exhibition registers no less than eight different but very imperfect essays toward its accomplishment. My own observation least year at the annual meeting of the Royal Agricultural Society of England, convinced me that a good reaping-machine was the great *desideratum* in British agriculture. In the immense and almost infinitely diversified collection of agricultural implements displayed there, no instrument of that kind was seen; and yet it was evident that, in a climate so humid and uncertain, some accelerated and at the same time economical process of getting in their harvest was a matter of the highest importance. I immediately wrote to our friend C. J. Meriwether (as he will doubtless recollect), that if the Virginia reaper were sent out to the Great Exhibition of the next year, for which the arrangements were then commencing, it would make the fortune of its inventor. It has not only done this, but it has *reaped a harvest* of honor and renown for himself, his native state, and the reputation of American genius in general, which is a result far more to be prized.

"With this encouraging example before us, are we not strongly invited to some change in the direction which has been heretofore so exclusively given to the youthful talent of our state? As soon as our young men leave college, they crowd by hundreds into what are called the learned professions, which are already filled to repletion; or they devote themselves to a still more sterile and unprofitable employment of their faculties, for both themselves and the country, in mere party politics. If the same amount of mind and energy were applied to those useful practical pursuits in which science is the auxiliary of art in indefinitely multiplying the results of labor, and unfolding the latent capabilities of nature, what a magical change would soon be manifested in the prosperity and power of our ancient commonwealth—rich, as all admit her to be, in every element of moral, intellectual, and material wealth!

"In reflecting upon this subject, as I often do with a solicitude ever alive to the honor and destinies of my native state, I have thought that some modification of the systems of education pursued in most of our public schools would greatly contribute, and is perhaps indispensable, to introduce the change which appears so desirable in the active direction of our mental resources. Could not that education be made more *practical,* without abating anything from the high standard of science and learning which should characterize it, simply by giving more development to the *applications of science* to the various branches of industry and art, as is done in the admirable institutions of this country, the *Ecole Polytechnique,* the *Ecole des Ponts et Chaussées,* the *Ecole des Mines,* and the *Ecole Centrale des Arts et Manufactures,* from which England, with her usual sagacity, has taken a hint in the establishment of her 'Government School of Mines and Science applied to the Arts,' not being able to engraft these new studies upon the ancient and *chartered* systems of her universities. Whether the object is to be accomplished with us by some modification in existing institutions, or by the establishment of new and special institutions, is a question on which I am not prepared to pronounce an opinion. Those who are more competent than myself, recognising the utility of the end, will, I trust, devise the proper means, and my prayers will be for the success of whatever they shall adopt, as they ever are for the happiness and prosperity, in all things, of my native land. Most truly and faithfully yours,

"W. C. Rives."

The wild birds which frequent the bosom and shores of the Potomac, are very numerous. Among them are the swan, the wild goose, the red-head shoveler, the black-head shoveler, the duck and mallard, the black duck, the blue-winged teal, the green-winged teal, the widgeon, and the far-celebrated canvass-back. This duck, which we believe is unrivalled in the world for richness of flavor, is one of a class called drift-fowl, from their habit of floating in the middle of the river when at rest. The two species of shoveler have the same habit, and are scarcely inferior in flavor. The canvass-back, it is supposed, breeds on the borders of the northern lakes, or on the shores of Hudson's bay; and in their migrations confine their pasture almost exclusively to the Chesapeake and Potomac. It is well ascertained that they feed on the bulbous root of a grass which grows on the flats in these rivers, and which is commonly known as wild celery. It is said, that during a hard winter, some forty years ago, a strong wind blew so much of the water off the flats of James river, that the remainder froze to the bottom, enclosing the long tops of this grass so closely in the ice, that when it broke up, and was floated off in the spring, it tore whole fields of it up by the roots, and destroyed the pasture. Since that time the canvass-back has never been seen on the river.

The bald duck feeds very frequently among these water-fowl; and not having the power to dive entirely under water in search of food, he watches for the rising of the canvass-back, and, by his superior quickness on the wing, seizes on the celery the moment it appears above the surface, and escapes with it to the shore.

The canvass-back is often shot from behind blinds of brush, which conceal the sportman, in the midst of the feeding ground. There is a practice, however, of "tolling them in," as it is called, by shaking a colored handkerchief tied to the branch of a decayed tree. On what propensity of the bird the success of this manœuvre is founded, it would be difficult to say. There is no doubt of the fact, however, that they are thus decoyed within gun-shot; and it is related of an old sportsman on the Potomac, that a long queue of red hair, which he wore in a brush, and shook over his shoulder, served the purpose admirably well. Perhaps we have yet to discover that birds have curiosity.

Among the many varieties of wild fowl found on the Potomac, below Harper's Ferry, is the wild swan. The young bird is considered a great delicacy; while the old one is hard and without flavor. In a book on the District of Columbia, by Mr. Elliott, there are some curious particulars respecting their habits, and the manner of taking them.

"This noble bird," says the author, "is seen floating near the shores, in flocks of some two or three hundred, white as the driven snow, and from time to time emitting fine, sonorous, and occasionally melodious songs—so loud, that they might be heard, on a still evening, two or three miles. There are two kinds, so called from their respective notes—the one the trumpeter, and the other the hooper; the trumpeter is the largest, and, when at full size, will measure from five to six feet from the bill to the point of the toe, and from seven to eight feet from the tip of one wing to the tip of the other, when stretched and expanded. They are sagacious and wary, and depend more on the sight than on the sense of smell. On a neck nearly three feet in length, they are enabled to elevate their heads so as to see and distinguish, with a quick and penetrating eye, objects at a great distance; and by means of this same length of neck, they feed in slack tides, by immersing, as is their habit, nearly all of the body, and throwing only their feet and tails out in three or four feet water, and on the flatty shores they frequent, generally beyond gunshot; the sportsman availing himself, however, of a peculiar propensity (of which we shall presently speak more particularly) prevailing with them, and some of the other water-fowl, often toll them within reach of their fire. The swans remain here the whole winter, only shifting their ground, in severe weather, from the frozen to the open part of the river, and dropping down into the salts, where it is rarely frozen. They get into good condition soon after their arrival in autumn, and remain fat until toward spring, when, a few weeks before their departure (about the first of March), they gradually become thinner in flesh; and in the latter part of their sojourn here, are found so poor and light, that, when shot, the gunner gets nothing fit for use but the feathers. Whether this circumstance be owing to their having exhausted the means of subsistence at their feeding-places, or that they are taught by Him who rules the universe, in small as well as great things, thus by abstaining, to prepare themselves for the long aerial voyages which they are about to undertake, we pretend not to determine with certainty; there is nothing more wonderful in this than in the fact, which is notorious, that they, by exercise, regularly and assiduously fit themselves for this continuous effort, to bear themselves through the air to the distance of perhaps a thousand miles or leagues. Large flocks are seen every day rising from the river, and taking a high position, flying out of sight, and apparently moving in a circuit to a considerable distance, again returning to or near the same place, during the last two or three weeks of their stay.

"The swan is 'tolled' by a dog that is taught to play about within easy call of his master, at the edge of the water; the hunter contrives to place himself behind a log, or some other cover well concealed, before he begins his operations, taking care to observe that the direction of the wind is not unfavorable to him, and that the flock he means to toll is near enough to distinguish such objects on the shore, and under no alarm at the time. By what motive these fowls are influenced, we have not heard satisfactorily explained; but certain it is, they are very commonly brought in from some hundreds of yards' distance, in this way, to within point-blank shot. It is said, and perhaps truly, in the case of the dog, that they fancy themselves in pursuit of some animal, as the fag or mink, by which their young are annoyed at their breeding-places.

"The wild goose is yet more wary and vigilant to keep out of harm's way than the swan. He too is sharp-sighted, but depends much on his sense of smell for protection: this is so well known to the huntsman, that he never attempts, however he may be concealed from this bird, to approach it from the direction of the wind; since he would assuredly be scented before he could get within gun-shot, and left to lament his error, by the sudden flight of the whole flock. These geese, toward spring, often alight on the land, and feed on the herbage in fields; and sometimes in such numbers as to do great injury to the wheat-fields on the borders of the river."

Geological Facts.—Some twenty or thirty feet below the level of the plain around Richmond, occurs one of the most remarkable deposites in this or any country. The place in which it has been found most fully developed, is where the small brook at the east end and on the north side of Clay street empties into Shockoe creek. On the bank of that brook will be seen a stratum from ten to fifteen feet thick, which most persons would call white clay; but Professor W. B. Rogers (the state geologist) of the university, has ascertained that it is made up almost entirely of *animalculæ* or *infusoria*—that is, microscopic animals. These skeletons, consisting of silex, are incredibly small, so that each cubic inch of this infusorial earth contains many thousand millions of them. How inconceivably numerous, therefore, must they be, to form a deposite at least ten feet thick, and extending many miles over the adjoining country! It has excited great interest among the learned naturalists of Europe as well as of our own country, and henceforth none of them will visit Richmond without at once searching for this deposite. Professor Ehrenberg, of Prussia, the most eminent of living microscopists, has examined specimens from this place, and discovered in them at least one hundred and thirty species of these minutest of animals. To discover them in this almost impalpable dust, requires a powerful microscope; and doubtless, therefore, many who look at specimens with the naked eye, will be very incredulous as to these statements. But they are considered as established facts by the scientific world.

The substance may be distinguished from clay by being much lighter when dry. It is not, indeed, much heavier than magnesia, when pure. In other parts of the world it is sometimes used for polishing-powder. From a slight trial, it is believed that the Richmond deposite would answer the same purpose.

Beneath the infusorial deposite is a greenish or bluish clay, containing numerous seashells, or rather casts and moulds of them, with sharks' teeth, &c.; but these, although of deep interest to geologists, will not excite much attention from others.

It can hardly be doubted, that when this region was covered by the ocean, the waters swarmed with microscopic animalculæ, whose skeletons, as the animals died, dropped to the bottom, and in the course of ages accumulated prodigiously. But when we recollect how astonishingly fast they multiply, we need not suppose many centuries necessary to produce even this extraordinary thickness.

Scenery and Climate.—So beautiful is that portion of the state which is encircled by the lofty summits of the Allegany, that scarcely can its inhabitants be charged with blinding prejudice in believing and styling it the "garden of the state," or even the "Eden of the world." The climate presents a pleasant medium between the extremes of heat and cold, occasioning particular prevalence to neither the fevers incident to the one, nor the pulmonary complaints belonging to the other. The mountains—still the haunt of game, and oftentimes re-echoing the sound of the hunter's gun, the baying of his hounds, or perchance the mirthful laugh of young equestrians, who seek amusement on their sides and summits, by the exhilarating exercise to which they invite—give healthful relief from the ennui of southern life; and at the same time, crowned with foliage, or capped with fire, reflecting and dispersing the rays of the rising or setting sun, they impart variety to the scenery, and render it grand beyond the power of description.

Reposing in their midst, are those medicinal waters, which give health to the pilgrim and pleasure to its devotee from the most distant borders of our land. The soil, in parts at least, of high fertility, adds beauty to the landscape, by the luxuriant covering which it spreads over the face of nature.

In the months of spring, the eye is everywhere met by wide fields of clover, colored by its blossoms, and loading the air with fragrance. Later in the year, scattered here and there, are seen plantations of tobacco, fields of corn of gigantic growth, and of hemp—the dark, rich foliage of the latter rising far above the barriers that would hem it in. Nor does the hoar frost of winter entirely despoil the landscape of its loveliness. Even then, lay revelling in the warm sunlight of each genial day, fields of grain, that, anticipating the early spring, have already put on their dress of green, in which to wait its coming.

But let us turn from this to another portion of Virginia—a portion far less favored in respect to soil and climate, still viewed, perhaps, with scarcely less partial satisfaction by those who have had long familiarity with its droughts and heats—have inhaled from infancy its pestilential breath, and with every autumn, greeting as old acquaintances, have lustily and, forsooth, involuntarily shaken hands with its chills and fevers. Scarcely does the traveller leave, with the setting sun, the blue lofty summits of the Allegany, as he is informed by the increasing uniformity of scenery, multitudinous marshes, forests of evergreen, and wide-spread plains of sand, that he is in verity entering upon the pine barrens of the South Atlantic coast. On every side he observes tracts of land lying waste, half overgrown with briers and thistles, or low underwood, which, he is told, is left to regain its strength, by the rest of several seasons, or perhaps has been "turned out"—that is, given over to a second growth of forest. Much of the wooded land around him, densely covered with full-grown pines, he will find to be of this last description.

Meager herds of cattle wander through the tall coarse grass, or feed on the refuse of cornfields. Tracts of corn and cotton are, at least to the planter's eye, relieving features of the landscape.

But aside from the peculiarities of natural scenery, there are others which can not fail to fix the eye of the stranger, in traversing this portion of Virginia. He will observe the singular appearance given to country houses, by the common custom of placing the chimneys exterior to the main building. He will also notice a scarcity of barns; and if, perchance, on the borders of some pleasant grove, or in the outskirts of a forest, he spies a rude shelter which he would mistake for a barn, he is at once informed that he sees before him a country church, where a periodical discourse calls together a multitude of wealthy planters from ten, fifteen, or even twenty miles around. But though in this warm climate, cattle require no lodging-places, still a destitution of out-houses will in no wise be observed to be a characteristic of a southern residence. Conspicuous enough will be seen a meat-house, and from this, as a centre, radiate many humble dwellings, constituting almost a village of themselves. Fine flourishing orchards, filling up the rear-ground of the picture, will for the most part be looked for in vain. Even figs, peaches, apricots, and grapes—which, in this favoring temperature, might be expected to multiply in profusion—are generally far from abundant.

To the prevalence of fevers we have already alluded. Regular as the pestiferous dews and decay of foliage in August and September, so regular are their ravages on human prey. Friend then anxiously watches the countenance of friend, in dread expectancy of tracing there the saffron mark of the king of terrors. Still, long familiarity with disease, and practical skill acquired for its control, have, to a considerable degree, given to the inhabitants a sort of recklessness and seeming insensibility to the extent to which it prevails; and question one of them if his locality be healthful, and you will probably be assured that, though pestilence strolls through surrounding districts, his own is the favorite abode of Esculapius. And you will not discover that it is otherwise, till, as the sickly season approaches, you see on every hand increasing symptoms of disease; one after another, in alarmingly rapid succession, sinking beneath its influence; and it sometimes happens, that in a neighborhood thus afflicted, there are scarcely a sufficient number of well persons to take care of the sick.

Turning northward from Virginia—not in spring, but in the last months of summer—a pleasing change of scenery is soon apparent to the observer. The fields contract in their dimensions, yet present to the eye a greater variety, and everywhere assume a more fresh and healthful aspect. The tall brown grass gives place to verdant meadows. Herbage becomes of a deeper green, and dense fields of corn and broomcorn wave gently to the breeze. Fruit-yards and orchards multiply in all directions, encircling every little country cottage, and weighed down with their luxuriant burdens, imparting to the landscape an air of peace and plenty. Towns and villages are of greater frequency. And in short, as you approach the great northern metropolis of trade, the whole appearance of things is changed; you are greeted in a different dialect; different habits and manners attract attention; and a certain something in the general air of all around, tells you that the hot haste of steam has in two short days conveyed you to another soil, beneath another sky, and among another people. Still you are yet, as it were, only in the great congress-place of states. Here citizens from both sides of Dixon's line meet, some on business, others in friendship. Peculiarities of diverse sections of our Union conflict with and modify each other; and altogether there is presented a sort of amalgamated medium or medley mass, retaining indeed much that is sectional, but intermingled with almost every variety of habits, appearance, and customs.

History.—Some writers are of the opinion that Sebastian Cabot discovered the coast of Virginia, in his voyage of 1498; but circumstances delayed the settlement, and even all particular acquaintance, with this part of the country until a much later period. In consequence of Martin Frobisher having taken back to England from Hudson river, as was pretended, a small piece of gold, the merchants of London, incited by the hope of enriching themselves as the Spaniards had done in South America, engaged in voyages of discovery with great zeal in 1578. But this spirit was short-lived, their enterprises being altogether unfortunate. The expedition of Sir Humphrey Gilbert in 1578, and that in 1583, had no better success, one of the vessels, with the leader of the expedition, being lost on the way home.

The next year, however, his step-brother, Sir Walter Raleigh, had better success, in a voyage he made to America, under one of the very liberal royal patents so easily obtained at that period. On the 13th of July the vessels entered Ocracoke inlet (now in North Carolina); and a landing was made at Wocoken island, where an amicable intercourse was opened with the natives. A colony was formed under Governor Lane; but as no gold was found, and prospects became discouraging, it was soon abandoned, but not until the important discovery had been made of Chesapeake bay. Passing by one or two other unsuccessful attempts of the same kind, we come to the year 1606, when Jamestown was occupied by the celebrated Captain John Smith.

Under the command of Captain Newport, on the 19th of December, three small vessels sailed for Virginia with one hundred and five colonists. The aggregate numbers of tons of all these vessels was one hundred and sixty; and they were detained on the English coast six weeks by the weather.

Taking the usual course of a southern passage at that day, they steered first for the Canary islands, and then stopped at the West Indies; and the consequence was, that the expedition did not arrive at the Delaware until April 26th of the following year. Dissensions had arisen during the voyage, which could not be pacified before making the land, because the instructions delivered them by royal authority were sealed, and not to be opened until after the landing.

The capes of the Chesapeake then received the names which they still bear, after the two sons of King James—Charles and Henry. The first landing was effected on Cape Henry, and there the instructions were read, which appointed a council for the government of the country, among which was Smith. Such, however, was the opposition made to him, that he was excluded by a vote, and Wingfield was elected president. The colonists soon re-embarked, sailed into the bay, and entered a fine river, which they named James, in honor of the king, though the natives called it Powhatan. Proceeding up the stream about fifty miles, they chose a spot for a town. The president, through some foolish jealousy of his people, refused permission to erect a fort or to allow military exercises, but sent Smith and a few other men to make discoveries; while, by the exertions of Kendall, a half-moon was constructed of the boughs of trees, as a feeble breastwork.

JAMESTOWN, seven miles from Williamsburg, is now a deserted spot containing only a few remains of its ancient importance. It is truly an interesting place, as the first ground occupied by a permanent colony within the boundaries of the country, and the scene of the principal events, before mentioned, connected with the early settlement.

James city was one of the eight original shires into which Virginia was divided in 1634, and is twenty-three miles long by about eight miles wide, being bounded on the north and south by York and James rivers. The population at the last census was 1,325 whites, 1,947 slaves, 507 free colored persons—in all, 3,779.

Jamestown is the spot which was occupied by Captain John Smith and his companions, and is a point of land belonging to the tract that extends into James river. The current is gradually wearing away the land. The only remains are the stone tower of an old, ruinous church, of unknown date, and the churchyard. The Westover manuscript says a church was erected here

Ruins of Jamestown.

very soon after the beginning of the settlement, but it cost only fifty pounds, and therefore must have been but a small and perishable building. The edifice of which the remains are now to be seen, must have been of a later date, and may have been the second which, as we learn from Smith's journal, was in ruins in 1617. If so, the venerable remains represented in the cut must be two hundred and thirty years old.

This vicinity is also remarkable for the invasion of Arnold, January 3, 1781, and for two actions fought here between General La Fayette and the troops of Cornwallis, June 25 and July 8, 1781.

But to return to the narrative of early events. While on his journey of discovery, Smith penetrated to the falls of the river, and found a native tribe seated near the present site of Richmond, under the command of the chief Powhatan, by whom he was kindly received. But during his absence, the colonists, while at work, had been assailed by the neighboring savages, who wounded seventeen men and killed a boy. The interference of the crews of the vessels alone saved them all from destruction. From that time watch was kept by day and night, and preparation made for defence by erecting a fort and otherwise.

Newport prepared to depart at the end of six weeks; but before he left the colony, Smith was tried by the council at his own request; and although great exertions were made to procure his condemnation, he received an award of two hundred pounds as damages for injurious treatment; but this he threw into the common stock. The vessels now sailed, leaving a feeble colony of about one hundred men, about one half of whom were "gentlemen," unaccustomed to labor, and ill qualified to endure privations and hardships; and so powerful were the effect of the climate and the circumstances around them, that at the end of a week hardly ten of the company were able to stand upon their feet. Fifty died between the months of May and September; yet the president felt so little sympathy with his companions, that he enjoyed every luxury within his reach, while they were living miserably on such food as they were able to procure, chiefly sturgeon and crabs taken from the water. Newport, however, being at length arrested, in an attempt to abandon the sufferers by sailing away in the pinnace, was deposed, and Ratcliffe was appointed president in his place.

He, however, proved so unpopular and so incompetent, that he was glad to place Smith in fact at the head of affairs; and by the energy of the latter, the colony was saved from starvation. Finding all other means to obtain provisions unsuccessful, he managed to terrify the Indian tribe dwelling at Hampton (then called Keochtan), so much that they furnished them with food. Soon after this, Smith was made prisoner by the savages, and after being sentenced to die, and led out for execution, was rescued by the celebrated princess Pocahontas; with the history of whom, and this singular act of humanity performed by her, we presume our readers are familiar.

In 1609, a new charter was granted by the king to the company, entitled "The Treasurer and Company of Adventurers of the City of London, for the First Colony in Virginia;" the powers and territory being enlarged, and a new council being formed in England, while the old president and council were abolished. Lord Delaware, or De la War, was appointed governor, and five hundred emigrants were collected, who embarked in nine ships, under the command of Captain Newport, who, with Sir Thomas Gates and Sir George Somers, was to exercise the government until the arrival of the governor. The vessel in which the three governors sailed was separated from the rest by a storm, and driven to Bermuda; and, when the others arrived at Jamestown, the emigrants proved so wild and insubordinate, and so unsuccessful in their attempts to form a government, that Smith, finding the colony exposed to an attack from the Indians, resumed his authority, imprisoned the most turbulent, and soon reduced things to a state of order. He then sent a band of settlers into the country, who began a new town; but, being alarmed at the hostile aspect of the natives, they soon sent to him for protection.

Smith, a short time after this, was shockingly mangled by the explosion of some gunpowder, and was compelled to go to England for surgical aid, whence he never returned. The colony suffered severely from his loss. Being left under the government of Mr. Percy, a man of less energy than goodness of heart, the motley band of colonists, consisting chiefly of broken-down tradesmen and profligate young men, soon fell into confusion and anarchy; and the Indians, emboldened by their weakness, threatened them so much that the settlement was abandoned, and the people were proceeding to sea, when, at the mouth of James river, they met Lord Delaware, and were encouraged to return. By remonstrances, threats, and promises, he reduced them to a state of order, and formed a council, consisting of Sir Thomas Gates, his lieutenant-general; Sir George Somers, his admiral; the honorable George Percy, one of his captains; Sir Fernando Weinman, his master of ordnance; and Christopher Newport, his vice-admiral.

But the state of things was very alarming; though the ships had brought out clothing and biscuit, they had not supplies of meat; the five hundred hogs left by Smith were all gone, and the Indians had driven away the deer from the forest on purpose to distress the foreigners; while the fish, though abundant, could not be taken for the want of good nets. The governor had found plenty of hogs at Bermuda, though there were no inhabitants, and sent there for a supply; while he took other means to procure provisions, though with little success, as most of the Indians refused all assistance, and Powhatan was openly hostile.

To terrify this chief, Delaware cut off the hand of one of his Indians, and sent him to threaten similar treatment to all who should attempt to injure the colonists; and this awed the savages into peace. The first exports were soon after made from the colony to England; and being only cedar and black-walnut wood and iron, instead of gold, the company were hardly persuaded, by Delaware's representations of the fertility of the soil and the prospect of success in agriculture, to sustain the settlement they had begun. Successive fluctuations in the political condition of the colony continued to retard its improvement for several years.

In 1613 the land was divided among the people, having before that been held in common, by which practice general idleness had been fostered. The following year, Argal was sent against the French colony of L'Acadie, and he took Port Royal, and also seized New York, on his way home, in the name of England. Tobacco began to be extensively cultivated in 1615.

Captain Argal was appointed governor in 1616, after the return of Governor Yeardly to England; but, in consequence of tyrannical conduct, he was superseded by Yeardly in 1619. In that year the first colonial assembly in America was convoked, and consisted of the governor, the council, and two burgesses, elected by each of the boroughs, which then numbered eleven. They assembled in one room at Jamestown, and the laws they adopted were sent to England for the approbation of the company, who soon after sanctioned the acts of the Virginia legislature, but reserved the power of appointing a council of state. The laws passed by the legislature were to be ratified by the court of proprietors, and the orders of that court were to be approved by the assembly, before they could be carried into effect.

The first slaves were brought into the colony in 1620, by a Dutch trading-vessel from Africa, which sailed up James river, and sold part of her cargo to the planters. Finding the climate more favorable to blacks, importations increased, and the traffic soon became extensive.

During the civil wars in England under the reign of Charles I., many of his opposers, after falling into his hands as prisoners, were transported to Virginia and sold as slaves. This was the fact with many of the captives taken in the battles of Dunbar and Worcester, and the leaders of the insurrection of Penruddoc. Besides, many poor persons were induced to emigrate from England, under promises to pay their passage by subsequent labor; and these were sold to the highest bidders after their arrival, and set to work for the benefit of their purchasers.

In 1620, ninety young women were sent from England to be sold for wives; and in the following year sixty more. The first sales were made for one hundred and twenty pounds of tobacco, and the last for one hundred and fifty.

Measures were soon after taken for the establishment of an institution for education, which at length resulted in the foundation of William and Mary college. A dispute arose, under Sir Geo. Yeardley's government, with the king about the exportation of tobacco; and great and imminent dangers were threatened by an Indian plot to extirpate the colonists, which was so far successful that three hundred and forty-seven persons' lives were sacrificed, and the number of settlements reduced from eighty to six. A war ensued, in which the savages suffered severely.

After a prolonged contest between King James and the colony, a new charter was exchanged for the old, while he prohibited the cultivation of tobacco in England, and gave the exclusive trade in it to Virginia and the Somers islands. Charles I., on the other hand, claimed the government to himself, and forbade the vending of tobacco to any but his own agents, appointing Yeardley governor, and twelve councillors to make laws and exercise other high powers, which led to new difficulties. The authority of Cromwell was disputed as long as possible, and the majority of the people, being episcopalians and loyalists, ever remained attached to the royal party, and received from Charles II., while in exile, Sir William Berkeley as their governor. After the restoration, Berkeley introduced several aristocratic features into the government, establishing the church of England by law, prohibiting the preaching of dissenters, depriving the poorer people of the right of suffrage, raising the salaries of officers, &c. The navigation-act was passed by parliament, by which new restrictions were laid on commerce; and Bacon's rebellion soon after broke out, which continued seven months, until the death of its ringleader, who had already succeeded in reducing Jamestown to ashes, and sustaining a rebellious government. Berkeley, with great humanity, soon reduced the colony again to quiet; but a variety of changes afterward followed, which may be passed by in a brief sketch of the history of this colony.

Virginia continued attached to the royal party in England through the struggles of the following generations. The French war, in the middle of the last century, had disastrous effects on the new western settlements, which were the scenes of massacres and of several military expeditions, especially the ill-fated one under General Braddock.

In that war, George Washington commenced that career which he pursued through the revolution with such unrivalled splendor, and with such great and beneficial effects to his country and to mankind.

Says a late writer: "I look upon Washington as the peculiar gift of God to the American people: I regard him as specially raised up as our political Joshua, to guide these people across the swellings of a war-vexed revolution to the fair inheritance of freedom which lay beyond. I behold in him the development of a character that has no equal in the annals of man; and I feel, therefore, that it is true, as has been stated by a distinguished nobleman of England (Lord Brougham), that, until time shall be no more, the progress of our race in wisdom and virtue will be tested by the veneration paid to the immortal name of Washington.

"A review of the many dangers to which Washington was exposed from childhood, makes it clear that nothing but the watchful providence of God—keeping him for some great end—could have protected him amid the dangers of youth, the vicissitudes of manhood, the perils of the wilderness, and the fortunes of a bloody war.

"It was God who so ordered the anxious fear of his mother, as to prevent

Portrait of Washington.

the lad of fourteen from accepting a midshipman's warrant in the royal navy of England. HE it was who marked out for his youth the occupation of a surveyor, by which his body was knit into strength—his mind inured to danger; so that much of his future success hung upon the knowledge gathered, while, with the chain and compass, he ranged the hills and valleys of western Virginia.

"It was God who protected him in all the perils of the French war, and particularly in that bloody battle of the Monongahela, when Braddock and one half of the army fell. Washington himself felt and acknowledged this, and said in a letter to his brother: 'By the all-powerful dispensation of Providence, I have been protected beyond all human probability or expectation; for I had four bullets through my coat, and two horses shot under me; yet I escaped unhurt, although death was levelling my companions on every side of me.' Not only was this protection known and acknowledged in the pulpit at the time, in that almost prophetic sentence of Davies where, speaking of that heroic youth, he adds: 'whom I can not but hope that Providence has hitherto preserved in so signal a manner for some important service to his country'—but even the Indians were persuaded that he was under the special guardianship of the Great Spirit; because, though they had singled him out in that battle for the aim of their sharpshooters, not a ball touched him, and they felt that he was the particular favorite of Heaven, who could never die in battle.

"Indeed, in all his exposures by land and sea—in open war and covered ambush—in the masked treachery of pretended friends, and the hireling assaults of pensioned murderers, it was God who 'covered his head in the day of battle'—who preserved him from danger—and who checked the hands and bridled the power of those who had vowed his destruction.

"The French war, which called out so large a share of his youthful prowess, and in which his military abilities shone so pre-eminent, he saw honorably closed by the defeat of his enemies and the possession of their lands. The revolution, which began in the oppressions of the British parliament, and the war which he conducted from its beginning to its end, he beheld terminated in peace; his enemies were driven from our shores; and the red cross of old England gave place to Freedom's banner, with its stars for glory and its stripes for foes.

"Others had often begun to battle for the rights of their country, but ended by fighting for themselves. Others had frequently unsheathed their swords for freedom, but soon had even cloven down freedom in their march to dominion. Others had attempted to guide a nation from monarchy to republicanism; but, having once grasped the reins of power, they soon became the charioteers of their own glory, and drove with scythe-armed wheels through the land they covenanted to redeem.

"But Washington accepted military authority with reluctance—used it with prudence—freed a nation from its oppression—drove from it its foes—established for it perfect freedom; and then, when an admiring army and his native state would have taken him and made him their king—when applause rang loudest and fame shone brightest, and Power threw herself a willing captive in his arms—when he was confessedly first and supreme, did he resign his commission, ungird his sword, and return a private citizen to his farms on the Potomac.

"Robertson, speaking of the abdication of Diocletian and of Charles V., remarks: 'To descend voluntarily from the supreme to a subordinate station, and to relinquish the possession of power in order to attain the enjoyment of happiness, seems to be an effort too great for the human mind.' But it was not too great an act for Washington—he did it—but not, like the abdicating emperors, with an impaired constitution, and the infirmities of age crumbling his heart within him. He did it in the prime and vigor of life and health, resolving, in his own manly language, 'to pass the remainder of his days in honorable repose, and place his glory beyond the reach of fortune.'"

The Birthplace of Washington.—The house which formerly occupied this spot, and in which the hero of America was born and spent his earliest years, was destroyed before the revolution. The place is in Westmoreland, in the county of Westmoreland, half a mile from the mouth of Pope's creek. This spot, though marked only by a simple monument, must ever possess an unspeakable degree of interest to every person who loves his country and the principles of that most exalted character which was here formed and matured, under the instructions of a pure and noble-minded mother. How strongly must every visiter to that spot feel that

"His name is his own best monument."

The plain stone, placed here by his relative, G. W. P. Custis, bears the expressive inscription:—

"Here, on the 11th of February (O. S.), 1732 George Washington was born."

The scenery around the place is very fine. The Maryland shore is in sight for a considerable distance, with the river Potomac, which flows along under the eye for many miles, on its way toward the capital. The house was of the old-fashioned kind, of wood, and two-two stories high, with four rooms on the first floor.

The following memorandum of the birth of Washington is copied from the

The Birthplace of Washington.

family record in the bible which belonged to his mother, and believed to have been written by her hand:—

"George Washington, son to Augustine and Mary his wife, was born yᵉ 11th day of February, 1732, about 10 in yᵉ morning, and was baptized yᵉ 3d of April following. Mr. Beverly Whiting and Captain Christopher Brooks, godfathers, and Mrs. Wildred Gregory, godmother."

Soon after the passage of the stamp-act, Patrick Henry introduced into the Virginia assembly the following resolution: "That the general assembly of this colony, together with his majesty or substitute, have, in their representative capacity, the only exclusive right and power to lay taxes and impositions upon the inhabitants of this colony; and that every attempt to vest such power in any person or persons whatsoever, other than the general assembly as aforesaid, is illegal, unconstitutional, and unjust, and has a manifest tendency to destroy British as well as American freedom."

The resolution was adopted, on which the governor dissolved the chamber. When election day arrived, however, the members who had voted for it were re-elected by the people, and its opposers were left out.

After the repeal of the stamp-act, the legislature of Virginia sent a vote of thanks to the king and parliament.

Governor Fauquier died in 1767, and the following year Lord Botetourt arrived from England as his successor. He soon dissolved the assembly, because they had adopted a resolution condemning the taxes on paper, &c.; but the members combined in a non-importation association. Lord Botetourt had much influence, but could not long suppress the dissatisfaction excited among the people at the course of the British ministry. He died in 1771, and the statue now standing in Williamsburg was then erected to his memory.

Lord Dunmore, the next governor, stooped to the fomenting of paltry dissensions, to divert the attention of the people from the designs of the king; but the news of the destruction of the tea at Boston called out a spirited resolution from the Virginia assembly, for which they were again dissolved; and on the following day the members assembled and agreed on an address to the people, pronouncing an attack on one of the colonies an attack upon all British America, and appointed deputies to attend a general congress.

Early in the days of the revolution, Thomas Jefferson became a leading man in Virginia, and he was for a long time afterward one of the principal men in the country. He was born at Shadwell, in the county of Albemarle, April 2, 1743, and receive from his father an ample fortune. He graduated with distinction at William and Mary college, and studied law under George Wythe. Soon after he became of age, he was a representative in the colonial assembly and had a seal with this motto, expressive of his liberal sentiments: "Resistance to tyrants is obedience to God." In 1772 he married Miss Wayles, who died ten years afterward, leaving two daughters.

In 1772 he organized the first system of colonial resistance, by appointing committees of correspondence; in 1776 he took his seat in congress, where he drew up the Declaration of Independence. In 1779–'80 he was governor of Virginia, during the days of the invasion. In 1783 he returned to congress, and drew up the address of that body to Washington on his taking leave of public life. In 1784 he went to France as minister, and was afterward secretary of state under Washington. In 1798 he retired to Monticello, and from 1801 till 1809 was president of the United States, having formed a democratic party, in opposition to the Washington or federal party, may of the principles and measures of which he opposed. He finally retired to Monticello in 1809, where he died July 4, 1826, at the age of eighty-three years. His grave is in a grove, near the road, at the foot of Monticello.

Monticello.—This elegant mansion, the seat of Jefferson, is situated on the top of a steep conical eminence, rising from an elliptical plain, three miles southeast from Charlottesville. Toward

Monticello, late Residence of Thomas Jefferson, now in possession of Capt. Levy, U. S. N.

the west, and partly north and south, it commands a view of Blue ridge, which stretches away one hundred and fifty miles; while on the east is seen a boundless plain. At different points rise several mountains of various forms and sizes, among which one of the most conspicuous and interesting is Willis' mountain in the south.

The approach to the house affords glimpses of this fine scene; and the spacious hall at the entrance was ornamented with objects of taste, arranged in an appropriate manner to gratify the eye. Mr. Wirt, in his description of the place, mentions that Jefferson had placed various specimens of sculpture in that hall, in such order as to mark the progress of the art from the rudest to the most perfect state: at the end being seen his own statue by Carracci. On other sides were displayed Indian remains, petrified bones, the horns of deer, &c. The grand saloon, in which the visiter is next ushered, is appropriated as a picture-gallery, and contains a great number of valuable productions of the pencil and the graver, comprising many historical events and distinguished men of all ages. The windows command charming views of the extensive scene below.

In September, 1774, the meeting of delegates was held in Philadelphia. The disaffections continued between the governor and the people, but they joined in an expedition against the Indians in western Virginia, who had assumed a hostile attitude, as was suspected, by the intrigues of the governor. On the 20th of April, 1775, he was so bold as secretly to remove the gunpowder from the colonial magazine, at Williamsburg, to Yorktown, where it was stowed in a British vessel. The people took up arms; but the governor threatened, in case of any resistance, to proclaim liberty to the slaves, and set the town on fire. Six hundred men were soon assembled at Fredericksburg to protect it, and to oppose any rash measure, while thousands prepared, throughout the colony, to render their aid if necessary. At this crisis, the two leading patriots of the time, Peyton Randolph and Edmund Pendleton, sent to the former a request that they would do nothing until congress should decide on some general plan of defence.

The assembly then held a council, consisting of more than one hundred members, who adopted, by a majority of only one, a resolution to disperse for the present, and draughted an address, in which they "firmly resolved to resist all attempts against their rights and privileges, from whatever quarter they might be assailed;" and firmly pledged themselves "to reassemble, and, by force of arms, to defend the laws, the liberties, and the rights, of this or any sister colony, from unjust and wicked invasion. God save the liberties of America!"

Patrick Henry, however, at the head of the volunteers of Hanover, marched from Doncaster to recover the powder, and, being joined by numbers from the counties of King William and New Kent, obtained ample compensation from Corbin, the king's receiver-general, and then returning dismissed the troops. The governor issued a proclamation against him two days after; but he left the state, about the same time, to attend the meeting of the continental congress, while a band of insurgents seized the arms in the magazine. Committees of safety were soon formed in the counties of Virginia, and "minute-men" were raised, who, as John Randolph, of Roanoke, afterward remarked, with characteristic humor, were raised in a minute, marched in a minute, and defeated in a minute.

Among the acts of the governor which fomented discord, was his sending for aid to the commander of the Fowey ship-of-war, off Yorktown, while Patrick Henry was on his march; in consequence of which forty marines and sailors were stationed at Williamsburg about ten days, while the ship threatened to fire upon Yorktown in case they should be molested.

Governor Dunmore convened the assembly on the 1st of June, and made an address, in consequence of which the house of burgesses had a correspondence with him, defending the rights of the colonies. He took refuge on board the

Fowey, on the 8th, with his family, under pretext that they were not safe on shore; and refused to sign any bills, unless the assembly would meet him under cover of the guns. He was then, by a resolution, declared to have abdicated his office, and the president of the council proceeded to act in his place. Near the end of the month the vessel sailed down the river: and thus closed the royal government of Virginia.

Delegates soon after met in Richmond, to form a provisional government; and a description of this beautiful town, now large and important, may be here introduced, as it began to rise into consequence at about this period of its history.

Richmond.—This is the capital and principal town of the state, the capital of Henrico county, and a port of entry, standing at the foot of the lower falls on James river, 117 miles from Washington, 342 from New York, 557 from Boston, 520 from Cincinnati, 423 from Charleston, 62 from Fredericksburg, 106 from Norfolk, 146 from Winchester, and 23 from Petersburg.

The spot on which this large and fine city stands was first visited by white men in 1609, when "Master West" penetrated to the falls in search of provisions for the young colony at Jamestown, but found nothing edible except acorns. He however began a settlement near the place the same year, with one hundred and twenty men. Smith attempted a settlement at "Nonsuch," but failed. Fort Charles was erected at the Falls in 1644–'5; and in 1646 the assembly offered extraordinary inducements to encourage a settlement on the south side of the river, opposite the fort.

Richmond was founded in 1742, and made the state capital in 1780, since which it has steadily increased. The population in 1800 was 5,737; in 1810, 9,785; in 1820, 12,067; in 1830, 16,060; in 1840, 20,153; in 1850, 27,483. The city is situated at the head of tidewater, and vessels drawing ten feet of water can come up to within one mile of the centre of the city, and those drawing fifteen feet to within three miles. A canal with locks extends around the falls (opened in 1794), above which boats navigate the river two hundred and twenty miles. A canal affords navigation also to Lynchburg, one hundred and sixteen miles.

The situation is healthy and pleasant; and the city has a pleasing appearance from several points of view, especially that from which it is represented in the cut. It is generally well built, and the streets cross at right angles. Richmond hill and Shockoe hill, rising from the opposite side of Shockoe creek, vary the surface of the ground, the town being situated between them, and up both acclivities. The latter eminence affords fine situations for dwellings, and is the favorite quarter, containing many handsome houses; while on its summit stands the state capitol, surrounded by a spacious square of eight acres, enclosed with an iron fence.

The city-hall, opposite, is a fine edifice in Grecian style; and among the other public buildings are three banks, two insurance offices, the armory, theatre, female asylum, penitentiary, thirteen academies and higher schools, the free Lancasterian school, and twenty-three churches.

The water-works, by which the city is supplied, raise the water, by hydraulic power, into three reservoirs, each containing a million of gallons, and from these lead off to all parts of the city.

The *Medical College* is a department of Hampden Sidney college, and has a building in the Egyptian style. It has a dean and five members of the faculty.

Richmond College, a baptist institution, is one mile west of the city, and contains about one hundred students.

St. Vincent's College, a Roman catholic institution, is situated one mile east of the city, and has about fifty students.

Richmond presents many varying aspects, from different points of the undulating surface above the banks of the creek. The falls, extending more than six miles, give liveliness to the water-scene; while the islands which lie upon the surface and the two bridges, which cross it, to connect the town with Manchester on the opposite shore, offer a constant and pleasing variety. The city

View of Richmond.

plot now covers about three and a half square miles, being seven and a half miles long; but only a small portion of this is thickly covered with buildings. A spot near the centre of the business part of the city is occupied by the basin of the canal.

The *State Penitentiary*, in the western suburbs, is in the form of a hollow square, three hundred feet by one hundred and ten, with several acres of ground attached.

The *Armory* contains a considerable supply of arms, and is three hundred and eighty feet by three hundred and twenty.

Manufactures are carried on to a considerable extent, by water-power obtained at the falls. Within two or three years, cotton mills have been erected and are in profitable employment. Richmond has many facilities for this species of industry, which must ultimately become advantageous to the whole neighborhood. The total amount of capital invested in manufactures in Richmond is about two millions of dollars. Richmond is a great commercial dépôt, having an extensive back country abounding in tobacco, wheat, hemp, and coal, which is reached by the James river canal and branches. The flouring mills of Richmond have a world-wide celebrity.

The Capitol.—This fine and chaste edifice occupies a lofty and commanding position on the summit of Shockoe hill, in the midst of the spacious public square before described. The front is ornamented with an Ionic portico, with lofty columns; and the effect of the building, from its elegant front, is very fine, when seen from the neighboring points of view. The building contains the halls of the senate and house of delegates, with numerous rooms for officers, committees, &c.; and here assemble the legislators of this great and influential state, to deliberate on the interests of its various sections.

From different parts of the capitol, as well as from the neighboring grounds, are presented many fine views over the surrounding country, and the city and river below; and the scene is the most imposing one of the kind to be found within the limits of the state. James river is seen, after flowing down the long falls and rapids which interrupt its course above the city, spreading wide its smooth surface, to float the boats, vessels, and steamboats, which ever enliven its course between this point and its mouth; while the two beautiful bridges which cross the stream and connect the opposite shores, afford passages from side to side.

The important figure which the capitol makes in the preceding general view of Richmond, gives a just idea of its importance, as a principal feature in the aspect of the city from many different points of view. Crowning the summit of the principal eminence, and rising far above the crowded city, it forms an appropriate and elegant trait to a scene otherwise possessing many beauties.

The Statue of Washington.—This interesting piece of sculpture, the work of a distinguished French artist of the last century, stands in the area of the capitol. It was made by Houdon, in Paris, a few years after the Revolution, at the order of the Virginia assembly, and under the direction of Jefferson. Washington is represented in the military costume of the country at the time, covered with a cloak, while one hand holds a cane, and the other the fasces; and on the pedestal is the following inscription, written by Mr. Madison:—

"George Washington. The General Assembly of the Commonwealth of Virginia have caused this statue to be erected, as a monument of affection and gratitude, to George Washington, who, uniting to the endowments of the *hero* the virtues of the *patriot*, and exerting both in establishing the liberties of his country, has rendered his name dear to his fellow-citizens, and given the world an immortal example of true glory. Done in the year of Christ one thousand seven hundred and eighty-eight, in the year of the Commonwealth the twelfth."

The Bust of LaFayette.—This handsome specimen of sculpture is appropriately placed near the statue of Washington.

The Monumental Church.—This edifice was erected in commemoration of the calamitous destruction, in 1811, of a theatre which stood on the same spot. About six hundred persons were assembled in the theatre on the fatal evening, when, at the conclusion of the play, the scenery accidentally caught fire, and a

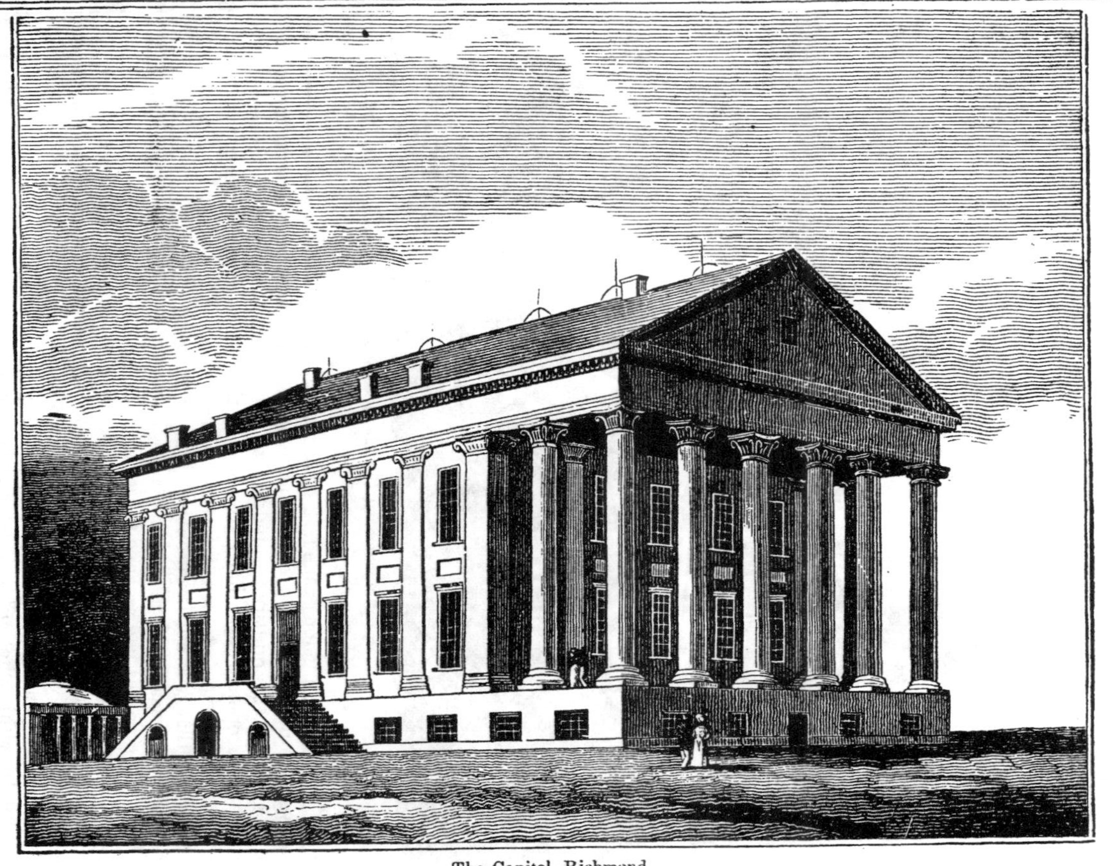

The Capitol, Richmond.

Monumental Church—Richmond.

scene of dreadful confusion ensued. The doors were so narrow as to prevent the ready egress of the multitude—indeed only one door opened into that part of the house where most of them were assembled, and that was not large enough to permit the escape of more than a few before the flames had reached those within. Many were scorched by the burning of their clothes; great numbers jumped from the windows, some with the flames all around them; and many died, chiefly within the building, which was soon enveloped in flames. The scene caused a dreadful shock throughout the country; but the gloom in the city itself was deep indeed. Hundreds of families lost their nearest members or friends, and the sad effects of the mournful calamity were general and lasting.

An episcopal society afterward erected the Monumental Church on the spot, to perpetuate the memory of the event; and the bones found among the ruins were collected and placed in an urn at the entrance.

The above cut affords a view of this edifice, the melancholy associations connected with which must ever continue to be of a nature peculiarly solemn and impressive.

We now return to the progress of events in the history of the state. On the 17th of July, 1775, delegates from the counties met at Richmond (as before remarked) to form a provisional government and a plan of defence, and the following persons were put on the committee of safety: Ed. Pendleton, George Mason, Jno. Page, Richard Bland, Thos.

Ludwell Lee, Paul Carrington, Dudley Digges, Jas. Mercer, Carter Braxton, Wm. Cabell, and Jno. Tabb. Preparations were made for raising troops, and the county committees were requested to provide colors bearing the motto: "Virginia for Constitutional Liberty." But the governor proceeded to several acts of hostility He landed a party at Norfolk, under cover of the men-of-war, and carried off the press and types of a patriotic newspaper; and soon after he marched to Kempsville to destroy a collection of firearms, and made prisoner the commander of the minute-men, Captain Matthews. Hampton was also attacked by British vessels under Captain Squires; but they were driven off without loss on the part of the patriots. A number of armed men now arrived at Williamsburg from the upper country; and Lord Dunsmore, having heard that the second Virginia regiment and the Culpepper battalion had been ordered to Norfolk, sent the Kingfisher and three large tenders up James river to Burwell's ferry, to prevent their crossing. A large boat was twice beaten off by the Virginia riflemen, as was also another boat, which afterward attempted to land at Jamestown. In the same month a colonel of Princess Ann militia was made prisoner by Lord Dunsmore, with some of his men, on their march. On the 7th of November he proclaimed martial law, and, with a considerable force at his command, raised his standard in Norfolk and Princess Ann.

Having ordered the militia captains to raise troops in opposition to the colonial army, he proposed to destroy the colonial stores of provisions at Suffolk; but two hundred and fifteen light troops were sent for their defence by Colonel Woodford. He then undertook to incite the western Indians to war in co-operation with him, and matured a plan with a Pennsylvanian, named O'Connelly, who was made a lieutenant-colonel by General Gage at Boston. A regiment of volunteers was to be raised at Fort Pitt, who, accompanied by several companies of royal Irish, were to march across Virginia to Alexandria, and take possession of the town, in co-operation with Lord Dunsmore, in the ships-of-war. The plot, however, was discovered and defeated after a time; for O'-Connelly, Cameron, and Dr. Jno. Smith, were arrested near Hagerstown (Maryland), on suspicion, and were found in possession of papers and money, which fully proved their guilt.

Colonel Woodford, on his march to Norfolk, found the enemy in a stockade fort at the Great bridge—the only way by which he could proceed; and, having thrown up a breastwork, was soon attacked, but repulsed the British with great loss to them, and drove them to their vessels. Lord Dunsmore cannonaded Norfolk on the night of January 1st, 1776, and having destroyed parts of it, Lieutenant-Colonel Howe was ordered by the committee of safety to burn the remainder. That city had contained six thousand inhabitants.

Nine regiments, in all, were now raised, of which six were placed on the continental establishment, of the first of which Patrick Henry was appointed colonel. He, however, soon resigned his commission, and was chosen a member of the new convention at Hanover, who appointed delegates to congress, instructing them "to propose to that respectable body to declare the United Colonies free and independent states, absolved from all allegiance to, or dependence on, the crown or parliament." A constitution was adopted on the 25th of June, and was the first formed without admitting any prospect of reconciliation with the mother-country. Patrick Henry was chosen governor; and from that time through the war, Virginia continued to sustain the cause of independence, harmoniously and efficiently co-operating with her sister-colonies, until the independence of the country was settled by the great and final victory on her own soil, at Yorktown.

The first constitution of the state was adopted on the 5th of July, 1776, and revised in 1830. The right of suffrage is restricted to heads of families paying taxes or owners of certain amounts and kinds of property. There are one hundred and thirty-four delegates in the house, chosen annually, and thirty-two senators, elected for four years. The governor is chosen for four years by the legislature, and ineligible the next three years.

As early as 1681, there was a dispute between William Penn and Lord Baltimore, respecting the construction of their respective grants, the debatable land being one degree, or sixty-nine English miles, on the south line of Pennsylvania, and extending west as far as the state itself. The matter was in litigation over sixty years, when Charles Mason and Jeremiah Dixon were appointed to run the line in dispute. This is the boundary line separating Virginia and Maryland from Pennsylvania, and known as "Mason and Dixon's line."

Education.—There is a literary fund in this state, to promote learning in general, established from escheats of all lands, militia and other fines, all forfeited lands, overplus of debt due from the United States, and some other contingent funds. A great part of this fund has been borrowed to establish the university of the state. About fifty thousand dollars are annually appropriated to the several counties, according to their number of white children. This fund is collected by the state auditor, and is under the direction of a corporation composed of the governor, attorney-general, treasurer, and the president of the court of appeals, who appoint an agent in each county to collect the funds. School commissioners are appointed by the county courts, who have power to determine what number of poor children shall be educated, and to draw orders on the treasurer for the amount of the tuition.

Printing.—The first newspaper in Virginia was printed at Williamsburg, August 6, 1736, by W. Parkes, at fifteen shillings per annum. The same man had printed Stith's History of Virginia in 1729, and the laws of the colony. His paper was under the influence of the government, and ceased at his death, in 1761, until revived by William Hunter in 1751. It was at first only twelve inches by six in size. In 1761 it was enlarged by John Royle, and continued to appear until some time in the revolutionary war. In 1766 William Rind was invited to come from Maryland and establish the second newspaper, which was the "Virginia Gazette." It was "open to all parties." His widow, Clementina Rind, continued it for some time from his death, in 1773, and was succeeded by John Pinckney. Another "Virginia Gazette" was commenced at Williamsburg in 1775.

The first printing-press in Virginia was erected in 1681, but was soon put down—Sir William Berkeley being opposed, like many other influential men in the colony, to the diffusion of knowledge. In 1671 he "thanked God there are no free schools nor printing (in Virginia), and hoped we shall not have, these hundreds of years to come."

Norfolk.—This is the most important seaport in the state. It occupies a commanding situation at the mouth of Elizabeth river, at the southern extremity of Chesapeake bay, only eight miles from Hampton Roads, by which it communicates with the Atlantic ocean; one hundred and six miles from Richmond; and two hundred and twenty-nine from Washington city. The ground on which it stands is low, and the same feature prevails for miles around the city. The streets are crooked, and the appearance of the town rather uninviting. The principal public buildings are the market, customhouse, theatre, four banks, eight churches, an academy, a Lancasterian school, orphan asylum, &c. The population is about fifteen thousand, and the commerce of the place considerable.

Large steamboats depart daily for Richmond, and others for Washington and Baltimore. A railroad leads south to North Carolina, on which cars run daily to Wilmington.

Portsmouth, on the opposite side of Elizabeth river, appears like a part of Norfolk. It is the site of the

U. S. Navyyard, which occupies a portion of the town called Gosport. A large and expensive dry-dock has been constructed there, and the storehouses, workshops, &c., occupy a large extent of ground. There is also the Virginia Literary and Scientific academy, founded in 1840, which has about forty pupils.

The *U. S. Naval Hospital* stands at a short distance from the town.

The other public buildings in Portsmouth are the courthouse, a bank, and six churches; and the population is about nine thousand.

The *Dismal Swamp Canal* leads from this place through that extensive and melancholy morass into North Carolina, and is an important channel of transportation. It is more particularly noticed under the head of North Carolina.

HAMPTON, situated near the mouth of James river, on the eastern bank, is a small town, in a poor region of country, but its position is important, just behind Forts Monroe and Calhoun; the former is the military post on the southern coast, which commands Hampton Roads, the channel leading from the ocean into the Chesapeake. The town contains four churches, a courthouse, and about fifteen hundred inhabitants.

Old Point Comfort, a low sandy cape, lies opposite the narrow part of the channel, which is there so narrow that the guns of the fortress completely command it. The adjacent part of the bay, called the Rip-raps, is so shallow that the surface of the water is kept in a state of agitation by the meeting of the currents and tide.

Fortress Monroe is one of the largest fortifications in the United States. It mounts three hundred and thirty-five guns, of which one hundred and thirty are in casemates, or subterranean chambers arched with stone and bombproof. Opposite stands Fort Calhoun, one thousand nine hundred yards distant, which, although of smaller size, will mount two hundred and sixty-five cannon, the greater part of them in casemates.

Montpelier, the seat of the late president Madison, is about four miles from Orange courthouse. On approaching it from the north, you turn to the left on leaving the main road, and after proceeding through a wood about a mile, the mansion of the late ex-president may be seen a mile distant, situated on a slight eminence. It is a large brick building, composed of a main body and two wings. In front of the body is a portico of wood, painted white, which is supported by four lofty Doric pillars. The interior of the house is furnished with plain but rich furniture, and ornamented with busts and pictures; in the right wing is a library of rare and valuable books, and a cabinet. In the rear of the mansion is an extensive lawn; after crossing this you come to the garden, which consists of several acres of ground, laid out with elegance and taste, and contains a great number of native plants and exotics, besides an abundance of grapes. Here, on the 28th of June, 1836, Mr. Madison died, at the advanced age of eighty-seven.

Mr. Madison was by birth a Virginian, and wholly educated in this country. He was intended for a statesman from his youth, and made himself master of constitutional law, when it was hardly known as a science either in England or in this country. He was born on the 16th of March, 1751, and was, of course, in all the ardor and freshness of youth on the breaking out of the Revolution. In 1775 he was a member of the Virginia legislature, and was soon appointed one of the council of the state. During the whole eventful struggle, he had the confidence of the state, and, as as a member of her legislature, was listened to with profound attention when he brought forward sundry resolutions for the formation of a general government for the United States, based upon the inefficiency of the old confederation. From these resolutions grew a convention of delegates from the several states, who, in conclave, prepared a form of a constitution to be submitted to the several states for their discussion, approbation, and adoption. Mr. Madison was a member of this convention, as a delegate from Virginia, and took an active part in the deliberations of that enlightened body, of which Washington, his colleague, was president. On the adoption of this constitution, Mr. Madison was elected a member of the first congress, and took an active part in setting the machinery in motion. At this period, public opinion was greatly agitated by the crude and false opinions scattered throughout the country, through the medium of the opposition presses;

Montpelier, late Residence of Madison.

this was grievous to the friends of the constitution, and Jay, Hamilton, and Madison, formed an alliance to enlighten the people upon the great doctrines of the constitution. The essays from the pens of these worthies were collected in a volume, called the "Federalist," which now stands a monument of the wisdom and patriotism of that age. In the debates of the first congress, Mr. Madison took a large share. It was an assemblage of patriots, among whom there often arose a difference of opinion in regard to political policy, but all were lovers of their country, and laboring for her best interests. Here Mr. Madison acted with the Cabots and the Ameses of the east in perfect harmony. It was reserved for an after-age to feel the withering effects of party feuds. These were hardly discovered as long as the Father of his country filled the presidential chair. In the administration of his successor, a separation into parties took place, and Mr. Madison ranked himself on the side of Mr. Jefferson and his party, and was secretary of state during the presidency of Mr. Jefferson.

In March, 1809, Mr. Madison became president of the United States. In 1812, war was declared. In 1817, when the reign of peace was established, Mr. Madison retired to his farm to enjoy the serenity of rural life; but here he was not idle. On the death of Mr. Jefferson he was made chancellor of the university of Virginia, and took a deep interest in the prosperity of the institution. When Virginia called a convention to alter her constitution, Mr. Madison, with Chief-Justice Marshall and Mr. Monroe, was found among the most prominent members.

James Madison was not an orator, in the common acceptation of the word; there were no deep tones in his voice—no flashes of a fierce and commanding eye—no elegant gestures to attract the beholder: all was calm, dignified, and convincing. He never talked for the love of display, but simply to communicate his thoughts. He spoke often in debate, when earnest in his cause, but was always heard with profound attention. His voice was deficient in volume, but it was so well modulated that its compass was more extensive than that of many speakers of stronger lungs.

Charlottesville.—This town, the seat of the university of Virginia, enjoys a beautiful situation in the valley of Rivanna river, on the right of which it stands, at the distance of eighty-three miles from Richmond. The principal buildings of the town are four churches, an academy, and a female seminary; and the population amounts to about two thousand.

Stagecoaches depart daily for Richmond, for Washington, and for the White Sulphur springs; and three times a week for Fredericksburg and Lynchburg.

Lynchburg stands on the right bank of James river, one hundred and sixteen miles from Richmond. The spot which it occupies is rough, the ground being an acclivity, surrounded by a variety of surface with striking scenery. The town contains one or two banks, three savings-banks, fifteen classical schools, a library, eight churches, several large flourmills, and about thirty tobacco manufactories, with about eight thousand inhabitants. It is a place of great trade, as well as of considerable manufactures. The town is supplied with water raised from James river by hydraulic power, and is distributed from a reservoir containing 400,000 gallons, and standing at an elevation of two hundred and fifty-three feet above the river; thence it passes through the city in iron pipes.

James River Canal.—This important work of internal navigation, at Lynchburg, extends to Richmond, one hundred and forty-seven miles.

Farmville, seventy-five miles from Richmond, is situated on the right bank of the Appomattox, and contains three churches, a bank, and ten tobacco manufactories. The population is about one thousand four hundred.

Fredericksburg, fifty-six miles from Washington, stands on the right bank of the Rappahannock river, and has a pleasant appearance, being regularly laid out, and surrounded by elevated grounds. The river makes a considerable fall at this place, by which the town is supplied with valuable water-

Birthplace of Ex-President Monroe.

power; and as the stream is navigable almost to the foot of the fall, in vessels of one hundred and forty tons, the trade of the place is active and important. The principal public buildings are the courthouse, two banks, the orphan asylum, five churches, and six academies. The population is about six thousand.

The railroad, passing through the town, affords daily communication in cars with Washington, Richmond, Wilmington, &c.

The Birthplace of James Monroe.—James Monroe was born in the county of Westmoreland on the 28th of April, 1758. He was seventeen years old, and in William and Mary college, at the time when the declaration of independence was made by congress, and he soon after entered the army as a cadet. He was with Washington, as a lieutenant, at Harlem, White Plains, and Trenton. At the latter place he was wounded in the shoulder, and was promoted to a captaincy for his bravery. After his recovery, he served as aid-de-camp to Lord Stirling in 1777–'78, in the course of which he was in the battles of Brandywine, Germantown, and Monmouth.

He then returned to Virginia, and endeavored, unsuccessfully, to raise a regiment; after which he entered the office of Mr. Jefferson as a student of law. In 1780 he was appointed military commissioner by Governor Jefferson; and in 1782 was elected into the Virginia legislature and made a member of the executive council. June 19, 1783, he was first chosen a member of congress at the age of twenty-four. He married Miss Kortright, of New York, in 1786, with whom he lived through a long life. Leaving congress after three years' service, he was again elected into the legislature of his native state, and soon after elected to the convention for the adoption of the federal constitution, which he opposed.

From 1790 to 1794 he was a senator of the United States, and was then appointed minister plenipotentiary to France; and having been recalled, toward the close of Washington's administration, was elected governor of Virginia. In 1803, he again went to France under Jefferson's administration, and, in conjunction with Mr. Livingston, negotiated the treaty for the cession of Louisiana. He was then appointed successor to Mr. King as minister to England; and, having been ordered to Spain, he soon after returned to England and back to Virginia. After serving again as governor of Virginia in 1811, he was appointed secretary of state by Mr. Madison, and continued in that office till, in the second term of the president, he was appointed secretary of war. On the return of peace he again entered the office of secretary of state, which he held until his election as president of the United States in 1817. He was re-elected in 1821; and at the expiration of his second term, in 1825, he retired to private life in Loudoun county, where he resumed the practice of an attorney-at-law, and was elected a magistrate of the county. In 1829 he was chosen a member of the convention for the revision of the constitution of Virginia, and made president of it. But before its close, his health failed; he lost his wife the following summer; and having removed to New York, to reside among his friends in that city, he died there after a few months, July 4, 1831.

A short time before his death, congress appropriated considerable sums of money to defray the debts under which he had for some time suffered, partly in consequence of advances made by him for the public account. He was uniformly a supporter of the policy and measures of Mr. Jefferson.

Hampden Sidney College.—This institution is situated ten miles southwest from Farmville. It was founded in 1774, and chartered in 1783, but for a long time did not prove very flourishing. It has five professors, and about seventy students, with eight thousand volumes in its libraries. Commencement is held on the fourth Wednesday of September.

The *Union Theological Seminary* is at a short distance from the college. It was founded in 1824, and has three professors, twenty students, and one hundred and seventy-five under-graduates, with about four thousand volumes in its libraries.

WHEELING.—This is the most important town in western Virginia. It is one hundred and four miles west of Philadelphia, on the Ohio, at the mouth of Wheeling creek. It is almost enclosed by considerable hills, which afford an abundance of bituminous coal. The public buildings are a courthouse, two banks, a savings institution, a theatre, twelve churches, two academies, masonic hall, and institute; and there are a great many manufactories. The population is about eleven thousand. Water for the supply of the town is raised from the Ohio. There is a daily communication with Pittsburg (Ohio), and the various places below on the river.

ELIZABETH.—This town is twelve miles below Wheeling, on a plain, once the habitation of a large population, whose remains are visible in numerous ancient tumuli scattered over its surface. The largest is one hundred and sixteen feet high, and surrounded by a ditch four hundred yards in circuit.

PETERSBURG, on the north bank of the Little Kenhawa river at its confluence with the Ohio, has a courthouse, two banks, nine churches, and fifteen thousand inhabitants. The celebrated Blennerhassett's island lies three miles below this place.

Point Pleasant is two hundred and twenty-six miles below Pittsburg, on the Ohio, at the mouth of the Great Kenhawa. On this spot the great Indian battle of October 10, 1774, was fought, and Logan, a celebrated chief, defeated.

FINCASTLE, in the southeast part of the valley of the Catawba, contains a courthouse, four churches, and about nine hundred inhabitants. It is seventy five miles from Richmond.

Botetourt Springs, twelve miles from Fincastle, have accommodations for a considerable number of visiters, being the resort of many in the warm season. The water contains magnesia, sulphur, and carbonic acid.

Daggers' Springs are eighteen miles from Fincastle, in the midst of a picturesque region. The waters contain the carbonates of soda, magnesia, and chlorides of the same, with sulphate of soda, &c.

ABINGDON, near Holston river, is the largest town in southwestern Virginia, with a courthouse, two academies, four churches, twelve hundred inhabitants.

WINCHESTER.—This town is one hundred and thirteen miles from Baltimore, and one hundred and forty-six from Richmond; it is situated in a fine and fertile valley, and has regular streets lined with handsome houses. The public buildings are the lyceum, masonic hall, twelve churches, two banks, one savings bank, and an academy. The population amounts to four thousand five hundred. The town is supplied with water, by iron pipes, from a fine spring in the vicinity. There is a daily communication with Baltimore in the railroad cars.

Jordan's White Sulphur Springs, six miles north of Winchester, have recently become known, and are annually the resort of many visiters. The waters are said to have a resemblance to those of the Greenbriar White Sulphur springs.

WOODSTOCK is sixty-two miles from Harper's Ferry, and stands on the north bank of the Shenandoah. It has one thousand inhabitants. The public building are a courthouse, three churches, and masonic hall.

The *Yellow, or Orkey Springs*, eighteen miles from Woodstock, give an abundant supply of chalybeate water, and enjoy a good reputation.

STAUNTON.—This town is situated at the headwaters of the Shenandoah, one hundred and twenty miles from Richmond, one hundred and sixty-two from Washington, and two hundred and seven from Baltimore. It has a courthouse, the Virginia asylum for the deaf and dumb, the Western lunatic asylum, two academies, four churches, two seminaries, and two thousand six hundred inhabitants.

The *Augusta Springs* are twelve miles northwest of Staunton, and are charged with sulphuretted hydrogen, resembling the Harrowgate springs in England.

The Cyclopæan Towers are remarkable rocks in this vicinity.

Wier's Cave, one of the greatest natural curiosities in this country, is seventeen miles northwest of Staunton.

MARTINSBURG is twenty miles from Harper's Ferry, stands on the line of the Baltimore and Ohio railroad, and contains a courthouse, six churches, two academies, and about one thousand seven hundred inhabitants.

Berkeley Springs, a favorite watering-place, is twenty-five miles from Martinsburg.

CHARLESTOWN.—This place is eight miles from Harper's Ferry. The public buildings are a courthouse, an academy, and three churches, and the population about fifteen hundred.

Shannondale Springs.—This favorite resort is represented in the vignette at the head of this description. Stage-coaches run daily to this place from Charlestown, which is five miles distant, and at which place carriages from the springs meet the railway.

The situation of the springs is near the foot of the Blue ridge, on Shannondale river. Shannondale is situated among the green hills, in a romantic bend of the Shenandoah, twelve miles from Harper's Ferry. The waters resemble those of Bedford, containing sulphate and carbonate of lime, sulphate and muriate of magnesia, muriate of soda, sulphate and carbonate of iron, sulphuretted hydrogen, and carbonic acid. The scenery around this spot is remarkably fine and varied. These springs are famous for the cure of spleen, hypochondria, and those gnawing, corroding ailments that weigh down the system, without confining the sufferer to his bed; and are highly medicinal in cases of disease.

Fairfax County—which contains a portion of tne territory lately included in the district of Columbia, viz., that part which was ceded to the United States by the legislature, and lately restored to Virginia—was named after Lord Fairfax, the proprietor of the tract called the "Northern Neck," and an individual much distinguished by his wealth and peculiar character, whose family was connected with that of Washington, who was a native of the county. It is bounded by the Potomac river, and crossed by the Occoquan and its branches; has a low and sandy surface, like most of the tide-water country of Virginia, but in some parts is fertile. Large tracts, however, have that aspect of desolation which is peculiar to "worn-out tobacco lands," in consequence of the bad system, long pursued, of raising tobacco as long as possible on one field after another, and then abandoning them successively, without an effort to restore the exhausted fertility. The result generally is a spontaneous growth of cedars and low pines, a sterile and forbidding appearance, and a general abandonment of the land by the inhabitants.

The soil, however, has proved valuable in the hands of farmers accustomed to a different system of agriculture, on both sides of the Potomac. Tracts have been rendered productive, especially in Fairfax county, where bodies of settlers from New York, principally of German extraction, purchased land at very low prices a few years ago, and are already in flourishing circumstances.

MOUNT VERNON, in Fairfax county—the estate of the Washington family—is nine miles south from Alexandria, and is remarkable as containing the tomb of General Washington. The road is somewhat intricate, and has but few inhabitants; so that the stranger, unless he goes in a steamboat, will need to make careful inquiries. The house stands on an eminence, looking down upon the Potomac. The buildings which project from each end are deformities, which greatly mar the effect.

The key of the bastile of Paris is hung up in the hall; and a miniature portrait of Washington, from an earthen pitcher, is preserved, which is considered by the family the best likeness of him ever made. A beautiful lawn, partly shaded by trees, extends from the front of the mansion to the verge of the precipice which overhangs the Potomac, and affords a delightful view upon the river and a tract of hilly country above and below.

This is the place to which Washington retired after he had accomplished the independence of his country, and again when he had presided at the consolidation of the government—voluntarily resigning the stations he had consented to accept, and the power he

Harper's Ferry, from the Patomac side.

had exercised, only for the good of his country. To an American this place is interesting, in a degree which no language can either heighten or describe. Whoever appreciates the value of private and social virtue, will rejoice to find it associated with the traits of a personage so distinguished and influential; the consistent politician will rejoice to reflect that the principles of natural freedom are not restricted to any portion of the world, or any part of the human race; while any one who can duly estimate the extent of the blessings he has conferred on his country, and the influence of his actions on the happiness of the world, will wish that his history may ever be cherished, as a model of sincere and disinterested patriotism.

Last Illness of Washington.—On Thursday, the 12th of December, 1799, while riding over his farms, Washington became exposed to a severe storm of rain, hail, and snow, with a sharp, piercing wind. He took a cold, but it did not exhibit any alarming symptoms till Saturday morning, the 14th, when his throat and chest were so severely affected that he could hardly speak, and breathed with difficulty. He continued to grow worse during the day. His medical advisers were sent for, and bleeding and other remedies adopted, without affording relief. The following account of his last hours is from a memorandum of his private secretary:—

"By Mrs. Washington's request, I despatched a messenger for Dr. Brown, of Port Tobacco. About nine o'clock, Dr. Craik arrived, and put a blister of cantharides on the throat of the general, and took more blood, and had some vinegar and hot water set in a teapot, for him to draw in the steam from the spout.

"About eleven o'clock, Dr. Dick was sent for. Dr. Craik bled the general again; no effect was produced, and he continued in the same state, unable to swallow anything. Dr. Dick came in about three o'clock, and Dr. Brown arrived soon after; when, after consultation, the general was bled again. The blood ran slowly, appeared very thick, and did not produce any symptoms of fainting. At four o'clock, the general could swallow a little. Calomel and tartar-emetic were administered without effect. About half-past four o'clock he requested me to ask Mrs. Washington to come to his bedside, when he desired her to go down to his room, and take from his desk two wills which she would find there, and bring them to him, which she did. Upon looking at one, which he observed was useless, he desired her to burn it, which she did; and then took the other and put it away. After this was done, I returned again to his bedside and took his hand. He said to me, 'I find I am going—my breath can not continue long—I believed from the first attack that it would be fatal. Do you arrange and record all my military letters and papers; arrange my accounts and settle my books, as you know more about them than any one else; and let Mr. Rawlins finish recording my other letters, which he has begun.'

"The physicians arrived between five and six o'clock, and when they came to his bedside, Dr. Craik asked him if he would sit up in the bed: he held out his hand to me, and was raised up, when he said to the physician: 'I feel myself going; you had better not take any more trouble about me, but let me go off quietly; I can not last long.' They found what had been done was without effect; he lay down again, and they retired, excepting Dr. Craik. He then said to him: 'Doctor, I die hard, but I am not afraid to go; I believed, from my first attack, I should not survive it; my breath can not last long.' The doctor pressed his hand, but could not utter a word; he retired from the bedside and sat by the fire, absorbed in grief. About eight o'clock the physicians again came into the room and applied blisters to his legs, but went out without a ray of hope. From this time he appeared to breathe with less difficulty than he had done, but was very restless, continually changing his position, to endeavor to get ease. I aided him all in my power, and was gratified in believing he felt it, for he would look upon me with eyes speaking gratitude, but unable to utter a word without great distress. About ten o'clock

Mount Vernon, late Residence of Washington.

he made several attempts to speak to me before he could effect it; at length he said: 'I am just going. Have me decently buried; and do not let my body be put into the vault in less than two days after I am dead.' I bowed assent. He looked at me again and said, 'Do you understand me?' I replied, 'Yes sir.' ''Tis well,' said he. About ten minutes before he expired, his breathing became much easier: he lay quietly: he withdrew his hand from mine, and felt his own pulse. I spoke to Dr. Craik, who sat by the fire: hn came to the bedside. The general's hand fell from his wrist; I took it in mine, and placed on my breast. Dr. Craik placed his hands over his eyes; and he expired without a sigh."

Washington's Tomb is a simple structure of stone, only the front of which is visible, the other parts being covered with the earth of a small sandhill which was excavated, and the surface of which was left covered with dwarf cedars and a few other trees with which it was naturally shaded. The whole is concealed from the view of the passer-by, by a neat and substantial stone wall of considerable height, with a gate, over which is a slab bearing this inscription:—

"Washington Family."

The surrounding scene is left nearly in the state of nature. The irregular surface of the ground and the numerous trees exclude the sight of every distant object; and there is nothing in view to disturb the mind, in the solemn and impressive reflections which naturally arise within it. Although the Potomac flows by at a short distance from the spot, and was in full view from near the door of the original tomb, every glimpse of it is shut out from this, and not a single sound intrudes to interrupt the solitude.

Few visiters to the spot obtain an entrance into the tomb, or even through the gate. The stone coffin, which contains the ashes of the venerable occupant, is engraved with the arms of the United States, and the simple name of "Washington."

The following description of General La Fayette's visit to the old tomb, was written by his companion and secretary, Levasseur:—

"After a voyage of two hours, the guns of Fort Washington announced that we were approaching the last abode of the Father of his country. At this solemn signal, to which the military band accompanying us responded by plaintive strains, we went on deck, and the venerable soil of Mount Vernon was before us. At this view, an involuntary and spontaneous movement made us kneel. We landed in boats, and trod upon the ground so often trod by the feet of Washington. A carriage received General La Fayette, and the other visiters silently ascended the precipitous path which conducted to the solitary habitation of Mount Vernon. In re-entering beneath this hospitable roof, which had sheltered him when the reign of terror tore him violently from his country and family, George La Fayette felt his heart sink within him, at no more finding him whose paternal care had softened his misfortunes; while his father sought with emotion for everything which reminded him of the companion of his glorious toils.

"Three nephews of General Washington took La Fayette, his son, and myself, to conduct us to the tomb of their uncle; our numerous companions remained in the house. In a few minutes the cannon, thundering anew, announced that La Fayette rendered homage to the ashes of Washington. Simple and modest as he was during life, the tomb of the citizen-hero is scarcely perceived among the sombre cypresses by which it is surrounded. A vault, slightly elevated and sodded over—a wooden door without inscriptions—some withered and green garlands, indicate to the traveller, who visits the spot, where rest in peace the puissant arms which broke the chains of his country. As we approached, the door was opened. La Fayette descended alone into the vault, and a few minutes after reappeared with his eyes overflowing with tears. He took his son and me by the hand, and led us into the tomb, where, by a sign, he indicated the coffin. We knelt reverentially, and rising, threw ourselves

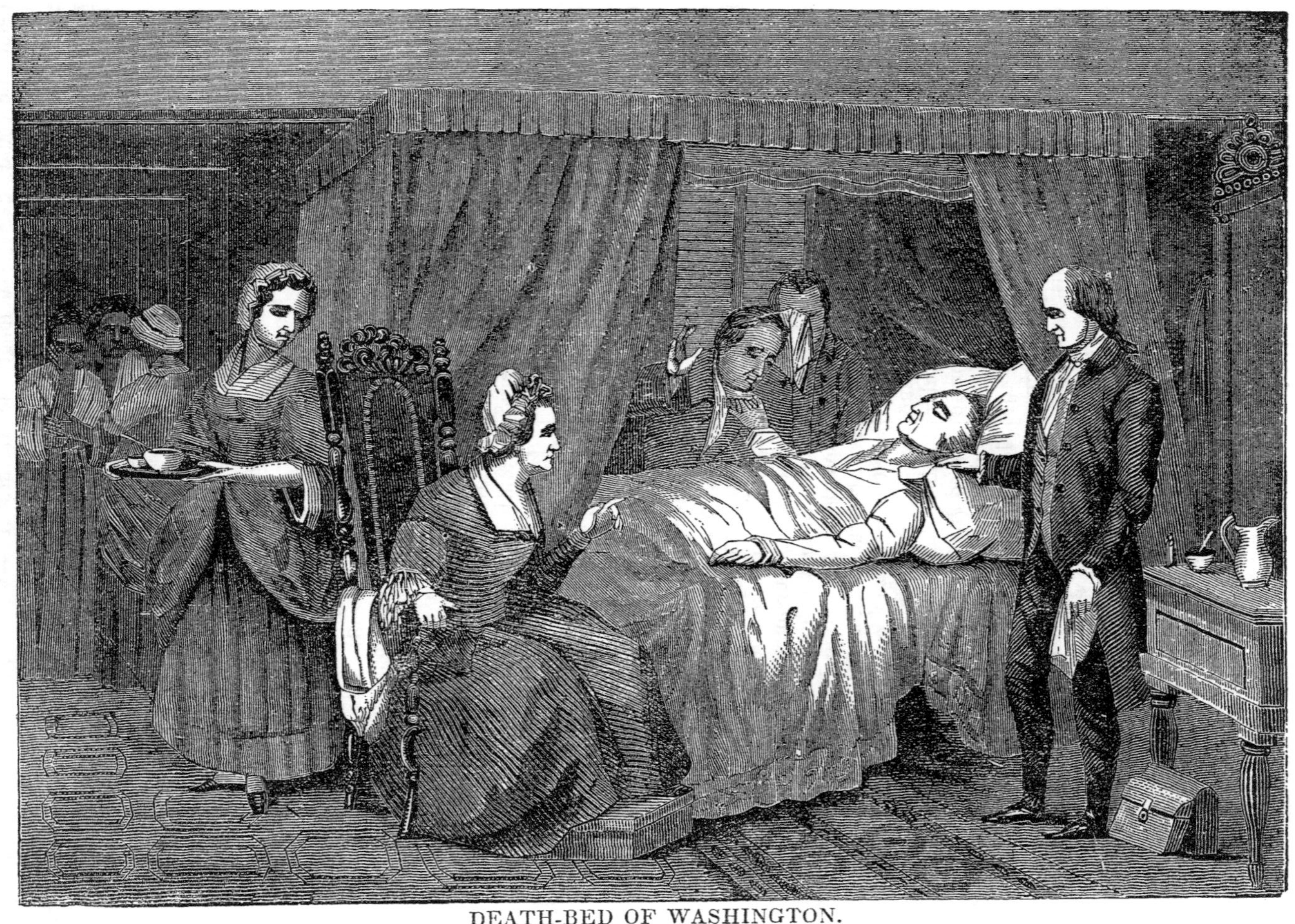

DEATH-BED OF WASHINGTON.

into the arms of La Fayette, and mingled our tears with his."

WILLIAMSBURG, though a small place, is the oldest incorporated town in the state, and was formerly the capital. It is fifty-eight miles from Richmond, and sixty-eight from Norfolk. It has three churches, a magazine, two seminaries, the eastern lunatic asylum, and William and Mary college. The number of inhabitants is about two thousand.

The Statue of Lord Botetourt stands in the square, which retains a portion of its original beauty, though much mutilated, having been a good specimen of sculpture. He was one of the first judges of the colony. It was erected in 1774, at the expense of the colony.

William and Mary College.—This was the first literary institution of the higher kind, in Virginia, having been founded in 1692, under the reign of the sovereigns whose name it bears. They were its liberal benefactors, granting it twenty thousand acres of land as an endowment. There are five professors, about one hundred students, and about four thousand volumes in its libraries. The institution embraces a law department. The commencement is held on the 4th of July.

This institution is the oldest of that name in the Union, with the single exception of Harvard university, but was long kept as a mere grammar school. Many of its graduates have been among the most distinguished men in the state and nation. Some of the books in the library bear the name of Robert Dinwiddie and his coat-of-arms, with his motto: "*Ubi libertas, ibi patria.*" Among the most valuable works is Catesby's Natural History of Carolina, Florida, and the Bahama Banks, two volumes folio, English and French—printed in 1754. The first building was erected in 1793, in Williamsburg; but it was not until some important changes were made in the plan of the institution, that it began to assume the character of a college. The two professorships in divinity and that for Latin and Greek, established in 1692, were substituted by professorships in other departments. Among the six formerly existing was one for the instruction and conversion of the Indians, founded by Mr. Boyle, of England.

The Old Capitol.—A few fragments only now remain of the building known as "the capitol." This, however, was not the first edifice erected for the capitol of the colony, which was consumed by fire in 1746. Its successor also was burned in 1832, and that is the one whose remains are to be seen. Within its walls some interesting incidents occurred. There Washington received, in his youth, an expression of the thanks of the colonial legislature, on his return from the French war, from the lips of Mr. Robinson, the speaker, who complimented him in such high terms, that, with characteristic modesty, he blushed, trembled, and stammered—unable to return a distinct answer. To relieve his embarrassment, the speaker kindly said: "Sit down, Mr. Washington; your modesty is equal to your valor, and that surpasses the power of any language that I possess."

In the same building, Patrick Henry made his first public speech before the house of burgesses; and although in a coarse dress, and with the air of "an obscure and unpolished rustic," he astonished the aristocratic members of the chamber, by his vigorous eloquence.

The old *Raleigh Tavern* is still to be seen, distinguished by a bust of Sir Walter Raleigh over the door. It is the place in which some of the most important committees of the legislature used to meet in the Revolutionary days; and there is said to have been first conceived and proposed, by Henry Lee and his associates, the system of correspondence which was carried on with so much success during the war.

Lord Dunsmore's Palace.—Two small buildings may be seen, which are the remains of the edifice occupied by Lord Dunsmore, the last royal governor of Virginia. They stand in a small court, which formed part of the extensive grounds which surrounded his mansion, and then embraced three hundred and sixty acres. There he maintained a splendid style of living; but, being opposed to the rising spirit of the people

The Tomb of Washington

at the approaching of the revolutionary period, he was deprived of his place and power.

The Old Magazine.—This is an ancient octagonal building, on the square, erected above one hundred and twenty years since, from which Governor Dunsmore, in 1775, removed the gunpowder of the colony on board the man-of-war Magdalen, then in the harbor. This act excited the people to form the first armed forces assembled in opposition to the British government.

YORKTOWN, seventy miles from Richmond, is situated on the right bank of York river, and is distinguished for the closing military scene of the American revolution, the surrender of Lord Cornwallis, which put a close to the struggle between Great Britain and the new states. It was founded in 1705, and was formerly much more flourishing than it now is. The number of inhabitants is very much reduced, so that it is hardly worthy of the name of a village, containing scarcely forty houses, and these marked by decay. York county was one of the eight original counties into which Virginia was divided in 1634. The situation is pleasant, and many of the scenes are fine.

The *York Tavern*, in the village, is believed to be the oldest in the state. The ruins of the old church have a sad and solemn aspect. It was built above one hundred and fifty years ago, and destroyed by fire in 1814. The bell is preserved, and bears this inscription:—

"*County of York*, *Virginia*, 1725."

The walls of the building were composed of marl, which was soft when first dug from the ground, but hardened like stone after a little time.

The *White Sulphur Spring*, in Greenbriar county, two hundred and twelve miles from Richmond, is situated in an elevated and beautifully picturesque valley, hemmed in by mountains on every side, and in the midst of the celebrated 'spring region." Its elevation above tidewater is two thousand feet. It bursts with boldness from rock-lined apertures, and is enclosed by marble casements five feet square and three and a half feet deep. Its temperature is sixty-two degrees Fahrenheit, and remains uniformly the same, winter and summer. The principal spring yields about eighteen gallons per minute, and is never increased or diminished by any changes of weather. The water is perfectly clear and transparent, and deposites copiously, as it floats over a rough and uneven surface of rocks, a white precipitate—sometimes, under peculiar circumstances, red and black—composed in part of its ingredients. Its taste and smell, fresh at the spring, are those of all waters so strongly impregnated with sulphuretted hydrogen gas.

The fountain is enclosed and covered by a circular edifice, about thirty feet in diameter, supported by pillars like the cupola of a church or other public building, except that in place of a weathercock, or some religious emblem, the summit is handsomely embellished with a large marble figure of Hygeia (the goddess of health), presented by the late Mr. Henderson, of New Orleans, in a spirit of gratitude for the benefit he had received at this noble fountain. Here visiters resort early in the morning, to quaff from two to six glasses of water impregnated chiefly with sulphate of lime, sulphate of magnesia, and sulphate of soda.

Within two hundred yards of the spring, in the centre of the valley, which here spreads out nearly to a plane surface, and at the lower end of a lawn of some eight or ten acres, stands the dining hall, near two hundred feet long, with tables to seat six hundred guests. From one hundred and fifty to two hundred cabins and cottages are ranged along at considerable elevation above the spring, in curvilinear form, adapted to the sinuosities of the mountain base that skirts the valley, and other irregularities of the site; but still making nearly an oblong square, and occupying a line of perhaps nearly a mile in its entire length, enclosing an area of ten or twelve acres, well set in blue grass, intersected with dry walks for exercise, and ornamented with that variety of trees which seems characteristic of this region. Here the native oak in all its grandeur; there the symmetrical sugar-maple; next again

View of Yorktown, from the old Windmill, as you approach from Williamsburg.

the hickory (that of the old stock), and hard by the locust.

These beautiful forest-trees have been so judiciously left and pruned, as not to conceal or smother what they were intended to shade and beautify; and make, with the cottages, especially when these are lighted up at night, altogether a fine panorama.

Lord Morpeth and other distinguished foreigners have, in their admiration, pronounced the bath at the Warm and the White Sulphur springs—for arrangement and extent of accommodations, scenery, and health-giving qualities of the water—far superior to any similar resorts in Europe.

The cabins are all of brick, or neatly framed, finished, and painted, with a nice piazza separately railed in for each. Many of them display handsome and chaste specimens of architecture.

Travellers leaving Baltimore in the morning, by the railroad, reach Winchester the same evening; thence travel by post-coach, along a Macadamized turnpike, one hundred miles up the valley of Stanton; sup and lodge the next night at Cloverdale; and the second morning breakfast at the Warm springs. The warm bath is forty feet in diameter and six feet in depth, ninety-eight degrees Fahrenheit, and withal clear as crystal and sparkling as champagne.

A Negro Cabin.—There is considerable difference in the form, size, and materials of the habitations of negroes in Virginia, especially if we include those in the principal towns. That represented in the cut may be taken as a specimen of the largest and best kind ordinarily seen in the country. The negro huts are usually built in clusters; those for the family servants forming a quadrangle in the yard, and others being placed at a greater or less distance from the house of the planter, according to the extent of his estate.

Most of them are built of logs or the bodies of small trees; the materials differ, however, in certain parts of the country; some of the poorer white people dwelling in huts of a similar description. The arrangements and furniture are of the simplest kind. The chinks between the logs or boards are filled, entirely or partly, with moss or clay; the chimneys are formed of small sticks and covered with mud; the floor is the ground, which often serves for beds at night.

The fol'owing is from a recent letter-writer:—

"Not long ago, I attended a funeral of an aged female slave. About the grave were gathered some two score of negroes; and as the coffin descended into the tomb, the moistened eye of every one bespoke the touched heart; and an old man, with half-choked utterance, said: 'Cry not, my friends, our sister has gone from us, but we mus meet her de oder side of de grave. De great Master has sent for her, and she is now at *home*. God grant we be dere too!' The chips made in constructing the coffin, were burned in a fire made for the purpose in the open air, as they believe that death will soon enter the family on whose hearth-stone they are burned. Several weeks after the burial the sermon is preached. Crowds of slaves attend, and all are treated abundantly to refreshments of every kind.

"An old servant, who often speaks of the surrender at Yorktown, and of the scenes that were witnessed at the time by him—and who told me that he 'learned to read' when he went with his 'young master to college'—now that he is exempt from labor, spends his time in reading his bible, and in 'fighting his battles over again.' I often see him of a Sunday evening, surrounded by an audience of his own race, reading and explaining the Scriptures to them; and they, in the meantime, manifest their appreciation of the sacred word, by looks of the most active interest, and expressions of joy and comfort."

Wellsburg, eighty-seven miles from Pittsburg, on the Ohio river, has a bank, a courthouse, five churches, with several manufactories, and about two thousand inhabitants.

Bethany is eight miles east from Wellsboro'. It is a small village, but is the seat of

Bethany College, an institution with about one hundred pupils.

Negro Cabin

POCAHONTAS.—No other Indian female ever rendered such a service to a white man as Pocahontas, under circumstances so well calculated to excite admiration. All have read the simple narrative of her intercession to save the life of Captain Smith, at that critical period when his death would probably have led to the extirpation of his little suffering colony. But perhaps many have lost sight of one circumstance which is calculated to enhance its effect upon the feelings. We refer to the tender years of the heroine: she was a child of only twelve or thirteen years of age.

From the accounts we have of the case, we see abundant reason to believe that nothing could have directed her in the course she pursued, but a strong natural dictate of humanity. Yet why she should have been so affected in that case, it is difficult to say, as it may be presumed, she had witnessed scenes of cruelty, bloodshed, and murder, among the savage race, and in the savage family to which she belonged. Many of the actions of Indians, we find on nearer acquaintance with them, are dictated by some of their strange superstitious notions. A dream, an unusual sight or sound, or some other trifle, they often believe to be connected with something which gives it importance. This is especially true of the men, whose dreams in their initiatory fasts decide some important point for life.

We have no particular reason, however, to assign such a motive to Pocahontas, any more than to the celebrated Indian princess who figures so remarkably in the early history of New England—the wife of Mononotto, the Pequod sachem, whose refinement and dignity, as well as her humanity, excited the admiration of Governor Winslow, familiar as he was with the manners of the English court.

It was in the gloomy year when the little colony at Jamestown (the first which survived the trials of the settlement) was reduced to such sufferings by the scarcity of food, that Smith, with the determination of relieving them, ventured among the Indians in the interior, and after proceeding up James river in a boat, left it with his companions at the landing, and went on toward the dwelling of Powhatan. This would, probably, have appeared only a bold step, if he had met with no difficulty; but we are so prone to judge of an act by its consequences, that when we see him falling into a snare, laid on a rock, and a war-club raised to dash out his brains, we are ready to call him inconsiderate and rash. He appeared to have retained his presence of mind through all his dangers, and by happy expedients twice obtained a short reprieve, viz.: by showing the savages his pocket compass, and by sending to Jamestown for medicine to cure a sick Indian. These and other circumstances may have had their influence on the feelings of the young princess. But, whatever was the cause, she behaved like a heroine; and not in one case only, or toward a single individual. By a timely message, sent no doubt with great personal risk, she warned the infant colony of the murderous plots of the savages.

Through her intercession, an English boy, named Henry Spilman, was saved from death, and afterward rendered the colonists much service. So strong was the friendship of Pocahontas for the whites, that she left her home, and resided with the Patamowekes, whose sachem, Japazas, was a friend of Smith's, that she might not witness the death of English prisoners, whom she could no longer rescue from the bloody hands of her father. Strange as it may seem, however, she was sold by that sachem to Captain Argall for a copper kettle, as he thought her father's attachment to her might prevent him from prosecuting his bitter persecutions of the colony. Her father sought to recover her; but, before any arrangement was made for the return of the interesting captive, she gave her consent to marry an Englishman named Rolfe, who had long before contracted an affection for her.

The character of Powhatan is a very marked one. His attachment to his daughter alone would be enough to vindicate the red race from the charge of being without natural affection. He at first opposed her marriage, but afterward gave his consent, despatched an officer to witness the ceremony, sent a deerskin to Pocahontas and another to her husband, and maintained thereafter the most friendly terms with the colonists.

Yet Powhatan refused to give his younger daughter in marriage to Governor Dale, though solicited by him and her sister—saying to the messenger:—

"Go back to your governor, and tell him that I value his love and peace, which, while I live, I will keep. Tell him that I love my daughter as my life; and though I have many children, I have none like her. If I could not see her, I would not live; and if I give her to you, I shall never see her. I hold it not a brotherly part to desire to take away two children at once."

Pocahontas was baptized, and received the name of Rebecca. In 1616 she made a voyage to England with her husband, where she was received with much attention. Her husband had just been appointed to an office in the colony, and was preparing to return when she died, at the age of twenty-two. Her only child, a son, was educated by his uncle in Virginia; and his daughter was the ancestor of the Randolphs, and several other principal families of the state.

John Randolph.—A writer in the Norfolk Beacon describes a visit to the grave of this remarkable man, and in speaking of his former residence, thus writes:—

"After a ride of two or three hours, we entered a forest of tall oaks, and were told by Mr. Cardwell that we were on Mr. Randolph's estate. Shortly the houses that were occupied by the great and eccentric genius appeared through the intervening trees, built up in the midst of the woods. Not a stump to be seen, not a bush grubbed up—all standing as if the foot of man had never trodden there. Mr. Randolph would not suffer the primitive aspect of things to be disturbed in the least. Not a tree, or a branch, or a switch, was allowed to be cut. During his absence in Europe, a limb of an oak, projecting toward a window of one of the houses, drew so near that old Essex, fearing the window would be broken, cut off the limb. On Mr. Randolph's return, he at once discovered the mutilation; old Essex was called up, and the reason demanded for cutting off the limb. The old negro told his master he feared the window would be broken. 'Then,' said Mr. R., 'why did you not move the house?'

The writer met John, the former body servant of Mr. Randolph, who treated him with great politeness. He says:—

"At my request, John directed us to his master's grave, at the foot of a lofty pine, just a few steps in the rear of the summer-house; the place was selected by Mr. R., just twenty years before his death, and by his direction his head was laid to the east instead of the west, the usual position. It was observed to John that his master had ordered his body to be thus laid, that he might watch Henry Clay. John replied that he had never heard him say anything of the kind. I suppose the position was preferred by Mr. Randolph because it is the Indian sepulchral posture; his descent from Pocahontas, the Indian princess, being one of the things he much boasted of. A rude unchiselled mass of white rock, found by him on a distant part of his estate many years before his death, and used by him at the door of one of his houses as a washstand, marks the head of the grave. A huge mass of brown stone, also selected by him and used as a stepstone to mount his horse, marks the foot of the grave. These rocks were procured and kept for the purpose to which they are now appropriated, and particular directions were given to John on the subject.

"I can never forget my emotion while standing over the unornamented grave of the gifted and eccentric Randolph. The tall, unbroken forest by which I was surrounded—the silence and gloom that reigned undisturbed amid the deserted place—the thought of the brilliant mind that once animated the remains then mouldering beneath the sod upon which I was standing—the vanity of earth's promises, hopes, and distinctions, impressed my heart and mind with a degree of solemnity and interest I was unwilling to dissipate."

NORTH CAROLINA.

Like the other southern Atlantic states. the coast of North Carolina is uniformly flat, low, and sandy, but little elevated above the water's level, and generally covered with pine forests. It extends 320 miles; and the low, sandy region referred to reaches from 80 to 100 miles westward, to the hilly regions, forming an area of 23,000 square miles. All this, with scarcely an exception, is a dead level, with but few spots of good soil, and showing but little cultivation, although the live oak grows readily in some parts, and figs and some other fruits are easily cultivated in the most favored positions. One of the principal occupations of the inhabitants has ever been the collection of turpentine, pitch, rosin, and tar, the first of which is a spontaneous effusion of the yellow pine when wounded, and the others the same substance in different degrees of inspissation, effected by the heat of fire applied to the trees when cut in pieces, and partly colored by smoke. This same business was carried on in many other of our states in their early periods, but in the most of them the supplies of turpentine have long failed, in consequence of the clearing of the pine land; but the vast extent of the terebinthine forests of North Carolina has perpetuated this branch of manufactures to the present day.

It may be presumed that such a soil and surface, and such a situation, could not prove favorable to the prosperity of the people. The monotony of the landscape corresponds too nearly with the monotony of life and stationary condition of society, in which the difficulties of elevating habits or education are almost insurmountable.

The hilly region of the state, which bounds the sandy region on the west, presents a marked and sudden change in climate, soil, and population. It occupies an area of 14,000 square miles, with a general, gentle slope to the southeast, cut through, at intervals, by rivers. The Roanoke, Yadkin, Catawba, Tar, Neuse, and Cape Fear rivers, are the principal streams of the state, but the Catawba and Yadkin, rising in the middle region, empty in South Carolina.

The Blue Ridge, which in several other states forms the eastern range of high land, is here in the rear of two other hilly ranges, if, indeed, the Blue Ridge can with propriety be said to cross this state. A large part of this region is varied in a pleasing manner by hill and valley; while the soil is good, the climate cool, and the productions those of the temperate regions, including wheat, grass, potatoes, apples, peaches, and Indian corn, which is the staple product. The villages are numerous and flourishing; the people industrious, intelligent, and prosperous; and literary institutions are founded with success. The more elevated parts, as in the adjoining states, have weather as cold in the winter, as in some of those much farther north. Iron is the only metal found in considerable quantities, and this is mined and manufactured to some extent. Gold has been found on the surface, in a range of counties at the dividing line of the two regions, in loose particles or quartz stones, apparently the debris of a stratum of the hilly region, and perhaps belonging to a long auriferous range, extending from Georgia to Virginia. Some geologists think it may be traced much further. About fifteen years ago, much interest was raised in the North Carolina gold mines, and several companies were formed, in New York and elsewhere, and mining operations were undertaken, partly with steam machines imported from Europe. The sanguine expectations of adventurers were, however, soon disappointed; but considerable quantities of gold are still annually derived from this state by the U. S. mint.

The western part of the state has a slope toward the northwest, and is drained by several of the branches of the Tennessee river.

Although settlements were begun within the territory of this state at an early period, they were retarded by a variety of untoward circumstances, arising partly from the nature of the country, and partly from the influence of unwise policy and evil men. The weakness of the colonists, and the fear of the Indians, long prevented the occupation of land in the interior; and the seacoast offered only tracts of poor, sandy soil, burdened with pine forests, almost incapable of improvement, and at a uniform low level, but little higher than the ocean. The higher regions, now so flourishing and populous, lie far in the interior; but they were long unknown, and longer unoccupied.

The first attempts to colonize this part of the country, were made by the French under Charles IX., from whose name (in Latin Carolus) the Carolinas derived their appellation. The interference of the Spaniards broke up the settlements. In 1586, Sir Walter Raleigh sent out a small colony from England, under a patent from Queen Elizabeth; but no trace was ever found of them, and the presumption is that they were destroyed by the Indians.

North Carolina was included in the patent granted to Sir Robert Heath, attorney-general of Charles II., in 1630, which extended from Louisiana to the 36th degree of north latitude, and, as usual with English patents in those days, west to the Pacific ocean. All this extensive region was named Carolina; but as circumstances did not favor the settlement within the specified time, it soon became null, and was afterward superseded by a grant obtained from the same monarch, by Lord Clarendon, and some of his other friends, which embraced all the territory between the 31st and 36th degrees of north latitude.

In the meantime, however, settlements had been made north of Albemarle Sound, by colonists discontented with the intolerant measures adopted in Virginia, and several families from Massachusetts arrived at Cape Fear, to engage in fishing. The latter, however, were soon obliged to apply for assistance to their friends at the north, which they received.

After the new charter had been granted, the colonists at Albemarle were placed under the jurisdiction of the governor of Virginia, Sir William Berkeley, who soon paid them a visit, and appointed Drummond to be their governor. In 1666, they chose the first assembly ever formed in this part of our country, and sent their new governor, Stephens, with a petition for the privilege of holding their lands on the same terms as their neighbors in Virginia, which was granted them. A new constitution was also made, which provided for an annual election of members of the assembly by the colonists, while the choice of governor and half of the council was left to the proprietors. The taxes were to be laid by the assembly. In 1669, the first assembly under this constitution held their first session.

A constitution for the colony was drawn up this year by the celebrated author John Locke, at the request of Lord Clarendon; but, as might have been expected, the general views on which it was founded, proved quite inapplicable to the people and the country, and the experiment remains as a warning to all men who would meddle with plans of government for communities with which they are unacquainted.

A new colony was formed south of Cape Fear, by a band of men from Barbadoes, under Governor Yeamans, who was created a baronet, and soon after a landgrave, and the district was named the county of Clarendon. This settlement was soon divided, and we may now begin to speak of North and South Carolina as partly distinct; for, while a part of the settlers removed to Charleston, which had just been occupied, the remainder were soon united with Albemarle.

But many obstacles awaited the northern division of Carolina. In 1677 a rebellion against the government was headed by Culpepper, a restless and troublesome man, who usurped the government and held it for two years, but was superseded by Governor Eastchurch, after which he went to England, to offer the submission of the colonists on conditions, but was saved from punishment by the favor of Lord Shaftsbury. He afterward purchased the interest of Lord Clarendon, took the government in 1683, and so disaffected the people by his corrupt policy, that they seized and imprisoned him in 1688, and afterward banished him for a year.

A band of Huguenots arrived from France in 1707, and settled on the Trent, a branch of the Neuse, who were succeeded in 1710 by a party of Palatines from Germany, and each received a grant of 100 acres of land. But most of these unfortunate colonists were soon after massacred, in a sudden and treacherous attack by 1,200 Indians, from several nations, and only a small number escaped, to tell the tale in the southern colony.

Passing over some years, for even a sketch of which we have no room, we shall barely note the period of the separation of Carolina into two provinces. In 1730, George Burrington was appointed governor of North Carolina, by the crown, and he assumed his office at Edenton, Feb. 25th, 1731.

To secure the friendship of the Indians, Sir Edward Cumming was sent to the Cherokee country, which embraced all the land between North and South Carolina and the Alleganies, and contained 20,000 persons, of whom 6,000 were warriors. The chiefs acknowledged King George their sovereign, on their knees, and sent a deputation to England.

As early as 1731 rice had become the staple production of the colony, and was exported in great quantities.

In 1738, commissioners appointed by the two colonies, began to run the boundary line, as fixed by royal command, from the northeast end of Long bay, northwestwardly to the 35th degree of latititude, and thence westwardly to the South sea! After running it 64 miles, it was agreed that the dividing line between the Cherokees and the Catawbas should, for the present, be considered the line of the colonies. The same year, the three counties, Albemarle, Bath, and Clarendon, into which the colony had before this been divided, were abolished, and the precincts were erected into counties.

Provision was made for placing buoys in the rivers, and otherwise improving the navigation.

Soldiers were raised in North Carolina in 1740, for the expedition sent against Pensacola from Charleston, and also to join the expedition against Cuba. The legislature, for the support of the war, laid a poll-tax of three shillings "proclamation money," to be paid in tobacco, rice, Indian-dressed skins, beeswax, tallow, pork, and beef. In Albemarle, the people were allowed to pay in bills of credit, at the rate of seven and a half pounds for one pound proclamation money. The ordinary taxes were also made payable in the above-mentioned articles, and warehouses to receive them were ordered to be built in all the counties. To encourage immigration, foreigners were offered the privileges of citizens, after seven years residence, by taking the oath of abjuration, and receiving the communion in a protestant church; Jews and quakers being excused from the last.

The same year, in consequence of complaints made by British merchants against the paper money, the legislature agreed to issue no more without the consent of the king. To the expedition against Havana, under Admiral Vernon, in 1741, North Carolina supplied 400 men. The legislature divided the colony into 14 parishes, regulated the election of churchwardens and vestrymen, provided for the erection of churches, the apprehension of fugitives, and the trial and punishment of slaves, defining the rights and duties of masters and servants, and laying restrictions on the emancipation of the latter.

The legislature, in 1743, although urged by the governor to make spirited preparations for defence against the Spaniards and French, in consequence of the threatening aspect of affairs, consented only to erect magazines in the different counties. The next year, John, Lord Carteret, afterward earl of Granville, had one eighth part of the original province of Carolina, which had been reserved to him by act of parliament, set apart to him, he resigning his interest in the government, and his title to the other seven. His territory extended from Virginia to a line drawn in latitude 35 degrees 34 minutes from the Atlantic to the Pacific! This tract was granted to Lord Carteret (except the powers of government),to be holden on the payment of thirty-three shillings and fourpence yearly, for ever, with one fourth of all the gold and silver ore.

War having been declared by England against France, in 1745, Fort Johnson was erected at the mouth of Cape Fear river, for 24 cannon. The village of Powerscreek, on that part of the river, was then expected to become an important port, but Wilmington has increased at its expense. Two years after this, a number of the adherents of the Pretender, after the failure of his attempt to seize the crown of England, settled in the vicinity of the present town of Fayetteville. The legislature took measures to have the laws printed for the use of the people. They had hitherto been circulated in loose manuscripts.

After the passage of the stamp-act by the British parliament, meetings were held in Edenton, Newbern, and Wilmington, to express the strong disapprobation of the people, and their concurrence with the northern colonies. A spirited address was published by an illiterate but patriotic man at Nutbush, Granville county, "containing a brief narrative of our deplorable situation, and the wrongs we suffer, and some necessary hints with respect to a reformation." The representatives of Massachusetts, in June, directed their speaker to address the speakers of the other colonial legislatures, inviting a meeting at New York, on the first Tuesday in October, at which North Carolina was not represented. The people, however, in all their public meetings, expressed warm approbation of the measures adopted by the northern colonies

Early in the year 1766, the sloop-of-war Diligence arrived in Cape Fear river, with stamped paper for distribution; but Colonels Ashe and Waddle assembled the militia at Brunswick, and informed the commander that they would resist the landing of the stamps. They seized one of the boats, and carried it in triumph through Wilmington. The next day, Col. Ashe led a party to the governor's house, and threatened to set fire to it unless the stamp officer gave them an audience. The latter was induced to resign his office. In February a riot took place in Wilmington, and a duel, in which an officer was killed.

In 1767, the two houses of the legislature joined in an address to the king, on the repeal of the stamp-act, after the lower house had resisted all the exertions of the governor to reconcile them to it. The document was written with ability, and disclaimed every disloyal intention. But the vanity of Governor Tryon led him this year to begin a project, which laid the foundation of serious difficulties to the colony. This was the erection of a palace for his residence, at the expense of the people. The houses were prevailed upon to appropriate £5,000, which he expended in purchasing ground at Newbern, and laying a foundation, the money having been wholly intrusted to him. He made himself ridiculous, also, by making an ostentatious military display, in leading a party westward, to settle the boundary with the Indians. The next year, £10,000 were added to the palace fund, and a mob was soon raised in the west, which set the government at defiance for several years, often overawing the officers and courts by a display of armed companies, sometimes to the number of 1,500 men; the people having bound themselves to pay no taxes, until they should have some security for the proper use of their money. They several times seemed satisfied, and made very humble acknowledgments, particularly to the king.

The governor's palace having been completed, in 1770 the legislature were received there, and the edifice is described as one of great magnificence, even for England. But the attempt to get an obnoxious friend of the governor into the lower house, again excited the mob (or regulators as they called themselves), who threatened to burn the town. A ditch was dug from river to river for defence, and the country militia were ordered to be in readiness to march in. The legislature had, before this time, addressed the king on the subject of taxation without representation, in the spirit of Massachusetts and other colonies, though in opposition to the repeated remonstrances of the governor. In 1770, the sheriffs were ordered to disperse every meeting of ten men, wherever assembled, and it was declared to be felony, without benefit of clergy, to disobey, or to undertake any unlawful acts.

The next year the public troubles came to a crisis. Governor Tryon, at the head of a few hundred militia, met a somewhat more numerous body of regulators at the great Almance river, and, after repeated attempts to bring them to an accommodation, had a sharp battle with them for an hour, which discipline and cannon decided in his favor. A few executions terminated the whole, and the governor soon sailed for New York.

In 1774, on the 25th of August, a meeting of delegates was held at Newbern, representing meetings of the people in all parts of the state, who had assembled to express their feelings on the condition of the country; and although the governor called the council, they refused to act, while the convention chose John Harvey, of Perquiman, for speaker, and adopted resolutions, expressive of unshaken loyalty, but firmly in favor of the country, and opposed to the north-port act, the taxes on tea, &c. They applauded the measures of Massachusetts, and resolved not to import, purchase, nor export, until American grievances were removed. They approved of the proposed congress at Philadelphia, resolved to hold no intercourse with persons or towns who would not co-operate with them, and agreed to contribute for the relief of Boston sufferers. They then appointed deputies to the congress, William Hooper, of Doange, Joseph Hewes, of Edenton, and Richard Caswell, of Dobbs county.

The legislature met at Edenton, on the 4th of April, 1775, at the time when the delegates of the people assembled to appoint members of the congress, many of the delegates being also members of the legislature, and John Harvey being chairman of both bodies.

Governor Martin, in a long speech, remonstrated against the proceedings of the people, and the deputies replied in the plainest and most decided tone. The council, at the proposal of the governor, struck off the name of John Harvey from the list of justices of his county; and he afterward collected cannon for the defence of his palace, endeavored to enlist the Highlanders and others in the west to take part with him, and wrote a letter to General Gage, at Boston, for arms and ammunition, which was intercepted. But the committees of safety were active throughout the colony, and that of Newbern took away the governor's cannon, and drove him, in fear, to take refuge in Fort Johnson.

A dangerous plot was discovered on the evening of July 7th, for a massacre of the people on Tar river, by their negroes, on the following day, and many of the latter were found armed. The people of Wilmington prepared to seize the arms, &c., at Fort Johnson, but found the governor had embarked with them on board the sloop-of-war Cruizer. They then burned the fort, headed by John Ashe, who had resigned his commission as militia colonel of New Hanover.

The congress authorized the levy of 1,000 men, in North Carolina, if necessary, to be regarded as part of an American army; the 20th of July was kept as a day of fasting and prayer, and the provincial congress met August 20th, to the number of 184 members; while the governor issued a proclamation, offering pardons &c.; 1,000 troops were raised, and 400 placed in Wilmington, the first regiment under James Moore, and the other under Robert Rowe, and 150,000 dollars was emitted in bills of credit, to be redeemed by a poll-tax of nine years, to commence in 1777. A battalion of ten companies of fifty minute-men, was ordered to be raised in each district. The congress also adopted an address to the inhabitants of the British empire, drawn up, it is said, by William Hooper. Other arrangements were made for defence.

On the 19th of April, 1775, a committee, appointed by the captains of militia of Mecklenburg county, met at Charlotte, and while in session, received news of the battle of Lexington, when, after hearing addresses from some of the members, they all cried out, "Let us be independent!" and Dr. Ephraim Brevard reported resolutions declaring themselves "a free and independent people." They were forwarded to the congress at Philadelphia, but the president said it would be premature to present them.

Governor Martin now sent emissaries to the regulators and the Highlanders in the southern counties, and a General M'Donald, to induce them to adhere to the royal cause; to counteract which, clergymen were sent to defeat his efforts to deceive them. Lord Dunmore of Virginia at the same time marched for the northern counties, with 120 regular troops, and some tories and negroes. He intrenched himself at the great bridge, and invited slaves to join him; but he was attacked by Lieut. Colonel Scott, while Lieutenant Tibbs, with his boat-guard, six miles off, was attacked by royal troops, which he repulsed.

General M'Donald, with 1,500 men, offered terms to Colonel Moore, encamped on Rocky river, and after some time passed him by a rapid march, but was defeated by Colonel Caswell near Wilmington, and made prisoner.

In May, 1776, Sir Peter Parker's expedition of about 30 vessels reached Cape Fear river, and on the 12th, Generals Clinton and Cornwallis landed at General Howe's plantation in the county of Brunswick, with 900 men, but failed in their object, which was to surprise Major Davis at Ostin's mills, for a sentinel on the shore gave the alarm, they were fired upon while crossing the causeway, and accomplished nothing but the destruction of the mills, and the beating, stabbing, and shooting of three women who fell into their power. They returned on board, with the loss of several men. The expedition failed, in consequence of the universal patriotism of the people, the defeat of M'Donald, and the refusal of the regulators to cooperate. After waiting in vain for their friends on shore, until they were obliged to kill several horses for food, they sailed on the 29th of May for Charleston.

The constitution of the state was adopted in December, 1776, and in 1835 was revised. There are 35 senators, and 120 members of the house of commons, who are elected once in two years, as is the governor. The houses elect an executive council of seven, for two years, and the judges of the supreme court, to act during good behavior. The attorney-general is appointed by the legislature for four years. All white males, 21 years of age, inhabitants of the state for 12 months, are allowed to vote, except for senators, for which a freehold of 50 acres of land is necessary. The legislature meets twice a year at Raleigh.

Little as the lower parts of North Carolina afford of variety, either in surface, soil, or natural productions, there is a region in the west, which vies with the most picturesque portions of the Union in rudeness and sublimity. The mountain region comprehends some of the highest land this side of the Rocky mountains, and towers far above the common table-land of the western counties. The latter is about 1,800 feet above the ocean, while Grandfather mountain is 5,556 feet, Roan mountain 6,038, and Black mountain 6,476: a little more than the reported height of Mount Washington, the loftiest peak of the White hills of New Hampshire.

The rivers, in the upper parts of their courses, wind through some pleasing and striking scenes; and in their lower parts, several are accessible to vessels, and now visited by steamboats.

Near the middle of the state, passes the boundary between the high and the low lands; and this line, which extends through several other adjacent states, is connected with some peculiarities of great importance. East of it extends the broad and sandy level to the seacoast, through which the rivers flow with a slow and uniform course, whose head-waters come through the high, cool, and more healthful region west of it, with a descent which precludes navigation. The occupations of the people, and the state of society, differ considerably in those two parts of the state, as well as the native products of the soil, and the objects of culture and of export. Near that line, also, are the gold mines, which, a few years since, began to excite much attention, and which are still wrought with some success.

The peculiar features of the coast of North Carolina, render it the scene of frequent shipwrecks, and of consequent sufferings to crews and passengers. The land is so level and low, as to render it difficult of discovery from a distance, except in clear weather; and the greatest desolation and solitude generally prevail there, which, with the difficulty of crossing the sounds that form so large a part of the eastern boundary of the state, often render the situation of unfortunate mariners almost desperate, even after they have escaped the perils of the sea, before they can obtain relief from the land. The temptation offered by the exposure of property thrown on shore by the waves, has too often led the solitary, ignorant, and indigent inhabitants, in some places, to theft and inhumanity: but such acts have been rare of late years, and instances of hospitality and kindness are much more common.

In some of the poorest parts of the low country, a habit prevails to a considerable extent, which is at once unnatural and injurious: clay-eating. A species of fine clay is found, which many learn to eat while young; and the practice leads to the formation of an inveterate habit, which at length produces a peculiar diseased and almost idiotic appearance and dulness of mind, with serious injury to the health, often terminating in premature death.

The Dismal swamp, lying partly in Virginia and partly in this state, renders a large tract in its northeastern corner uninhabitable, and almost entirely useless. It lies nearly on a level with the ocean, and presents only a dreary and repulsive wilderness of cypress, and other trees and plants able to live in water or marshy soil, with patches of somewhat drier land here and there, rising from the immense morasses, and a large pond in the middle called the Lake of the Dismal swamp. The whole tract is 22 miles in length, and it connects the waters of Albemarle sound with Chesapeake bay. There is no passage through it, except the canal which has been cut from Virginia, to bring the produce of that part of the state to Norfolk. It is a work of considerable importance and value: but a more unattractive region can hardly be imagined, than that through which it passes.

The Gold Mines.—According to traditions in some parts of the gold regions (which may embrace a tract of a thousand square miles), that precious metal has been found from early times, and sometimes in large masses. It now occurs in small lumps and grains, down to minute points, invisible even to the microscope; for the auriferous quartz often yields a considerable quantity when submitted to the separating process, even when no indication of its presence can be detected by the highest magnifiers.

The books of the U. S. mint first record the receiving of gold from North Carolina in the year 1814, when 11,000 dollars' worth was obtained. Between that time and 1824, an annual average of only $2,500 was received; in 1825, $17,000; 1826, $20,000; 1827, $21,000; 1828, nearly $46,000; and 1829, $128,000. The best gold-washings (as deposites in sand are called), are in the counties of Burke and Rutherford. The miners believe that streams of water formerly flowed where the gold is now found in this condition. The richest mines, properly so called, where the metal is found in rocks and stones, are in Mecklenburg, Rowan, Davidson, and Cabarras counties. There the particles are usually invisible to the naked eye, and are separated by the aid of quicksilver. The best veins have a dip of 45 degrees to the horizon, and are from a few inches in thickness to several feet. The process of obtaining it pure is laborious, tedious, and expensive. In some places excavations have been made 120 feet deep.

The stones are beaten to fine dust, either by common hammers, or by sledges moved by steam, and the mass is then placed in wooden troughs, called rockers, with a quantity of quicksilver, and a small stream of water is made to flow in, while the troughs are kept in continual gentle motion. The quicksilver readily combines or amalgamates with gold when brought into contact with it, and after this process has been kept up for a time, a lump of the united metals is taken out, and pressed in a deerskin bag, through the pores of which the quicksilver is forced in minute globules, while the gold is left behind in a state of purity. The separation is effected at some foreign gold mines by heat, which distils over the quicksilver.

During the height of the gold speculations, 6,000 persons were employed by one company, and it was supposed that 20,000 were occupied in the business in all parts of the gold counties.

The annual product of gold was once estimated as high as $100,000 a week, or at the rate of five millions annually. The chief part of the laborers were Germans, Swedes, and other foreigners, speaking not less than thirteen different languages, and most of the gold was exported to Europe. The village of Charlotte, in Mecklenburg county, which is near one of the largest mines, experienced a sudden growth and a great increase of business: but the influence of mining, as carried on in the state generally, has not been favorable to the moral interests of the people.

In the course of the excavations, evidences have been found of former mining operations, on the same ground. Many pieces of machinery have been discovered, and crucibles, of considerable size, and, in the opinion of some of the miners, of superior qualities to the best Hessian crucibles of the present day.

Internal Improvements.—Exertions have been made to improve the very defective channels of trade in this state, and to prevent the products from being carried to the ports of South Carolina and Virginia. In 1815, an extensive system of canals and roads was planned, and much expense has been incurred in connecting the principal rivers by canals, the draining of marshes, &c. Railroads have since been constructed, which add much to the prosperity of the state.

Education.—The institutions for education have been much increased since the year 1804, when there were only two academies. They are now established in different parts of the state; and the university of North Carolina, at Chapel Hill, 28 miles from Raleigh, is a respectable and flourishing institution.

Religious Denominations.—The baptists are most numerous, and the methodists the next. After these are the presbyterians, Lutherans, episcopalians, united brethren, and friends.

The Manufacture of Tar and Turpentine.—The following description of the process of making tar and turpentine, we copy from a letter from a traveller in the South, which appeared in a late newspaper:—

"This turpentine business has become, within the last two years, a very lucrative one indeed. The boundless forests of fir which cover North Carolina, offer material to the enterprising for a couple of centuries to come. The forests can be purchased for a dollar an acre. Some farms have been sold for ten cents an acre! and the highest I have heard did not exceed two dollars.

"Many speculators have latterly entered into this turpentine manufacture. One negro man will collect 200 barrels in a season, which will sell for about $800; about $100 will feed and clothe the negro; thus there is a pretty full margin of profit for the capital embarked in the land and negroes. It is better by far than cotton-raising—many cotton planters are going into it, and the expansion of manufactures and arts, at home and abroad, keeps pace with the increased number of those who are entering into this profitable business.

"For the benefit of those who have never been in a turpentine country, I may describe the process of gathering and distilling this subtle spirit. The trees are cupped in the spring; about eighteen inches square of the bark is peeled of; the cupping is made by one or two cuts of an axe, of peculiar shape, near the root. In the summer and fall the turpentine oozes out through this vent. The negro comes round from tree to tree, and gathers this oozed matter into his bucket. The trees are continually exuding during the season. The ensuing year they are cut a little higher than before, when a new crop is obtained. The process may be repeated for five or six years, cutting higher up the trunk each year; after which the trees are cut down and chopped into short logs, and piled together in peculiar heaps, called "kilns," when a slow fire is put under the heap, and thus pitch and tar are obtained from the heated pile. The fatty matter, or raw turpentine, is packed into barrels—brought to the distilleries, boiled and evaporated in the common way in which spirit is extracted in the alcohol distilleries, the steam passing through a large worm or refrigerator, which is set in an immense vat of cold water. The surface of the water, being the hottest, passes off, while the attendant keeps pumping cold water through a pipe that forces it to the bottom, causing the hot water, created on the surface, to pass off. The steam comes out in spirits of turpentine below, and is barrelled tightly and sent to all the markets of the world, and the residue is rosin.

"North Carolina sends out an immense quantity of Indian corn, staves, turpentine, pitch, tar, and rosin, besides which, she is beginning to manufacture cotton and woollens."

Raleigh, the seat of government, is situated nearly in the centre of the state, 6 miles distant from the river Neuse, 164 southwest from Richmond, and 288 southwest from Washington. It was named in honor of that conspicuous statesman of Queen Elizabeth, who makes so interesting a figure in the history of her reign, and displayed so much zeal in prosecuting discoveries, and planting protestant colonies in this part of America.

Raleigh is a small town, containing only about 3,000 inhabitants, but it is pleasantly situated, and laid out with taste, having a square of ten acres in the centre, called Union square, from which the four principal streets, of a fine breadth, viz., 99 feet, diverge at right angles. Between these are four smaller squares of four acres each. There are two academies, and several other public buildings. The capitol, which was destroyed by fire several years ago, contained the finest and most

The Old State House at Raleigh.

valuable piece of sculpture ever seen in America: a statue of Washington, by Canova. With a degree of taste and patriotic spirit which are highly creditable to the state, the legislature employed that greatest of modern sculptors to execute the noble work, on which he was employed as early as 1819. It was placed in the capitol, and excited general admiration, being made of the finest Carrara marble, in a dignified sitting posture, with an expression and features much like those of the Father of his country. The costume was that of a Roman senator. In the destruction of the statehouse, this most valuable of its contents was ruined; but although it can never be replaced, the history of it will reflect lasting honor upon the character of the state.

The old statehouse (which is represented in our engraving) was a well-proportioned edifice, of plain architecture, and consisted of a main building and a projection at the centre, with a basement of hewn stone, and a front of four Ionic half-columns, while a large dome, with a cupola, rose from the middle of the roof. A broad yard in front, offered a fine approach; and the building was of sufficient size to afford large halls for the legislature, and various offices, and other appropriate apartments for public purposes.

The present statehouse is of granite, on the plan of the celebrated temple of Minerva at Athens, called the Parthenon, 166 feet in length, 90 in breadth, with a range of noble columns of granite, 30 feet high, and five and a half in diameter.

The other public buildings are the courthouse, the governor's house, five churches, four academies, two banks, and a theatre.

Wake Forest College is at Forestville, 15 miles from Raleigh. It has three professorships, and a library of 4,700 volumes, and was founded in 1838. The number of pupils is yet small.

Edenton is a small town, situated on the bay at the mouth of Chouan river, and contains a handsome courthouse, two churches, an academy, and a bank, with a population of about 1,600. Stage-coaches go to Norfolk three times a week, distant 86 miles.

Tarborough stands on the south side of Tar river, and contains a courthouse, two churches, a bank, and an academy, with about 800 inhabitants. Stage-coaches go every other day to Raleigh and Washington.

Warrenton, 62 miles northeast from Raleigh, is a small town, containing about 800 inhabitants, now frequently visited on account of its proximity to a favorite watering-place, which is resorted to, in the warm season, by many travellers. This is the

Shocco White Sulphur Springs, 12 miles from Warrenton, with which there is a daily communication by stage-coaches. The water is charged with sulphuretted hydrogen and carbonic acid gases, and contains the sulphates of lime and magnesia, oxyde of iron, muriate of soda, and carbonate of lime, and is recommended for diseases of the skin and the liver.

Wilmington.—This is the principal town in the state for trade and most other kinds of business. It contains a population of about 12,000, of whom 9,000 are whites. It stands on the eastern bank of Cape Fear river, just below the confluence of the two branches, 13 miles from the ocean, at the head of navigation for vessels of 300 tons, although steamboats go up to Fayetteville a part of the year, 120 miles. The town is chiefly built on four streets, and in some parts shows some of the ruins caused by several destructive fires, from which it has successively suffered. The houses are built of pitch pine, which renders it difficult to arrest the progress of the flames when once enkindled. Much lumber is brought down the river, and sawed up by steam-mills erected on the shore, where vessels receive their freight for the West Indies, and some of the northern ports. The railroad has increased the population in six years, about 6,000.

Great quantities of turpentine, tar, &c., are also brought here from the country. Considerable quantities of spirits of turpentine are made, about twenty manufactories having been recently erected.

We must conclude our sketch of North Carolina with a brief account of one of the most courageous acts in the history of the revolutionary war in this state.

In Ramsay's history of South Carolina, mention is made of an engagement, which took place at Williams' plantation, in the upper part of South Carolina, on the 12th of July, 1780, between "a part of the corps commanded by Col. Sumter," and a detachment of British troops and tories under the command of Captain Huck. The historian does not inform us, however, who commanded this "*party*" from the corps of Col. Sumter, nor are we told by him the particulars of this brilliant little engagement, which was the first check given to the royal forces after landing in South Carolina on the 11th of February, 1780. The following account of it is from the speech of Col. W. C. Beatty of Yorkville, delivered on the anniversary of the battle, in 1839.

Captain Christian Huyck was said to be a native of Philadelphia. He bore the commission of a captain in the British army and was distinguished for his profanity and bloody deeds in the upper part of South Carolina. His enmity to the presbyterians displayed itself in burning the library and dwelling-house of their clergyman, Mr. Linyman. At the moment of his attack and defeat, "a number of women," says Dr. Ramsay, "were on their knees, vainly soliciting his mercy, in behalf of their families and property." He had been despatched by Col. Turnbull, the commander of the British forces at Rocky Mount, with the following orders: "You are hereby ordered, with the cavalry under your command, to proceed to the frontier of the province, collecting all the royal militia with you in your march, and with said force to push the rebels, as far as you may deem convenient."

Previous to the issuing of the above order, Colonel Bratton, Major Wynn, and Captain M'Clure, had attacked and defeated a body of tories assembled at Mobley's meetinghouse in Fairfield district. This gallant adventure on the part of a few bold whigs, had induced Col. Turnbull to send Captain Huyck into York district to chastise the rebels —"push them as far as he might deem convenient." "The evening before his defeat he arrived at the house of Col. Bratton and demanded of Mrs. Bratton where her husband was. She replied that he was in Sumter's army. He then proposed to her, if she would get her husband to come in and join the royalists, he should have a commission in the British service. Mrs. Bratton replied with heroic firmness that she preferred her husband's remaining and dying in the army of his country." For this bold and spirited reply, a soldier, under the command of Huyck, attempted her life, and was prevented executing his purpose by the interference of an officer second in command. She was then ordered to prepare supper for Captain Huyck and his officers. While doing so, the idea occurred to her that "she might play," in the language of Col. Beatty, "a Roman's part and take a deadly revenge on the enemies of her country." She had poison in the house and could mix it with the food. But a moment's reflection taught her that this food might fall into the possession of the whigs, who were closely watching the footsteps of the enemy. Her own brave husband might, by some mishap, be the victim of her treachery, instead of his enemies. The idea was quickly abandoned.

Huck and his officers slept in Williamson's house the night preceding the battle. His troops lay encamped around it. A road enclosed in a lane passed the door, and sentinels were posted along the road. The guard kept negligent watch, and the troops lay in fancied security—undreaming of to-morrow's scenes—unknowing that they were already marked for defeat and death. On that same day, Col. Bratton, with one hundred and twenty-five men, principally his neighbors, left Mecklenburg county, North Carolina, under the conviction that some royal force, would shortly visit their neighborhood to avenge the defeat of the tories at Mobley's meetinghouse. During the march, about fifty of the men dropped off, and thus only seventy-five were left to attack the enemy, instead of one hundred and thirty-three, as stated in the history of Carolina. With this force, Col. Bratton arrived that night near their encampment. Intelligence of the enemy had passed up, and their number, had been received during the day. After concealing their horses in a swamp, the whigs impatiently awaited the dawn of day, to commence the attack. At length it came, and with it victory. One half of the men, led by Col. Bratton and Capt. Moffit, came up the lane, while the other half, commanded by Capt. M'Clure, of Chester, a brave and daring officer, were sent round to the head of the lane. Thus the enemy were enclosed, speedily routed and conquered. When the attack commenced, Huck and his officers were in bed, and were aroused from their slumbers by the roar of the American guns. The captain quickly mounted his horse and attempted to rally his men. This he several times effected, but all his efforts were unavailing—the determined spirit of the whigs carried all before them—and as soon as Huck fell, his men threw down their arms and fled. Huck, Col. Ferguson of the British army, and thirty-five or forty men, lay dead on the field or were wounded unto death. How many perished in the woods is not known—the rest escaped. Of the whigs, only one was killed—whose name was Campbell, as stated by Col. Gill. The rest, though in the thickest and hottest of the fight, escaped unhurt, to fight other battles and do further service in the cause of their beloved country. This battle is said to have lasted one hour.

This victory was not only brilliant and glorious in itself, but it had the most salutary and important effect on the destinies of the state. It was the first time since the fall of Charleston, that any power dared to meet the hitherto victorious enemy. This victory reanimated the drooping spirits of the country. The citizens were buoyed up with new life and fresh hopes. It brought them confidence, and taught the enemy to dread the vengeance of freemen, fighting for their liberties, their lives, and domestic altars. It had the direct and immediate effect of embodying the whigs, and in a few days afterward, six hundred new troops joined the army of Sumter. Thus reinforced, on the thirtieth of the same month, Gen. Sumter made a spirited attack on the British forces at Rocky Mount, and in eight days afterward gained a complete victory over the enemy at Hanging Rock.

After the engagement was over, the officer who had saved the life of Mrs. Bratton the evening before, was about being put to death by the whigs. He asked the favor of being carried into the presence of Mrs. Bratton, who immediately recognised him, related her obligation to him, and implored that his life might be spared, which was done. Thus she had an opportunity of proving that she was as grateful in the hour of triumph, as she had been bold and spirited in the time of danger.

Col. W. Bratton, who was chief in command on the occasion, was a gallant officer throughout the American revolution. He was in the battles fought at Guildford courthouse, Hanging Rock, Blackstocks, Rowsam's mills, and Mobley's meetinghouse, beside the one already recounted. In all of these engagements, he fought with great spirit, courage, and determined bravery. In the darkest period of his country's distress, he stood firm in her cause, and by his influence and example, encouraged and cheered on his whig neighbors, and "bid them hope for brighter and better days." As an evidence of his uncommon daring, it is said, that on the night before the battle at Williamson's, he reconnoitred the encampment and advanced entirely within their line of sentinels. By this bold adventure, he acquired information which greatly contributed to the victory which they gained.

The distinction and honor of having killed the famous Captain Huck, or Huyck, as his name was more properly written, belonged to John Carroll, who greatly distinguished himself in many engagements by his extraordinary boldness and daring. Huck was shot while endeavoring to rally his men. This battleground is now known as Brattonsville.

SOUTH CAROLINA.

This state, although presenting many of the leading features which characterize North Carolina, enjoys some counterbalancing advantages, of much importance to commerce and agriculture. There is a good harbor at Charleston, and several of the rivers and inlets along the coast are more accessible, and navigable to a greater distance. The low land which borders the ocean has many tracts of good soil, among which are numerous rice-fields. The line between the high and the low lands is still more marked than in North Carolina, in its influence on trade and the position of towns. Rice and cotton in the low grounds, and cotton and grain in the middle regions, and apples and other northern plants in the mountains, mark their appropriate sections, while maize yields abundantly in all parts. The oak and palm, as well as the pine and walnut, are prevailing native trees, and many others have been introduced.

A few of the events in the early history of South Carolina have been given in the preceding pages, in speaking of the first settlements of North Carolina, with which it was for a time connected. Oyster Point, near Charleston, was first occupied by a colony under William Sayle, who, having made a survey of the coast some years previously, arrived on the coast in 1670, and after several changes of place, finally chose the spot at the confluence of the Ashley and Cooper rivers, near that now covered by the large and flourishing city of Charleston. The number of the colonists was soon increased, as we have before remarked, and the name of South Carolina was conferred on the new settlement.

In 1674, Joseph West was elected governor, and exercised the chief authority for several years, with much ability. The principal offices were filled by the cavaliers, although the puritans were in greater numbers; and considerable additions were soon made by the arrival of English dissenters and protestants, driven by religious intolerance from several Roman catholic countries.

The site of the present flourishing city of Charleston, was first occupied in 1673, by a number of Dutchmen from the New Netherlands, now New York, and, the advantages of its situation becoming at length obvious, it was finally taken by the colonists at Oyster Point.

The year 1680 was unfortunately signalized by the first Indian war. A considerable number of prisoners were taken, who were sold as slaves by the governor to West India planters; for which inhuman policy he was removed by the proprietors, in 1683, and Governor Morton was appointed his successor. An Irish and a Scotch colony came out the same year. The latter at first settled on Port Royal island, but were soon driven to Charleston by fear of the Spaniards at St. Augustine. They afterward returned, when their settlement was laid waste in 1686. Governors West, Kyrle, Quarry, and Morton, in turn succeeded to the chief-magistracy, but in the short space of three years, gave place to Colleton, in 1686. The inhuman practice of kidnapping and selling Indians was allowed, to the discredit of the colony.

A large and valuable addition was made to the colony at this time, by the arrival of many French Huguenot families, who, having been deprived of the protection of the laws in their native country, by the revocation of the edict of Nantes, sought an asylum in the new world. Some of the principal families of South Carolina at the present day, bear the names of some of those refugees; and there, as elsewhere, they have done honor to their principles, and the land of their adoption, by the characters they have sustained in the country of their choice.

One chief source of difficulty between the colonies of South, as well as North Carolina, and their governors, had been the payment of quit-rents to the proprietors; and Colleton was deposed, in 1687, in consequence of his attempt to enforce it. After a period of anarchy, Seth Sothel assumed the chief-magistracy, in the character of a friend of the people, who unwisely trusted him after his misconduct in the northern colony. They soon however found it necessary to banish him, and elected in his place Ludwell, who had succeeded him in North Carolina.

The introduction of rice into the colony, an event of particular interest, took place during the administration of Governor Smith, the successor of Ludwell. A vessel from Madagascar stopped at Charleston, and the captain presented a bag of that grain to the governor, who distributed it among his friends, and the culture of that valuable staple was thus commenced, with results most important to agriculture and commerce.

Governor Blake, a dissenter (son of Admiral Blake), with great liberality, sustained religious liberty; but after his death, in 1700, Governor Moore, sustained by Lord Granville, one of the proprietors, by intrigue induced the assembly to pass a bill establishing episcopacy, and thus introduced religious persecution. The majority of the people being dissenters, many of them prepared to leave the colony; but the house of lords having voted against the law, and Queen Anne having annulled it, the threatened evil to the colony was prevented.

In 1702, England being at war with Spain, Governor Moore undertook a wild expedition against St. Augustine, and sailed from Port Royal with a part of the force raised. Colonel Daniel and his enlisted Indians, took and robbed the town: but, while the governor was waiting for cannon to batter the fortress, into which the enemy had retired, two Spanish ships appeared, and he made a hasty retreat. To meet the expense of this expedition, six thousand pounds, the first paper-money, was emitted in Carolina, which depreciated after a few years.

A happy termination was at length

View of Charleston.

put to the old difficulties between the people and the proprietors, by the wise, moderate, and conciliatory policy of Archdale, a quaker, who arrived from England in 1695, with authority to bring the matter to a close; he was succeeded in the government by Blake; but from his death, in 1700, under Governors Moore and Johnson, the colony was distracted by wars with the Indians and Spaniards. In 1703, the savages commenced hostilities, instigated by the Spaniards, but were conquered by Gov. Moore, who destroyed about 800. In 1706, the Spaniards made a new attack upon Charleston, but were unsuccessful, and retired with much loss; while the colony failed in an attempt on St. Augustine.

The Tuscarora and Cosee Indians assaulted the western settlements in 1712.

A great advantage was gained over them by Col. Barnell, and a decisive victory by Col. Monro soon after, both of them being aided by large bodies of friendly Indians. The Tuscaroras were so discouraged, that they migrated to the north, in 1713, and settled on lands granted them by their ancient allies, the celebrated Five Nations, or Iroquois of the present state of New York; with whom they were incorporated, as the sixth member of the confederacy. They are now in a state of much improvement, under the influence of missionaries, by means of schools and churches; and many of them are respectable farmers. (See Schoolcraft's Census of the N. Y. Indians, 1846.) Their residence is a few miles from the falls of Niagara.

After the departure of the Tuscaroras, the other Indians proposed terms of peace with South Carolina, and never again caused any disturbance.

The close of the wars with the savages, formed an epoch quite important in the histories of both of the Carolinas. It was not till that time that the nature of the interior lands became known. The fear of Indians being passed, and no obstacle now existing to the establishing of settlements inland, considerable numbers of colonists came from Pennsylvania, and other northern parts, to occupy them. The nature of the country, and the character of the climate, combined to encourage a different system of agriculture; and the state of society has naturally been much influenced by the circumstances which surrounded the people. Manual labor is not regarded as intolerable or discreditable to the owners of the soil, who often go to the fields with their slaves, and work at their side. They do not demand so large a number of servants, to perform the work on an upland farm as on a lowland plantation, and more simplicity and economy are observed in the style of living.

Our limits do not allow us to give even so much as an outline of the French or revolutionary wars in this state. In the latter, the people suffered exceedingly from the conflict of parties nearly equally divided, and the repeated prevalence of the royal authority; as well as from the want of power or firmness among the friends of the country. Charleston was once saved from capture, by the bravery of a few men in Fort Moultrie. Marauding parties were occasionally sent out under Tarlton and others, from that city, when it afterward lay in the power of the British; and these were repeatedly harassed or checked by small bands of patriots. Among the partisan leaders who became prominent and useful in those trying times, was General Marion, who established a high character for skill and bravery, in a long course of irregular military operations in the interior. A characteristic anecdote is told of him, which does peculiar honor to the American character.

A young English officer, in wandering through the woods, unexpectedly found himself among the soldiers of Marion, and was kindly received by the generous outlaw, who hospitably invited him to partake of his fare. His food was of the plainest kind, and his lodging was upon the bare ground. The foreigner, fascinated by the character of his host, remonstrated with him, in the most urgent terms, against the desperate and dangerous course of life in which he had engaged, offering to procure him a pardon and rewards, if he would join the party of the king. The soldier declined in the most spirited manner, declaring that he would not exchange his poverty and humble fare, with his faithfulness to his country's cause, for all that the king had to bestow. He then took leave of his new acquaintance, whom he allowed to retire without hinderance. But it is related that the interview so far enlightened the mind of the young officer on the real nature of the American war, and so deeply affected his heart, that he soon obtained leave to return to England, and took no further part in the contest.

Two of the principal battles fought in this state, were at Columbia: one in 1780, August 7, by General Gates against Lord Cornwallis, and the other between General Greene and Lord Rawdon, April 23, 1781. A third was at the Cowpens.

Such was the unsettled state of South Carolina during a great part of the war, that many cases occurred, in which men of different classes changed from side to side, and many took the oath of allegiance to the king, after having been for a while on the side of the revolution. In order to present, in a striking manner, some of the events of those disastrous times, with a picture or two of the scenes which they produced, we make the following abridgment of a history of "the Cunninghams of South Carolina," from the appendix to the second edition of the "Journal of Kirwen," by Mr. Ward.

The first decided outbreak of the civil war, originated in the unjustifiable arrest and imprisonment of Robert Cunningham, in November, 1775, at Charleston. There he was destined to remain till the ensuing July, when the English having been expelled from the country, the council of safety, deeming it prudent to try the effect of conciliatory measures, released him and the other state prisoners, without any conditions whatever as to their after conduct. He repaired immediately to the headquarters of an army under the command of General Williamson, which had been collected to repel a threatened invasion of the Indians, and offered his services as a volunteer. To prevent a mutiny in the camp, Williamson was obliged to decline his proffered services.

After this time, till the year 1780, no public mention is made of any of the Cunninghams. They had all removed to the city of Charleston, where they lived quietly attending to their private affairs.

In the spring of 1780, Charleston capitulated to Clinton, and nearly the whole of South Carolina returned to their allegiance. In December of this year, Patrick Cunningham was made colonel of the Little river regiment, and he seems to have had superintendence over some of the confiscated estates. Robert was made a brigadier-general in the British service, and sent to command a fort about seventeen miles from "Ninety-six," called Williams' fort, with a garrison of 150 men. After the surprise and slaughter at Hammond's store, which was about thirty miles distant, many of the fugitives arrived, on the evening of the same day, at Fort Williams, on their way to "Ninety-six," the stronghold of the British in the country. They reported that Washington was at Hammond's store, having a large force under him, with which he intended to march directly on "Ninety-six," taking Fort Williams on his way. These reports were confirmed by many arrivals of wounded men and stragglers during the night, and General Cunningham determined to retreat upon "Ninety-six," so as to increase the force of the garrison, while there was yet time to carry off as much arms and ammunition as each man could bear, rather than, by a fruitless opposition to an overwhelming force, not only lose *all* his military stores, but cause also a useless sacrifice of human life. They accordingly marcned the next morning, leaving only a few men to take care of such of the sick and wounded as were unable to go with them.

In July, 1781, when Lord Rawdon returned to "Ninety-six," from a short pursuit of General Nathaniel Greene, whom he had forced temporarily to retreat, he called the chief of the loyalists together, explained to them the necessity of abandoning the district, and advised them all to retreat within lines which the British troops were able to maintain. Every preparation was accordingly made by Colonel Cruger for immediate departure. Half of all the British force was left with him to cover their retreat, which was commenced on the 8th of July. All would then have left, but for a letter addressed to them by General Greene, in which, declaring himself to be their protector, he promised all who should remain his favor and support. Relying on these assurances, some were induced to remain, but soon had cause bitterly to regret their determination.

It would be in the highest degree unjust to impute bad faith to General Greene in this matter, but it was impossible for him to restrain his subordinates, and to guard against their excesses. But no sooner did he hear of them, than General Sumter was despatched to restore order and capture the ringleaders; in the meantime, much mischief had been done, and many cruel and disgraceful outrages perpetrated. In November, General Cunningham was sent with 700 men into the neighborhood of Orangeburg, where he encountered General Sumter's brigade of equal force. The latter was obliged to fall back, and met with some loss, in consequence of one of his officers having allowed himself to be drawn into an ambuscade; he continued, however, to act as a check on Cunningham's further advance into the country. After the capitulation of Charleston, a great many whigs renewed their oaths of allegiance to the king, and yet when success appeared to favor the whig cause, they reassumed arms against the British. Cornwallis issued orders that all such, when taken, should be put to death as rebels, who had forfeited their lives by breaking the oaths of fealty they had so short a time previously taken. Major William Cunningham, then an officer in the British service, was one of those who received these orders, and who executed them rigorously on all such offenders as fell into his power.

After the retreat of the loyalists from "Ninety-six," in July, 1781, those who had been induced by General Greene's proclamations to remain, were treated with the greatest barbarity. Among the whigs who distinguished themselves by their cruelties toward these helpless tories, were a Colonel Hays, and a Mr. Turner. Complaints having been made to Major Cunningham, of injuries committed by these men against the innocent wives and children of some of the soldiers of his corps, who had adhered to him in every danger, he did not hesitate to leave the English camp at Charleston, and to pass into district "Ninety-six," with a party of not exceeding one hundred and fifty men, for the purpose of inflicting punishment on those against whose inhumanity neither age nor sex had afforded any protection. Both Turner and Hays occupied military "stations." Turner's was the first encountered. It was taken, and the men put to death. On their way to Hays' "station," some of the men, led on by one "Elmore," seizing the opportunity of Cunningham's being at a considerable distance behind, proceeded to Captain Caldwell's house, and finding him at home, they killed him, and burned the house. When Cunningham came up, he regretted what his men had done, but it seems doubtful whether, even had he been present, he could have restrained them, bearing as they did, such determined hatred toward their victim. The party then proceeded on their way to Hays' station. Col. Hays had been warned of his danger the night before, by a Captain Brooks, who sent an express advising him to disband his men, and leave the ground instantly, as Cunningham was in the country, had taken Turner's station, and killed nineteen men. Hays, distrusting this information, as he had just returned from scouring that part of the country, and had heard nothing of Cunningham, did not think fit to follow the advice, but merely sent off to another station for assistance in case of need.

It was on a fine morning toward the end of November, when, at 10 o'clock, the party of loyalists, led on by Captain John Hood, rode up to the station at full gallop. This Hood was a very daring fellow. He went close to the piazza in front of the house, and called out in a loud voice, that "none should fire from within, or they should all be put to death." Those within, disregarding this warning, fired through the openings, and killed one man. Major Cunningham arriving shortly afterward, sent a flag of truce with a written message, demanding "instant surrender," and promising, if they did so, "to spare all their lives," but declaring at the same time, that "if they should resist, and so cause the spilling of his men's blood, he would give them no quarter, but put them all to death." Col. Hays, trusting to receive a reinforcement before the station could be carried, refused to surrender, and answered, "he should hold out to the last, at the risk of the lives of his whole party." After some shooting on both sides, Cunningham succeeded in setting fire to the "station," which was of wood, by means of a ramrod wrapped round with tow, dipped in pitch, and thrown in a blazing state on the roof. Half-suffocated, Hays and his party at length surrendered at discretion. Cunningham immediately hanged Hays and another man called Daniel Williams on the pole of a fodder-stock, the former for his cruelty to women and children, and the latter for having murdered in cold blood his favorite follower, Thomas Ellison, whose death he had sworn to avenge. Before they were dead, the pole broke, and Cunningham, drawing his sword, slew them both with his own hand. Being told that Cook, the man who with Ritchie and Moore had whipped his brother to death, was among the prisoners, he ordered him out from the rest, and slew him with his sword.

He then gave permission to his men to do as they pleased with the rest. All who had rendered themselves obnoxious by acts of cruelty and plunder, were slain without mercy. The others were saved. Each of Cunningham's men singled out whomsoever among the prisoners had been guilty of murdering any of his relatives, and killed him forthwith. The execution took place about sunset.

At the affair of Turner's station, there was no surrender made, nor quarter asked, and of course such a party as Cunningham's could not burden themselves with prisoners. At the time they were attacked, the people of that station were busy cutting up some beeves of which they had just plundered the tories. To conceal their occupation, they had fastened up blankets before the windows. The call for vengeance upon these marauders, which had reached Cunningham and his followers in Charleston, received an additional impulse from learning their present employment. The house was surrounded, and the inmates cut down as they attempted to fly. Only one man escaped the general massacre. Seven were saved at Hays' station, and were next morning set free without terms or conditions.

On their way back to Charleston, the party encountered one "Oliver Toles," famous for stealing tory cattle. Cunningham had him hanged with a thong cut from a tory cow's hide.

By this time the country had become fully alarmed. Parties under Pickens, Leroy Hammond, &c., commenced a vigorous pursuit, and before they arrived at Charleston, Ringtail's mettle was well tried. Seven fresh parties started in pursuit of Cunningham, one after the other, but Ringtail carried his master safe off from the whole of them. It was at the expense, however, of his own life, for he died twenty-three days after they reached the city, of fatigue, and the violent exertions he had been forced to make. Major Cunningham, "Bloody Bill," "the heartless, unfeeling monster," "the coldblooded demon," as they called him, wept like a child over his poor favorite and friend, as he was wont to term him. He had him buried with all the honors of war, the bells of Charleston were tolled and volleys were fired over the hero of many fights.

When the English evacuated Charleston, Major Cunningham, instead of embarking with them, chose to proceed to Florida by land, accompanied by five of his followers. One day having pitched his tent near the region of Greenville, in the fancied security of a deep wood, they laid aside their arms, unsaddled their horses, and began to cook and get ready their dinner. In the midst of this interesting occupation, they were suddenly interrupted by the unwelcome appearance of a Captain Butler and twenty men of the revolutionary party. Taken thus by surprise, each man sprung as he was, without arms, on his unsaddled horse, and made off, as he best could. The tent, arms, and everything, except themselves and their barebacked horses, fell into the hands of the gallant captain and his band. The odds of twenty-one, well armed, to six unarmed men, was rather too great, even for Bloody Bill; so, thinking in this case that discretion was decidedly the better part of valor, he and Captain Hood, who kept close to him, made off as fast as their horses' legs could carry them, and were soon beyond the reach of danger.

He arrived safely in Florida, and afterward went to England with General Cunningham. He was presented at court, and during the rest of his life, enjoyed the half-pay of a major in the British service.

Cotton, the principal product of South Carolina, is of three kinds: the long-staple or black-seed, the short-staple, green-seed or upland, and the nankeen.

The first of these is the most valuable kind of cotton, and is raised on the small, low, fertile islands, and on the immediate coast, in South Carolina and Georgia. The fibres are much longer and finer than those of the other kinds, and it is highly prized for the manufacture of some of the finest fabrics, in Europe as well as in this country.

The second kind is extensively cultivated in the interior, and in much the greatest quantity: but the culture and supply were greatly restricted for many years, in consequence of the difficulty of separating the seeds, to which the fibres adhere very closely. There was no other way known to effect the necessary separation, until the invention of the cotton gin, by Mr. Eli Whitney, of Connecticut, which was soon extensively introduced, and is now in universal use, to the incalculable benefit of the culture, commerce, and manufacture, of cotton, by greatly reducing the cost and the time devoted to its preparation for market. The inventor of this invaluable machine was, however, long unrewarded for his skill and ingenuity; for, while on a tour of visitation in the south, after it had become extensively introduced, he was informed that it would be unsafe for him to prosecute a claim for violations of his patent. He afterward, however, received sums of money from some of the states most benefited, as a small return for the favor he had conferred upon them.

The nankeen cotton is of a clear and lasting buff color, and has been introduced with success into the middle and northern parts of the state, where it is much employed for home use. It is that kind of which the nankeen cloths of China are made.

Rice, as we have before remarked, is one of the principal productions of South Carolina. Being a water plant, its culture is confined to the lowlands, to which water can be brought in. It is a crop which requires peculiar care and attention, as may be presumed from the various processes necessary in its cultivation.

On the tide-lands, or those which lie on the coast and are open to the ocean, so that the supply of water is obtained from it, rice is sown about the 20th of March, while on those inland, which are irrigated from fresh-water streams, the sowing-time is about three weeks later. The soil is turned up with the hoe or plough, and then formed into drills or trenches. From one to two bushels are sown upon an acre, and then the water is let in, and left standing from two to four days, to kill the worms, and make the grain germinate. The water is then drawn off, and the hoeing commences, which is soon repeated, the grass being now picked from among the young grain by hand. The water is again let in after the third hoeing, for ten days and often more, sometimes for twenty. The water is then suffered to run off by degrees, and the rice branches out, each branch at length bearing an ear of from 100 to 300 grains. Three months after sowing it begins to blossom, and then the floodgates are again opened and the

View of Keōwee Lake.

water flows in, where it remains till harvest, which takes place in August on the coast, and in September inland. But the great obstacle in the way of rice-culture, is the unhealthiness of the neighborhood, caused by the miasma raised by the heat of the sun, which is most deadly to white men, and very injurious also to the negroes. The rice-planters generally leave their homes during the summer, and take their families to the cities, or to the uplands, to avoid this evil.

From 600 to 1,500 pounds of rice are obtained from an acre inland, and on the coast from 1,200 to 1,500, and even sometimes 2,400.

The separation of families from each other, in a country where the plantation system is universal, and the scarcity of villages and even smaller settlements, necessarily throw many obstacles in the way of social improvement. Children can hardly be collected in schools, or the people in churches, while social intercourse must be limited, even though there may be much hospitality, leisure, and love of society, such as are generally found in this and other southern states.

Railroads.—South Carolina distinguished herself by her early enterprise, in constructing one of the first great railroads in the Union, on a plan whose success has proved its sagacity. It was constructed across an extensive region, offering indeed few obstacles of surface, but encouraged by few of the advantages found in a thickly-populated country. The grand object lay in opening a communication with the Savannah river overland, by which the delay and exposure of the sea voyage might be avoided; and a large part of the great cotton crops, annually gathered on its banks, is now carried in safety and at a rapid rate to the city of Charleston, the great commercial port of the south, to be shipped for New York and Europe.

KEOWEE LAKE (see page 373).—This secluded little lake lies among the wild scenes of a region little changed by cultivation or the neighborhood of man. A bold and wooded hill rises on the right with a sudden swell, while a path, winding along the left bank, is shaded with a variety of trees, presenting a diversity of form and foliage. A white sail, seen at a distance, intimates that the placid waters are sometimes disturbed by a passing boat, while the group of visiters in the foreground, reminds us, that the beautiful scene has attracted the attention of the admirers of nature.

THE FALLS OF THE CHARASHILACTAY.—This view is inserted here, to give an idea of the bold and picturesque scenery which abounds in some parts of the high, western regions of the state. The stream, whose singular, aboriginal name has been preserved, after flowing some distance, meets an abrupt, mural precipice in its course, and falls, in a beautiful sheet, interrupted by two successive projecting shelves of the rock, to the bottom of the gulf which opens beneath. The effect is very striking, especially when viewed from below, the bare ledges in front, whitened by the glistening foam of the falling stream, being crowned with foliage, and half shaded by trees, which line the banks, and spring from the crevices.

CHARLESTON is the principal Atlantic seaport of the southern states, and a large and flourishing city. It stands upon a peninsula, at the mouths of Cooper and Ashley rivers, which empty into a spacious bay, with depth of water sufficient to form an excellent harbor. By the aid of several islands, advantageously situated, it is well protected from the waves of the ocean, and fortified against foreign attack. The population, including the Neck, in 1850, was 42,806.

Although the site of the city is level and low, like the neighboring land, its appearance is favorable from the water. The buildings, however, are chiefly of wood, and the streets are narrow, except the two principal ones, which cross each other, and traverse the city in its length and breadth. The principal public buildings are the city-hall, courthouse, college, orphanhouse, medical college, guardhouse, hospital, poorhouse, customhouse, jail, St. Andrew's hall, and state building, with several churches. The city suffered from a great conflagration in 1835, which laid waste a

Falls of the Charashuactay.

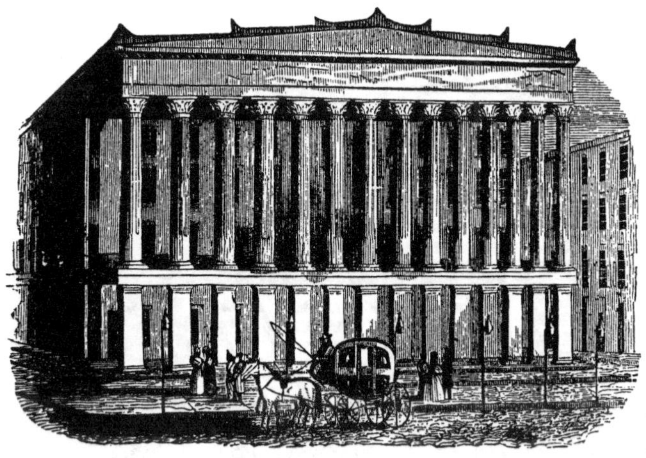

Charleston Hotel.

considerable extent of ground. The private houses are generally of a plain style, but many of them are neat and substantial; and the appearance of the city is much improved by many gardens, in which some of the finest fruits are cultivated, with a success which well rewards the taste and care of the inhabitants. Oranges, figs, pomegranates, grapes, &c., abound, with a great variety of flowers and ornamental shrubs. Of these a charming display is annually made, in the exhibitions of the horticultural society.

The inhabitants, who amount to about 43,000, include many persons from the eastern states, and a considerable number of French. In the summer months the city is the residence of many of the planters from the neighboring estates and the interior, who are driven from home by the unhealthiness of the country.

Our engraving of Meeting street presents two churches in the distance, while Charleston Hotel (a front view of which is given above) is seen on the left. This edifice has a fine colonnade of fourteen tall Corinthian pillars, rising from the second story, and supporting the roof above the fourth, with a broad piazza within, while the tall pediments below, afford between them entrances to the basement story from the street.

The *Charleston College*, the oldest institution of the kind in the state, was founded in 1795, and has four professors, with a library of 3,000 volumes, and about 50 or 60 students.

The *Medical College* of the state was founded in 1833, and has eight professors and about 150 students, and enjoys a high reputation.

The *Orphan Asylum* is an interesting and highly useful institution, containing about 200 friendless children.

Free Schools have been supported in all parts of the state, at considerable expense, by the legislature. The annual appropriations of money, as early as 1828, were nearly 40,000, the number of schools 840, and of pupils 9,000.

The *Guardhouse*, which has been mentioned among the public buildings, is large, and the headquarters of the city guard, a part of which consists of mounted men, who form the regular night patrol.

The *Citadel*, which was formerly used as the gnardhouse, is now occupied as the state military school.

The *Literary and Philosophical Society* is an association creditable to the state, and possesses a valuable collection of specimens in the different departments of science.

The *City Library* contains about 20,000 volumes.

The *Apprentices' Library* contains about 10,000 volumes, and supplies the members with a course of lectures.

View in Meeting Street, Charleston.

Among the objects in the vicinity of Charleston worthy of particular attention, is *Sullivan's Island*, which was the scene of important military operations in the revolutionary war. *Fort Moultrie*, which commands the entrance of the harbor, was gallantly defended by a very feeble force, against a British squadron sent to take the city.

The harbor now presents a scene of great activity. Besides the regular foreign and coasting vessels, which are numerous, steamboats and packet vessels arrive or depart every day, chiefly for the transport of passengers. There is a daily line of steamboats to Wilmington, North Carolina, and other lines to Savannah and St. Augustine. Regular lines of fine ships sail at stated times for New York, &c., &c. Railroad cars start every day on the great track, for several important cities, to which the branches lead, Columbia, Augusta, and Savannah, and onward to more distant places beyond the last two: Mobile, Montgomery, Ala., and Memphis, Tenn. Stage-coaches offer the means of conveyance to other towns, near and distant.

Beaufort, 75 miles from Charleston, is situated on Port Royal river, and has one of the largest and best harbors in South Carolina. With a population of about 1,600, it contains an academy, a library, and three churches; and has communication with Charleston and Savannah by steamboats.

COLUMBIA, 130 miles from Charleston, is the capital of South Carolina, and stands on a large plain, about 200 feet above the level of the Congaree river, which flows at a little distance south of it, crossed by a bridge. The town makes a handsome appearance, being laid out with regularity, in long and broad streets, planted with shade trees. Steamboats and railroad cars keep up a daily communication with Charleston.

The *Statehouse* is a handsome edifice of two stories, and 170 feet in length; and the town contains two banks, a theatre, an academy, and several other public buildings, including six churches of different religious denominations. The population amounts to 6,100.

The *College of South Carolina*, at Columbia, was founded in 1801, by an act of the legislature, and has been supported in a great degree by the treasury, which, previously to the year 1833, had expended about $200,000 in erecting edifices, procuring a library and apparatus and other contingencies, besides an annual sum of $15,000. There are six tutors, about 150 students, and a library of 15,000 volumes. The commencement is held on the first Monday in December.

The *Southern Theological Seminary*, which also is situated in this place, has a library of 4,000 volumes, two professors, and as yet, only a small number of students. It was founded in 1831.

Cheraw stands on the great Pedee river, 93 miles from Columbia, and, like it, at the dividing line between the high and the low regions, at the head of navigation. The town is on a considerable elevation, about 100 feet above the water, but is small, containing only about 1,400 inhabitants. The public buildings are the bank, the town hall, five churches, and two academies. Steamboats come from Georgetown, and stage-coaches daily to Columbia and Raleigh.

Camden, 33 miles from Columbia, stands on a plain on the left bank of the Wateree, and contains several fine public buildings; the city-hall, courthouse, masonic hall, bank, library, academy, and four churches.

The *Monument*, in De Kalb street, was founded in 1825, when the cornerstone was laid by General Lafayette, in honor of Baron De Kalb. The Indian mound, a few miles west of the town, is said to be one of the remains of the Catawbas, formerly a powerful tribe.

Spartansburg is a pleasant town, in a hilly part of the state, much resorted to by travellers, on account of the watering places in the vicinity; the Limestone, Pacolet, Cedar, and Glenn Sulphur springs.

Greenville stands near the bank of Reedy river, which has several falls. The town is laid out with taste, and enjoys a healthful situation. It contains a courthouse, two academies, a library, and several churches. It is 107 miles from Columbia.

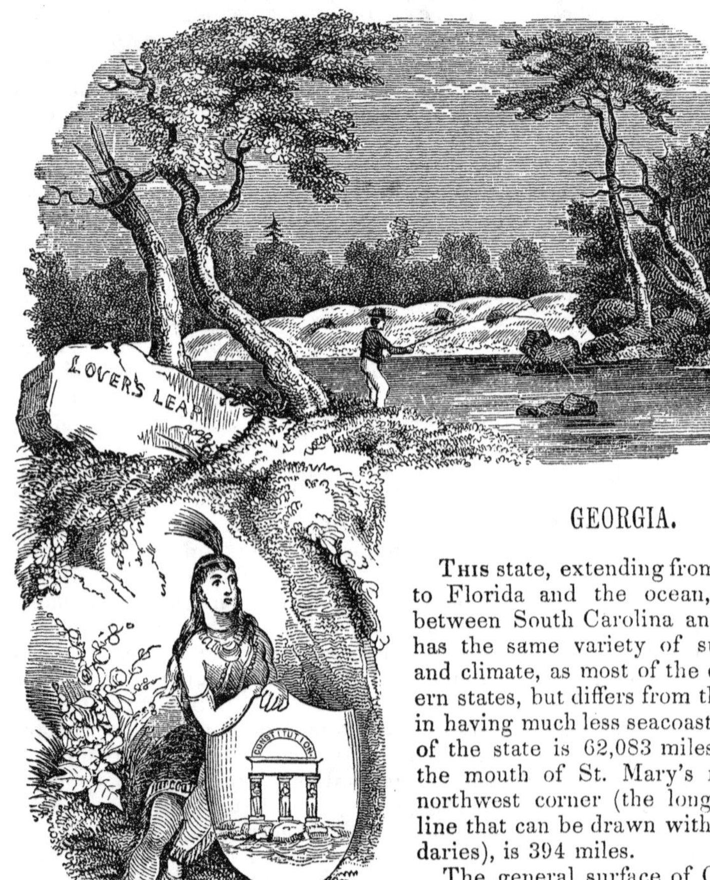

GEORGIA.

This state, extending from Tennessee to Florida and the ocean, and lying between South Carolina and Alabama, has the same variety of surface, soil, and climate, as most of the other southern states, but differs from the Carolinas in having much less seacoast. The area of the state is 62,083 miles; and from the mouth of St. Mary's river to the northwest corner (the longest straight line that can be drawn within its boundaries), is 394 miles.

The general surface of Georgia presents a great slope toward the south, of which the peninsula of Florida is a mere continuation. The rivers which descend it flow eastward into the Atlantic, or westward into the gulf of Mexico. On the coast, the slope descends to the very level of the salt water, forming the rich islands and shores which produce the celebrated sea-island cotton; while in the north it presents a general elevation of 1,200 feet, which is overlooked by the still higher mountain ranges. It is remarkable that the temperature is two degrees higher on the Atlantic coast than on the gulf, where the latitude and elevation are equal; and this is proved by the vegetation, as well as by scientific experiments. The great length of the state, with its variety of surface, gives Georgia a greater extent of vegetable production that any other state in the Union, producing wheat in the north, and sugarcane in the south, with the various plants, in different parts, between these two extremes.

The nature of the surface requires us to distinguish three zones in this state, like those of North and South Carolina. The sea-border has an almost tropical climate, and is so nearly on the water level, as to be in part overflown by the daily tides; and where the soil is rich and dry enough, sugarcane flourishes, as well as the orange, date, and other palms, with a variety of plants not found further north. The islands and shores on which the long-staple cotton is cultivated, above alluded to, are bordered by narrow, and often intricate channels, navigable by vessels, which appear from a distance as if moving upon the land. This species of cotton is well-known, and most highly valued in all the ports and manufacturing cities of Europe, as well as of this country; and all attempts made, at home and abroad, to produce a rival have proved unsuccessful. The length and fineness of the staple or fibre fit it for some of the most costly fabrics; and the demand is always great, and the prices high. A considerable proportion of this first and lowest region of the state, however, has a poor and even barren soil.

The second district, which is both sandy and hilly, has considerable tracts of worthless land, though other parts yield corn and cotton; but the most valuable portion of the state is the higher region beyond, which presents a more varied surface, and a soil of superior fertility, well watered by numerous streams; while the sultry and unhealthy atmosphere of the lower country is replaced by cool, pure, and wholesome air.

The grand primitive formation of the United States commences at Milledgeville, in this state, and extends, with the highest ridge of the Allegany mountains, through several northern ones, forming the boundary between the great western valley of the Mississippi, and the eastern slope to the coast of the Atlantic. This range is distinguished through a great part of its length, by a remarkable feature. It terminates abruptly at the border of the extensive alluvial region which forms the broad band between it and the ocean. This character accompanies it as it passes west of Washington and Philadelphia, to the Hudson river, and is attended with several circumstances and effects, of great practical importance, which have been referred to in our notices of the geography of North and South Carolina. Beyond the Hudson the same primitive range extends eastward, and spreads over the New England states, reaching down to the coast, and lining the shore with a range of rough granite rocks.

Westward, the same primitive range extends almost to Tennessee, being bounded beyond by a transition range, which intervenes between it and the secondary region of the Mississippi.

The Chatahoochee river is said to have derived its name from a rock of a peculiar appearance, which stands on its bank, a short distance above Columbus. It is marked with various bright colors, so intermingled as to make it appear as if overgrown with various plants, in full bloom. Hence the Indians bestowed upon the stream the name which it has retained, and which signifies the "flower-rock waters." Many parts of this fine stream are interesting, on some account or other, between its source, in the north-east quarter of Georgia, and Appalachicola bay, which is four hundred and thirty miles below Columbus. The scenery just above that city is remarkably wild and picturesque; rocks projecting from the banks, and many rising from its bed, impeding the current, and increasing the roughness of the stream, rendered hasty by the descent of the channel. Its course is, for several miles, a succession of falls and rapids, within four of which the declivity is more than one hundred feet.

Along its shores have been some of the most rapid improvements made in the state. Columbus has already become a considerable town, although but a few years ago an Indian village. Below its site many villages are to be seen from the steamboats, in which the traveller makes his way through the heart of the state.

The Lover's Leap.—The place bearing this name is a romantic spot on the Chatahoochee, and is represented in the vignette at the head of this state. It is a high and ragged cliff, which is the termination of an ascending knoll of dark rocks, and projects boldly into the river. One of the most beautiful scenes of nature can be viewed from this rock. In a straight line on the left, the river pursues its downward course to the city. The water foams and frets over the

Tullulah Falls.

rocks, in angry surges. A deep ravine forms the bed of the stream, and it is walled by lofty and irregular cliffs, covered to their tops with forest-trees of beautiful growth.

The falls of Coweta are enveloped in a thick mist, which partially obscures all the surrounding objects, among which are the steamboats which constantly ply upon the river, and the bridge which stretches across the river.

The river at the leap suddenly turns so as to form a right angle with its course below, flowing in a narrow channel, which is so regularly lined on each side with rocks, and of so uniform a width, as greatly to resemble a canal; but a little distance above, it again forms a right angle, and moves onward in its old course. The beauty of the view which we have described, does not exceed that of the other parts of the landscape, for the scene on the right, and in the foreground, is scarcely less beautiful and picturesque.

"Dr. F., the guide and life of our party," says Richards, "remarked, that a surprising change, indeed almost magical, has come over the scene upon which we gaze, since 1828, when the Indians lighted their council fires in the town of Coweta, an Indian settlement, where now the fair city of Columbus, obedient to the will of civilization and commerce, erects her noble head. Then, the fields over which we have rambled to-day, had never felt the ruthless share ploughing their virgin soil. The trees, which now spread their bare and decaying arms to the sky, were enrobed in their primeval greenness and strength. The cliff, which we now behold, had rarely echoed to the woodman's axe. Its voices were responsive to the occasional rifle of the wild hunter, and the more frequent yell of the savage, and roar of the wild beast."

The spot derives its name from an Indian tradition: A young woman of the tribe having fallen in love with a youth of a neighboring one, just before hostilities occurred between them, she was pursued as a traitress, and the lovers threw themselves into the stream, and were carried to destruction down the falls.

The Falls of Tullulah.—In the midst of the picturesque region which forms the county of Habersham, in the northeastern corner of the state, we find the falls of Tullulah, twelve miles from Clarkesville. The road is rough, and almost dangerous to carriages; and there is not a single habitation to be seen, except a log house, two miles from the spot, where visiters stop for refreshment.

A small stream, called by the Indians the Terrora, rushes impetuously from a remarkable rent in the Blue Ridge, which extends several miles, and everywhere presents a most impressive, and often a terrific scene. The granite rocks which compose the banks are precipitous, and about a thousand feet in height; though the breadth of the narrow gulf between hardly exceeds that distance. The engraving on page 381 presents the reader with the view from the most favorable point, which is a mass of rock called "the Pulpit," that projects from the face of a precipice overhanging the narrow valley, and looking down, from a considerable height, upon the roaring brook, as it pours furiously over three of the principal cascades in its course.

Some distance above, a steep and broken path leads down the bank, and ladies have sometimes descended to the margin of the stream, though it is not free from danger, and the return is laborious. The visiter may also find access to the foot of the second fall, by a path too hazardous to be prudently passed, namely, by creeping on his hands and knees along the brow of a precipice, a fall from which would be almost certain death. A gentleman, as we are informed, once fell in making this experiment, plunged into the stream, and was carried rapidly along till he reached the cataract and was swept down it, sixty feet, yet escaped without serious injury.

The Indian name of this stream, which is written by Americans Terrora and Tellula, is said to signify *terror*, presenting a singular, though doubtless an accidental resemblance to its meaning in English and Latin.

Rock Mountain.—Within view of the Blue Ridge, and at a short distance from the course of the Chatahoochee,

Rock Mountain.

rises the Rock mountain, a tall and conspicuous eminence, nine hundred feet high, with a gentle slope toward the west, and a precipitous termination toward the east. The road winds along the base, till it reaches the foot of the eastern bluff, where the sublime eminence, rising far above, produces an impression of wildness and grandeur, difficult to describe. The rock above presents a convex surface, with a rapid descent to the plain, channeled by numerous ravines, down which, in every storm, pour numerous torrents, whose channels again become as speedily dry. We present the reader with a handsome engraving of this mountain, on page 383.

On the summit of the mountain has been erected an octagonal tower, built of wood, one hundred feet square at the base, and one hundred and sixty-five feet high. This singulaı construction, so convenient to the visiter, and elevating his eye to a superior sphere, has already stood several years, although it rests upon the bare rock, without anything except its own weight to keep it in its position. In the lower part is a small hotel, which contains even a piano. The view from the top of the tower is very extensive and interesting, ranging over a long extent of the blue ridge, with varied tracts of country below, chiefly covered with forest.

The Cross-Roads are two remarkable fissures in the rocks, which cross each other at a point where they are five feet wide; and at that spot they are covered by a large, flat rock, twenty feet in diameter.

The Fort.—The whole summit of the mountain is enclosed by the remains of an ancient entrenchment, of the history of which the Indians disclaimed all knowledge, except that it was of a date prior to that of their ancestors.

The circumference of Rock mountain is about six miles, and the height of its summit 2,230 feet above the level of the ocean. It exhibits, in different parts, a great variety of vegetation; plants, flowers, and berries of many different kinds, presenting themselves to the visiter, as he winds along its base, climbs the rocky sides, and wanders over its lofty eminences, amid the exhilarating atmosphere of a superior region.

HISTORY.—Georgia was one of the original thirteen states of the American Union, but the youngest in respect to the time of settlement. Its increase in population, however, has been among the most rapid since the revolution. The first colonies were planted under authority of a patent granted by George II., in 1732, to twenty-one persons, who were called "the trustees for settling the colony of Georgia," a name bestowed in honor of the king. The first party of emigrants reached Charleston in 1733, under the direction of General James Oglethorpe, and the settlement of Savannah was begun in the spring. In consequence, however, of injudicious restrictions laid on the colonies, the increase of the population was checked, and its prosperity retarded for some years.

Unfortunately, this part of the country was easily accessible to the Spaniards, who claimed it as their own; and the fear of invasion, as well as the actual attempts made to gain possession, greatly retarded the increase of the colony. Retaliation on the part of the English served to increase the difficulties of the community. In 1742, General Oglethorpe made his unsuccessful attempt to capture St. Augustine; and two years after, the Spaniards invaded the colony, but were in their turn defeated. The Georgians were thus burdened by heavy debts, like the Carolinians, and by the same causes, from which they were soon able to recover, in consequence of the more favorable circumstances in which they were placed by coming under the royal government, as a colony of the king. This occurred in 1752.

A general representative assembly was formed in 1755; and in consequence of the cession of Florida to Great Britain, the country between the Altamaha and St. Mary's rivers was ceded, much to the advantage of Georgia. Symptoms of increasing prosperity soon began to appear; but the Cherokees, a powerful and warlike nation of Indians, occupied the western and northern parts of the territory; and several others were near them; and a period of danger and

Pulaski Monument—Christ Church, Savannah.

wars soon commenced, which caused great sufferings, and greatly checked the increase and extension of the settlements.

During the revolution, Georgia suffered in common with the country at large; and since the close of that war, she has ceded to the general government a larger extent of territory than any of her sisters, except Virginia, embracing all Alabama and Mississippi, north of latitude 31°: about 100,000 square miles.

The first constitution was adopted in the year 1777, and the second in 1785. The latter was amended in 1789; and the present was adopted in 1798. The senators and legislators are elected annually. A senator must be twenty-five years of age, nine years a citizen of the United States, one year a resident of the district, and the owner of an estate of five hundred dollars, in the county, or of taxable property of one thousand dollars. Each county sends one senator. The number of representatives is proportioned to the number of whites, and three fifths of colored persons, of whom an enumeration is made every seven years. Each county has one member, but none can elect more than seven. A representative must be twenty-one years old, seven years a citizen of the United States, three years an inhabitant of the state, a resident in the county the preceding year, and owner, for a year, of a freehold of two hundred and fifty dollars, or five hundred dollars' worth of taxable property, cleared of incumbrance.

The governor is elected by the assembly, for two years. He must be thirty-six years old, have been a citizen of the United States for twelve years, six years a citizen of Georgia, and the owner of five hundred acres of land in Georgia, and four thousand dollars in other property. A voter must be a citizen, twenty-one years of age, and a payer of taxes.

Education was quite neglected in Georgia before 1811, about which time academies sprang up in almost every town. Since that period, few persons have grown up in entire ignorance, while thousands, born before the year 1800, it has been said, "know not a letter." The baptists and methodists are the most numerous denominations in the state, and after them the presbyterians and episcopalians.

Printing was first introduced into Georgia in 1762, by James Johnston, a Scotchman, who commenced the publication of a newspaper, called "The Georgia Gazette," in the following year. The first number of it was published on the 17th of April. He continued the publication twenty-seven years, after which it was published by his successors. This was the only newspaper printed in the limits of Georgia before the revolution.

SAVANNAH.—This chief town and principal seaport of Georgia is situated on the western bank of the river of the same name, fifteen miles from its mouth, one hundred miles southwest from Charleston, and one hundred and sixty-seven miles southeast by east from Milledgeville; in latitude, 32° 5′, and west longitude, 4° 18′. Population 30,000.

The streets of Savannah are sandy, but shaded by China-trees, and the houses are generally of wood. There are eighteen public squares in different parts of the city. The commercial advantages which it enjoys, from the abundant crops of cotton, &c., raised along the banks of the river, and the free access of ships drawing not more than twelve or thirteen feet of water, rendered it an important town, even while the place was made unhealthy by the practice of wet culture on the neighboring rice-plantations, which has been abandoned since the year 1817, in consequence of an act of the legislature, passed at that time. In 1820, Savannah suffered to the amount of four millions, from a devastating fire, which swept irresistibly over a large part of the city.

Care has been taken to embellish the city, by providing abundance of shady trees for the numerous public squares. Among these the celebrated Pride-of-India is conspicuous, whose graceful form and delicate foliage, with its semi-tropical aspect, render it peculiarly appropriate to such a use. Among the houses, the city now presents a consid-

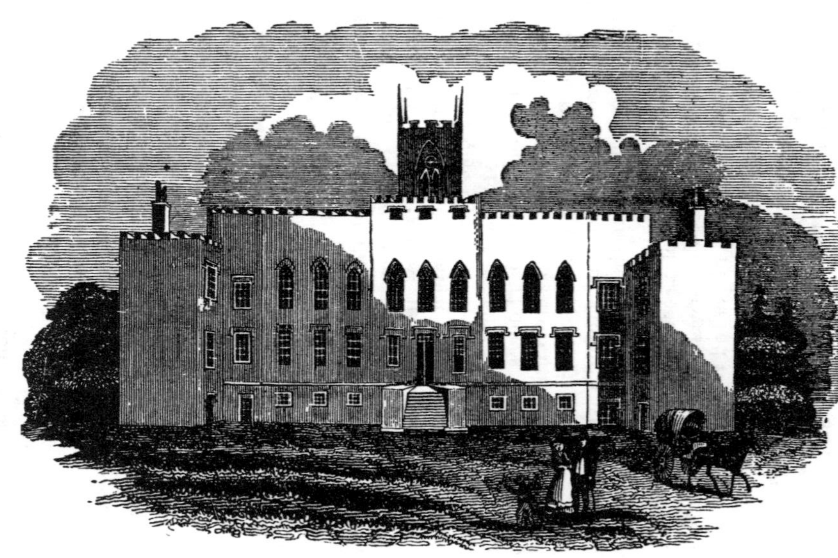

The Statehouse Milledgeville

erable number of handsome, well-built dwellings, while the following are the principal public edifices: the arsenal, exchange, courthouse, barracks belonging to the United States, theatre, hospital, market, banks, public library, three academies, thirteen churches, &c.

The Pulaski Monument was erected in the year 1825, in memory of Generals Pulaski and Greene, of the revolutionary army. It is a neat and simple obelisk of white marble, fifty-three feet high. The base of the pedestal is ten feet four inches by six feet eight inches, and its height thirteen feet, the needle which surmounts the pedestal being thirty-seven feet in height. It is built upon a platform of granite, three feet above the ground, and the whole is enclosed by a cast-iron railing. It has a very advantageous position, in the middle of one of the public squares. See p. 385.

MILLEDGEVILLE.—This town is the capital of the state. It stands on the southern side of the Oconee, one hundred and fifty-eight miles from Savannah, on an irregular surface, at the head of steam navigation. The streets cross each other at right angles; those running in one direction lying parallel to the river. At the distance of three quarters of a mile from its banks is a fine public square, on the summit of a hill, which is adorned with the statehouse. This is a building in the Gothic style; and the representatives' hall, which is sixty feet in length, and fifty-four in breadth, is ornamented with full-length portraits of Generals Oglethorpe and Lafayette, while those of Washington and Jefferson are in the chamber of the senate.

In different parts of the city are the arsenal, magazine, market, academy, three banks, three churches, and the governor's residence.

COLUMBUS, two hundred and eighty-four miles from Savannah, stands on the left bank of the Chatahoochee, at an elevation of sixty feet above the water. The falls, which extend for three miles above the town terminate steamboat navigation. They are a succession of rapids, descending, in all, one hundred and eleven feet. The two principal streets are one hundred and sixty feet wide, and run north and south, crossed by twelve others, ninety-nine feet wide. The academy, market, schoolhouses, five banks, and five churches, are among the public buildings, and the place contains a number of cotton-factories, mills, &c. The population is about eight thousand. A flourishing trade in cotton employs several steamboats, and it is a place of much business, although so late as 1827 it was a council-town of the Coweta Indians, and the commissioners appointed to apportion the lots of the city began their work so late as the 10th of July, 1828. The Cowetas, who inhabited this region, and made this spot the chief settlement, were one of the seven tribes of the Creek nation.

The Courthouse is a fine building, with a basement, two stories, and a steeple one hundred and ten feet high, and two Grecian porticoes on the front.

The Planters' and Mechanics' Bank has a portico, in the style of the celebrated Temple of the Winds, in Athens.

The private buildings of Columbus display a good degree of taste, as do the decorated yards and flower-gardens which are here and there displayed.

The Cotton Warehouse, on the bank of the river, is one of the largest in Georgia, an extensive fireproof building, covering an acre and three quarters. In the year 1838, 42,000 bales of cotton were shipped here, and the amount has increased considerably

ATHENS, on the right bank of the Oconee, contains about three thousand inhabitants, and has a pleasant and healthy situation, seventy five miles from Milledgeville. It is the seat of

The Georgia University, founded in 1785, which has six professors and about eighty students, with a large philosophical apparatus, and libraries containing about twenty thousand volumes.

The railroad affords the means of a daily communication with Augusta.

MADISON SPRING.—This fashionable resort is named after the county in which it is situated, and is found in the midst of a wild region, near Oconee river, seven miles distant from Danielsville,

View of Columbus.

Entrance to the Madison Springs.

the county town. It is convenient to go in a stage-coach from Athens. The nature of the water has been known about twenty years, but the place has but recently attracted much notice, since accommodations have been provided for visiters. A large hotel has been erected, surrounded by small tenements, for the summer residence of families; and an avenue, several hundred yards in length, leads through the forest to the spring, which is provided with conveniences, as represented in our engraving. The water, which flows from a marble curb, is chalybeate, in a greater degree than the springs of Cheltenham and Brighton, in England. A *sulphur spring* has been discovered at three miles' distance.

MACON is already a considerable and flourishing place, with seven thousand inhabitants, although so lately as the year 1822 there was but a single house on the spot. The situation is favorable for business, being at the head of steam navigation on the Ocmulgee river, which flows through the middle of it, and is crossed by a fine bridge, three hundred and eighty feet long. A great quantity of cotton is annually received at this place, and sent down the river, while there is a daily communication with Savannah by the railroad.

An institution for female education was opened here in 1839, under the name of the Georgia Female College, which is in a flourishing condition, having about one hundred pupils, under the charge of a president, three professors, and several other instructors.

AUGUSTA.—This town is situated on the Savannah river, one hundred and thirty-five miles from its mouth, and one hundred and twenty north of Savannah. It is a place of much trade, receiving large quantities of produce from the neighboring country, especially cotton, and being connected with Charleston by the great railroad, which extends beyond it, still further into the interior. During a certain part of the year, the river is navigable by steamboats.

The streets are regular, and planted with shade-trees, and the houses are generally of brick. Among the public buildings are the courthouse, city-hall, medical college, hospital, theatre, arsenal, female asylum, several academies and churches.

The Medical College of Georgia.—The first proposal to establish a medical school in this state was made by Dr. Antony, in 1827; but active measures for it were not taken until the year 1830, when the legislature passed a bill, incor-

Medical College of Georgia.

porating this institution, and authorizing them to confer the degree of Doctor in Medicine on persons who have complied with the requisitions of the most respectable institutions in the United States. In 1835, the faculty addressed a circular to all the medical schools, proposing a convention in Washington city, which has not been held, but the honor of the project is due to this state. In 1833, a donation of $10,000 was made by the legislature, and another of $5,000, by the city council of Augusta, on condition that the college should supply the hospital, for ten years, with attendance and medicines. These sums enabled the trustees to erect the fine edifice which they at present occupy. It is a large structure, in the Doric style, with accommodations and arrangements well adapted to the nature of the institution, and which has been pronounced by good judges, equal, in this respect, to any other in the Union. It enjoys a fine and pleasant situation, admirably adapted to its use, in the vicinity of the town, on a lot appropriated to it by the trustees of Richmond academy.

In 1834, ten thousand dollars were raised by the faculty, who sent one of the professors to Europe, to purchase an anatomical museum, chymical apparatus, and surgical cabinet. In 1835, the legislature conferred on the institution a second grant, amounting to about twenty-five thousand dollars, which afforded them a fund for contingent expenses. The first class was instituted 1833–'4, and amounted to thirty; and the members have been increasing almost every year, although the institution suffered a severe reverse, in consequence of the fatal epidemic of 1839, when, among many other losses, the valuable life of Dr. Antony fell a sacrifice to his humane exertions for the benefit of the sick.

The lectures begin on the second Monday in November, and close early in March; and the expense of the whole course, including practical anatomy and matriculation, is only twenty-five dollars. In the first ten years of its existence, the medical college of Georgia had three hundred and ninety-seven students, of whom one hundred and nineteen received degrees.

Georgia Female College.—The various religious denominations in this state, by combined contributions, having collected more than six hundred thousand dollars, for the support of education, which has been appropriated to different institutions, in all parts of the state; and this college, so creditable to the intelligence of Georgia, and so well calculated to confer upon it the highest benefits, owes its existence to the enlightened spirit and indefatigable labors of a few individuals in the city of Macon. Twenty thousand dollars were raised, to found a female college, in conformity with a resolution passed at a public meeting, and soon after, placed at the direction of the annual conference of the methodist episcopal church. In 1836, the legislature incorporated the trustees appointed by that body, and granted twenty-five thousand dollars to the institution.

The college edifice enjoys a commanding situation, on a fine eminence between Macon and Vineville, overlooking the former (which lies upon the plain beneath), and the surrounding hills, beautified by many neat and tasteful edifices. On the west is the village of Vineville; and on the north Fort Hawkins shows its remains, consisting of old blockhouses and trenches, while the forests spread far away on the east, and bound the distant horizon. The college building is one hundred and sixty feet long, and sixty in breadth, four stories high in the middle, with a cupola. Four large columns, in the centre of the front, support a roof over the entrance; and the building contains fifty-six rooms Most of those in the basement are occupied as recitation-rooms. The steward's apartments are also below, where some of the officers have accommodations. The chapel is forty feet by sixty, on the second story, where are also the library, music-room, and president's apartments. The young ladies attending this institution provide their own furniture; and their lodging-rooms, which occupy the third and fourth stories, accommodate four each.

Oglethorpe University.

The yard extends over four acres; and the rest of the section of land devoted to the institution is judiciously left covered with groves of fine oak-trees, so that ample opportunities are afforded for agreeable and healthful exercise. Six acres of ground opposite have been reserved for a botanical garden—the gift of the city council.

The college was opened in 1839, and has a president, three professors, with the principal of the primary department, professors of music and drawing, a matron, and a superintendent of domestic economy. The methods of instruction are thorough and practical. The regular course includes the French language; but Latin, Greek, and Spanish, are taught, only in extra classes. There is but one term in the year: from the first Monday in October, for ten months. Pupils are not received under twelve years of age.

OGLETHORPE UNIVERSITY.—This institution is situated at Medway, in Baldwin county, on account of its central position, in a pleasant and healthful region, being a place easily accessible from all directions. The spot is elevated, on a ridge lying east and west, two miles and a half south of Milledgeville, and ending at the bluff on Oconee river, on which are the ruins of old Fort Wilkinson. The foundation of the edifice is on a level with the top of the cupola of the statehouse; and the view is extensive on every side, embracing an undulating surface of twenty miles round, including Milledgeville.

The erection of the principal building was begun in 1836, and completed in 1838. It is of brick, two stories high, with a basement, in the Doric style; and being painted white, and of great extent, makes a striking appearance. The chapel occupies the centre, forty-eight feet by sixty, with a colonnade and vestibule. The wings are each thirty feet in front, and three stories high, with professors' and recitation rooms, while other rooms are appropriated to the library, museum, apparatus, &c. Two ranges of small buildings stand at some distance on each side, each containing two students' rooms; while the house of the president stands on the south side of the campus.

The institution commenced operation in January, 1838, with six professors; and the first class was graduated in 1839. It is under the direction of the presbyterian synod of South Carolina and Georgia, but its advantages are free to all. There are two sessions in the year: one from the first Monday in January to the second Wednesday in May; after which is a vacation of four weeks. Commencement is held on the Monday succeeding the second Monday in November.

Oglethorpe university owes its origin to two manual labor schools, under the Education society of Georgia. That association was dissolved, and in 1835, the trustees of the Medway seminary, which was one of those institutions, offered it to the Hopewell presbytery, who received it, and soon constituted it a college, under their government and control, with a charter from the legislature. That charter forbids any shop to be opened, within a mile and a half of the institution, on penalty of five hundred dollars, or more; while deeds of university lots provide for the forfeiture to it of lots on which such shops may stand. This feature has since been introduced into other charters, and has doubtless prevented many of the evils to which other literary institutions are often liable.

THE FALLS OF THE TOWALIGA, eight miles from Indian springs. This picturesque scene is presented by the little river whose name it bears, at the spot where it pours down a rocky ledge, which there disturbs its generally gentle course, and gives it an aspect of wildness, elsewhere foreign to its shores.

The Towaliga has an Indian name, of uncertain import, pronounced with the accent on the last syllable. The stream has its origin in Henry county, and pursues a course of seventy miles, to the Ocmulgee, of which it is a tributary. Just before it reaches the falls (which are represented in the engraving on page 123), the bed has a rapid descent for some distance, where the surface of the water is broken in rapids, overlooked

Falls of Towaliga.

from the summit of a hill, over which passes the road leading to the spot. A mill occupies one of the banks; and a lofty bridge, erected across, was partly destroyed, a few years since, by a flood.

The falls, seen from below, make an impressive appearance. The breadth of the bed is there about three hundred feet, and a mass of rock, at the brow of the first precipice, divides it into two sheets, which descend perpendicularly about fifty feet, in beautiful foam, made in the course of its tumultuous passage down the rapids. Here it is received by a deep gulf, which suddenly checks its fury; but, before it has time to recover its tranquillity, it reaches the brow of the second rapids, down which it hurries, with roar and turbulence, a distance of two hundred feet, and then pours over the second fall, in a current broken into several cascades, when it soon subsides, below, to comparative quietness. The height, roughness, and thick shade of the banks, greatly increase the effect of the scene. The reader may form some correct conception of the interesting spot, by a glance at the accompanying engraving, which is copied from a print in that elegant work, "The Scenery of Georgia," to which we have been indebted for many interesting facts on these pages. The drawing was made from the northern bank of the stream, a spot rather difficult of access, and not easily attained by many spectators, who generally find it more convenient to content themselves with a view from the opposite side. There are, however, many favorable points of view, both near and more distant, especially from some of the rude rocks which border and overhang the water, in different parts of its romantic and terrific course.

A short distance below the falls, a little island occupies the middle of the river, dividing it into two currents, which are narrow, but rapid. This vicinity was formerly a favorite resort of the deer, which visited it in considerable numbers, to feed on a peculiar kind of long and delicate plant, resembling moss, which grows to the length of two feet, in the sluices of the falls. They have, however, been destroyed or driven away by the hunters.

Tockoa Falls.—The most remarkable waterfall in this state is that of the Tockoa creek, which flows from the southern extremity of the Alleganies, at Cunawhee mountain. It descends one hundred and eighty-seven feet, from a precipice, in a narrow stream, twenty feet in breadth, which, in the rainy season, forms an unbroken sheet of foam to the bottom. At the ordinary height of water, the supply is so small, that it is said to be dissipated in vapor before it reaches the level below.

Remarkable Incidents in the History of Georgia.—As we have not room to give a connected history of this state, it may be interesting to our readers if we recount a few incidents relating to some of its most important periods.

Yamacraw, the Indian name of the bluff on which Savannah now stands, was the spot on which the treaty was held with the Creek Indians by General Oglethorpe, at which the first tract of land was ceded to him. The place was then occupied by a small tribe of that nation, called the Yamacraws.

In 1733, General Oglethorpe brought out from England a band of one hundred and thirteen colonists, who landed at Charleston. They were there kindly assisted, and furnished with boats, &c., by which they were enabled to proceed to the place of destination, and soon reached the Savannah river. The following year they were joined by five or six hundred more, who were provided with tracts of wild land, but soon proved ill-qualified for the task they had undertaken, and ere long difficulties arose, as many of them had been collected from among the poor and idle population of European cities. The trustees of the colony therefore took measures to secure emigrants of a better class; and, in 1735, about four hundred arrived in Georgia, from Scotland, Switzerland, and Germany.

Mary Musgrove was the name of an Indian woman, or half-breed, who rendered material service to General Oglethorpe, in promoting his plans for the

Tockoa Falls.

benefit of the colony. She was able to speak both languages, and appears to have been a woman of much address, acting as interpreter at several important treaties which terminated favorably. In gratitude, he bestowed upon her a hundred pounds a year, in addition to the presents with which he had secured her interest. Fifty Creek chiefs presented themselves at the treaty of Savannah, at which the great land-grant was obtained, and among these was Tomochichi, who, in the name of the others, thus addressed Oglethorpe, in reply to the general's speech, in which he had dwelt on the power and wisdom of the British king:—

"Here is a little present. I give you a buffalo-skin, adorned on the inside with the head and feathers of an eagle, which I desire you to accept, because the eagle is an emblem of speed, and the buffalo of strength. The English are swift as the bird, and strong as the beast; since, like the former, they flew over the vast seas to the uttermost parts of the earth, and like the latter, they are so strong that nothing can withstand them. The feathers of the eagle are soft, signifying love; the buffalo's skin is warm, and signifies protection: therefore I hope the English will love and protect their little families."

But, although this treaty terminated in so amicable a manner, difficulties, ere long, began to arise, being fomented by one of those restless, unprincipled, and dangerous men, so often the bane of young colonies. Thomas Bosomworth, the chaplain in Oglethorpe's regiment, for his own selfish and ambitious views, wrought upon a petty prince, named Malatchie, king of Frederica (near Savannah), till he persuaded him to assume the ridiculous title of Emperor of the Creek Nation. Bosomworth then married Mary Musgrove, and set up for her a claim to the empire, on pretence of her being the elder sister of Malatchie. The Indians were incited to support her, and escorted her to Savannah, to establish her claim.

The president of the colony, and his council, were alarmed at their approach, and at first knew not what course to pursue. The militia, however, were soon under arms, and Captain Noble Jones, by his resolute conduct, induced the Indians to lay by their weapons, when Bosomworth, with his queen, escorted by the chiefs and their warriors, solemnly paraded the streets, and struck the feeble colonists with fear. They, however, made such fair promises, that their arms were returned. Bosomworth was soon after seized and confined, which so irritated his wife that she threatened vengeance, and excited the savages to hostile demonstrations. By great prudence and coolness, the governor succeeded in tranquillizing them, two or three successive times, though Mary and Malatchie as often again enkindled their passions, and misled their judgment. The storm was at length dispelled by the decision of Captain Noble, who entered the council-room with a guard, and made the Indians surrender. Bosomworth was subsequently induced to lay aside his ridiculous claims, and received a pardon, while the Indians departed in peace. It was not long, however, before Bosomworth presented his case in England, which remained pending in the courts for twelve years. The result was, that the island of St. Catharine was granted to him and his wife, of which they took possession. She, however, died soon after.

In the year 1778, Savannah was occupied by General Howe, with six hundred regular troops and a few militia, when it was attacked by a British army of six thousand men, under Lieutenant-Colonel Campbell, who had arrived from New York by water. The defenders were in too small force effectually to resist such numbers, but did not yield without a severe struggle. An obstinate battle was fought, in which our countrymen lost about six hundred men killed, and thirty-eight officers and four hundred and fifteen soldiers prisoners, with forty-eight guns, twenty-three mortars, and all the vessels lying in the river.

The enemy remained in possession of the city until 1779, when Count d'Estaing, commander of the French fleet, then in the West Indies, being invited by General Lincoln to make a combined attack upon Savannah, proceeded to the river with twenty ships-of-the-line, two of fifty guns, and eleven frigates. Lincoln, with the militia of Georgia and South Carolina, proceeded toward Savannah; but, before his arrival, Count d'Estaing, after demanding a surrender, had granted a suspension of hostilities for twenty-four hours, before the expiration of which, a reinforcement of eight hundred troops arrived at Savannah, from Beaufort, who encouraged the garrison to reject the demand of a surrender. The siege of the town was therefore commenced on the 4th of October, with thirty-seven cannon and nine mortars, on land, and fifteen cannon from the water. An assault was, however, determined on; and on the 9th, at daybreak, a strong force attacked the Spring Hill battery, which was taken, and held for a short time, but soon recovered, and the invaders retreated, abandoning the enterprise. A regular siege, it is believed, would have soon reduced the place; but the French officers objected to hazarding their fleet so long on the coast.

Count Pulaski, a Polander, distinguished by his birth, and exploits in Europe, who had recently been made a brigadier-general in our army, received a mortal wound in that engagement. In memory of him, Congress ordered the erection of the monument, which is described on page 388.

We will close our brief account of that interesting period, by mentioning a remarkable exploit performed by six Americans, just before the attack on Savannah. It is equally remarkable for the sagacity of the plan and the coolness and bravery of the execution.

On the Ogeeche river was a British force of about one hundred and forty men, of whom one hundred were under Captain French, of the royal army, and forty were sailors, composing the crews of five small vessels lying in that stream, four of them armed, and the largest with fourteen guns. The six men above referred to, formed an ingenious plan for capturing this force. They made preparations for kindling numerous fires, at short distances from each other, and lighted them all at once, in the evening, presuming the Englishmen would mistake them for the camp-fires of a large body of troops. In order to countenance such a deception, they resorted to other measures which their ingenuity dictated; and then, in due form, and in a peremptory manner, summoned the enemy to surrender.

Colonel John White, of the Georgia line, and Captain Elholm, were the leaders in these movements, which required so much skill and caution; and with such success did they perform their parts, that the British were completely blinded, and their commander, "to prevent the effusion of blood," promised to surrender. It was now extremely important for the captors to avoid the exposure of their weakness; and Colonel White represented to Captain French, that he was afraid to bring forward his troops, because they were exasperated against the invaders of their country, and offered to give him three faithful men, as guides, who would conduct them to safe and comfortable quarters. The offer was thankfully accepted; and the Englishmen marched off in haste, leaving the colonel, with his whole "reserve" (his servant and one other man), to bring up the rear. To perform this last-remaining duty required a little time, for he immediately hurried away to call out the militia; but he soon followed on, and made his appearance with a respectable force, which had been collected rather later than the enemy supposed.

General Lee declares, that this exploit was of so extraordinary a nature, that he could never have persuaded himself to record it, if it had not received general credit, without ever having been contradicted.*

* For the pictures which accompany this article, we are indebted to the pencil of T. Addison Richards, Esq. the first, if not the only artist, who has sought themes of study amid the beautiful scenery of the south. It is to his works, which have been engraved on steel, wood, and stone, and widely circulated, that we owe our acquaintance with the beautiful mountains, valleys, and cascades of the southern states. No work of the kind, in this country, has equalled in beauty his interesting publication, "Georgia Illustrated."

Among the numerous men who performed important parts in the early periods of our colonial history, there are few more remarkable for activity, enterprise, and purity of principle, than Oglethorpe. He performed a variety of duties, and generally with equal skill and success. As circumstances required, he could confer with the friends of America in England, on plans for planting colonies, then, collecting bands of emigrants, and placing himself at their head, conduct them across the Atlantic, and transport them to the places assigned for their habitation. He would conduct negotiations with the savages, provide for the sustenance and defence of the community, encourage his companions under adversity, protect them from invaders, and even march, with a band of white men and Indians, through the wilderness, to seize the post of a dangerous enemy, or to intimidate them, when an attack was to be apprehended.

Oglethorpe combined in his character much strength of purpose, and boldness and perseverance, with philanthropy and active zeal. Had he been of a less manly disposition, he might have chosen a less exposed and less dangerous theatre to act upon; but the peculiar position of the country now forming the southern part of Georgia, offered attractions for such a spirit as he possessed. It was wholly unoccupied by civilized men; for, although it was included in Heath's old patent, that instrument had been declared void, on account of the failure to fulfil the terms on which it had been granted, viz., that settlements should be made on the land. But the time had now arrived, when it was highly important that some of the principal military points should be occupied: for the Spaniards in Florida, and the French in Louisiana, had the power to traverse it at will, and were at liberty to enter it with whatever force they could command, and might soon annex it to their own territories.

The exposed situation of that district excited much solicitude in England; and to interpose a protecting power between it and the rival Spanish neighbors, whose antipathies were religious as well as national, was the principal motive for the first settlements made in the territory of Georgia. A charter was therefore granted to Sir James Oglethorpe, and several other noblemen and gentlemen, in 1732, of the country lying between the Savannah and Altamaha rivers; and they proposed to form a colony of criminals taken from the prisons, on the plan afterward practised on a larger scale in New Holland. The project was approved by the benevolent, and a considerable sum of money was collected in different parts of England, while the house of commons granted, at several times, appropriations to the amount of thirty-six thousand pounds, to the enterprise. We have already given a brief outline of some of the principal events, and shall now only attempt to supply some of the important particulars, not included in our cursory glance.

On his first visit to Savannah, Oglethorpe in a short time erected a fort, formed his colonists into a military company, consummated his treaty with the Creek Indians, and, appointing two of his officers, named Scott and St. Julian, to exercise the government of the colony during his absence, returned to England. He gave them charge to make a treaty with the Choctaws, which they successfully accomplished, and thus secured the friendship and protection of another powerful native nation, of great importance in the infancy of the colony.

The principal chief of the Creeks accompanied the governor to England, with his wife and several of his inferior sachems. They were received with much honor in London, being introduced to the king and nobility, and enriched with numerous presents, estimated to be worth four hundred pounds. After a stay of four months they returned with Oglethorpe, in a vessel which brought out a new band of colonists. Among the numerous emigrants who soon after arrived from Germany and Switzerland, were several of the associates of the celebrated Moravian missionary, Count Zingendorf; and a no less famous individual of that age, John Wesley, came from England in the same year, 1735. The character and history of this man, then in his youth, are worthy of a much more particular notice than can be given in a work like the present. It is pleasing to recur to this early enterprise of one so eminently distinguished by Christian philanthropy, directed to a class of men, and a region of the New World, presenting so little to incite the interest of any person not devoted to doing good.

John Wesley, with his brother Charles, had become known to Oglethorpe, in London, in consequence of their labors in the prisons, for the instruction and improvement of criminals. They had formed a society, in company with George Whitfield and a few pious young men, while in college, for that truly benevolent object, in which they persevered, in spite of the jeers of some of their acquaintance, who called it in contempt the Godly Club. What important effects have resulted from that association! It may have been the original model of those societies since formed for kindred purposes, especially of those for the reformation of delinquents and criminals, whose influence has been so salutary and extensive.

It was through Oglethorpe's persuasion that the two Wesleys were induced to visit the new colony; and they were accompanied by three or four of their associates, and a company of three hundred other persons, including a hundred and seventy more Moravians. After a short period of religious exertions, he returned to England: and Whitfield soon after came out, with similar objects. He proposed the foundation of an orphan asylum, which, as appears from his published letters, was a favorite plan, and pursued with his characteristic zeal and perseverance. It exists at the present day; but it has never proved successful in the degree anticipated by its founder. This may be partly accounted for from the fact, that comparatively few orphans, in our country, need such provision for their support. Vice, rather than the mere loss of parents, reduces children to destitution and distress; for the means of living are easily obtained in our new settlements and smaller towns; and no great number of children are cast off wholly unprovided for. Public or private charity steps in for their relief.

A fort was soon built at Augusta, for the defence of the Savannah river; a second at Frederica, which was a considerable work with four bastions; and a third on Cumberland island, to command the entrance of Jekyl sound, the only ship passage to Frederica. These were constructed at the expense of parliament, which appropriated ten thousand pounds for their erection and maintenance. Before they were completed, a message was received from the Spanish commander in Florida, that a conference was desired with the governor, and the news came that a reinforcement had arrived from Havana. A peremptory demand was made for the immediate evacuation of the territory south of St. Helena sound, with a threat that the king of Spain would seize his own possessions by force of arms in case of refusal. Oglethorpe, being unprovided with adequate means as well as authority, immediately embarked for England, and there received the appointment of major-general of all the forces of South Carolina and Georgia, and a regiment of military emigrants, with whom he hastened back.

On his arrival, he learned that the Spaniards had been busy in attempts to draw off the Indians from his interest, and that some of the Creek chiefs were then at St. Augustine. But he had the address to counteract the enemy; he sent invitations to the Indians to visit him at Frederica, whither they repaired after their return from Florida, and by his influence were easily confirmed in their friendly relations with the English.

But it was not long before alarming symptoms of treachery were discovered among the English troops. One of the soldiers had served at Gibraltar, and there acquired an acquaintance with the Spanish language, through the medium of which he had held a traitorous communication with the enemy; and, after being corrupted himself, he had found means to excite disaffection among his comrades. The first intimation received by the general, was made in an attempt to assassinate him, which fortunately failed, and the conspirators were executed.

By a report made to the trustees of the colony in 1740, it appears that at that time twenty-five hundred persons had been sent out as settlers, and that the amount of money expended was half a million of dollars; but it was so far from yielding any returns to the proprietors, and even from supporting itself, that it still required annual aid. The character of the colonists was far different from that of many of the earlier settlements; though when we consider the natural advantages of the country, we may well be surprised at the discouraging result. A mixed population, however, especially with a large proportion of the dregs of European cities, and even of the prisons of England, could not rationally be expected to bring a colony to such a condition as was early attained by the Pilgrims in the north, the Friends in Pennsylvania, the patient, economical Hollanders at New York, or the bands of farmers and others, who at different periods occupied different points along our extensive seacoast. Perhaps, we might rather be surprised that Oglethorpe was able to accomplish as much as he did for the benefit of the colony, amidst the numerous obstacles which surrounded him.

We have before mentioned his attempt to seize St. Augustine, and his want of success, in consequence of an unexpected reinforcement of the Spanish garrison at that place. We have also spoken of the invasion made in retaliation; but a few particulars may here be added, which show at once the perilous condition of affairs at that juncture, and the military abilities of the general.

The expedition which sailed from Havana for the Altamaha river in 1742, consisted of six thousand men; and its object was finally to destroy the southern colonies, and to seize upon the territory for the crown of Spain. An energetic demand was immediately made upon South Carolina for troops; but all assistance was refused, and he was left to his own resources. His policy was therefore to be adapted to his weakness; and, instead of offering such resistance as he would have wished on the frontiers, he retreated as far as Frederica, having only about seven hundred Europeans under his command, with a body of Indians. After this show of timidity, or of prudence, however, he boldly, but secretly, moved on toward the enemy, intending to take them by surprise, and had already marched within two miles of their camp, with every prospect of success, when a French deserter among his ranks, fired his musket and fled back to the enemy. Although thus disappointed, Oglethorpe's ingenuity still found a resource, and sitting down, he wrote a letter to the deserter, in terms calculated to lead the Spaniards to suspect the runaway as faithless to them, in the style of instructions to him, for his guidance in the enemy's camp. In this he requested him to represent that Frederica was defenceless, and ought to be immediately taken. If the Spanish commander should appear unwilling to take that step, the Frenchman was instructed to use his utmost exertions to persuade him to remain three days longer in his present position, as that would allow time for the removal of six thousand troops, who, he pretended, were on their way to reinforce the British army, and six ships, expected on the coast. The letter insisted particularly on the greatest caution being used, to avoid any allusions to Admiral Vernon's plan of attack upon St. Augustine, as a secret of the utmost importance. The letter was then put into the hands of a Spanish deserter, who was set at liberty under a promise to deliver it to the Frenchman. On reaching the Spanish camp, however, he took it to the commander, who was completely imposed upon by the ingenious device, and thinking he had happily obtained important information, seized the Frenchman, and put him in irons. In the midst of doubts and fears, into which this letter had thrown the enemy, a fortunate event occurred, which turned the scale in favor of Oglethorpe. South Carolina had slowly yielded to the request he had made for assistance, so far as to send three vessels with troops; and these arrived off the mouth of the Altamaha just in season to be mistaken by the invading general, for a part of the naval reinforcement alluded to in the intercepted letter. Such apparent confirmation of the document convinced him of its truth; and he immediately destroyed his fortifications, and embarked for Florida in consternation, leaving, in his haste, a number of his cannon, &c., and some military stores.

The success of this stratagem, the ingenuity of which is certainly very remarkable, secured the deliverance of the colony, when it was in its most critical condition, and threatened with final destruction. Without the loss of life, and at a small expense of money, the sagacious Oglethorpe was thus able to deliver the colony of an enemy far too numerous to be resisted, and from the threatening prospect of falling irretrievably into the hands of a foreign power, opposed to that of Great Britain in policy, laws, and religion.

Having accomplished so important a service, and finding nothing important to demand his future presence, he embarked for England for the last time, and spent the remainder of his life in tranquillity. On the commencement of hostilities in America in 1775, he received the offer of the command of the British forces, prepared to suppress the spirit of opposition, but accepted only on condition of being authorized to assure the colonies that they should have justice done them. This reply appears to have been unsatisfactory to the ministry, for Sir William Howe was appointed commander in his stead. Oglethorpe remained in retirement until the close of his life. He attained an extraordinary age, surviving the unhappy contest between his native country and the colonies which he had so faithfully served. He witnessed the first nine years of peace which succeeded the revolution, during which, the colony that he had planted, nursed, and defended, became an independent state, connected with a young republic which already showed signs of that rapid increase, in population, wealth, and improvement, which it has since experienced, and is likely long to enjoy.

Among the numerous striking changes which have been produced in our country by the lapse of a short period of time, that effected on the ancient seat of Yamacraw may be appropriately mentioned. One hundred and eighteen years ago, a small band of settlers lately from England, driving a few "hogs and cows," which had been given by people at Charleston, "to begin their stock," arrived near the spot, escorted by "the rangers," and aided by "the scout-boats," sent by the governor of South Carolina.

"Oglethorpe and Bull explored the country; and, having found a high and pleasant spot of ground, situated on a navigable river, they fixed on this place as the most convenient and healthy situation for settlers. On this hill they marked out a town; and from the Indian name of the river which ran past it, called it Savannah. A small fort was erected on the banks of it as a place for the defence of the colony. The people were set to work in felling trees and building huts for themselves; and Oglethorpe animated and encouraged them, by exposing himself to all the hardships which the poor objects of his compassion endured. He formed them into a company of militia, appointed officers from among themselves, and furnished them with arms and ammunition. To show the Indians how expert they were in the use of arms, he frequently practised them.

"Having thus put his colony in a good state of defence, the next object of his attention was, to treat with the Indians for a share of their possessions. The principal tribes that at this time occupied the territory were the upper and lower Creeks: the former were numerous and strong; the latter, by diseases and war, had been reduced to a smaller number; both tribes together were computed to amount to about twenty-five thousand, men, women, and children.

"At a little distance from Savannah, is a high mound of earth, under which the Indian king lies interred who held a conference with Sir Walter Raleigh."

FLORIDA.

The history of Florida, from the earliest expedition of discovery almost to the present hour, has been but a record of disappointments and disasters. Having neither mines of gold, nor any peculiar advantages for agriculture or commerce, the Spanish character of the people, while occupying it for three hundred years, had a full opportunity to display its imbecility; while our own government, since entering upon the possession a few years ago, have exhibited, in a manner no less lamentable, a disregard to humanity in their treatment of the poor remains of the original red race.

Florida is one of the few great peninsulas of America, and presents several peculiar features, one of which is its very important position. As has been remarked, in speaking of Georgia, this long point is only the continuation of the southern slope of that state. It nowhere presents any considerable elevation; and the greatest part of the surface is a level, raised but little above the ocean, with vast tracts too wet for use, and even wholly or chiefly impassable, or submerged in water.

The western coast of Florida extends six hundred miles, from the Perdido river to Cape Sable; while the eastern, from St. Mary's river, including the southern, to Cape Sable, is four hundred and fifty. The Atlantic ocean bounds the eastern coast, and the southern extremity is washed by the Bahama and Cuba channels. The northern boundary runs from the mouth of St. Mary's river to the mouth of Flint river, up the Chatahoochee, to latitude 31 deg. 40 min., separating it from Georgia. Thence the line proceeds along the limits of

Alabama, two hundred and forty miles, to Perdido river, and down that stream forty miles, to its mouth. The whole outline of Florida is about fifteen miles, and it extends through six degrees of latitude.

The climate is more uniform than in any other tract of equal extent, north and south, in the United States. This is owing to the little variation of surface, and the proximity of the sea. Pine prevails among the forests, as the soil is generally poor; but the variety of other trees is very great. Rice and Indian corn, sweet potatoes, cotton, indigo, and sugarcane, are the chief productions of agriculture, while oranges, limes, pomegranates, and figs, grow in abundance.

The surface of Florida presents a great proportion of waste land and water, with all the varieties of bays, creeks, and lagoons, along the coast; and inland, of hammocks, savannahs, and everglades. The hammocks vary in their nature from dry to wet, and many of them are impassable, or with a few intricate intervals of hard and shallow grounds, wholly under water; never known to any except the Indians, whose superior acquaintance with the country, during the late lamentable Florida war, often gave them advantage over our troops, in the hammocks and everglades. The various plants which grow abundantly in some parts of those swamps and lakes, often add their obstacles to the traveller; especially saw-grass, which soon cuts in pieces the clothes of men, and even their flesh. It would be difficult to give an adequate idea of the forbidding aspect of those extensive and desolate regions. Yet, in some places, verdant tracts occur even among those low and swampy districts, where flowers in profusion display their beauties throughout the year.

The eastern coast is dangerous for large vessels, in easterly gales, as the numerous inlets are generally too shallow for ships, having water only for vessels of a light draught. On the west, however, are the harbors of Perdido, Pensacola, Choctawhatchee, St. Andrew's, St. Joseph's, Appalachicola, Appelachee, Tampa, Carlos, and Gullivain. St. John's river is very crooked, and in some parts, four or five miles wide.

Pensacola, in north latitude 30 deg. 23 min., and longitude 10 deg. 19 min. west from Washington, stands on the northwestern shore of the bay of the same name, and enjoys the advantages of a fine and safe harbor, with a bar passable by vessels drawing twenty-one feet of water. The anchorage is good, but the water is shallow near the land.

The city was founded in the year 1699, by a Spanish officer named Don Andre de Riola. The entrance to the bay of Pensacola is narrow, between St. Rose's island and Barrancas point, eight miles from the city.

St. Augustine is the principal town and seaport on the Atlantic coast of Florida, in north latitude 29 deg. 48 min., and longitude west from Washington, 40 deg. 21 min. It is the oldest settlement in the limits of the American Union, and even older than the first Canadian colony, having been founded in 1565, by the Spaniards. The harbor has twenty-eight or thirty feet of water, and is safe and commodious, being protected from the sea by Anastatia island. The town extends along its side, on a peninsula, elevated only twelve feet above the level of the sea, and is of an oblong form, about a mile in length, but not very compactly built. The shell-limestone which forms the coast is the building material. It presents a very attractive appearance from without, as orange-trees in abundance grow in the yards and gardens; but many of the streets are crooked and narrow. The climate is as mild as that of southern Europe, and this city is therefore a resort of many invalids from the north. The sea-breezes by day, and the land-breezes by night, co-operate to keep the temperature mild and uniform. Steamboats go to Savannah and Charleston. Population about 3,000.

The square near the water is ornamented with an obelisk of stone, erected in the centre by the Spaniards, in the days of the constitution. It is surrounded by two churches, the courthouse, and a number of handsome private buildings.

View of the Public Square and Obelisk, St. Augustine.

Fort Marion, at the mouth of the harbor, is intended for seventy guns and one thousand soldiers.

The harbor of Pensacola receives the two rivers, Yellow Water and Escambia; Choctaw river falls into the bay of the same name; while the Appalachicola forms a delta, and the Suwanee empties into Vacasausa bay, in latitude 29 deg. 25 min. The St. John's differs from all the other rivers in the Union, in taking its rise from low, flat grassy plains, which extend to about latitude 28 deg. It then flows a little westward of north, for a considerable distance parallel to the coast, and has the appearance of a sound.

The low and uniform character of the coast of Florida renders it very dangerous to navigation, especially on the eastern side; and the perils of the seaman are greatly increased by the numerous shoals and banks which line the southern coast.

THE FLORIDA KEYS are celebrated for the numerous shipwrecks which have occurred upon them. They are now the resort of wreckers, who often afford important assistance to vessels in distress, for rewards proportioned to the value of their services. They have heretofore been infested by pirates, at different periods, and stained with the blood of many of their unfortunate prisoners. The Keys consist of a long line of sand-banks, reefs, rocks, and small islands, some bare, and others thickly overgrown with grass, reeds, or bushes, which formerly gave complete shelter and concealment to the outlaws who lay in wait for prizes, and the last of whom were destroyed and captured by some of our armed ships, a few years ago.

TALLAHASSEE.—This town, the capital of Florida, 210 miles from St. Augustine, stands on a considerable eminence, and contains above two thousand inhabitants, with several public squares, a courthouse, statehouse, masonic hall, land-office, market, and three churches. There is a valuable mill-stream which passes along the eastern side of the town, and has a fall of sixteen feet, a short distance from the place where it sinks into the earth, and disappears.

JACKSONVILLE, thirty-eight miles from St. Augustine, and thirty from the sea, is a pleasant town, on the bank of St. John's river, with less than one thousand inhabitants.

APPALACHICOLA stands at the mouth of the river of the same name, on the gulf of Mexico. It contains about fifteen hundred inhabitants, and has considerable trade in cotton. Steamboats go to New Orleans, and Columbus, Geo.

CURIOSITIES.—Among the natural curiosities of Florida are :—

The White Sulphur Spring, on the bank of the Suwanee river. The water makes its appearance in a large basin, thirty feet in diameter, and ten feet deep, from which it flows in a strong current. It is so highly impregnated with sulphur, that the taste and smell are very disagreeable; and it is celebrated for its efficacy in various cutaneous and other diseases.

Subterranean Streams.—Williams, in speaking of this state, says, Florida is, in itself, a natural curiosity. It is (as all who are acquainted with the outline of the United States will allow), a singularly-formed peninsula. Mr. Seagrove alleges that it is a sand-bank; but Mr. Williams supposes it to be a calcareous fragment of the Appalachian mountain, clothed with some sterile sand-banks, some rich, variegated clay-banks, and some beautiful coralines. It is remarkable that, although Florida has many beautiful streams, some of them are found pursuing a considerable part of their course under ground. Pretty streams of sweet and pure water often rush headlong into some wild opening in the rocks, and entirely disappear; and it is quite common to see streams jet forth from the earth. Mr. Williams gives the following description in his work on Florida, published in 1837 :—

"*The Wakully River* rises about ten miles northwest of St. Mark's, from one of the finest springs in Florida, or, perhaps, in the world. It is of an oval form, the largest diameter of which is about six rods. It is of an unknown depth, and perfectly transparent. In looking into it, the color resembles a clear blue sky, except near the border, where it has a slight tinge of green, from the reflection of the surrounding verdure, which hangs over it in drooping branches and waving festoons. The eastern side presents a rugged, rocky precipice; all else is an abyss of boundless depth. Squadrons of fishes are seen careering round their own world, in perfect security. The water is moderately cold, and highly impregnated with lime. The beauty of the fountain, the luxuriance of the foliage around it, and the calm retirement of the whole scene, render this one of the most charming spots that West Florida affords."

Lime-Sinks.—All over the territory are scattered lime-sinks, or sink-holes, which mark the course of the subterranean rivers. Holes in the ground, where the earth caves in, and where the hollow is filled with water, form these lime-sinks. Williams says: "They are often very deep, and from them I have often taken fine strings of trout. Two instances have occurred, within our knowledge, where persons have camped under the pines for one night, and the next, earth, trees, and all, have disappeared, and an unfathomable sink has supplied the place."

Caves.—A large part of Florida (that is, the limestone region) abounds in caves. The rock is porous and soft, and slowly dissolves in water. Swift-running streams rapidly wear and tear away mass after mass, and from time to time new channels are formed, by which means the old are left dry. In many places, channels are worn under ground, and there considerable rivers pursue their way, for greater oı less distances, beneath the surface, some of which reappear, and others fall into the sea by unknown passages. Such is the nature of a number of streams in Europe, some of which have been connected with mythological traditions and poetical associations. Wherever an old subterranean channel is deserted, a cavern is left; and among those which have been discovered in Florida, the most curious, perhaps, is

The Arch Cave.—This remarkable excavation is about three miles from Chipola river, in Jackson county. At the foot of an immense limestone bluff is an opening, only five feet in height, and thirty feet wide. Having entered, the visiter finds a descending passage of fifty feet, when he perceives that he has reached a spacious apartment, a hundred feet across and fifty in height, along the southern side of which flows a stream of pure, cold water, which soon disappears. A narrow passage leads onward to the northwest, with a pointed arch overhead, like a Gothic aisle. After proceeding sixty yards, a stream, twenty feet wide and five feet deep, crosses the path, which abounds in white cray-fish. The passage next turns northeastwardly, to a chamber one hundred feet long, with a floor of red clay, scattered with fragments of fallen rock, and blocks of stalagmite, formed by the water dripping from the numerous stalactites above. These, of different forms and sizes, almost conceal from view the lofty roof; while a collection of the longest, united in one undivided mass, extends from the ceiling to the floor, forming an immense, but well-proportioned column, which seems erected to support the rock above. The entrance of visiters into this hall with torches, disturbs a large flock of bats, which have their residence far above; and on their rapid wings, after fluttering about awhile, they disappear among the inner recesses of the extensive cavern, making a sound like that of a rushing wind.

A narrow and winding passage next opens, to conduct the stranger to a new hall, from which several paths branch off in different directions, where several streams are observed rushing through crevices of different sizes, and annually producing changes in their subterranean courses. The stalactite formations, at the same time, gradually fill up some of the chambers in which they are found; and the beauty of these it is difficult to describe, and even to imagine. They are masses of small crystals, more or less regular, though endlessly varying in form. The sides of the cavern are covered with them in many parts, while the pendants above, like icicles, usually have a corresponding mass of the same material forming on the floor below; and thus the light of the torches is reflected in a thousand spangles, from every quarter.

This cavern has been explored about six hundred yards, and many more hollows are known to exist in its vicinity. Several wells, sunk by Colonel Stone, opened into dark caves, by which the workmen became too much alarmed to continue their labors.

The Ladies' Cave is another remarkable opening in the earth, about a mile distant, in a southeast direction. The entrance is large, and the interior more spacious. The passage at first divides into two, of which that on the left soon leads the visiter to a deep stream, which disappears under an arched rock, covered with crystals. The other, after a longer course, and leading through several halls, is interrupted by water, beyond which is seen a large room.

The Everglades.—This peculiar feature may be ranked among the natural curiosities of Florida. South of the twenty-eighth degree of north latitude, Florida has very much the shape of a dish, the border of which is raised toward the coast. Near to the cape this border lies at the distance of from twelve to twenty miles from the shore. It is composed of the same calcareous rock which forms this peninsula. This extensive basin is intersected by numerous lakes and lagoons, and is filled by marshes and wet savannahs, which form a labyrinth, and are called the everglades. It is drained on the north by the St. John's, on the east by the St. Lucia, Greenville, Jupiter, New river, Rattones, and Miami, and by the Snake, Swallow, Delaware, Caloosahatche, and Macaco, on the west. As one approaches the level of the glades, he is surprised by the appearance of a field of grass before him, which seems like the ocean, without bounds. He may then pass on westward, from six to twelve miles, till, by degrees, the grass disappears, and he is left in an unexplored, grassy lake, the limits of which his eye can not discover. The grass is so tall and thick, that, although the borders of the lake are usually covered in winter with water, it is never so deep as to cover it. For ten miles from the timbered land, the earth is generally hard and dry in summer. This tract of country would afford a fine place for cattle to range, and is always well stocked with wild game. La Vega tells us, that pearls were known to abound in this region, at the time of the invasion by De Soto. Mr. Williams says: "An old manuscript in my possession asserts, that a governor of Florida appointed a commission, for the purpose of seeking pearls in these lakes, which was successful." Mr. Williams seems to infer from this and other facts, that it would be of much advantage to drain this portion of the country. He asserts, that if the waters could be lowered ten feet, it would probably drain six hundred thousand acres; and if this should prove to be a rich soil, as it appears to be, what a field would it open for tropical productions!

History.—We have only room for a few leading events in the history of Florida:—

1497.—Discovery by Sebastian Cabot, under the English flag, who merely saw the coast, without landing.

1512.—Visited by Ponce de Leon, in search of "*the fountain of health*," reported to him by an Indian girl. He landed from Hispaniola at Cape Sable, on Easter day, and gave it the name of Florida, which the Spaniards afterward used to embrace all the country to Canada. After a long search for the fountain (which may have been the Sulphur Spring), he returned, with the loss of many men.

1516.—He made a second search for gold, and was driven away by the Indians.

1524.—The king of Spain having granted Florida to Guerray, his successor, Allyon, attempted to seize the country, but was repulsed by the natives.

1528.—Pamfilo de Narvaez, with four hundred foot and forty horse, after many sufferings, and much perfidious conduct toward the Indians, lost almost all his men; eighty only reached Mexico in boats.

1539.—Fernando de Soto next attempted to occupy the country, having sold his claims on the Peruvian conquest, to which he had contributed, for one and a half millions. Landing at Tampa bay with one thousand men, and assisted by Ortez, a survivor of the last expedition, who was a favorite with a chief in the interior, he proceeded far without interruption, treating the natives with kindness, until he had won their confidence, and had an opportunity to seize one of their large towns. A numerous body of Indians ambushed him some time after, but were repulsed in an obstinate battle. He pursued his way through Florida, though bravely and powerfully resisted; and, led on by the hope of finding gold, two years afterward died on the Red river, having crossed the Cumberland mountains and the Mississippi.

1562.—A Huguenot colony, sent out from France by Admiral Coligny, arrived on the coast, but proceeding north, landed at Beaufort. After extreme sufferings, however, they abandoned their undertaking.

1564.—A second and larger colony was established at May river, supposed to be the St. John's, where they built Fort Caroline, six leagues from the sea. General Menendez sailed from Spain to destroy them, as heretics, as his catholic majesty had received from the pope a grant of the new world, on condition that he should convert the Indians to the Romish faith. He succeeded, partly by perfidy, in butchering the colonists; and in revenge, the Chevalier Dominique de Gourges, though born a Romanist, led an expedition to Florida, and, with the assistance of a body of Indians, cut off the Spaniards at Caroline. Finding the remains of his countrymen hanging on trees, with the inscription: "*Not as Frenchmen, but as heretics,*" he hung the Spaniards in their places, and put up signs bearing these words: "*Not as Spaniards, but as devils.*"

1574.—Menendez, governor of Saint Augustine, sent out many friars among the Indians.

1583.—The last of the Indian nations formed treaties with the Spaniards, and a missionary system was established for all Florida, the head of which was at the Franciscan convent in the capital. The convents, whose ruins are now seen in different parts, were built about this time.

1702.—Governor Moore's unsuccessful siege of St. Augustine, with the troops of the southern English colonies. Two years afterward, by a land-expedition, he seized the north of Florida, and excited the Indians to revolt and massacres. After various Indian wars, in

1718—M. Chateauque, from Louisiana, captured the fort at Pensacola with eight hundred Indians, twenty-two years after its erection. It was soon retaken by a Spanish fleet, but fell again into the hands of the French, who demolished it.

1725.—Governor Palmer, to retaliate for a Spanish and Indian invasion of Georgia, laid the country waste to St. Augustine.

1740.—Governor Oglethorpe's expedition, mentioned in our description of South Carolina and Georgia. After an invasion of Georgia by the Spaniards, in

1763—Florida was ceded to Great Britain, when only six hundred poor Spaniards were found inhabiting the country, and these soon removed to Cuba. The land was therefore parcelled out among half-pay officers and disbanded soldiers, who had served in the American war; while colonists of different classes arrived from Great Britain.

1767.—New Smyrna, seventy miles south of St. Augustine, was settled by 1,500 Greeks, Corsicans, and others, under Dr. Turnbull, who for several years treated them with great injustice and barbarity. In 1776, they were placed in an independent situation by the government, and took up their residence in St. Augustine, where many of their descendants now reside.

1781.—Pensacola was besieged and taken by the French from Louisiana.

1783.—Florida was ceded back to Spain, and the manufacture of sugar, and other enterprises introduced by the English, were abandoned, the British subjects leaving the country. The Greek colony alone preserved signs of prosperity.

1811.—Seven commissioners were sent to Pensacola by the president of the United States, to obtain, if possible, a cession of Florida, but were unsuccessful. The next year, Fernandina and Amelia island were captured by Com. Campbell and an American force; and the place was a great resort of smugglers and slave-traders, during the American embargo.

1813.—The place was restored to the Spaniards.

1814.—Colonel Nichols, with an English fleet, took Pensacola, and armed the Indians against the Americans. On the 6th of November, in that year, Gen. Jackson appeared before Pensacola with a strong force, and soon took the place, but the British escaped in their ships. Gen. Jackson destroyed the fortifications and evacuated the place, leaving private property wholly uninjured.

1819.—A treaty of amity, settlement, and limits, was concluded between Spain and the United States, by which Florida was ceded to this country. Gen. Jackson was appointed governor.

1822.—Florida was made a territory; and the following year Tallahassee was made the seat of government.

The improvements made in population, agriculture, arts, and commerce, have been rapid since that epoch, though much retarded for several years by the war with the Indians, who, in spite of their claim to their own country, and the bravery and skill with which they defended it, have been removed beyond the Mississippi.

A careless and wasteful plan of agriculture, too common in some of the southern parts of the Union, has exhausted great tracts of land in Florida. Williams says it "has destroyed the native fertility of the soil, from the Chesapeake bay to the St. Mary's river, with few exceptions. The object has been to cultivate as much land and with as few hands as possible; to exhaust the soil and turn it common, and then to remove and pursue the same course again, upon new land." He remarks that abundance of seaweed and marsh mud are to be found all along the coast of Florida, and that all experience proves that it is much less expensive to manure old land than to clear the timber from new.

Sea-island cotton on the sea-border, and green-seed cotton inland, have heretofore been the principal crops; but the cultivation of sugar is now fast gaining the ascendency in the middle and eastern parts of the country; and experiments have proved that the cane will flourish anywhere, while it is more certain and valuable in most places, and there can be no danger of glutting the market with this article.

There are three kinds of sugar-cane cultivated in Florida: the Creole, the Otaheite, and the Ribbon; the first of which is thought to yield more sugar, though slower in ripening. The Ribbon is better adapted to a more northern climate, as it ripens in a short time; but the grinding is more laborious, on account of the superior hardness of the stalk. It has another advantage, in not fermenting as speedily as the Creole. The yellow varieties are preferred south of thirty degrees latitude. Transplanting is best performed at the season of ripeness. Excellent stalks have been raised six successive years from the same roots; and we are yet unable to say how much longer it might be done with depreciation.

In the spring it is useful to cut off the tops several times, to make the plant spread and destroy the weeds; and the heads cut off are excellent food for cattle and horses. Williams assures us that the culture and manufacture are carried on with full success on small farms, as well as on the largest estates: for a press may be made by the farmer, at little cost, which will perform the work as well or even better, than a mill costing ten thousand dollars. This branch of business has some peculiar advantages, particularly in the small amount of labor required in the cultivation of a sugar plantation. No work upon it is necessary from midsummer until harvest, though at that time many hands must be employed.

Indigo was the principal product under the British, and silk might be well made in the northern districts.

ALABAMA.

This state lies between thirty degrees ten minutes, and thirty-five degrees, north latitude, and between eight and eleven degrees, west longitude from Washington. From north to south it occupies a tract of land three hundred and seventeen miles long, and one hundred and seventy-four miles broad, containing forty-six thousand square miles. In 1850, the population was numbered at 771,650.

Alabama is situated in the valley of Tennessee, and the basin of Mobile, except its southeast and southwest angles. The southern part borders on the gulf of Mexico for the space of fifty or sixty miles, and is nearly covered with pines, and low and level. In the central part it is hilly and varied by prairies, and broken and somewhat mountainous in the north. The soil, in the northern portion of the state, is excellent; but in the southern, it is sandy and barren. The native trees in the northern and middle sections are black and white oak, hickory, poplar, cedar, chestnut, pine, mulberry, &c. The arable land of southern Alabama, may be found mostly on or near to the water-courses, and is called by two different names, alluvion and intermediate. The intermediate has a kind of soil between the open pine woods and the alluvial river-bottoms. Although it comprises the much greater part of the state, it is sterile. It abounds more in the southern than in the northern sections.

Alabama has a number of fine rivers, of which the Mobile is the principal. The Alabama is a very fine river, and is navigable to Claiborne, sixty miles above its junction, for vessels drawing six feet of water. At the mouth of the Cahawba, one hundred and fifty miles further, it has four or five feet of water, and in the shallowest places, to the junction of the Coosa and Talapoosa, the rivers by which it is formed, it is never less than three feet.

The Tombigbee is four hundred and fifty miles long, and is navigable for schooners to St. Stephen's, one hundred and twenty miles, and for steamboats to Columbus, Mississippi. Indeed, it is boatable for the greater part of its course.

It has a large branch which is called the Black Warrior. This river is navigable to Tuscaloosa.

Another river, the Chatahoochee, forms a boundary of Alabama; and the northern part is watered by the Tennessee.

Mobile river, properly the lower part of the principal stream in the state, is formed by the confluence of two others, the principal of which is the Alabama, and the second the Tombigbee. And the Alabama, in its turn, is formed by the Coosa and the Talapoosa. It is to be regretted that this incorrect plan in naming streams has been adopted here, as in some other places, as it leads to confusion and often to false impressions. A stream should bear one name from its source to its mouth, and each branch should be named in the same manner.

The Coosa, which is regarded as the main branch of the Alabama, ought to have been named as the main stream; and we shall so consider it, and follow the order of nature, and the proper practice of geographers, in our brief description. It rises in Tennessee, between the sources of the Hiwassee and Chatahoochee, in latitude thirty-five degrees five minutes south, the highest point of all the waters flowing directly into the gulf of Mexico, east of the Mississippi. The head stream bears the name of the Conessauga, and flows first in a westwardly direction, and then southwestwardly and south. At the distance of seventy miles in Georgia, it receives the Etowah, and there assumes the name of Coosa. About ten miles beyond it crosses the line of Alabama, and turns southwest, south, and southeast, till it receives the Talapoosa and changes its name again, as beforementioned, to Alabama river, at Coosanda, in latitude thirty-two degrees twenty-eight minutes, longitude nine degrees twenty-two minutes west from Washington. In this part of its course, the Alabama (or Coosa) flows about four hundred miles, including its windings, while it gains only two hundred and forty, measuring in a straight line, draining an area of about nine thousand square miles.

The Alabama now flows westwardly until it receives the Cahawba, and then turns south-southwest, until it is joined by the Tombigbee, and changes its name to the Mobile. The lower part of the channel is no less crooked than the upper; for while the distance in a direct line from the Talapoosa is but one hundred and twenty miles, the navigation is not less than two hundred and fifty.

Mobile bay is of a triangular shape, about thirty-two miles across, and into it empties the Mobile river, by several mouths. The outer bar has sixteen feet water; but Dog river bar, which is seven miles below the harbor, has only eleven. The principal entrance is between Dauphin island and Mobile point. There is another: the pass of Heron, which affords a communication between Pascagoula sound and the harbor, between Dauphin island and the continent. This has six feet of water at middle tide, and is taken by steamboats and coasting vessels on the way to New Orleans, by the Rigolets, Lake Pontchartrain, and Bayou St. John. Anchorage can be found in any part of that route, in mud, shells, and sand.

The basin of Mobile river contains an area of 37,120 square miles, in the draining of which that stream and its branches perform their parts. It extends north to the borders of the basin of the Tennessee, and east to that of the Chatahoochee.

When we consider the variety of surface, soil, and productions, in Alabama the extent of its navigable routes, and the facilities for commerce, together with the mildness of its climate, it might seem strange that it should so long have remained almost uncultivated and uninhabited, if we were not aware of the various unfavorable circumstances connected with its situation. It has been shown, in our notices of the Carolinas, that the colonists near the coast remained for a generation ignorant of the advantages of the upper country in the interior: those elevated regions, which enjoy a climate more favorable to health and bodily exertion, and abounding in productions unknown among the low, hot, and often sandy and barren plains on which they had pitched.

The feebleness of the young colonies, the distractions caused among them by ignorant and evil counsellors and rulers, the danger of foreign invasion by sea, and still more the fear of the powerful Indian tribes on their western frontiers, afforded sufficient explanation for this delay in extending their borders in that direction. These reasons apply with double force to Alabama, for it lay still further beyond; and, in addition to this, the territory was in the vicinity of another enemy or rival of the English: the French on the Mississippi. A portion of it, indeed, and that the most important part, in fact, the key of the whole, was early occupied by them: we mean Mobile; which, being placed at the mouth of the chief river, and on a good harbor, commanded the whole accessible portion of the country.

Since Alabama has come into the possession of the United States, and has risen to the dignity of a state, it has had to struggle with obstacles arising from its backwardness; and by the superiority of New Orleans as a great mart of commerce, long established, the difficulty of concentrating business at a small place in its neighborhood is much increased. The natural obstacles of the interior are in many parts great, as may be perceived from some of the particulars we have given; and thus several circumstances combine, which are likely to retard the rapid increase of settlements for some time to come.

The prolonged disputes and contests for territory between England, Spain, and France, brought an innumerable host of evils upon the early colonies, and especially upon those most accessible to invasion. Alabama lay so far from the Atlantic coast, so near to the French settlements on the Mississippi, and so totally within the Indian territory, that an occupation of any part as a British colony, or even a visit to it, was not to be regarded as a possible thing, for a long time. Until the year 1667, there had never been any treaty or understanding entered into between England and Spain, for the prevention or arrangement of difficulties arising out of conflicting claims to territory in America.

It was then, however, happily agreed, in due form, between those two powers, in a treaty framed by Sir William Godolphin, that, "the king of Great Britain should always possess, in full right of sovereignty and property, all the countries, islands, and colonies, lying and being situated in the West Indies, or any part of America, which he and his subjects then held and possessed, inasmuch that they neither can nor ought to be thereafter contested on any account whatsoever." The buccaniers were suppressed, and the navigation of the American seas was freely opened to both nations. It was also agreed, that all ships in distress entering any of the ports, should be admitted and treated with humanity, and freely permitted to depart. The Spaniards then gave up, by this treaty, all claim to the Carolinas; and the prosperity of the British colonies would have been increased by it, had that power observed it in good faith.

Soon after this event, a treaty of neutrality was concluded between Great Britain and France, by which limits were fixed, with greater precision than before, to the various possessions of these three powers in America, and the freedom of commerce and navigation was better secured.

But the happy results which might naturally have been expected from these measures, were greatly diminished by the arrogant pretensions advanced by one of the religious orders in Spain. The Franciscan monks, claiming the authority of the pope as paramount to international agreements, found means to gain a footing in Florida, where, under the protection and favor of Spanish fortresses and troops, they soon gained over to their direction the Indians, and established a missionary system throughout that country, by which they raised up a power hostile to Great Britain, as a protestant nation, from which a long series of evils resulted, that continued through several generations. Hence arose the hostility of the Florida Indians and some of the more northern tribes, with many of the disasters which they produced; and hence, and from a similar cause, viz., the long and continued intrigues and open military expeditions of the French Jesuits in Canada, the sad scenes of fire, murder, and captivity, which spread a gloom over the history of the colonies of New England and New York.

The planting of the colonies along the Mississippi, in the year 1709, is worthy of notice as one of the great causes of the delay in the occupation of the territory of this state by the English. Louis XIV. of France having granted a large tract of land about the mouths of that river to Secretary Crozat, the settlement was soon commenced; and, although the place was considered by the southern British colonists as lying within their patent, no attempt was made to interrupt the intruders, and the steps they were taking were not even protested against. The French gradually won to their interest some of the Indians, and extended plantations in different directions, while they established forts and trading stations still further in advance. In 1725, they built a fort on Alabama river, at a considerable distance above its mouth. That position, called Fort Alabama, afforded them facilities of intercourse with the Creek nation, whose hunting grounds extended to that vicinity; and when a friendly standing had been established with them, the Cherokees were, ere long, brought into correspondence; and thus the foundations were laid of an extensive rival interest to the British colonies, the evil effects of which were long felt.

To oppose the intrigues of the French, who soon brought the Choctaws, Chickasaws, and other tribes, under their influence, the president of Carolina employed Captain Tobias Fitch, to act as his agent among the Creeks, and Colonel George Chicken among the Cherokees; but they were unable to prevent all connexion between those nations and the French, who generally supplied them with tomahawks and firearms, which they adopted instead of their bows and arrows, and thus became far more bold, formidable, and destructive enemies than they would else have been.

In 1730, after the colony of Carolina, with the extensive territory which it then included, had been purchased by the crown, Sir Alexander Cumming came from England to America, to secure the friendship of the Cherokees by a formal treaty; and met the chiefs of the nation at Nequassee, a place about three hundred miles in the interior, where he was received on the most friendly terms. Five of them accompanied him to England, where they made a treaty of peace and amity, agreeing never to trade with any other people but the British, to aid and fight for them, &c.; "not to permit the white men of any other nation, to build any forts or cabins, or plant any corn among them, upon lands which belong to the great king, to restore runaway negroes, to submit to English laws in case of murder on either side," &c. The Indians returned the following year, highly satisfied with their success. Governor Glen, in 1755, had the treaty confirmed, and obtained a vast cession of land. But this promising aspect of affairs was not of long duration; and the scenes of war and distress which followed, as we have briefly stated in our accounts of the older colonies, condemned the territory of Alabama to the long neglect which it suffered, in consequence of the hostile state of its savage inhabitants.

Thus we have seen that a small portion of the present state of Alabama was occupied by the French, early in the last century, when, soon after the founding of Louisiana, they built a fort at Mobile, and settled at several points upon the river; while the English left the territory unoccupied, and made no attempt to settle any part of that large portion of it which was included in the charter of Georgia, so that nearly the whole territory remained in the undisputed possession of the Indians. In 1802, it was ceded to the United States by Georgia, and annexed to the Mississippi territory. In 1817, it was made a distinct territory, and on the 2d of August, 1819, admitted as a free and independent state into the American Union.

The constitution of Alabama is remarkably liberal it its provisions for the support of education, as it contains a long section on the subject, of which the following is the commencement :—

"Schools and the means of education shall for ever be encouraged in this state." It requires the legislature to take measures to preserve the lands appropriated for the support of education, to apply the funds, &c. The income from the lands is devoted to the support of a university. The number of common schools is already six hundred and fifty, and there are one hundred and twenty academies and grammar-schools.

The constitution likewise secures to slaves, accused of any crime higher than petty larceny, a trial by a pettit jury.

Printing was commenced in this state sometime between 1810 and 1820; but as early as 1821 there were no less than eleven newspapers.

State of the Country, &c.—In so new and extensive a region as Alabama, improvements must necessarily be backward, especially where the inhabitants are few, and the means of communication difficult, where facilities have hardly been introduced. Commendable enterprise has already been displayed, by both the legislature and the people, in introducing important improvements, and in devising more. That the progress of the state, in many important respects, will hereafter be great, we have flattering reason to expect, when we recollect the provision made for the general and lasting support of education in the constitution. Intelligence, literature, and science, united with religion, must necessarily render a people great and happy; and it is gratifying to see that means are employed in Alabama for their diffusion. Steam has already begun its career of civilization and improvement on both land and water.

The establishment of steamboats on the Alabama river, affords one of the principal channels of travelling and trade in the state of Alabama. A safe and rapid passage is afforded by that route from Mobile to Montgomery, the head of navigation. Wetumpka, fifty miles higher up the river, by water, but only eighteen by land, is the highest point accessible in light boats. From Montgomery to Atlanta, a railroad extends 185 miles, whence a stage-road of one hundred and thirty miles leads to Notasulga, and there the traveller finds himself on the Augusta railroad, one hundred and thirty-six miles in length. The part of this route which lies in this state, and most of that part in Georgia, is wild and almost uninhabited. A traveller in 1846 thus describes some of the features of this unreclaimed wildness and the primitive state of society existing among the few people who inhabit it :—

"The whole country through which we passed, from Augusta to Montgomery, is as dull and deficient in interest, as the most misanthropic could desire. It was sufficiently rolling, sometimes stony, and had numerous clear rivulets meandering on it. But the *improvements* were mostly a sad blotch on nature. It is bad enough to find log-shanties, slipshod fences, &c., in a decidedly fresh and untamed country; but to see these, so old as to be already in their dotage, and comparatively little to redeem the general forbiddingness of the scene, is, to say the best, the reverse of gratification to a traveller.

"The log-houses on their best estates consist of a room at either end, with a passage between (but seldom enclosed with doors), through which a loaded team could be driven, and the enclosed rooms would generally afford a tolerably distinct view of the opposite scenery through the *unchuncked* double walls. The chimneys in most of the country, and some of the city houses, from Maryland to the Gulf, are placed on the outside of one or both ends, and are built entirely independent of the houses, though connected with the first floor by a single fireplace. This may abate a little the intense heat of summer; but it has a most unsightly and forbidding appearance. The best houses are sometimes painted, and the chimneys are well laid up in brick and mortar, while those attached to the poorest are more frequently made of mud and sticks, and the surrounding buildings are limited to a rough hovel or two, about as closely housed in, as a field under a well-laid worm fence.

"The *shuck* provided for the winter forage of the cattle, is one or more stacks of corn-blades or husks, some twelve or fifteen feet high, and five or six in diameter. The working mules or horses are fed with corn; but all the remainder of the quadrupeds betake themselves to the woods for brouse. As the range is illimitable, and vegetation has a torpid existence through the winter, they will frequently do very well on it, though they have in many cases to go so far for it, that they do not think it worth while returning to report progress till the feed has again become deserving their attention at home. Of course, milking the cows is out of the question, unless half of one's time is used in pursuit of them.

"Where there are canebrakes, as is frequently the case on rich bottom lands, the animals have a good winter subsistence on the young shoots of this gigantic grass. Its rich evergreen leaves acquire a palatable nutritiveness after the frosts, which it does not possess during the summer and autumn, and when abundant, cattle will fatten on this alone. The swine through this country are the vilest brutes a farmer's eye ever rested on. They are of all colors, but principally black, gray, red, blue, or striped and dotted like a hyena, which comely beast, and its congener, the wolf, they more nearly resemble than any of their own well-bred family. Even the fattening porkers are only in a passably-growing condition, while the nomads could hardly lay claim to hide enough to hold their bones together. As the stages rattled along, they rushed out of the woods in all directions, to follow the horses. I asked the driver the cause of their leanness when the woods were full of oaks and chestnuts. He said the former bore no acorns, and the people gathered the latter.

"We were glad to get on a boat at Montgomery. Had the river been at moderate height, we should have passed down the four hundred miles to Mobile in two days instead of five, owing to our frequently grounding.

"The Alabama is a fine winding stream, hemmed in by banks from twenty to eighty feet high. These are sometimes worn, and shelve off from the action of the stream; but are generally fringed with a great variety of forest-trees, shrubs, and frequently the cane, which, springing up from the water's edge, surmounts the banks, and extends for miles in one impenetrable mass. It grows from fifteen to twenty feet high; straight as an arrow and almost as thick as standing wheat. It throws out delicate branches near the tops, whose gracefully tapering foliage, at a distance, nearly resembles a field of luxuriant hemp, and these become so closely interwoven at their tops as to resemble one vast carpet of resplendent green. A variety of beautiful branching evergreen, and deciduous oaks, are found on the banks and bordering tablelands, and occasionally the pine and other resinous trees. Here and there a magnolia may be seen shooting up with perfect symmetry for fifty to seventy feet, and bearing the dark-hued evergreen leaves, in a beautiful cone. In May and June, this is gemmed over its entire surface with beautiful snowy flowers, five to seven inches in diameter and of great fragrance. The cypress that everywhere fills up the low grounds south of Virginia, is always to be found in its appropriate place here; and from nearly every tree, of whatever species, the clinging moss hangs in graceful festoons. This appears to be exclusively an air-plant. Its slender stem throws out minute tendrils or branches, some two inches long, and about the same distance from each other, and it is suspended from the twigs solely by the mechanical attachment of the stem. When this has become dead for a long distance from the point of its origin, the fresh shoots continue to multiply and grow on with undiminished vigor. Cattle are said to be fond of it, and if suited to impart nourishment to them, it seems improvident that such vast quantities of it are hung so far above their reach. This moss is exported largely to the northern states, and is used for stuffing cushions, beds, &c.

"The soil on both sides of the river is almost invariably good, as is much of that in central Alabama."

MONTGOMERY, the capital of the state, is built on a high bluff, on the left bank and at the head of steamboat navigation, on Alabama river, three hundred and thirty-eight miles from Mobile by the course of the river, and two hundred miles in a direct line; one hundred and twelve miles southeast from Tuscaloosa, and eight hundred and fifty miles from Washington city. Its contains a courthouse, seven churches, two academies, and about seven thousand inhabitants. The cotton shipped from this place amounts to forty thousand bales annually. Montgomery has recently been made the capital of the state, and preparations are already in progress for building an elegant statehouse.

MOBILE stands on a low plain, only about fifteen feet above the water at high tides, but commands a view over the spacious harbor, and lies open to the sea-breezes. The distance from the coast of the gulf of Mexico is thirty miles, and from New Orleans, one hundred and sixty-four. The population is about twenty thousand, and the principal public buildings are the United States naval hospital, courthouse, city hospital, three banks, seven churches, theatre, and Burton academy. Provision has been made for a supply of water for the city from Spring Kill, two miles distant. The cotton trade of this port is very great, the amount received and exported annually being larger than that of any other city in the Union except New Orleans.

The entrance of the harbor is defended by Fort Morgan, on a sandy point opposite Dauphin island; and a lighthouse is erected for ships entering. Mobile has been in possession of the United States only thirty-four years, having been ceded by Spain in 1813.

Spring Hill College, two miles from Mobile, has about four thousand volumes in its library, and seventy students.

Steamboats depart daily for New Orleans, Columbus, Miss., and Montgomery.

TUSCALOOSA, lately the capital, is situated on the left bank of the Black Warrior river, in latitude thirty-three degrees and twelve minutes, and longitude ten degrees and forty-three minutes, one hundred and fifty-five miles southwest from Huntsville, two hundred and seventeen miles a little north of east from Mobile, and eight hundred and fifty-eight miles southwest from Washington, by post-route. Its position is at the foot of the lower falls, at the head of steamboat navigation, on an elevated plain. The old statehouse, courthouse, land-office, masonic hall, ladies' athæneum, four churches, academy, and institute, are the public buildings. The streets are broad, straight, and regular, and the inhabitants about five thousand.

The University of Alabama, founded in 1828, is situated at the distance of one mile from Tuscaloosa. It has a library of six thousand volumes, seven professors and tutors, and about sixty students. The commencement is held on Wednesday after the first Monday in December.

DEMOPOLIS, on the Tombigbee, two hundred and twenty miles from Mobile, situated a little below the mouth of the Black Warrior river, communicates daily with Columbus, Miss., and Mobile, by steamboats. Stage-coaches go three times a week to Tuscaloosa and Mobile. The principal public buildings are three churches, two academies, and the land-office; and the population is about one thousand.

GAINESVILLE, a small town, about two hundred and eighty-three miles from Mobile, is on the Tombigbee, and a place of much trade in cotton. It contains only about two hundred inhabitants, but is daily visited by the steamboats from Columbus and Mobile, and stage-coaches go three times a week, to the latter place and Jackson in Mississippi.

ST. STEPHEN'S, with a population of one thousand, is the second settlement in the state in point of age. It stands on the Tombigbee, one hundred miles from Mobile, and has two churches, a land-office, and an academy.

CAHAWBA, on the west side of Alaba-

View of the City and Harbor of Mobile.

ma river, two hundred and forty miles from Mobile, and once the capital town, contains about one thousand inhabitants. It has a courthouse, an academy, and two churches, and the river steamboats touch there daily, while stage-coaches go to Mobile, Tuscaloosa, and Huntsville.

SELMA, sixteen miles above Cahawba, on the right bank of the river, has two academies, three churches, and about one thousand inhabitants.

FOSSIL BONES, &c.—Alabama, more than most other parts of our country, abounds in ancient bones, which are found in various positions, but most abundantly in a peculiar stratum, which in some places lies many feet beneath the natural surface, but in others, is laid bare, or cut through by the wearing away of streams of water, &c. In certain districts, these remains of ancient and often unknown animals, have been long familiar to the present inhabitants, as well as to their predecessors the Indians; but their remote situations have prevented many of them from being either generally seen or accurately described.

Dr. Koch of Germany made a tour of exploration in this and several other states, three years ago, and discovered and brought away a collection of bones, many of which were exhibited by him in our principal cities. A great number of them were arranged by him, in the order in which he supposed them to have been naturally placed, judging from their relative positions when discovered in the earth. When thus placed, they seemed to form the skeleton of an immense serpent, which the discoverer named the *Hydrargos Sillimanii*, and described, with a sketch of its probable habits, food, &c., after the manner of many of his predecessors, some of whom have published pictures of the animals of extinct species, as when restored, by the addition of the decayed flesh, &c.

Naturalists, however, did not generally adopt the opinions of Dr. Koch; and more evidence is thought necessary before the existence of such an animal can be admitted. The lighter bones connected with this skeleton, were found in a state of dislocation, particularly those which he placed as ribs. The vertebræ are so entirely separate, and generally so much worn away, by decay or attrition, that no evidence of their relation to each other, could be obtained from their form or size; and their alleged proximity when discovered, is not of itself sufficient ground on which to proceed in constructing an animal of such an extraordinary kind. Besides, the bones placed as the head, and which are said to have been found lying at that end of the skeleton, but inverted, have little or no resemblance to those of a serpent's head.

The parts of which this collection consists are unquestionably natural remains of some gigantic animal or animals, and were taken from the earth in Alabama; but to what kind of animal, or to how many individuals they belonged, we pretend not to decide. They present a striking specimen of innumerable remains of a similar kind existing in abundance in some parts of Alabama: and future discoveries and researches may probably shed important light upon the interesting subject.

The following statements we derive from a letter of Professor Silliman:—

"Dr. Koch, the proprietor of the skeleton now in this city, made a journey of discovery a year since, into Alabama and other southern regions, with particular reference to this animal. He had the rare good fortune, as the result of his perseverance, aided by the kind assistance of the inhabitants, to disinter the stupendous skeleton which is now set up for exhibition here.

"It has evidently been done at great expense and personal toil; and the public, while they owe a debt to Dr. Koch, will, when paying it, receive a high gratification in contemplating the remains of a race of animals whose length exceeded that of all other creatures hitherto discovered; the spinal column of this skeleton as now arranged measures one hundred and fourteen feet in length. The skeleton having been found entire enclosed in limestone, evidently belonged to one individual, and there is the fullest ground for confidence in its genuineness. The animal was marine and carnivorous, and at his death was imbedded in the ruins of that ancient sea which once occupied the region where Alabama now is; having myself recently passed 400 miles down the Alabama river, and touched at many places, I have had full opportunity to observe, what many geologists have affirmed, the marine and oceanic character of the country.

"Judging from the abundance of the remains (some of which have been several years in my possession), these animals must have been very numerous, and doubtless fed upon fishes and other marine creatures—the inhabitants of a region, then probably of more than tropical heat; and it appears probable also, that this animal frequented bays, estuaries, and seacoasts, rather than the main ocean. As regards the nature of the animal, we shall doubtless be put in possession of Professor Owen's more mature opinion, after he shall have reviewed the entire skeleton. I would only venture to suggest, that he may find little analogy with *whales*, and much more with *lizards*, according to Dr. Harlan's original opinion.

"Among the fossil lizards and saurus, this resembles most the *pleisiosaurus*, from which, however, it differs very decidedly.

"Most observers will probably be struck with the snake-like appearance of the skeleton. It differs, however, most essentially from any existing or fossil serpent, although it may countenance the popular (and I believe well-founded) impression of the existence in our modern seas, of huge animals to which the name of sea-serpent has been attached. For a full and satisfactory statement of the evidence on this subject, see a communication by Dr. Bigelow of Boston in the second volume of the American Journal."

Projected Improvements.—Among the projects for improvements which now attract the attention of the people of this state, is the establishment of a line of transportation on a grand scale. A glance at the principal river and its branches, is sufficient to discover, that thousands of miles lie along and near their borders; and that, even were the proportion of land susceptible of cultivation much less than it is, sufficient would still remain to furnish support for an immense population, if judiciously managed, and furnished with convenient means of sending the products to market. The steamboats already plying daily upon the main stream, and the railroads now in use, with the advantages which they afford, intimate what further benefits might be secured by extending the improvements to every part of the state which may be accessible to them. But something more than this is contemplated, by a system of public works proposed to the people.

The western parts of Georgia and South Carolina are still unprovided with adequate channels of transportation; and the slightest examination of the maps, will go far to justify the assertion of those who maintain, that it is easy to adopt measures now which shall bring all their trade to Mobile. The extension of steamboat routes as far as possible upon the streams, then a resort to railroads, and finally the improvement and multiplication of common roads, it is insisted, will accomplish this; while the profits can hardly fail to justify and richly to reward the expense, and in a moderate period.

But this is not all. The valley of the Tennessee river is separated from that of the Alabama by only a narrow ridge; and if that barrier can be surmounted, another very rich and extensive region will be added to the vast commercial territory of Mobile. It is proposed to construct a railroad across that tract; and thus to draw off the trade which seeks a slow and difficult channel down the Tennessee to the Mississippi. But the system of improvements projected stops not here. The route may be extended northward; and it is seriously proposed to carry it to the mouth of the Ohio.. From Selma to the Tennessee, a railroad route has been surveyed, and part of it graded; but the work has been abandoned, at least for the present. Such favorable views, however, are held forth, that it is supposed the project will yet be accomplished. From some of the recent publications on the subject, we derive the following facts respecting the country along the route. It will be perceived that the mineral treasures now embosomed in the earth, and of little or no value on account of their inaccessible position, are among the chief advantages promised by the advocates of the plan of improvement. The coal lands abounding in that region, are capable of affording abundant supplies of fuel for the use of steamships in all parts of the gulf of Mexico, and steamboats on the rivers, as well as for the locomotives on railroads, so far as it may be wanted.

The distance from Selma to the Tennessee river, by a line running north, is about one hundred and fifty miles; and the point at which it would be reached is at Decatur. Such a line would pass through the midst of the coal region, and those parts of it which border on the Cahawba and Warrior rivers. Between Mulberry creek and Cahawba river, the line passes along the water-shed; and there the soil is peculiarly favorable for the construction of a substantial road, consisting of cretaceous lime-rocks, of a very solid description. The Cahawba coal-field commences at Centreville, and is crossed by the line, as is that part of the coal-region called the Warrior coal-field, which lies just beyond the Mulberry fork, in the eastern part of Walker county.

From that part of Decatur the country is of a different formation, but of a very solid, firm nature for a railroad, being of granite. Decatur is a town of considerable business, being advantageously situated for trade, at the head of the falls of the Tennessee, at the foot of an extensive line of navigation on that river above the falls, and with the advantages of a railroad to Tuscumbia, on the part of the river below the falls.

But another route is also proposed, which offers some important advantages to recommend it, not promised by that just described. There is a railroad already formed and in use, between Montgomery and Westpoint, to which we have before alluded. A route laid out from some convenient point on that, to Tennessee river, would be about one hundred and forty miles long, only one hundred of which remains to be provided for, and this would cost but about ten thousand dollars a mile, including machinery, &c. Of course, the whole expense of the one hundred miles, at this estimate, would be but a million of dollars; which the results would well warrant, if the anticipations entertained should prove well founded. If the proposed work should commence at Mount Jefferson (a point on the Montgomery and Westpoint railroad), it would pass through the counties of Chambers, Tallapoosa, Randolph, Talledega, and Benton, to the Double Springs, on Coosa river, and thence forty miles to Gunter's Landing, on the Tennessee, on which part a railroad has already been projected, and funds appropriated. This route has therefore but one hundred miles of railroad to be provided for, is much shorter than the other (from Selma to Decatur), and passes through a more fertile and populous part of the state, and a region rich in minerals of value.

A chief object proposed by the friends of these improvements is, to connect the interests of the two parts of the state. Northern and southern Alabama are now so far divided, by having different channels of trade, that but little of that sympathy exists between them, which is so desirable in the same state, and necessary to its harmony and prosperity. Plans are proposed in Georgia, for the opening of new routes of transport, by which the trade of the north-eastern counties is likely to be permanently drawn off into other channels. The railroad just described would effectually counteract such measures, and at the same time prove so convenient to the northwestern parts of the adjoining state, that several large counties of Georgia would become tributary, in a commercial point of view, to the city of Mobile.

Alabama has thus much to expect from the extension of internal improvements. Although, by circumstances, she has been long prevented from making rapid progress, and was even so situated, as to be unable to begin for a century or more after her older sisters of the Union, her exertions made since she has had the power, are very creditable to her leading men, and the results have been such as to stimulate her to new projects and new labors. Notwithstanding the obstacles and discouragements presented to the extension of internal navigation and railroads, there are doubtless streams remaining, on which steamboats may hereafter be run with advantage, and numerous tracks may be laid through the most important districts, by which places now unprovided with the means of transport, may be rendered accessible. There are, fortunately, large deposites of coal and other minerals in different parts of the state, which must afford a rich reward to the enterprise of those who shall open channels of transportation, by which they can be brought to the manufactory and the steam-furnace; while the important advantages to be expected from the opening of intercourse between distant points of the state and other districts more distant, will annually increase, and become stronger incitements to men of business to give them an improved direction, and to bring them within their own reach.

However important may be this department of the public interest, and however much praise the state may deserve for her early and spirited attention to it, it is but of a physical kind, and, from its own nature, necessarily inferior to the intellectual and moral objects for which, as we have before remarked, provision is made in the constitution of the state. If the spirit of that article should be carried into operation, as promptly and efficiently and with as much perseverance as has been displayed in the introduction and extension of steam-routes by land and water, greater real advantages would be secured, and a still more substantial foundation would be laid for the future greatness of the state. Industry, commerce, and wealth, may be pursued too exclusively, to the neglect of education. Such must be allowed to be the case in our country generally. If any one of our states should have the wisdom to choose the opposite course and to pursue it, what evidences of fundamental improvement would ere long begin to appear. Schools would not only be opened, but well-filled, well-furnished, and well-taught. Academies and colleges would enjoy the patronage and respect of the public, as well as an occasional donation from the state treasury. Men would be placed in the general direction of education, not because of their political connexions, ability in intriguing, or want of office; but for their intellectual and moral merits, and their known qualifications to perform well and faithfully those important duties. And they should be secured against the evil influence of change in politics. They should be protected against those subversive movements, which have more than once overthrown systems of education, devised and put in operation in other states, merely because they were the works of a party no longer in power. In short, the best men in Alabama, should be at once called upon to take into their hands this great business, invested with all authority necessary, and furnished with every facility requisite to favor the most extensive and rapid improvement, and insure the greatest regularity and permanency. Even the fear of improper interference should be prevented; and then, with such measures as good men might devise, such zeal and perseverance as they might be expected to display, and such cooperation and support as the people might be soon brought to afford to them, the whole face of society must soon be essentially improved, and, in a single generation, every department of business, and every town, village, and family, would share in the benefits.

Although some other regions are more attractive to the masses of emigrants, Alabama has received a large increase of population since the commencement of her short history as a territory and a state. The northern counties, between 1810 and 1820, experienced an increase of inhabitants of two hundred and twenty-two per cent. These are the counties of Franklin, Jackson, Lauderdale, Lawrence, Madison, Morgan, and Limestone, and belong to what we have before spoken of as the Tennessee section of the state. On the five thousand and sixty square miles which they comprise, the population which, in 1810, was only forty-six thousand, in 1820 had increased to one hundred and two thousand. Like our other states, especially the new ones, Alabama experiences the various evils arising from the mixture of people of different, and often foreign origin; and these may be most speedily and effectually overcome by a universal, sound, and thorough system of common schools, operating simultaneously and harmoniously with high schools and universities. Men who have been educated together in childhood and youth, will feel more like fellow-citizens through life; especially if the education be good, and more especially if it be the best. The public interests of all descriptions, imperiously demand such a system for the whole country; and whatever state shall lead the way, first and best, will most wisely consult its own permanent good, and inevitably secure, for the future, the highest place for itself among the benefactors of the nation, and the directors of its destiny.

THE MAGNOLIAS.—Having described some of the chief vegetable productions belonging to some of the states, before closing our account of them, on the preceding pages, we may perhaps properly introduce here a description and history of the magnolias, the finest of which are common to most of the southern states. For the following facts, respecting this elegant genus of plants, we have been largely indebted to a late work: "The Trees of America, by D. J. Browne."

The several species, ranged under the genus Magnolia, form a splendid collection, which it would perhaps be impossible to rival in the world. They are indigenous to the southern parts of North America, but nowhere on our southern continent; while in the eastern hemisphere they are not to be found as natives either in Europe, Africa, or Australia. In Asia, are several species, but only in China and Japan, unless, perhaps, in Hindostan. The most hardy species are some of our own; and these are extensively cultivated in England and the middle and southern countries of Europe, and are able to endure the winters without protection. Even the less hardy species usually succeed there. But in the north of Europe they can not live through the year, out of the greenhouse. In England, the seeds will not often come to maturity; but in France they ripen well. All the species are much admired, for the beauty of their forms and their flowers. The most elegant, however, is the grandiflora, which abounds in the southern states of the Union, and will be the last described.

The Glaucous-leaved Magnolia (*M. glauca*), called the white bay and the sweet bay in our southern states, is known in more northerly parts of our country by various names; swamp-sassafras, swamp-sorrel, swamp-magnolia, beaver-wood, and small laurel. It bears the specific name of *glauca*, among botanists, on account of the sea-green color of its leaves; and the name of beaver-tree, given it in certain parts of the Union, is owing to its roots being eaten with great avidity by beavers. According to Micheaux, those animals prefer it, when felling timber to construct their dams, because the softness of its woods renders it very easy for them to gnaw.

This species is sometimes found forty feet in height, and ten or twelve inches in diameter; but not usually above twenty feet. The trunk is crooked, and divides into several limbs. The bark is gray and bitter to the taste; the leaves are five or six inches long, of a shining bluish green above, and greenish beneath. It is often an evergreen; and even when not strictly so, sometimes retains many of its leaves through the winter.

The flowering begins in the South late in April or early in May, and often continues in autumn. In New England it begins about six weeks later. The flowers grow from the extremities of the shoots of the previous years, and are two or three inches broad, with six white concave petals. The fragrance is peculiarly rich and powerful, being perceptible at a distance; and, when kept in a close room, soon becoming almost insupportable. The seed-vessel is of a conical shape, about an inch and a half in length, full of little cells, which open and let the seeds drop out. They are, however, attached to slender threads, which hold them hanging for some time in the air. This peculiarity belongs to all the magnolias.

The glaucous-leaved magnolia has two varieties: the *arborea*, or tall, and the *sempervirens*, or evergreen; and there are several others, some of which are supposed to be hybrids.

This species is the most extensive in its geographical range near the sea, being found further north than any other of the magnolias. The highest spot where it has been observed, is said to be a sheltered swamp in Manchester, Cape Ann, about thirty miles beyond Boston. It is there but a small tree, and is frequently cut down to the ground by severe frosts. In Florida and Louisiana, it is abundant in wet situations, and in Georgia and the Carolinas is confined to the pine barrens.

The wood is sometimes used for joiners' tools, while the bark is sometimes administered in cases of fever.

The Umbrella Magnolia (M. tripetala), often called the umbrella-tree, and, in Virginia, elkwood, is remarkably uniform and graceful in the arrangement of its leaves. The shoots have a resemblance to the young horns of the elk; and hence probably the origin of the name by which it is known in the mountainous regions of Virginia. The leaves are deciduous and lanceolate, petals nine, the outer ones pendant. It is very seldom higher than thirty-five or forty feet, or thicker than five or six inches, and usually much smaller. The stem is commonly inclined. The leaves are oval and acuminate at both ends, near twenty inches long, and seven or eight wide. Being thus long and narrow, and often growing around a centre, they give the appearance of an umbrella; and, when adorned with the flowers, which are about eight inches in diameter, in May and June, present an object of great beauty. The fragrance emitted is strong.

In October the fruit becomes ripe, and it is five inches in length, of a rich rose color, with thirty or more seeds. It is found as high as the northern counties of New York, and with the M. grandiflora on the alluvial grounds of Georgia. Since its introduction into England in 1752, it has been extended in Europe, and is said to be the most common of the magnolias on the continent. It requires a sheltered and shady position. It is best propagated from seeds, which must be planted very soon after they fall. It is short-lived, and its wood is of no use; but it is one of the most ornamental trees.

The Large-leaved Magnolia (M. macrofylla) has very large deciduous leaves, oblong-ovate, of about the same size as the preceding, but much more rare. The bark is smooth and white, by which it is easily known in the winter. The leaves are not less than thirty-five inches long in the forests, slender and pointed, and of a light green. In May, June, and July, it puts forth large flowers, sometimes eight or nine inches in diameter, with a purple spot in the centre, and a rich odor. The fruit nearly resembles that of the preceding variety.

This plant was discovered by the elder Michaux in 1789, and first sent to Europe in 1800. The largest individual in England is at Arley Hall, which, in 1837, was twenty-eight and a half feet high. It is raised from seeds with greater facility and certainty than in any other way.

The Pointed-leaved Magnolia (M. acuminata), called the cucumber-tree in this country, and the blue magnolia in England, grows most abundantly on the rivers of upper Georgia and western South Carolina. This is one of the noblest of our forest-trees, growing to the height of sixty feet, and in May, adorned with bluish or yellowish white flowers, five or six inches broad, with a delicate odor. It is called the cucumber-tree, from the resemblance of its fruit or seed-vessel to cucumbers when green. There are several varieties of this species, chiefly distinguished by the shape of the leaf. Of these the principal is the heart-leaved cucumber-tree. It was introduced into England in 1801. It attains the height of forty or fifty feet, and bears leaves from four to six inches in length, and from three to five in breadth. It blooms in April, and the flowers are yellow, streaked with reddish within, and three or four inches in diameter.

The acuminate magnolia grows as far north as Niagara, and abounds in the Cumberland mountains. It was discovered in 1736, by John Bartram, sent to England to Peter Collingson, and soon propagated in Europe by layers. Trees of large size are now numerous in England, France, and northern Italy, forty and sixty feet in height, which bloom abundantly. In the old Bartram botanic garden, near Philadelphia, is one eighty feet high, and three feet in diameter, which was brought from Lake Erie in 1753, and furnishes most of the seeds of this species annually sent to Europe. Moist situations on declivities or narrow valleys are favorable to this species.

The wood is remarkably light and chosen for canoes. Where it abounds it is used for joiner-work.

The Ear-leaved Magnolia (M. auricolata), or longleaved cucumber-tree, is also known in some parts of the United States by the name of Indian physic and washoo. The leaves are deciduous and smooth, spatulately obovate, cordate at the base, with blunt approximate auricles. It grows to the height of thirty or forty feet, straight, with wide branches pointing upward. The leaves are eight or nine inches in length, four or six wide, and of a light green; and, on young trees, often much larger. There is a round lobe on each side of the petiole. The footstalks are short and radiating, which gives the clusters of leaves the form of an umbrella. It flowers in April and May, and the petals are white. It is found on a portion of the Allegany range, in North Carolina; and a variety of it in the western parts of Georgia and Carolina. The bark is infused in spirits for a sudorific in fevers.

The Conspicuous-leaved Magnolia is a Chinese tree, and the *Purple-Flowered Magnolia* is a native of Japan; and neither of them has been extensively introduced into the United States.

The Magnolia Grandiflora, or large-leaved magnolia, we have yet to notice, and this is the most splendid species of the kind, the most admired and the most cultivated. It is known by several other names in different parts of this country: as the laurel-leaved and large flowering evergreen magnolia, bay-tree, laurel-bay, and big laurel.

It is an evergreen, with oval-oblong leaves, shining on their upper surface, and rusty beneath. The flowers are erect, with from nine to twelve petals, expanding. "Of all the trees of North America," says Browne, "the large-leaved magnolia is the most remarkable for the majesty of its form, the magnificence of its foliage, and the beauty of its flowers. It claims a place among the largest trees of the forest, varying from one hundred feet and upward in height, and from two to three in diameter. Its head often forms a perfect cone, placed on a clean, straight trunk, resembling a beautiful column; and, from its dark green foliage, silvered over with milk-white flowers, it is seen at a great distance."

The leaves are from half a foot to a foot in length, and three or four inches broad, smooth and polished, and varying considerably in form, being oblong, oval, acuminate, &c., &c. In our southern states, the flowers appear in April or May, but in the north, as in England and France, in June or July; and some of the varieties continue in blossom until the frost. In the size of the flowers, as well as that of the entire plant, this splendid species excels its congeners: their diameter being from six to ten inches. The length of the flowering season, is another very great advantage: most of the other species of magnolia giving out their flowers at once, and soon dropping them. In autumn, when the seed-vessels are left bare, they exhibit a beautiful and delicate appearance, being conical, and, when they open, dropping out a few seeds, which remain for several days hanging by slender filaments. Being of a blood-red color, they make a very rich and striking display.

Peculiar attention has been directed to the M. magniflora by foreign gardeners, and numerous varieties have been produced, which have been regarded by some as distinct races. Among these are distinguished the obovate, round-leaved, Exmouth, rusty-leaved, lanceolate-leaved, elliptic-leaved, &c.

The native regions of the splendid tree is comprised within the maritime districts of South Carolina, Georgia, Florida, Alabama, and Louisiana; and up the Mississippi to Natchez, extending a little way into North Carolina and Texas on the Brazos. It was introduced into France in 1732, but not extended until after 1760. It was admired by the Indians, who used the bark of the roots, mixed with snakeroot, in fevers.

The propagation of this noble and elegant tree may well excite particular interest in Alabama, as well as in other of our southern regions, to which the soil and climate adapt it. As twenty or thirty years' growth is necessary to bring one of the plants from the seed to the first flowering season, that manner of propagation should never be resorted to, for purposes of ornament. If layers are resorted to, they must remain two years before they are ready to be potted. Care is required, in transplanting them, to place the earth well about the roots, and to keep it well shaded for several weeks. The Exmouth varieties sometimes bears flowers the second year, with great care.

Among the objects worthy of the attention of men of taste and public spirit in Alabama, and our other new states, is the planting of shade-trees in the towns and villages: among which the magnolias hold a prominent place, especially the grandiflora.

Natural Bridge in Alabama.—The Natural Bridge over Cedar creek, near Lexington, in Virginia, has been noticed at length on a previous page, in our description of the beautiful scenery of that state. Alabama, too, possesses a "natural bridge," which is spoken of as rivalling the far-famed one of Virginia. Professor Toumey of Alabama, state geologist, and an associate, have recently been traversing that state, investigating its geological character. While their attention was attracted to many natural wonders in the more mountainous regions, the most conspicuous among them was the "natural bridge" which they described as follows:—

"It is situated in Walker county, about a mile from the road, and on the property of a man by the name of West, but yet would well repay a traveller by the beauty of the scenery for deviating a little from his regular route. It occurs in that geological deposite termed the millstone grit, the lowest one in the coal measures—the only rock which, in Alabama, exhibits the truly wild and romantic grandeur of Nature. Before reaching it, our imaginations had been considerably elevated by the descriptions given by our guide; but, notwithstanding, when the reality broke upon us in its full magnificence, we found that our expectations fell very far short of the truth. This grand structure of the Great Architect spans about one hundred and twenty feet, while its height is about seventy. A smaller bridge connects it with the bluff beyond.

"The symmetry of the main arch will make it almost indestructible, though of course its regularity has only been produced by the undermining and breaking down of the rock which, at some bygone time, existed below it. The cleavage marks of the massive sandstone of which it is formed cause it, even in the more minute construction, to resemble an artificial bridge, as these lines make it appear as if built with regularly-worked blocks. Beneath it are many pieces of broken and partially water-worn rocks—materials, as it were, left by the builders; and these, together with the mighty escarpments round about, would impart a most grand aspect, even if that were not produced by the bridge itself. A little spring trickling from between these broken masses make it a frequent resort of the deer, which abound in that part of the country, and whose numerous footprints on the soft soil indicate a favorite lick. Lofty hemlocks and beech trees growing on the bridge, and near by, shade it from the rays of the sun."

A Wooding Station on the Mississippi.

MISSISSIPPI.

This state is bounded north by Tennessee, east by Alabama, south by the gulf of Mexico and Louisiana, and west by Louisiana and Arkansas, from which it is separated by the Mississippi river. It lies between 30° 8′ and 35° north latitude, and 10° 12′ and 12° 42′ west longitude, from Washington. Its entire outline measures 1,203 miles, of which large portions lie along the Mississippi and the Tennessee. Extreme length from north to south, 337 miles; mean breadth, 135 miles; area, 45,760 square miles.

There is a gentle declivity in the east part of the state toward the Tombigbee river; but the grand general slope is toward the Mississippi, having abrupt bluffs at a considerable distance from the bank, and leaving a wide, low tract of land between them, which is subject to inundations. That part of the state is crossed by the following streams, which are small tributaries of the great river of North America, viz.: Yazoo, Big Black, Bayou, Pierre, and Homochitto. Pearl river, a considerable stream, has its source in the central part of the state; and flowing south-southwest, nearly parallel with the Big Black, for a distance of eighty miles, then turns south-southeast, runs one hundred and fifty miles, and empties into the Rigolets between Lake Pontchartrain and Boyne.

The soil of the state is generally thin, but in some places very rich, especially on the narrow border of lowlands along the bank of the Mississippi, above mentioned. Cotton, indigo, and tobacco, flourish so well, that they have been, in turns, the staple productions. Indian corn, potatoes, and various other useful plants, are also cultivated with great success.

Among fruits, peaches and figs are the most abundant; but the climate is favorable to almost every kind except those confined to the tropics. The indigenous trees most abundant are the pine, oak of different varieties and species, hickory, sweetgum, liriodendron, tulip-tree, beech, persimmon, blackwalnut, blacklocust, honeylocust, redmaple, dogwood, chinquipin, spicewood, papau, &c. The great reedcane *(arundo gigantea)* formerly abounded in the low grounds; but it has been nearly rooted out.

The temperature at Natchez is variable, and, although usually mild in winter, has sometimes been as cold as twelve degrees, Fahrenheit, above zero. Frost is always experienced there, in some degree, in the course of the cold season, and snow is occasionally seen; so that it is not surprising that neither sugarcane nor orange-trees are to be found above thirty-one degrees of latitude. The climate is about two degrees colder than on the Atlantic. In summer, heats and drought are often unintermitted for a long period. The state is generally healthy, although intermittent fevers are common along the banks of some of the streams. The prevailing winds, as in the southwestern states generally, are westerly, and chiefly from the northwest.

The first settlement made in this state by Europeans was by the French at Natchez in 1716, when a fort was built by permission of the Indians, a powerful tribe, who inhabited the bluff. In 1723 the foreigners were involved in a war with the natives, which was terminated by a body of French troops marched from New Orleans by Governor Bienville, who were too powerful to be resisted by the savages, and they submitted.

In 1729, the French having become very numerous at Natchez, the commandant (Choteau), by ill-treating the Indians, excited them to revenge; and by a sudden attack, while the garrison were secure and unprepared, they cut off about seven hundred persons, of both sexes, leaving alive scarcely enough to carry the news. The Indians, however, were soon driven from their homes by the fear of their powerful enemies; and as the French made no further attempt to occupy the place, it was left desolate until the year 1763, when it was ceded to Great Britain. From that time a few respectable settlers arrived from Europe, New England, and elsewhere; but the events which took place for some years subsequently were very unfavorable to the populating of the country.

The fort at Natchez was taken several times by the Spaniards, English, and Americans. In 1781, Governor Galvey, of Louisiana, conquered Florida, and by the treaty of Paris it was ceded to the United States.

On the 7th of April, 1798, congress, by an act, authorized the president of the United States to appoint commissioners to adjust the claims between Florida, Louisiana, and the acquired territory north of latitude thirty-one degrees and west of Chatahoochee river; and on the 10th of that month made provision for a territorial government. A territory was therefore formed, and named Mississippi territory, which included, not only the present state of Mississippi, but also that of Alabama. An act of congress was passed on the 9th of July, 1808, admitting a delegate from Mississippi; and on the 17th of June the assent of Georgia was demanded to the formation of two states out of Mississippi territory. But, although the demand was acceded to, it was not until December, 1817, that any change was made. A petition had been presented on the 21st of January, 1815, from the Mississippi legislature, praying that a state might be constituted. A favorable report on this petition was made in December, 1816; and by an act passed March 1st, 1817, the people were authorized to hold a convention, which assembled in July following. A constitution having been drawn up, it was adopted August 15th, and was confirmed by congress in December following.

The government consists of a governor, and a general assembly of two houses (a senate and a house of representatives). To be a candidate for the senate, a man must be twenty-six years of age, a citizen of the United States, for four years previously an inhabitant of the state, and one year an inhabitant of his district; he must hold, in his own right, three hundred acres of land in Mississippi, or an interest in real estate of one thousand dollars' value, at the time of election and for six months previously. Senators are elected for three years. To be candidate for a seat as a representative, citizenship of the United States is required; two years' residence in the state, and one year's residence in the county, city, or town of which he is candidate; an age of twenty-one years; and the ownership of one hundred and fifty acres of land, or five hundred dollars in real estate for six months.

Voters must be free white citizens of the United States; twenty-one years of age; residents of the state for the last year, and of their district for the last six months; enrolled in the militia, or exempts; or have paid a state or county tax.

The governor is elected by electors, and holds his office two years, and until his successor shall be duly qualified. He must be thirty years of age; twenty years a citizen of the United States; a resident of the state five years; and the owner of two thousand dollars for the past year.

There is a supreme court, and from four to eight judges of the supreme and superior courts, who hold office during good behavior, but may be removed by address to the governor of two thirds of both houses of the legislature, or by impeachment by the house before the senate. The age of sixty-five limits the term of judgeship. The sixth article of the seventh section of the constitution forbids any minister of the gospel or priest to hold the offices of governor, lieutenant-governor, or a place in the legislature. No officers of the United States, except postmasters, are admitted to offices in the state.

The geology of the western border of Mississippi has some most remarkable features. The land on the bank of the great river appears to have undergone wonderful revolutions; and recent investigations in the vicinity of Natchez have brought to light curiosities of the most interesting nature.

On the shore, at the foot of the bluff, are strewn great numbers of tubes, resembling, at first sight, the bodies of old trees, formed of iron ore, and filled with earth, and which appear to have fallen from the bank. The remains of numerous kinds of extinct animals are contained in the ground at different depths; while on the present surface a mound has been opened, which contains bones and implements of men of a race anterior to the present red men; and trees of great age were growing over the spot.

Population.—According to the census of 1850 the population of Mississippi was 605,488, by counties, as follows:—

Northern District.—Attila, 10,999; Bolivar, 2,577; Carroll, 18,485; Chickasaw, 16,368; Choctaw, 11,403; Coahoma, 2,780; De Soto, 18,052; Itawamba, 13,311; La Fayette, 14,069; Lowndes, 19,547; Marshall, 29,690; Monroe, 21,131; Noxubee, 16,257; Oktibbeha, 9,171; Panola, 11,459; Pontotoc, 17,112; Sunflower, 1,060; Tallahatchee, 4,643; Tippah, 20,740; Tishomingo, 15,148; Tunica, 1,314; Winston, 7,986; Yallabusha, 17,260. Total, 300,561; of which number 133,672 were slaves.

Southern District.—Adams, 18,621; Amite, 9,624; Claiborne, 14,903; Clarke, 5,477; Copiah, 11,710; Covington, 3,348, Franklin, 5,904; Green, 2,018; Hancock, 3,672; Harrison, 4,875; Hinds, 25,310; Holmes, 13,930; Issaquena, 4,478; Jackson, 3,196; Jasper, 6,174; Jefferson, 13,393; Jones, 2,135; Kemper, 12,517; Lauderdale, 8,708; Lawrence, 6,485; Leake, 5,535; Madison, 18,173; Marion, 4,410; Neshoba, 4,560; Newton, 4,466; Perry, 2,438; Pike, 7,357; Rankin, 7,227; Scott, 3,979; Simpson, 4,735; Smith, 4,071; Warren, 19,998; Washington, 8,389; Wayne, 2,892; Wilkinson, 16,638; Yazoo, 13,582. Total, 304,927, of which 174,495 were slaves.

Natchez, the principal town, is advantageously situated on the summit a side of a high bluff, on the eastern ba of Mississippi river, three hundred an one miles from New Orleans by the river; about five hundred miles from St. Louis, and one thousand one hundred and forty-six from Washington city.

The soil is rich, and the climate delightful in the winter. The vicinity is adorned with many fine residences, where elegant houses are seen embosomed in luxuriant groves, amid a wonderful profusion of flowers and fruits. The streets, which are straight and regularly laid out, are chiefly on the high ground, which is elevated from a hundred and fifty to two hundred feet above the river. The nature of the soil, however, is unfavorable for the situation of a town, as a loose sandstone-rock, which lies so low as to be observable only at low water, is the only substratum of a high bluff composed of clay, intermingled in some parts with sand. Violent rains, therefore, sometimes form large cavities in the surface, which is irregular and often changing. A large part of the lower town was destroyed a few years ago, by the falling of the bank near the water.

The houses are generally of wood, and many of them are constructed with taste, and adorned with trees and gardens. There are four churches, a courthouse, three banks, an academy, a female seminary, a masonic-hall, theatre, orphan asylum, hospital, &c. The population, at the present time, probably exceeds five thousand.

The wharves are the scene of active business, as an extensive trade is carried on in cotton, which is produced in great quantities in the neighborhood; and numerous boats, rafts, and steamboats, lie or touch at the wharves. The situation of the town, on a prominent elevation, distinguishes it as the principal place on this part of the Mississippi, where the banks are generally low, and almost invisible from the waters. It was as much distinguished in former times as at the present day, having been the residence of the most powerful Indian tribe in this region, whose chief, denominated the Great Sun, was undisputed ruler over the surrounding country, which he overlooked from his lofty fort on the summit of the bluff. This was the chief who permitted the French to erect Fort Rosalie on that eminence, but afterward massacred the garrison.

Steamboats arrive daily from New Orleans, and others depart for that important city; and a similar communication is kept up with St. Louis, Cincinnati, and the other principal places above, on the mighty river and some of its branches. Stagecoaches depart three times a week for Jackson and for St. Francisville, Louisiana.

The *Mississippi Railroad* leads to Washington, sixteen miles, and Malcolm, fourteen miles beyond.

The distance from Natchez to New Orleans by land is only two hundred and eleven miles. The route is first by stagecoach to Coldspring, twenty miles, and Woodville, fifteen miles; thence by railroad to Laurel hill, eleven miles, and St. Francisville, seventeen miles. The route then passes Port Hudson, Baton Rouge, Manchac, Iberville, New River, Donaldsville, Bringier's, Bonnet Carré, and Lafayette, two miles from New Orleans. From Natchez to Cincinnati (Ohio) the land-route is first by the railroad to Washington and Malcolm, then by stagecoaches through Gallatin, Jackson, Springfield, Louisville, Choctaw Agency, Columbus, Florence, and Nashville, to Cincinnati, seven hundred and sixty miles.

Some of the most remarkable features of the Mississippi river—the greatest stream of North America, and one of the largest in the world—are most easily observable from the elevated position which Natchez affords to the spectator. The tortuous course which it pursues, through a considerable part of its length, causes numerous eddies, one of the largest of which is in this vicinity. These eddies, when known and properly used by pilots, afford important facilities to vessels passing up the stream, as in some places they run northward for a considerable distance, at the rate of one, two, or more miles an hour. When not known, or when the navigator is deceived by the weather, they sometimes cause great embarrassment and loss of time. Some years ago, a flat-bottomed boat was passing down the river, with a load of produce for New Orleans, when the boatmen heard music at night on the neighboring shore. The air was then so misty, that it was impossible to distinguish distant objects; and they floated on for some time, until their ears were again greeted with a similar sound. At about an equal interval, music was again heard; and they came to the conclusion that the inhabitants of the bank were celebrating some general festival, presuming that they were passing one village, or hamlet, after another. Thus they continued to move on through a great part of the night, and judged they were making rapid progress on their voyage. Morning, however, at length dispelled the mists and their delusion. They found themselves in the great eddy, which has a regular sweep of about five miles at a particular stage of the water; and they had been floating round and round its wide circle for several hours, passing a solitary house, then distinguishable on the shore, where a small party had spent the time in mirth and music.

The looseness of the earth along the banks, and the low level of land in most places, give occasion to some surprising phenomena. The channels are continually liable to changes, as the current is strong enough to wear away the earth in any direction to which it may be turned, either by an obstruction or the removal of an obstacle. The earth thus torn away in one place is deposited in another, together with some of the particles brought down from the upper parts of the stream, or its branches, in the annual floods. A bank undermined soon falls, often with a mass of timber; and trees then float along, until stopped by some shoal, or entangled at the bottom. These, becoming imbedded by the rapid accumulation of sand, often stand fixed for years, and, if allowed to remain, expose the numerous rafts and boats to danger. The boatmen designate these obstructions by different names, according to the manner in which they are placed in the ground. A log or tree fixed upright in the bottom of the river is called a planter; one pointing upward in a slanting direction, and moveable by the current, is called a sawyer; one with numerous prongs or branches is denominated a snag. Of these the planter is often an object of the greatest dread, when wholly sunken, as it may penetrate a boat's bottom in an instant. A sawyer, also, is very dangerous; for while a boat lies against it, and is pressed upon it by the current, the motion of the water keeps the end of the log alternately rising and sinking, which may quickly cut through the side or upper works, and cause material injury.

Such, however, have been the labor and expense devoted by the United States government, for years past, to the clearing of the channels from obstructions, that few of these now remain in situations where they are likely to cause injury—though new changes, of course, require new care.

Natchez has frequently been visited by the yellow-fever, and with fatal effect; for although the state generally is far more healthful than Louisiana, some parts of it are not safe from this scourge of our southern regions, and this its principal town has suffered most severely. This must be assigned as one of the principal causes of the slow increase of population. The neighboring low ground, much of which is inundated by the river, must be the principal source of the contagion.

Jackson, the capital, is situated on Pearl river, on a plain about a quarter of a mile from its left bank, and is accessible in small vessels. The streets are regular, and the town contains several public buildings worthy of particular notice. The statehouse is a handsome edifice, and there are also the state-penitentiary, the governor's house, and the United States land-office. The number of inhabitants in 1850 was four thousand five hundred.

Centennary College, founded in 1841, is a methodist institution, and has a president, five professors, and about one hundred and seventy students.

A railroad leads to Vicksburg, and cars arrive and depart daily; and stage-coaches go to Nashville (Tennessee) via Columbus and Florence (Alabama), and to Gainesville. Those for Natchez go three times a week.

GRAND GULF.—This town bears the name of a remarkable bend in the Mississippi, on which it is built, three hundred and fifty-two miles above New Orleans. It has a townhall, an hospital, two churches, and a theatre. The population is about fifteen hundred. It has a daily communication with New Orleans by steam.

WASHINGTON.—This town has a pleasant situation, on a gentle elevation, six miles east of Natchez, and contains a few detached but neat and handsome dwellings. It has two churches, and is distinguished as the site of

Washington College.—This institution was founded in 1802, and received from congress an endowment in a grant of land. The buildings are of brick; and it contains a library of about one thousand volumes, a chemical apparatus, a geological collection, and specimens of various fossil remains, such as we have before referred to as being found in this vicinity.

Ellicot's spring is a fine source of water rising on the college grounds; several other springs in this neighborhood are remarkable for their excellent water.

PORT GIBSON.—This is a small town on Bayou Pierre; it is eight miles from Grand Gulf, and twenty-five miles from the Mississippi by water. It has three churches, a courthouse, an academy, and over two thousand inhabitants.

VICKSBURG.—This town is on the Mississippi, five hundred and thirteen miles from New Orleans by water, and is quite flourishing, though of recent date. It contains a courthouse, five churches, three academies, and a theatre, with about five thousand inhabitants. The surrounding region is very fertile, and the town makes a very picturesque appearance, presenting many clusters of dwellings, scattered along the declivity of several eminences, just below the Walnut hills. Steamboats from New Orleans arrive and depart daily, as well as from St. Louis (Missouri).

YAZOO CITY.—This town stands on Yazoo river, at the distance of four hundred and ninety-three miles from New Orleans, and is connected with it by steamboats. Stagecoaches go to Holly Springs three times a week. The population is only about eight hundred, but it is a place of considerable business, and contains several large stores.

HOLLY SPRINGS.—The situation of this town is elevated, on the summit of a range of hills near the headsprings of Yazoo river. The surrounding country is rich and pleasant. The number of inhabitants is about one thousand seven hundred, and the town contains a courthouse, an academy, and three churches. Stagecoaches go to Memphis every day, and depart three times in the week by several routes for La Grange, Tuscumbia (Alabama), Columbus, Jackson, Yazoo City, and Commerce.

COLUMBUS.—This town is one hundred and forty-one miles distant from the seat of government, on a hill on the left bank of Tombigbee river, one hundred and twenty feet above its level. The stream is crossed by a handsome bridge. The public buildings consist of a courthouse, an academy, two banks, five churches, a market, a theatre, and a female seminary. The population is about ten thousand.

Steamboats run from Columbus to Mobile, and stagecoaches depart every day for Jackson and Vicksburg, as well as for Nashville (Tenn.), through Tuscumbia, and three times a week for Pontotoc, Holly Springs, and Memphis.

The inundations of the low grounds adjacent to the lower parts of the Mississippi, are among the most striking phenomena connected with it. The bed of the stream is, in some places, much higher than the level of the adjacent fields, and whole plantations are actually below the surface of the river. The flood begins on the lower branches of the Mississippi, some time before the warm season is sufficiently advanced to melt the deeper snows in the more distant northerly parts, near its upper sources. The regions from which the floods are derived lie between latitude forty-two and fifty degrees, and at different elevations from twelve hundred to five thousand feet above the ocean. The heat of summer prevails at New Orleans some time before any change of elevation is made at the mouth of the river by the water derived from its head streams. About the end of February the waters begin to arrive from the lower tributaries which flow from regions of frost and snow. By gradual but irregular increase, the surface continues to rise from the end of that month, when the Red river pours in its early flood, until late in the summer, when the last surplus waters arrive from the snows melted long before on the elevated surface near the northern lakes.

The loneness of the bank of the Mississippi, along a great part of the western border of this state, with the loose nature of the alluvial soil, renders it almost impossible to erect even a single building near the water's edge, except at particular places, many of which are at considerable distances from each other. Yet along this part of the river it is peculiarly important to have depositories of wood for the use of steamboats, which consume fuel in such quantities that a full supply can not be taken in at the commencement of the voyage. So great is the demand, that, in spite of the numerous obstacles interposed by nature, *wooding stations*, as they are called, have been established in considerable numbers, some by driving piles into the bank, and laying platforms on the top, elevated sufficiently to be above the floods; and there quantities of wood, cut for the steamers' furnaces, are piled, and small tenements erected barely sufficient for the habitation of a few persons, and sometimes designed only for a single man. These are the only stopping-places for steamboats in long distances, where towns are rare; and only here has the traveller any opportunity to observe the river's banks, or any of the productions of nature, sometimes so attractive to a naturalist.

The reader is referred to the vignette at the head of this description, for an accurate representation of a Mississippi "wooding station;" as a view of it will naturally impress the mind with ideas of the great loneliness of such a retreat, especially at seasons when least visited by passing boats; and with those of gloom and danger during the inundations, when the inhabitants are situated in the midst of a wide expanse of water, with an irresistible current sweeping along, wearing away the unstable foundations of their fabric, and threatening to scatter its parts over the face of the waters, leaving them no ark for safety.

ANTIQUITIES. — Some persons have fancied a resemblance between some of the remains of former inhabitants found in the western mounds, and those discovered in the pyramids, catacombs, and other depositories of ancient times in the old world. The following remarks on the subject we abbreviate from the remarks of Mr. Squier, who has been successfully engaged in examining many of the remains in the west:—

"There are many coincidences between the remains of antiquity in the old and new worlds; but coincidences do not necessarily imply community of origin, or even regular or accidental intercourse. . . . The wants of man, his hopes and ambition, have always and everywhere been very much the same, and have, almost of necessity, resulted in common methods of gratification. . . . . . The comparisons which I shall make between the ancient remains of our own country and those of Egypt, are instituted with no view to prove an identity of origin, but as a new and curious illustration of the philosophical axiom already laid down. Upon one hand, we have the monuments of a people whose hieroglyphical annals are now resuscitated by the Champollionists, around whom cluster the recollections of more than five thousand years, the subject alike of sacred and profane history; upon the other, the relics of a race respecting whom the voice of History is mute, and whose very name is lost to tradition itself. . . . . The pyramid is but a *developed mound*, marking in its superior structure only a more advanced stage of man's progress. Many of the large mounds of the Mississippi valley were places of sepulture—not for the mass of the people, as has been generrally supposed, but for chieftains; and, like the pyramids, had sepulchral chambers—not lined with polished granite in massive blocks, but built of timber or of unhewn stones. As in the pyramids, these chambers were constructed at the base, and the dead body, after proper envelopment, deposited within them, with its ornaments and badges of power and authority. The great mound at Grave creek, like the great pyramid of Ghiza, had two chambers, one placed thirty feet above the other—occupying, indeed, the same relative positions in respect to each other and the structure in which they were contained. The explanation of the circumstance is undoubtedly the same in both cases—the upper part containing a subsequent deposite, perhaps the son or successor of the occupant of the lower and earlier chamber. . . .

"We need not go out of our own country to mark the gradual development of the mound tombs. As we go southward, we find them increasing both in size and regularity. In Louisiana, *brick* enters into their construction; and in Mexico, they pass into the regular pyramidal form, are built of stone, and rival the monuments of Egypt in size. The large pyramid of Teotihuacan is not less than two hundred and twenty-one feet in height, with a base six hundred and eighty-two feet square. It is built of stones cemented together, and the whole was originally coated with a layer of pure white cement. The second pyramid, which has been most thoroughly investigated, has interior chambers, communicating with the exterior by narrow passages, lined with brick. Surrounding these, as the tombs cluster around the Memphite pyramids, are thousands of small monuments, which were significantly designated, by the ancient inhabitants, the *Micoatl*, or Path of the Dead.

"The mound-builders used copper axes, identical with those of Egypt, Peru, and Mexico."

Mr. Squier has collected several copper axes from the mounds, in contrast with those of the several nations above named, between which it was difficult, if not impossible, to distinguish. He also possesses some axes of flint and green stone from Denmark, and others from the mounds, which display an identity of shape and workmanship; also, some copper bracelets from the mounds, perfect counterparts of some in Mr. Gliddon's collection from Egypt; also some beads of blue and green enamel or glass, the production of one of the western Indian tribes of the present day, hardly distinguishable from similar Egyptian ornaments. He also adverted in further illustration to the subject of pottery.

"In their pottery," he continues, "we also observe marked resemblances, both in shape, material, and finish. In all primitive earthen vessels (found only in alluvial countries in ancient times), we recognise the gourd as the model: the vessel, in the first instance, being formed over the shell, which was afterward removed by fire. Upon this natural suggestion—a hint which nature everywhere holds out—man has improved in his course of development, and the elegant vase has supplanted the gourd-shaped vessel of his primitive artisanship. In some of the sculptures found in the mounds, we have singular, but undoubtedly entirely accidental, coincidences in form with those to which peculiar significance was attached by the Egyptians. The hawk with a human head, sculptured from the hardest porphyry, closely resembles the symbolical representation of the *soul* which appears sculptured on Egyptian tombs. The crane in the attitude of striking a fish, also exquisitely sculptured in porphyry, is the universal hieroglyphical symbol, signifying to fish, fishing, or fisher. . .

"It has been a very favorite theory to derive the ancient or early Americans, in whole or part, for Egypt and Hindostan; and an equally favorite one to transport them from Palestine, from Tartary, and even from the north of Europe! Volumes have been written in support of these theories, and the most sweeping conclusions have been advanced, based upon coincidences less striking than those here pointed out."

In relation to the various quadrupeds which once existed in this region, recent scientific observations have brought to light evidences more definite and certain. The mastodon, mammoth, &c., have left their bones here; while the origin of the ancient race of men is conjectural.

LOUISIANA.

This state is, in many respects, the most peculiar country on the globe. Its southern border rests upon the gulf of Mexico, a vast inland sea, in latitude below twenty-nine degrees north; its northern boundary reaches to thirty-three degrees; its eastern boundary is the Pearl river, which separates it from Alabama, to latitude thirty-one degrees, when the great Mississippi becomes the dividing line from the state that receives its name; while its western extremity is limited by the Sabine.

The whole southern portion of this state, over three hundred miles in length by an average width of nearly seventy-five miles, is exclusively an alluvial deposite. If to this be added similar deposites on the great river and its tributaries above, it presents a delta of comparatively recent formation, far surpassing any other, within the same compass, in any quarter of the world. Even those of the Nile, the Euphrates, and every other large river except the Ganges, are inconsiderable formations in comparison with this magnificent encroachment on the ocean bed. And still the struggle is onward and irresistible. The vast body of water which debouches into the gulf from several mouths, has its rise more than five thousand miles above, by the course of the stream; and from its remotest source, and by every one of its innumerable branches, it is bringing down the ancient elevations, and spreading them over the tidewaters, the future fruitful abode of civilized man.

Opposite the city of New Orleans, the trunk of the river has a breadth of two thousand five hundred feet, with an average depth of one hundred, through which the water passes with a mean velocity of two feet per second. During a flood, this velocity is greatly augmented, and the water contains about a thousandth part by weight, and a two-thousandth part by bulk, of purely earthy matter, yielding a daily deposite of nearly one million, four hundred thousand tons! The effect of this immense floating alluvion is seen in the gradual deposites and elevation of the lowlands bordering the principal stream, and its numerous bayous and collateral branches, the accretions on the levée opposite the centre of the city (which have extended the bank several hundred feet within a few years), and the constant and rapid extension of the land at the mouth. The late Judge Martin states that "the old Balize, a post erected by the French in 1724, at the mouth of the river, was two miles above it in 1827."

Everywhere on the banks of the passing stream the land is highest; as the water charged with floating matter overflows its brim, and becomes comparatively stagnant, allowing a large portion of the solid material to subside, while the partially-purified water passes onward through other channels to the gulf. The result of this is to give a higher arable surface for some distance from the banks, while that portion of the land remote from them subsides into irreclaimable swamps, and frequently navigable lakes and lagoons. The natural elevation of the banks is not yet sufficient to prevent the overflow from floods; and this object is secured by artificial levées, or embankments, on both sides, which extend in a continuous line for hundreds of miles on the main stream and its collateral channels. The slow accumulation and consequent elevation of the surrounding country from deposites, which would otherwise have been going forward, is thus arrested; and the present low swampy surface must forever continue unreclaimed, till embankments on the lower sides, and the artificial removal of the waters, bring portions of it into a condition for future cultivation. Could the hand of civilization and modern improvement have been arrested for a few centuries longer, till nature had finished what she has so auspiciously commenced, large additions, and in a state far more fitted to reward their efforts, would have been subjected to their control.

The delta of the Mississippi is similar in its character, though on an immeasurably larger scale, to that formed around and below the junction of the Alabama and Tombigbee rivers, and extending into Mobile bay. Here it is apparent that the waters of the bay once extended high up the stream, and embraced what are now the low, level banks on either side. The same is true of the mouths of the Pearl, Pascagoula, and other smaller streams, which lie between those larger rivers; and we are thus inevitably forced to the conclusion, that the inner channels which lie within the islands stretching from Mobile to Lake Borgne, inclusive of this, and Lakes Pontchartrain and Maurepas, and the innumerable other smaller lakes and bayous which intersect the whole delta of the Mississippi, have been rescued from the tidewaters within a recent period. And there is scarcely a doubt that this former arm of the gulf once extended up the Yazoo, the Red river, and some other of the smaller rivers, all of whose banks are intersected by numerous channels, through which the waters flow into the adjoining streams, as either has the ascendency from recent floods on its upper branches. These interlocking with each other in every direction, and all at last terminating in the gulf, separate the entire delta into a perfect network of islands. The land seldom rises beyond a few feet above lowwater-mark, and, from the banks, gradually subsides into the swamps, lagoons, and lakes in the rear. The latter are sometimes deep, but are usually shallow, with the slightest declination from a level as they recede from the shore; while the shorter and more direct channels, through which the water flows to the gulf with fearful rapidity in times of floods, are generally narrow and of immense depth, frequently exceeding one hundred feet. The coast is usually a low receding line, so obscurely defined as to leave it questionable, for miles, where the water ends and the land begins.

The condition of the surface clearly indicates that *draining* is the first and paramount object in the cultivation of the alluvial land of Louisiana. This has accordingly been practised to an extent far beyond anything elsewhere in the United States. Large ditches running from the banks of the river and bayous to the swamps in the rear, intersected by numerous cross excavations of a less depth, effectually drain off the surface-water.

GEOLOGY.—The following is an interesting detail of observations, made during an experiment of boring for fresh water to the depth of two hundred and six feet below the surface, at the mouth of Bayou St. John, New Orleans, by the superintendent of the work :—

"From the surface to 18 feet, vegetable mould, wood, &c., very impure—so much so, that, although in the month of February, the smell was almost insupportable; from 18 to 28 feet, blue clay or vegetable mould, but not so impure as the first 18 feet; 28 to 33, sand, shells; 33 to 40, dark, fine sand, free from shells; 40 to 43, sand, clay, shells, and vegetable matter, but a very large portion of shells; 43 to 66, blue clay, sand, and shells, but mostly clay—the last 10 feet, clear clay, and very hard, dry, and adhesive, the strata growing lighter to pale yellow; 66 to 77, fine, beautiful yellow sand, containing a large quantity of mica, also petrifactions and indurated clay—this stratum was very strongly impregnated with sulphur, so much so as to render the water offensive to the smell; 77 to 87, pale clay, vegetable mould, and sand, very compact and hard; 87 to 118, blue clay or mould, intermixed with some sand; 118 to 119½, sand, clay, and shells; 119½ to 137, the same strata of blue clay or mould, intermixed with some fine sand, the color growing a little paler, intermixed toward the bottom with many shells.

"In passing this stratum from 120 to 137 feet, we found a great number of pieces of limestone; in some parts of it we found it difficult to get our tube down to them, they were so numerous; in fact, the whole stratum is evidently rapidly becoming a limestone-rock. 137 to 140, sand, very fine, of a brown color, containing a large portion of mica; 140 to 145, alternate thin strata of sand and clay—the clay extremely hard, firm, and beautiful, when fresh not unlike chocolate in appearance; 145 to 171, clay, or mould, of a variety of colors, intermixed with some sand, likewise a substance much resembling fuller's earth. This stratum at first was nearly white. After penetrating it about two feet, it became darker and extremely hard and compact, also very adhesive, and capable of being cut in very thin pieces with a knife.

"In this stratum, at 168 feet, passed a few inches of sand, but below to 171 feet, the stratum the same again; 171 to 184, strata same as above; 184 to 192, sand, shells, and mould: in this stratum we found shells of almost every variety found in this vicinity; also, what appeared to have been a whole crab, but broken by the instrument in getting it up; the claws were very perfect, so that the joints might be worked by the finger; also a bone of about two inches in length, and evidently broken, supposed to be a bone of a deer; also pieces of wood, in a high state of preservation, apparently cypress. 192 to 194, sand and mould intermixed, two inches of sand and stones, apparently in a rapid state of formation; 194 to 196, mould and sand, very hard, of a greenish color; 196 to 199, alternate strata of mould and sand, containing many stones, apparently forming rock; 199 to 201, sand and clay, in alternate veins, containing much water; 201 to 202½, clay of a light pale color; 202½ to 203½, clay and mould of a dark color, very hard and beautiful—the division in the color was very distinct; 203½ to 206, the same as from 201 to 202½.

"The soil alluded to called clay, is in all probability a formation of vegetable and mud of the Mississippi. I have found that when dry it becomes very light, and some of it has much the appearance of wood or other vegetable substance."

New Orleans is the principal city of

Louisiana, and great commercial emporium of the southwest, enjoying advantages possessed by few cities in the world. Indeed, there is probably no other which can be considered equal to it, in the several leading points of being the grand mart of a river so extensive, with so many navigable branches, flowing through regions of fertility, occupied and fast peopling by a race possessing all the arts of civilization, and all the advantages of our united, free, and powerful government. Under the direction of modern science and art, the rapid current of the Mississippi has been rendered eminently subservient to the commerce of this city; for, without steamboats, the immense productions of the great valley would still have been retarded, in their way to their only natural market, by the dangers of the descending navigation and the difficulties and delays of the return. It is scarcely twenty years since the corn, hogs, and other articles, annually sent to New Orleans, were taken down in arks and on rafts, by men who could hope to arrive in safety only by incessant watchfulness and frequent labor, among the shoals and snags of the river, and who had no resource left them, after reaching the city, than to break up their vessel (if such it might be called), sell it for lumber, and then travel home on foot.

Cotton.—The immense cotton trade of the United States, of which a large portion is carried on at New Orleans, has so important relations with the manufactures, commerce, and condition of Europe, and is liable to so many fluctuations, that much of the attention of merchants is annually turned to this city. The following facts will assist the reader in appreciating the present importance of our great emporium of the west, though its prospects are so great as to fill the mind with astonishment, when we look forward to the increase of population, and indulge the hope that divine Providence will perpetuate our Union, and continue our national prosperity.

Europe is almost entirely dependent on the United States for cotton, although England and France have endeavored to secure supplies from other sources. Formerly North Carolina and Virginia formed our principal dépôts for American cotton; under the influence of receding prices, these states had to yield to the greater fertility of new land, and Georgia became the largest cotton-growing state in the Union. In its turn, however, Georgia has declined before the productions of Mississippi; and the right bank of the Mississippi river may, in its turn, supply that production, which the cultivation of corn and sugar may supersede, if proved to be the more remunerating crops. There is, however, a limit to this. So far as we know, cotton can only be grown, to any extent, in that portion of the United States known as the southwestern states. In other countries, the cultivation has not succeeded to the desired extent—a weak and useless fibre being the result of much enterprise and capital. But whatever be the amount of cotton hereafter raised in Louisiana, Alabama, and Mississippi, an immense annual supply of produce must be brought to New Orleans.

Civil Divisions.—Louisiana is divided into parishes, after the old French plan, as follows:—

Eastern District.—Ascension, Assumption, Baton Rouge (West and East), Feliciana (West and East), Iberville, Jefferson, La Fourche, Livingston, Orleans, Plaquemine, Point Coupee, St. Bernard, St. Charles, St. Helena, St. James, St. John Baptist, St. Tammany, Terra Bonne, Washington.

Western District.—Avoyelles, Bienville, Bossier, Caddo, Calcasieu, Caldwell, Carroll, Catahoula, Claiborne, Concordia, De Soto, Franklin, Jackson, La Fayette, Madison, Morehouse, Natchitoches, Ouchita, Rapides, Sabine, St. Landry, St. Martin, St. Mary, Tensas, Union, Vermillion.

Population.—In 1785, while under the government of Spain, Louisiana contained 27,283 inhabitants. In 1810, under the government of the United States, it had 75,556. In 1820, 153,407; in 1830, 215,575; in 1840, 352,411; and by the census of 1850, 500,762.

Surface and State of the Country.—Three quarters of the whole state is said to be destitute of everything that might be called a hill. A hilly range commences at Opelousas and extends toward the Sabine river, running about equally distant between that stream and Red river. Gradually rising, it assumes at length the aspect of mountains. Another ridge lies between Red river and the Dudgemony. The whole state, however, with small exceptions, may be regarded as a succession of pine woods with a gently rolling surface, prairies, alluvions, swamps, and hickory and oak lands. The prairies, in many places, present the peculiar characteristics of those extensive level tracts properly known by that name in other parts of the west and southwest, being unvaried even by a single elevation, and in summer overgrown with a uniform coat of grass, richly besprinkled with flowers of various hues.

Large quantities of swampy land remain unreclaimed, which is of a rich soil, capable of yielding abundant crops of sugarcane; but various obstacles still prevent its improvement. Draining is the first step necessary: but the backwardness of emigrants in choosing the plains of Louisiana, caused partly by the fear of disease and partly by unsettled land-titles, prevents that advance in prosperity which could be desired. The sickliness of the climate is exaggerated; for, although the yellow-fever has often been fatal in some parts of the country as well as in New Orleans, the general impression at a distance doubtless exceeds the reality; and some parts of the state are as healthful as any parts of our country. This is particularly the fact with the pine hills; and that unwholesome miasmata of the lower, marshy lands would doubtless be in a great degree destroyed, if a good system of drainage were once formed.

Sugar-making.—The making of sugar on a large scale, in this state, is of but recent date; yet it already forms a most important and lucrative branch of business, and is so rapidly increasing, with so great improvements in the different methods and processes, that it threatens almost to absorb the attention, labor, and capital of the state. Science was early called in, and practical experience was not overlooked, when this branch of production and manufacture was first zealously commenced in the United States. When it had been ascertained that much of the soil of Louisiana was adapted to the growth of the cane, and that it could be raised with great pecuniary advantage, the government of the United States had the judgment to employ the distinguished chemist Professor Silliman, of Yale college, to examine the subject in its various aspects; and his report presented a most valuable collection of facts, for the guidance of congress in making regulations for the encouragement of the business, as well as of the agriculturists and manufacturers entering into it.

The following brief description of the manufacturing processes, is copied from a series of letters published in the New York Express, in June and July, 1847:—

"In the northern states comparatively little is known as regards either the culture or growth of the cane, or the many and varied principles of manufacturing its rich juice into sugar; yet we may anticipate that a more perfect knowledge of this branch of industry will soon be apparent. Texas and all parts south of South Carolina are adapted to the planting of cane, and for several reasons all those places will become sugar-growing districts. Cotton-planting, which used to be prosecuted with such vigor, is now gradually dying away; the staple article, sugar, is fast usurping its place; the cottonfield is changed to the sugar-cane, and the ginhouse to the sugar-house. The production of sugar has gradually increased up to the crop of 1845–'6; but the crop of 1846–'7 fell short of even 1841, being only about one hundred and thirty thousand hogsheads of a thousand pounds each, and about four and a half millions of gallons of molasses. Although this was a very small crop, it sold for more money than the largest crop ever produced in America, probably on account of England now admitting slave-grown sugar. The short crop of last year may be partly attributed to the unpropitious season. This year, so far, has the most auspicious appearances; the planters have planted upon new principles; the season has been very dry, but the extraordinary height of the Mississippi has amply made up for it, the transpiration water having found its way through the lands. According to Creole theory, this is a good omen: 'A high river, a great crop.' There are near two thousand plantations in operation this year; and as I have lately visited the majority of them, from what I can see and learn, the crop of next gathering (all well) will amount to three hundred thousand hogsheads of one thousand pounds each, and nine millions of gallons of molasses. To give some idea to those unacquainted with the manufacturing of this domestic article, I will give some data, which I trust will prove interesting.

"One gallon of cane-juice generally makes one pound of sugar; therefore, three hundred millions of gallons of cane-juice must be expressed to obtain this quantity of sugar. To give some idea of this quantity of liquid, provided it was water, and supposing the city of New York in a state of blockade, it would be sufficient to serve the inhabitants for four years' subsistence.

"A large quantity of white and refined sugar will be made direct from the cane next grinding, some planters having procured very expensive machinery and apparatus for that purpose. The insides of most of the sugarhouses on the Mississippi are quite familiar to me, some of which have cost over fifty thousand dollars in improvements. A much less quantity of molasses will be made next crop, according to the quantity of sugar produced, than is customary.

"It is of little use to enter into a description of the old mode of sugar-making. Cane, like other things, may in time become acclimated; consequently, experience teaches us how to humor it. We now plant cane in rows eight and nine feet apart instead of, as originally, four and five feet. It thrives better; receives more fresh air, more sun, more nourishment; grows larger and stronger; requires less seed and labor; and gives more sugar to the arpent.

"After the cane is cut, it is brought to the mill, where it is ground to express the juice. However, the best of mills do not take out all the juice, some sixteen or eighteen per cent. remaining in the baggasse or frosh. A second two-roller mill was introduced at considerable expense, requiring much power, the drawbacks on which will prevent its general adoption; however, to obviate this, and obtain fifteen per cent. of the lost juice, a revolving-doctor is about to be adopted, which, though cheap, will answer every purpose, when applied to old or new mills. The cane-juice is now carried into large wooden boxes called clarifiers, where it is heated to two hundred degrees Fahrenheit, by steampipes, and receives a small dose of flake-lime; this regulates acidity, and cleans the juice to a certain extent. The juice is now at about nine and a half or ten degrees saccharometer; it is now run off into open boxes heated by steampipes, where it is boiled and scummed, passing from one box, called the grand, to another, called the battery, where it is concentrated until its boiling point reaches two hundred and eighteen degrees Fahrenheit; it is now let off into an elevator, so as to be risen up into a cistern of considerable altitude previous to its going through the further operation of filtering, &c.

"I would here state the reason of its having to go into an elevator: the mills are set too low for the juice to run from one vessel to another, for the purpose of its going through the various processes, according to the new plans of sugar-manufacture. This elevator is a kind of cylinder-boiler set on end; when this is full, steam is turned into it, which, pressing on the surface of the syrup, forces it through a pipe attached to the cotton leading up to the receiver above. This is far from being an economical mode of raising fluids, but it is better than pumps, as it does not oxydize the syrup. However, a more simple, cheap, and effective mode, upon the principle of waste steam forming a vacuum in the upper cistern, will soon come into general use. The next process through which this concentrated cane-juice has to pass is the bag-filters; these are a series of large fine-duck bags, neatly folded up, and placed in a cylindrical small case of the same material; they are suspended by the neck on metal rings, and hang down in a square wooden box, where the juice drips through, leaving dirt, sediment, &c., inside the bags. This is rather an old-fashioned process. A new plan will shortly take its place, upon a hydrostatical principle—the pure liquid passing through compressed sponge.

"The next process through which syrups pass is that of the vacuum-pan, of which there is a great variety. The original and perhaps the best one is known as the Howard vacuum-pan—Mr. Howard being the inventor and patentee. In fact, all others are mere modifications. Another, called De Rosne's, is both simple and good, and very much used; it is this which I will describe, although there are several others daily coming into use, viz.: the Bevan pan, Morgan pan, and Rillieux pan. This last stands rather high—sugar made by it having received awards and premiums from the Louisiana Agriculturists' and Mechanics' association more than once. Yet the pans of De Rosne and Howard, simple and cheap as they are, have produced the best sugar ever made in Louisiana.

"The De Rosne pan is a cylinder of cast-iron, with a wrought-iron steam-jacket, for the purpose of admitting steam for boiling the charge. It has also copper pipes passing up and down its inside for the same purpose—that is, to accelerate evaporation. This pan being air-tight and filled with syrup, steam is turned on for the purpose of boiling. At the same time the steam-engine is started to work the airpumps, the vacuum being formed and maintained in the following manner: a pipe attached to the dome of the pan, of sufficient capacity to carry off all the vapor given off by ebullition, leads into a large, tight iron vessel, constantly supplied with cold water. This is the condenser. The air-pumps remove all the vapor cold-water, and draw in fresh to renew and carry on condensation, and thus is the vacuum kept up as indicated by the barometer, from thirteen to fourteen pounds per square inch. The surface of the liquid thus relieved from pressure boils at about one hundred and thirty degrees Fahrenheit. Thus a large grain and fair sugars are obtained."

New Orleans.—This city is situated on the left bank of Mississippi river, which has here a singular curve, that places the city on its northwest side, and facing to the southeast. It is one hundred and five miles from its mouth, by the course of the river, but only ninety in a direct line. It is about eleven hundred miles from St. Louis, fourteen hundred from New York, and twelve hundred from Washington. New Orleans is the fourth city, in point of population, and the third in commerce, in the United States. Its rapid increase in population has not been equalled, probably, by that of any other city in the Union. In 1810, it was 17,242; in 1820, 27,176; in 1830, 46,310; in 1840, 102,193; in 1850, 119,285.

The old city proper is in form a parallelogram. Above the city are the suburbs of St. Mary and Annunciation, and below are the suburbs of Marigny, Franklin, and Washington. These are called fauxbourgs. Between the city and the bayou St. John's are the villages of St. Claude and St. Johnsburg. The old city proper was laid out by the French, and now forms not more than one eighth of the city limits, and not more than one fourth of its thickly-settled parts. The coup d'œil of the city when seen from the river is extremely beautiful. Many of the principal streets making a curve, from the shape of the city, New Orleans has been called the "Crescent city."

The public buildings are the United States branch mint, which is an edifice of the Ionic order of architecture, merchants' exchange, commercial exchange, city exchange, city-hall, courthouse, the statehouse, formerly the charity hospital, sixteen churches, some of them elegant buildings, four orphan asylums, three theatres, and several large and splendid hotels.

The situation of New Orleans for commerce is very commanding. The length of the Mississippi river, and its

View of New Orleans.

connected waters, which are navigated by steam, is not less than 20,000 miles, and the country which they drain is not surpassed in fertility by any on the globe. Its advantages for communication with the country in its immediate vicinity are also great. By a canal four and a half miles long, it communicates with Lake Pontchartrain, and its connected ports. This canal cost $1,000,000. There is also a canal, one and one fourth miles long, which communicates with Lake Pontchartrain through bayou St. John. A railroad, four and a half miles long, connects it with Carrollton. A railroad, four and one fourth miles long, connects the city with Lake Pontchartrain one mile east of bayou St. John. The Mexican gulf railroad extends twenty-four miles, to Lake Borgne, and is to be continued to the gulf, at the South pass. The Mississippi, opposite to the city, is half a mile wide, and from one hundred to one hundred and sixty feet deep, and continues of this depth to near its entrance into the ocean, where are bars, with from thirteen and a half to sixteen feet of water.

An embankment, called the Levee, is raised on the river's border, to protect the city. The Levee is from twenty to forty feet broad, but in front of the second municipality is extended to five or six hundred feet broad. This forms a splendid promenade, and a very convenient place for depositing the cotton and other produce from the upper country, which can be rolled directly from the decks of the steamers to the bank of the river.

The harbor presents an area of many acres, covered with flat-boats and keel-boats in its upper parts. Sloops, schooners, and brigs, are arranged along its wharves, and present a forest of masts; and steamboats are continually arriving or departing. The amount of domestic articles exported exceeds $12,000,000 annually, being greater than those of any other city in the Union, excepting New York. The houses of the city proper have a French and Spanish aspect, are generally stuccoed, and are of a white or yellow color.

The city proper contains sixty-six complete squares: each square having a front of three hundred and nineteen feet in length. Few of the streets, excepting Canal street, are more than forty feet wide. Many of the seats in the suburbs are surrounded with spacious gardens, splendidly ornamented with orange, lemon, magnolia, and other trees. No city in the United States has so great a variety of inhabitants, with such an astonishing contrast of manners, language, and complexion. The French population probably still predominates over the American, though the latter is continually gaining ground.

A mistaken impression prevails in some sections of the Union, in relation to the moral character, and healthfulness of the climate, of the Crescent city. But while not free from those evils incident to all large and crowded populations, still, in proportion to its size, New Orleans is as free from vice as any other city of the Union. The yellow fever is but little more to be dreaded than those pulmonary complaints which yearly sweep away so many thousands of victims at the north. And as to the dampness of the land, that is yearly becoming of less account as the cultivation and second soil more and more dwindle away its evil effects. For personal safety, men, women, and children, are as secure from insult or injury there, at all times, and under all circumstances, as in any city in the world.

The Battle of New Orleans.—This city has been rendered memorable as being the scene of the last battle in the war of 1812–'14, with Great Britain, a brief detail of which will close our notice of New Orleans.—In the month of December, 1814, fifteen thousand British troops, under Sir Edward Packenham, were landed for the attack of New Orleans. The defence of this place was intrusted to Gen. Andrew Jackson, whose force was about six thousand men, chiefly raw militia. Several slight skirmishes occurred before the enemy arrived before the city: during this time, Gen. Jackson was employed in making preparation for his defence. His front was a straight line of about one thousand yards, defended by upward of three thousand infantry and artillerists. The ditch contained five feet of water, and his front, from having been flooded by opening the levees, and by frequent rains, was rendered slippery and muddy. Eight distinct batteries were judiciously disposed, mounting in all twelve guns of different calibres. On the opposite side of the river was a strong battery of fifteen guns.

At daylight, on the morning of the 8th of January, the main body of the British, under their commander-in-chief, General Packenham, were seen advancing from their encampment to storm the American lines. On the preceding evening they had erected a battery within eight hundred yards, which now opened a brisk fire to protect their advance. They were suffered to approach in silence, and unmolested, until within three hundred yards of the lines, when the whole artillery at once opened upon them a most deadly fire. Forty pieces of cannon, deeply charged with grape, canister, and musket balls, mowed them down by hundreds, at the same time the batteries on the west bank opened their fire, while the riflemen, in perfect security behind their works, as the British advanced, took deliberate aim, and nearly every shot took effect. Through this destructive fire, the British left column, under the immediate orders of the commander-in-chief, rushed on with their fascines and scaling ladders, to the advance bastion on the American right, and succeeded in mounting the parapet; here, after a close conflict with the bayonet, they succeeded in obtaining possession of the bastion; when the battery, planted in the rear for its protection, opened its fire, and drove the British from the ground. On the American left, the British attempted to pass the swamp, and gain the rear, but the works had been extended as far into the swamp as the ground would permit. Some who attempted it, sunk in the mire and disappeared; those behind, seeing the fate of their companions, seasonably retreated, and gained the hard ground. The assault continued an hour and a quarter; during the whole time, the British were exposed to the deliberate and destructive fire of the American artillery and musketry, which lay in perfect security behind their breastworks of cotton bales, which no balls could penetrate. At eight o'clock, the British columns drew off in confusion, and retreated behind their works. Flushed with success, the militia were eager to pursue the British troops to their intrenchments, and drive them immediately from the island. A less prudent and accomplished general might have been induced to yield to the indiscreet ardor of his troops; but General Jackson understood too well the nature of his own and his enemy's force, to hazard such an attempt. Defeat must inevitably have attended an assault made by raw militia, upon an intrenched camp of British regulars. The defence of New Orleans was the object; nothing was to be hazarded which would jeopard the city. The British were suffered to retire behind their works without molestation. The result was such as might have been expected from the different positions of the two armies. Before eight o'clock, the three generals were carried off the field, two in the agonies of death, and the third entirely disabled; leaving upward of two thousand of their men dead, dying, and wounded, on the field of battle.

On the 9th, General Lambert and Admiral Cochrane, with the surviving officers of the army, held a council of war, and determined to abandon the expedition. To withdraw the troops in the face of a victorious enemy, would have been difficult and hazardous. To withdraw in safety, every appearance of a renewal of the assault was kept up, till the night of the 18th, when the whole army moved off in one body, over a road which had been previously constructed through a miry slough, in which a number of the troops perished by sinking into the mire. On the 27th, the whole land and naval forces which remained of this disastrous expedition, found themselves on board of their ships, with their ranks thinned, their chiefs and many of their companions slain, their bodies emaciated by hunger, fatigue, and sickness.

Baton Rouge.—This town, the capital of the state, is one hundred and forty miles above New Orleans, on the left bank of the Mississippi, standing chiefly on a plain elevated about thirty feet above the water, except the business streets, which are on the low ground along the shore.

The public buildings are the court-house, state-penitentiary, United States land-office, a college, an academy, three banks, and four churches. The population is about four thousand five hundred.

The college was founded in 1823, and has four professors, one thousand volumes in its library, and about fifty students. Steamboats communicate daily with New Orleans, Vicksburg, &c., and stagecoaches run to New Orleans and St. Francisville.

DONALDSONVILLE, ninety miles above New Orleans, stands on the west side of the river, at the point where the La Fourche fork leaves the main stream.

GALVEZTOWN stands on Bayou Manchac, and is in the village of Iberville, at a short distance from the place where it enters Lake Pontchartrain. It is a small town, twenty miles north-northeast from Donaldsonville, and twenty-five southeast of Baton Rouge.

SPRINGFIELD is a post village in the southeast part of the parish of St. Helena, eleven miles southeast of St. Helena, and eighty miles northwest of New Orleans.

MADISONVILLE.—This village is also a seaport, and belongs to the parish of St. Tammany, at the mouth of Chifuncte river. It is about twenty-eight miles north of New Orleans, on the opposite side of Lake Pontchartrain, in latitude thirty degrees twenty minutes.

The situation is so healthful that the place has been much resorted to by citizens of New Orleans during the warm and sickly seasons, and it contains several houses designed for the accommodation of visiters. Some years ago the government attempted to establish a navyyard a few miles above, on the river's bank.

COVINGTON, seven miles above Madisonville, is a considerable village, and stands on a branch of the Chifuncte, called the Bogue Falaya. It is the seat of justice for the parish of St. Tammany, and at the head of navigation in schooners. A considerable quantity of cotton is, therefore, annually shipped here. General Jackson's road, from Lake Pontchartrain to Nashville, passes through Covington. It is one of the favorite places of resort from New Orleans in the sickly months.

OPELOUSAS, two hundred and seventy miles from New Orleans, is the seat of justice of the parish to which it belongs, had a rapid growth a few years since, and is surrounded by a flourishing region. It stands on Bayou Bourbee, the head branch of Vermilion river, and a branch of Teche river rises just in the rear of the village. Large heads of horses and cattle, abounding on the extensive plain in the neighborhood, with the abundant and varied productions of the earth, give an interesting aspect to this place. Before the addition of Texas to the United States, Opelousas was the most southwest village in the country.

New Iberia and St. Martinsville are two other villages on the banks of the Teche, both on the west side; the latter, being at the head of schooner navigation, and surrounded by a fertile country, promises much increase.

ALEXANDRIA, on Red river, seventy miles from the Mississippi, is situated half a mile below the falls, at the mouth of Bayou Rapide. It is in the centre of several extensive and fertile cotton districts, and is a seat of justice. The village is thickly shaded by groves of China-trees, in the midst of a beautiful plain. It is the scene of an active trade in cotton.

COUNTRY LIFE IN LOUISIANA.—We copy from a late writer the following description of the house of a Louisiana planter, which applies to those common on the banks of the Mississippi:—

"The house was quadrangular, with a high stoop, a Dutch roof, immensely large, and two stories in height; the basement or lower story being constructed of brick, with a massive colonnade of the same material on all sides of the building. This basement was raised to a level with the summit of the Levée, and formed the groundwork or basis of the edifice, which was built of wood,

View on the Mississippi, at Bend No. 100.

painted white, with Venetian blinds, and latticed verandas supported by slender and graceful pillars, running round every side of the dwelling. Along the whole western front, festooned in massive folds, hung a dark-green curtain, which was dropped along the whole length of the balcony in a summer's afternoon."

THE MOTH.—The cotton crops are liable to extensive injury by a noxious insect, called the cotton moth, of which the following description was recently published:—

"The cotton moth, or *noctua xylina*, appears in the spring, when the cotton-plant is in a fit state to receive the eggs. She places these on the leaves of the plant to the number of from two to six hundred; these hatch in from two to five days, according to the weather. The young larvæ are very minute, but grow rapidly, attaining their full size of one and a half inches in from fourteen to twenty days, during which time, like their congeners, they moult every eight days. The difference in the color of the worms is owing to their moulting, as a slight change takes place after each skin is cast off. Their duration in the larva state is six weeks, in which time they feed voraciously; they then spin their cocoons, and remain in the pupa state a longer or shorter time, according to the season of the year. The moths that remain in the pupa until the following spring, will be those whose larvæ will destroy the summer's crop. Should the fall and winter be favorable to the premature development of the moth, the planters may be grateful, as it will be their greatest safeguard, unless they will gather and destroy the pupa.

"Mr. Affleck states that the caterpillars frequently spin on the old plants."

VIEW ON THE MISSISSIPPI AT BEND No. 100.—So numerous are the curves or bends of this river, and so difficult is it to distinguish them from each other by any natural features, in consequence of the uniformity of the surface, that they are marked on the maps by the numbers one, two, &c., and are commonly spoken of, by pilots and travellers, by that designation. The same may be said of the numerous islands, many of which are hardly to be known apart, except by their position.

The scene represented in the print is at one of the most considerable "bends" on the lower part of the Mississippi. The land is low and flat, wearing that appearance which has before been described, rising but a few feet above the river's level at low-water-mark, and composed of such loose materials as to be in constant danger of removal by some of the frequent changes of the currents. The curve which the stream takes at this place, where it sweeps away to the right, is so great, that, if the isthmus were cut through at its narrowest part, the passage would be reduced a great many miles. Preparations have been made to diminish the distance considerably, by cutting down the trees near the left-hand side of the print, to permit the river to find an unobstructed passage across at the time of flood, by which means it may probably wear for itself a new channel.

The tall tree which forms the most conspicuous object in the foreground, is a cypress, of a species which, with the cotton-tree, forms the principal growth in the native forests on this part of the shores. It is much used in building, and often covered with the moss, which is here represented as forming a thick canopy on its upper branches.

This parasitical plant does not grow north of latitude thirty degrees, but is well known in the northern states as a very useful article, being purchased in great quantities for the stuffing of mattresses, cushions, &c., by upholsterers and coachmakers.

Canebrakes form a prevailing feature in many of the marshy regions of Louisiana, as well as in other of the southern states. The peculiar nature of the plant which there occupies the soil, renders a canebrake different from every other kind of growth. It is well known, in its dry state, throughout most parts of our country, being extensively used for fishing-poles, and to some extent in manufactures.

The cane grows in one long, slender, upright stalk, from ten to twenty feet in height, giving out but a few thin leaves, especially when close together. Though hollow, it possesses great strength; for it is jointed, and the texture is compact, and the external part is formed of a hard shelly substance containing silex. When green, it is also tough; and the difficulty of penetrating a canebrake at any season of the year is so great as to be but seldom attempted, except where paths have been formed, by either cutting away or trampling down the canes when young. Paths once opened, and frequently travelled, remain passable, except when overflown by the water—a state in which many of them often lie for a considerable part of the time. But when several paths cross each other, nothing is more easy than for a passenger to lose his way; for the tops of the canes often bend over and meet above his head, so as to shut out a view even of the sky. Some idea may be formed of the peculiar appearance of a canebrake, by the sketch given in the vignette at the head of this description of the state.

The value of Cotton, the staple production of this and the adjacent states, is shown in the following extract from a late English paper, giving a brief history of the progress of *a pound of cotton*:—

"There was sent off for London, lately, from Glasgow, a small piece of muslin, about one pound in weight, the history of which is as follows: The cotton came from the United States to London; it was thence sent to Manchester and manufactured into yarn; thence it was sent to Paisley, where it was woven; thence to Ayrshire and there tamboured; thence conveyed to Dumbarton and handsewed, and returned to Paisley; thence to the county of Renfrew, bleached, and again returned to Paisley; thence sent to Glasgow, finished, and sent per coach to London. It is calculated that in two years from the time the muslin was first packed in America, its cloth arrived at the merchant's warehouse in London, having been conveyed 3,000 miles by sea, and 920 by land, and contributed to the support of at least 150 people, employed in its carriage and manufacture, by which the value has been advanced 2,000 per cent. Such is descriptive of a considerable part of the trade."

TEXAS.

TEXAS was formerly a part of the republic of Mexico, but became independent in 1836, and was annexed to the United States by a joint resolution of Congress, passed in March, 1845, and confirmed by a convention of the people of Texas, in July, 1845. It was finally admitted into the Union as a state, by act of Congress passed in December, 1845.

The boundaries of Texas, as defined by an act of the Texan congress, were as follows: "Beginning at the mouth of the Sabine river, and running west along the gulf of Mexico, three leagues from land, to the mouth of the Rio Grande; thence up the principal stream of that river to its source; thence due north to the forty-second degree of north latitude; thence along the boundary line, as defined in the treaty between the United States and Spain, to the beginning." An act of Congress, the terms of which were accepted by Texas, in 1850, established her northern and western boundaries as follows: "The state of Texas will agree that her boundary on the north shall commence at the point at which the meridian of one hundred degrees west from Greenwich is intersected by the parallel of thirty-six degrees and thirty minutes north latitude, and shall run from said point due west to the meridian of one hundred and three degrees west from Greenwich; thence her boundary shall run due south to the thirty-second degree of north latitude; thence on the said parallel of thirty-two degrees of north latitude to the Rio Bravo del Norte; and thence with the channel of said river to the gulf of Mexico. . . The United States, in consideration of said establishment of boundaries, will pay to the state of Texas the sum of ten millions of dollars in a stock bearing five per cent. interest, and redeemable at the end of fourteen years, the interest payable half-yearly at the treasury of the United States. Immediately after the president of the United States shall have been furnished with an authentic copy of the act of the general assembly of Texas, accepting these propositions, he shall cause the stock to be issued in favor of the state of Texas, as provided for in the fourth article of this agreement."

The gulf of Mexico forms a line of seacoast of about four hundred miles in extent, on the southeastern boundary of Texas.

The seacoast is very level, but free from marsh or swamp; the soil is a rich alluvion of great depth. This region extends into the interior seventy-five miles. Most southern staples can be produced in this section in the greatest abundance and of the finest quality. The only peculiar diseases are bilious distempers, and these by no means universal or extremely severe.

Above the level region commences the "rolling country." The soil is of an excellent quality, a rich sandy loam. The water is pure and healthy, streams clear and rapid, and the atmosphere purer than in the low country. This region covers the greatest proportion of Texas above the level district, and northeast of the Brazos river. No local causes for disease exist; the facilities for farming are unrivalled; most kinds of grain and fruit grow luxuriantly; and it is unnecessary to exercise any further care over cattle and other stock than the herding and marking of the increase during the whole year.

The northwestern and western portion is mountainous and broken, to within one hundred and fifty or one hundred and seventy-five miles of the coast. The valleys are rich, and the mountains abound in a variety of mineral productions. Several valuable silver mines, once worked by the Spaniards, but abandoned on account of the hostile Indians, have been recently discovered; and some fine specimens of virgin gold. This region abounds with fine streams of crystal water.

It is a remarkable feature of Texas that the bulk of the timber is immediately on the water-courses. Nearly every stream is lined with an abundance of timber, while the intervals between the streams are mostly prairie land, with groves, having the appearance of a park.

The numerous rivers of Texas, running in a parallel course, indicate the general surface to be one inclined plane, with a slope to the southeast. None of the rivers are of much importance for navigation, being in the dry season extremely low, and during the floods impeded with floating timber.

The Rio Grande, or Rio del Norte, which forms the western boundary of Texas, is the largest river, having a course of from fifteen to eighteen hundred miles; it is much impeded by rapids, and can be forded in nearly all parts of its course except for a distance of about two hundred miles from its mouth. The Sabine is three hundred and fifty miles, the Nueces three hundred, and the Trinity river four hundred miles in length; all navigable a part of the year. The Rio Brazos is considered the best navigable stream in Texas; vessels drawing six feet of water can ascend it to Brazoria; and steamboats of light draught to San Felipe de Austin, ninety miles higher. The Rio Colorado rises in the high prairies east of the Puereo river; and after a course of five hundred miles, falls into Matagorda bay. It is obstructed by a raft, of a mile in extent, about twelve miles above its mouth; beyond which light vessels may ascend two hundred miles. The city of Austin, the seat of government, is situated on its left bank, near the foot of the mountains. La Baca and Navidad rivers are secondary streams, flowing into the La Baca bay. The Guadaloupe is a large stream of pellucid water; two of its tributaries, the San Marcos and the Coleto, have their origin in fountains at the foot of the mountains. The San Antonio enters the Guadaloupe some distance above Espiritu Santo bay, and much resembles the Guadaloupe, though the forest on its banks is not so dense. It receives the Cibolo, the Medina, the Salado, Medio, and Leon creeks, all rapid and clear streams. The San Jacinto is a minor river, flowing through much good land, abounding in pine timber; it falls into Galveston bay, which receives also the Trinity river, and Buffalo bayou (a small stream navigable to the city of Houston). Galveston bay is a large body of water, having twelve feet on the bar at the entrance, and good anchorage inside. The Trinity river, its principal contributor, is one of the largest rivers in Texas, and is navigable further up than any other of these rivers. Its banks are lined with the choicest land and the best of timber. Numerous settlements are springing up on its banks. Several beds of coal, and some saline springs have been recently discovered on its margin. The river Nueces is a beautiful and rapid stream of considerable magnitude, and flows into Corpus Christi bay, which is accessible to vessels drawing six feet, with deep water inside. Below Espiritu Santo bay lies Aransazua bay, with a good entrance and twelve feet of water on the bar. It receives several small streams and one considerable river, the Aransas. The estuary of the Sabine river is a large bay, with sufficient depth of water for vessels of an ordinary draught, and a soft mud bar at the entrance. There are several thriving towns on the banks of the Sabine, which are frequently visited by steamboats.

The climate of Texas is mild and agreeable, and, as the country is free from swamps, is more healthful than the corresponding sections of the southern United States. The dry season lasts from April to September, and the wet season prevails during the rest of the year. The cold weather lasts a short time in December and January. The surface of the country is in most parts covered with luxuriant native grasses, affording excellent pasturage. As already mentioned, timber is abundant, and among the varieties are live oak, white, black, and post oak, ash, elm, hickory, musquite, walnut, sycamore, bois d'arc, cypress, &c., and in the southeast parts pine and cedar of fine quality abound.

Texas is amply supplied with fruits and garden products. The climate of the low lands is too warm for the apple, but almost every other fruit of temperate climes comes to perfection. Peaches, melons, figs, oranges, lemons, pineapples, dates, olives, &c., grow in different localities. Grapes are abundant; vanilla, indigo, sarsaparilla, and a variety of dying and medicinal shrubs and plants are indigenous, and on all the river bottoms is a thick growth of cane.

Cotton is the principal staple of the state, and generally of a superior quality, mostly cultivated on the Brazos, Colorado, Red, and Trinity rivers, and Caney creek, but advancing in other quarters. Cotton-planting begins in February and picking in June. Indian corn and wheat are the principal grains cultivated. The sugar-cane has attained great perfection in Texas, also tobacco, common and sweet potatoes, and the mulberry-tree. The raising of live stock is the occupation of most of the people, and many of the prairies are covered with cattle, horses, mules, and sheep; hogs are plentiful, and large quantities of pork are raised for market. Vast herds of buffaloes and wild horses are seen on the prairies, and deer are everywhere abundant. Bears, cougars, panthers, peccaries, wolves, foxes, and raccoons, are among the other wild animals.

To illustrate the manner of capturing the wild horses, called by the Spaniards *mustangs*, on the prairies of Texas, we insert the following description by one who has often engaged in the exciting chase, as well as an engraving of the scene:—

"The pursuer provides himself with a strong noosed cord, made of twisted strips of green hide, which, thus prepared, is called a lazo, the Spanish word for a band or bond. He mounts a fleet horse, and fastens one end of his lazo to the animal, coils it in his left hand, leaving the extending noose to flourish in the air over his head. Selecting his game, he gives it chase; and as soon as he approaches the animal he intends to seize, he takes the first opportunity to whirl the lazo over his head, and immediately checks his own charger. The noose instantly contracts around the neck of the fugitive mustang, and the creature is thrown violently down, sometimes unable to move, and generally for the moment deprived of breath. This violent method of arrest frequently injures the poor animal, and sometimes even kills him. If he escapes, however, with his life, he becomes of great service to his master, always remembering with great respect the rude instrument of his capture, and ever after yielding immediately whenever he feels the lazo upon his neck.

"Being thus secured, the lazoed horse is blindfolded; terrible lever, jaw-breaking bits are put into his mouth, and he is mounted by a rider armed with most barbarous spurs. If the animal runs, he is spurred on to the top of his speed, until he tumbles down with exhaustion. Then he is turned about and spurred back again; and if he is found able to run back to the point whence he started, he is credited with having bottom enough to make a good horse; otherwise, he is turned off as of little or no value. This process of breaking mustangs to the bridle is a brutal one, and the poor animals often carry the evidence of it as long as they live. After service during the day, they are hoppled by fastening their fore-legs together with a cord, and turned out to feed. To fasten them to one spot in the midst of a prairie, where neither tree, nor shrub, nor rock, is to be found, is quite a problem. But that is accomplished by putting on a halter, tying a knot at the end, digging a hole about a foot deep in the earth, thrusting in the knot, and pressing the earth down around it As the horse generally pulls nearly in a horizontal direction, he is unable to draw it out.

"When a number are caught, they are generally driven to market, where they are purchased for three or four dollars, branded, hoppled, then turned out and abandoned to themselves, until needed. At some future time they will doubtless become a valuable article of export."

The present population of Texas is estimated to amount to over two hundred thousand, nearly all of whom are Americans—emigrants from the other United States. The population, according to the census of 1850, was 187,403, of whom about one fifth were slaves. By the act of Congress admitting Texas into the Union, that state had two members of the house of representatives and has the same under the census of 1850. Texas was of course entitled to two members in the senate of the United States at the date of her admission.

Texas, at the period of her admission, had but thirty-six organized counties; she now (1851) numbers ninety. In many of these counties the increase of population, principally by emigration, has, it is estimated, since her admission, been equal to fifty per cent.

The principal towns in Texas are Galveston, the principal seaport, Houston, San Augustin, San Felipe de Austin, Nacogdoches, Austin, the present seat of government, Washington, for a while the temporary capital, San Antonio de Bexar, and a few others.

In the eighteenth century Texas was nearly unknown, having only been occasionally traversed by the Spaniards, in their way from New Orleans to Mexico. About 1800, there were only two or three small military establishments, near which a few Spaniards had settled. In 1807, Pike made it known that this country was distinguished by fertility of soil. From that time many citizens of the United States wished to form settlements in Texas, but the policy of the Spanish court was not favorable to their designs. When Mexico obtained her independence, the government of the republic adopted a liberal system of colonization, inviting (in 1824) natives and foreigners to settle within the territories of the republic, under very advantageous conditions. The first settlement was made by Colonel Austin, of Missouri, in his grant on the Rio Brazos, and called San Felipe de Austin. About this time the stream of emigration from the United States turned toward Texas. In 1833, the people of Texas formed for themselves a separate constitution, and insisted on a separation of their country from the state of Coahuila, to which it was united by a decree of the Mexican government. This being re-

Catching Wild Horses on the Prairie.

fused, and a central government established in Mexicc, the Texans took up arms in 1835, in defence of their rights and liberties, and the republican principles of the federal constitution of Mexico of 1824. The few Mexican soldiers stationed at Bexar were compelled to leave the country in December, 1835, after sustaining considerable loss in a battle with the Texans. The president of the Mexican republic, Santa Anna, however, marched into Texas at the head of a small army, and succeeded in getting possession of Bexar, the garrison of which he put to the sword; but in 1835 he was defeated on the banks of the river San Jacinto, with great slaughter, by a small body of Texans (Americans from the United States), under General Houston. Santa Anna was taken prisoner, but released on certain conditions, among others, that the Mexican troops were to evacuate Texas, passing beyond the Rio Grande. No effective attempt was afterward made by the Mexicans to conquer Texas, and it became an independent republic, being soon acknowledged as such by the United States, France, Great Britain, and some other nations.

Galveston, two hundred and fifty-five miles from Austin, and three hundred and fifty west by north of the Southwest pass of Mississippi river, is situated on rising ground, compactly built, on the east part of Galveston island, with many good houses and several conspicuous churches and other public buildings. Galveston makes a favorable appearance from the water, and is rapidly extending its population and business. The settlement was begun in 1837, and has some large stores, several cotton presses, a university, two high schools, and a population of about 7,000. The streets are wide and straight. The harbor is fine, and the bar has twelve feet of water. A regular communication is kept up with New Orleans by steam-packets, a daily line of boats runs to Houston, and other boats go to the Brazos, Trinity, and Sabine rivers.

At Galveston, in the month of October, the air has a temperature like mid-September. As you enter the harbor through the crooked channel studded on both sides with shoals and breakers, the gloomy pelicans saluting you on every side, the approach is both difficult and dangerous. The low, level, and sandy, but grass-covered island of Galveston, on which the city is situated, is about thirty miles long, and has on it but three small groups of native trees—though of fruit-trees there are plenty in the city, planted by the inhabitants. It is tolerably fertile, and, owing principally to the industry of the German emigrants that have settled there, gardens of all kinds abound. It is healthy for all but those who expose themselves to the hot mid-day summer sun, and bring on attacks of the fever. It is considered more healthy at any season than New Orleans. Galveston bay is about sixty miles long and thirty-five wide, and in its deepest parts there is about twelve feet of water; on its greatest, unavoidable shoals, there is about three feet. There are various islands in different parts of it; the largest is "Pelican," opposite the city of Galveston. This is, from one extremity to the other, about four miles long. It is destitute of timber, as are all the islands on the coast; nevertheless, it is, during the spring season a great resort. Some visit it for the purpose of making pic-nics or chowders (for the last it is famous), others go for the sail, but most go for the purpose of gathering the myriads of eggs deposited by gulls and other aquatic birds.

In Galveston bay about eighteen miles from the city is situated Red-fish bar. It is created by the influx of the Trinity and other rivers and extends entirely across the bay. It consists of a number of small islands through there are several navigable passes. Of these, the most esteemed at present is called the "East," but there is a better one still more easterly, not much used at present, but which is superior to any other, having deeper water, and being more direct. It is called "Possum pass," partly because it is a feasting ground for that animal which, swimming from one island to another of the chain, repairs there for the purpose of devouring the eggs laid in the vicinity, and partly because

View of Galveston.

it is hidden from sight until approached very near. Here there are spots, of acres in extent, covered with eggs of all flavors, colors, and sizes—and in every state of incubation, small boats make a trade in collecting them for market, and as the robbed birds, with the greatest perseverance, commence laying anew after each depredation, the egg-hunters reap an unfailing harvest while the season lasts. When the *squabs* are hatched they make one of the most delicious items in the boatman's bill of fare. Sitting round their savory supper, these care-free rovers quaff their drams of whiskey, smoke their pipes, sing songs, and tell stories of wild life, beneath the clear sky, until tired, when, with their blankets around them, they seek a soft spot upon the sand. At the dawn, the shrill cry of the eagle in pursuit of his prey awakes the egg-hunters to business. Having laid in their stock of eggs, they commence the second but no less pleasant part of their trade—this is fishing, for which this place is famous.

The red-fish is the desired animal to the fishermen; mullet, buffalo, cat-fish (a species of salmon), and countless numbers of less important classes of fish abound. The fisher, with a small spear, commences searching in the various water-holes in the sand for crabs for bait; then, fastening a crab to his hook, he casts it in, and in an instant some red-fish is hauled out flouncing upon the sand. Sometimes it is a closely-contested question whether the fish shall quit his element or the fisherman take a bath. Red-fish often weigh twenty-five pounds They are a very vigorous fish, and of delicious flavor, either fresh or dried and salted, which is a favorite way of curing them. About eight miles above Red-fish bar, there is a group of islands famous for the great inducements they hold out to the sportsman—they are called the "Veintiuno," or Twenty-one isles. In the winter season their little harbors are filled with small craft and the craft with sportsmen, who make a little fortune during that season by the vast numbers of geese, brant, duck, and swan, they kill here—selling their carcasses at Galveston, and curing their feathers for various markets. A swan skin will at any time bring a dollar. The appearance of a flock of these stately water-fowls is that of a floating island of half a mile square moving gracefully along over the water, now swiftly, now almost stationary, but pouring forth a continual boisterous bird-language. In spite of their own din, however, they catch the slightest hostile sound. Should the sportsman crack a twig, move a bush, or crush a shell beneath his foot, the noisy conclave stops instantly, and, *en masse*, both their propellers and their throats. For an instant all is silent and motionless—bang! then go the fowling-pieces, and perhaps one thousand of these birds, so graceful in the water but so awkward in flight, will stretch their wings, knocking each other down in their confusion, and, amid loud cries and great splashing of water, take themselves off as soon as possible, probably leaving thirty or forty of their comrades to be gathered up by the sportsmen.

HOUSTON, on Buffalo bayou, at the head of tide-water, is eighty-five miles from Galveston, and one hundred and eighty-eight from Austin. The situation of this town is not only favorable and convenient, but, when seen from certain points, quite picturesque. The summit of the gentle eminence on which it is built is crowned by several churches, and the slope is thickly covered with houses, many of which are small and simple in their construction, as in most new, interior towns of Texas. The stream which flows at the base of the hill, meanders peacefully along, flowing under a handsome bridge of a single arch, and beneath the shade of some of the trees of the forest which have been spared in clearing the land. The distant scenes are varied by ridges of high ground, which extend far away, with winding valleys between them. An extensive prairie adjoins it, and it is a place of much trade in cotton. Steamboats run to Galveston, and stage-coaches to Washington. It contains four churches, a courthouse, a number of large manufactories, and 6,000 inhabitants.

AUSTIN, the capital of Texas, is situated on the east side of Colorado river,

View of Houston.

two hundred miles from the gulf of Mexico, on a plain elevated about thirty feet. The capitol, on the summit, is conspicuous from its position, and overlooks an extensive region. At a short distance from it is the governor's house. The population amounts to about 4,000.

The governor of Texas is chosen by the people for two years, but is eligible only two years in six. He must be thirty-two years old, and have been a resident of the state three years previous. The lieutenant-governor is eligible under the same restrictions. There is a supreme court, and such district and inferior courts as the legislature shall appoint. The legislature appoints the judges of the supreme court for six years, with the advice and consent of the senate. The senators are chosen by the people for two years, half being chosen each year. They must be thirty-two years old, and residents for the last three years. The representatives are chosen for two years, by the people, and must be twenty-one years old, citizens of the United States, and residents of the state of Texas for one year, and of the county for the last six months. The legislature meets once in two years.

Matagorda, one hundred and ninety-eight miles southeast from Austin, and thirty-five from the Caballo pass, stands on the Colorado, and has a customhouse, two churches, an academy, and 700 inhabitants. Steamboats run to New Orleans and Galveston.

San Felipe de Austin, on the west bank of the Brazos, is one hundred and twenty miles from Austin, and contains 2,000 inhabitants. It was burnt by the Texan army, in the war, but has been rebuilt.

San Augustin, twenty-seven miles from the Sabine, and three hundred and sixty east-northeast from Austin, is built on the Ayish bayou, and contains about 2,500 inhabitants. It is one of the best-built and best-situated towns in Texas, in a healthy region of rolling country.

The *University of San Augustin* is in this place. It was incorporated in 1837, and has two professors in the male department, and three instructors in the female.

The *Wesleyan college* has four instructors and a president, with departments for the two sexes.

Washington.—This town is situated at the head of ordinary navigation on the Brazos, one hundred and thirty-three miles from Austin, and contains about 3,000 inhabitants, with a courthouse, four churches, and a number of large manufactories.

Nacogdoches, is sixty miles west of the Sabine and two hundred and fifty distant from Austin, near the head of Angelina river. It was formerly a military post, but is now a town of 2,000 inhabitants, and contains a university of the same name, with two professors.

San Antonio de Bexar.—This place, celebrated for the destruction of a band of Texan soldiers in the Alamo or citadel, in the Mexican war, is ninety miles south by west of Austin, on the upper part of San Antonio river, and formerly contained 8,000 inhabitants, but has now only about 2,000.

Corpus Christi, two hundred and fifty south of Austin, stands at the head of a bay, and contains a population of about 800, being connected with other towns on the coasts by steamboats.

Bastrop.—This town stands on the east side of Colorado river, where it is crossed by the road to San Antonio, in the midst of a rich prairie, and has about 700 inhabitants.

Brazoria is on the right bank of the Brazos river, about thirty miles above the sea. It is a place of considerable trade, and has about 900 inhabitants.

From April to September the thermometer, in different parts of the state, has been found at a general average to range from sixty-three to one hundred degrees. These great heats, however, are tempered by continual and strong breezes, which commence soon after sunrise and continue till three or four o'clock in the afternoon, and the nights are cool throughout the year.

Among the natural curiosities of Texas are the "Cross Timbers," consisting of two lines of continuous forest, varying in width irom five to fifty miles, extending in almost a direct line from the sources of the Trinity northward to the Arkansas.

ARKANSAS.

This state is bounded north by Missouri, east by the Mississippi river, and south by Louisiana.

It is naturally divided into three districts. The east part is generally level; and, lying along the Mississippi, White, St. Francis, and Arkansas rivers, is subject to inundations in the spring. Some portions of this section are prairie land, but most of it is covered with forests. When cleared, the soil is generally good. The second or middle district is watered by some of the upper tributaries of the White and Ouachitta rivers, and the main part of the Arkansas and Red rivers. The surface is broken, but has large prairies. The third district, in the north and northwest, is mountainous, but with extensive prairies intermingled.

This state is remarkably well supplied with navigable streams. The St. Francis comes in across the northern boundary, and after flowing one hundred and twenty miles, falls into the Mississippi about sixty miles above the mouth of White river. White river, which is a stream of much superior size, has its rise in two branches north of this state, and, after a course of one hundred and twenty miles, enters the Mississippi fifteen miles above the mouth of the Arkansas.

The Arkansas is navigable far into the interior, though considerably impeded by falls. The Ouachitta is formed by the confluence of numerous branches, rising in the Masserne mountains, between the Red river and Arkansas. It is navigable, when the water is high, for a distance of two hundred miles, including the windings of the stream, in large boats. Red river has but a small part of its course in this state, crossing the northwest corner.

Several very extensive salt-prairies in the interior affect the water of many of the streams, which has a brackish taste. Salt-springs are numerous.

The scenery along the Mississippi, in this part of its course, is well described in the following extract from the journal of a late English traveller:—

"The American forests are generally remarkable for the entire absence of underwood, so that they are easily penetrable by a foot-traveller, and generally even by a mounted one. But in the neighborhood of the Mississippi there is, almost uniformly, a thick undergrowth of cane, varying in height from four or five to about twenty feet, according to the richness of the soil. Through this thicket of cane I should think it quite impossible to penetrate; yet, I have been assured, the Indians do so for leagues together, though by what means they contrive to guide their course, where vision is manifestly impossible, it is not easy to understand.

"It has been the fashion with travellers to talk of the scenery of the Mississippi as wanting grandeur and beauty. Most certainly it has neither. But there is no scenery on earth more striking. The dreary and pestilential solitudes, untrodden save by the foot of the Indian; the absence of all living objects, save the huge alligators which float past, apparently asleep, on the drift-wood; and an occasional vulture, attracted by its impure prey on the surface of the waters; the trees, with a long and hideous drapery of pendent moss, fluttering in the wind; and the giant river, rolling onward the vast volume of its dark and turbid waters through the wilderness—form the features of one of the most dismal and impressive landscapes on which the eye of man ever rested. . . . . No other river in the world drains so large a portion of the earth's surface. It is the traveller of five thousand miles, more than two thirds of the diameter of the globe. The imagination asks, whence come its waters, and whither tend they? They come from the distant regions of a vast continent, where the foot of civilized man has never yet been planted. They flow into an ocean yet vaster, the whole body of which acknowledges their influence. Through what varieties of climate have they passed? On what scenes of lonely and sublime magnificence have they gazed? In short, when the traveller has asked and answered these questions and a thousand others, it will be time enough to consider how far the scenery of the Mississippi would be improved by the presence of rocks and mountains. He may then be led to doubt whether any *great* effect can be produced by a combination of objects of discordant character, however grand in themselves. The imagination is, perhaps, susceptible but of a single powerful impression at a time. Sublimity is uniformly connected with unity of object. Beauty may be produced by the happy adaptation of a multitude of harmonious details; but the highest sublimity of effect can proceed but from one glorious and paramount object, which impresses its own character on everything around.

"The prevailing character of the Mississippi is that of solemn gloom. I have trodden the passes of Alp and Apennine, yet never felt how awful a thing is nature, till I was borne on its waters through regions desolate and uninhabitable. Day after day, and night after night, we continued driving right downward to the south; our vessel, like some huge demon of the wilderness, bearing fire in her bosom, and canopying the eternal forest with the smoke of her nostrils. . . . I passed my time in a sort of dreamy contemplation. At night I ascended to the highest deck, and lay for hours gazing listlessly on the sky, the forest, and the waters, amid silence only broken by the clanging of the engine. All this was very pleasant; yet, till I reached New Orleans, I could scarcely have smiled at the best joke in the world; and as for raising a laugh—it would have been quite as easy to square the circle.

"The bends or flexures of the Mississippi are regular in a degree unknown in any other river. The action of running water, in a vast alluvial plain like that of the basin of the Mississippi, without obstruction from rock or mountain, may be calculated with the utmost precision. Whenever the course of a river diverges in any degree from a right line, it is evident that the current can no longer act with equal force on both its banks. On one side the impulse is diminished, on the other increased. The tendency in these sinuosities, therefore, is manifestly to increase, and the stream which hollows out a portion of one bank, being rejected to the other, the process of curvature is still continued, till its channel presents an almost unvarying succession of salient and retiring angles.

"In the Mississippi the flexures are so extremely great, that it often happens that the isthmus which divides different portions of the river gives way. A few months before my visit to the south, a remarkable case of this kind had happened, by which forty miles of navigation had been saved. The opening thus formed was called the *new cut.* Even the annual changes which take place in the bed of the Mississippi are very remarkable. Islands spring up and disappear; shoals suddenly present themselves where pilots have been accustomed to deep water; in many places, whole acres are swept away from one bank and added to the other; and the pilot assured me that in every voyage he could perceive fresh changes.

"Many circumstances contribute to render these changes more rapid in the Mississippi than in any other river. Among these, perhaps the greatest is the vast volume of its waters, acting on alluvial matter, peculiarly penetrable. The river, when in flood, spreads over the neighboring country, in which it has formed channels called bayous. The banks thus become so saturated with water, that they can oppose little resistance to the action of the current, which frequently sweeps off large portions of the forest.

"The immense quantity of drift-wood is another cause of change. Floating logs encounter some obstacle in the river, and become stationary. The mass gradually accumulates; the water, saturated with mud, deposites a sediment; and thus an island is formed, which soon becomes covered with vegetation. A few years ago, the Mississippi was surveyed by order of the government, and its islands, from the confluence of the Missouri to the sea, were numbered. I remember asking the pilot the name of a very beautiful island, and the answer was, 'Five-hundred-and-seventy-three,' the number assigned to it in the hydrographical survey, and the only name by which it was known.

"A traveller on the Mississippi has little to record in the way of incident. For a week we continued our course, stopping only to take in wood, and on occasion to take in cargo.

"One of the most striking circumstances connected with this river-voyage was the rapid change of climate. Barely ten days had elapsed since I was traversing mountains almost impassable from snow. Even the level country was partially covered with it, and the approach of spring had not been heralded by any symptom of vegetation. Yet in little more than a week I found myself in the region of the sugarcanes.

"The progress of this transition was remarkable. During the first two days of the voyage, nothing like a blossom or a green leaf was to be seen. On the third, slight signs of vegetation were visible on a few of the hardier trees. These gradually became more general as we approached the Mississippi; but then, though our course lay almost due south, little change was apparent for a day or two. But after passing Memphis, in latitude thirty-five degrees, all nature became alive. The trees which grew on any little eminence, or which did not spring immediately from the swamp, were covered with foliage; and at our wooding-times, when I rambled through the woods, there were a thousand shrubs already bursting into flower. On reaching the lower regions of the Mississippi, all was brightness and verdure. Summer had already begun, and the heat was even disagreeably intense.

"Shortly after entering Louisiana, the whole wildness of the Mississippi disappears. The banks are all cultivated, and nothing was to be seen but plantations of sugar, cotton, and rice, with the houses of their owners, and the

Rocky Bluffs on the Mississippi.

little adjoining hamlets inhabited by the slaves. Here and there were orchards of orange-trees, but these occurred too seldom to have much influence on the landscape."

Rocky Bluffs.—In some parts the banks of the Mississippi present an aspect widely different from that of the prevailing scenery in this state. At that point especially which is represented in the above engraving, the eye is struck by bold outlines rising far above the ordinary level of the alluvion. The three rocky bluffs here seen standing side by side, at equal distances and of nearly equal size, are terminated in small horizontal terraces, which seem to indicate that they are the remains of an ancient high plain, elsewhere torn away or sunk by some tremendous convulsion of nature. These eminences stand like castles, fabricated by gigantic hands, or cut out of the living rock, with sides remarkably perpendicular, smooth, and uniform; and the crevices which here and there mark the surface, occur at such points and of such forms as to bear a considerable resemblance to windows, loopholes, and embrasures.

The picturesque effect of these bluffs is much increased by their singularity, and the extreme rarity of eminences of all kinds along the lower parts of the river's course. The narrow belt of lowland which intervenes between the water and the bases of the rocks, with the scattering trees and groves by which it is partly shaded, and the masses of forest-foliage which form the background, combine to render this wild scene one of the most striking and pleasing to the eye of the traveller.

In the water is seen one of the flat-bottomed boats before mentioned. They are constructed with skill, and well serve the purpose for which they are designed, although formed of boards fastened by a few timbers. Being filled with large quantities of various articles, they float down to New Orleans with the current, and seldom suffer injury on the way.

There is an Indian tradition that the Kansas tribe were utterly destroyed at this place by their enemies. Their totem, or pretended guardian spirit, was a white fawn. An animal of this description, it was said, afterward haunted the spot at night.

DESCRIPTION OF A PRAIRIE, BY ALBERT PIKE.—The world of prairie which lies at a distance of more than three hundred miles west of the inhabited portions of the United States, and south of the river Arkansas and its branches, has been rarely, and parts of it never, trodden by the foot, or beheld by the eye, of an Anglo-American. Rivers rise there, in the broad level waste, of which, mighty though they become in their course, the source is unexplored. Deserts are there, too barren of grass to support even the hardy buffalo, and in which water, except in here and there a hole, is never found. Ranged over by the Camanches, the Pawnees, and Caiwas, and other equally wandering, savage, and hostile tribes, its very name is a mystery and a terror. The Pawnees have their villages entirely north of this part of the country; and the war parties, always on foot, are seldom to be met with to the south of the Canadian, except close in upon the edges of the white and civilized Indian settlements. Extending on the south to the Rio del Norte, on the north to a distance unknown, eastwardly to within three or four hundred miles of the edge of Arkansas territory, and westwardly to the Rocky mountains, is the range of the Camanches. Abundantly supplied with good horses from the immense herds of the prairie, they range, at different times of the year, over the whole of this vast country. Their war and hunting parties follow the buffalo continually. In the winter they may be found in the south, encamped along the Rio del Norte, and under the mountains; and in the summer on the Canadian, and to the north of it, and on the Pecos. Sometimes they haunt the Canadian in the winter, but not so commonly as in the summer. It is into this great American desert that I wish to conduct my readers.

Imagine yourself standing in a plain to which your eye can see no bounds. Not a tree, nor a bush, not a shrub, nor a tall weed, lifts its head above the barren grandeur of the desert; not a stone is to be seen upon its hard-beaten surface; no undulations, no abruptness, no break, to relieve the monotony—nothing, save here and there a deep narrow track, worn into the hard plain by the constant hoof of the buffalo. Imagine, then, countless herds of buffalo, showing their unwieldly, dark shapes, in every direction as far as the eye can reach, and approaching at times to within forty steps of you; or a herd of wild horses feeding in the distance, or hurrying away from the hateful smell of man, with their manes floating, and a trampling like thunder. Imagine here and there a solitary antelope, or perhaps a whole herd, fleeting off in the distance, like the scattering of white clouds. Imagine bands of white, snow-like wolves, prowling about, accompanied by the little gray collotes or prairie-wolves, who are as rapacious and as noisy as their bigger brethren. Imagine, also, here and there a lonely tiger-cat, lying crouched in some little hollow, or bounding off in triumph, bearing some luckless little prairie-dog, which it has caught straggling about at a distance from his hole. If to this you add a band of Camanches, mounted on noble swift horses, with their long lances, their quiver at the back, their bow, perhaps their gun, and their shield ornamented gaudily with feathers and red cloth, and round as Norval's, or as the full moon; and imagine them hovering about in different places, chasing the buffalo or attacking an enemy—you have an image of the prairie, such as no book ever described adequately to me.

I have seen the prairie under all its diversities, and in all its appearances, from those which I have described, to the uneven, bushy prairies which lie south of Red river, and to the illimitable Stake prairie, which lies from almost under the shadow of the mountains to the heads of the Brazos and of Red river, and in which neither buffaloes nor horses are to be found. I have seen the prairie, and lived in it, in summer and in winter. I have seen it with the sun rising calmly from its breast, like a sudden fire kindled in the dim distance, and with the sunset flushing in the sky with quiet and sublime beauty. There is less of the gorgeous and grand character, however, belonging to it, than that which accompanies the rise and set of the sun upon the ocean, or upon the mountains; but there are beauty and sublimity enough to attract the attention and interest the mind.

I have also seen the *mirage*, painting lakes, and fires, and groves, on the grassy ridges near the bounds of Missouri, in the still autumn afternoon, and cheating the traveller by its splendid deceptions. I have seen the prairie, and stood long and weary guard in it, by moonlight and starlight, and in storm. It strikes me as the most magnificent, stern, and terribly grand scene on earth. A storm in the prairie is much like a storm at sea, except in one respect—and in that it seems to me to be superior—the stillness of the desert and illimitable plain, while the snow is raging over its surface, is always more fearful to me than the wild roll of the waves; and it seems unnatural—this dead quiet, while the upper elements are so fiercely disturbed! it seems as if there ought to be the roll and roar of the waves. The sea, the woods, the mountains, all suffer in comparison with the prairie—that is, on the whole; in particular circumstances, either of them is superior. We may speak of the incessant motion and tumult of the waves of the ocean; the unbounded greenness and dimness, and the lonely music, of the forests; and the high magnificence, the precipitous grandeur, and the summer snow of the glittering cones of the mountains: but still the prairie has a stronger hold upon the soul, and a more powerful, if not so vivid an impression upon the feelings. Its sublimity arises from its unbounded extent—its barren monotony and desolation—its still, unmoved, calm, stern, and most impressive grandeur—its strange power of deception—its want of echo—and, in fine, its power of throwing a man back upon himself, and giving him a feeling of lone helplessness, strangely mingled at the same time with a feeling of liberty and freedom from restraint. It is particularly sublime as you draw nigh to the Rocky mountains, and see them shoot up in the west, with their lofty tops looking like white clouds resting upon their summits. Nothing ever equalled the intense feeling of delight with which I at first saw the eternal mountains marking the western edge of the desert.

The constitution of the state of Arkansas was adopted in 1836, in which year it was admitted into the Union. The governor is chosen for four years, and prohibited to hold office more than eight years in twelve. Senators are chosen for four years by the people, and representatives for two years. Elections are made *viva voce*. The senate can never consist of fewer than seventeen members, or more than thirty-three; the house of representatives from fifty-four to one hundred. The legislature meets once in two years. Judges of the supreme court are appointed by the legislature for eight years, those of the circuit court for four years. The judges of the county courts are chosen by justices of the peace.

Every white male citizen of the United States is entitled to vote after a residence of two years.

There are ten academies and one hundred and fifty common schools in the state.

Little Rock.—This town is the capital of Arkansas, and is situated on the right bank of the Arkansas river, on an elevated and rocky bluff, one hundred and fifty feet above its level. The distance from New Orleans by the course of the stream is nine hundred and five miles. This is the first place, west of the Mississippi, where rocks present themselves above the surface of the immense alluvion which lies on its western border.

The town contains the statehouse, the penitentiary, an arsenal of the United States, a land-office, two banks, five churches, a theatre, an academy, and over four thousand inhabitants.

Steamboats go to New Orleans, and up the river to Fort Gibson. Stage-coaches leave the town three times a week for Washington; and also for Van Buren, St. Louis via Batesville, and Fredrickstown (Missouri); and twice a week for Rock Koe, whence steamboats go to New Orleans.

Arkansas Post is on the left bank of Arkansas river, six hundred and eighty-five miles above New Orleans. It stands on an elevated piece of ground, and has a courthouse with about two hundred inhabitants. Steamboats run hence to Little Rock and New Orleans.

Helena.—This is a small town on the bank of the Mississippi, and contains about five hundred inhabitants. It has a land-office and a courthouse. Steamboats touch from New Orleans and the principal cities of the Mississippi and its branches.

Hot Springs is six miles north of Ouachitta river, and sixty miles distant from Little Rock. It contains about one hundred inhabitants with a courthouse. It is situated near a mountain, from the base of which, on the western side, flow the springs which have given a name and celebrity to the place; they are about fifty in number, and empty into a small stream, which is one of the branches of the Ouachitta. The springs are warm, differing in temperature from one hundred and ten to one hundred and fifty degrees Fahrenheit, and bear a high character for their restorative qualities, especially in chronic rheumatism, scrofula, gout, and several cutaneous affections.

Good accommodations are provided for visiters, who resort to the place in considerable numbers.

The *Chalybeate Springs* are three miles northeast of the Hot springs, and are no less esteemed. The water is cold, and impregnated with iron.

The *Sulphur Springs*, thirty miles from Hot springs, have been known only a short time.

Statistics.—According to the census of 1840, the whole amount of the population of the state was 97,574; of whom there were 42,211 white males, 34,963 white females, 19,935 slaves, and 465 free colored persons. By the census of 1850, the population of Arkansas was, 162,225 whites, 590 free-colored persons, and 45,075 slaves; total 207,890.

Indians.—Some poor remains of tribes once inhabiting the fertile fields of Arkansas, are still to be seen, but in a degraded and wretched condition. The following translations of speeches made many years ago by two chiefs, one of them belonging to the Arkansas nation, too plainly indicate the destructive effects of demoralizing intercourse on the one hand, and of the wars by which they were reduced to subjection on the other.

The following is a speech of an Indian, from the Arkansas tribe, directed to Bossu, a Frenchman. In the year 1770, Bossu, of whom we have a good account of his travels through North America, visited the Arkansas tribe, among whom he had formerly lived many years. They received him in the most friendly manner. After dinner, an Indian orator arose, and showing his respect to the chief and the nation, thus addressed Bossu: "It is a long time, Father, that we have not seen thy face. Our whole nation rejoices to see thee walk again on our earth, which is white, and has never been stained with the blood of thy nation. All thy children, the Arkansas, have wept for thee, not knowing what fate, since fourteen harvests and six moons, had met thee. We hope now that thou wilt no more cross the great salty sea, in order to return to the great village of the Frenchmen, where thou hast been, and where, according to reports, thou wast imprisoned in a locked cottage (called Bastile), because bad reports were raised against thee through the *speaking bark*," meaning letters. "If thou hadst remained with us, this would not have happened to thee. Here the strong does not oppress the weak. The malicious is not happy, and good men are not punished. Here the red men do not kill their brethren, as the white men do, for land and yellow iron," meaning gold, "which we despise. Here the earth nourishes us, which we cultivate, without trouble. Those to whom it gives the most, do not treasure up their harvest of potatoes, maize, or Indian corn, in order to obtain advantage from the misfortunes of others, and to rob them of their provisions, like the Europeans. On the contrary, the Arkansas rejoice if they can support widows, orphans, the aged, and the helpless. Here we live contented, without being tormented by burning passions, like the white men, and without committing murders or terrific crimes. Every one is here subject to the will of the great Spirit. Here, every man serves him, in the best manner, in a plain temple without decorations, under the shade of an ancient green tree, from which flows an odoriferous gum. Remain for ever with us, and let our people be thy people."

In the year 1720, a savage, from the Chitimachas nation, had murdered a French missionary. Bienville, governor of Louisiana, declared and made war against the whole nation. Peace was obtained, on presenting the head of the murderer. In producing the calumet of peace, one of the Indians addressed the governor thus: "My heart laughs for joy to see thy face. All of us have heard the word of peace which thou hast sent. The heart of the whole nation laughs so for joy, as to hear it beat. Our women, in this moment, have forgotten the past, and have danced, and our children have jumped like young fawns. On thy command, we will run and jump, like deer, to please thee. O how beautiful is the sun to-day, in comparison with that time when thou wast angry at us! How dangerous is a bad man! Thou knowest that only one has killed the praying chief," the missionary, "whose death has brought our best warriors to the grave. We are only left with old men, women, and children, who stretch forth their hands to thee as a good father. The gall which formerly filled thy heart has been changed into honey. The great Spirit is no more angry against our nation.

"Thou hast requested the head of the bad man, to make peace, and we have sent it. Heretofore the sun was red, the road was covered with briers and thorns, the clouds were black, the water thick and colored with blood. Our women wept, without cessation, over their dying men and relations, and were afraid even to fetch wood, to prepare our food. Our children wept for fear; our warriors were under arms, at the least screech of the night-owl, and they slept in no other manner than with their tomahawks in their hands. Our wigwams were forsaken, and our fields were uncultivated. We all appeared with empty stomachs and long faces. The venison took flight before us; the serpents hissed for anger, and lengthened their stings; the birds, nestling near our wigwams, by their mournful voices sang obituary tunes. But to-day, the sun is brilliant, the sky is clear, the clouds have moved, the roads are covered with roses, our gardens and fields will be cultivated, and we will offer to the great Spirit the firstlings of their fruits. The water is so clear that it represents to us our image; the serpents take flight, or are changed into eels; the birds rejoice as by their sweet song; our women and children dance and jump, that they forget to eat and drink. The heart of the whole nation laughs for joy, that, at present, we thy people can walk united on the same road. The same sun will give light to us both. We will have but one united word, and our hearts shall be one. Whoever will kill the Frenchmen, them will we kill. Our warriors shall go hunting to kill venison for them, and then we will eat all together. Is this not good? What dost thou say to this, father?"

When we take into view the extent of the territory of this state, with its variety of surface and soil—the number, directions, and navigable character of its streams, and the favorable nature of the climate—we can not but anticipate a rapid increase in population and wealth. Unfavorable circumstances indeed exist, but not greater than in many older states in its neighborhood, which have made, and are still making, great advances.

Early and due attention to public education and moral improvement, can hardly be overlooked by the intelligent, virtuous, and public-spirited inhabitants of Arkansas; and here, as elsewhere, they will prove the most solid foundations of permanent prosperity. With so many sad warnings as are here presented, on the one hand, of the dangers of delay, and, on the other, the noble examples set by some other states, the Americans have enough to show them "in what their great strength lieth."

TENNESSEE.

THIS state is bounded north by Kentucky, northeast by Virginia, east by North Carolina, southeast by Georgia, southwest by Mississippi, west by the Mississippi river, which separates it from Arkansas, and northwest by Missouri. The main Appalachian ridge forms the boundary line for one hundred and sixty-eight miles, from the south border of Virginia to Macon county; and the entire outline is 1,171 miles. It is between 35° and 36° 7′ north latitude, and 4° 39′ and 13° 14′ west longitude from Washington. The longest straight line that can be drawn in this state, is from the northeast to the southwest corner—south seventy-seven degrees by calculation—almost five hundred miles. The mean length of the state is four hundred miles; the mean breadth, one hundred and fourteen; and the mean area, forty-five thousand six hundred, or above twenty-nine millions of square acres.

This state is divided into two natural sections. The first and smaller occupies a large part of the valley of Tennessee river, and is two hundred and eighty miles long from southwest to northeast, with a medium breadth of fifty-seven miles, which embraces a little less than one third of the state. Its southern limit is the ridge of Cumberland mountains, and it is elevated, cool, and diversified in surface, with a good soil, pure air, and an abundance of excellent water. It deserves to be ranked among the most attractive portions of the United States. The climate forbids the culture of the staples of the lower and warmer parts of the more southern districts, and grasses and grain are more natural to it. This section has a rapid declivity toward the southwest, and is, in fact, the reverse side of the southern and highest section of Kentucky, which occupies the north slope of the same ridge.

The western section, embracing above two thirds of the state and called Western Tennessee, is subdivided by its rivers into two parts, the northern of which embraces parts of the Cumberland and Tennessee valleys, the area lying in the former being eleven thousand nine hundred square miles, and that in the latter ten thousand square miles. Central Tennessee has a declivity toward the west, though Tennessee river has there a north course. Beyond that region, Western Tennessee slopes toward the Mississippi, into which it is drained. That portion of the state has a superficies of seven thousand, seven hundred and forty square miles, and contains the following rivers, which empty into the Mississippi: the Obion, Forked Deer, Big Hatchee, and Wolf. These streams have a remarkable resemblance in their courses, all of them flowing in parallel curves, first northwest, then west, and finally southwest. The declivity down which they flow rises at about the distance of twenty-five miles west of Tennessee river, and descends westward by a gentle slope.

This state, when first known to white men, was covered with a thick forest, in which the growth varied greatly, according to the various elevation, soil, and relative situation of different parts. These are very diversified, from the highest points of Cumberland mountains to the rich valleys beside the principal rivers, and the low, inundated banks of the Mississippi.

History.—The whole territory of Tennessee was embraced by the second charter of North Carolina, granted by Charles the Second in 1664; but the first settlement was made in 1754. This was not a permanent one; for the few families composing it, being much exposed to the Indians in their remote position on Cumberland river, were obliged to abandon it in the French war. In 1757, Fort London was erected on the Little Tennessee river, about a mile above the mouth of Tellico river, now in Blount county. This was attacked and taken by the savages in 1760, when two hundred persons, of different ages and both sexes, were killed. In the following year, however, Grant's expedition reduced the Indians, and established a permanent state of tranquillity by treaty, which encouraged the peopling of the country. In 1765, settlements were commenced on the Holston, which increased rapidly in spite of the opposition made by the natives.

When the revolution began, the inhabitants, led by Colonel John Sevier, made a successful resistance to the encroachments of the savages; and, assisted by a few Virginia troops, defeated them in the month of June, 1776. Difficulties, however, continued through the war.

Delegates from Tennessee appeared in the first assembly of the state of North Carolina, and some of her soldiers assisted in the defeat of the British and tory army at King's mountain, on the 7th of October, 1780. So great, however, were the obstacles in the way of a settlement of West Tennessee, that the site and vicinity of Nashville were a wilderness in 1779.

North Carolina made a provisional cession of the territory of this state to the United States in 1784. This act was soon repealed, but the people adhered to their favorite plan; and, as North Carolina persevered in her opposition to their independence, the country suffered from the evils of an uncertain and unsettled government. The people adopted the name of Frankland for the country; but in 1790 the territory was ceded to the United States, and disorders ceased. It received the name of the territory southwest of the river Ohio.

The first printing-press was introduced at Rogersville in November, 1791, and on the 5th of that month the Knoxville Gazette appeared—the first newspaper in Tennessee.

Minerals.—Tennessee abounds in gypsum and marble of different colors; and burr-millstones are quarried in some parts of the Cumberland mountains. Iron mines are numerous, and several lead mines have been worked. Salt-springs are known in many places, but they are not of sufficient strength to be very valuable. Saltpetre abounds in caves.

Harpeth Ridge.—In a recent exploration in this region (which is in Davidson county), in company with the geological class of the college, new evidences were discovered of the correctness of what has been said of these formations—in the American Journal of Science, No. 2, new series, p. 222—in relation to their relative age, position, and identity with the corresponding formations of Ohio and New York. The rocks in this vicinity correspond with the blue shaly limestone of Cincinnati and the surrounding region, above which, in the knobs and ridges in Middle Tennessee, we find a stratum, of a few feet in thickness, corresponding with the red encrinital limestone of the Niagara group, New York; succeeding which, in most places, are the water-lime, Onondaga limestone, and Marcellus shale, of the New York geologists, which correspond with the water-lime, cliff-limestone, and black shale, of Louisville, Kentucky. Immediately upon the shale was found a stratum composed almost entirely of the columns of encrinites, and occasionally a beautiful head, which, from the disintegration of the rock, may be found detached and upon the surface. In this formation at Louisville have been found eight or ten undescribed species of encrinites, some of which Dr. Troost, state geologist of Tennessee, has figured and described for the memoirs of the Geological society of France.

Above the lastmentioned rock occurs a layer of dark-brown slate, a few feet in thickness, containing the *strophomena setigera*, and *tentaculites fissurella*, probably corresponding with the Genesee slate of New York. This is succeeded by olive shales and sandstone, corresponding with the portage group of New York.

In the year 1846 a skeleton was discovered in Tennessee, which was at first reported to be a fossil giant. An examination of it, however, by scientific men, soon detected the error. We copy the following "remarks on the fossil bones recently brought to New Orleans from Tennessee."

"The 'Gigantic Fossil.'—Considerable interest has been recently excited by the announcement of the discovery in Tennessee of the remains of a man eighteen feet high. The papers teem with accounts of the prodigy, and public confidence was secured by the assertion that the distinguished physicians of the west had testified that they were human remains. About the last of December these remains reached this city; and on the first of January I was requested by a distinguished surgeon here to go with him, on the invitation of the proprietor, to examine them, and give an opinion. They had been erected in a high room; the skeleton was sustained in its erect position by a large upright beam of timber. At a glance it was apparent that it was nothing more than the skeleton of a young *mastodon* (one of Godman's tetracaulodons, with sockets for four tusks). The bones of the leg and ankle were complete, the metatarsal bones wanting. The bones of the anterior extremities were complete to the metacarpal bones, which were present in one leg, the phalanges wanting. Most of the vertebræ were present; the ribs mostly of wood. The pelvic arrangement was entirely of wood; the scapulæ were present, but somewhat broken, and were rigged on with a most human-like elevation, pieces of ribs supplying the want of clavicles. The osseous parts of the head were portions, nearly complete, of the upper and lower jaws. Some of the molars were quite complete; of the tusks, only one little stump remained, but the four alveoli of the upper jaw had large incisive-looking wooden teeth fitted into them, and the lower jaw supplied to correspond. The cranium was entirely wanting from the lower margin of the orbits, back; but a raw-hide cranium was fitted on, which was much more becoming to the animal in his new capacity than the old one would have been.

The artificial construction was principally in the pelvis and head; and, taking it as thus built up—in its half-human, half-beastlike look, with its great hooked, incisive teeth—it certainly must have conveyed to the ignorant spectator a most horrible idea of a hideous, diabolical giant, of which he dreamed, no doubt, for months. To one informed in such matters, it really presented a most ludicrous figure.

"The person who had it for exhibition was honest, I believe, in his convictions as to its being the remains of a man, having been confirmed in them by numerous physicians, whose certificates he had in his possession; and, having asked and received my opinion, he determined to box it up, never again to be exhibited as the remains of a human being."

Dr. Troost endeavors to show that the bodies which have been found in the caves of Tennessee are not probably mummies, but merely dried *cadavers*, exhibiting no marks of embalming or artificial preparation. He doubts whether one of these, which he examined, was even of remote antiquity. The other question is respecting the numerous graves found in the western states some years ago, and which were said to contain the remains of an extinct pigmy race of human beings. Dr. Troost supposes these graves to contain the collected bones of the slain in battle. The Indian custom was to carry their slain to their own towns, and hang them up in mats on trees. At their general burning festivals, the bones thus preserved were collected and buried, "and thence in my opinion," says the doctor, "those numerous small graves which are attributed, but I believe erroneously, to pigmies. I have opened numbers of these small graves, and have found them filled with a parcel of mouldered bones, which, judging from some fragments I have seen, belonged to common-sized men. In one of them I found, among these mouldered bones, *two* occipital bones; of course, it was a mere mixture of bones belonging to more than one body. These bones lay without any order." The doctor then considers the circumstances attending the ancient and extensive burying-grounds found in Tennessee. He mentions one near Nashville, about a mile in length and of unknown breadth, in which is found stone coffins so close to one another, that each corpse is separated from its neighbor by only a single stone, the side of one coffin forming one of the sides of the next. In a circle of about ten miles in diameter, there are six extensive burying-grounds. These graves are supposed to contain the remains of an extinct race. The extinct race is supposed to have been less civilized than the Indians who were found here at the time of Columbus. This is inferred from the trinkets and utensils found in the graves being of a very rude construction, and all formed of some natural product—none of metal. Dr. Troost says that the examination of these trinkets, &c., has created in him an opinion that the people to whom they belonged, and in whose graves they are found, came from some tropical country, and adduces many cogent reasons for thinking so. That they were idolaters, and, from their idols—several of which are in the possession of Dr. Troost—acquainted with some of the idolatrous mysteries of the Egyptian and other eastern nations, is very evident. This would seem to indicate that the earliest inhabitants of this continent had an *eastern origin*, and is corroborative of a common opinion.

Caverns.—The caves may well be ranked among the natural curiosities of the country. One is four hundred feet deep, with a stream of pure water at the bottom; and one cave, on one of the peaks of Cumberland mountains, is of greater extent than is yet known. Some of them are several miles in extent, and present sides and roofs of remarkable uniformity, with the appearance of having been cut by art, or worn by the washing of streams. One has been explored for a distance of ten miles.

Statistics.—According to the census of 1840, the population of the state was 829,210; of whom there were 325,434 white males; 315,193 white females; 183,059 slaves; 2,796 free colored persons. According to the census of 1850, the population was 767,319 whites, 6,280 free colored persons, and 249,519 slaves; total 1,023,118.

Furnaces.—An official report to the

legislature of Tennessee sets down the capital employed in the iron business at $4,100,000, and the annual products at the same amount. Three fourths of this capital is employed in Middle Tennessee. On the Cumberland river, near Nashville, there are "twenty-one blast-furnaces, eleven forges, and three splendid rolling-mills, which yield annually about $800,000." On the Tennessee river "there are twelve furnaces, and eight forges and bloomeries, which produce about 180,000 tons annually."

The agricultural products of Tennessee are in value $57,551,820; while those of Ohio are only $57,899,390, and of New York 57,685,400: showing Tennessee to be the third state in the Union in productive wealth.

The ordinary revenue of the state in 1850 was $200,000.

"The original settlers," says a late intelligent letter-writer, "came of a good stock. A strong religious, puritan-like character was that of the leading men among them; and although multiplied sects have since sprung up, there is a leaven of it still remaining.

"East Tennesseans are sometimes called the yankees of the south. They have strong sense, shrewdness, and patience in labor, like your New-Englander. There is probably some degeneracy, however, from the heroic age of this people.

"The early days of Indian fighting, and of manifold struggles and privations, were the days of peculiar energy and fortitude—the like of which are not exhibited now in the various departments of peaceful life. There is an aspect of newness visible here and there; there are indications of progress, but there are also signs of decay. Some things are waxing old and ready to vanish away in this state, which has lived as a state but fifty years.

"Near the Holston is a hill, at the foot of which the first-appointed governor of the southwestern territory landed and selected his residence. President Washington had sent him out. Peace established with Great Britain—the constitution formed, and states settling down quietly under it—had not given peace or protection to the vast region west of the mountains. Conflicts with Indians, collisions with Spaniards—then our powerful neighbors south and southwest—went on for years, with bloody forages and wild adventures on both sides. The federal governor came—a man prudent in policy and conduct. At that time the town where I am writing was commenced; it took the honored name of Knox, after the then secretary of war. Andrew Jackson, then a young lawyer recently from North Carolina, was made United States district attorney. On this spot the state government was first set up, and here was its seat for many years. The eastern part, for some purposes, is really a state within itself. One day it made the attempt to set up for itself. With a little corner of Virginia, and another fragment of North Carolina, East Tennessee constituted itself the state of Frankland, but the effort was premature. It is the Switzerland of the south. The Cumberland mountains, which divide the state on a part of its northern boundary from Kentucky, turn sheer out of their straight course, and, sweeping across the state, terminate abruptly in Georgia. The Unakas, coming down from North Carolina on the east, meet them there, and both ranges together hem in this mountainous district.

"But, with the tokens of retrogression and decay above adverted to, what shall be done to secure permanence together with true progress? Perhaps a fresh infusion of vital force is needed. No portion of the Union, I think, would better please the industrious farmer of New England; and such men, as a class, would be acceptable to this population. Both would be benefited by the accession. Elements of agricultural and manufacturing skill found among them are needed here; they would do substantial service, and would find their reward.

"This soil yields a fine increase with no great labor bestowed upon it—without scientific, not to say careful cultivation. In corn, no state equals Tennessee. On these hills sheep could be raised in great numbers, if only the dogs were reduced in number at the same time. The climate is very agreeable—most grateful to invalids. People were crossing the ice at Albany and on Lake Champlain, when the peach-trees had long since bloomed with us; gardens were beginning to look well; in some places, it was already late to make them here, when snow was lying ten feet deep in Vermont the last season. Fruits, flowers, and crops, come some five or six weeks earlier than in your vicinity, and there is abundance for all. Without the oppressive heat of more southern climes, this region has a bland atmosphere, and the freshness and vigorous life of more northern countries. Its position, southern and elevated, gives it that combination.

"These mountains have sent out no small part of the active men of the entire southwest. Many of their foremost men were trained among these hills."

Among the curiosities of Tennessee are the celebrated foot-prints on some parts of the Cumberland mountains. The rocks on which they have been observed are of limestone, and some of them have been supposed to be the tracks of men, others of horses and oxen, and all of recent date. Some observers, on the other hand, have regarded them as the tracks of bears and other wild beasts, and probably very ancient.

Petrifactions of various kinds abound in some parts of the state. Near the southern line are three petrified trees, nearly entire. One of them is a cypress, another a sycamore, and the third a walnut. They were discovered in consequence of the falling of a bank on the south shore of the Tennessee river. Claws, teeth, and bones, of different large animals, have been found in numerous placos. Logs, too, in various stages of change, have been dug up at various depths; and both mineral coal and charcoal have been found at from sixty to one hundred feet below the surface of the ground.

Cascades.—These are numerous, and many of them very picturesque. One of the most beautiful is the "Falling Water," on a branch of Caney creek, eight miles from its mouth, and sixty miles from Carthage. The stream has a rapid course for some distance before it reaches the cascade, having a descent of one hundred and fifty feet within a short distance, when it makes a precipitous leap of one hundred and fifty or two hundred feet, in a single sheet, eighty feet broad.

The fall on Taylor's creek is still more remarkable, as the scenery is more wild, and the approach attended with much danger, while the perpendicular descent is greater, being, as some say, from two hundred to two hundred and fifty feet. What adds to the impressive, gloomy, and terrific effect of the scene, is a large overhanging rock, three or four hundred feet high, which almost excludes the sight of the sky, and throws its shade over the wild and foaming sheets of falling water, which are half converted into foam and spray by the height of the fall and strong currents of air, which rush and whirl through the deep and frightful gulf.

Another fall, only twenty yards distant from this spot, toward the south, offers to the spectator a scene of a very different nature. A precipice, about three hundred feet high, crosses the channel of another and smaller stream, which, in descending it, is divided into innumerable little rills, each of which forms separate cascades, and all together, in the contrast of the dark rock down which they pour, present a scene remarkable for its richness and beauty.

Along some of the streams of Tennessee, where they flow through rocks of limestone, wonderful effects have been produced by the cutting out of deep channels between high and ragged banks. Some of the larger and navigable rivers present scenes of this description to the admiration of the traveller, who is borne with rapidity along the bases of lofty natural walls, inaccessible to human foot, and sometimes apparently overhanging the stream, and threatening destruction to everything below. When contemplated from above, the rivers in some places appear to flow through deep channels cut by the labor and skill of man, so uniform is the original surface of the ground, and so smooth and perpendicular the rocky precipices which descend from the level.

KNOXVILLE.—This town is the principal one in East Tennessee, and stands on Holston river, four miles below the mouth of French Broad creek. It has about five thousand inhabitants, some of whom are engaged in manufactures. The situation and appearance of the town are pleasant; and it is the site of a very respectable literary institution, East Tennessee university. Here is the head of steamboat navigation, and stagecoaches run three times a week for Washington (D. C.), via Abingdon (Virginia) and Staunton; for Raleigh (N. C.); for Charleston (S. C.) via Warm Springs; for Savannah (Georgia) via Atlanta; for Nashville; and for Lexington (Kentucky) via Cumberland gap.

East Tennessee University.—The buildings of this institution are situated on the summit of a considerable eminence, half a mile west of Knoxville, and near the bank of the Holston. The principal edifice, which occupies the centre, has on each side a fine building, three stories high, for the accommodation of students. There are also three residences of the professors.

The institution possesses a philosophical apparatus, a chemical laboratory, a mineralogical cabinet, and a library of about four thousand volumes. Commencement is held on the first Wednesday of August.

JONESBOROUGH is a small town, with about one thousand inhabitants, and the site of Washington college. It is on the bank of a branch of Holston river, ten miles south of the latter, and has a courthouse, three churches, and two academies.

Washington College was founded in 1794, and has a president, three professors, about one thousand volumes in its library, and about fifty students.

MAYSVILLE.—This is also on the bank of the Holston, eighteen miles from Knoxville, and has a courthouse, a church, and about five hundred inhabitants.

The *Southwest Theological Seminary*, which is situated here, was founded in 1821. It is under the presbyterians, and has in its library about six thousand volumes.

NASHVILLE.—This town, the capital of the state, stands at the head of steam navigation, on the left bank of Cumberland river, one hundred and twenty miles from its junction with the Ohio. Near it are three lofty bluffs. The situation is fine, the climate healthful and inviting, and the town has been rapid in its growth.

One of the most striking of the public buildings is the markethouse, which is one of the finest in the western country. There are 13 churches, a lunatic asylum, the state penitentiary, three banks, a lyceum, and many handsome houses. The population in 1850 was eighteen thousand. The distance from Washington is seven hundred and fourteen miles southwest; it is five hundred and ninety-four northeast of New Orleans, two hundred and ninety-four southwest of Cincinnati, two hundred and eighty-eight south of Indianapolis, and nine hundred and thirty-seven southwest of New York.

The *Capitol* is constructed of pure white limestone, and upon a plan of the most liberal magnificence, challenging the admiration of the Union. Chaste, yet grand, it will stand through all time, as a noble monument of the taste and patriotism of this age: and to the youths of the state who gaze upon its complete and faultless proportions, it will irresistibly convey a lesson in architectural symmetry and beauty, that books may never teach them.

Nashville University.—This institution was founded in 1806, and has four professors, two tutors, about three hundred alumni, one hundred students, and ten thousand volumes in its libraries. The principal building is two hundred feet long, fifty wide, and three stories high. Commencement is held on the first Wednesday in October.

MEMPHIS, one of the most busy and flourishing towns in the state, is situated on the bank of the Mississippi, in front of an extensive and productive region, which is naturally tributary to it; it has lately been selected as the site of the United States navyyard on the river.

View of Nashville.

COLUMBIA, forty-two miles from Nashville, stands on Duck river, and has a courthouse, three churches, an academy, a bank, and about two thousand inhabitants. There is a daily communication by stagecoaches with Nashville.

Jackson College, situated in this town, was founded in 1830, and has four professors, and about one hundred students, with one thousand two hundred and fifty volumes in its libraries.

FRANKLIN.—This town, eighteen miles from Nashville, on the left side of Harpeth river, contains a courthouse, five academies, four churches, and about fifteen hundred inhabitants. Stagecoaches start three times a week for Nashville.

CLARKSVILLE is sixty-five miles from Nashville by the Cumberland road, on the right bank of which it stands, and contains about two thousand inhabitants. There are a courthouse, three churches, two banks, and an academy. It is a place of much business, an active trade being carried on in cotton and tobacco. Steamboats run to Nashville and New Orleans, and stagecoaches start three times a week for Nashville and Smithland.

MURFREESBORO'.—This town was formerly the state capital. It stands on a small branch of Cumberland river, and has a courthouse, three churches, an academy, and fifteen hundred inhabitants.

KINGSTON, on the right bank of Tennessee river, and at the mouth of Clinch river, has a courthouse, two churches, and about seven hundred inhabitants.

CLIMATE AND PRODUCTIONS.—The seasons are generally much milder than in Kentucky. On the higher regions the summer heats are moderate, and apples, pears, peaches, and other northern fruits, are successfully cultivated. In West Tennessee, cotton forms the staple production. Indian corn is planted, in the middle portions of the state, early in April. Where stagnant waters abound in some of the valleys, disease is generated, and the alluvial regions on the larger streams are unhealthy.

Among the forest-trees, juniper, red-cedar, and savine, prevail in the more elevated regions; and in the various soils and exposures in this extensive territory may be found all the forest-trees known in the southern states. The laurel tribe, however, is rare. The products of agriculture are very numerous and abundant—chiefly cotton, tobacco, flour, indigo, &c.

Tennessee presents us with a very peculiar form, and a surface, climate, and variety of soils, varying on almost every side. Under a judicious system of moral and intellectual as well as physical improvement, how general—how rapid—how permanent might its prosperity become, in every department necessary and desirable! The most intelligent and truly patriotic of her citizens have long shown their high regard for learning, refinement, and religion, by the establishment and support of institutions which have already reflected honor on the state, while they have contributed to the benefit of the people. That enterprise is not wanting with many of the inhabitants, is farther proved by the abundant products annually obtained by agriculture, floated down her rivers and launched upon the Mississippi. The appearance of the principal towns, also, bears witness to the good taste and refinement of many of the citizens, no less than do the iron-works and other manufactories to the industry, skill, and success of the mechanics.

Much, however, remains to be done, as well in Tennessee as in other states, and especially our southwestern states, to counteract the unfavorable tendencies of regions in their peculiar circumstances. The debilitating effects of a warm climate in some parts, with the luxury spontaneously introduced by wealth; and, in others, the obstacles in the way of improvement among a thin population scattered over a rough and wilder country, demand great and combined exertions on the part of the friends of education, public intelligence, pure habits, and real national advancement, to counteract and overcome them. That such men may arise, duly impressed with the importance of the duty before them, and with a spirit fitted to cope with all the obstacles they encounter, is the earnest desire of every friend of the state.

BANK LICK.

KENTUCKY.

THIS state is bounded north by Ohio, from which it is separated by the Ohio river; east by Virginia, from which it is separated by Cumberland mountains and Sandy river; south by Tennessee; southwest by Mississippi, from which it is separated by Mississippi river; west by Illinois, from which it is separated by Ohio river; and northwest by Indiana, from which it is separated by the same river. It lies between the parallels of 36° 30′ and 39° 6′ north latitude, and the meridians of 5° 3′ and 12° 38′ west of Washington. The superficies is about forty thousand five hundred square miles.

The longest line that can be drawn in this state is from the southwest corner to the place where Sandy river crosses Cumberland mountains, and is four hundred and thirty-one miles in length. The greatest breadth is from the northwest corner along latitude seven degrees forty-five minutes, and is one hundred and seventy-one and a half miles.

This state forms but a part of the great declivity of Cumberland mountains, sloping northwest toward Ohio river. A minor slope, however, toward Tennessee river, first turns Green, Cumberland, Salt, Kentucky, and Licking rivers, west or southwest; but those waters afterward obey the grand slope, and, running northward, pour into the Ohio. The tillable surface in different parts of the state has a great diversity of elevation, from three hundred and fifty to twelve hundred feet above the gulf of Mexico.

There is, therefore, a considerable diversity of temperature and productions; and these are farther increased by certain peculiarities of the surface.

The channels of the rivers are generally cut remarkably deep into the earth, and have formed, in some places, broad valleys, partly shut out from the full influence of the sun. One third part of the descent, beginning with the first part of the descent from the foot of the Cumberland mountains, is very hilly and broken for about one hundred miles, comprising one third part of the state, from the Tennessee line to the Ohio. Beyond this another section extends north, about ninety miles in width and two in length, which may be called the hilly part of the state. It contains about eighteen thousand square miles, and is in the form of a rhomb. The middle part of it, however, is much less uneven than the two extremes. But all parts of it are alike in two important respects: they belong to one extent of uneven table-land, with a similar substratum of limestone, and with a soil generally good, but a frequent scarcity of good water.

The southwestern section, which is the smallest of the three divisions, is almost level.

"The Barrens" is a tract of considerable extent in the southern and mountainous section, with isolated rounded elevations, bearing stunted oak, chestnut, and elm-timber. The soil, however, even there, is much better than appearances indicate. The more level and unchannelled portions of the central section were covered by nature with full-grown forest-trees, and abundance of the reed-cane, the limestone soil being there remarkable for its strength and fertility.

History.—The first settlement of this state by white men was effected by men of great hardihood, and attended with severe privations and extreme dangers. A map of the middle British colonies was published in 1755, by Lewis Evans; and in 1775, J. Almon, of London, published an edition of it with a statistical account of the country. At that time, as appears from these, settlements had been extended as far as the heads of the great Kenhawa, Roanoke, Clinch, and Holston rivers; but that part, including Kentucky, was left entirely blank, as a region of *terra incognita.*

In 1767, John Finley visited it from North Carolina, and he was followed by Daniel Boone and several other men in 1769. Boone remained there until 1771, and returned in 1775 with a small band of resolute settlers.

Kentucky River, as well as the state, derives its name from the language of the Indians, who called it Cutawa. It is formed by numerous branches, which have their sources in the west slope of Cumberland mountains, interlocking with the head-streams of Sandy, Powell's, and Cumberland rivers. The upper streams of the Kentucky flow northwest from the counties of Pike and Perry, and uniting in Estill county, then turn west from the boundary between the counties of Clarke and Madison. The stream, next turning southwest, runs between Madison and Lafayette counties, and Jessamine and Garrard, when it receives Dick's river from the southeast. Finally, turning north-northwest, it keeps that course until it falls into the Ohio at Port William. Its general course is nearly northwest.

The valley of the Kentucky lies between latitude 37° and 38° 40′, and longitude 5° 40′ and 8° 10′; it measures one hundred and seventy-five miles in length, and has a medium breadth of forty miles, with an area of seven thousand square miles, being about one sixth part of the whole state. It contains the following counties, in whole or in part: Anderson, Clark, Clay, Estill, Franklin, Gallatin, Garrard, Henry, Jessamine, Lafayette, Lincoln, Madison, Mercer, Montgomery, Owen, Perry, Pike, Scott, Woodford.

This great stream flows in a channel remarkable for its depth, it being a great chasm, cut far down below the level of the country which it waters. Steamboats navigate it from Estill county downward, though the current is rapid, and has a considerable descent, although not broken by falls.

Cumberland River rises in this state,

but, after a course of one hundred and twenty miles, leaves it, and crosses the boundary of Tennessee, on its way to the Mississippi.

GOVERNMENT.—The legislative power is vested in a senate and house of representatives, which together are styled the general assembly.

The senators are thirty-eight in number, chosen, one half of them biennially, by the people from single districts for a term of four years. Representatives, one hundred in number. are chosen by the people, for a term of two years.

A governor and lieutenant-governor are elected by the people for a term of four years. The governor is ineligible for the four years succeeding the expiration of his term. The lieutenant-governor is president of the senate, and on him the duties of governor devolve in case the office of the latter becomes vacant.

The governor may return a bill passed by the legislature, but a majority of the members elected to each house may pass the bill afterward, and it then becomes a law notwithstanding his objections.

The state officers, viz., the treasurer, auditor of public accounts, register of the land-office, and attorney-general, are elected by the people, for a term of four years.

The judicial power is vested in a court of appeals, circuit courts, and county courts; the judges of each election by the people.

The general election takes place on the first Monday of August biennially, and the legislature meets on the first of November biennially, at *Frankfort.*

Every white male citizen 21 years of age, or over, resident in the state two years, or in the county where he offers to vote, one year next preceding the election, may vote at such election. Elections by the people are *viva voce,* and not by ballot.

PRODUCTIONS.—Grain is the staple production, but hemp and flax are produced of excellent quality. Flour, spirits, salted meat, and live stock, are sent to New Orleans every year, by the Mississippi, in great quantities.

POPULATION.—According to the censes of 1850, the population consisted of 770,061 whites, 9,667 free colored persons, and 221,768 slaves; total 1,001,496.

THE MAMMOTH CAVE.—The following brief description we copy from a letter in the New York Recorder. This wonderful cavern is the largest in the world:—

"During the summer of 1845 I was called into the vicinity of the Mammoth cave, and I determined to devote a few hours to a visit to this renowned curiosity.

"Leaving the main road at Mumfordsville, we are conducted to the right by a path lately opened for the accommodation of visiters. As we approach the cave, the country assumes a wild and picturesque appearance, rising abruptly in precipices, covered with verdure and wild flowers, or stretching away into the distance its fruitful valleys, diversified with the neat farmhouse of the planter reposing among flowers, and the cabins of the poor peeping humbly forth from the luxuriant fields of corn. Sometimes the road leads up the steep mountain's side; then, winding around its summit, suddenly conducts us again to the vale below. After a succession of these ups and downs, the traveller ascends the mountain in which the cave is situated. The first object of interest to the visiter is the entrance to this underground world; but for this he looks in vain. He sees only a large white building, surrounded by a variety of outhouses, occupying the centre of a clearing of small extent.

"Having procured a guide at the hotel (without whom no one is permitted to enter the cave), I was conducted down a steep declivity to the right of the house, until we entered a deep gully, through which courses a small stream of water, among broken fragments of rocks, scattered about in wild confusion. Following this ravine for a number of rods, we turn suddenly to the right, and the mouth of the cave is before you. But little effort seems to have been made to change its natural appearance, and that little has greatly marred its beauty

Entrance to the Mammoth Cave.

and interest. The sublime in nature, like great men and noble deeds, should be left to appear in its own native ornaments. The descent is somewhat abrupt and unpromising—a confused mass of unsightly rocks is all that meets the eye. We advance until the appearance is like the gray mists of the early dawn, when the lamps are lighted, and preparations made for the subsequent exploration. Soon after the descent, the passage is through a door built of rough stones, through which rushes a strong current of air, that at first produces an unpleasant chilliness; this, however, gradually wears off, as we advance into the more extended galleries of the cave. The bottom over which we pass was once, evidently, the bed of a river. It is now deeply marked by the feet of oxen, and the wheels of carts, once employed here in the manufacture of saltpetre. The avenue gradually increases, until the eye, unaccustomed to the surrounding gloom, tries in vain to trace the outline of the lofty ceiling. The first object of more than ordinary interest is the 'Giant's Coffin'—a large rock, sixty feet in length, that, from the point where the beholder stands, presents the perfect outline of a coffin. Next we pass the dilapidated saltpetre works, which greatly detract from this sublime work of nature. Progressing onward three quarters of a mile, we enter the 'Church,' a vast dome where a pulpit and seats have been erected; and as invalid clergymen often come here to seek a restoration of health, the opportunity is improved, and religious services are conducted in this subterranean chapel. I ascended the rude pulpit while the guide was igniting a quantity of saltpetre; and as it threw its livid glare over the place, revealing the dark openings of the various avenues branching out on every side—the vaulted dome sparkling with crystals of various forms and hues—the effect was almost overpowering. I have stood on the verge of Niagara, and beheld its whirl of waters, and listened to the wild, deep music of its voice—I have seen the ocean, in its fury, beating the sounding shore; the storm of fire, as, with the wings of the wind, it swept over the wild prairies of the west; and the father of waters when he spurned the narrow bounds of his native channel: but never did I comprehend the nature of true sublimity until this moment. It was not the fire, the earthquake, nor the wind; but it was the *still small voice of God*, speaking in this temple made with his own hands, as he spoke to Elijah. It was one of those moments, few and far between, when the soul appears to catch one glimpse of its future and tranquillized existence.

"Having mentioned the name of Marshall, the guide informed me that he was employed then as now when Marshall came to the cave. At my request he conducted me to the spot where the shanty was erected for his accommodation. It is situated a little more than a mile from the entrance. Here the poor invalid, with his devoted wife, took up his abode, with a hope that the peculiar atmosphere of the place would restore him to health. Vain hope! His Master said: 'Come up higher'—and he passed from the darkness of this living tomb, to the glories of the upper paradise. Here the affectionate wife watched by the couch of her afflicted husband, leaving him only once a day (as the guide informed me), and then only for a short time, to enjoy the light and sunshine of the outer world above. Portions of this little cabin still remain. I lingered around the spot with a melancholy pleasure.

"We will pass hastily through 'Purgatory;' take a peep into 'Limbo;' tarry a few moments in the 'Hall of Independence;' cross the 'Dead Sea;' make a speech in the 'Whispering Gallery'—all of which have their peculiar and indescribable beauties—and we are come to the river 'Styx,' beyond which, as I was informed, are situated the more interesting portions of this immense grotto. But as I could not devote the time necessary for further examination, I declined employing the modern Charon who here plies the oar—who, I must say, demands an exorbitant price for his services.

"To appreciate fully the beauty and sublimity of this wonder of nature, the visiter must devote several days to the work of exploration.

"The body of Marshall lies near the hotel, in its unassuming grave, unnoticed by the pleasure-seeking throng, who here congregate to squander away their precious time in idleness and dissipation."

Indian Curiosities.—We have always—says a western paper—regarded any event or circumstance, calculated to throw light upon the history of the aborigines of this country, as peculiarly interesting and worthy of record. As a nation, we are fast losing sight of the old original landmarks which distinguished the two different races who inhabited and occupied this beautiful country; and as one of those races is as rapidly disappearing as the other is increasing in numbers and power, it becomes a sacred duty with us to preserve as much as we can, for future generations, of their singular character—a character distinctive in itself from all other races of the earth—and whatever evidences may, from time to time, be discovered as we progress in civilization. Some discoveries have recently been made in Kentucky, and were reported in the Louisville Journal.

"Last fall, when it was first resolved to remove the mound, it had not been dug into more than nine or ten feet before several fine specimens of isinglass were discovered. This excited much curiosity, and strict attention was paid to all subsequent removals. The cold weather, however, setting in, stopped the project until the opening of spring, when the work was again commenced, and has been going on ever since. Several skeletons have been dug up at different times in a good state of preservation; the teeth, particularly, had the enamel on them apparently as perfect as ever. They were buried without any uniformity, some with their heads toward the south, and some sitting up. There were thought to be considerable discoveries; and indeed they are, for they prove incontestably that the mound is of artificial origin; but, in speaking of them, the half is not told.

"Some six weeks ago, near the centre of the mound, on the original surface, the appearance of two skeletons was discovered. The dirt was then carefully taken away from one, and there was found about its neck a great number of small sea or lake-shells about the size of periwinkles, and the small end ground off so as to string them for the neck. The most superficial examination of them will convince any intelligent man that they have had their origin in the sea or lakes. After the removal of this one, the other was carefully exhumed, and a like quantity of beads was found upon its neck and breast, but of an entirely different kind. They are round, with a hole through them, and are made of a solid ivory-like bone, with a very fine polish. There has been great ingenuity, too, in their make: they begin with a very large hole in the middle of the strand, which has one edge much narrower than the opposite one, the rest being strung on at each end of the strand, and made pretty much of the same fashion, but, gradually diminishing in size, formed a round ring precisely fitted to the neck. The number found shows that the same neck wore several strands. But upon the breast of the same skeleton was found a breastplate of copper, having a beautiful piece apparently of marble, worked to fit upon it very neatly and mechanically. It is an oblong square, scolloped on the sides and ends, and rounded on the corners, weighing seven ounces and a half precisely. It is six inches and a half long, and four inches and three eighths in width at each end. There are two holes in the middle of it about an inch and a half apart. The piece of stone weighs seven ounces and a quarter. It is five inches and a half in length, and one and an eighth in width at each end, and two in the middle. It has two holes through it corresponding to those upon the breastplate, and fits down upon it with a flat side, the upper part being oval. The holes are an eighth in diameter on the flat side, but, coming through to the upper oval surface, a pin-head would fill either of them; they are drilled so smooth and neatly, it would beggar human ingenuity to excel them at the present time. Immediately under the back of the skeleton a whetstone was found, three and a half inches long, and two and a half broad. It is an excellent piece of sandstone, and has the appearance of having been greatly used."

LEXINGTON.—This is the most populous town in the state, and one of the most beautiful in appearance and situation, as well as most distinguished for its flourishing condition, and intelligent and refined society. It stands near the sources of Town creek, which is one of the branches of Elkhorn river, twenty-four miles southeast by east from Frankfort, eighty south of Cincinnati, and five hundred and seventeen a little south of west from Washington, in latitude 38° 3′, longitude 7° 28′ west.

This place, notwithstanding its substantial appearance, was hardly a village in 1785, and in 1795 contained only about fifty dwellings and three hundred and fifty inhabitants. The population in 1820, was 5,279; in 1830, 6,404; in 1840, 6,997; and in 1850, about 9,500. It is the oldest town in the state and was once its capital.

It is a place of considerable manufactures, especially in cotton, woollen, linen, copper, tin, and ironware; and gristmills, papermills, tanneries, ropewalks, &c., are numerous.

Transylvania University, situated at Lexington, was founded before the separation of Kentucky from Virginia, reorganized in 1798, and brought under the present system in 1818. In 1820 it contained one hundred and forty-three academical, two hundred medical, and nineteen law students. The college buildings were partly destroyed by fire some years since, but they are now much enlarged.

The Canal.—A short but noble canal surmounts, by a cut-off, the rapids of the Ohio, two miles from Louisville. The locks and bridges of this work are on a grand and massive scale. The noble three-arched bridge, under which a large two-decked steamer can pass, is the first attraction. From this point Louisville and its environs present a charming panorama. The country is slightly rolling, and richly diversified by forest, field, and habitation. The canal cuts through it in a straight line, with its gliding show of steamboats, apparently self-impelled through the meadows. The Ohio, with its sparkling rapids and distant waving outline, and the city, imbowered in trees, fill up the picture. Out of the scores of fine buildings, some imposing public edifices and three or four stately churches rise and detach themselves; presenting, altogether, a scene truly beautiful and inviting.

LOUISVILLE.—This city stands on the south bank of the Ohio, just above the rapids, and below the mouth of Beargrass creek, in latitude 38° 18′ north, and 5° 42′ west longitude from Washington. It is the most important commercial town in the state. The navigation of the Ohio, interrupted by nature, except only during high water, about ten months in the year, has been improved by a canal constructed round the falls.

The distance from Frankfort is fifty-two miles, a little east of north; one hundred and twelve from Cincinnati; six hundred and thirty-two from Pittsburg; and one thousand four hundred and eleven from New Orleans. The ground is seventy-five feet above low-water mark, and the streets cross at right angles, giving a favorable appearance to the city from without, and a fine display to the public buildings. The principal of these are the cityhall, the courthouse, marine-hospital, medical institute, city-hospital, two savings-banks, four insurance-offices, two orphan asylums, four markets, a school for the blind, eighteen public schools, thirty select schools, a Magdalen asylum, three banks, and twenty-six churches. The city is lighted with gas, and expensive works are in construction to supply it with good water. This being the principal place of business in the state, and, to a great extent, of the neighboring country, a very extensive trade centres here; and where an unknown number of flatbottomed and keel-boats are constantly employed in the transportation of goods, about three hundred steamboats are also in constant activity, running in different directions, to and from the city.

View of Louisville.

The growth of Louisville has been very rapid. In 1800 the inhabitants amounted to only 1,357; in 1830 they were 10,196, and in 1850 about 44,000. Many kinds of manufactures are carried on here. The canal, leading round the falls, is one of the earliest and most important works of improvement undertaken in this part of the country. The charter was granted in 1825, and the canal was opened for use in 1829. The stock was $600,000, of which congress took $100,000. The canal is nearly three miles in length, and in that distance overcomes a descent of twenty-two and a half feet, by five locks.

The *Medical Institute* at Louisville is a very important institution, founded in 1837, with six professors, and about two hundred and fifty students. The lectures commence on the first Monday in November.

The Kentucky Historical society has a considerable library with numerous manuscripts. The Merchants' library contains 8,500 volumes. The Agricultural and Horticultural society has been founded within a few years.

Communication is daily had by steamboats with Cincinnati, Maysville, Guyandotte (Virginia), Wheeling, and Pittsburg, up the Ohio; and with St. Louis, New Orleans, and the intermediate places below. Stagecoaches go daily for Maysville via Frankfort and Lexington, for Cincinnati, for St. Louis through New Albany (Indiana), for Vincennes, for Nashville, &c.

Frankfort, the capital of the state, is twenty-two miles west-northwest from Lexington, fifty-one east from Louisville, one hundred and two south-southwest from Cincinnati. It stands on the right bank of Kentucky river, sixty miles from the Ohio, on a level, elevated piece of ground, nearly two hundred feet above the neighboring surface. The river is subject to great and sudden floods; being comprised in a narrow channel, it sometimes swells in a short time to a height of sixty feet above its ordinary level. The river divides the town into two parts, one called Frankfort, and the other South Frankfort.

The *Statehouse* has a fine portico, in the Ionic style, and makes a conspicuous appearance. It is built entirely of marble, and contains halls for the chambers of the legislature, the court of appeals, and the federal court. The staircase has a fine effect, being placed under the dome.

A chain-bridge crosses the river near the middle of the town, where the banks are four or five hundred feet high.

Among the public buildings are the courthouse, state-penitentiary, market-house, bank, academy, theatre, and five churches. There are several manufactories of different kinds, and the population amounts to about two thousand.

The Stateprison.—The following extracts from a late report of the officers will afford the reader correct ideas of the condition and prospects of this important institution:—

"We have availed ourselves of every possible means in our power to carry out the wishes of the legislature, and of every true philanthropist, in regard to the moral and religious instruction of this unfortunate portion of our race; and we most heartily acknowledge that it is a source of much gratification to us, to see the manifest disposition on the part of nearly all the prisoners to conform to law and good morals, submitting to the laws of the prison with that character of submissiveness which ought to be gratifying to every true lover of man.

"We look forward with pleasure to a day early in next season, when we will be prepared with a suitable school-room and chapel, where we can carry on the work of moral and religious instruction more perfectly, and where those ministers of the different denominations who have labored with us can be rendered more comfortable than we have been able to make them heretofore, while they further aid us in the most pleasant part of our duties; and although a fair proportion of our best energies have been constantly engaged in endeavoring to promote the moral and religious interests of the prisoners, yet, for want of suitable buildings and other means, we have not been able to do what we would wish; but sufficient provision having been made, we most confidently promise to present to your honorable body, at the meeting of your next session, their condition in a much more favorable light. Ministers of the different denominations of our town and its vicinity, generally, have contributed to aid us in advising the prisoner for his good, to whom we feel thankful.

"The disbursements for the year past were as follows: for hemp, iron, lumber, leather, &c., $29,375 02; victualing prisoners, 5,719 57; clothes and bedding for prisoners, 1,281 63; wood and coal for engine, blacksmith shop, &c., 2,473 74; wagons, hauling hemp, stone, lumber, wood, &c., 1,800 56; pay of officers, physicians, and guards, 4,387 35; cash paid to prisoners ($5 each), as directed by law, 285 00; tools and implements of trade for workshops, 966 41; brick and lumber for new buildings, 388 24; cash paid town of Frankfort, water privilege for use of engine, and repairs of pipe, 68 70; travelling expenses to various points, including trip east, on business of the institution, 227 55; cash paid ferriage and turnpike for wagons, hauling stone, hemp, &c., 176 02; medicines and medical instruments for use of prison-hospital, 60 69; rewards and expenses incident to arrest and return of escaped convicts, 83 45; lot purchased for extension of prison-wall, as authorized by act of assembly, 2,400; cash paid stonemasons engaged in the erection of prison-wall, 836 63; moral and religious instruction, 237 38; stationery for use of office, 52 20; printing office-blanks, advertisements, &c., 44 37; postage, letters sent and received on business of institution, 9 05; tobacco for use of prisoners, as directed by law, 166 25; two yoke of oxen purchased for use of prison, 75 00: total, $51,114 81.

"The receipts were as follows: By Craig and Henry, advanced for institution, $2,311 20; cash received for the sale of bagging and baled hemp, and for the manufacture of bagging, 30,299 11; cash received for the sale of articles at prison, 6,287 47; cash loaned by the state, per act approved February 23, 1846, 6,000; cash received for lock-up fees, for safe-keeping of slaves, 195 00; by barter (manufactured articles given in exchange), 6,022 03: total, $51,114 81.

"The number of prisoners in confinement on the first day of December, 1845, was 176; received into the prison from 1st December, 1845, to 1st December, 1846, 71: total, 247.

"The number discharged during the same time were: by expiration of sentence, 32; by pardon of Governor Owsley, 22; restoration to rights of citizenship by pardon of the governor, one day previous to expiration of sentence, 3; by death, 2; escaping, 1: total, 60.

"Leaving in confinement, on 1st December, 1846, 187. Of this number, there were 166 white male, and 21 colored males.

"The crimes for which they were convicted were as follows: for manslaughter, 13; burglary, 9; larceny, 72; horse-stealing, 32; intent to kill 4; assisting slaves to run away, 8; felony, 12; passing counterfeit money, 13; forgery, 3; highway robbery, 4; arson, 3; counterfeiting, 3; perjury, 3; bigamy, 2; rape, 2; mailrobbery, 1; poisoning, 1; slave-stealing, 1; mayhem, 1.

"The terms of their sentences were: for 40 years, 3; 22 years, 1; 15 years, 1; 12 years, 1; 10 years, 15; 9 years, 2; 8 years, 7; 7 years, 10; 6½ years, 1; 6 years, 10; 5½ years, 1; 5 years, 11; 4½ years, 2; 4 years, 38; 3½ years, 1; 3 years 4 months, 1; 3 years, 33; 2½ years, 2; 2 years, 25; 1 year 10 months, 1; 1 year 6 months, 1; 1 year 1 day, 1; 1 year, 19.

"*Education.*—Superior, or those who have a classical or scientific education, 3; good, or those who have received a general English education, 20; common, or those who can read, write, and cipher, 49; poor, or those who can only spell and read, 53; none, or those who are entirely destitute of education, 62.

"*Ages.*—From 15 to 20 years, 20; 20 to 30, 87; 30 to 40, 44; 40 to 50, 19; 50 to 60, 14; 60 to 70, 2; 70 to 80, 1.

"*Previous Habits.*— Habitually intemperate, 62; occasionally intemperate, 95; temperate, 30.

"Married, 75; single, 96; widowers, 11; separated, 5. Total, 187.

Blannerhasset's Island.

OHIO.

THIS state is bounded north by Lake Erie, northeast, by Pennsylvania, east and southeast by Ohio river, which separates it from Virginia, south and southwest by the same stream, which there separates it from Kentucky, west by Indiana and northwest by Michigan. The noble river from which the state has derived its name, extends along its boundary for 440 miles, viz., from the mouth of the Beaver to that of the Great Miami, and its coast on the lake is 150. The entire outline is 933 miles, and area nearly 44,000 square miles, or above 26,000,000 of statute acres.

This state lies between 37° 25′ and 41° 58′ north latitude, and between 3° 30′ and 7° 48′ west longitude from Washington. A line drawn nearly straight from the west boundary of Pennsylvania, at a point between the sources of the Ashtabula and the Shenango branch of Big Beaver, southwest by west, would cross the summit level of the Ohio canal and the ridge dividing the waters flowing into Lake Erie from those flowing north into the Ohio. The northern division of the state thus made, is an inclined plane, widening from twenty-five miles, in the northeast, to eighty miles in the northwest, and contains about one fourth of the whole area. The southern declivity is much more gentle; while the north has a descent of 405 feet, that of the south is only 509 in a mean breadth of 247 miles, being only two feet per mile instead of thirteen.

The southern division might rather be regarded as originally a plain, as high grounds near the Ohio river which appear like a range of hills when viewed from the south, are only the declivity of the broad table-land there broken down. The south slope before spoken of, properly belongs only to the valleys of the streams flowing in that direction into the Ohio. These streams are generally free from falls, except the Muskingum and a few others; but those which flow into Lake Erie, passing down a ridge about eight hundred feet high, are too much broken for navigation. Some of them make that descent within five miles. This ridge is visible to a person sailing up the coast, and is seen gradually receding inland until it disappears in the distance near Sandusky.

The course of the Ohio forms nearly a perfect semicircle along the outline of the state. If one point of the dividers be placed on the map at Worthington, nine miles north of Columbus, and the other at the mouth of Big Sandy river, it will sweep round on or very near the course of the great river. Like its tributaries, it flows through a deep channel, cut down below the original plain. The breadth of this valley varies, above Louisville, from one to two miles, and its temperature is so much warmer than that of the neighboring high land, that vegetation is about six weeks earlier in the spring; but the cold is greater in winter.

On account of its rapid increase in population, and the general extension of the improvements of civilization, as well as the intelligence, industry, and thrift, of its inhabitants, the state of Ohio is inferior to no other country of equal extent. Indeed, it may be safely asserted, that none has been equally distinguished in all the points we have enumerated.

In consequence of a singular and peculiarly favorable concurrence of events and circumstances, the energy of our nation here found an opportunity to display itself, while in its early youth; and the results show something of the tendencies and power of the principles and habits implanted by our ancestors, when left at liberty to develop themselves.

The surface, soil, and climate of Ohio are all highly favorable to agriculture; and her situation, with the natural facilities offered to navigation, afford opportunities to many parts of it to communicate with markets.

The soil of Ohio is in general very fertile; and the productions are afforded in immense quantities. These are wheat, rye, oats, Indian corn, live stock, and salted meat. Indian corn ripens in all parts, and apples and peaches flourish well, as do nectarines, cherries, plums, grapes, and berries of all kinds. Flint says Ohio "is the appropriate empire of Pomona."

The principal tributaries of the Ohio flowing in this state are Muskingum, Hockhocking, Scioto, and Great and Little Miami. Their head streams interlock with those running into Lake Erie: the Ashtabula, Grand, Cuyahoga, Huron, Sandusky, and Maumee. Numerous smaller streams are omitted in this enumeration.

The Ohio canal extends from Cleveland, on Lake Erie, up the valley of the Cuyahoga south, about thirty miles, crosses Portage summit to the Muskingum or Tuscarawas river, whose valley it follows to Dresden, within fourteen miles of Zanesville, and then, in a southwestern direction, crosses the ridge to the Scioto, twelve miles south of Columbus, then south down the valley to Circleville, Chillicothe, Piketon, and Portsmouth, where it enters the Ohio, being three hundred and six miles long.

The Miami canal extends from Cincinnati north through the Great Miami valley, through Hamilton, Middletown, Franklin, and Miamisburg, to Dayton, a distance of sixty-seven miles.

The population, in 1800, was 45,365; in 1810, 230,760; in 1820, 581,434; in 1830, 935, 884; in 1840, 1,519,467; and in 1850, 1,977,031.

The original constitution of Ohio was formed at Chillicothe, in 1802, and continued in operation until 1851, when a new constitution was framed at Columbus, by a convention, March 10th, and adopted by the people, June 17th, 1851.

By this constitution, the senaters and representatives are elected biennially, and meet at Columbus on the first Monday of January following.

The senate consists of thirty-five members chosen by single districts, except the first, the county of Hamilton, which is entitled to three senators. The whole numbers of representatives is one hundred, who are apportioned among the several counties by a plan laid down in the constitution, on the basis of population, according to the federal census, or such other mode as the general assembly may direct, once in every ten years, which is to continue for the ten years next succeeding such apportionment.

The executive department consists of a governor, lieutenant-governor (who is president of the senate), secretary of state, auditor, treasurer, and an attorney-general, who are chosen by the people at the biennial election, on the second Tuesday in October. These officers hold their offices for two years, except the auditor whose term is four years. The respective terms commence on the second Monday in January. The board of public works, consisting of three members, is elected by the people, one annually for the term of three years.

The judicial power is vested in a supreme court, in district courts, courts of common pleas, courts of probate, justices of the peace, and in such other courts, inferior to the supreme court, as the general assembly may establish; the five supreme court judges hold their office five years, the term of one of the judges expiring annually. There are nine judges of the common pleas, elected by districts for five years. A judge of probate court is elected in each county for three years; a competent number of justices of the peace in each township are elected for the same term. All these elections are by the people.

The elective franchise is enjoyed by every white male citizen of the United States, of the age of twenty-one years, who shall have been a resident of the state one year next preceding the election, and of the county, township, or ward, in which he resides, such time as may be provided by law. All elections are by ballot. No person in the military, marine, or naval service of the United States, shall by being stationed within the state, be considered a resident.

No new debts may be contracted by the state, exceeding in the aggregate $750,000. The credit of the state shall neither be given nor loaned to any individual association or corporation whatever, nor shall the state hereafter, become a joint owner or stockholder in any company or association. The general assembly shall never authorize any county, city, town, or township, by vote of its citizens, or otherwise, to become a stockholder in any joint-stock company, corporation, or association whatever: or to raise money for, or loan its credit to, or in aid of, any such company, corporation, or association. The state shall never contract any debt for purposes of internal improvement. The general assembly shall pass no special act conferring corporate powers; corporations may be formed under general laws, subject to alteration or repeal. Stockholders in corporations are individually liable for all dues therefrom over and above their stock to a further sum equal in amount to such stock. No act authorizing associations with banking powers shall take effect until it shall be submitted to, and approved by, the people at a general election. Lotteries and the sale of lottery tickets are for ever prohibited. No license to traffic in intoxicating liquors shall hereafter be granted in the state.

History.—The time when the settlement of the state of Ohio commenced, was that when the close of the revolutionary war promised permanent peace and security, even to that then distant and wild portion of our territory. A considerable part of the territory had been granted to the soldiers newly disbanded; and tracts of considerable extent to persons who had been sufferers from the destructive marauding incursions of the enemy, in the course of the war, when several Connecticut towns were reduced to ashes.

The Connecticut claim was founded on the royal charter of the colony, which, after fixing the northern and southern boundaries of Connecticut, carried them through to the Pacific ocean. Under this authority, Connecticut had settled the Wyoming valley in Pennsylvania, and long exercised jurisdiction over it, but finally abandoned it, together with all other parts of the tract thus conceded to her, in consideration of a valuable portion of Ohio, afterward called New Connecticut, or the Connecticut Reserve. It was from that part of the present state of Ohio that the legislature of Connecticut gave the "fire lands," as they were termed, to the sufferers above referred to.

Under the several inducements above enumerated, the settlement of Ohio began in the year 1788, since which, its increase in population and wealth has been such as may well astonish the world, while it affords reason for gratitude, as well as for self-congratulation, not only to its inhabitants, but to all those who feel a becoming interest in the solid growth of our common country.

Early Surveys.—The Great Miami river was surveyed for one hundred miles, in 1751, by Christopher Gist, agent of the old English Ohio company; and the English had a fort, or trading-post, on Loramie's creek, forty-seven miles north of Drayton, which was taken by the French. In 1778, the Miami valleys were examined by Daniel Boone, during his captivity, and by Bowman and Clark, on their military excursions. In 1784, '5, and '6, the Indians ceded the regions of the Muskingum, Scioto, and Miamis, and the settlement was immediately commenced.

Benjamin Stiles, of Redstone (now Brownville), Pa., first proposed to John Cleves Symmes, of New Jersey, the joint purchase of a large tract of land in Ohio, which was afterward made by the latter for himself, and embraced nearly 600,000 acres. Portions having been sold, parties of emigrants left New York and New Jersey in 1788.

Harmer's Expedition.—In 1790, nearly twenty persons were killed by the Indians near Cincinnati; and in the autumn General Harmer proceeded against the savage enemy, with 320 regulars, 833 Kentucky and Pennsylvania militia, and 600 volunteers. After a severe loss in an ambush, he returned without accomplishing anything important. In 1791, General St. Clair, with a force of 2,300 men, was attacked in his camp, fifty miles from the Miami villages, and after a severe battle, driven from his position, and pursued four miles, with the loss of about 900 men in killed, wounded, and missing. The following year, the Indians murdered several of the commissioners sent by the United States government to treat for peace.

Fort Harmer was first occupied in 1785 by a part of the first regiment of United States troops, under Major John Doughty, and named after their military commander. In the same year, Gen. Benjamin Tupper, of Chesterfield, Mass., was appointed surveyor, under the surveyor-general of that state, to begin the survey of the country northwest of the Ohio, and went that year as far as Pittsburgh. The survey was postponed by the hostile movements of the Indians. In the following year, he and General Israel Putnam (the celebrated revolutionary officer) published an invitation to disbanded soldiers. who had received deeds of land in Ohio in payment of their services, to proceed with them to the Ohio region. "The Ohio Company" was formed, at their proposition; and, on the 7th of April, 1788, Gen. Putnam landed at the mouth of the Muskingum, with a party of laborers and artificers, and began to make preparations for the first settlement designed by that association, at Marietta.

At that period, the Shawnees were inhabitants of a large part of the best land in the bounds of the present state, especially the valleys of Scioto, Miami, and Wabash. Their principal chief was Cornstalk, who had distinguished himself by his faithfulness to our countrymen, by his successful opposition to the league formed against them by the nations beyond to assist the British in the war.

In 1794, *General Wayne*, after many delays, and the erection of several forts, routed a large force of Indians and Canadians near Fort Deposite, and after destroying the various villages and positions of the enemy along the Miami, brought them to consent to a treaty of peace, which was concluded August 3d, 1795.

The next settlement after that at Marietta, was made at Columbia, six miles above Cincinnati, Nov. 16, 1789, by Major Stiles and twenty-five others, chiefly from Redstone, as before mentioned, and partly from New York and New Jersey, under Judge Symmes. This colony was formed under circumstances of peculiar danger, the Indians being numerous and hostile around them, so that the settlers were compelled to take turns as laborers and sentinels, while erecting a block house.

The third settlement was made by Frenchmen, at Gallipolis, in 1791. They had been induced to come from France by the "Scioto Land Company," so called, an association of men who hoped to obtain from Congress a large grant of land, but were unsuccessful. Many of the settlers afterward dispersed, but the remainder at length obtained a grant of 24,000 acres, in the southeast part of Scioto county, on the Ohio. The tract is now called the French grant.

The fourth settlement was at Cleveland, on Lake Erie, in 1796. Another was made at Conneaut, the same yea· Both these were made by emigrants from the eastern states.

Settlers afterward came in, in great numbers, from different parts of the country, and from several parts of Europe.

The first territorial legislature met at Cincinnati, Sept. 24, 1799, whose jurisdiction extended to all the territory northwest of the Ohio. Gen. Wm. Henry Harrison was the first delegate to Congress. In 1802, Nov. 1, the convention to form a state constitution assembled at Chilicothe, which was formed and adopted in three weeks, and remained till 1851, though never formally ratified by the people. One of the provisions of the constitution, in compliance with a suggestion made by Congress, was, that section sixteen of every township (or a substitute where that was not disposable) should be reserved for the support of public schools. The first general assembly of the state met at Chilicothe, March 1, 1803. The second, the same year, passed a law allowing aliens to hold land.

The victory of Tippecanoe, by Gen. Harrison, was gained in 1811. The first steamboat voyage was made that year from Pittsburgh to New Orleans.

The first resolution in favor of a canal, was introduced into the legislature in 1817; and in 1825 an act was passed "to provide for the internal improvement of the state by navigable canals." In that year, also, a general system for common schools was adopted, which was followed by another in 1829, laying a tax, for their support, of three fourths of a mill on the dollar, and authorizing householders to lay taxes for certain school purposes, in their districts. None but negroes and mulattoes are excluded from the schools.

Ohio presents all varieties of surface, in different parts, except the mountainous. The most hilly part is in the southeast, on the Ohio. Along that stream and its tributaries are many tracts of level meadows, of the finest soil. Some of the largest and richest of these are watered by the Miamis. Prairies, or meadows of a particular kind, are found in several parts of the state, especially near the sources of the Muskingum, Scioto, and the Miamis. They are almost destitute of timber, and some are marshy, others high and poor, while most of them are covered with high, coarse grass.

Bituminous coal abounds in some of the eastern parts of the state, and salt springs and iron mines are also found in several counties. There is usually good sleighing for several weeks, in the northern part of the state, along Lake Erie. The winds are generally from the west and southwest.

There were found no signs of Indian settlements in the limits of the state, though an ancient trail, or Indian road, came down and crossed the Ohio river, at the mouth of the Licking, and led on through the Cumberland gap, being the grand route of travel through the vast western forest, between the north and the south. The preceding race, however, of whom so little is known, had left very interesting traces on the very site now occupied by Cincinnati, which have been obliterated. A number of considerable works, of different forms, extended between Ludlow and Mound streets, and between Third and Northern row. These were, first, an oval

Scene in the early Settlement of Ohio—Adam Poe and Big Foot.

embankment, 830 feet by 730, and from 3 to 7 feet high, with an eastern opening of 90 feet. It was from 30 to 40 feet wide at the base, and had evidently been much higher. A raised path led from near the opening to the top of a flat mound, at some distance beyond Main street. A similar work, and a small circular one, may also be enumerated; but these were inferior to another oval, 760 feet by 40, lying nearly north and south, with a southern opening, beyond which was a pit 50 feet wide and 12 feet in depth. At the corner of Fifth and Mound streets was a mound, 35 feet high, and several smaller elsewhere, in some of which were found pottery, various shells, &c.

The mounds in Ohio form part of the long chain which extends from the middle of New York, southwesterly to the Mississippi, and down its course, as is said by some, to Mexico. They are supposed by some writers to mark the progress of a numerous and partially civilized people, on their gradual retreat before powerful enemies. Amid abundant materials for general conjectures, and with few hints of anything positive, it is not surprising that a variety of theories should have been proposed, to account for their existence.

One cause of this variety of opinions has been the mistakes made by persons who have investigated the subject too hastily. The Grave Creek mound, fourteen miles below Wheeling, about 70 feet high, and 33 rods in circumference at the base, is one of the largest known to be wholly of artificial origin. A shaft was sunk from the top to the bottom, which exposed to view two rude tombs, one a few feet above the other, and each containing the remains of a human skeleton, several flat stones, and parts of decayed logs, with a number of implements, or weapons, and ornaments, like those often discovered in other mounds. A small stone, with an inscription resembling Runic and some other ancient alphabets, said to have been taken from the place, has recently excited the curiosity of the learned in Europe, as well as in America.

At Circleville existed one of the most curious and wonderful collections of ancient works in the state. The streets of the town are laid out in curves, corresponding with the two concentric circles of a fine, large, ancient work in which it is situated. The interior circle is 47 rods in diameter, and distant from the outer 3 rods, with a ditch between them. The outer wall was of clay, which must have been brought from a distance, and was used to make bricks in building the town. There was but one entrance through the walls, and that led into a large square, which had seven other openings. The walls were 20 feet high. Several smaller circles, &c., existed in the vicinity.

"Fifty-five years ago," said General Harrison, in his discourse before the historical society of Ohio, "there was not a Christian inhabitant within the bounds which now comprise the state of Ohio; and if, a few years anterior to that period, a traveller had been passing down the magnificent river which forms our southern boundary, he might not have seen, in its whole course of eleven hundred miles, a single human being, certainly not a habitation, nor the vestige of one, calculated for the residence of man. He might, indeed, have seen indications that it was not always thus. His eye might have rested on some stupendous mound, or lengthened lines of ramparts, and traverses of earth, still of considerable elevation, which proved that the country had once been possessed by a numerous and laborious people. But he would have seen, also, indubitable evidences that centuries had passed away since these remains had been occupied by those for whose use they had been reared."

He concluded that their departure must have been a matter of necessity; for no people would willingly have abandoned *such a country*, after a long residence, and the labor they had bestowed upon it, unless, like the Hebrews, they fled from a tyrant, or unfeeling taskmasters.

"If they had been made to yield to a more numerous, or more gallant people, what country had received the fugitives? and what has become of the conquer-

View of Cincinnati, in 1800.

ors? Had they, too, been forced to fly before a new swarm from some northern or southern hive?" What was their fate? and why has so large a portion of country, so beautiful, inviting, abounding in all that is desirable, been left to the wild beasts, or for distant tribes of savages to mingle in mortal conflicts?

We learn from the extensive country, covered by their remains, that they were a numerous agricultural people, congregated in considerable cities, but in possession of no domestic animals. It seems probable, if not certain, that they possessed a national religion, "in the celebration of which, all that was pompous, gorgeous, and imposing, that a semi-barbarous nation could devise, was brought into occasional display; that there were a numerous priesthood, and altars, often smoking with hecatombs of victims." They had made much progress in the art of building; their habitations were probably small, inconvenient, and composed of slight and perishable materials, as few remains of them are to be discovered.

General Harrison concluded that they were assailed both from the north and the south, receded from both directions, and made their last effort at resistance, on the banks of the Ohio.

The engineers who directed the execution of the Miami works, he says, must have known the importance of flank defences; and, "if their bastions are not as perfect, as to form, as those which are in use in modern engineering, their position, as well as that of the long line of curtains, are precisely as they should be."

He denies the occupation of the banks of the Ohio for centuries before its discovery by Europeans, but thinks there are indubitable marks of its having been thickly inhabited by a race of men inferior and subsequent to the authors of the great works. Pottery, pipes, stone hatchets, and other articles, are found in great abundance, inferior in workmanship to those of the former people.

The tribes within the bounds of this state, when the white settlements commenced, as General Harrison informs us, were the Wyandots, Miamis, Shawanees, Delawares, a remnant of the Mohegans (who had united themselves to the Delawares), and a band of the Ottowas. "There may also have been some bands from the Senecas and Tuscaroras remaining in the northern part of the state. But, whether resident or not, the country, for some distance beyond the Pennsylvania line, certainly belonged to them." As has been before remarked, however, the red men appear to have had no permanent settlements in any part of this extensive region, at least in a long course of time, as none of the usual or supposable marks of their fixed residence were perceptible.

How different is now the aspect of the country! Flourishing villages and scattered farmhouses on every side, amid fields of corn, sometimes extending farther than the compass of vision; large towns and cities at the principal exits of trade, extending their crowded streets along the shores of the rivers, and crowning the neighboring eminences with villas; houses for the education of the young, and for the worship of God, sprinkled over every part of the territory; and steam laboring with all its power to bear rich freights over the land and the water!

There are 87 counties, 784 town-plats, 1010 postoffices, 5 incorporated cities, 45 chartered railroad companies, about 30 canal companies, 30 banking companies, 20 colleges and principal seminaries, an asylum for lunatics, one for the deaf and dumb and another for the blind, and a complete system of common schools. What is, perhaps, of equal importance, Sunday-schools are universally established, as in most other parts of our country, every week, and often every day, bringing the minds of the old and the young to the mutual study of the word of God, and practically training the people to the observance of the Sabbath, its occupation in work appropriate to its institution, and training the people to the important duty of teaching, under circumstances most favorable to its success.

The population in 1790 was about 3,000; in 1850, 1,977,031, above 65,000 per cent.

View of Cincinnati, from the River.

The Connecticut Reserve is one of the most flourishing parts of the state. It contains the seven northeastern counties, 120 miles east and west, and 52 north and south, with four millions of acres, and was settled chiefly from Connecticut and Massachusetts.

A striking view of the rapid and solid growth of Ohio is presented by the following statistics:—

The first permanent settlement was made in 1788, and the following are among the returns made to the legislature forty years afterward, in 1836: Land for taxation, 16,460,029 acres; value of the above, exclusive of town property, $55,242,254; value of the town property, excepted, $16,906,854; houses, 280,562; cattle, 402,376; merchants' capital, $8,899,994; pleasure-carriages, 2,986. The taxes on the above, for state, county, town, and road purposes, were $995,376. The revenue of the state that year, $301,057. As early as 1837, there were 450 miles of navigable canals, with expectation of 1,000 by 1839.

CINCINNATI.

Cincinnati is the largest city in the western states, and enjoys a situation distinguished by several advantages, on the north bank of the Ohio river, which there rises, with a bold, but not too abrupt ascent, to the height of 108 feet above low-water mark, affording a convenient and commanding elevation to the upper streets. The latitude of the city is 39° 6′ 30″ north, and the longitude, 7° 24′ 45″ west. It stands half way between the head of the Ohio, at Pittsburgh, and its confluence with the Mississippi, at Cairo, being 465 miles distant from each, measuring the course of the stream. From the following cities the distances by the roads are as follows: Indianapolis 120, Columbus 115, Lexington 90, Nashville 270, Pittsburgh 298. By the steamboat routes it is 198 miles from Louisville, 655 from St. Louis, 1335 from Natchez, 1631 from New Orleans. By the stage routes, Washington is 502 miles, Baltimore 518, and Philadelphia 617. By the lakes, the distance to New York is 650 miles.

Cincinnati stands near the head of one of the largest and most fertile of the valleys watered by the Ohio. It is twelve miles in circumference, and enclosed by hills of moderate elevation, which afford a succession of varied and pleasing scenes, though the approach to the city by water affords no striking view.

The climate is very variable, and the cold in winter severe, but Cincinnati is a healthy city. The want of pavements is a serious inconvenience in wet weather, although the sloping ground on which the city is built is favorable to draining.

Geology.—The rocks at Cincinnati are mountain limestone, below which, as elsewhere, are found beds of coal. They are, however, at a considerable distance beneath. The vicinity appears to have been once a plain, 600 feet above the river at low water, and 1200 above the Atlantic, but cut down by streams, in the course of ages, which expose alternate strata of blue clay, marl, and fossiliferous limestone, nearly pure, and of a bluish color. At different elevations, in alluvial deposites left by the streams, at different ages, in their former beds, are found old trees, and the remains of elephants. On the larger streams are fine bottom lands, or meadows, of a very rich soil, of an amber color, which, in floods, tinges the river. Wells are sometimes filled with carbonic acid gas, or choke-damp, which proceeds from the limestone. Numerous marine fossils abound in the rocks.

Railroads and canals, as well as steamboats, greatly subserve the business of Cincinnati. In 1841, there were estimated to be 1,125 miles of these three kinds of routes concentrating at this city, to cost, when completed, twelve millions of dollars.

Cincinnati, notwithstanding its present importance, and the great advantages of its position, was not occupied until most of the other principal points on the western rivers had been planted with towns.

The first surveys were begun by Mr. Filson in 1788; but he soon disappeared in the woods, and was never seen again. Israel Ludlow, Robert Patterson, and

Cincinnati Landing.

Mathias Denman, occupied a part of the land at the close of that year and the next, and they gave the place the name of Losantiville, which was fortunately soon changed to that which it still bears. Jan. 7, 1789, thirty men drew lots for portions of the land, but about a year afterward, Joel Williams purchased two thirds of the town. The original price of the whole was $500, in continental certificates, then worth only five shillings on the pound. In June, 1789, Fort Washington was erected by Major Doughty, with forty men, and consisted of four blockhouses, with a stockade and barracks. In 1790, General Arthur St. Clair arrived, as governor of the "territory northwest of the Ohio."

"When I first saw the upper plain on which Cincinnati stands," says General Harrison, "it was literally covered with low lines of embankments. I had the honor to attend General Wayne two years afterward, in an excursion to examine them. The number and variety of figures in which the lines were drawn were almost endless. The cause I take to have been continued cultivation; and the probability is, that the people were the conquerors of the original possessors."

Judge Burnet says, that when he went to Ohio, in 1796, the country was literally a wilderness. The entire population between Pennsylvania and the Mississippi, from the Ohio to the lakes, was fifteen thousand. Cincinnati was a small village of log-cabins, including, perhaps, a dozen of frame houses, with stone chimneys, most of them unfinished. Not a brick had been seen in the place.

Cincinnati in 1800.—This view of our western inland emporium, while in its infancy, possesses a great degree of interest. See page 493. How much more cheerful to the eye than the sight of many an ancient European city, in which no trace of improvement is visible, and where no thought of enterprise is found! In our western towns, industry, directed by intelligence, and stimulated by hope, displays itself in prodigies, and strides on like a giant. In this city, however, if anywhere, our countrymen have surpassed themselves; and even those of us best acquainted with their energy and success may compare this print and the frontispiece, with astonishment. The particulars of the changes which have taken place between 1800 and the present time, we need not repeat; but we will refer the reader to the preceding pages, where they are recorded.

Cincinnati in 1848.—The transition from the view on page 493, to the one depicted on p. 495, seems like an illusion. Such a growth, in less than half a century, appears impossible. Cities have indeed been suddenly erected by monarchs who had absolute power over their subjects; but these changes have been produced by the spontaneous labors of individuals. The growth of the place has been natural, and the impulse will be continued. The noble display of steamboats, drawn up in line, is still inferior to what might actually be made; and the long ranges of stores in front, as well as the crowded buildings beyond, give but an imperfect idea of their real numbers.

The streets of Cincinnati are generally wide, straight, and well-built. They cross at right angles, and seven of them are sixty-six feet in breadth. The spaces enclosed between them are 396 feet square; and one of these is appropriated to public buildings and public purposes. A portion of another is also devoted to the same use. Main street, Broadway, and Fourth streets, are the finest streets; but Pearl street, between Market and Walnut, has a fine block of buildings, in a uniform style, terminated by a large hotel.

The Landing-Place. See page 497.—This nearer view of the river's side will give a more just idea of the spacious street which borders the shore, and of the size of the buildings, though it shows but a small part of the front line of the city. The reader will readily perceive, that the landing-place is convenient, as it extends far along the bank, up and down the river. It is indeed a landing-place well adapted to the extensive and increasing trade of this commercial metropolis of the west.

The principal public buildings are the courthouse, jail, four markets (one of

New Catholic Cathedral, at Cincinnati.

which is 400 feet in length), the Bazaar, Cincinnati college, the Catholic Athenœum, the Medical college, the Mechanics' institute, two theatres, two museums, the hospital and lunatic asylum, the Woodward high school, and nearly thirty churches. The town is chiefly built of brick.

Manufactures.—Within a few years, the amount and variety of manufactures have greatly increased. The principal business is done in heavy iron castings, for steam-engines and machinery. A great deal of cabinet-work is also produced, and numerous steamboats and canal-boats are built every year. The Cincinnati Manufacturing Company have a collection of large buildings on Deer Creek.

Great quantities of pork are prepared and shipped at Cincinnati. In 1848, not less than 500,000 hogs were killed in the city. The price was then only about two and a half cents a pound. One of the consequences of this business is the manufacture of great quantities of lard and oil.

Numerous steamboats have annually been built at Cincinnati. In 1843 the number was 43, whose tonnage was 8,571, and cost $618,000; in 1844, 89.

Canal-boats proceed from Cincinnati through the canal, over Lake Erie, to Buffalo. Tolls on the Ohio canals in 1850, about $800,000.

Orphan Asylums.—There are three:—

1. St. Peter's orphan asylum, managed by the sisters of charity.

2. St. Aloysius's orphan asylum, another Roman catholic institution, for boys.

3. The Cincinnati orphan asylum, erected by contributions of the citizens. It is 64 feet by 54, four stories high, and cost $18,000. It stands in Elm street. The children are taught at a good school, and have a good library, and extensive playgrounds. Morals and religion are carefully inculcated, and the future interest of the pupils provided for.

The Roman Catholic Church.—The building is of simple form, and in a neat style of architecture. The walls are straight and smooth, with seven windows on each side, and a portico projected in front, with ten Corinthian columns. The steeple, which is disproportionately high, is conspicuous from a distance. (see engraving, p. 499.)

The Commercial Hospital and Lunatic Asylum of Ohio is situated in the north-western part of Cincinnati, in a retired and airy situation. The building is of brick, with three stories and a basement, and can contain 250 inmates. The poor-house occupies a separate part of the edifice; and there are two medical departments. Boatmen who have paid hospital money, those who have not, and the town poor, are provided for gratuitously in this institution, by different funds. Other sick persons are admitted at two dollars a week.

The House of Employment for Female Poor, and the *Savings Bank*, are also valuable institutions.

Benevolent Societies.—The Cincinnati Total Abstinence Temperance society; the Colonization society; the Ohio Anti-Slavery society; the Scots' Benevolent society; St. George's society; the Cincinnati Typographical assocation; and the Hibernian Benevolent society.

The Cincinnati Astronomical Society, organized in 1842, have an observatory, with a large telescope, on Mount Adams, under the care of Professor Mitchells.

The Western Academy of Natural Sciences was incorporated in 1838, and has a valuable cabinet.

The Apprentices' Library was founded in 1821, by private contributions, and is open to all minors in the city, brought up to laborious employments.

The Young Men's Mercantile Library Association has its library and reading-rooms in the Cincinnati college, which are open daily. It was organized in 1835, and chartered the following year.

EDUCATION.—1. *Common Schools.*—The common school system of Cincinnati was founded in 1830–'31, and the number of children taught is very large. The number of districts is ten, which are now supplied with brick school-houses, with cupolas, and furnished with common apparatus, with seats for from three to five hundred pupils, each, at a

Lane Seminary, Walnut Hills, near Cincinnati.

Kenyon College.

cost of more than $100,000. They are under three boards, viz.: 1, the trustees; 2, the examiners; 3, the corps of teachers.

2. *Academies, or Classical Schools.*—There are several in different parts of the city.

COLLEGES.

Cincinnati College was chartered in 1818–'19, with university powers, and has been endowed chiefly by private contribution. It has a building in the middle of the city, with chymical and philosophical apparatus.

St. Xavier College, a Jesuit institution, enjoys the privileges of a university, and has a mercantile, as well as a classical department. It has a library of 6,000 volumes, and a cabinet of natural history. The expenses are $160 a year, including board.

Woodward College was founded in 1812, by William Woodward, one of the early settlers, who gave the land on which the building is erected.

The Medical College of Ohio, on Sixth street. Students are admitted to the lectures for $15, and for $5 more to the hospital, which is large.

Lane Seminary, a presbyterian theological seminary, is situated at Walnut Hills, a short distance from Cincinnati. Rev. Lyman Beecher is president. The course of study occupies three years, and is gratuitous, while room-rent is only $5 a year, and incidental expenses $5. This seminary enjoys a fine and conspicuous situation. The building for the lodgings of the students is of four stories and a basement, and has an entrance in the middle, with five windows on each side of the door, and sufficient depth to afford numerous apartments. On a line with it, at the right, is a very neat edifice for the chapel and other purposes, in simple Grecian style, with six Doric columns supporting an architrave, forming a portico, to which rises a broad range of steps. In the rear are the houses of the president and professors; and the whole is backed by a fine wood, while spacious grounds in front and around are laid out in yards, walks, and gardens.

GAMBIER.

Gambier is the seat of Kenyon college. Connected with this are Bexley Hall (the principal episcopal academical and theological institutions of this part of the country), Milnor Hall (the junior preparatory school), and Rosse chapel. They are situated in the midst of a large tract of land, belonging to the diocese, in a secluded and pleasant place, and are under the direction of a board of trustees. In the vicinity are the bishop's residence, the president's house, and the dwellings of five professors, with a number of other buildings, including farmhouses, storehouses, &c.

Kenyon College.—This edifice is of a plain, Gothic style, built of stone, 190 feet in length and 44 in breadth, with a spire in the centre. Funds for its erection having been collected from the contributions of friends in England, by Bishop Chase, in spite of much opposition, the main building and spire were finished in 1828. The wings were added in 1834 and 1835, under the direction of Bishop M'Ilvaine, by whom further subscriptions were obtained in 1833. (see engraving, page 502.)

All the buildings, with 4,000 acres of land surrounding them, belong to the institution, which affords theological instruction gratuitously, and is supported chiefly by the products of the soil. The whole was estimated, in 1843, to be worth from $175,000 to $185,000.

The institution was placed in the midst of this tract of land to secure it from all exposure to intrusion. An unsettled region was selected, in the midst of the forest, and the trees have been cleared off since the commencement of the undertaking.

Bexley Hall is a well-proportioned building, for the residence of the theological students of Kenyon college. It was constructed with funds raised in England by Bishop M'Ilvaine, after a plan proposed by an architect in London. It is 100 feet long and 50 deep, and affords accommodations for a large number of students. It bears the name of Lord Bexley, a distinguished and efficient friend of the institution, and well known for his enlightened and Christian zeal.

Milnor Hall is the preparatory school for Kenyon college. It is of brick, and was erected by money contributed in 1833, under the direction of Bishop M'Ilvaine.

Rosse Chapel was raised in 1836, on the site of a larger one, commenced by Bishop Chase, and serves both as the college chapel and the parish church.

MARIETTA.

The situation of this village is not unpleasant, but low, yet its institutions and society have given it a distinction worthy of the oldest settlement in the state. It is the capital of Washington county, and stands on the west bank of the Ohio, immediately above the mouth of the Muskingum. It is 61 miles southeast of Zanesville, 109 southeast of Columbus, 93 east by north of Chillicothe, and 178 from Pittsburgh. The college, and several academies and schools, give a very respectable literary standing. Shipbuilding was formerly carried on.

Here, as we have before mentioned, was planted the first permanent colony of civilized men within the bounds of the present state of Ohio. Here, on the 7th of April, 1788, landed a party of adventurers, with the celebrated veteran, General Israel Putnam, at their head. The fort, erected by United States' troops, had been some time constructed, the site of which is still pointed out.

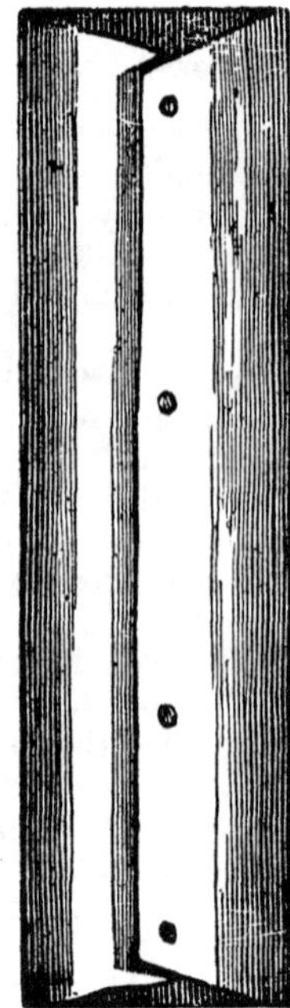

Silver sword ornament.

Antiquities.—Near the fort, on high ground and a dry soil, was an ancient mound, which was dug away some years ago, and several curious relics were brought to light. Dr. S. P. Hildreth, of that place, published drawings and a description, from which we have derived the following particulars. The objects were buried with a dead body, the remains of which existed.

The object of this form (see engraving, page 22), made of silver, was found lying beside the remains of the body. It is about six inches long, and two in breadth, and weighs an ounce. It is smooth, with three longitudinal ridges, and four holes for rivets, probably to attach it to the scabbard.

Remains of the blade were found, but they were mere iron rust; a portion of which was in the corroded fragments of the copper tip.

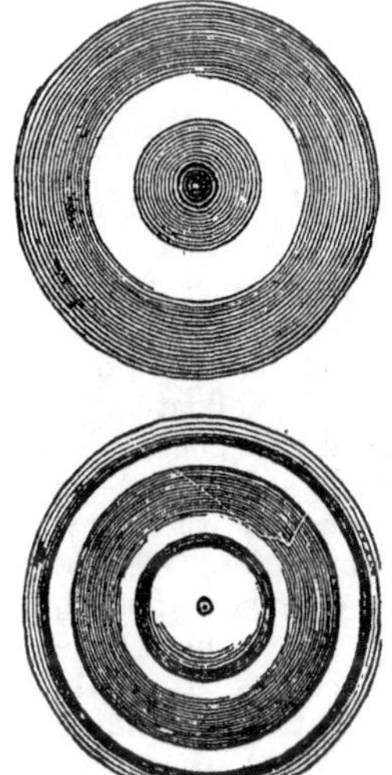

Front and back view of a boss of the sword-belt.

Three of these were found lying on the forehead of the skull, and one of copper, thickly plated with silver. They are plain, with a circular depression round the centre, and measure two and a quarter inches across. A bit of leather remained between two of the bosses, preserved by the oxyde of copper.

Near the feet of the body was found a small piece of copper, of this shape,

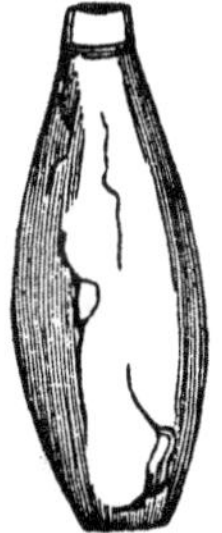

A copper plumb, or pendent.

weighing three ounces. It appears to have been formed of small pieces of native copper, pounded together, and in the cracks are several pieces of silver, one about the size of a sixpence.

There were also found a piece of red ochre, and one of iron ore, partly vitrified.

The body lay with the back on the surface of the ground, and its head toward the southwest. Fragments of charcoal and mineral coal, half burnt, lay about the body; and over and around the whole was a circle of thin, flat stones, which seemed to have been laid while the fire was burning. It seemed that the mound had been formed over this tomb, by heaping up the earth from the neighborhood, being of clay, sand, and gravel. It was six feet high, and thirty or forty feet in diameter; but had been reduced in height by the action of rain, &c. The remains of the skeleton were imperfect, and some of the bones soon crumbled. It was about six feet in length; the skull was very thick.

The mound was found by the first settlers covered with trees as ancient as those which grew around it, and everything indicated antiquity.

Several other ancient works existed at Marietta, from some of which, bits of pottery have been taken. Dr. Hildreth mentions several specimens in his possession, which appear to have lain long exposed to the elements, on the surface of the ground, yet retained their structure and hardness. They consist of clay and pounded flint. Such as are found on the meadows are composed, he tells us, of clay and broken clam-shells; and these he refers to the present race of redmen.

Ashtabula county is remarkable for containing the first settlements in the Western Reserve, and, indeed, in all northern Ohio. The first surveying party of the Reserve landed at the mouth of Conneaut on the 4th of July, 1796. It consisted of fifty-two persons, two of whom were women; and the family of Judge James Kingsley was the first which ever wintered within the limits of that region, now so populous.

Conneaut Landing, the scene of the above events, is now an important place of transhipment, and has a pier with a lighthouse, with a few buildings. The village, or borough, of the same name, stands at the distance of two miles north. It is twenty-eight miles from Erie, Pennsylvania, and contains four churches, an academy, and about 4,000 inhabitants.

Toledo, on the left bank of Maumee, and on the Wabash and Erie canal, is one hundred and thirty-four miles northwest from Columbus, two hundred and forty-six miles, by the canal, from Cincinnati, and fifty south of Detroit. It extends along the river more than a mile, with two landings, the upper and the lower, where most of the business is done, and where are many large stores and warehouses. The view down the river, from the upper landing, is remarkably fine, being extensive, bounded by headlands, and often enlivened with numerous vessels.

Fort Industry was built on the site of this town, in 1800, near the present Summit street, in which the Indian treaty was held, on the fourth of July, 1805, at which the Indian title to the "fire-lands" was extinguished. The tribes represented were the Ottowa, Chippewa, Pottawatomie, Wyandot, Shawnee, Munsee, and Delaware.

Toledo was incorporated in 1836 as a city, and has five churches, two banks, and about 4,000 inhabitants.

Cleveland has one of the best harbors on Lake Erie, it being formed by the mouth of Cuyahoga river, and improved by two piers, each four hundred and twenty-five yards in length, running into the lake on both sides. The Ohio canal, which extends from this place to Ohio river, continues the line of navigation commenced by the Erie canal, from the ocean to that great tributary of the Mississippi, which washes the southern border of this state, and gives it its name. Immense quantities of wheat and other productions are annually sent through Cleveland to New York, and the exports to Canada are large, through the Welland canal. The Ohio and Pennsylvania canal offers a ready communication with Pittsburg; and railroads are proposed to extend from Cleveland to Wellsville, on the Ohio, and to Columbus.

The Medical College, though of recent establishment, is flourishing, and has seven professors, with all the necessary apparatus.

Preparations were made in 1837 for a marine hospital, on a tract of nine acres of land on the heights overlooking the lake. The edifice is to be of hewn stone, and in the Ionic style.

The number of churches is twenty-one, and population which in 1796 was only three, in 1840 was 6,071, and in 1850, 17,094, of whom 9,000 were natives of the United States.

Akron, thirty-six miles from Cleveland, and one hundred and ten northeast of Columbus, stands on the Ohio canal, at the Portage summit, and at its junction with the Pennsylvania canal. The numerous locks and Little Cuyahoga river afford an abundance of water-power for manufacturing purposes. There are a courthouse, five churches, an academy, a number of mills and manufactories, and about 4,000 inhabitants. It was laid out in 1825, and at first the inhabitants were all confined to South Akron, just below. It is now a very flourishing place.

Cuyahoga Falls, five miles from Akron, stands on the river of the same name, and possesses extraordinary advantages for a manufacturing town, being well supplied with water-power by the stream, which makes a descent of two hundred and forty feet in a short distance. The banks and bed of the stream are rocky, and present a wild scene, with a succession of cascades. Here are four churches, and 1,500 inhabitants.

ELYRIA.—This town is one hundred and thirty miles northeast of Columbus, and twenty-four west of Cleveland, and is the capital of Lorain county. It stands on a level piece of ground, seven miles from Lake Erie, and near the junction of the forks of Black river, which affords abundance of water-power, by making falls of forty feet. The population is only about 1,500 inhabitants, but there are several manufactories, six churches, and an academy. The first settlement was made in 1817, by Heman Ely, of West Springfield, Massachusetts. One of the presbyterian churches is of sandstone, cost $8,000, and is one of the most elegant in Ohio.

OBERLIN, the seat of a collegiate institute, is eight miles distant from Elyria. This institution was founded in 1834, and contains a male and a female department, with a president, fifteen professors and teachers, and about five hundred pupils. It is a manual-labor institution. Stage-coaches run every day to Elyria. The village resembles those of New England, consisting of houses of two stories, painted white.

MANSFIELD, sixty-eight miles from Columbus, and sixty-nine from Sandusky, has an elevated situation, and contains a courthouse, seven churches, an academy, and a population of about 2,800. It has a daily communication with Sandusky by the railroad, and stage-coaches run to Columbus, Wooster, &c., three times a week.

SANDUSKY CITY.—This is an important commercial place, standing on a fine bay, three miles from Lake Erie. Many vessels enter here. The population is about 5,500, and fast increasing. It contains five churches. Much valuable building-stone is quarried in the vicinity. Railroad cars arrive and depart daily for Cincinnati, through Cleveland, and for Mansfield, while stage-coaches run in several directions.

STEUBENVILLE stands on the western bank of the Ohio, twenty-two miles above Wheeling, and one hundred and forty-seven east by north from Columbus, and is regularly laid out. It is thirty-five miles below Pittsburg, by water, and contains six churches, a courthouse, a bank, and two academies, as well as a number of manufactories. Stage-coaches start daily for Pittsburg, and frequently for Washington, Cambridge, Canton, &c.

This town is named from Fort Steuben, which was erected in 1789, near the site of the present female seminary, in High street. It consisted of several block-houses, connected by palisade fences. It was occupied by United States infantry, commanded by Colonel Beatty, until Wayne's victory, after which it was dismantled. Another block-house stood on the opposite side of the river. The town was laid out in 1798, by Bezaleel Wells and James Ross, of Pennsylvania. It was incorporated February 14, 1805.

The situation of Steubenville is handsome, as it occupies an elevated plain; and the neighboring country is rich and well cultivated, the soil being esteemed the best for wheat in Ohio. The surrounding region is also remarkably well adapted to the raising of wheat. Merinoes, were introduced here, at an early period, by Messrs. Wells and Dickerson; and a woollen manufactory was erected in Steubenville in 1814, which led to the establishment of various manufactories in the place. It now contains five of woollen, one of paper, one of cotton, one of iron, and two of glass, besides others; and in the neighborhood are seven copperas manufactories. All these employ between eight hundred and one thousand hands, and consume more than a million bushels of coal annually. This important kind of fuel is derived from mines at a short distance from the town. The population, in 1810, was 800; in 1820, 2,479; in 1830, 2,964; in 1840, 4,247; and in 1850, about 7,000.

Steubenville contains five public schools and four select ones, besides a male and a female seminary. The former is named Grove academy, and is a flourishing institution, containing about eighty pupils. The latter, situated on the bank of the Ohio, was commenced in 1829, at an expense of nearly $40,000, has ten or twelve teachers, and about one hundred and fifty pupils. The edifice presents a fine and imposing front,

View of Steubenville.

having a central building of four stories, with a piazza, and two long wings of three stories. A broad lawn, shaded with trees, slopes toward the river.

PORTSMOUTH, on the right bank of the Ohio river, at the mouth of the Scioto, one hundred and five miles from Cincinnati, is at the head of the Ohio canal, and contains a population of about 5,000 inhabitants. The public buildings are the courthouse, a bank, and four churches. Iron ore is found in the upper parts of Scioto county, and in Lawrence country, and there are several mills and manufactories. Water, for the supply of the town, is raised from the river by steam. Steamboats depart daily for Wheeling, Pittsburg, &c., and stage-coaches go daily to Columbus. Portsmouth is the capital of Scioto county. A company of eastern capitalists are forming a basin in the old channel of the Scioto, for the building and repairing of steamboats.

PAINESVILLE.—This town has a high situation on the left side of Grand river, three miles from Lake Erie, and 31 miles from Cleveland, with a population of about 1,500. There are four churches and a courthouse. Stage-coaches start daily for Buffalo.

FAIRPORT, the harbor of Painesville, is three miles farther north, nearly at the mouth of the river.

WILLOUGHBY.—This is a small village, eleven miles southwest from Painesville, the seat of Willoughby medical college. This institution was incorporated in 1834, and has nine professors, and about one hundred and thirty students. The lectures commence on the last Monday in October.

ZANESVILLE enjoys a very handsome situation, on the left bank of Muskingum river, seventy-three miles from Wheeling, opposite the mouth of Licking river. The principal public buildings are the courthouse, a market, two academies, a bank, fourteen churches, and the athenæum, with a reading-room and mineralogical cabinet. A fine bridge crosses the Muskingum, over which passes the national road. The population is about 11,000.

A succession of dams and locks renders the navigation to the Ohio uninterrupted along the valley of the Muskingum; and water-power is obtained for several large flour-mills and iron-works. The first settlement was made here in the year 1799, when the village was laid out. The site of the town was granted to Ebenezer Zane (after whom it was named) as a reward for opening a bridle-road from Wheeling to Maysville.

There is a daily communication between Zanesville, and Maysville, Kentucky, by stage-coaches, as well as with Cincinnati and Wheeling, and twice a week with Marietta and Cleveland.

GALLIPOLIS, ninety-seven miles from Cincinnati, and three hundred from Pittsburg by water, stands on the left bank of Scioto river. It has a population of about 2,600 inhabitants, and contains three churches, a courthouse, a bank, and an academy, and is the capital of Gallia county. Some of the inhabitants are of French descent.

CHILLICOTHE.—This town, the capital of Ross county, was formerly the seat of government of Ohio. It is situated ninety-three miles from Cincinnati, on the left bank of the Scioto, extending south to Point creek, a distance of about three fourths of a mile. It contains a United States land-office, two banks, two academies, and thirteen churches. The population is about 8,000. A number of ancient mounds formerly stood in the town and its vicinity. The Ohio canal passes through the place, and stage-coaches go daily for Zanesville, Columbus, Maysville, and Portsmouth.

Chillicothe has been compared to Philadelphia, in situation and plan, as it stands on a plain, and the streets are regular, and the Scioto and Paint creeks bounding it on both sides, as the Delaware and Schuylkill. But the surrounding scenery is far superior, and equalled by but few other cities. The seat of government of the Northwest territory was established here in 1800, by an act of Congress, and the business was done in a log-house. The old statehouse (now the county courthouse) was commenced in 1800, and is believed to be the first stone building erected in the territory. In 1816, the seat of government was removed to Columbus.

Pickaway County was formed in 1810, from Ross, Fairfield, and Franklin counties, and contains the Pickaway plains, said to be the richest body of lands in the state. The name is derived from that of the Piqua Indians, a tribe of the Shawnees. Here resided the celebrated chiefs Logan and Cornplanter. The county abounds in plain and fertile country, and the eye may frequently overlook an extent of five hundred acres of corn. The four varieties of Ohio soil, however, are to be found in different parts of the county, viz., woodland, barren, plain and prairie. The barrens were formerly covered with shrub-oak, and received their name from their supposed worthlessness. They have, however, proved to be very good for grass and oats. The first settlers came principally from Pennsylvania and Virginia. The chief productions are corn, wheat, oats, grass, pork, wool, and neat cattle. Many of the inhabitants of the west side of Scioto river are tenants. Population in 1850, 21,286.

In 1774, Lord Dunmore marched from Virginia with 3,000 men, to attack the Indian towns on the Pickaway plains, but one of his divisions was assaulted in his camp, at the mouth of the Kenhawa, now Point Pleasant, and barely succeeded in repulsing the savages after a severe loss. The Indians at length sued for peace, after the army had reached Old Chillicothe; and on that occasion Logan made the speech which has been so much celebrated as a specimen of simple but pathetic eloquence. His last days were melancholy. He became addicted to intemperance, and wandered about the country, until he was killed by an Indian whom he had offended.

Among the principal towns in Pickaway county is Circleville which is elsewhere described. The ancient inhabitants, the builders of the mounds, appear to have made this part of the Scioto valley one of their most favorite abodes, as the remains of their works are abundant. For a most authentic and complete description of these, the reader is referred to the first number of the Transactions of the Smithsonian Institute, now in the press, which contains a memoir by Messrs. Davis and Squier, by whom many of the works in Ohio have been recently and carefully surveyed and excavated.

Lancaster is the county seat of Fairfield county, and is situated on a beautiful and fertile valley, on the Hockhocking river and canal, and on the Zanesville and Chillicothe turnpike. It is twenty-eight miles southeast of Columbus, and is a very flourishing town. It has seven churches, each one belonging to a different denomination. In 1840, it numbered 2,120 inhabitants, and has since then rapidly increased.

The land upon which this town now stands, was, when first known to the settlers of Marietta, in the possession of the Wyandot Indians. Their principal town occupied a large part of the tract on which Lancaster has since been built. It is said that, in 1790, this town contained five hundred inhabitants, and a hundred wigwams. Its name, which was Tarhe, or, in English, Crane town, was named after the principal chief of the tribe. Near the fourth lock on the Hockhocking canal, and not far from the junction of a beautiful spring with the Hockhocking river, the hut of this chief stood. It was formed of the bark of trees set on poles, with one square opening, large enough to admit a man. At this time the tribe numbered five hundred warriors. In 1795, the territory was ceded by them to the United States, in the treaty of Greenville; after which the larger number removed with their chief, to Upper Sandusky.

In 1797, a communication having been opened with the eastern states, by what was called Zane's trace, many who were probably desirous of improving their condition in life, removed to this spot, where, finding everything they could wish to make them comfortable, they determined to fix their abode. Captain Hunter, who in 1798, settled on the bank of the prairie, about one hundred and fifty yards northwest of the present turnpike, is considered as the founder of Fairfield county.

April 30th, 1803, Franklin was formed from Ross, and named from Benjamin Franklin. The land is generally level, and the prevailing character of the soil is clay, and is very well adapted to grazing, more so than to the cultivation of grain, though on the water-courses, which are very numerous, there are many well-cultivated and flourishing farms. The staple productions are potatoes, hay, oats, corn, wheat, pork, and wool. In 1820, the population of Franklin was numbered at 10,300, and in 1840, it had increased to 24,880; in 1850, 43,000.

This tract of country was once occupied by the Wyandot Indians, who cultivated the river bottoms and raised extensive fields of corn, opposite their town, which stood where the city of Columbus now stands.

In the year 1780, a party of whites pursued some Indians from the mouth of the Kanawha river, and overtook them near Columbus, gave them battle, and overcame them. During the fight, two squaws were observed to hide themselves in a hollow tree; after the skirmish was over they were drawn out, and carried captives to Virginia. As lately as 1845, this tree was standing on the west bank of the Scioto river.

An old Wyandot chief, named Leatherlips, was executed in this county, in 1810, on a charge of witchcraft.

Coshocton, the capital of Coshocton county, has a fine situation on Muskingum river, at the junction of the Tuscarawas and Walhonding, eighty-three miles northeast of Columbus, and thirty from Zanesville. The buildings are much scattered over a fine piece of ground lying in four terraces, each rising about nine feet above that below it, and the upper being one thousand feet in breadth. The public square is sixty rods from the Muskingum, and contains four acres, planted with trees, and containing the county buildings.

This town was laid out in 1802, by Ebenezer Buckingham and John Matthews, having been first settled a few years previously. It contains four churches, two printing-offices, one woollen factory, and a flour-mill, and in 1850 had 800 inhabitants. Steamboats occasionally come up to this place at high water.

Roscoe stands opposite Coshocton, on the west bank of the Muskingum, and is connected with it by a bridge. It was laid off in 1816, with the name of Caldersburg by James Calder. The Walhonding canal extends from this place to Rochester, twenty-five miles distant. Roscoe is a great depôt for wheat, and has abundant water-power, supplied by the canal.

The following villages are in this vicinity: East Union, West Carlisle, Newcastle, Rochester, West Bedford, Keene, New Bedford, Evansburgh, Birmingham, Chili, Jacobsport, Lewisville, Plainfield, Van Buren, and Warsaw.

Bucyrus, the capital of Crawford county, was laid out in 1822, by the first settler, Samuel Norton, who came from Pennsylvania in 1819. The country then abounded in wild animals.

Massillon.—This village is situated on the left bank of the Tuscarawas river, and on the route of the Ohio canal. The public buildings are a bank and seven churches, and the population is about 2,000.

Granville, six miles from Newark, has a college of the same name, situated at the distance of a mile. It was founded in 1832, and has four professors, twenty-five students, and a library of about three thousand volumes. The commencement is held on the second Wednesday in August.

Newark stands at the confluence of the three branches of Licking river, and on the line of the Ohio canal, and also on that of the railroad from Sandusky city to Columbus. A branch of the latter it is intended to construct from this point to Zanesville. The public square is the most spacious and elegant in the state. The town was laid out in 1801, on the plan of Newark, New Jersey, by General William C. Schenk, George W. Burnet, and John M. Cummings, who were proprietors of this military section, embracing four thousand acres. The first house of hewed logs was erected in 1802, and the first regular church edifice was built in

1817, by a presbyterian congregation, both on the public square. There are now nine churches, three newspapers, two grist-mills, one foundry, and a woollen factory, and the population in 1850 was 4,000.

DAYTON.—This town is the capital of Montgomery county, and is situated on the east side of Great Miami river, at the mouth of Mad river, and one mile below the southwest branch. The distance from Columbus is sixty-seven miles west, from Cincinnati fifty-two, and one hundred and ten from Indianapolis. It was proposed to build a town here as early as 1788, by the name of Venice, the land lying within the contract of John Cleves Symmes: but the project failed in consequence of the revolutionary war. In 1795, soon after Wayne's treaty, a company purchased the land of Mr. Symmes, and the town was laid out on the 14th of November of that year. It was named after General Jonathan Dayton, Springfield, New Jersey, the leader of the enterprise. The first nineteen settlers arrived on the 1st of April of the year following. Some of the settlers were afterward obliged to purchase titles from the government, in consequence of the inability of Symmes to fulfil his contract. The Miami canal, commenced in 1827, which has been of great benefit to the town. Both the town and the country stood the second in the state, in point of taxable property, in 1846.

The first canal-boat from Cincinnati arrived at Dayton on the 25th of January, 1829, and the first from Lake Erie on June 24, 1845. The first line of stage-coaches from Cincinnati to Columbus, weekly, was established in 1825, and were two days on the way. There are now three daily lines.

URBANA, forty-two miles west-northwest from Columbus, is the capital of Champaign county, and was laid out in 1805, by Colonel William Ward, who gave lots for public buildings. The first church was of logs, and built by methodists in 1807.

Some handsome houses are now built in the environs of the town, which contains four churches, two printing-offices, one woollen factory, one iron foundry, and two machine shops. In 1850, the number of inhabitants was 2,000.

BATAVIA, the capital of Clermont county, is twenty-one miles east from Cincinnati, and one hundred and three southwest of Columbus, on the north bank of the east fork of Little Miami river. It was laid out about the year 1820, by George Ely, and made the county seat in 1824. It contains two churches, and two printing-offices, and had, in 1850, 800 inhabitants.

WILLIAMSBURG, seven miles east of Batavia, stands on the east branch of the Miami, and is a pleasant village.

There are several other small towns in Clermont county: NEW RICHMOND, MOSCOW, POINT PLEASANT, NEVILLE, and CHILO, all on the Ohio river: also BETHEL, FELICITY, and MILFORD.

WILMINGTON.—This is the capital of Clinton county, and a village belonging to the township of Union. It stands on Todd's fork, and is seventy-two miles southwest from Columbus, on a tract of undulated ground. It contains five churches, a printing-office, a high-school, and about 1,500 inhabitants. It was settled chiefly by families from North Carolina, and the first church was built by baptists.

The following villages are in this neighborhood: CLARKESVILLE, nine miles southwest of Wilmington; MARTINSVILLE, nine miles south; PORT WILLIAM, nine miles north; NEW VIENNA, eleven miles southeast; and BURLINGTON, eleven miles northwest. SABINA, SLIGO, BLANCHESTER, CUBA, LEWISVILLE, WESTBORO', CENTREVILLE, and MORRISVILLE, are small.

CLINTON COUNTY was organized in 1810, and named after Governor George Clinton, of New York, vice-president of the United States. It has a level surface, and a rich soil, well adapted to grass and corn, with some prairie land. The streams afford a good supply of water-power. The chief productions are corn, oats, wheat, wool, and pork. The population, in 1850, was 18,837, or fifty to a square mile. It was first settled in about 1803, chiefly by people from Kentucky, Pennsylvania, and North Carolina. William Smally was the first white inhabitant, in 1797.

SPRINGFIELD, forty-three miles west of Columbus, is the county town of Clarke county. It stands on the national road, and the river road from Cincinnati to Sandusky City passes through it. It was laid out in 1803, by James Demint, and is remarkably beautiful and advantageously situated. The adjacent region is fertile and picturesque, and the people are very intelligent and moral; so that it is one of the most agreeable places for residence in the state. The east fork of Mad river, which borders it on the north, is an excellent mill-stream, never failing in the driest seasons. The Lagonda, or Buck creek, flows through the town, which also affords good water-power; and there are more than twenty mill-seats within three miles of Springfield.

The main street is broad and fine, being ornamented with the courthouse, a church, and the academy. The high-school is flourishing, and under the direction of the Methodist conference of Ohio. There is a lyceum, which has existed about fifteen years; and the public libraries contain about four thousand volumes. There are nine churches, two printing-offices, and a variety of manufactories. The population is about 6,000.

Wittemberg College, situated half a mile from Springfield, has twenty-four acres of fine grounds, and stands in the midst of beautiful scenery. It is a Lutheran institution, and is organized on a broad plan, with collegiate and theological departments, and provision for six professorships. It commenced operations in 1846, with about seventy students.

XENIA.—This town, the capital of Greene county, is situated sixty-four miles north of Cincinnati, and sixty-one from Columbus, and has broad streets with fine houses, and considerable advantages for business. It was laid out in 1803, on land belonging to John Paul, who gave a large square for public buildings. The first cabin was erected the next year, by John Marshall, in the southwest corner of the town. The first meeting of the grand jury was held October 3, 1804, under a sugar-tree.

Zenia now contains eight churches, a bank, a classical academy, two newspaper printing-offices, and about 4,000 inhabitants.

SIDNEY, the capital of Shelby county, was laid out so recently as 1819, on the farm of Charles Starrett, on a piece of table-land, on the west side of Miami river. The court was held there the following year, and the first frame building was erected in 1820. The first newspaper was printed in 1836. The courthouse stands on a fine square in the centre of the town, and the number of churches is five. There are three flour and four saw-mills, and two carding and fulling-mills. The population probably now amounts to about 2,000.

VAN BUREN, a township in Shelby county, is remarkable for containing a large and prosperous settlement of colored people, numbering about four hundred. The land is not well situated, being low and wet; but the inhabitants are industrious, moral, and careful for the education of their children, being as prosperous as their white neighbors. They have also churches of their own. In 1846, the slaves emancipated by the will of the celebrated John Randolph, came to this place, and attempted to settle permanently, after they had been driven from Mercer county, but the white neighbors drove them off by violence, and compelled them to scatter about the country.

PORT JEFFERSON, five miles northeast of Sidney, stands at the head of the feeder supplied by Miami river to the Miami canal, a distance of thirteen miles. It contains about fifty houses, two churches, &c.

The following villages are in this vicinity: HARDIN, five miles west of Sidney; NEWPORT, twelve miles west; BERLIN, sixteen miles west-northwest; HOUSTON, eleven miles west-southwest; LOCKPORT, eight miles south; and PALESTINE, nine miles east.

HAMILTON, the capital of Butler county, is twenty-two miles north of Cincinnati, stands on the left bank of the

Great Miami. It contains seven churches, a flourishing female academy, two newspaper printing-offices, three flour-mills, three saw-mills, three cotton factories, and two machine shops, and had a population of 2,000 in 1850; since which it has increased considerably, and seems destined to be a large manufacturing town. Large hydraulic works have been erected, which rank among the best west of the Alleganies. The water is brought four miles, from the Great Miami, by a canal, and is sufficient for two hundred run of four and a half mill-stones.

Maumee City, the capital of Lucas county, is one hundred and twenty-four miles northwest from Columbus, and eight south of Toledo. It was laid out in 1817, in the old reservation of twelve miles square, at the foot of the rapids of the Maumee, which was granted to the Indians in 1795. The site of the town is at the head of navigation opposite Perrysburg and Fort Meigs, on the Wabash and Erie canal. The ground is about one hundred feet above the Maumee, which here makes a fine, broad bend, from which the banks rise like a vast amphitheatre, about two miles long and one mile wide. A beautiful island of two hundred acres, and several smaller ones, ornament the surface of the river.

The French had a trading post a little below the town, as early as the year 1680, where the English built a fort in 1794; the place was a favorite resort of the Indians. The ruins of the latter fort still remain. A part of Wayne's battle was fought within the limits of this town; and the British erected several batteries below the town, in the late war, during the siege of Fort Meigs. These were taken by storm by Colonel Dudley, on the 5th of May, 1813; but he was afterward driven back and defeated.

The Pork Trade of the West.—More than four hundred thousand hogs had been packed in Cincinnati, up to the month of January, 1848, for the season of 1847–'8—an unprecedented number, even for that place. With the exception of a very few places, the same rate of increase has occurred in the west generally.

The pork packed at Cincinnati comes exclusively from Ohio, Kentucky, and Indiana. The supplies from all these quarters were immense. On one road leading to Cincinnati from Indiana, about 70,000 hogs crossed the Miamitown bridge. There are other bridges over the Miami, on roads leading from Indiana.

For about two months, the passage of hogs up the leading streets, from the Ohio river, seemed to be almost constant. So, also, the turnpikes coming in from Ohio indicate the same state of facts.

That we may have an idea of the capacity of these states to increase the number of hogs brought to market, take the following statement. The first table contains the amount for 1840, the second an estimate for 1850.

1840.	Hogs.	Corn.
Ohio,	2,099,746	33,668,144 bush.
Kentucky,	2,310,533	39.847,120 "
Indiana,	1,623,608	28,155,887 "
Total,	6,033,887	101,671,131 bush.

In 1840, then, the farmers of these three states had six millions of hogs, and more than a hundred millions of bushels of corn. They could have fatted two millions of those hogs, and sent them to market, on forty millions of bushels of corn.

1850.	Hogs.	Corn.
Ohio,	2,500,000	50,000,000 bush.
Kentucky,	2,500,000	45,000,000 "
Indiana,	2,000,000	40,000,000 "
Total,	7,000,000	135,000,000 bush.

There are in the United States 30,000,000 of hogs. This is about fifteen times the number usually slaughtered in the whole country for market in one year. Hogs grow upon full size in less than two years. It follows, then, from these facts, that there must be at least five times as many hogs in the country that *might* be fatted for market, as really are.

The west being peculiarly adapted to the cultivation of Indian corn (the best food for fattening hogs), renders the raising of hogs a very profitable business.

MICHIGAN.

This state consists of two great peninsulas, and presents a form and position unlike any other state in the Union. It might be compared with Maryland and Virginia, in respect to the separation of its parts by water; but it is different from them in lying far in the interior, and in having for its principal boundaries the borders of three great lakes. It has Lake Superior on the north, with its outlet and the Saut de Sainte Marie on the northeast; Lake Huron on the east, with the west end of Lake Erie on the southeast, with Lake Clair and the outlet of Huron, Ohio and Indiana on the south; Lake Michigan and Wisconsin on the west.

The advantages offered to commerce and trade by the natural features of the country, and to internal improvements, are equalled only by the agricultural facilities and mineral wealth of some parts of the territory. There are several good harbors along the borders of the lakes and their coves, which also abound with fish; copper mines, of great extent and richness, abound along the shores, on Lakes Huron and Superior; and railroads have already been constructed nearly across the isthmus of the grand peninsula.

This grand peninsula is divided into two inclined planes, by a continuation of the ridge of land which separates the water of the Wabash and the great Miami and Maumee—one of them sloping toward Lake Huron, drained by the rivers Raisin, Huron, Erie, Rouge, Huron of St. Clair, Bell, Black, Saginaw, Thunder, Cheboiang, &c.; and the other sloping toward Lake Michigan, and crossed by the St. Joseph's, Kalamazoo, Grand river, and many of smaller size. All the rivers have a fall from the table-land. The mouths of these streams generally afford harbors of different depth and size, while few other parts are to be found along the shores, although the depth of the lakes is sufficient for all the purposes of commerce, and canals to facilitate the passage, Detroit river, &c., will hereafter render commerce still more extensive. The whole line of coast on the different lakes, including the sinuosities, is probably one thousand miles. The shores of Superior and Huron are much more irregular than those of Michigan. Saginaw bay is a gulf, sixty miles in length.

In point of soil, the best part of the grand peninsula is in the south, toward Ohio and Indiana, the upper portion being rather barren. The surface is but slightly varied, with a succession of oak-openings and rolling country, often spotted with small hollows and ponds called cat-holes.

History.—This state was first visited by the French from Canada; and Detroit (or "the strait") was founded in 1670. But it was a small town when ceded to the United States by the treaty of Paris. It was not before 1796 that this country was given up to the United States; it was formed into a territory in 1805; in 1812 was occupied by the British troops; recovered in 1813 by General Harrison; and soon after the return of peace, became one of the principal objects of emigration, and was greatly favored by the opening of the Erie canal. Fort Brady was built in 1822, when the settlement of Chippeway county, the north part, commenced.

Population.—In 1820 Michigan contained only 8,896 inhabitants; but in 1830, 28,000; and in 1850, 395,576.

The following remarks on the soil and agriculture of the state, are from a recent number of the American Agriculturist:—

"A considerable portion of the eastern part of Michigan consists of a clay soil, and is well adapted to grass and grazing. This quality of land extends from a point some thirty miles south of Detroit, to near Lake Huron on the St. Clair river, and for about thirty miles in the interior. As we advance westward, the soil, with more or less exception, gradually changes to a gravelly or sandy loam, and in some instances acquires these characteristics to so decided an extent as seriously to interfere with its permanent fertility. This is universally true of the large quantities of the oak-openings, which so generally pervade the interior and western part of the state. These lands will bear a few good first crops; but manures must follow close upon their heels, or exhaustion and sterility are as certain as blighted leaves after autumnal frosts. There are some moderately good corn lands among this class of soils, and most of it excellent for wheat; but all the agricultural vigilance of a long-cultivated country must be generally adopted, or diminished crops will soon drive the occupants into the uncultivated regions still farther west. There are many exceptions to these remarks, and none more so than a considerable part of the beautiful valley of the Kalamazoo, whose rich and gracefully undulating fields, clad with their native burr-oak, give unfailing promise of abundant wheat-fields for years to come.

"There are other and extensive portions of the state, possessing considerable fertility, which yet remain to be occupied, and which, in the inevitable progress of things, will ere long be settled, and swell the tide of her population and wealth, to a respectable approximation toward her elder sisters.

"Sheep husbandry is making considerable progress in the state, and promises soon to furnish no inconsiderable proportion of the aggregate of her occupation. Depredations from wolves seem already to offer no serious impediment to this department of the farmer.

"Wheat is the product of the state, and on this the farmers principally rely for their available exports. Never did their efforts receive a greater reward than the present season. The estimate of several judicious citizens is, that the crop fully averaged twenty bushels per acre over the state. I was informed of a wheat field containing one hundred acres, which averaged over forty-five bushels per acre, and one measured acre of which produced over sixty bushels. A cargo of this year's crop from Michigan averaged one barrel of flour for every two hundred and twenty-four pounds of wheat."

Within eight years the population of Michigan must have increased at least fifty per cent., while its area of land under cultivation and the amount of its annual product have probably more than doubled. The export of its great staple wheat (either in the berry or in flour), from the last crop will more than quadruple that from any crop prior to 1839. Its annual production of corn and other grains, of cattle and sheep, of wool and the products of the dairy, of ashes, &c., is also very considerable; but wheat is the great staple of Michigan, and will doubtless continue so, unless the ravages of the Hessian fly, now reported as terrible, shall be perpetuated.

The situation of this state is peculiar. Almost surrounded by water, *old* Michigan—the grand peninsula—is bounded on three sides by the lakes Erie, St. Clair, Huron, and Michigan, with the straits connecting them, and having Indiana on the south. The face of the country is remarkably level, and the soil mainly of a decided fertility. The latter may be said to be naturally divided into dry and wet prairie, 'timbered openings' (upland) and a heavy proportion of low, flat, wet land, most of which will be dry enough when thoroughly cleared and cultivated, but which is, as yet, rather swampy—often decidedly so. All around, on the three sides bordering on the lakes and straits, there is a belt of flat land, a little elevated above the water level, and very heavily timbered. Inside of this, the land gradually rises and becomes gently rolling, being divided into "oak-openings (having two or three dozen small and middling oak-trees to the acre, with any quantity of oak-bushes and roots, and an indifferent show of wild grasses); "timbered openings" (on which the oak-trees are much more, and the bushes less numerous); and open "prairies," or vast natural meadows, with heavy belts of forest intersecting and dividing them, usually on the courses of the streams, or on wet marshy ground. The prairies, especially all the largest and finest, are generally found in the southern half of the state, and more of them west than east of a line drawn through its centre. These are pretty easily subdued and abundantly fertile; the oak lands are "brought to" with more labor, but also yield largely both wheat and corn.

Aside from its general depth and fertility, much of the soil is strongly impregnated with lime, which accounts for its partiality to wheat. The low and luxuriously timbered lands (usually with elm, cucumber, basswood, &c.) have not to any great extent been cleared as yet, being most stubborn and least inviting; but here also the soil in the main is strong. Yet even Detroit appears to be closely hemmed in to landward by the primitive forest, which still covers probably five sixths of the nearest hundred square miles.

On the west side of the state, especially around Saginaw bay, there are extensive forests of choice pine; and far in the North is a great abundance of poor land—extensive sterile swamps and marshes, checkered by barren knolls and hillocks. But nobody thinks of settling in that bleak, forlorn region, and the great portion of the soil north of a line drawn through the centre of the state is good, as nearly all south of that line is. Very few states exceed this in agricultural capacity, either in the aggregate, or acre to acre.

The absence of mountains or anything like them through the greater part of the state, is by no means an unmingled good. It is the cause of a palpable deficiency of springs and running streams through the better portion of the state, and of a decided deficiency of navigable waters within the state, though it is so nobly provided with them externally. But this again is compensated to a great extent by the signal facilities everywhere presented for the construction of canals and railroads, especially the latter.

Thus tempted, the state undertook, about the year 1836, the construction of three lines of railroad across the peninsula—the central, stretching hence to Lake Michigan near the mouth of the St. Joseph; the southern, from the Maumee near Toledo due westward; and the northern. On the two former a very considerable beginning had been made when the state fell into pecuniary embarrassments, in part owing to the magnitude of her undertaking, and somewhat to a change in the times. The southern road was arrested; the central road was feebly and haltingly prosecuted, fed by the sale of state lands and the issue of treasury warrants, which sold at a ruinous depreciation; and of the revenue accruing on the completed portion of the road or roads, nearly all was absorbed. Such was the condition of these works when, more than a year since, the state decided to offer the central road, just as it stood, for sale for two millions of dollars of her acknowledged debt, which then was worth in the market something less than one million dollars. The offer was accepted by a club of Bostonians, the payment made, the road transferred, and instantly placed under very different management. The receipts of the completed portion rapidly increased, expenses were curtailed, and the work on the unfinished portion vigorously stimulated, payment therefor being made promptly and in cash. Already the road is in operation to Kalamazoo, more than half way across the state, and it is to be entirely completed at farthest within the next year. Already the finished portion pays a liberal and rapidly increasing profit on its cost to the company, whose stock is at a high premium, and can rarely be bought at all. Already preparations are being made for relaying the old track, now very imperfect, with a new and improved rail; while in the city large purchases of real estate have been made by the company, mainly on the river or strait just below the present centre of trade, including a water-front of sixteen hundred feet, on which a gigantic freight and a passenger dépôt are to be erected, while the track of the railroad to its decreed terminus is to occupy, for a considerable distance, what is now part of the river, which is to be filled in for the purpose. By this means vessels will load and unload directly from the dépôt, whereas now there is a necessity of carting every barrel and bale some two hundred rods, involving serious expense and waste. On these works a large number of men are now employed here.

The southern railroad (a much ruder and less promising work) has been or is to be sold for half a million of dollars of state liabilities, in order that it likewise may be pressed onward to completion.

The usual time of departure from Buffalo is in the evening. Lake Erie is traversed in about twenty-four hours, stopping at Cleveland and Detroit. Passing the beautiful Detroit and St. Clair rivers, and the wide-spreading and difficult flats of the latter, you enter Huron, and stretching along an unbroken wilderness coast for hundreds of miles, passing Saginaw bay and the Thunder bay islands, reach Mackinaw, the resort of all who delight to enjoy a glimpse of its solitary loveliness, or to breathe its pure, cool, and invigorating atmosphere. This (including the time to wood) occupies two days and a half. Thence passing the straits of Michilimackinac, and the Manitou islands, the boat pushes either across Lake Michigan to Sheboigan, Milwaukie, &c., or passing up Green bay, and stopping at, or catching glimpses of, its innumerable islands in all their greenness and beauty, reaches Navarino. Returning through the passage called "Death's Door," and again entering Lake Michigan, the voyage is pursued to Chicago, stopping at Milwaukie, Racine, and Southport—the populous and rapidly-growing creations of the lake commerce and western settlements: thus terminating the voyage where nature and art combine to fix the seat of a great city—now rapidly rising as such, and combining in a remarkable degree the elements of commerce, business, society, and refinement. In short, nothing can exceed the upspringing vigor of such cities as Buffalo, Milwaukie, Racine, and Chicago; and no one can predict perhaps with too glowing a prospective the destiny of the mighty region now just springing into life and being.

The voyage to Chicago, via Green bay, may be made in five days or less, according to the delays at the places and points of interest on the route. The distance is about 1,350 miles.

Returning, the excursion may be extended, with additional gratification, from Mackinac to the Sault St. Marie, or even far up into Lake Superior and the mineral region. At least the trip to Chicago should be taken by all who desire to understand, not only the breadth and scope of these inland waters, and the cities on their borders, but the teeming population—the great and rapidly-advancing free states—to which they afford the avenues of a commerce and intercommunication, already of gigantic extent, and the mighty progress of which the most sanguine may not fully predict.

Lake St. Clair.—The St. Clair flats are formed by the division of the waters which issue from Lake Huron through the St. Clair river, by two or three low marshy islands, forming three or four channels or branches, within and just below which division the water, being wide, has in some places a depth of only six or eight feet, or something less than a steamboat will draw, if built stanch enough for the lake trade and tolerably loaded. Of course they generally get aground, and, there being no tide in the lakes, have no choice but to remain aground until a good part of their freight can be transferred to flatboats termed "lighters," which are on hand, ready to be serviceable for a consideration. Fifty thousand dollars well applied here would dredge out a deep and wide channel, and the current is so very gentle that it would not move the sand back again. Yet for want of this fifty thousand dollars (vetoed in the harbor bill), the farmers, whose produce, and the emigrants, whose families, as well as the merchant, whose goods, must traverse the lakes—are put to an expense, including that of delays, probably not less in one year than the entire cost of dredging out a clear and durable channel. Such is one of the many grievances which impelled the people of the west to ask their fellow-citizens generally to meet them in convention at Chicago, in 1847, to consider the general subject of river and harbor improvement.

The banks of the St. Clair river are low and level, generally well wooded, except where settlement has driven back the forest for a mile or less. The British side appears highest, driest, and most settled. A part of it has been peopled by white men for fifty or sixty years—as a good part of *our* bank of the Detroit river and Lake St. Clair has for even a longer period. The old settlers are of French origin, and are wedded to old customs; they are seldom seen out of their settlements. The largest and most active village on either side for a hundred miles above Detroit is Newport, in St. Clair county, famed for steamboat and ship building. Saginaw, a thrifty lumbering village at the bottom of Saginaw bay, much further up, is larger, but far away from the steamboat route to Mackinac or the Sault.

Detroit.—This city is situated in latitude 42° 20′ and longitude 6° west of Washington, on the shore of Detroit river, which is the outlet of Lake Huron into Lake St. Clair, which lies midway between it and Lake Erie. The river is above a mile in breadth, and divided into channels by Peach island, and below by Grand Turkey island.

The town stands on an inclined plane, rising thirty feet; most of the streets are regularly laid out at right angles, but obliquely to the bank of the river; there are several fine, broad avenues, and the situation for trade is highly advantageous. It contains the old state-house, city-hall, a markethouse, eleven churches, four banks, masonic-hall, a land-office, two orphan-asylums, three female academies, several literary societies, and twenty-five thousand inhabitants. The first steamboat arrived here in 1818.

The growth of this city has taken the healthy form of expansion in every landward direction, instead of the too common mode of accommodating an increasing population by filling up the interstices between old houses with new

View of Detroit.

ones, and putting one on the top of another. Nearly all the dwellings stand healthfully apart, and each surrounded by its little garden or grass and flower plat, evincing a fondness for shrubbery and the minor poetry of nature. Many of the streets are thickly set with rows of young maples, in some instances two rows on one side of a wide avenue, which will in a few years add greatly to the beauty and comfort of Detroit, especially of its favorite promenades. All around are signs of growth and prosperity, to which the development of the mineral wealth of the Lake Superior region has already, though in its infancy, given some impetus, and is destined to give far more. The only counterpoise to this is the removal, last winter, of the state government to a township in Ingham county, named Lansing, seventy miles northwest of Detroit, wherein is the confluence of the Red Cedar creek with Grand river, which latter, however, does not become navigable until far below this. The location on a corner of a county, in a township as yet mainly in primitive wilderness, remote from natural or artificial, present or prospective facilities of travel and transportation, created much surprise at first. Yet the site is pretty central to the whole state, not specially objectionable on any ground, and the selection seems at present to be pretty generally acquiesced in.

Agents transport flour hence by way of the Welland canal, Lake Ontario, the St. Lawrence to Montreal, the railroad, Lake Champlain and the Champlain canal, to Albany and New York, for the present charge from Buffalo to New York.

Monroe is on the right bank of the river Raisin, two and a half miles from its mouth and Lake Erie, and thirty-seven miles from Detroit. It has two banks, a land-office, a courthouse, seven churches, two academies, a reading-room and library of fifteen hundred volumes, and a number of manufactories. The number of inhabitants is about 5,000. Cars set off every day for Hillsdale, through Adrian; and stage-coaches daily for Detroit, and for Toledo, Ohio.

A branch of the university of Michigan is established in Monroe.

Marshall, on Kalamazoo river, at the mouth of Rice creek, is one hundred and thirteen miles west of Detroit. It contains a bank, four churches, an academy, and a number of mills and manufactories, with about 4,000 inhabitants. Cars start daily for Detroit and Kalamazoo.

Kalamazoo.—This town is situated on the left bank of the river of the same name, at the distance of one hundred and forty-six miles west from Detroit, with which it has a daily communication by the railroad. There are three churches, a land-office, a courthouse, and a branch of the university.

St. Joseph's is two hundred miles west of Detroit, on the bank of the river of that name, at its mouth in Lake Erie. A part of the town looks out upon the lake, where is a good harbor. It is a place of increasing importance, and contains a courthouse, three churches, a bank, and a population of about 900. It has daily communication with Chicago by steamboat, and stages run to the Detroit railroad; and stage-coaches run to Chicago through "Michigan city."

Mackinac.—This town is situated on the southeast extremity of Mackinac island. The public buildings are the courthouse, two churches, a school of the American board of commissioners for foreign missions, a Roman catholic missionary school, and a branch of the university. It has over 1,000 inhabitants. The harbor is large enough for one hundred and fifty vessels, and a valuable fishery is carried on, which supplies a considerable export trade, above three thousand barrels of white-fish and trout being sent out annually. A considerable amount of business is annually done in the fur trade.

Mackinac consists of three slight wooden piers, a water street and a back street, with perhaps sixty houses on both. The fort stands to the right of the village, on the brow of the eminence, is built of a porous, shelly limestone, and has a tolerable command of the main passage out of Lake Michigan into Lake Huron; but it happens to be it-

Mackinac Bluffs.

self commanded by a higher eminence, a mile west of it, which the British silently seized and fortified at the outbreak of the war of 1812, placing guns there in battery and summoning our commandant to surrender before he suspected even that war was declared.

Mackinac has a commanding view of Lakes Michigan and Huron, with the surrounding isles, headlands and bays. The air is very pure, and there is some timber, but it is mainly covered with low, shrub-like evergreens—fir, spruce, &c. It is among the coldest spots within the limits of our Union. The apple-tree blossoms, but does not bear there, any more than at the Sault.

The soil is mostly gravelly and rock of a limestone nature. In traversing the island, which is about ten miles in circumference, we find but three farms, and they not much laid under cultivation. Farming, however, must be profitable; a ready market being at hand in the village, which now contains by estimation not far from 1,000 inhabitants, who are mostly engaged in fishing.

The village, within the past five years, has begun to wear a greatly improved appearance, several good buildings having been erected, which are neatly painted, and several new ones now going up. All the upper lake steamers and sail craft stop at the wharf for an hour or two to wood.

Usually there are a number of Indians visiting the village from the main shores. They come in their bark canoes, freighting poles, bark, and matting, for a temporary wigwam. They pitch their tent on the beach during their stay, and are gazed at most intently by the passengers. Apparently they are all happy. Songs and laughter emanate from them in the evening, echoing over the broad expanse of waters. Many of the "curiosity" wares are made by the squaws, and bartered with the merchants for provisions. The sales of these curiosities to strangers can not be less than $15,000 annually.

The imports of the place are now estimated at $150,000 annually. The exports for a great number of years have been mostly furs. This trade declining, fish has taken their place. The merchants are interested in the business—all of them more or less. But few of them, however, are engaged in catching them. They generally sell or let nets, furnish barrels and salt, and then purchase of the fishermen after they are packed.

FISH PACKED AT MACKINAC AND VICINITY.

Year.	White-Fish. bbls.	Trout. bbls.	Total. bbls.
1835	1,200	—	1,700
1837	—	—	1,600
1840	3,250	750	4,000
1841	4,500	500	5,000
1842	6,275	1,425	7,700
1843	9,800	2,110	11,910
1844	12,200	3,575	15,775
1845	15,150	4,270	19,420
1846	16,000	4,000	20,000

These fish were packed and shipped from this place, and were taken at St. Croix, Grande Traverse, Little Traverse, L'Arbre Croche, and fishing grounds adjoining. It will be seen that the trade is flourishing, and in a little over ten years has increased from 1,700 barrels to 20,000.

The fishing, however, on the upper lakes, is not confined to this place and vicinity. Other points on Lakes Huron and Michigan are profiting by it. We append the statistics of the business at

SAULT ST. MARIE AND LAKE SUPERIOR.

Year.	White-Fish. bbls.	Trout. bbls.	Total. bbls
1835	—	—	2,300
1837	—	—	6,100
1840	8,000	4,000	12,000
1841	7,000	3,000	10,000
1842	7,500	3,000	10,500
1843	2,500	500	3,000
1845	2,100	250	2,350
1846	1,550	175	1,725

During the years 1841 and 1842, the American Fur Company met with heavy losses in the fish trade on Lake Superior, and they abandoned the business. Since then it has been carried on by various individuals on a small scale, and will not probably regain its former flourishing condition until a canal is constructed around the falls of St. Marie.

On the St. Mary's river, in the neighborhood of St. Joseph's, on the British side, the business is carried on largely, which goes to the Canada market. The catch is generally from 6,000 to 8,000 barrels yearly.

At Beaver island and vicinity, on Lake Huron, a large quantity is taken annually. A gentleman in the trade is of opinion that 10,000 barrels will be packed this season.

At False Presque isle, Thunder bay, and vicinity, last season, 12,000 barrels were furnished for the Ohio market.

Of the business at Green bay, Drummon's island, Three rivers, the Manistee, Shoboigan and Racine rivers, Saginaw bay, and other grounds, we are without particular information. An old fisherman estimates the quantity packed at these places last season at 20,000 barrels. This is considered a low estimate.

The following is a recapitulation for 1846, in barrels: Mackinac and vicinity, 20,000; St. Marie and vicinity, 1,725; Beaver island and vicinity, 10,000; Presque isle, Thunder bay, &c., 12,000; other places on Lakes Huron and Michigan, 20,000; Canada side, estimate, 15,000; total, 78,725.

In addition to barrelling, at several points, large quantities are boxed daily in ice and shipped to Chicago, Milwaukie, Detroit, Toledo, Cleveland, and Buffalo, on sale. The sales at Mackinac for the consumption of steamers passing, is no small item. It amounts to not far from one hundred dollars' worth per week. The whole catch of all the lakes may, therefore, be safely estimated at 100,000 barrels. When an access to Lake Superior is easy by canal, that almost unexplored lake will annually furnish an equal quantity.

The number of barrels required gives employment to at least three to four hundred persons in their construction. The salt consumed is an item of consequence to commerce, and the freight is worthy of note. The business may now be considered at *half a million of dollars per year*. A canal completed at the Sault would swell it in five years to a million.

Ann Arbor is situated on both sides of Huron river, forty miles west of Detroit, with which it has daily communication by the railroad, and also with Kalamazoo. It is divided into the upper and lower town by the river, and the elevated ground which it occupies makes the situation a fine one. It contains a bank, courthouse, six churches, and a number of manufactories, with about 3,500 inhabitants.

The *University of Michigan*, situated here, was founded in 1837, and has three professors, about eighty students, and libraries containing about five thousand volumes. The cabinets contain valuable collections made by the state naturalists.

Ypsilanti.—This town also stands on Huron river, which furnishes valuable water-power at this place. Here are several mills and manufactories, four churches, and about 2,500 inhabitants. Railroads afford daily communication with Detroit and Kalamazoo.

Jackson stands on the right bank of Grand river, seventy-nine miles west of Detroit, and contains about 3,000 inhabitants. The public buildings are a courthouse, four churches, an academy, and the state penitentiary, with a branch of the university. Cars go daily for Detroit and Kalamazoo.

Adrian.—This town is on the right bank of Raisin river, at the distance of sixty-seven miles from Detroit, and contains four churches, a courthouse, an academy, a number of manufactories, mills, &c., and a population of about 3,500. Railcars go daily to Toledo, Hillsdale, and Monroe.

Saut de Sainte Mary, or falls of St. Mary (familiarly called the Soo) stands on high ground on the right bank of St. Mary's strait, just below the falls, or rapids. Here are Fort Brady, the trading-house of the American Fur company, three churches, and a courthouse. The population is about one thousand.

The organization of copper companies commenced here in 1845, and during the past year at least one hundred were formed. Many of them are good, but not a few of them will prove mere bubbles. Those who have commenced working on their locations meet with great encouragement. Eight hundred and ninety-six permits for location have been granted by government. The companies that have actually commenced work, or have left men in charge as settlers, are entitled to pre-emption, under the late law for the sale of the lands. Of this class, there are not probably more than twenty-five companies, and they cover much territory, some of them as many as twenty-five permits, or sections. Those that hold pre-emptions get their lands at two dollars and a half per acre; the others at five dollars. Rising of twenty companies have expended much money in mining operations—one company over one hundred thousand dollars, and others from five to fifty thousand. Of the ultimate success of their operations, few who have visited the country have any doubt. The enterprise is necessarily attended with heavy outlays at the commencement, for machinery and mining implements.

It is but a few years since nearly all the iron and lead consumed in this country was imported. It was with the utmost difficulty that capitalists could be persuaded to embark in it. The lead mines on the Mississippi lay dormant for years, for want of confidence in their productiveness. The experiment, however, of mining it was tried; and now this country exports the article to various parts of the world, and the stockholders are amassing a great interest on their investments. The copper business is more promising at this time than even lead or iron. Many more have visited Lake Superior and gone into it. The Cliff mine has raised 2,495 tons of native copper and vein-stone containing copper. A portion of it was sent to Boston and Roxbury for smelting. According to a statement based upon the portion smelted, the amount of pure copper is about three hundred tons, at four hundred dollars a ton, worth one hundred and twenty thousand dollars in the aggregate. A shaft has been sunk one hundred and sixty feet below the bed of Eagle river, and a vein of native copper, four feet wide, was found of great richness.

The Eagle Harbor company have opened twenty veins containing native copper and sulphurets. Native silver has been found in the copper ores as tested by Professor Mather. Two hundred tons of ore has been raised from one vein; forty tons of it was shipped to New York last fall, of which the Waterbury (Connecticut) brass foundry smelted five tons and obtained forty-five per cent. of pure copper. An ingot of it was rolled there for platers' use without annealing, which can not be done with even English refined cake-coppers. A smelting establishment has been erected.

The Northwestern company have sunk a shaft to a considerable depth, and a large quantity of vein-stone, containing copper, has been raised.

The Bohemian company commenced exploring their location in 1846. A vein of gray sulphuret, of great richness, was found.

Prince's mine raised a considerable amount of ore, which has been sent to England for analysis. It is supposed that it contained much silver. The bed is worked vigorously this season.

A company in New York and Philadelphia have sent a German geologist up the country, to erect smelting works and a laboratory. There is now a sufficient ore on the shores of the lake, to keep a large establishment at work a year.

The Bruce mine begins in or very near the St. Mary's river, a little above the point at which its name is lost in that of Lake Huron, and where its outlet winds among and is divided by the thousands of islands which chequer the north end of that lake. It is on the British mainland, opposite St. Joseph's island, which is also British territory. The usual route of steamboats is on the other side of this island.

The course of the vein is north forty-five degrees west—neither parallel nor at right angles with the river, but about half way between; the principal development has been made sixty rods from the water's edge. The average width of the whole is over eight feet. It is said to grow richer as it descends.

The ease of quarrying it is wonderful, and can not be overstated; ten thousand tons of this ore may be mined and placed on a dock at the river side, ready for shipment, for less than the cost of transporting as much ore already raised and dressed from almost any Lake Superior mine to Saut St. Marie, so as to be ready for shipment below. It certainly must be a large estimate to make the cost of delivering ten thousand tons of this ore on shipboard, fifty thousand dollars, or five dollars per ton. If the ore yield but ten per cent. of copper—and it can not be worth less than twenty or twenty-five dollars per ton on shipboard—the profit to be made from working it may thus be roughly computed.

Another vein just opened on this location, not fifty rods west of the vein just described, is about six feet wide on the surface. Nearly a mile further west, on the same location, is a vein eighteen feet wide on the surface, but this is less rich than the worked vein.

The Bruce mines, belonging to the "Lake Huron and St. Mary's river company," are situated on the north shore of Lake Huron, about seventy miles below the Saut, within thirty hours' run by steamer from Detroit; they were discovered, during the early part of last summer, by an exploring party under the direction of Captain Keating, late of the Indian department, her Britannic majesty's service. In addition to the location on which they are situated, the same company have three others, situated either on the shores of Lake Huron or on the banks of the St. Mary's river, and all below the Saut. The Lake Huron and St. Mary's river company was first organized in Montreal, in the early part of November last, and immediately afterward, Captain Keating, accompanied by Mr. Arthur Rankin, of Sandwich, proceeded to the island of St. Joseph, whence the latter gentleman, accompanied by an experienced practical miner, proceeded to the location. After spending two days in examining the veins, &c., he set out in an open boat, for the Saut, on the morning of the 20th of November, in order to take the steamer Champion on her last downward trip for the season, having in one day got out a sufficient quantity of ore to fill sixteen barrels, besides several large blocks, one of which weighed six hundred pounds; another weighed about two hundred. Part of the ore was taken to Montreal, and the remainder to New York, whence about a ton was sent to Baltimore to be smelted, where it was found to contain twenty and a half per cent. of pure copper. On the 12th of December last, Captain Keating, with one regular miner and four laborers, commenced operations by sinking a shaft in one of the veins on the location.

LANSING.—The new capital of Michigan is just beginning to assume the appearance of a town, and is pleasantly situated in the northwest part of Ingham county, near the confluence of Cedar and Grand rivers. Population 2,500.

Its recent aspect—the smoking heaps of wood, the blackened surface of the ground, the standing girdlings and board shanties—more readily suggest the idea of some immigrating colony, than the capital of a great sovereign state.

At first view it seems strange that a dense forest, with only here and there an opening, should have been selected as the site for the city. But when understood, one will not think so. The advantages to the state in general by the removal of the capital from Detroit, will be very great. There it was at one side; here it is in the centre of the state, and surrounded by a territory, which, in point of fertility and all other agricultural facilities, is scarcely anywhere equalled.

On the river near the town is abundance of water power.

The new statehouse is not designed for the permanent one, and its plan is therefore not very magnificent. The spot selected for the site is on a pleasant elevation above Grand river. The foundation of it is laid, fronting on the river ninety-seven feet, and sixty deep. The basement story is of stone, and is designed for offices, &c.; the superstructure is of two stories, for the two houses of the legislature.

There is no stone on the soil; but an abundance of stone convenient for building is found in the river.

New roads are opened, and settlers fast coming in; and what was formerly regarded an obscure by-place, will soon be the point for news and intelligence for all this vicinity. A line of stages now communicates between this place and the railroad at Jackson, and the trip from Detroit is easy.

The *Illinois and Michigan Canal* extends from Chicago, on Lake Michigan, to La Salle, at the head of steamboat navigation on the Illinois river, a distance of one hundred and five miles. The canal is constructed the same size as the proposed enlargement of the Erie canal of New York—the water being six feet in depth and sixty feet wide at its surface. The locks are one hundred and ten feet long between the gates, and eighteen feet wide, admitting the passage of boats conveying one hundred and fifty tons burden. Upon the original plan, this canal was to be supplied with water drawn from Lake Michigan. It is now constructed with the summit level raised eight feet above the surface of the lake; and the supply of water is obtained, in part, through a feeder about seventeen miles long, from the Culmet river, and in part by introducing the Des Plaines river, which runs a considerable distance along the side of the canal, and the surface of which is on a level with the water in the canal at the summit.

These two sources will supply, in all ordinary seasons, a sufficient quantity of water for a maximum trade on the canal; but in seasons of extreme drought there will be a deficiency of 3,300 cubic feet per minute; and to supply this periodical deficiency, two steam-engines of one hundred and sixty-three horse power each, are in course of erection at the junction of the canal with the Chicago river, five miles south of the city of Chicago. The power of these engines is to be applied in part to cast-iron cylinder-pumps of four and a half feet diameter, and in part to a wheel with float-boards, working in a tight chamber, to raise the water from the river (which is here on a level with the lake) eight feet in height upon the summit level. The surplus power, above that which may be required to these pumps, &c., as well as when the pumps are not required, it is proposed to apply to some kind of manufactures.

The canal occupies the channel of the Chicago river for five miles from the lake; it then rises by a lock of eight feet lift, to the summit level; thence to the first lock at the south end of the summit, is twenty-seven miles, or three miles above Lockport. From this point the canal descends along the valleys of the Des Plaines and Illinois rivers, by fifteen locks, overcoming a fall of one hundred and forty feet. At the distance of twenty-four miles from Chicago, the extensive rock excavation commences, and extends nine miles in length, varying in depth from four to twenty feet, making an average depth of fifteen feet. The excavation of this amount of rock has cost an immense sum, but by raising the summit level eight feet, a very great additional amount of rock excavation has been avoided.

On the final completion of the canal, the immense piles of rock, which had lined the canal banks, became available for the people of Chicago to Macadamize and improve their streets, pave their sidewalks, and in brief, for building purposes generally.

This canal has very few mechanical structures in proportion to its length. There are but four aqueducts, and only ten stone arch culverts, of eight to twenty feet span, and two stone dams, one across the Des Plaines, and one across the Du Page river. The whole of the canal has been constructed in the most thorough and permanent manner, and reflects great credit upon the skill and scientific acquirements of the engineer-in-chief, William Gooding, Esq.

One important feature of this canal, and of canals in general, over other modes of communication, is the water power which they create for manufacturing purposes, the effect of which is to increase directly the amount of business on the canal, by the transportation of the raw materials and of the manufacturing products, but it has a further effect in its influence upon the more speedy settlement of the country, and the development of the agricultural and mineral resources of the country adjacent to these lines of improvement.

It is estimated that above the town of

Joliet there will be eighty-four runs of stone, on a fall of sixty feet; and below that place, forty-five runs, on a fall of the same amount; making one hundred and twenty-nine runs of stone. This quantity of power may be increased by using the whole force of the steam power, to raise the water eight feet high from the Chicago river, and discharging this additional quantity of water at the south end of the summit level over a fall of sixty feet.

Of course it is impossible, from the rapidity with which this western country is filling up with inhabitants, and not of being able to foresee to what extent changes may take place in the present roads and routes for the transportation of the great interior commerce of the west, to make any definite calculations as to the amount of business which may be done on this canal. The following exhibit has been prepared by a person who is well acquainted with the subject. It is intended as an estimate of the amount of business and toll on this canal for the second year after its completion:—

		Tolls.
Lumber -	33,472,000 feet.	$33,472
Salt - -	207,700 bbls.	37,386
Flour - -	400,000 "	60,000
Wheat -	2,257,000 bush.	100,650
Sugar, molas's, and tobacco	8,625 hhds.	10,781
Merchandise	38,298 tons.	76,576
All other articles -	- -	45,000
Total - - - - -		$364,865

Sheep.—Grain has been considered the principal staple of export. To this we may now add wool-growing. As early as 1834, the farmers of Macomb county gave attention to it—particularly in the towns of Shelby, Washington, Bruce, and Armada. They led in the introduction of sheep into the territory, and have continued ever since to increase their flocks in quality and number. The state census of 1837 gave the number in that county at 5,365 head, which was then over one quarter the number in the state; the whole then being but 21,684.

The United States census taken in 1840, only three years after, gave the number at 89,934. During the years of 1840 and 1841, a company of gentlemen from Vermont took into the counties of Kalamazoo, Van Buren, and Eaton, over 25,000 head, and left them with the farmers on shares. During the same years, many of the more thrifty farmers sent out to Ohio and obtained many thousands, and sold them in the western counties. Among others, Rev. John D. Pierce was zealously and patriotically engaged in getting into Calhoun and vicinity the best breeds. Mr. Pierce sent east and to Ohio for some four or five thousand, which he sold to his poorer neighbors, on time sufficient for the fleece that could be obtained, would enable them to pay. In those times, a majority of our farmers were poor, for it took two or three years to get a dollar surplus. Most of those to whom Mr. Pierce sold, are now large growers. The increase since 1840 has been almost beyond belief. Thousands after thousands have been driven from other states—western New York sending her full quota of the best of Merinoes and not a few Saxonies.

During this time a large number of cloth-dressing establishments have been erected, and some dozen woollen factories, in various parts of the state. The largest are at Pontiac, Ypsilanti, Ann Arbor, Jackson, and Marshall. The wool now manufactured into cloth in the state can not be far from 500,000 pounds, including the home-made flannel.

The present number of sheep can not be estimated at less than 600,000. The crop averaging three pounds each, would give 1,800,000 pounds. The whole averaging twenty-four cents to the pound, give a total of $432,000. Of this quantity, say—home consumption 500,000 pounds; for export 1,100,000 pounds.

We are borne out in this conclusion by the exports of past years, and increase of sheep.

The exports were—in 1841, 23,000 pounds; in 1844, 256,407; in 1845, 412,081; in 1846, from Detroit, 506,103; from Monroe, 84,424; from St. Joseph, 4,000; from Toledo, 124,600: making a total of 716,587 pounds.

This season a large number of eastern manufacturers are in market, particularly for the coarser kinds, the new tariff having done away the duty of five per cent. on foreign coarse wools, that cost abroad seven cents and under, and made a uniform duty of thirty per cent., which tends to keep the harsher qualities from coming from South America to compete with ours. Another branch of manufacture of which wool of the coarser qualities is a component part, has sprung up at the east—*Mousseline de Laine.* Eight or ten large factories have been erected. For years this class of goods has been supplied from France and England. One of these establishments at Nashua, New Hampshire, will use a million of pounds annually. This new branch of industry will add five millions of pounds to the consumption yearly. The Bakewell, English, and South Down sheep, having long wool, are preferred, as it has to undergo a combing process.

Farmers say it is more profitable to raise wool, at present prices, than to grow wheat at sixty-two and a half cents a bushel. Sheep do not exhaust land, but, on the other hand, fertilize it. If it can be grown at the east with profit, where the very interest on the land is more than the purchase of pasturing in this state, the west, in a short time, will supplant the east in its production entirely. Since the west has gone into the business, mark the increasing quantity that has passed through the Erie canal.

The following is a statement of the arrival of wool at tide water on the Hudson river, and average price:—

Year.	Pounds.	Value.	Price.
1840,	2,876,000	$1,150,400	40 cts.
1842,	3,355,000	1,004,554	30 "
1843,	6,216,400	1,678,428	27 "
1844,	7,672,300	2,519,474	38 "
1845,	9,504,039	2,946,252	31 "
1846,	8,866,376	2,571,415	29 "

The amount of wool which arrived at Buffalo from Michigan, in 1844, was 256,407 pounds; in 1845, 412,081; and in 1846, 716,587.

Wool has also become an article of foreign export, there being no duty on it in England. The project was never tried till 1844, when about 300,000 pounds went from Boston and New York. The quantity has annually increased since.

In almost every village of this state there are wool-buyers. In the principal ones, eastern manufacturers have agents.

The Pictured Rocks of Lake Superior.—The southern shore of Lake Superior is distinguished by long ranges of inaccessible rocks, which form a hopeless obstacle to the unhappy navigator driven before a northerly storm. For miles there is not a spot to be found where even a canoe can effect a landing, or where a man could climb up the lofty perpendicular banks, to escape destruction. The water is deep quite up to the base of the cliffs, and the region is shunned, especially in bad weather.

In some places, however, where a small accessible point has been found, the Indians formerly made their landing-places; and remains of their rude drawings are still traceable upon the precipices far upon the shore. One of the most remarkable of these is represented in the vignette. The cliffs are high, bold, and apparently perpendicular; but their faces are marked with drawings of different figures, explicable only by members of the tribe or nation by which they were inscribed, but all significant parts of a record capable of distinct interpretation only by those acquainted with the secrets of the system.

The figure of an animal is usually the token, or armorial representative, of some tribe, family, or individual; and rude drawings of objects are expressive of things or actions connected with them. By the aid of native interpreters, the inscriptions on some, it is said, have been discovered to refer to a great Indian military expedition against a nation on the north side of the lake, to which the pictured rocks of the Mississippi also relate.

The following description of a visit to this remarkable spot, by a gentleman engaged in surveying the upper peninsula of Michigan, for the United States government, will be interesting to the reader:—

"I had passed and repassed the 'Grand Portal' of the pictured rocks, three different times, and had once made a sketch of it, but it seems I had never ascertained the extent of its interest. In passing it lately, all the circumstances being favorable, we determined to enter the arch with our boat; and though our mast was only about sixteen to eighteen feet high, still the feeling, as we approached, was, that we must take it down to be able to pass under the apex of the arch; but drawing nearer, the mast seemed to shrink, and the arch to tower upward, until our sail shook under a vault one hundred and twenty feet high! So much is the eye deceived by a general proportionate grandeur. Entering, we found ample room for a vast ship-of-war, with sails all standing, to conceal herself, turn round, and come out without impediment. Although the water is deep for three fourths of the way, yet at the far end of the cave there is, first, a pile of huge fallen blocks of sandstone; and, beyond these, a sand-beach, fifty to sixty feet wide. Excited by a work so magnificent, I determined to make it my observatory until I had ascertained the form and dimensions as accurately as expedition would permit. For this purpose, and to enjoy the romantic luxury, I resolved on spending a night where I need not call upon the mountains to hide me.

"As there was a spice of danger in passing a night in this palace of the winds and waves, I landed the party to encamp on the sands, near the Doric rock, and was then transported and led in the cave with my nephew and instruments, the voyagers returning with the boat to the encampment. Here we were more securely imprisoned than Napoleon on St. Helena, the only means of escape being to climb over hanging rocks two hundred feet high, or swim half a mile of the lake, with water so cold as to stiffen us in one eighth of that distance, and our provisions, a few sticks of wood which we brought in the boat, and a bucket of bean-soup. But we gave ourselves no anxiety, for we had too much work to perform. Immediately we measured our base line for triangulation, five hundred feet long, all within the cave of the great arch. At this part of the Pictured Rocks there is a table of sandstone about two hundred feet high, presenting to the lake a perpendicular wall of waving and angular outline for several miles. At the Grand Portal, the rock juts out into a short peninsula by two curves which come up like the curves from the shoulders in each side of the neck; at the end it is abruptly truncated as if the head had been cut off. Into this truncated end enters the Grand Portal arch, about one hundred and twenty feet high, and, pentrating about three hundred feet, terminates in two smaller arches. Near the far end, a cross arch, opening on each side of the neck, traverses the main cavern. Thus the ground plan, like that of ancient cathedrals, is a cross; in the portal, however, the head of the cross is double. We ventured to give names to the various apartments: First, the Grand Dome opening in the Grand Portal; second and third, the first and second dormitories; fourth and fifth, the right and left wings of the cross; sixth, the vestry with columns, groined arches, and Gothic windows communicating with the right wing; seventh, the Egyptian labyrinth, consisting of cylindric and groined galleries, supported by peculiar columns, having a distant resemblance to the Egyptian, communicating both with the right wing and with the Grand Dome. The form of the columns is that of two elongated bells, with the two small ends joined to form the middle of the shaft; or, to detail the figure, it is expanded at the top like an inverted bell, contracts rapidly as it descends, and by a gradual curve becomes nearly cylindric for some distance; and again it contracts on a gradual curve till it comes almost to a point, where it meets the same figure reversed. This form is essentially beautiful, being a solid generated by rotation of Hogarth's sigmoid line of grace. To explain the mode of its formation would lead to too long a discussion.

"Our most active and frolicsome half-breed voyager had waded the water, and, without our perceiving him, had entered the labyrinth. To our surprise he thrust his head out of a hole in the Grand Dome, and uttered a hideous growl. His companions instantly took up the drama of the beast in his den, and hurled a volley of stones at him. Darting back, Legarde presented his head at another opening, and defied his pursuers with a still fiercer snarl; instantly there followed another volley, another evasion, and another peal of laughter echoed back from the dome, I labored hard until dark, and then discovered a new danger in making it my place of rest. I found a great part of the cave to be lined with a shell of stone loosened by the last winter's frost, and ready at all points to fall with crushing force. Going back to the farthest recess of the dormitory arch, I knocked off all the loose stones, propped up my cot on piles of rocks, and composed myself to sleep, not unmindful, as I lay down, that the canopy of my bed was of solid stone, two hundred feet thick, with a forest of fir-trees on top as the ornamental fringe. About midnight I arose, lighted a candle, built a fire, and walked forward with my lantern to the farthest block of stone. Here I gazed at the great star-lighted window presented by the portal arch, and as I stood, the polar star just twinkled on the verge of the opening, making the angular altitude equal to the latitude of the place. Again I lay down in the dormitory and listened to the dirge-like music of the ripple, as it kissed the rocky fragments and danced into the labyrinths. In such situations there is often a mirage of sound as wonderful as that of sight; the discords seem to be absorbed, and the harmonious notes are echoed and reverberated with more enchanting spells than belong to the Æolian; commingled with the dirge one imagines imitations of cascades, hail, rain, and storms. This was the pianissimo; while the fortissimo would be witnessed when the northern storm should drive the thunder of the great lake directly into the Grand Portal. Suppose this to have happened while I was a tenant—it was really what I desired. An avalanche of rock sufficient to have crushed a city, had fallen just outside of the left arch, and laid rudely piled to the height of fifty feet. Thither would I have retreated to witness the bloodless battle of the elements; for a long war has been waged between waves and rocks, in which the rocks have so far been obliged to yield. Morning came, and with the dawn myself and nephew were at our work of triangulating. Having completed the survey, and obtained geological specimens of great interest, we returned in the boat which had come from the party on shore, in the afternoon.

"I shall calculate my observations, make drawings of ground-plan and elevations, and include them in my report to Dr. Jackson, and through him to the government, that, if they are found worthy of it, they may be published. I need hardly say, that such a curiosity, in such a climate, deserves a visit from the Cincinnatians during the hot months. Within half a mile is a boat harbor, a fine camping ground; and still another half a mile along the land beach, is the Chapel rock, and still nearer, a cascade. Beyond this again is a cascade leaping the top of the Pictured Rocks clear into the lake, and blowing a blast of wind in all directions from where it strikes the water sufficiently to propel a sail-boat. The Grand Portal is less extensive than the mammoth cave, being a mere fraction of it, but it has some compensating beauties. It has light and a fine breeze, and is at the same time as cool. You arrive at all of its beauties without fatigue, and enjoy, through its three open arches, the most extraordinary landscapes. Through the Grand Portal you see only the shoreless lake; through the western opening of the cross arch a limited but magnificent view of the lake and the Pictured Rocks overhanging its dark blue waters, on whose surface, when calm, those rocks are reflected into a symmetrical counterpart of the original. Through the eastern wing is seen also the lake and the Pictured Rocks dying away in well-marked perspective, as one point sinks behind the other, to the distance of ten miles. In the course of this perspective is the cascade of Chappel river, the Chappel rock, and the cascade of the winds. This cross arch is five hundred feet long, and so straight that light is seen through it from one side to the other. Mr. Schoolcraft passed through it with his boat: but the lake having fallen about four feet it is nearly dry, and the only entrance by water is by the Grand Portal."

The emigration to Michigan is now larger than for years past. Every part of the peninsula wears a new aspect to what it did five years since. The log houses have given way to fine brick and pine dwellings, ornamented with paint, and the windows bedecked with blinds or tasty curtains. The slab sheds are hardly known. Large barns have taken their places. Where the wolf prowled undisturbed, herds of sheep are seen—the bleating of the frolicsome lambs is heard, where the doe had full sway. You can scarcly ride on any road that has been open for five years, that is not lined on either side with grain. The whole country has the appearance of a fifty years' settlement. Enterprise and industry are everywhere prevalent.

The advantages that Michigan offers to the emigrant, are clearly set forth in the following statements :—

"First. We are surrounded with water communication for hundreds of miles, with noble streams that are navigable, and from its tributary waters into the lakes. From the mouth of each the canvass wafts the staff of life to the east.

"Second. We have avenues of art, binding with solid iron, as by links, the centre and southern counties from one extremity to the other, while the north for some distance equally enjoys the benefit of iron horses to forward their surplus to a shipping point.

"Third. No state can boast of better hydraulic power—the summit level being near the centre of the peninsula and its never-failing streams diverging to several points, as though the hand of an engineer had planned their serpentine courses to accommodate every county. View the lines of all the streams of every state in the Union, as laid down on their respective maps, and it is unequalled.

"Fourth. The soil is calculated for the production of almost every species of culture that could be desired north of the tropics.

"Fifth. Our school and university fund exceeds most of our neighbors, for land already sold and that remaining is mostly of the choicest kind. We have our school districts and rapidly-increasing school libraries, in every direction settled. Our state university is already in operation, with professors of the rarest talent for the higher branches. In point of advantages for education, New England or New York are not ahead. In point of intelligence, the last census of the United States places us ahead of nearly every sister state, with two exceptions, as having the least number who can neither write nor read.

"Sixth. A majority of our present population are mostly from New England and New York. The rapid increase of our exports exhibit their industry. No state in the Union, from the organization of the confederacy, has made such rapid strides. It is unparalleled in ancient or modern history.

"Seventh. Our state indebtedness, by the sale of state improvements, has been reduced. The interest on all acknowledged bonds will be paid on the first of January next, and a tax law has been passed to meet it hereafter.

"Eighth. Our exports exceed our imports the past year by over a million of dollars.

"Ninth. Our advantages for marketing our surplus products are far superior to any and all other states west of Buffalo, and they bear a much better price.

"Tenth. We have two months the advantage of our neighbors in the navigation of Lake Erie for eastern shipments, always at a season when produce bears the best prices. In the spring there is generally four weeks after the opening of the lower lakes, that the straits of Mackinac are obstructed with ice, which is invaluable either in a rising or falling market, and some four weeks after the first of November, when the passage to the upper lakes is hazardous, and craft going thither are in danger of not being able to return until the following spring. During all this time, both spring and fall, most of the craft make trips from Detroit to Buffalo, which throws hundreds of them in competition for freight, and transportation is thereby cheapened while it advances at the upper ports."

Cut-Off River, near New Harmony.

INDIANA.

THIS state is bounded on the north by Michigan, east by Ohio, south by Kentucky, from which it is separated by Ohio river, west by Illinois, and northwest by Lake Michigan. The Ohio forms the boundary for 340 miles from the mouth of the Great Miami to that of the Wabash. The entire outline is 990 miles. The greatest length is along the west border, 272 miles, the main length nearly 260 miles, the mean breadth 140 miles, and the area about 36,000 square miles. It lies between north latitude 37° 50′ and 41° 47′ and longitude 7° 48′ and 11° 48′ west from Washington. Population, 988,734.

About five sixths of this state is drained by the Wabash river. In surface it is intermediate between Illinois and Ohio, being less monotonous than the former, and less hilly than the latter. A range of rough and abrupt hills rises on the banks of the Ohio; but these are formed by the cutting down of the channel, while on the opposite side there is only a gentle declivity of the surface toward the northwest, where the waters are drained into the Wabash. The White river, a minor stream, rises within half a mile of the Ohio, opposite the mouth of the Kentucky, at the Great Bend. The region crossed by the branches of this stream and by the Wabash is remarkable for the amenity of its surface; beyond which extends the wide plain or table-land. Here rise the Tippecanoe and Eel rivers, which flow into the Wabash, as well as the Kankakee and Pinkimink, tributaries of the Illinois; the Elkhart, Pigeon, and others, flowing into the St. Joseph's of Lake Michigan, and the St. Joseph's branch of the Maumee. The

Wabash, the principal river in the state, is five hundred miles long; and, rising in Ohio, flows into Indiana in the northeast part, crosses it, and forms the western boundary for one hundred and forty miles.

The great western plain commences on Lake Erie, between the Maumee and Raisin rivers, and extends to the junction of the Illinois with the Mississippi river. It is about four hundred miles in length, from northeast-by-east to southwest and west, and is chiefly prairie. The surface and subsoil abound in marine and river shells, and numerous trees are found imbedded. Prairies abound also along White river, and present every variety of these peculiar kinds of lands, viz., the dry, wet, level, rolling, barren, and fertile prairie. The rich, however, preponderate, and many tracts are luxuriant.

Climate.—That part of the state nearest to Lake Michigan is subject to copious rains; and as much of the land in that section is low and marshy, a considerable portion of it is thus unfit for cultivation; while sandhills, bearing small juniper-trees, are numerous in the rear. The low tracts have generally proved very unhealthy, especially near swamps, ponds, and streams; and fever-and-ague has sometimes prevailed; the warmer regions have also suffered from the same cause. The rapid increase of the population, however, shows that this evil has not materially checked the prosperity of the state.

The winters are mild compared with those of New England and even Pennsylvania—as winter lasts only about six weeks from the end of December. The rivers which are not the most rapid are then frozen; and sometimes even the Wabash has been bridged with ice. Frequently snow falls in the northern parts to the depth of eighteen inches; but in the south it is seldom ever more than six inches. Peach-trees bloom early in March, and the forests grow green from the 5th of April to the 15th; and, as numerous shrubs put forth their flowers before their leaves appear, the appearance of the country is delightful early in the season.

The governor is elected by the people, for four years, ineligible next term. A lieutenant-governor is also chosen in the same manner, and for the same term. The senate, not to exceed fifty members, elected for four years. The representatives, not to exceed one hundred, chosen for two years. Elections are held biennially. Elections by the people are by ballot; by the assembly which meets biennially, *viva voce*. The judicial power is vested in a supreme court of from three to five members, elected by the people, for six years; in circuit courts, the judges of which are elected by the people for six years; and in such minor courts as the assembly may establish. This right of suffrage extents to every white male citizen, twenty-one years of age, six months a resident of the state.

Literary Institutions.—In this state are the following: Indiana university, at Bloomington; Hanover college, at South Hanover; Wabash college, at Crawfordsville; Indiana Ashbury university; the University of Notre Dame du Lac, at South Bend; Franklin college, at Franklin; and St. Gabriel college. The number of academies is sixty, and that of common schools one thousand six hundred.

Indianapolis, the capital of Indiana, stands on the west bank of the west branch of White river, one hundred and twenty-two miles west of Cincinnati. It is at the head of steamboat navigation on that stream, and is already a large and flourishing town, although the spot was in the midst of the forest as late as the year 1821. The river is crossed by a fine bridge.

The position of the town is near the centre of the state, and it enjoys the advantages offered by a large river, which waters as great a portion of fertile land, in proportion to its size, as any other in the United States. The surrounding country has been settled with great rapidity; and the town is laid out with much taste, and presents a fine appearance. Several broad streets meet from different points, at a beautiful circular public green, situated on a gentle elevation, on which conspicuously stands the governor's house. Population, 8,000.

Capitol of Indiana.—This edifice is situated in an open square of the city. It is of the robust or ancient Doric order, and is considered the nearest approach to the classical spirit of the antique on the western continent.

The building is eighty feet wide, and one hundred and eighty feet long, and contains rooms on three floors—a basement below the level of the portico and peribolus, and two stories above. The great halls of legislation, chambers of the senate and representatives, are on the upper floor, which renders them lofty in the ceilings, and the committee rooms, which are on the first floor, more accessible by the free passage from end to end of the building, which passage could not be admitted were the great rooms below. The senate-chamber is thirty-six by seventy feet; the hall of representatives, forty-eight by seventy, or near these dimensions; and the rotunda, thirty-six feet, with dome and skylight. The halls are rectangular oblongs on the plan, but have a semi-hemispherical concavity, or half dome in the ceiling, resting on a semicircular colonnade, which forms the "bar of the house" (so termed), within which the members' seats are placed, all facing inward, fronting the focal point and speaker's chair. This general arrangement is favorable to the extension and inflection of sound, which, here made sonorous, is yet found free from reverberation, distinct and clear. It affords variety, with an architectural character to the apartment, while the columns contribute an additional support to the roof.

As an exhibition of classical architecture, we have in the capitol of Indiana each of the three orders appropriated by Greece: the Doric, Ionic, and Corinthian—the robust, chaste, and magnificent. In the body of the edifice we have a resemblance to the Parthenon of Athens; in the interior, the rich Ionic of the Erectheion; in the dome, the circular temple of Vesta, at Tivoli; and the lantern is a model of the Corinthian monument of Lysicrates.

The other public buildings are the courthouse, state-prison, deaf and dumb asylum, lunatic asylum, a female institute, and ten churches. The population amounts to about three thousand.

Stage-coaches depart daily for Cincinnati, Wheeling, Columbus, and Zanesville; and for several other places there times a week. The communication with Madison is also daily, being all of the way by railroad.

VINCENNES, one hundred and fifty miles from the mouth of the Wabash, is the second western town in point of antiquity, having been settled by Frenchmen from Canada as early as 1735, at a time when Kaskaskia was the only place inhabited by white men in those extensive regions. Here, in the midst of a fertile district, and in the heart of a wilderness, a small colony remained, for a long time almost entirely excluded from the world, and mingling only with the savages, to whose habits they in some respects accommodated themselves. It was for a time the seat of the territorial government.

The ground is level, regularly laid out in squares, and the houses generally have fruit gardens attached to them. Steamboats come up to the town most of the year. The adjacent prairie is large and fertile, and five thousand acres of it are in common, according to the provision of the old French inhabitants.

During the early part of its history the French and Indians carried on a predatory warfare against the Kentuckians and other border settlers.

NEW HARMONY, fifty-four miles below Vincennes, on the east bank of the Wabash, and over one hundred from its mouth, was settled in 1814 by a band of eight hundred Germans, of a sect called Harmonists, who had previously made a settlement in Pennsylvania on Beaver creek. They were led by Joseph Rapp, and held their property in common, under certain strict regulations. They formed a large and flourishing village, with a large house for public meetings, a botanic garden, and green-house.

About the year 1826, the people having become somewhat discontented with the place, and disposed to return to Pennsylvania, sold to the celebrated theorist, Robert Owen, of Lanark, Scotland, who here brought some of his vis-

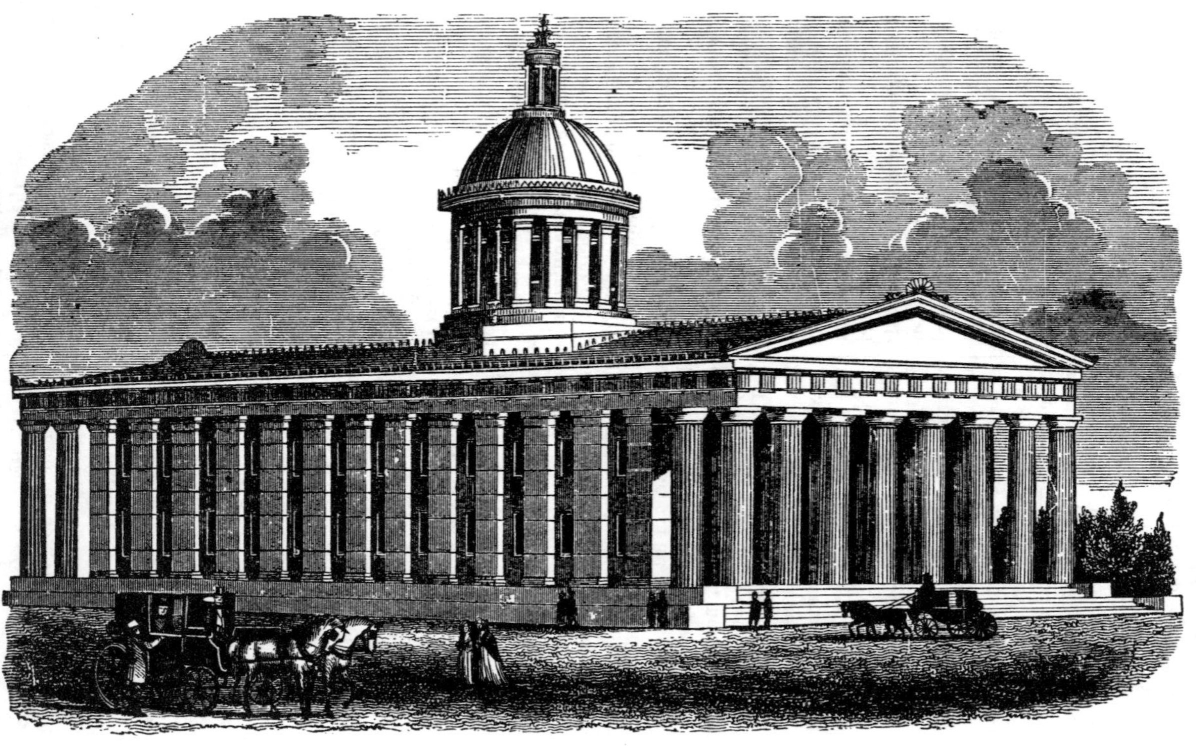

The Capitol of Indiana, Indianapolis.

ionary plans to experiment. A community was established, who spent the sabbath in listening to his discourses, and occupied their time in various modes, with very little profit to themselves or the public. The experiment at length failed, and the place may hereafter rise to the rank for which nature seems to have fitted it, under the management of persons of better sense and sounder principles.

LOGANSPORT stands on the bank of the Wabash, at the mouth of Eel river, and each of these streams is crossed by a fine bridge. This place enjoys the commercial advantages afforded by the Wabash and Erie canal, and by the water-power obtained from the rivers. Manufactories of several kinds are in operation. Stage-coaches run three times a week to Lafayette and Niles, as well as to the capital of the state.

SOUTH BEND, on the bank of Maumee river, is well situated for a manufacturing place, though partly built on a lofty bluff. It contains a courthouse, four churches, and about 2,000 inhabitants.

The *Roman Catholic college* of Nôtre Dame du Lac was founded in 1844.

MICHIGAN CITY.—This town, at the south end of the lake of that name, has the only harbor in the state. It was laid out in 1835, but is already a considerable village, of about 2,900 inhabitants, with some trade, and a communication with Chicago, Niles, and South Bend, by stage coaches, three times a week.

TERRE HAUTE.—This town, as its French name indicates, occupies an elevated position. It is on the left bank of the Wabash, and seventy-three miles west of Indianapolis, where the river is crossed by the national road on a fine bridge. A courthouse, six churches, a market-house, bank, and a seminary, are the principal public buildings. The population is about 4,000. The situation is advantageous for trade, and the place is flourishing. Stage-coaches go daily to Indianapolis, St. Louis Shawneetown, and Danville, Illinois.

CRAWFORDSVILLE stands on the left bank of Rock river, forty-five miles distant from Indianapolis, and contains seven churches, a courthouse, a seminary, and 4,000 inhabitants.

Wabash college, which is situated in Crawfordsville, was founded in 1835, and has four professors, more than one hundred students, and about four thousand five hundred volumes in its libraries.

LAFAYETTE.—This town stands at the head of steam navigation on the Wabash, three hundred and ten miles from its mouth, by the course of the stream. It has seven churches, a courthouse, and several other public buildings, with a population of about 4,000. The Wabash and Erie canal affords a communication between this place and Lake Erie. Stage-coaches go three times a week to Indianapolis and Logansport.

Indiana occupies an important portion of the vast central valley of North America, drained by the Mississippi and its numerous branches, while it touches, at its extreme northwest corner, the south end of one of the great northern lakes. As a large part of the state lies between the Ohio and the Wabash, it partakes of the general features of the Mississippi country; and to Indiana, in common with her neighboring sister states, the following impressive statements and views justly apply:—

The Peculiar Characteristics of Western Mind.—Says a late writer: "There have been, I apprehend, in no country in its early settlement, precisely the elments in forming the public mind, which are found in the western regions of our own. The colonies that went out from Phœnicia, and that laid the foundations of empire on the shores of the Mediterranean, had a homogeneousness of character, and transferred the principles and feelings of the mother-country at once to the new lands where they took up their abode. The colonies that went out from Greece to occupy the maritime regions of Asia Minor, carried with them the love of the arts, of literature, and of liberty, which distinguished Corinth and Athens; and Ionia became merely a reflected image of what Attica and Achaia and Argolis had been. The colonies which landed on Plymouth rock, and at Salem, and Boston, also had an entire homogeneousness of character. There was no intermingling of any foreign elements contemplated or allowed. They were, when they landed, and when they laid the foundation of Harvard university, and when they spread over New England, what they were in Holland and in England, with only the modifications which their new circumstances made, but with none from any foreign admixtures.

"When we turn our eyes, however, to the great west, we discern an entirely different state of things. There is no homogeneousness of character, of origin, of aim, of language. There are elements already mingled and struggling for the mastery, any one of which, if alone, would have vital and expansive power enough to diffuse itself all over that great valley.

"There is a large infusion of the puritan mind.

"There is a large infusion there of a foreign mind, with little homogeneousness of character or of views, except in the single reason which has precipitated it on our western shores. There are different languages; different manners and customs; different modes of faith and worship. It is alike in this, that it is a foreign mind, little acquainted with our institutions; bred up mostly under a monarchical government; restrained at home less by an intelligent public sentiment than by the bayonet; tenacious in most instances of the religion in which it was trained; and having, to a large extent, little sympathy with the principles and the achievements of protestantism. There is at the west, as a consequence of this, a great intermingling of those minds which are likely to be most adventurous, energetic, and bold. In the vast valley there are representatives from nearly all the nations of Europe, and all the forms of religion which prevail there. Ireland, and France, and England, and Germany, and Italy, have their representatives there; and they appear there, not as amalgamated with our republican and protestant institutions, but as still imbodying the sentiments which they cherished in their native land.

"A second characteristic of the western mind, as it is now, is, that it is as yet unsettled. A demagogue, a propagator of error, a rejector of religion, here, must begin his work by a covert or open attack on these associations; he must weaken their power over the soul; he has a long work to do to detach the mind from its fastenings, before he can move it according to his will. But, in a new region, he finds all this, to a great extent, done to his hand. There is no ancient sanctuary, or sabbath-bell, or sepulchre of the dead, or schoolhouse, or established public sentiment, that can hinder his purposes; and his work begins at a point, to reach which elsewhere might cost the labors of his life.

"A third observation which may be made in relation to the characteristics of the western mind, is, that there are circumstances which make it certain that it will be developed.

"From the character, also, of the elements which compose society there, there will be intellectual strife; there will be earnest conflict; there will be impassioned eloquence; there will be a struggle of mind with mind.

"Everything in the natural scenery is on a scale so vast and grand—the majestic rivers, the boundless prairies, the deep forest, the very immensity almost of the rich domain which is spread out there as if to make man vast in his schemes, gigantic in his purposes, large in his aspirations, and boundless in his ambition.

"I may notice a fourth characteristic of the western mind, in its relation to religion. Strange as it may seem to one who looks on the heterogeneous and unsettled mass, the result of the experiments there made has shown that the west is not a favorable field for planting communities destitute of all religion.

"The question, then, if these are just views, is not whether there shall be any religion, or none—but whether the religion which shall prevail there shall be true or false; enlightened or ignorant; a miserable fanaticism, or a large and liberal Christianity; a low and drivelling superstition, or principles that commend themselves to reason and common sense; the religion of tradition, or the religion of the Bible; a religion of excitement, and feeling, and variableness, or the religion of principle."

The following statements, recently published, give an interesting view of the advantages offered by the Ohio for ship-building:—

An intelligent gentleman, formerly of Boston, but who has spent most of the last twenty years in the west, in 1805 explored the west, with a view to the establishment of a ship-yard there, and in 1806, a Mr. Jarvis, of Boston, on his recommendation, built one or two large ships at Marietta. One of the largest and best bodies of oak in the United States is on the banks of the Ohio, stretching along the highlands of Virginia, Ohio, and the more mountainous region of Kentucky, for several hundred miles. There are inexhaustible beds of coal and iron ore directly on the river bank from Pittsburgh, some four hundred miles westerly, and within which distance there are now nearly two hundred and fifty furnaces and forges engaged in producing and manufacturing the raw material. Several large ships have since been built at the above and other places on the Ohio, and at an average of from twenty to thirty per cent. less than they could have been built for on the Atlantic. The Ohio is an unsteady stream, but all who are acquainted with it know, that at least two months in the spring, and for the same period in the autumn, there is sufficient water, as high up as Marietta, for a ship-of-the-line to pass down to the Mississippi. It is also true, that for six or eight months, one year with another, there are times when the largest merchantmen can traverse this river in perfect safety. By so arranging as to bring out the ship so that she would make her descent in the spring or autumn, she could load with the products of the country, and make, on her homeward passage, more than sufficient to compensate for any loss of time or other inconveniences for being built at a distance from her place of final destination, while the timber crop and means of subsistence can be obtained in the greatest abundance, and at a comparatively small price to what they would cost on the seaboard. It is to be borne in mind, that Kentucky and Ohio produce the best of hemp, which, if called for, would be manufactured on the spot, to complete the rigging up, and at a great saving in expense.

The only difficulty to be encountered in the commencement of an extensive yard in the interior, would be the want of workmen; but this would be remedied so soon as an assurance should be given for constant employ. It is observable, too, that in this mild and genial climate, the same force can accomplish more in the year than at New York, Boston, or anywhere at the north, a fact showing that both principal and labor have greater advantages here than elsewhere; besides, the workman can support his family for one third what it will cost him at the east.

A Western River-Town.—Many of the principal river-towns in the west bear more or less resemblance to that represented in the accompanying engraving; and in several points some of those of Indiana enjoy situations much like it. The banks of the Ohio and the Wabash, in several parts, are as elevated as the land seen on the opposite side of the streams, while the clusturing houses near the shore, the signs of navigation on the water, and the general aspect of active and prosperous business, on the one hand, and of a varied and fruitful country, on the other, may afford an impression of one of the western towns rising so rapidly on the borders of those large and beautiful rivers. The roofs of large public buildings are seen above the numerous private habitations, and the number of church steeples, which present the most conspicuous objects, indicate that various Christian denominations in the country are represented in our distant regions, and carry with them their zeal and their industry.

There are salt-springs in different parts of Indiana; but the people were formerly wholly supplied with salt from the United States saline, near Shawneetown, and the salines of Kenhawa. Coal beds exist in some places, and copper

View on the Wabash River.

ore is found in the north. From early times a report has prevailed that a silver mine existed near Ouitanon ; but the uniform surface of the country and the deep soil which covers a large part of it, are unfavorable to the discovery of mines, and to the abundance of minerals of any kind. Large tracts of the state, as in many other extensive regions of the west, are destitute of rocks, stones, and even pebbles.

The navigable waters of Indiana are very numerous and extensive ; the principal rivers being accessible in large steamboats, and many of their branches being boatable. The entire extent of navigable waters has been variously estimated at from two thousand five hundred miles and upward.

So numerous are the streams which approach the shores of the lakes, so high are they navigable in boats, at least a part of the year, and so many convenient ponds lie between, that more than twenty portages have formerly been used on various routes between the waters of the Ohio and Wabash and the lakes.

1. The oldest of these used by white men is that between St. Mary's and the little river of the Wabash, which was used by the French from Canada, in communicating with their early posts on the Wabash. 2. By the short Chicago and Kickapoo of the Illinois. 3. By the Big Miami and a branch of the Maumee, by which canoes proceed from the Ohio to Lake Erie. 4. To Lorimer's fort, between the Miami and Maumee. 5. By Hudson river of Lake Erie and Grand river of Lake Michigan. 6. By the Muskingum and Cuyahoga of Lake Erie, during spring floods. 7. The four-mile portage, between St. Joseph's of Lake Michigan and the Theakiki. 8. The two-mile portage, between Theakiki and the Great Kenomic. 9. The half-mile portage, between the Great and Little Kenomic. 10. The three-mile portage, between the Chicago and the Plein. There are also many others between the branches of the Wabash and Lake Michigan.

There were formerly many tribes of Indians residing within the bounds of this state : the Mascotins, Piankeshaws, Kickapoos, Delawares, Miamies, Shawnees, Weeas, Ouitanons, Eel Rivers, and Pottawotamies.

In 1791 General Wilkinson invaded their country, and destroyed their great town, in which were one hundred and twenty houses, eighty of which had shingled roofs.

The country about the upper parts of the Wabash is of the best kind, the soil being black, deep, friable, and highly productive, and the surface extending in wide and beautiful prairies, of an undulated form. They are less uniform and flat than most of the prairies further west, often being varied by hills, some of considerable elevation. The region thus abounds in fine scenes, which afford a delightful relief to the eye.

These regions were formerly well stocked with game ; and wild animals are still common in some places : bears, deer, wild turkeys, prairie-hens, partridges, grouse, wild pigeons, rattlesnakes, and copper-heads. Abundance of fish of different kinds are found in the streams and lakes. The first settlers, as well as the Indians, depended for their subsistence, to a great extent, upon the chase and fishing; and the pursuit of bears and deer, especially, gave frequent exercise to their skill and activity.

A Bear Hunt.—The accompanying engraving offers a very interesting scene of a nature quite common in the early period of the settlement. In a still and clear winter's night, when the animal, ravenous with hunger, sometimes proceeded from his den in search of food, the bold and hardy settler was also awake and abroad. With his trusty rifle in his hand, a cautious step and a watchful eye, his ear attentive to every sound, he sought a station from which he might discover and observe the approach of the fierce wanderer of the forest. The cracking of the frozen surface of a lake or river, or the falling of a twig overladen with ice, was the only sound that, for a time, broke the solemn silence of the night. But a rustling of the bushes, or the motion of a dark figure slowly emerging from the gloom, betrayed the approach of the prowler.

Bear-Hunting—Winter scene.

After the discovery of a bear, the primary object of the hunter is to avoid his observation, until he comes within the reach of the rifle; and the second is to make sure work at the first shot. The savage beast, though usually inclined to avoid a rencontre with his human enemy at a season when his nature is tamed by full feeding on vegetables, is rendered bold and fierce by hunger, seems raised above all fear, and rushes even upon an armed man to devour him. Unlike most other wild animals, also, he is almost inevitable in the pursuit, when the hunter turns to fly. There is scarcely any surface, however yielding, over which his soft and spreading foot will not bear him; and he climbs the tree with far greater facility than the most agile man, following him to the extremity of the limbs, and falling, on occasion, more safely to the ground.

But such men as the settlers of Indiana would seldom find themselves reduced to seek escape before the bear, even in the severest season. Having discovered his game, he resorted to all the arts which ingenuity and experience could dictate, until he found himself within rifle distance; and then, with unerring aim, he sent the fatal ball into the savage heart of the beast, which would gladly have found his way into the little log-house, and devoured the sleeping family: and now the monster's flesh is to serve them for food, and his warm and shaggy skin is to shield them from the cold.

Many a scene like that represented in the engraving has been witnessed in the prairies of Indiana, which in winter present a dreary and chilling aspect, though in summer blooming in the richest fertility, enlivened with graceful deer, smiling with a thousand flowers, and resounding with songs of musical birds.

The first newspaper in Indiana was published at Vincennes, the seat of government, sometime before 1810. In 1828 there were twenty-eight newspapers in the state.

The historical society of Indiana was organized in 1820, and incorporated in 1831.

LAWRENCEBURG is a small town on the bank of the Ohio, one mile below the mouth of the Great Miami. There are four churches and a courthouse, and the number of inhabitants is about 2,500. Three times a week stage-coaches depart for Cincinnati, Madison, and Indianapolis.

MADISON.—This town, eighty-nine miles below Cincinnati, occupies a beautiful position on the bank of the Ohio. The surrounding country has fine hills, and the streets are laid out with regularity, and built with taste. There are ten churches, a courthouse, a market-house, a bank, and a savings bank, and a population of about 5,000. The hills in the rear of the town rise to an elevation of two hundred and fifty feet, and there are several fine views from their sides and summits. Steamboats land at the wharves, stage-coaches run three times a week to Cincinnati, Louisville, and Frankfort, and the railroad forms a constant and easy communication with Indianapolis.

NEW ALBANY, one hundred and forty miles above Cincinnati, and two miles below the falls, is the largest town in Indiana, containing six thousand five hundred and sixty inhabitants. The public buildings are nine churches, a bank, a male and a female seminary, a lyceum, and the theological college.

The streets are from seventy to one hundred feet in breadth, and laid out with regularity. Much ship-building is carried on here. There are several large ship-yards; and from ten to fifteen steamboats are annually built, besides a considerable number of sloops and schooners. Besides several stage-routes, much travelling is performed on the river.

EVANSVILLE, two hundred and thirty-three miles below Cincinnati, stands on an elevation on the bank of the Ohio, and contains several large manufactories, with ten churches, and several other public buildings. The population is two thousand five hundred. One mile distant from this place are

The Pigeon Springs.—This is a favorite resort for visiters in the summer months. The waters contain muriate of soda, bicarbonate of iron, and magnesia, carbonic acid, and carburetted hydrogen gases, with nitrogen. Their medical properties are aperient, alterative, diuretic, and diaphoretic.

BLOOMINGTON, forty-nine miles from Indianapolis, is situated at the head of a branch of White river, and contains nearly 3,000 inhabitants. It has five churches and the Indiana university.

Cut-off River.—This wild scene, represented in the engraving, is on the course of a stream of this singular name, which is a branch of the Wabash, flowing into that river at New Harmony. The banks are high, steep, and very remarkable for their picturesque character, being steep, and thickly grown with gigantic oaks and other trees of large size, while the surface is broken by rocks and ledges. The stream in some parts is beautifully variegated with small islands, which add a most pleasing character to the scene; while the high, rude, and frowning banks, crowded with thick, natural forests, give an air of wildness and sublimity, strongly contrasting with the smooth surface of the stream; and the gentler aspect of some of the islets which seem to float on the water.

Evergreen-trees are rare in these regions; but the catalpa-tree and plane, with the maples, rise from an undergrowth of pawpaws, spinewood, and redbud, presenting a rich variety of form and color, remarkably agreeable to the eye.

Circumstances have led to some peculiarities in the settlements of large portions of Indiana. The cheapness of the land attracted many settlers from Pennsylvania and further south, as well as Germans and foreigners from several nations in Europe. These did not generally meet and mingle in one mass: they were not drawn to particular points, but usually scattered and planted at distances from each other. Later immigrants, therefore, naturally obeyed the laws of affinity, and bent their steps to the neighborhoods where they found the languages or the customs in which they had been educated. Thus the process of amalgamation has not gone as far in this state as in many other newly-settled regions; and in some parts it hardly appears to have yet commenced. The traveller on some of the routes through Indiana, meets in succession with small communities which offer striking pictures of several distinct European nations, alternating with others marked with the peculiarities of the east and the south, the west, the middle and the northern parts of our own country.

The history of New Harmony, already given, presents a striking picture of one community of a peculiar nature, and essentially different from any other within the limits of the state; but there are others, of different kinds, which are hardly more exclusive, and but little less affected by surrounding influences. Such circumstances are unfavorable to some of the best interests of the state, and must tend to retard such improvements as the public need. They may, perhaps, be best counteracted by the universal diffusion of education, and primarily by the multiplication of good public schools. Unhappily, Indiana has not yet shown becoming zeal in this important department of public improvement; and she must expect to see some of her more sagacious neighbors leading the way in solid progress, in prosperity, wealth, and numbers, as well as in general intelligence, refinement, and power. She must, notwithstanding, continue to increase, and with rapidity. Her soil, situation, and various natural resources, will constantly attract new-comers, while they will well reward those who have already adopted the land as their own. With the strong inducements which the state has to lay wide and deep the foundations of public intelligence and virtue, and the strong stimulus offered by the examples of some of her sister states, it may be hoped that she will hereafter become not less conspicuous for her patronage of learning, than for her numerous and superior natural advantages. Certain it is, that whenever such a period shall arrive, Indiana will find her career attended with many facilities and improvements; and such of her citizens as may anticipate the change of public opinion, will find their active and persevering exertions rewarded by great and honorable and lasting results.

Cave-in Rock, near Shawneetown

ILLINOIS.

This state is distinguished by natural peculiarities, which give it a marked distinction among its sisters of the American Union. In the rapid increase of its inhabitants, it is unsurpassed, having a population in 1850 of 858,234. In 1771 it was only 1,460; in 1800, 3,250; in 1810, 12,282; in 1820, 55,211; in 1830, 157,445; in 1840, 484,500; in 1845, 668,000.

Various authentic sources, of the latest dates, furnish the following particulars respecting this extensive, fertile, and growing state.

The extreme length of Illinois, from north to south, is 375 miles, and the extreme width 215, averaging about 160. It lies between 37° and 42° 30′ north latitude, and 10° 25′ and 14° 25′ west longitude from Washington. The area is about sixty thousand square miles, or 38,400,000 acres. The public land surveys give 35,235,200 acres, or 55,055 square miles, leaving 4,945 square miles chiefly occupied with navigable waters. All the waste lands, including those so broken as to be useless (there are no mountains), irreclaimable swamps, &c., may amount to two millions of acres, or 3,125 square miles; leaving of arable lands and small water-courses, which are necessary for farming purposes, 51,930 square miles.

Illinois is the third state in the Union in extent; and in its proportion of good land by far the first. Another such tract of equal size and quality can not be carved out on the globe. It is larger in area than all New England, deducting one tenth of Maine; greater than England and Wales united; has two acres of good land to their one; and, in productiveness, two acres of Illinois land are equal to at least three of their cultivated ones on the average, and with good husbandry will continue so for many years. And with such agricultural capabilities, unsurpassed by any other state or nation great or small, not a state in the Union, except a few small ones on the seaboard, possesses equal natural advantages for marketing its surplus.

The mineral riches beneath the soil are perfectly exhaustless. No geological survey has been had, so that we know not what the resources in this respect may be. But coal mines, limestone, and granite, are found in all parts; lead in immense quantities at the north and south; iron at the north; salt springs at the south and centre; and potter's clay, waterlime, and various kinds of marble, in the different sections.

In general it is well watered with springs and running streams, though some of the large prairies in the northern part are somewhat deficient in this respect. Even there, however, it is not common to find a section* without a spring. Closely in connexion, come in the manufacturing advantages. The greatest lack of nature's bounties, and indeed the only one of consequence, is a limited supply of timber. This objection, however, lies only against portions of the north, and is easily remedied by culture. There is enough for present purposes. As yet the best can be bought in all parts of the state for from three to ten dollars per acre; and twenty to forty acres, well husbanded, suffice for a large farm. The future will take care of itself. Black-locust will grow in two years from the seed, to make fencing material; and if the fires on uncultivated prairie be kept down for a few years, the surface is speedily covered with a young forest growth. There will be more timber in Illinois twenty years hence than now.

Illinois will be—must be—one of the noblest branches of the confederacy. No one of her sister states enjoys equal natural advantages; and with honesty and ability to direct her public affairs, which her citizens can supply, she will take a most honorable position.

The "timbered openings" are most delightful to the eye, though the intimate combination of them all is requisite to satisfy the highest ideal of utility or beauty. Were Illinois all prairie, though inconceivably fertile, it would be uninhabitable by man, by reason of the lack of fuel, fencing and building materials; were it all timbered, there would be slender temptation to desert in its favor the more accessible new lands of Ohio and western New York. But this natural intermingling of grain-field and pasture, meadow and grove, is more inviting than any aspect worn by nature elsewhere. He who traverses this region will never again wonder at the mighty tide of emigration which sets with resistless, ever-increasing volume from the Atlantic westward.

There is extreme difficulty in realizing that this adaptation is indeed the work of nature. Before and beside you rolls an "inland sea" of verdure and luxuriance—hundreds of acres of wheat, corn, and oats, darkly waving in early summer; while behind them stretch the immeasurable meadows, coeval with Eden, their untold wealth of herbage and flowers undulating in the fresh breezes like a gently-troubled ocean; and still behind these, at points not very far distant, and again far as the eye can reach, or farther, swells the graceful outline of the nearest woods, marking the winding way of some sluggish watercourse, or, more commonly, crowning some scanty elevation with the glossy foliage of the scattered oaks, beneath whose protecting shade a thick growth of clustering shrubbery, mainly oak also, commingled with hazel, repels the grass and withstands the fire of the prairie, maintaining a precarious and stationary existence. The little that man has yet done here blends so naturally and easily with the work of nature, that the forest outline seems the limit of his transformations. The open prairie, often dotted with extensive herds of cattle or

* A section is a square mile, or six hundred and forty acres. The public surveys divide the lands into townships six miles square, sections, quarter and half quarter sections.

sheep, and everywhere inviting their presence—everywhere proffering a harvest to the mower's scythe—seems, alike with the neighboring expanse of corn and wheat, too bounteous, too beneficent, to have waved there spontaneously, through summer after summer, since the deluge. The new and the old do not palpably wrestle here as in the forest clearings, where the narrow field of man's victory stands out in scathed and blackened contrast with the verdure and stateliness surrounding it; but all seems peaceful, genial, and bounteous. The prairies are the Capua of nature. May they not lure into indolence and sensuality the Hannibals of our continent—the hardy pioneer race, whose rapid and mighty conquests have been more truly wondrous, and far more beneficent, than those of any warrior!

The best natural dispositions of prairie and timber, and the most tasteful improvements, are on the cross-roads and by-ways, quite aside from the three or four great roads leading west from Chicago, which are mainly travelled. These routes are injured by land speculation and non-resident ownership; they traverse immense breadths of treeless prairie, threaded by narrow ridges of scattered and scanty timber; while in crossing diagonally from one western road to another, especially in the valley of the Fox, the Sycamore, or the Blackberry, the country is better timbered, better improved, and every way more inviting.

As to cattle and sheep, they cost literally nothing here. From April to November they thrive and fatten on the broad, unappropriated prairies uncared for, and the settler will cut hay enough in a fortnight, within half a mile of his cabin, to carry a large herd through the winter. Good cows might be raised here for five dollars a head, and a yoke of well-broken oxen turned off at a net cost of twenty. Herds of a hundred head are no rarity, new as are the settlements here, and they bid fair to be soon swelled to thousands. Sheep are brought in by thousands and loaned to settlers, on covenants with good security to pay one and a half to two pounds of wool annually per head, and return a flock equal in all respects after a term of years; and, exorbitant as is the usury, the settler, unable to pay for sheep, may better take them on these terms than do without them. Nearly every cabin is surrounded with hogs, which run at large in summer, and convert the superabundant corn into pork in the fall.

The pioneer who erects his shanty in the midst of a forest, must struggle long or very efficiently before he lets in sunshine enough to give him a surplus of grain, or justify him in keeping a herd of cattle. But here be can not have too many cattle, even though his cabin is not yet built; a hundred head would enrich and could not embarrass him; while, give him but team enough, he may grow his own grain the first year, and a surplus of a thousand bushels the next. The wet lands (termed 'sloos,' or 'sloughs'), at first unavailable, are richest of all, and need but a little drainage to render them the most productive Even the higher timbered lands, thinly covered with patriarchal oaks, overlooking a thick undergrowth of bushes—though here termed "barrens"—are really only less fertile than the prairies. They produce abundantly when broken up and planted.

And now let us look at the other side of the picture, and see what are the disadvantages of settlement and life on the prairies.

Deficiency of timber is the first to strike the eye of one familiar with rural or pioneer life at the east. The denizen of a log cabin in western New York or Ohio may at times be short of meal or of meat, but he has always good fuel in abundance within a stone's throw of his door, fencing stuff as near, and building timber not much less so. But here he finds the accessible sections embracing portions of timber and prairie, all clutched by speculators, or appropriated by earlier immigrants, and he can obtain land at government price only by pitching his tent on the broad, treeless prairie, where not even an armful of wood can be picked up within a mile. Hither he must haul his building materials (pine) from Chicago, his fuel

The Pioneer of the Western Forest.

and fencing from some adjacent grove or "barren," after buying or stealing them; so that the time saved to him in having no timber nor stumps between him and a crop, is nearly all required to cut or haul timber and fuel. As to eligibility and comfort, a little rude pioneer's cabin looks better, and is more habitable, in an opening of the forest than in the glaring sunshine of an unshaded prairie.

Ill health is another drawback on the charms of prairie life. The settler has hardly erected his cabin, and begun to break up the earth around it, when the detested ague jumps upon him, just when his time is most precious—when his winter wheat should be got in. His family, one after another, are taken down with bilious disease, and a hard season they have of it—in a strange land, with means and neighbors scanty, and the nearest physician perhaps miles away. Of course all are not so visited—many escape, through previous acclimation, fortunate location, or constitutional hardihood; but these are truly exceptions, and the settler from New England, or any region not cursed with the ague, should go expecting a siege of it, and thoroughly prepared with medicines, &c., for its proper treatment.

But these discouragements to prairie settlement are not so formidable as they appear to many. Ill health must be braved almost anywhere in settling a new country; and, though more general here than on a more rugged and less fertile soil, if seasonably and properly treated, it is not often fatal. On the other hand, many diseases common at the east are said to be unknown here, and even curable by a timely removal hither, including that fatal blight, consumption. When the prairies shall have been thoroughly brought under cultivation, whereby the "sloughs" will have been easily drained, especially if good water shall be procured, Illinois will probably prove as healthy as western New York now is, and, in time, as New Hampshire.

So of the scarcity of timber. There is enough of its kind (oak and hickory) now, if it were only a little better distributed, and cultivation is gradually beating back the annual prairie fires, and planting groves and thickets. A little care and labor work wonders in this respect. A few acres ploughed and sowed to locust afford fuel and fencing after five or six years, and timber of slower growth may thus be as easily though not so quickly obtained. If speculation would now undertake to buy up the centres of the great prairies and plant them with trees, it would for once do a good thing, and abate somewhat of the just odium created by the purchase of large tracts to remain sheer waste and obstacles until other men's hard labor has quadrupled their value.

The great, formidable, permanent, drawback on the eligibility of the prairie region for settlement, is the *deficiency of water*. This, perhaps, can never be fully remedied. Though the face of the country is by no means a dead level, but undulating, the inequality is so slight that springs are very, very rare, and running brooks hardly less so. You may ride twenty miles across the country without seeing water enough in all to turn a gristmill; and what you do find a well-bred horse will only drink in his last extremity of thirst. A whole county, which in New England would give rise to half a dozen good mill-streams, and be threaded all over with sparkling trout-brooks, will here send off scarcely water enough in summer to run a single pair of burr-stones. This, in a region so wonderfully adapted to the production of grain and cattle, is a sore deficiency. Following down the valley of the Fox, some twenty miles, by the thriving villages of Elgin, St. Charles, Geneva, and Aurora (each well supplied with mill-power by the river), although the scarcity of running streams was here by no means so absolute as in the prairies on either hand, yet we may doubt whether the river gains as much by tributaries as it loses by evaporation within that distance. And, though water is generally obtained with facility by simply digging a few feet through the prairie soil, we can not in conscience recommend the drinking of it, whether by man or beast. The abundance of lime, which renders the soil so fertile, exerts a far less desirable influence on the water. Here is the main source of the prevailing diseases. With pure, cold water bubbling up at every door, and the vile liquors so prevalent here consigned to the bottom of the ocean, this would soon be a healthy country.

In time, the want of water on the prairies will in part be remedied by sinking deep wells through the nearest stratum of rock, and raising the fluid by means of a windlass or otherwise. In villages, the Artesian wells may not be too expensive.

At *Jacksonville* the country begins to lose that level appearance that it has exhibited in the north, and, as we proceed to the south, is more wooded, with more up-hill and down-hill. There is, however, still much prairie land to pass over, and the soil is, if possible, richer than it is further north. Everything will grow here, and the settlers have taken some pains to plant trees, particularly the locust and the rock or sugar maple. In the valleys and on the hillsides we find oak, and walnut, and the hazel-nut. On the hills are the blackberry and other bushes known in New England—the mustard, the mullein, the whiteweed, &c. We are now in a part of the country that is "fenced in," and we behold on every side the most luxuriant farms, good houses, and large barns. As we proceed south, the corn grows taller and taller, with ears, in the silk, higher up in the air than a tall man can reach. We see beautiful fields of rye, and thick tall grass of the various descriptions. As we pass through a more generally settled district, we find the prairie grass is nearly run out, and in its place is the timothy, and the redtop, and the clover.

Galena, the great dépôt of the mineral region of southern Wisconsin, is situated on Fever river, about six miles from its mouth. It presents a very metallic appearance, inasmuch as its wharves are lined with piles of pig-lead, as far as the eye can reach. In June last, the lead lying on the river bank awaiting exportation amounted to four hundred and fifty thousand pigs, averaging seventy-five pounds each, making about seventy-five cords, weighing over three millions of pounds, and worth at New York twelve millions of dollars! This lead region occupies the northwestern portion of Illinois, and the southwestern corner of Wisconsin, together with a strip of a few miles in width on the opposite side of the Mississippi in Iowa, equal to a surface of nearly three thousand square miles. In riding over the country from Galena to the Wisconsin river, the most remarkable feature presented is the numerous "diggings." One might imagine himself in the vicinity of some huge burrowing animal, with its holes scattered in countless multitudes on the sides and tops of the hills for many miles around. Here originated that slang phrase: "The greatest man in these *diggings*."

The peculiar method of discovering and working these mines has introduced another new word into the language—that of "prospecting." One or two men, with a pickaxe and shovel, commence digging on the top or side of a hill, opening a hole from three to ten feet deep or more; if they find no indication of mineral, they abandon it and commence prospecting in another place. If successful, they either continue to work it or sell the prospect. These prospect holes are seldom filled up. The usual method of raising mineral is very simple, and very much like the primitive system of working the silver mines in Mexico. A shaft is sunk to the required depth, and while the man below gathers the fragments of ore, the one outside, by means of a rude windlass, raises it to the surface in buckets. In Mexico they raise the gold and silver ore in oxhide bags. In no instance has a seam of ore been exhausted. As soon as the diggings are carried so low as to reach water, they are generally abandoned. With one or two exceptions, no attempt has been made to drain the mines by means of pumps worked by steam—a process absolutely necessary in nearly all the European mines. Dr. Owen, in his "Report of a Geological Examination of Iowa, Wisconsin, and Illinois," made in 1839, estimated the annual produce of the mines at that time at thirty millions of pounds. This was regarded as an over-estimate, the greatest amount reported by the government agents being above ten, or at most twelve millions.

A different order of things has since arisen; the mines are constantly increasing in productiveness, and there is now no interest in concealing the amount produced. The number of pounds actually registered at Galena the last year was over fifty millions, and it is not improbable that the amount which found its way to market without passing through Galena may have been several millions more. It is estimated by those whose knowledge and experience render them competent to judge, that if the mines already opened were well worked, they are capable of producing one hundred and fifty millions of pounds annually for ages to come, which is more than is now produced by all the world beside. It is without doubt the richest lead district in the known world. Neither is the wealth of this region confined to its mineral productions. It affords an exception to the general rule that "mineral lands are too barren for cultivation." This is the case in England, Wales, and indeed nearly all other countries; but here I find a mineral country of unequalled richness, covered with a soil fully equal to that of the good farming districts of other states; and, judging from the appearance of the country between here and the Wisconsin river, this fact is duly appreciated. New farms are brought under cultivation in every direction. The old ones have an improved aspect, and the whole district presents an appearance of thrift equal to the most favored agricultural regions of the west.

In *Henry county* is a settlement of Swedish emigrants, who, like our puritan fathers, were driven from the land of their nativity by bigotry, persecution, and intolerance. These people sought and found an asylum in this happy land of civil and religious liberty, where they can sit under their own vine and figtree, without any one to molest or make them afraid, and worship God according to the dictates of conscience. How such valuable citizens, such pious and exemplary Christians, could be persecuted in a protestant land like Sweden, under a king we so much esteem for his literary attainments and excellences as Oscar, we can not conceive, unless that he is controlled or deceived by a graceless priesthood. There are now at Bishop's hill, so named from a town in Sweden, whence many of them emigrated, about four or five hundred Swedes. According to Dr. Baird, they are from the best citizens in Sweden. About four hundred more of their brethren are expected to join them in this prairie land.

Their community is one of the best regulated that was ever visited. There is among them no lordly, arbitrary control, sustained by a few leaders over the many, but all is equality and brotherly love. Everything goes on among them in perfect harmony and with regularity, and there is every indication of industry and happiness in their little village.

In a few years—in a country so abundantly fertile as this, owners as they are of the soil, in large and extensive fields, composed as their body is of mechanics in almost every branch of industry—they can soon become vastly rich if they desire it. They have already two English schools among them, and intend soon the establishment of a literary institution. They need men among them of the first scientific attainments, to take charge of such an institution, as well as men of talent and energy, conversant with our laws, to defend their rights when infringed upon.

The general intelligence which pervades this band of our adopted brethren, is equal to that of the people of any part of the United States. Neatness, modesty, and sweetness of temper, are the characteristics of their females; the women all seem to glory in doing their part of the labor that is necessary to earn a livelihood.

Their houses are more cleanly and comfortable for winter than those of most new settlers. They dress well—not a ragged or ill-dressed person is to be found in the whole community. Their tables are abundantly supplied with a great variety of wholesome and well-dressed food, to which is added, as a beverage, very excellent small beer. Visiters are received with that warmth, cordiality, and confidence, which at once secure respect.

The best farmers have already begun to carry in wool and flax in abundance, to be manufactured by their superior skill, and to obtain the fruits of their mechanical labor, which is performed with the greatest faithfulness.

In their religious creed, they profess to take the Bible as their guide. They assemble every morning and evening for divine service, when they have prayer, singing, preaching, and the reading of the Scriptures. Religion among them seems to be in a high state of revival. The Rev. Mr. Jonson and their other preachers seem to be eminently pious, and in a few months more will probably be able to preach in English. The influence of these strangers in a republic like ours, where the people govern, must ultimately be very considerable; and, from what we can see and learn, we are led to believe that their influence will always be found operating in favor of virtue and intelligence.

CHICAGO.—This is one of the most flourishing towns of the west, of the most rapid growth and flattering prospects, as it enjoys a situation perhaps surpassed by none, and certainly equalled by few. Lying at the head of Lake Michigan, and possessing a good harbor, the extent of its trade, even for a short period, it would be difficult to limit. The navigable waters which must be tributary to it may already be estimated at thousands of miles, and the artificial means by which other regions are to be brought into near relations with it, are sufficient to double the amount. The fertility of these vast regions, and the rapid increase of their various products, which they annually pour through this outlet, secure to Chicago a rapid, solid, and permanent increase of population and wealth.

It stands on the shore of the lake, almost at its extreme southwest corner, and on the borders of one of the prairies which constitute so large and important a part of this and the adjacent states. The view of this young and thriving town, exhibited in our accompanying engraving, is taken from the land side, at a short distance on the prairie, whose level surface extends far and wide, on a level almost as unvarying as the surface of the lake at whose shore it terminates, and a glimpse of which is seen near the extremity of the picture, on the right. The accuracy of the drawing exhibits much of the freshness which naturally marks so new a town. The houses appear small and scattering, compared with those of a city in an older part of the country; but several are observable of larger size, and the number of churches and other public buildings, with the numerous masts of lake-vessels, and the smoke of steamboats and furnaces, are sufficient indications of the superior importance of the place, and the extent of business already carried on in several branches.

The population of Chicago has increased not only at a great, but at an astonishing rate. In 1846 it was, according to a census taken, 14,169. That the people are generally industrious, and possessed of property, may be easily inferred from the fact that, at the same time, the assessments on the tax-list amounted to four millions five hundred thousand dollars, and the taxes to thirty-seven thousand dollars. The number of inhabitants, according to the census of 1850, was 28,269, being an increase over that given by the census of 1840, of 23,790, over five hundred per cent.

Chicago is now a large city. At the close of the Black Hawk war, not more than fourteen years ago, the site now covered by a city of many thousand inhabitants, and with all the arts and elegancies, the substance and the comforts, of long civilization and settlements—was a frontier military outpost, which had no habitation without its pickets, and few or none but for the accommodation of a small garrison within.

Chicago is the seaport of Illinois—the point opposite to the *terminus*, at St. Joseph's, of the railroad across Michigan, and, therefore, in a direct line, affords the shortest cut from the Atlantic seaboard of the east to the Mississippi river, in traversing Lake Erie, the peninsula of Michigan, and the fertile state of Illinois.

The Illinois canal, which connects through the Illinois and Mississippi rivers, the waters of the lakes with those of the gulf of Mexico, is the connecting link of an unbroken water-communication, from the Atlantic ocean off Sandy-Hook to the gulf of Mexico off the Balize, on which line Chicago is a principal city. This canal, which has been lately finished, is one of the most magnificent works ever undertaken. It is sixty feet wide, and six feet deep. It is one hundred and five miles in length, and cost over eight millions of dollars. This canal is described at greater length on a previous page.

The town-plot of Chicago is a level plain, the prairie pushing up to the lake; a broad belt of wood runs along the margin of the lake, and marks the course of the Chicago river, as it comes from the interior.

Chicago is built on the dead level of the prairie, scarcely elevated above the the surface of Lake Michigan, and is commanded from no point unless from the roof of some edifice. Its harbor is but the narrow, bending channel of an inconsiderable creek, and greatly needs extension and improvement. Eastward, on the lake shore, is the most airy, agreeable section of the city, covered with tasteful dwellings.

Rapid as the growth of Chicago has been, large as it now is, whoever proceeds westward or southward across the prairies, and notes the unequalled capacities of the soil, its universal fertility, its susceptibility of easy culture, and the rapidity of its transformation from a waste to a garden, can hardly doubt that it will increase rapidly. The spacious Illinois canal will also add immensely to the trade of its northern emporium; but a railroad to Galena has also followed, and will prove even more beneficent and remunerating. The very deficiencies of the prairies—that of timber especially—renders this railroad across them more productive, supplying an abundance of heavy return freight to the trains which convey to Chicago the grain of the interior. The expense of grading and of bridging proved very light. The energetic and enterprising character of the population of Chicago and northern Illinois—in great part composed of emigrants from New England and New York—is an element not to be overlooked in estimating the productiveness of this road, by which the lead of Galena and very much of the trade of the upper Mississippi are to be drawn to New York and Boston.

Crossing the southern extremity of Lake Michigan, passengers for the east are landed about daylight at the mouth of the St. Joseph. A majestic hotel, erected in the year 1836, stands there in desolation, and there are some other monuments to the vanity of human calculations. The late decision of the directors of the Central railroad, making New Buffalo instead of this place their western terminus, would seem to seal the doom already written on its faded walls.

A stranger might not be very favorably impressed with western Michigan. The stage-road from St. Joseph to Kalamazoo (fifty-five miles) does not pass through a very good section of it. It is timbered mainly with oak, though hickory appears at intervals, with very large whitewood, &c., on some of the streams. The clearings are sparse and scanty. At Pawpaw (the capital of Van Buren county) there is a good water-power, well improved, and a thriving country village. But, throughout all this region, there is a scarcity of springs and brooks. The soil seems less natural to grass than to grain.

The impression of Chicago, as seen from the lake, is, on the whole, unfavorable to the beholder, owing to the level site, which gives a character of sameness to its aspect not observable as viewed from the land, whence you perceive not only the mere outline of the city, but its shipping, churches, and other public buildings, which impart variety and animation to the scene. The harbor, like many others on the lake, is an artificial one, consisting of two piers extending in parallel lines out from the Chicago river into Lake Michigan. The

View of Chicago, from the Prairie.

difficulties which are encountered here, in the effort to overcome by art the deficiencies of nature, are necessarily very great. To say nothing of the danger to which the harbor is subjected from the ice and storms of winter, the action of the winds and waves accumulates a deposite of sand which forms a bar not only across the mouth of the channel, but within the harbor itself. Yet there is no place on the lake equal in adaptation or advantages for the cheap and lasting construction of harbors of this description. So recent and rapid have been the settlement and growth of Chicago, that the mind can with difficulty avoid the supposition that the advantages of its geographical position must have been long overlooked. But these, like those of St. Louis, were appreciated by the French, who, as early as 1673, explored this portion of our country, but without, however, establishing any permanent occupancy of it.

Chicago was for a long time the hunting-ground of the Pottawatomie tribe of Indians, who, in the beginning of the present century, came from the islands near the entrance of Green bay, and expelling the Miamies, occupied the best portions of northern Illinois and Indiana. All the beautiful tract of country lying around the little chain of lakes in Steuben and other counties in the latter state, was the chosen abode of the warriors and hunters of this tribe.

As recently as 1830, Chicago consisted (exclusive of the residents required by the garrison, which government had established), of only three frame buildings and five or six log houses. It has now a population of 28,000! The number of new buildings erected during the past year, was fifteen hundred. Upward of two thousand vessels, of all classes and descriptions, enter and leave the harbor during each month of the navigable season. Its exports are supposed to exceed its imports, which latter amount to upward of two millions of dollars annually. Upward of twenty churches, of different denominations, attest the religious influences at work among its busy population. Of these, the baptists have two, one of which, the first baptist church, is perhaps the finest edifice in the city. It was built in 1844, of brick, and is fifty-five by eighty feet, with a handsome portico, columns, and spire, which contains a bell and a clock with five dials.

The commercial and agricultural interests of all the states bordering upon the lakes are indissolubly associated with Chicago, as a place of deposite and transhipment. Situated at the head of lake navigation, and at the termination of the Illinois and Michigan canal, by which a continuous water route has late been established from New York to New Orleans, she grasps in her embrace the increasing direct trade of the great northwest, and stands at the door of that granary, where a peaceful commerce exchanges and discharges the productions of both hemispheres. That the wonderful rapidity with which Chicago has substituted, for the miserable huts of a mere trading station, the comfortable dwellings and busy aspect of a commercial city, is attributable mainly to the natural advantages of its position, can not be denied. But much is due to the enterprise and intelligence of its inhabitants, evinced in their very emigration here, and also in their appreciation of the advantages with which a beneficent Providence has distinguished them, as well as in the efforts which they are constantly making to improve and extend them.

A railroad, for which subscriptions had been made, is completed between Chicago and Galena, by which intercommunication with different parts of the state must be greaty facilitated, and the mineral riches of the latter place find another outlet to the seaboard. Another railroad is already in successful operation between Detroit and New Buffalo, on the opposite side of Lake Michigan, and this it is contemplated to extend round the head of the lake to Chicago. This, in connexion with the first named, would bring the Mississippi within a day's journey of Detroit.

The labor of the husbandman has added to the riches of the soil in every direction in the vicinity of the city, which is generally a prairie, elevated and undulating, and as productive as any other portion of the west.

In the formation of society in Chicago, levies seem to have been made upon every nation and country. Yet this diversity is unfriendly to the growth of prejudices, which acquire such rankness in older communities, while it releases the hold of the caste, and arbitrary systems. Man comes to be regarded as man. The mind is disposed to receive readily, and to appreciate fully, great truths in morals and science, and this disposition pervades not a part, but the whole of society. "We are Illinois," was proudly said by the aborigines, to to the first white man with whom they came in contact upon the soil, which meant in their language, "We are men." Those who now occupy their places partake of this spirit.

SPRINGFIELD.—This town, the capital of Illinois, is ninety-five miles from St. Louis, and nearly in the centre of the state. It is situated four miles south of Sangamon river, on the margin of a wide and fertile prairie, and has had a rapid growth since it was first laid out, in the year 1822. But thirty families were residing on the spot the following year, when there were no habitations better than log-cabins.

It is now a large, handsome, and flourishing town, containing 6,000 inhabitants, and a fine, large statehouse, a courthouse, market, bank, land-office, three high-schools, several large manufactories, and eight churches. Railcars run daily for Meredosia, and three stage-coaches go to Quincy. Stage-routes lie in several other directions—for St. Louis, Chicago, Lafayette (Indiana), Terre Haute, Shawneetown, Burlington (Iowa), Lexington, &c.

JACKSONVILLE.—This town, thirty-three miles from Springfield, is on a beautiful and fertile prairie, and contains a courthouse, market, lyceum, mechanics' association, two academies, seven churches, and a population of about 3,500. It has a daily communication with the capital and Meredosia by the railroad.

Illinois College, situated at Jacksonville, has eight professors in the academical and medical departments, and about one hundred students. The libraries of the institution contain two thousand five hundred volumes, and the philosophical and chymical apparatus are complete and valuable. The commencement is held on the last Thursday of June.

ALTON is situated on the east side of the Mississippi river, two miles above the mouth of the Missouri, and twenty-one miles below that of the Illinois. It is twenty miles distant from St. Louis. The town is regularly laid out, the streets are broad and straight, and it contains six churches, a lyceum, a bank, mechanics' association, and a population of 6,000. The place is one of the best for commercial purposes on the Mississippi, having a good landing-place, formed by a flat rock, with a rich country around it; and timber, coal, freestone, and limestone, abound in the vicinity. Steamboats keep up a constant communication with the towns on the Mississippi, the Illinois, the Missouri, and the Ohio; and stage-coaches run to Vincennes and Jacksonville.

KASKASKIA, on the right bank of the river of that name, is one hundred and forty-two miles from Springfield, and seven from the Mississippi. It was settled about the year 1683, by the French, and a large portion of the population is of that origin. It contains two churches, a bank, a land-office, and about two thousand inhabitants. It is on the decline.

SHAWNEETOWN, about two hundred miles from Springfield, and ten below the mouth of the Wabash, stands on the Ohio, on an acclivity, but not high enough to be safe, from the highest floods in the river. It was laid out in 1814, and is one of the best places for trade in that part of the state.

Our vignette represents a spot well known to travellers on the western waters. This remarkable natural curiosity is situated on the Ohio river, a few miles below Shawneetown. The approach to it, as you descend the stream, is picturesque. Bold bluffs running out into the current, diversified here and there with green valleys opening between, afford a constantly varying scene of rock, meadow, and midland. Above and below the cave are high precipices of limestone, principally covered with cedars. The scenery still retains much of the wild aspect it wore before civilization had intruded on it, and when nothing broke the silence of the traveller's voyage except the dip of his oars, the scream of the eagle, or the whoop of the hostile savage.

The entrance to the cave is nearly semicircular, and is on a level with the river when the latter is high. The passage is about twenty feet in altitude, and, a few yards from the mouth, leads into a spacious apartment about twenty feet in height, one hundred and twenty feet in length, and of a breadth nearly equal. In the roof is seen an opening, which, if report speaks true, leads into an upper room, remarkable for its natural ornaments. The passage leading to it may be compared to a chimney; but few persons have enough of the spirit of adventure to attempt an entrance. The natural fretwork on the walls is said to give them the appearance of Gothic ornaments.

At one end of the cave is a deep hole, which has never been explored or fathomed to its termination. Its direction is downward, and the undertaking of a descent would be hazardous. Stones thrown in are heard to strike the rocks far below, after the lapse of several seconds.

About the close of the last century this cave was the habitation of a band of robbers, whose leader, named Mason, headed them in attacks upon boats and arks, as they drifted down the Ohio. In some cases the crews were not only robbed and ill treated, but even murdered. The criminals and their retreat becoming known, however, the gang were attacked in the year 1797, and broken up, so that peaceful navigators have not since been interrupted in that neighborhood.

Vandalia, on the right bank of Kaskaskia river, was formerly the capital of the state. The streets are regular, and the place has a handsome appearance. It contains two churches, a land-office, and several manufactories. The population is about 800. Here is the termination of the national road. Stage-coaches go daily to St. Louis and Cape Girardeau.

Peoria, on the right bank of the Illinois river, at the outlet of Peoria lake, is seventy miles from Springfield. The first bank of the river is from six to twelve feet above high-water mark, and is a quarter of a mile wide. Beyond it rises the second bank, which is five or six feet higher; and this extends to the bluffs, which are from sixty to one hundred feet high. Here are six churches, several manufactories, a courthouse, and about 2,500 inhabitants.

Galena.—This town, so intimately connected with the mining and trade in lead, is situated on the La Fevre, or Bean river, six miles from its mouth, and one hundred and fifty-eight miles from Chicago. Steamboats of the largest size go up to the town at all seasons, and the amount of exports is annually very large, especially in the staple article, lead. It contains five churches, and a population of about 8,000. The first settlement was made in the year 1826. Stage-coaches go daily to Chicago, and three times a week to several other places. In 1846 the arrivals of steamboats were three hundred and thirty-three, amounting to fifty-eight thousand, five hundred and seventy-five tons.

The exports, in 1850, were as follows: Lead, 672,620 pigs, worth $2,225,000; copper, $22,000; lumber, $100,000; hides, $14,800; wheat, 150,000 bushels.

Rock Island City is a small town on the Mississippi river, a little above the mouth of Rock river. The population is now about 2,000.

Belleville, fourteen miles from St. Louis, is the seat of justice for St. Clair county, and contains three large flour-mills, and various other manufactories. One half of the population of the town and county are industrious Germans. The number of inhabitants was 1,207 in 1840, and is now about 2,800.

Rock Fort.—This is a prominent bluff on the left bank of Illinois river, and rendered doubly interesting by an In-

Rock Fort, on the Illinois River.

dian tradition. It is about two hundred and fifty feet high, with steep, precipitous sides, wholly inaccessible in all parts except one, and presenting a peculiar striped appearance, caused by a number of strata of sandstone, of different shades, running in a horizontal direction. With the wide prairie on one side, and the river, flowing through it, on another, the perpendicular sides of this remarkable eminence rise like an immense watchtower, or rather castle—a work of gigantic hands; while, at the places where the neighboring range of highland is connected with it by a narrow ridge, a little path conducts the stranger to the summit, with great toil and difficulty.

There he finds a level spot, about three fourths of an acre in extent, overgrown with young trees, many of which stand upon an ancient ditch and a mound, which appears to have once served as a breastwork round the circuit of this natural fort. In the soil are remains of mussel-shells, pottery, and stones, that appear to have been heated; and the views from the edge of the precipice are extensive and delightful.

Strong and almost inaccessible, this natural battlement has been still further fortified by the Indians, and many years ago was the scene of a desperate conflict between the Pottawatomies and a band of the Illinois Indians. The latter fled to this place for refuge from the fury of their enemies. The post could not be carried by assault, and tradition says that the besiegers finally succeeded, after many repulses, by cutting off the supply of water; to procure which, the besieged let down vessels, attached to ropes of bark, from a part of the precipice which overhangs the river; but their enemies succeeded in cutting off these ropes as often as they were let down. The consequence was a surrender, which was followed by a total extirpation of the band.

The channel of the Mississippi is constantly shifting, and the only safe chart is the lead. The pilots, most of them, know every nook and corner of the river, and can judge by the surface current when the channel has shifted. The cause of this shifting is the strong current, nearly four miles an hour, which wears away a point of land here and there, washing the earth and trees out into the old channel and creating a new one. The mosquitoes at the "wood-up" stations come on to the steamer in swarms, and nothing but a strong breeze will drive them off. But little land has been cleared on the banks of the Mississippi. With the exception of Louisiana, which is pretty generally cultivated, and a few cities and towns scattered like guide-boards to civilization, through the wilderness, there is nothing but forest for over twelve hundred miles. Yet the soil looks rich, and is so, and only needs the axe of the pioneer to make the whole country a garden.

The river navigation of the great west is the most wonderful on the globe, and, since the application of steam-power to the propulsion of vessels, possesses the essential qualities of open navigation. Speed, distance, cheapness, magnitude of cargoes, are all there, and without the perils of the sea from storms and enemies. The steamboat is the ship of the river, and finds in the Mississippi and its tributaries the amplest theatre for the diffusion of its use, and the display of its power. Wonderful river, connected with seas by the head and by the mouth—stretching its arms toward the Atlantic and the Pacific—lying in a valley, which is a valley from the gulf of Mexico to Hudson's bay—drawing its first waters, not from rugged mountains, but from the plateau of the lakes in the centre of the continent, and in communication with the sources of the St. Lawrence and the streams which take their course north to Hudson's bay—draining the largest extent of the richest land—collecting the products of every clime, even the frigid, to bear the whole to a genial market in the sunny south, and there to meet the products of the entire world. Such is the Mississippi! And who can calculate the aggregate of its advantages, and the magnitude of its future commercial results?

Many years ago, the late Governor Clark and others undertook to calculate the extent of the boatable water in the valley of the Mississippi, and made it about fifty thousand miles, of which thirty thousand were computed to unite above St. Louis, and twenty thousand below. Of course they counted all the infant streams on which a flat, a keel, or a batteau, could be floated—and justly, for every tributary, of the humblest boatable character, helps to swell not only the volume of the central waters, but of the commerce upon them. Of this immense extent of river navigation, all combined into one system of waters, St. Louis is the centre, and the entrepot of its trade, presenting even now, in its infancy, an astonishing and almost incredible amount of commerce, destined to increase annually. It is considered an inland town. Counting by time and money, the only true commercial measure of distances, and St. Louis is nearer to the sea than New Orleans was before the steam-towboat abridged the distance between that city and the mouth of the Mississippi. St. Louis is a seaport as well as an inland city, and is a port of delivery by law, and has collected fifty thousand dollars of duties on foreign imports during the current year; and with a liberal custom would become a great entrepot of foreign as well as of domestic commerce. With the attributes and characteristics of a seaport, she is entitled to the benefit of one, as fully and as clearly as New York or New Orleans.

At a distance of 1,400 miles from the gulf of Mexico, is a new starting point for a further inland navigation to the north, of 1,000 miles by the Mississippi; to the west, of 2,000 by the Missouri; to the northeast, 1,000 by the Wisconsin, and 400 by the Illinois; and to the east, 1,200 by the Ohio. Through all of these and their countless tributaries, is the mighty west continually pouring out its teeming products to the seaboard. Through the Mississippi alone, only one of the outlets of this valley, there will probably be transported to a market more than $100,000,000 in the surplus agricultural products of last season, and that not an abundant one. If such are the results of a single half century's enterprise, by the surplus progeny of a people numbering but little more than 3,000,000 at its commencement, what must be the results of future centuries of similar enterprise, with the accumulating ratio of our skill and population?

In going up the Mississippi from the mouth of the Missouri, we take a final leave of the muddy waters that mar the beauty of the stream, the whole distance to the gulf. The Illinois is a miniature Mississippi, especially at its lower extremity; while higher up, its numerous bluffs, now approaching and now receding from the banks, remind one of the bolder scenery between its mouth and the Ohio. The banks, which are generally from six to twelve feet above low water, are frequently overflowed through a great part of their course. They descend from the edge of the river to lowland, or swamps, in their rear, evidently marking this valley as a delta formation. The conformation of the remote or primitive banks of this river, and those of the Aux-Plaines, one of its principal tributaries, which flows within eight miles of Lake Michigan, indicate conclusively that they formerly discharged a vastly larger body of water than they now contain. It is conjectured, and with a good deal of probability, that they were once the outlet of one or more of the large northern lakes, and possibly those of Michigan, Huron, and Superior. If this were the case, we can conceive of no adequate cause short of the upheaval of the western shore of Lake Michigan, which should have sent the waters that formerly met the Atlantic at Cape Sable, in latitude twenty-five degrees, through the gulf of St. Lawrence, that communicates with the ocean at its northern outlet in fifty-two degrees.

Most of the banks of the Illinois are densely wooded; after ascending about one hundred miles above its mouth, however, the prairies frequently come down to the edge of the water. Peoria is beautifully situated on one of these, two hundred miles from the outlet of the river, whose rolling bank, ascending inland, rises twenty feet above the water, which here expands to a tiny lake. The town of Henry, a few miles above and on the same western bank, is similarly situated, but on a higher bank, and the prairie stretches off sixty miles toward the Mississippi.

There are numerous small thriving towns along the stream, which are already the dépôts for immense quantities of corn, wheat, flour, pork, beef, &c. Some fifteen or twenty small steamboats are employed with the traffic and passengers on this river, besides scows and flatboats that are used in freighting the produce. Two of the latter, each capable of carrying one thousand barrels of flour, were loading at Hennepin, some three hundred miles above St. Louis. There are numerous steam saw and flouring mills on the banks, by which lumber and grain are largely manufactured, the latter only to any extent for exportation.

From Peru to Chicago, one hundred miles, the course is over fertile and undulating prairies, most of which, though unoccupied a dozen years ago, are now under cultivation and thickly studded with tasteful villages.

Mount Joliet.—Mr. Schoolcraft, in his travels in the central portions of the Mississippi valley, gives us an account of his visit to this place. It is a hill or mound, a few miles from Fox river, and near Lisbon, on an immense prairie. It is about 1,300 feet long, 225 broad, and 60 high; oblong at the base; and covers 500,000 square feet. It is far from any other elevation, and is conspicuous from a great distance on every side, commanding views in all directions which are bounded only by the horizon. We give an extract from Mr. S.:—

"We entered the strip of woods which form a margin to the Aux Sables, one of the tributary streams of the Illinois, during the most intense heat of the day, and enjoyed its refreshing shade for a few moments. Ten miles beyond this pellucid little river, we halted, and dismounted in the plains, and made a short excursion on foot to Mount Joliet. This monumental elevation takes its name from Sieur Joliet, who was sent by M. Talon, the intendant of New France, to accompany Father Marquette, in his search of the Mississippi, in the year 1673. They entered this stream through the Wisconsin, and then followed its current. It is not certain how far they descended, but it is evident they passed the junction of the Missouri, and some assert that they went to the mouth of the Arkansas. On their return to Canada, they followed up the Illinois, and have left us the first notice of this mound, which they ascended.

"Any prominent swell in the surface of the soil would appear interesting and remarkable in so flat a country, but this would be considered a very striking object of curiosity in a region of inequalities. It is, strictly speaking, neither a mountain nor a hill, but rather a mound, and the first impression made by its regular and well-preserved outlines is that of a work of art. This alluvial structure is seated on the plains, about six hundred yards west of the present channel of the river Des Plaines, but immediately upon what appears to have been the former bank of this river. Its figure, as seen at a distance, is that of a cone truncated by a plane parallel to the base, but we find, on approaching, its base describes an ellipsis. Its height we computed to be sixty feet. Its length is about four hundred and fifty yards, and its width seventy-five yards. These measurements have relation only to the top. Its base is of course much larger. The sides have a gradual and regular slope, but the acclivity is so great that we found the ascent laborious. There are a few shrubby oak-trees on the western side; but every other part, like the plain in which it stands, is covered with grass. The materials of this extraordinary mound are, to all appearance, wholly alluvial, and not to be distinguished from those of the contiguous country from which, it would appear, they have been scooped out. It is firmly seated on a horizontal stratum of secondary limestone. The view from this eminence is charming and diversified. The forests are sufficiently near to serve as a relief to the prairies. Clumps of oaks are scattered over the country. The lake Joliet, fifteen miles long and about a quarter of a mile wide, lies in front. There is not perhaps a more noble and picturesque spot for a private

Mount Joliet, near the Des Moines River.

mansion in all America. Few persons will choose to pass it without devoting an hour to its examination; and few will, perhaps, leave it without feeling a conviction that it is the work of human hands. It has been remarked by Dr. Beck, that this is probably the largest mound within the limits of the United States."

EMIGRATION.—We have introduced here two illustrations, exhibiting a family emigrating to the west. The one opposite is a day scene, in which is seen the emigrant, with a gun upon his shoulder, and his faithful dog by his side, leading the way, followed by a single horse and wagon, bearing his family, and perhaps all his earthly possessions. It is a picture of but one among thousands who leave the endearments of home, the luxuries of cultivated and commercial regions, teeming with population, for the wilds of the west. The rough road, the umbrageous forest, the gushing stream, and the treeless prairie, are no impediments to deter him from his purpose of finding some eligible spot where he may pitch his tent, rear his cabin, sow his seeds, and reap rich harvests, thus forming a nucleus for a thriving community and finally a new state to be added to the confederacy—a new star to our national banner. How many, very many, in humble life, have thus left the Atlantic states, where they were scarcely known amid the multitude, pitched their tents upon the virgin soil of the Mississippi valley, where the foot of the white man had never before trodden, and in a few years found themselves surrounded with all the comforts of life, called upon to take an active part in the political affairs of the state or territory wherein they had settled, and frequently again sent eastward to sit in the national council. There are many, very many, who "go to the west," with high anticipations of making speedy fortunes, without counting the cost. In their estimate of results they omit the many privations to which they will be exposed, and value too lightly the lessons of experience read to them by predecessors. They forget, in their day-dreams of gain, that they are about to exchange a pleasant mansion for a cheerless log-cabin; the privileges of social intercourse and religious association, for almost utter solitude; and a life of comparative ease for the most arduous physical labor. They look upon the bright tints of the picture, and seldom glance at the umber to which the finger of experience would point them. These are they who return from the west sadly disappointed in their hopes and expectations, and are for ever croaking about its unhealthy climate, barren soil, and other equally grievous complaints. But he who goes with the expectation of laboring hard, living prudently, managing wisely, and selects his locality with judgment, may be sure of receiving a bountiful return for his sacrifices.

There are millions of acres of land in our western states and territories, with a garden-like soil, that yet remain untouched by implements of culture, which may be purchased at the government price (one dollar and a quarter per acre), where no greater objections to the climate can be made than against any other sections of the Union; and far better would it be for the individuals and the public, if the *floating* population of our cities would act wisely and suffer themselves to *drift* westward with what little pecuniary means they may have. Many foreigners will land upon our shores with sufficient ready money to purchase land enough to yield them a comfortable subsistence; but instead of availing themselves of this advantage, they unwisely seek employment in our cities, soon spend their small means, and live year after year amid the miseries of hopeless poverty.

The cost of transition from the Atlantic states to the fertile regions of the western states, is now quite trifling for so great a distance, and hence emigrants who come with some money in their pockets, have no excuse for enduring the miseries of obtaining a precarious existence in our cities.

The second illustration, on page 565, represents the halt of the emigrant family for the night. They may be seen preparing their frugal meal, and arrang-

Emigration to the West.

ing themselves for rest, to be ready at break of day to start again on their journey, cheered amid the privations and vicissitudes to which they are subject on their toilsome way, by the consciousness that each day lessens the distance between them and the land of promise, and that the fertile soil of the west will recompense them for all their troubles.

Growth of the West.—The following remarks on this subject were made by a former resident of the west, now established in the profession of law in Portsmouth (N. H.), at a public meeting in Boston to take measures in relation to the late Chicago convention:—

"I say you can not have been indifferent to the political strength of the west; but have you, until quite recently, comprehended the vast commercial resources of that region?

"Of these you are now compelled to take notice. Every paper that comes to us, tells of the mighty energies of the west. One speaks of a line of canal-boats fifty-three miles in length; another tells us a ship has just left Chicago, spreading its white sails to the western breeze, and that it is to find no rest for its keel until the flag of our country shall wave in the port of a foreign land; another tells us that there are at this moment ten millions of people in the great valley of the Mississippi. How can it be? we exclaim. Fifty-five years ago the first settler of Ohio (in the person of Dr. Cutler, of Beverly, Mass.) bade adieu to his friends here, to go to a place upon which at present is built Marietta, a town which is now engaged largely in shipbuilding, for the commerce of the ocean. Michigan, thirty-five years ago, had scarcely an inhabitant; now, more than three hundred thousand warm hearts are beating upon her soil; and her sons count up the profits of their ample fields in the year that is past, in eight millions of bushels of wheat. Such has been the growth of the whole west. A few years since, in a birchen canoe, I was paddled all along the shores of Wisconsin, from Chicago to Green bay—a distance of several hundred miles—seeing scarcely a white man. Last year it was my good fortune to go along the same shore, and over the same waters, and I passed the large towns of Sheboygan, Southport, and Racine; and when far off, on the waters of Lake Michigan, I beheld the city of Milwaukie, looking like a sea-sybil with its 'tiara of proud towers.' But I can not, in the brief time allowed me, describe the change that has taken place in the lakes. The traveller may leave Buffalo to-day, in one of the lake steamers, and in seventy-two hours the keel of his noble vessel shall scrape the golden sands of Illinois—nearly one thousand one hundred miles to the westward. His eye will have gazed upon the soil of five of the states of this Union, as well as upon the possessions of Queen Victoria.

"In 1818 appeared the first steamboat upon the lakes; now there are more than one hundred of the largest class; and the Griffin, a vessel of seventy tons, launched by the daring La Salle, in 1769, has multiplied, until now the lakes are white with sails, and literally murmur with the rush of keels. The commerce of the lakes at this time may be safely estimated as worth one hundred and fifty millions of dollars per annum, requiring the constant employment of over three thousand sailors, as brave as ever dwelt on the ocean, and who would be as efficient if summoned to the gun-deck. The cities of Detroit and Buffalo have more tons of shipping afloat than are owned in the four planting states of North and South Carolina, Georgia, and Alabama; and these are but two of the seven cities along the lakes. It is estimated that there are on the western waters eight hundred and fifty steamboats, and that 13,440 persons are engaged in navigation. These are some of the random statistics that occur to me; but we must remember that the statisties of 1844 will not serve as a basis of calculation in 1847. The growth of that region far outstrips the wildest imagination of the poet, who has said:—

"'A thousand years scarce serve to form a state.'

"We behold them in our day leaping from our western forests into the bosom of this confederacy, almost before we can give them a 'habitation and a name.'"

Emigration—Encampment for the Night.

Elk Horn Pyramid, on the Upper Missouri.

MISSOURI.

MISSOURI is one of the largest states in the Union, covering an area of 69,100 square miles; some compute it as high as 70,000. It extends from 36° to 40° 30′ north latitude, and from 11° 45′ to 17° 30′ west longitude. To form some idea of its extent, we have only to reflect that the Mississippi washes five hundred miles of its eastern boundary, while the Missouri runs more than five hundred miles along its western border, and through its centre. It is bounded north by Iowa, south by Arkansas, and west by Indian territory. The banks of each of these rivers are dotted all along with towns, rapidly growing into importance by the commerce of its waters. Besides these great highways of trade, there are the Osage, Gasconade, and Grand rivers, navigable for one or two hundred miles within its borders. The great prairie, which extends over Indiana and Illinois, stretches through Missouri on to the Rocky mountains, interspersed, in this state, with heavy bodies of timber along its numerous water-courses. The soil, climate, and productions, are like those of most of the western states.

Generally, where the country is too rough and barren to be cultivated, there are inexhaustible mines of lead, copper, and iron. In connexion with these mineral ores, there are vast beds of coal, the great moving power of the world, the indisputable index of approaching greatness. It is worthy of remark, that within a few miles of the eastern border of Missouri is the first place west of Wheeling where this article is found in large bodies. All along the Missouri, on both sides, it is found in abundance.

The sickness of Missouri is a prominent hinderance to its growth. Although there have been prevailing sicknesses, the number of deaths by no means corresponds to the extent of the disease. Intermittent fever, the almost universal form of sickness, is little understood by the scientific, and is cured by specifics whose "*modus operandi*" is still shrouded in mystery. Nearly all who emigrate to this state have to undergo acclimation. Congestion sometimes supervenes, and the disease in this stage often proves fatal. Young men seldom suffer from this stage, unless they have been very imprudent in exposing themselves to its causes. Strange as it may seem, it is often the means of removing chronic complaints and establishing the health of the patient. And after enduring a thorough seasoning, they are seldom attacked again.

The importance of Missouri, from its agricultural resources, and vast mineral wealth, the large population it is calculated to sustain, from its peculiar advantageous commercial situation, is beyond calculation. Situated at the confluence of two of the mightiest rivers that water any continent, draining more than half of the territory of the United States —how vast the resources of this region when peopled by teeming millions! Where is the centre that is to have the greatest influence in this great valley? The Roman catholic bishop of St. Louis has more ecclesiastics under his control than any other in the country. The only university they have within the United States is at St. Louis.

The mineral wealth of the southwest is greater than many would imagine. Capital and skill, properly applied, will develop resources of wealth undiscovered and now slumbering in unknown beds. It may not be generally known that Murphy and M'Clurg have now a smelting establishment in full and successful operation, where they are enabled to supply any demand for lead which the country can possibly require.

Lead abounds in various parts of the southwest, but particularly in the vicinity of those waters which are tributary to White river. Much capital might be profitably employed in opening and working these mines. But the great misfortune is the obstruction in the navigation of the rivers. There are the Osage on the north, White river on the southeast, and the Neosho or Grand river on the west, draining an extensive, rich, and fertile country, with but few equals in mineral and agricultural wealth. These streams, with the improvement of which they are susceptible, would open an outlet to market at seasons of the year when the more northern outlets are closed.

Missouri has increased rapidly in population, improvements, and wealth. Its tobacco, which is one of its staples, is quoted at the highest rates in the European markets. Hemp is an article of increasing growth and of the first quality.

The population of Missouri in 1771 (by Hutchings), was 850; in 1804 (by Stoddard), 10,340; in 1810 (including Arkansas), 19,833; in 1820, 66,586; in 1830, 140,074; in 1840, 383,702; in 1850, 684,132.

Towns and cities along the waters of the Missouri, above "Boone's Lick" settlement, are increasing. The state is subdivided into 101 counties.

The River Missouri.—The Missouri is one of the largest rivers in America, so famous for the greatness of its streams. Its principal branch rises in the Rocky mountains, in about the latitude of forty-three degrees and thirty minutes north, and the one hundred and twelfth degree of western longitude: its head spring is said to be not more than one mile distant from the source of another great river—the Columbia—which flows in a contrary direction into the Pacific ocean. This branch has been termed by the American travellers, Captains Lewis and Clarke (who explored the whole course of the Missouri), *Jefferson's river*, in compliment to Mr. Jefferson, who was then president of the United States; and three of its tributaries have, in the same spirit, been dignified with the appellations of Philosophy, Philanthropy, and Wisdom. When Jefferson's river has run a course of about two hundred and seventy miles, it is joined by two others, called Gallatin's and Madison's, after the statesmen so named; and their united waters flow together for nearly three thousand miles, under the name of Missouri, until they pour themselves into the channel of the Mississippi.

At the distance of about one hundred and eighty miles from this junction—or of four hundred and fifty miles from the source of the Jefferson branch—the river escapes from among the Rocky mountains, and loses the character which, till shortly previous, it had borne throughout, of a foaming torrent. The spot at which it emerges, is remarkable for the sublimity of its scenery; for nearly six miles, precipitous masses of rock rise perpendicularly from the water's edge, to the height of nearly twelve hundred feet. "They are composed," says the official narrative of Lewis and Clarke, "of a black granite near its base, but from its lighter color above, and from its fragments, we suppose the upper part to be flints of a yellowish brown and cream color. Nothing can be imagined more tremendous than the frowning darkness of those rocks, which project over the river, and menace us with destruction. The river, of three hundred and fifty yards in width, seems to have forced its channel down this solid mass, but so reluctantly has it given way, that during the whole distance the water is very deep, even at the edges, and for the first three miles there is not a spot, except one of a few yards, in which a man can stand between the water and the towering perpendicular of the mountain. The convulsion of the passage must have been terrible, since at its outlet there are vast columns of rock torn from the mountain, which are strewed on both sides of the river, the trophies, as it were, of the victory. Several fine springs burst out from the chasms of the rock, and contribute to increase the river, which has now a strong current; but very fortunately we are able to overcome it with our oars, since it would be impossible to use either the cord or the pole. This extraordinary range of rocks we called the Gates of the Rocky mountains."

About one hundred and ten miles from this tremendous chasm, the "Falls of the Missouri" occur; and for the space of seventeen or eighteen miles, the river presents a succession of rapids and cataracts. At the "Great fall," as the largest of these is termed, it is three hundred yards wide; and for about a third of this breadth, the water rolls in one smooth, even sheet, over a precipice of nearly ninety feet in height. The remaining portion of the stream precipitates itself with a more rapid current, and being broken in its fall by projecting rocks, "forms a splendid prospect of perfectly white foam, two hundred yards in length," with "all that glory of refracted light, and everlasting sound, and infinity of motion, which," to use the words of a modern writer, "make a great waterfall the most magnificent of all earthly objects." The fall which is next in height, is perhaps a more remarkable object still. It extends completely across the river, where its width is at least a quarter of a mile; "the whole Missouri," says the narrative of Lewis and Clarke, "is suddenly stopped by one shelving rock, without a single niche, and with an edge as straight and regular as if formed by art," over which the volume of its waters is precipitated "in one even, uninterrupted sheet, to the perpendicular height of fifty feet, whence, dashing against the rocky bottom, it rushes rapidly down, leaving behind it a spray of the purest foam. The scene which it presented was, indeed, singularly beautiful, since, without any of the wild, irregular sublimity of the lower falls, it combined all the regular elegances which the fancy of a painter would select, to form a beautiful waterfall."

From the falls down to the very mouth of the Missouri—a distance of more than two thousand five hundred miles—there is no obstacle to the navigation of this river, but what arises from the rapidity of its current. In this long course, its waters are increased by the junction of many other streams, both great and small: among the largest are the Yellow Stone, La Platte, Kansas, and Osage, the first of which is one thousand eight hundred and eighty, and the last one hundred and thirty-three miles above the union with the Mississippi. It would be difficult to comprise in any general description, the characteristics of a river so extensive in its course, and fed by so many various streams; still, the Missouri is sufficiently powerful to give to all its waters something of a uniform character—and one extremely remarkable. Its prodigious length, its uncommon turbidness, its impetuous and wild character, and the singular country through which it runs, impart to it a natural grandeur belonging to the sublime. "We have never crossed it," says Mr. Flint, "without experiencing a feeling of this sort, nor without a stretch of the imagination, to trace it along its immense distance, through its distant regions, to the lonely and stupendous mountains from which it springs."

The Mississippi is remarkable for the clearness of its waters, which are of a light blue, not unlike the hue of the deep sea, or of the Rhone at Geneva. The Missouri, on the other hand, is described as being "nearly as thick as pea-soup," and of a dirty muddy-whitish color. A glassful of the former appears as clear as any spring-water; one of the latter is perfectly turbid, "worse than the rain-puddles on a highway-road," and in a few minutes deposites a stratum of mud; yet this turbid water, according to Mr. Flint, after the settlement of the whitish earth, which soon falls down, is remarkably pure, pleasant, and healthy; and another American geographer says, that it is more easily preserved cool, and fit to drink, than other waters are. The surface of the Mississippi, above the junction, is generally clear of drift-wood, while that of the Missouri is all covered with half-burnt logs, trees with their branches torn off, and great rafts or floating islands of timber, drifted from the interior, sweeping and whirling along at a furious rate.

The Missouri enters the Mississippi from the westward, nearly at right angles to it; and such, says Captain Hall, is the impetuosity of its current, that it fairly divides the Mississippi even to the left or eastern bank. "There were literally," he says, "not above ten or twelve yards of clear water on that side of the river, while all the rest was muddy. The line of actual contact was particularly interesting; it seemed as if the dirty Missouri had insinuated itself under the clear Mississippi, for we saw it boiling up at a hundred places. First, a small curdling white spot, not bigger than a man's hand, made its appearance near the surface; this rapidly swelled and boiled about, till, in a few seconds, it suddenly became as large as a steamboat, spreading itself on all sides in gigantic eddies or whirlpools, in a manner that I hardly know how to describe, but which was amazingly striking. At other places the two currents ran along, side by side, without the least intermixture, like oil and water; but this separation never continued long, and the contaminating Missouri soon conquered the beautiful Mississippi—indeed, the stain is never got rid of for one moment, during the twelve hundred miles that the united stream runs over, before it falls into the gulf of Mexico."

The Missouri carries down a great quantity of sand; this, with the aid of what is derived from the neighboring banks, forms sand-bars (as they are called), projecting into the river. By forcing the stream toward the opposite bank, these sand-bars aid materially in the process of undermining its loose texture, yet they are themselves constantly removing. Travellers mention an instance in which this shifting character was likely to have produced serious results. A party had encamped upon one of these sand-bars, and in the middle of the night, the sergeant on guard alarmed them by crying that it was sinking. "We jumped up," say they, "and found that both above and below our camp the sand was undermined and falling in very fast; we had scarcely got into the boats and pushed off, when the bank under which we had been lying fell in, and would certainly have sunk the two perioques (open oared boats), if they had remained there. By the time we reached the opposite shore, the ground of our encampment sunk also." This incident occurred as they were making the circuit of the

Great Bend. From the shifting of these sand-bars the bed of the Missouri is constantly changing; a chart of the river as it runs this year, says Mr. Flint, gives little ground for calculation in navigating it the next. The change, however, is not confined to its bed; the rapid and sweeping current of this river is constantly undermining its banks, large masses of which frequently fall in. The soil through which it flows is of a very loose texture, and the waters are perpetually scooping away the banks at one place, and depositing mud and driftwood at others. Lewis and Clarke mention two spots, at some distance lower down than the junction with the Platte, at which a portion of the cliff or hill, in each instance nearly three quarters of a mile in length, and in one two hundred feet in height, had fallen completely into the stream. "We reach," they say, in another passage, "a very narrow part of the river, where the channel is confined within a space of two hundred yards, by a sand point on the north and a bend on the south, the banks in the neighborhood washing away, the trees falling in, and the channel filled with buried logs." Only a short distance from the mouth of the Missouri, as they were passing near the southern shore, the bank fell in so fast as to oblige them to cross the river instantly, between the northern side and a sand-bar which was continually moving with the violence of the current; the boat struck on it, and would have upset immediately, if the men had not jumped into the water and held her till the sand washed from under her.

It has been contended by some, that from the length of the Missouri, the volume of its waters, and the circumstance of its communicating its own character in every respect, to the Mississippi below the junction, it ought to be considered as the main river, and to impart its name to the united stream during its course to the sea. Malte Brun states it to be now known that the Missouri is the principal branch, and has the better claim to the magnificent title of "Father of Waters," which the Indians have conferred upon the smaller one; and Balbi, a still more recent authority, has a similar remark. An American geographer, however, Mr. T. Flint, remarks, in opposition to this claim, that the valley of the Missouri seems in the grand scale of conformation to be secondary to the Mississippi—that the Missouri has not the general direction of the lower portion of the Mississippi, but, on the contrary, joins it at nearly right angles—that the valley of the Mississippi is wider than that of the Missouri, and the river broader—and that the course of the river, and the direction of the valley, are the same above and below the junction. "From these," he says, "and many other considerations, the 'Father of Waters' seems fairly entitled to his name." Captain Hall also supports the claim of the more direct river of the two, to give its name to the joint current.

Missouri has every description of soil and of surface, from mountainous and rocky ridges, dense and rolling forests, beautiful undulating prairies, extensive tracts of inferior rugged soil, and low inundated swamps. Extensive districts in the counties of Jefferson, Franklin, Washington, St. Francis, Madison, Crawford, and the adjacent regions, are vast mineral regions, and abound in lead, iron, copper, and a variety of other minerals.

St. Genevieve is the oldest town and permanent settlement in Missouri. The village church was situated two miles from the river (with its extensive "common field" of several thousand acres in front on the river, extending along its rich bottom land), and was commenced about 1754. On the arrival of Laclede, in 1763, "it was a town of some note," and the point to which the lead was brought from the mines in the interior on deposite. The landing on the river was at a rocky bluff two miles above.

The lead mines of Missouri were discovered by Philip Francis Renault and M. de la Motte, agents under a branch of the "Company of the West." La Motte discovered the mines that go by his name, on the waters of the St. Francis. Renault left France in 1719, with two hundred artificers and miners, to explore the Illinois, and the adjacent country on both sides of the Mississippi.

Jefferson City, the capital of the state, is situated on the right bank of the Missouri river, on elevated and uneven ground, one hundred and twenty-eight miles from St. Louis. It contains the statehouse, penitentiary, an academy, and about four thousand inhabitants.

Government.—The constitution of this state was formed by a convention at St. Louis, in June, 1820. In January, 1846, a new constitution was formed by a state convention at Jefferson; which was submitted to the people on the first Monday of August in the latter year, and rejected. The constitution adopted in 1820, is therefore still in force, and the outlines thereof are as follows:—

The legislative power is vested in a senate and house of representatives, styled together *the General Assembly*. The senators, in number not fewer than fourteen, nor more than thirty-three, shall be thirty years old, have the qualification of representatives, be inhabitants of the state for four years, and shall be chosen by districts, for four years, one half every second year. The representatives, in number not more than one hundred, shall be chosen in counties every second year; they must be free white male citizens of the United States, twenty-four years old, inhabitants of the state for two years and of the county for one year next before the election. Every free white male citizen of the United States, twenty-one years old, resident in the state one year before the election, and three months in the place where he offers his vote, may vote at elections.

The elections are held biennially, on the first Monday in August. The legislature meets every second year, on the first Monday in November, at the city of Jefferson.

The executive power is vested in a governor, who is elected by the people, for a term of four years, and is ineligible for the next four years. A lieutenant-governor is also chosen, for the same term, who is, *ex officio*, president of the senate. They must be thirty-five years old, natives of the United States, or citizens thereof at the adoption of the constitution. The governor may veto a bill, but a majority of both houses may pass it, notwithstanding his veto. If the office of governor be vacant, it shall be filled by the lieutenant-governor, and after him by the president of the senate *pro tem*.

The supreme court consists of three judges, appointed by the governor and senate, and has appellate jurisdiction only. Circuit courts have exclusive criminal jurisdiction, unless deprived of it by law, and hear all civil cases not cognizable by a justice of the peace. The equity jurisdiction is divided between the circuit and supreme courts. Judges of the supreme court must be thirty years old, may hold office until sixty-five, and may be removed upon address of two thirds of both houses of the legislature.

One bank, and no more, may be established, with not more than five branches, and a total capital of not more than five millions of dollars, one half, at least, reserved to the state.

The general assembly, by a vote of two thirds of the members, may propose amendments to the constitution, and if, at the first session thereafter, they are confirmed by a vote of two thirds of the members, they become part of the constitution.

St. Louis was founded by Laclede, Maxam, & Co., Feb. 15, 1764. Laclede obtained from M. D'Abadie, "director-general, and civil and military commandant of the province of Louisiana," under the French government, a grant, in 1762, for the exclusive privilege to trade with the Indians in Missouri, and those west of the Mississippi above the Missouri, as far north as the St. Peter's. He fitted out an expedition and started from New Orleans August 3, 1763, and on the third day of November, after a three months' voyage in keel-boats, reached St. Genevieve. He proceeded to Fort Chartres, stored his goods, and remained for the winter in that vicinity. Laclede was associated with Madame Choteau, the wife of a Frenchman in New Orleans, and had her two sons, Auguste and Pierre, young lads, with him. In February, 1764, Laclede with the young Choteaus and others, started to search out a spot for their projected trading post. St. Louis, eighteen miles below the mouth of the Missouri, was the spot selected and named. Several families of Cahokia accompanied Laclede. The first trading-house and cabins were erected near the river, on the spot of the centre market-house. A skirt of timber, tall oaks without under-brush, beautiful as an English park, skirted the river, while immediaiely in the rear an undulating prairie extended into the country for ten miles. The soil at the river was based on stratified limestone, forming a rock formation for four miles in extent. The ground ascended in a gradual slope for three or four hundred yards; when at an elevation of sixty or eighty feet, it continued in an undulating form for ten or fifteen miles into the interior. Springs broke out in various places, affording delicious water. Nature never formed a plateau of ground more admirably adapted to the site of an immense city. The river opposite, now one and one third of a mile in width, from the washing away of the deep alluvion that forms the Illinois shore, was then so narrow that persons could be heard distinctly from bank to bank. Such was the *site* of St. Louis eighty-seven years gone by. Pierre Choteau, one of the boys who accompanied Laclede, was still living, and at the age of nearly one hundred years, presided at the great meeting held in February, 1847, in honor of the founding of the city.

The transfer of the Illinois country from the French to the British government, by the treaty of 1763, which was consummated by a change of government in 1765, caused many of the inhabitants of Cahokia, Kaskaskia, and Fort Chartres, to remove to the new village west of the great river. A *secret* treaty had conveyed Louisiana to Spain, but a transfer of government did not take place till 1769. During this time St. Louis grew fast.

In April, 1785, the Mississippi rose to the height of thirty feet above the highest water mark then known, overflowed the whole of the American bottom, deluged the villages of Cahokia and Kaskaskia, destroyed a considerable portion of the walls of Fort Chartres, and was never equalled except by the great flood of 1844. St. Louis (except at the landing) is at least fifty feet above these highest floods. The year 1785 is styled by the old French people, "*L'Année des grandes eaux*"—the year of the great waters.

From 1769, or rather 1770, St. Louis, with the whole province of upper and lower Louisiana, was under the government of Spain, though French customs, language, and population, prevailed.

By the treaty of St. Ildefonso, October 1, 1800, under stipulated conditions, Spain retroceded Louisiana to France, and in December following, the transfer was made by the proclamation of M. Laussat. April 30, 1803, Louisiana was sold by the French government to the United States, for fifteen millions of dollars, and on the ninth of March, 1804, Major Amos Stoddard took possession of Upper Louisiana, and hoisted the American flag at St. Louis.

The first newspaper printed west of the Mississippi, was the "*Missouri Gazette*," by the late Joseph Chaross. It was on a sheet of "cap" paper, and dated July 12, 1808. A book of laws of the territory was printed the same year. The Missouri Gazette was the progenitor of the Missouri Republican, now published daily, tri-weekly, and weekly.

The *second* paper was started by a company of gentlemen in 1815. It was called "The Western Emigrant," and in 1818, the St. Louis Enquirer, and for several years edited by Colonel Thomas H. Benton, late of the United States senate.

The first steamboat that ever ascended the Mississippi above the mouth of the Ohio, and reached St. Louis, was a small boat called the "General Pike," which reached St. Louis, August 2, 1817, commanded by Captain Jacob Reed. The second steamboat was the "Constitution," commanded by Captain R. P. Guyard, which arrived October 3d, the same year.

The "Western Engineer," a keel-

View of St. Louis.

boat with a steam-engine and stern-wheel, was the first steamboat to ascend the Missouri river, in April, 1819. It accompanied the scientific expedition under Major S. H. Long. The next steamboat that ascended the Missouri was the "Independence," Captain Nelson, that reached Franklin, in the Boon's Lick country, May 19, 1819. This was followed by the "Calhoun," and the "President," two other steamers, which attempted to take troops and military stores to the "Council Bluffs," established that year. Neither boat reached the mouth of the Kansas.

A voyage from New Orleans to St. Louis in keel-boats, before the introduction of steam, was from three to four months. In 1819, a voyage by steamboats was from twenty-five to thirty days. Of late it has been run in less than *four* days!—usually from six to ten days.

The city of St. Louis is the *base* of navigation of all the upper Mississippi and its tributaries, the Missouri and its tributaries, and the *head* of navigation for the larger boats from the Ohio and the lower Mississippi. Here are now concentrated the trade of the upper Mississippi, the Missouri, and the Illinois rivers, and a large portion of that of the Ohio and the lower Mississippi. From a mere fur-trader's post, it has grown to be the *second* commercial city in the great central valley. *It is now the greatest steamboat port, next to New Orleans, in the world.* In capital, commerce, and active business, it is in advance of any city on the Ohio river.

The government business, and various extra branches of trade in St. Louis, are greater than in any other city in the United States—as the military and contract department—the Indian agency business—the Indian and Spanish trade (before the war)—the trapping business to the Rocky mountains—the fur trade, &c., &c.

The United States government has an arsenal two miles south of the city, which consists of stone buildings and extensive stone walls, of great value and durability. Jefferson barracks are twelve miles south of the city, and constantly occupied by United States troops whether in war or peace, capable of accommodating two regiments. The two comprise a government property equal to $1,750,000, and the permanent improvements are on the increase and will be for many years to come, as from this point all the military stores and forces must go out to the wide regions of the west, southwest, and northwest. During the Mexican war, there were manufactured at the arsenal, gunpowder, munitions, and other ordnance stores, amounting to over twelve hundred tons, and at a cost of several millions of dollars; between four hundred and five hundred tons of shells and shot—about seven millions of cartridges for small arms; all which furnished employment to about six hundred hands.

St. Louis has a United States sub-treasury, superintendency of Indian affairs, surveyor-general's office, and custom-house, and is the general military dépôt for all the vast region of the west.

Population.—On this subject there has been a most serious mistake in all the published statistics since 1840. At that time the *chartered* limits of the *city* did not extend over one third of its present area. Nearly half of the population lived out of the chartered limits, and the population of this portion, in the United States census, was placed under the head of the *county*. The population of the chartered limits was only 16,469—but the population then within the present chartered limits would have equalled 26,000.

The following table shows the population at various periods:—

Year.	Pop'n.	Year.	Pop'n.
1804,	800	1835,	10,500
1810,	1,400	1837,	15,300
1815,	1,800	1840,	26,000
1820,	4,598	1844,	34,140
1828,	5,000	1845,	36,255
1830,	5,853	1846,	47,833
1833,	8,397	1850,	82,744

The discrepancies between the year 1840 and the United States census are explained above. The number for 1850, is by the United States census.

Lots in the business part of the city sell from $300 to $500 per linear foot, in front—toward the suburbs, from $5 to $60 per linear foot.

There are in the city of St. Louis, about fifty churches, a courthouse, two hospitals, two orphan asylums, several brass and iron foundries, two universities, two medical colleges, many splendid hotels (one of which, the "Planter's House," is not exceeded by any in the United States), and public and private schools and academies. And here we may incidentally remark, that its public schools are hardly exceeded by those of any city in the Union. Among the public buildings the catholic cathedral, with a fine peal of six bells, and the courthouse, are the most noticeable. There are also in the city an elegant theatre and a concert-hall.

The courthouse, though incomplete, is not exceeded in the west, and is situated on the most elevated ground, and commands one of the finest prospects, from its immense cupola. The city is supplied with water from the river, which is elevated by steam to a reservoir constructed on an immense ancient mound, and situated above the highest buildings; and should its population (destined as it is, to become one of the largest cities in the United States) require it, Merimac river, larger than four Croton rivers, of pure, delicious water, can be brought from the distance of twenty miles, to an unlimited extent, for all purposes, including that of manufactures, on an immense scale.

There is a floating dock, and a railway for the repair of steamboats. From forty to fifty steamboats are daily moored to the wharves, and many of them of the largest size.

EDINA, the county seat of Knox county, is located in a rich and beautiful section of country, about forty miles from Tully and Canton.

MEMPHIS, the county seat of Scotland county, is one of the loveliest locations for an inland town in Missouri. It is located in a rich prairie, surrounded by beautiful groves of forest trees, the most attractive of which is a white-oak in the town, the top of which resembles in shape the top of an umbrella: it is not high, and the top measures upward of three hundred feet in circumference.

BETHEL, is the name of a village five or six miles north of Shelbyville, in Shelby county. It is located on North river, and populated by a body of Germans, who live together on the common stock system. They have a splendid steam-mill in operation (which grinds and saws extensively), a tanyard, and workshops of various kinds; the buildings are neat, and comfortably arranged.

They have a farm of several hundred acres in a superior state of cultivation. The body consists of several hundred persons, all Germans, who appear to be comfortable and happy.

TULLY AND CANTON.—These two towns are located on the west bank of the Mississippi, about forty miles above Hannibal, in a beautiful prairie bottom, three quarters of a mile in width, and rich beyond description. They are within half a mile of each other. Six or eight counties in Missouri, and a large scope of country on the Illinois side of the river, trade at that point.

ST. CHARLES, twenty miles west from St. Louis, occupies a commanding situation, on the left bank of the Missouri, at a place where a rocky shore gives place to a low alluvial region just below. The appearance of the town from the water is imposing, as it extends about a mile and a half along the bank of the river. The principal buildings are the courthouse, market, nunnery, and two churches. The population amounts to about 1,000. Stage-coaches start every day for St. Louis and Jefferson City, and three times a week for Burlington, Illinois, through New London.

St. Charles College.—This is a methodist institution, founded in 1839. It has about one hundred students.

PALMYRA, eight miles from Missouri river, is one hundred and twenty-nine miles distant from St. Louis, and has 1,200 inhabitants. There are three churches, built of brick, a courthouse, and a land office. Stage-coaches go to St. Louis three times a week.

Masonic college is an institution founded in 1831. It is situated twelve miles from Palmyra, and has about fifty students.

Fulton.—This town stands on Riviere aux Vases, twenty-two miles east of Jefferson City, and twelve north of the Missouri. It has about 800 inhabitants, with two academies, two churches, and a courthouse.

Columbia is a town of about 2,000 inhabitants, on a branch of the Missouri.

Missouri university situated in Columbia, was founded in 1840, and has three professors and about fifty students.

Booneville, one hundred and seventy-three miles from St. Louis, is situated on the bank of the Missouri, on a foundation of limestone rock, and contains a population of about 1,800. Cattle and provisions are here supplied in considerable quantities, and the trade of the place is active. A communication by land with Jefferson City, Independence, and Columbia, is maintained by stage-coaches, which run three times a week.

Glasgow.—This town, situated one hundred and seventy-two miles from St. Louis, contains 800 inhabitants, several large stores, and two churches.

Independence, six miles distant from the Missouri, is two hundred and ninety-two from St. Louis, and contains about 900 inhabitants. The place is important as the point from which the overland emigrants to California start, with their long trains of wagons. Of course it is often the scene of much business.

Liberty is a town about three times the size of Independence, two hundred and seventy-six miles from St. Louis. It stands on the bank of the Missouri, and has five churches, a courthouse, and two academies. Daily coaches run to St. Louis, passing through Glasgow, Columbia, and Fulton. Others go three times a week to St. Joseph.

St. Joseph, four hundred and seventy-eight miles from St. Louis, contains 2,000 inhabitants, and is a place of considerable trade, with large storehouses, &c. It stands on the Missouri, and, like the other towns so situated, is visited by steamboats.

The town commences at the foot of a high bluff, just at the upper extremity of the Seven-mile prairie bottom, which lies between the range of the "Black Snake hills" and the river. One of the said ranges of hills lies in about the centre of the town plat, and is about seventy-five feet above the level of the river. They are mostly destitute of trees, but covered with grass. From their base gushes forth the purest water. The country around this thriving village is equal to any in Missouri.

Springfield, two hundred and fifty-eight miles from St. Louis, stands on the head streams of James's fork of White river. The population is about 500. There is a land-office here.

Cape Girardeau, one hundred and thirty-four miles below St. Louis, is one of the river towns, standing on the right bank of the Missouri.

St. Mary's college, founded here in 1830, has five professors, and about two thousand five hundred volumes in its libraries. The commencement is held on the last Thursday of August.

New Madrid, on the right bank of the Missouri, is two hundred and forty-seven miles below St. Louis, at a bend of the river, where the ground is elevated, but gradually undermined by the stream. The population is about 800. By land, a stage communication is kept up three times a week with Cape Girardeau.

Hannibal.—This place is situated north of St. Louis, at the distance of one hundred and sixteen miles, and contains several manufactories, as well as stores, of considerable size, and a population of 1,200.

Potosi is another small but busy town, lower down, sixty-seven miles from St. Louis. It stands in the rich mining district in that part of the state, and an active business is done in iron, lead, and copper. It has 900 inhabitants, with four churches, &c.

Lexington, one hundred and twenty-four miles from Jefferson City, is on the right bank of the Missouri, and has about 2,000 inhabitants. There are three churches, a land-office, and an academy. Stage-coaches start three times a week for St. Louis, passing through Jefferson City.

Buffaloes and Elks.—The accompanying engraving affords a fine view of such a scene as is very common on our extensive uninhabited western regions. Extending his migrations to the northward, as the summer advances, the buffalo (or bison, as he is more correctly named) passes successfully over the hunting-grounds of several different nations of Indians, all on the alert to discover, pursue, and slaughter him for his valuable skin, as well as to make food of his flesh.

The buffalo is a very timid animal, and shuns the vicinity of man with the keenest sagacity; yet, when overtaken, and harassed or wounded, turns upon its assailants with the utmost fury, who have only to seek safety in flight. In their desperate resistance the finest horses are often destroyed; but the Indian, with his superior sagacity and dexterity, generally finds some effective mode of escape.

During the season of the year while the calves are young, the male seems to stroll about by the side of the dam, as if for the purpose of protecting the young, at which time it is exceedingly hazardous to attack them, as they are sure to turn upon their pursuers, who often have to fly to each other's assistance. The buffalo-calf, during the first six months, is red, and has so much the appearance of a red calf in cultivated fields, that it could easily be mingled and mistaken among them. In the fall, when it changes its hair, it takes a brown coat for the winter, which it always retains. In pursuing a large herd of buffaloes at the season when their calves are but a few weeks old, the hunter is often exceedingly amused with the curious manœuvres of these shy little things. Amid the thundering confusion of a throng of several hundreds or several thousands of these animals, there will be many of the calves that lose sight of their dams, and being left behind by the throng and the swift-passing hunters, they endeavor to secrete themselves, when they are exceedingly put to it on a level prairie, where naught can be seen but the short grass of six or eight inches in height, save an occasional bunch of wild sage, a few inches higher, to which the poor affrighted things will run, and, dropping on their knees, will push their noses under it, and into the grass, where they will stand for hours, with their eyes shut, imagining themselves securely hid, while they are standing up quite straight upon their hind feet, and can easily be seen at several miles' distance. It is a familiar amusement for those accustomed to these scenes, to retreat back over the ground where they have just escorted the herd, and approach these little trembling things, which stubbornly maintain their positions, with their noses pushed under the grass, and their eyes strained upon their pursuers, as they dismount from their horses and pass around them. From this fixed position they are sure not to move until hands are placed upon them, and then for the shins of a novice we can extend our sympathy; for if he can preserve the skin on his bones from the furious buttings of its head, we know how to congratulate him on his signal success and good luck. In these desperate struggles, for a moment, the little thing is conquered, and makes no further resistance. "I have often," says a writer, "in concurrence with a known custom of the country, held my hands over the eyes of the calf, and breathed a few strong breaths into his nostrils; after which I have, with my hunting companions, rode several miles to our encampment, with the little prisoner busily following the heels of my horse the whole way, as closely and as affectionately as its instinct would attach it to the company of its dam. This is one of the most extraordinary things that I have met with in the habits of this wild country."

The elk was one of the most useful animals to the Indians, in those regions where it abounds. It is a large, and sometimes a rather formidable animal, though its first impulse is to escape, when it discovers the approach of man. Elks abounded in New England at the first settlement; and they have been hunted within half a century, or a little more, among the White hills of New Hampshire. It is the largest of the

Herd of Buffaloes and Elks.

deer tribe; but fossil animals of the kind, found in the earth in several places in Europe, far exceed it in size. The form is far from graceful, and the gait in running is remarkably awkward, owing, apparently, to the great weight of the horns. The head is carried in a horizontal position, the neck is stretched out straight forward, and the pace or trot throws the body from side to side with a rolling motion. When brought to bay, it sometimes makes dangerous blows with its heavy and projecting horns.

The flesh of the elk is esteemed for food, but is less common in the west than buffalo meat.

Hunting the Buffalo.—There are several modes and several different weapons by which the buffalo is slain by the Indians of different tribes, and at different seasons. The gun is not, however, preferred, so generally, as might be expected, nor so extensively adopted as it might be. Several of the nations in the western plains are excellent bowmen, and are furnished with bows and arrows, which serve them admirably against these swift and powerful animals. It is a well-established fact, that an arrow sent by a strong and dexterous hand, and striking at a favorable instant between the ribs, occasionally passes through the body of the buffalo, and falls to the ground beyond him. When, therefore, we recollect the shortness and lightness of the bow (the best of which are only three or four feet in length), and rapidity with which arrows can be thrown (sometimes an Indian in sport will keep ten arrows in the air at a time), we may perceive that the use of this simple weapon is not retained without reason.

The Camanches, on the borders of Texas, often prefer their lances, in the chase as in war; riding up by the buffalo's side, and with a sudden, sidelong thrust, penetrating his heart. Passing on, another and another is thus mortally wounded, and several are seen dying at once, from blows inflicted in rapid succession, by one weapon.

The lasso is used by some tribes in certain circumstances; and, when not in immediate use, the long cord is sometimes allowed to drag behind on the ground, so that if the horseman is accidentally dismounted, he may seize it and recover his steed and his seat.

Mr. Catlin gives the following description of other methods sometimes practised:—

In the dead of winter, which is very long and severely cold in this country, where horses can not be brought into the chase with any avail, the Indian runs upon the surface of the snow by the aid of his snow-shoes, which buoy him up, while the great weight of the buffaloes, sinks them down to the middle of their sides, and, completely stopping their progress, insures them certain and easy victims to the bow or lance of their pursuers. The snow in these regions often lies, during the winter, to the depth of three or four feet, being blown away from the tops and sides of the hills in many places, which are left bare for the buffaloes to graze upon, while it is drifted in the hollows and ravines to a very great depth, and rendered almost entirely impassable to all these huge animals, which, when closely pursued by their enemies, endeavor to plunge through it, but are soon wedged in and almost unable to move, where they fall an easy prey to the Indian, who runs up lightly upon his show-shoes and drives his lance to their hearts. The skins are then stripped off, to be sold to the fur-traders, and the carcasses left to be devoured by the wolves. This is the season in which the greatest number of these animals is destroyed for their robes—they are easily killed at this time, and their hair or fur being longer and more abundant, give greater value to the robe.

The Indians generally kill and dry meat enough in the fall, when it is fat and juicy, to last them all winter; so that they have little other object for this unlimited slaughter, amid the drifts of snow, than that of procuring their robes for traffic with the traders. The snow-shoes are made in a great many forms, of two and three feet in length, and one foot or more in width, of a hoop or hoops bent around for the frame, with a netting of web woven across with strings

Buffalo Hunting.

of raw hide, on which the feet rest, and to which they are fastened with straps somewhat like a skate. With these the Indian will glide over the snow with astonishing quickness, without sinking down, or scarcely leaving his track where he has gone.

The poor buffaloes have their enemy, *man*, besetting and besieging them at all times of the year, and in all the modes that man in his superior wisdom has been able to devise for their destruction. They struggle in vain to evade his deadly shafts, when he dashes among them over the plains on the wild horse —they plunge into the snow-drifts where they yield themselves an easy prey to their destroyers, and they also stand unwittingly and behold him, unsuspected under the skin of a white wolf, insinuating himself and his fatal weapons into close company, when they are peaceably grazing on the level prairies, and shot down before they are aware of their danger.

The Elkhorn Pyramid.—This remarkable object, represented in the vignette at the head of the description of this state, is to be seen on Two-Thousand-Mile river, one of the branches of the Missouri, so named by Lewis and Clarke, at that distance from its mouth in the Mississippi. The surrounding country is an extensive level, called the *Prairie à la Corne de Cerf.* The numerous paths made in all directions through the artemisia bushes, indicate an abundance of elk and deer, which roam freely through the broad and fertile pastures there offered them by nature.

It has long been the practice with the Indians, to collect some of the cast-off horns of those animals from the vicinity of the spot, and add them to a heap, which was commenced at some unknown period. A few buffalo-horns are mingled with the rest. Mr. Bodmer, who visited and examined it, describes the heap as sixteen or eighteen feet in height, and twelve or fifteen in diameter, and probably containing about twelve or fifteen hundred horns. He found great difficulty in disentangling a large horn with fourteen antlers, so compactly are all parts of this fabric laid together. He made a drawing of the pyramid before leaving the spot, from which that in the vignette has been reduced. Every hunting and war party that passes near the spot makes an addition to the heap, probably under some superstitious idea.

Missouri Iron Mountains.—There are two or three iron mountains, situated not far distant from each other, and forty or fifty miles west of the Mississippi. One of them is seven hundred, and the other over three hundred, feet in height, above the surrounding plain.

The iron with which they abound is a *peroxyde*, consisting of twenty parts iron, and fourteen parts oxygen—thus constituting a very rich ore of iron. As you approach either of these mountains, and before you get to it, you find lumps and masses of this form of iron, scattered much like the stones of New England. Advancing, you find the masses in larger numbers and greater size; and so on up the mountains, till you approach their summits, where you find one *vast capping* to the mountain of these iron rocks and stones, whose depths have never been explored.

Of course, how far they go down we do not know, nor what proportion of the substance of these mountains is iron, but we perceive the quantity there to be immense, almost beyond calculation; enough to supply the whole human race, even under the present vast consumption of iron, with the metal for ages to come! The base and sides of the mountains are thickly and beautifully wooded; even after you come to the immense cappings with which the mountains are rounded off, you find the trees everywhere shoot up among those iron rocks, although you can discover scarce a trace of soil.

These vast deposites of ore, so long discredited, although repeatedly asserted to exist, are doubtless destined to contribute a large share of that material, so important to every branch of art, and so indispensable an article to civilization. Distance, the thinness of the population, and other circumstances, have hitherto prevented the extensive reduction of the ore. But the increase of inhabitants will make a rapid change.

Emigration.

IOWA.

Iowa is bounded north by the Minnesota territory, east by the Mississippi river, which separates it from Wisconsin and Illinois, south by Missouri, and west by Missouri river, which separates it from Nebraska. It lies between 40° 20′ and 43° north latitude, and 90° 20′ and 96° 50′ west longitude, with a length of about two hundred and fifty-six miles, a medium breadth of one hundred and ninety-eight, and an area of about fifty thousand nine hundred square miles.

The state is well watered by numerous navigable rivers and streamlets flowing into the Mississippi and Missouri rivers which bound the state. The principal of these are the Red Cedar and Iowa, and the Des Moines, which empty into the Mississippi. The rivers falling into the Missouri are comparatively unimportant.

Up to the year 1836, Iowa and Wisconsin, as well as Michigan, were embraced in the territory of Michigan.

Iowa was Indian territory as lately as in 1832, except a claim at Du Buque's mines. About five hundred persons, chiefly miners, had entered and labored on the Dubuque tract two or three years previously. The first emigrants who made farms in this now growing state, entered the territory in February, 1833, in the settlement a few miles back of Burlington. The first Christian church gathered was a baptist one, in 1834.

The growth of Iowa has been more rapid than that of any other western state. Its population now equals 200,000. It will soon be one of the great states of the west. No country on the globe is better situated for farming purposes.

IOWA CITY, the capital of Iowa, on the left bank of the river of the same name, at the head of navigation, is thirty-one miles from Muscatine, and enjoys a pleasant situation. The number of inhabitants is about 3,000. The public buildings are the capitol, courthouse, and several churches. Stage-coaches go three times a week to Burlington and Rock Island, Indiana.

The *capitol* is a fine building, chiefly in the Doric style, with a dome rising from the centre on twenty-two Corinthian columns.

BURLINGTON.—This flourishing town stands on the Mississippi, two hundred and twenty-two miles above St. Louis. The situation is pleasant and picturesque, on a rising ground, stretching up toward a range of hills which almost surround it. The streets run at equal distances and at right angles. The population is about 6,000. Daily communication is had by steamboats with near and distant river towns above and below, and by stage-coaches three times a week with Dubuque, &c. Burlington was originally the capital of Iowa, and contains many fine public buildings. The site was formerly known as the Flint-halls, an old Indian trading post, and was the residence of the celebrated Indian chief Black Hawk, whose remains are buried here.

MUSCATINE (formerly Bloomington) ninety-six miles south of Dubuque, is one of the most thriving towns in the state. Population, at the present time, about 4,000.

KEOKUK, a few miles north of the mouth of the Missouri, is becoming rapidly a place of importance, and has, of late years, increased in population and wealth, perhaps more than any other town in the state. It has a large commerce, and many advantages in situation and topography, which must ultimately make it a most flourishing mart. The present population is about 5,000.

Some years ago an ancient wall of large dimensions was discovered, at what is now called Azatlan, in Wisconsin, between the Four lakes and Milwaukie. The antiquarian may now find an additional field for his researches in Iowa. In Lee county, about ten miles from Burlington, a stone wall was accidentally discovered on the farm of Mr. William Heiter, while he was sinking posts for a fence.

It is about two feet wide, two feet deep, and laid regularly, the stone lapped after the fashion of foundation walls. It appears to have been the foundation of some ancient building or superstructure of square dimensions, about twenty-two feet either way. It is on the highest point of the prairie, the ground receding from it in every direction. Not a stone or a pebble except those in the wall, can be found in half a mile of the place. Most of it is now uncovered, and a part of the northern wall removed. There is a middle or partition wall. Many of the stones are greatly decayed.

DUBUQUE is also a river-town, and is four hundred and twenty-six miles from St. Louis, and three hundred and six from the falls of St. Anthony. The bank of the Mississippi is elevated and level for several miles above and below Dubuque, forming an advantageous position for a town. There are about 5,500 inhabitants. The public buildings are five churches, a land-office, a bank, &c.

JANESVILLE.—In this fine town, the county seat of Rock county, numerous evidences of rapid and prosperous growth everywhere meet the eye. On both sides of the river many buildings are going up; the streets are crowded with teams; business of all kinds appears brisk, and there is an air of enterprise, activity, and advancement, pervading the whole town, which must impress and surprise the most indifferent observer. Conspicuous among the buildings is a large flour-mill on the west side of the river. This substantial structure is eighty feet by fifty, five stories high, seventy feet from the ridge to the water-line, and rests upon solid stone-walls five and a half feet in thickness, designed for six run of stone. No expense has been spared in making this mill equal to any in the western country. The total cost can not be far from forty-five thousand dollars. Even in a dry season there is abundance of water, in the rock, at Janesville, to keep all the wheels of this mill in constant motion.

One significant circumstance in the growth of Janesville (and this is equally true of almost all the towns and village in the territory) is, that the surrounding country has grown even more rapidly than the town. On Rock prairie some two years since, for a distance of ten or twelve miles, the improvements were slight and the houses scarce. Now, the roads are fenced in nearly their entire length, and bordered by improved farms under skilful cultivation, with comfortable tenements, and every appearance of an industrious and thriving population. This is it which renders the growth of Janesville substantial as well as rapid, and which makes the increase and rapid improvement of the state a marvel in the history of civilized settlements.

A Log Cabin and Saw-Mill.—One of the most useful of all "improvements" that can be introduced into a new district where timber is to be found, is a saw-mill; and many an extensive region has long suffered from the want of one. The deficiency is more frequently supplied, however, of late years, since settlements have been more frequently undertaken by companies of capitalists. Under their care many conveniences are at once introduced, not within the reach of single emigrants or of a few poor families, whose pecuniary means are apt to be exhausted before they reach their new homes, or who at least can not transport to so great a distance anything more than the most simple necessaries.

But where capital is furnished, and preparatory measures taken, for the occupation of a new point in the wilderness, and the founding of a new town, the explorers first report all the necessary steps to be made, and plans are laid, tools, materials, and workmen, sent out, and constructions commenced before the settlers arrive. And then one of the very first points secured is a mill-site, where a saw may be set in motion, and the neighboring forest-trees cut up into timber, plank, and boards. For this end a rapid stream must be found; and, in extensive regions in our western prairies, this is not to be had. Such favored spots, therefore, in their neighborhood, as possess water-power, are rendered doubly important by the extensive demand.

The saw-mill, simple as it is, is invaluable to a new settlement. Without it not a plank, board, timber, or other piece of wood, can be obtained, for any purpose, except by the laborious process of sawing by hand, or the still more laborious one of hewing, more commonly resorted to. Many a table has been made, by slowly cutting a broad plank out of the middle of a log, with the axe alone; and the extreme difficulty of procuring wood in convenient forms, has long delayed the advance of society from the rudest state to a grade of comfort worthy of the name of civilization.

How different a state of things is immediately introduced by the busy motion of the saw-mill! The shapeless logs, felled in the neighboring forest, or brought down by the current of the river, take every form desired; and the tight frame-house rises, with all its superior advantages of floors, partitions, second stories, good doors, stairs, and furniture. In short, the saw alone adapts the rude trees of the woods to the convenient use of man.

Description of a Prairie in Iowa.—"When for the first time," says a writer, "I stood upon the edge of the prairie upon which I now reside, it was about noon of a beautiful October day. We emerged from the wood, and for miles around saw stretched forth one broad expanse of clear, open land. I stood alone, wrapt up in that peculiar sensation that man only feels when beholding a broad, rolling prairie for the first time—an indescribable, delightful feeling. O, what a rich mine of wealth lay outstretched before me!

"No plough or spade has broken the sod for ages; no magician has appeared with the husbandman's magic wand, and said to the coarse and useless grass that has grown for centuries, 'Be gone; give place to the lovely Ceres with her golden sheaves.'

"Little does one know or think, as

Log-Cabins and Sawmill at the West.

he digs in the corn among the stones of New England, what vast quantities of such land lie waste in the west, and how few are there to improve them; and what is worse, how indolent a great portion of that few are. Talk of the country being sickly! why, the worst epidemic that ever raged in any country is that idleness which fixes itself, incubus-like, upon the whole population of an extraordinary fertile soil.

"But who that ever undertook, ever satisfied his inquirers as to how a prairie looks while in a state of nature? The reason is that there is nothing analogous, to which one can compare it, in a thickly-settled country. But let the reader fancy the country with which he is best acquainted in an old settled region, entirely destitute of buildings or fences, or, in fact, any mark of civilization, with all the hills reduced so as to make a gently-rolling surface, the woodland to remain as it is, and the entire surface of cleared land covered with grass, that upon the upland thick and short, in the low lands one or two feet high, and in the swamps four or five feet, and he may have a very faint idea how a prairie looks.

"Gently undulating, applies to all prairie countries within my knowledge. Sometimes, though rarely, hills occur that are too steep to cultivate conveniently, and sometimes rocky bluffs. But a general characteristic is destitution of stone.

"The streams have generally muddy bottoms. The timber in the groves or islands that abound throughout this sea of grass, is most commonly short, and grows thin upon the ground, without underbrush, except at the edges, where the hazel-bush seems to be the advanced guard, and is constantly encroaching upon the prairie. There are large tracts of timber land called 'barrens,' which are about half way between prairie and timber land—the trees standing apart like an orchard, and the ground covered with grass, the sod of which is much less tough than that on the prairie.

"One very prominent feature of a prairie is the constant and ever-varying succession of flowers from spring till fall."

The whole valley of the upper Mississippi was almost wholly unknown to American geographers twenty years ago, though the French Jesuits and "coureurs des bois" were acquainted with it for a century and a half before. Bradford remarks that the whole region between the mouths of the Illinois and Missouri, and Lake Michigan and Council Bluffs, and further west, is one vast plain, slightly sloping to the south and east. The land between the Mississippi and the lake is only five hundred feet above the level of the Atlantic. Among the best portions of the upper Mississippi, is reckoned the whole of Iowa, the northern part of which, by reason of an admixture of sand, is rendered more moist and later in forwarding crops than the climate would lead us to expect. Carbonate of lime exists in the prairie soils, from twenty to forty per cent., but in much smaller proportion in the timber lands. Forests grow up spontaneously on the prairies, when fire is kept out. St. Louis county was changed from an open prairie to a thick forest in this way, in thirteen years.

The following general geological strata are found in the whole of the eastern upper Mississippi country, as truly as in Iowa: 1st, vegetable mould, eight to thirty inches; 2d, pure yellow clay, three to eight feet; 3d, gravelly clay with pebbles, four to ten feet; 4th, limestone, two to twelve feet; 5th, shale; 6th, bituminous coal; 7th, soapstone; 8th, sandstone. The limestone exists everywhere. Every well and other excavation, which penetrates deep enough, discloses it, and it is exposed by many streams.

The western part of Iowa is chiefly mountain limestone, with strata of fossil chalk formations, wholly or chiefly of shells. Such is the summit of the bluff at Burlington, and of this is formed the fine whitish marble of Iowa City. In the south, between the Des Moines and Iowa rivers, are several varieties of marble, some of them black, variegated, &c. Agates and cornelians are washed out on the banks of the Mississippi in abundance.

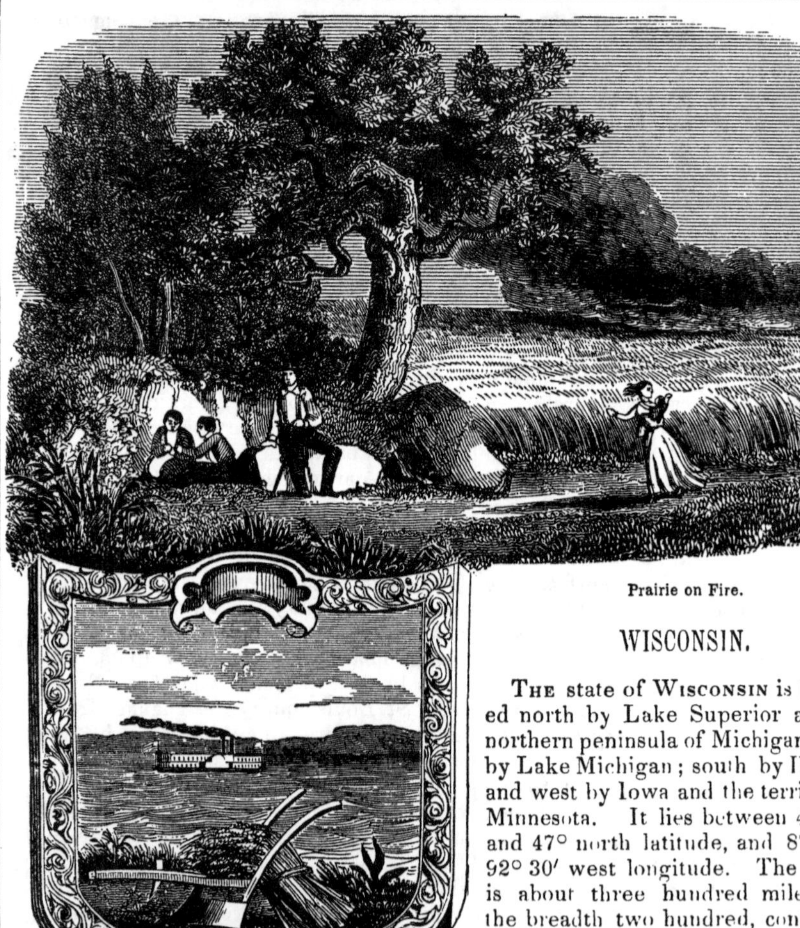

Prairie on Fire.

WISCONSIN.

THE state of WISCONSIN is bounded north by Lake Superior and the northern peninsula of Michigan; east by Lake Michigan; south by Illinois; and west by Iowa and the territory of Minnesota. It lies between 42° 30′ and 47° north latitude, and 87° and 92° 30′ west longitude. The length is about three hundred miles, and the breadth two hundred, containing about fifty-four thousand square miles. The population in 1840, was 30,945, and in 1850, 304,121. Those parts of the state that lie south of Green Bay, Fox river, and the Wisconsin, present a variety of prairie and timber land, with some swamps and wet prairies, and a rich soil, varying from one foot to ten feet in depth. The north part is mountainous, declining into hills and a swelling surface, which terminates at Wisconsin river. The streams in that part of the state are often wild, and much broken by falls and rapids. That part of the state in which some of the head streams of the Mississippi have their origin, is an elevated table-land, abounding in swamps, which produce wild rice, and ponds well stocked with fish. The forests are extensive and thick along the banks of the Mississippi and Wisconsin rivers, the land being rich.

The rivers are large. The Mississippi lines the west border. The Wisconsin is five hundred miles long, and the Chippeway is further north. Rock river is also a large stream. The Neenah, or Fox river, flows near the Wisconsin, through land in some places so low, that boats may pass between them in times of light floods. The former is navigable one hundred and eighty miles in boats.

Black river rises in the interior of Wisconsin, and after running a southwesterly course about two hundred and fifty miles, flows into the Mississippi about eighty-five miles above Prairie du Chien. Below the falls, which are about ninety miles from the mouth of the river, the country is mostly a hilly prairie. The predominating rock, which is the *base* of hills at Prairie du Chien, rises in ranges of hills, or single bluffs, of all shapes, and running in every direction; varying in height from one hundred to five hundred feet above the plain. The soil, which appears to be formed by the gradual denudation of these hills is light and sandy, and, for the most part, possesses but little fertility. The alluvial deposites on the bank of the river, however, are rich natural meadows, covered with a most luxuriant growth of grass. These meadows appear to be entirely undisturbed by the foot of man or beast, and the traveller is almost led to imagine that they must be under the protection of an owner, who is cultivating hay on a large scale, and the appearance of an extensive hay-pressing establishment would appear almost as a thing of course.

On the prairie berries and a variety of flowers grow in profusion. The strawberries are small. Among the flowers is a species of *phlox*, exceeding in splendor any of the family in an uncultivated state. The large yellow moccasin-flower, or ladies' slipper, is very common, and gives quite a variety of color to the prairies. In addition to their rich and varied coloring, most of these possess fragrance. There is an occasional grove to be seen, and the streams are generally skirted with timber, among which are several species of oak, white and black birch, maple, poplar, &c., but as a whole, this part of the country is deficient in fencing material, and, with the exception of the choice situations, must, for farming purposes, remain unoccupied for many years. For a distance of ninety miles there is but one house near the river, and this is at a mill-site at the mouth of one of the numerous streams which flow into it. This being about forty-five miles from the mouth of the river, and an equal distance below the falls is a stopping-place for raftsmen, and those persons visiting the upper country in search of employment or to make claims. About five miles distant from this house, and settled by the same family (Douglass and sons), is a farm of fertile land under a good state of cultivation, though it is but two or three years since the settlement was made. The road through this part of the country is still a very primitive one, and is travelled only by footmen and horses; no vehicle of any description except such as were merely for transportation to the upper country, having as yet found their way along it. The mode of ferrying is equally primitive; passengers and their baggage being taken across in a canoe at a dime a head, while the horses are allowed to swim beside it. From the mouth to the falls, small flat-bottomed boats are used to transport provisions, but even this sort of navigation is frequently suspended during the low water in summer, on account of the numerous sand-bars with which the river abounds.

From latitude forty-five degrees north to near Lake Superior, and from the head waters of the St. Croix to those of the streams flowing into Green bay, about one hundred miles in length and breadth, the whole country may be regarded as a series of swamps, lakes, and rivers, with just sufficient dry land interspersed to serve for the summer residence of a few hundred Indians, who still hold it as their hunting-ground. Seven eighths of the entire country north of forty-five degrees is one immense swamp, interspersed with narrow sandy ridges; and not over one tenth of it suitable for cultivation. Some of this swampy land may ultimately become valuable for the timber it affords, being covered with a beautiful growth of *cedar*, very straight and tall, and from one to two feet in diameter. The *tamerack*, if it were near the coast, might be in demand for masts and spars, being superior to any other species of pine in height as compared with size, and in the firmness, elasticity and durability of its timber; but this central region of eternal swamp has no navigable rivers to float it out. Hemlock, fir, and spruce, are the growth of perhaps the greater part of this low, wet tract of country. Many of these swamps have in their middle lakes of from half a mile to several miles in extent; some of these are connected with streams of water, forming chains for many miles in length. Comparatively few among the Indians, and scarcely any of the whites, have ever penetrated these gloomy water-courses so as to have become at all familiar with their outlets.

For many years past a portion of the Chippewa or Ojibwa tribe of Indians have had their summer residence around a chain of lakes, the largest of which is known as "Lake de Flambeau," situated about the middle of this low flat country; they have drawn their summer subsistence from the waters, and in winter have spread over the frozen surface of the forest and marsh, in search of bear, deer, fox, beaver, otter, marten, and other valuable peltries and furs, which find a ready market at the various trading posts on the Mississippi and its lakes.

Swamps form a very considerable portion of the territory of northern Wisconsin. From these sources flow the head-waters of the numerous streams with which the whole country is abundantly supplied, and which, uniting, form the tributaries of the rivers which flow into the Mississippi on the west, and the great lakes on the northeast.

Of those most difficult to pass, the alder-swamps are perhaps the most common, such having nothing larger than the alder growing in them. Most of these are exceedingly miry, and many of them for horses quite impassable. On foot and without a load, a man may easily step from clump to clump of the alders, and thus get safely across; but a misstep may let him into the mud to the depth of several feet. It is fortunate for the traveller that these are the smallest in size of any, for though frequently many miles in length, they are seldom over half a mile wide.

When absolutely necessary to get pack-horses across these morasses, the most favorable crossing-place is selected, and a road made by cutting away the alders, which are sometimes so disposed across the worst places as to form some support for the foot. The Indian ponies used for packing soon get accustomed to these matters, and it is interesting to observe the caution and willingness with which they encounter difficulties of this kind. When the path is prepared, one of the horses is led over. On entering the swamp, he places his foot with great care, moving it a few inches at a time, until he feels that his footing is sufficiently firm to bear him up, when another foot is advanced in a similar manner. If, however, despite his care, he sinks into the mire beyond the power of extricating himself, he takes it as coolly as can be imagined, remaining perfectly quiet until all arrangements are made for his assistance, and then, at a word, using the greatest possible exertions to second the efforts of those endeavoring to extricate him. When the horses are all over, their packs are carried across, and they are reloaded as before.

The black-ash swamps are also very miry, and differ from those already described, in having that species of tree thinly scattered through them, while the alder is merely an undergrowth.

Those swamps in which the cedar predominates, however, are the most formidable, and are quite impassable for a horse, which must either meander, or turn back. The fallen but undecayed trunks of the trees, some of them perhaps the growth of four ages, lie across each other in every direction. As these become covered with moss, young trees commence growing on the tops of the trunks, sending their roots down the sides and into the ground, thus sometimes forming the novel sight of a large tree standing erect over the trunk of perhaps its fallen ancestor. The undergrowth is entirely of cedar, and is so dense, that an unencumbered man would be obliged, in addition to climbing the logs, to cut nearly his whole way through this bristling underbrush, in order to cross it. They are not miry, but are often miles in width, with water under the roots of the trees as clear as crystal and very cold.

The tamarack, a species of pine, is a very common production. The swamps producing this are sometimes miry, in which case they have an undergrowth of alder. In other instances the whole surface of the ground is covered with an aquatic plant resembling moss, which grows to the height of from eight to twelve inches, holds water equal to a sponge, and though no water appears upon the surface, the foot of the traveller sinks into the soft, yielding, sponge-like moss so as to bring it around his ankles and frequently higher.

The hemlock, fir, larch, and spruce swamps have little to distinguish them, other than the species of tree which they produce. Many of them have lakes in the middle, the water being of a reddish-brown color, and not the most palatable. They may all be penetrated during the dry summer-months; all are mud during wet weather, and all abound in musquitoes and other pestiferous insects.

Racine, the capital of Racine county, is a thriving town, situated on Lake Michigan, at the mouth of Root river. It is one hundred and twelve miles from Madison, and seven hundred and eighty from Washington. It contains a court-house and jail. There are here two academies, with about one hundred students. The population is increasing very rapidly, at present numbering nearly 6,000. There are about $200,000 invested in trade and manufactures.

Madison, one hundred and fifty-nine miles from Chicago, is the capital of Wisconsin. It stands on a peninsula between two lakes. The situation is very favorable, the ground rising gradually from the water on both sides to a moderate elevation in the middle, where a spacious square is laid out, the site of the statehouse. This is a large building of stone, with a fine dome rising from the centre. The population is over 1,200; and there are several churches of different denominations. Stage-coaches run to Milwaukie, Rockfort (Illinois), Galena, and Fort Winnebago, three times a week.

The city of Milwaukie commences about a mile above the mouth of the river of that name, at a place called Walker's Point, and extends about a mile and a half along the river. Below Walker's Point the river is bordered by impassable marshes. The ground occupied by the town is uneven, rising from the river to the height of from fifty to one hundred feet, thus affording very beautiful situations for residences, commanding a full view of the town and bay, with its shipping. But few of these sites have yet been occupied and improved as their great importance and interesting views would lead us to expect. Along the base and front of these hills are a great number of springs of pure water, sufficient, if collected into a reservoir, to supply the wants of a considerable population. The river is sufficiently wide and deep to accommodate a large amount of shipping, and continues so for some distance above the city. At the head of this navigable portion of the river, a dam has been built by the "Milwaukie and Rock River Canal-Company," which raises the water twelve feet above high water, and causes a slack-water navigation extending two miles further up the stream. A canal of one mile and a quarter brings this water into the town on the west side of the river, and creates there a water-power which is estimated to be equal to about one hundred runs of millstones; and the canal has a width and depth sufficient to pass almost the whole body of water into the river. The manufactories erected on this canal have the advantage of being located on the immediate bank of the river, and may be approached by the largest steamboats navigating the great lakes: thus affording advantages not usually found associated in the western country. The city is ninety-seven miles from Chicago.

The settlement of Milwaukie was commenced in 1835. The village was laid out the same year. In less than fifteen months its population amounted to 1200. A land-office was opened there in 1836, at which the amount of money received in ten years was $2,221,359 73. This, it is stated in "Lapham's Wisconsin," was about two thirds of the whole proceeds of sales of public lands during that time in the territory. Till the season of 1835 the waters of Milwaukie bay were undisturbed by any craft save the Indian's canoe, or perhaps the rudely-con-

View of Milwaukie.

structed boat of a fur-trader or fisherman. Now more than a thousand entrances are made there annually by vessels and steamboats. The amount of merchandise, flour, pork, wheat, lard, furs, lead, copper, &c., shipped from year to year, is immense, and is rapidly increasing.

The present population of Milwaukie is supposed to be between twenty and thirty thousand, and was never multiplying faster. Almost every water-craft from the east that enters that port, has one or more new settlers on board. The number of buildings now going up would indicate thrift and prosperity. And here we might mention that a large part of the houses and blocks are built of brick, which, in this place, is of a light cream color (owing, it is said, to the absence of iron), and presents a strikingly-beautiful appearance. It draws the attention and excites the admiration of all strangers.

PRAIRIE DU CHIEN, on the Mississippi, is the most prominent point on that river. It is situated a few miles north of the Wisconsin river, and has its name from the beautiful prairie on which it is located. It is one of the oldest settlements in the west, and has been the scene of many battles. Population about 3,000.

SHEBOYGAN is well situated, on the Wisconsin side of the lake, and exhibits a vigorous, and, to all appearance, a permanent growth. Everything is new; the site is elevated and pleasant. The country back of it is well adapted to produce wheat, and the rapids in the river, a few miles out, afford a cheap power to convert it into flour.

The harbors of both these cities (Milwaukie and Sheboygan) require appropriations, to remove obstructions, and to render access to them easy. A few thousand dollars applied to the construction of piers will effect the object.

SOUTHPORT.—This is a town of so recent a date, that, as in the case of some others, it is impossible to find a description of it even in the latest publications, geographical or topographical. It stands on the border of a prairie of great extent, and its position gives it important commercial advantages, although the harbor is too shallow near the shore for the access of vessels. Two long piers of timber have therefore been constructed, extending far into the water, where vessels must load and discharge. The town is already large, busy, and prosperous, considering its recent date, and has every prospect of a rapid and continued increase. P. 3000.

FOND DU LAC.—In 1844 there were but two houses on this spot; but so rapid has been its growth, that it now looks much like a New-England village. The scenery about Fond du Lac is very fine, and the site of the village is beautiful: it is on the western edge of a prairie, in the sunset shade of a narrow strip of timberland which separates it from another prairie.

The prairie on which the village is situated extends eastward four and a half or five miles, and is nearly the same distance in width. On the east and south it is hemmed with timber-lands and oak openings, on the west by the strip of timber-land above mentioned, and on the north lie the clear blue waters of the Winnebago lake. The people are generally the enterprising, intelligent descendants of the eastern states.

AZTALAN is a small town, of about two hundred inhabitants, situated upon the east bank of the Crawfish, and about twelve miles southwest from Watertown. It has acquired some notoriety from being on the site of the "ancient city," as it is called throughout the state. It is true, that there is enough to be seen here to satisfy any one that the country has once been inhabited, and that, too, anterior to the present race of Indians, by a race that had made some progress in the arts; but there is nothing to show any considerable civilization or knowledge of science. The remains of a brick wall, enclosing about twenty-five acres, are distinctly visible. The enclosure is upon the west bank of the river, and the west wall is seventy or eighty rods long. At the north end it forms a right angle, and runs perhaps twenty or twenty-five rods to the river; it then follows down the river immediately upon the bank, for about forty rods, and there disappears. Near the

View of Southport.

south end of the west wall, it makes an angle to the west of ten or fifteen degrees, and pursues this course a few rods, and then makes an obtuse angle toward the river, and, before it reaches it, makes another angle, so that the south wall approaches the river nearly parallel with the north. The remains of the wall are about four, and in some places six feet high. The bricks are of red clay, and burnt, and in some places the clay of which they are composed is mixed with straw, only fragments of bricks having been found. Without as well as within the wall, may be seen regular and irregular formations on the surface of the ground—some appearing like cellars, and some are elevations. These appearances are visible nearly the whole length of the wall. There are only three or four elevations that may be called mounds, within the enclosure, and the most prominent of these is in the northwest corner, and is about ten or twelve feet high. On the bank of the river, without the wall, and nearly at the water's edge, are the remains of what appears to have been the end of a sewer, or an under-ground drain, to the enclosure. It is of limestone, and regularly arched.

In the vicinity of the enclosure are about one hundred and thirty mounds, varying in height from six to forty feet. The greater portion of the mounds are arranged in a line, nearly parallel with the west wall of the enclosure, and about thirty rods west of it, and extend at least fifty rods further north than the wall does. The mounds that are thus arranged touch at their bases, and are conical—some having a base two hundred and fifty feet in circumference, and some not more than one hundred feet. Around the northwest angle of the enclosure, and at a distance from it, is a curved line of mounds, and so at the southwest corner of the enclosure. Besides these, are other mounds, irregularly located on different eminences, at a great distance from the wall. One, in particular, is very prominent, about two hundred and fifty rods southwest from the wall, and it is different in formation from the others, having a crater formed in the top. Many of these mounds have been opened, and in some a regular stone structure has been found, in form like an oven—the stone cemented solidly together, having a perfectly smooth surface within and without. In one of these vaults was found a copper coin, with an impression upon one side, of two birds, and upon the other were unintelligible hieroglyphics. Metallic hatchets, axes, and knives, have been found, and pieces of cord and coarse cloth, and fragments of pottery.

Upon some of these mounds are trees a hundred years old. The present race of Indians have been using the enclosure for a planting ground, as the corn hills are very plain to be seen. The enclosure is upon a level piece of ground elevated about eighteen feet above the river, and the mounds are upon ground fifty feet higher than the enclosure. The mounds and enclosure were most undoubtedly the work of the same people. Here is to be found evidence of a progress in the arts, that no American Indian, of which we have any account, ever made. Mounds north of Fox lake, also upon the borders of Highland prairie, in Dodge county, are very similar in their formation and appearance to these.

At Summit, in Waukesha county, are a different class of mounds. They are formed like a house-roof, are about two rods long, and five or six feet high, and are scattered about over the plains in groups, resembling military companies in the different movements of marching by platoon, echelon, and in file.

Other antiquities of interest have been recently discovered in Fond du Lac, that are represented as being nearly as extensive as these of Aztalan.

A Clearing and Log Cabin.—This is a faithful representation of the dwelling of every settler in our western regions; and humble dwellings of this form and size now shelter the heads of thousands, whose families will be among the most wealthy of our citizens in a single generation. A log-cabin, in a new territory, may be regarded as a most striking emblem of enterprise well directed. Economy and industry, sound calculation and manly resolution, are expressed by its

A Clearing and Log-Cabin.

small size and rude aspect; for it is the cheapest dwelling-place which ingenuity can invent, in a country where wood abounds; and, when constructed with sufficient pains, is warm in winter and cool in summer.

The custom generally prevails among settlers to aid each new-comer in the erection of a house; and the simple plan of a log-cabin enables every one to become a competent builder, after a little practice. Where logs are not to be had, poles are sometimes used; and then the fabric is frail and loose, so that it is difficult to make the walls tight, even with all the clay, moss, &c., with which the interstices can be stuffed. When round logs are used, such means are generally effectual, if carefully applied and often renewed.

The first furniture usually introduced into a dwelling of this kind, is a table, made of four stakes driven into the ground, a bedstead of the rudest kind, and a few blocks cut from the ends of logs for seats; while the utensils are such as the family have brought in their wagon.

With such a roof over him as the engraving represents, and such food as he can procure in the forest, the settler proceeds with cheerfulness to the clearing of a little land, and the planting of his first crop, which is usually the harbinger of a series of fruitful seasons, and a course of continued and increasing prosperity.

A Prairie on fire is a scene of an impressive character, and sometimes terrific, dangerous, and destructive. It has been the practice of the Indians, in different parts of North America, from time immemorial, to set fire to the dry grass on the prairies, meadows, and other fertile grounds fitted for pasture; and the same custom has prevailed in some other parts of the world. According to Leichhart, the first explorer of Australia, it is common in the interior of that vast island, or continent. The object is usually twofold, so far as the motives of the American Indians can be ascertained, viz., to prevent the growth of young trees, and to enrich the pastures with the ashes of the burnt crop, that it may prove most attractive to the deer or other game in the succeeding warm season.

The fire, however, sometimes spreads much further than is desired, and forests of great extent, with houses, and even cattle and men, are sometimes destroyed. A strong wind, aided by a dry season, or accident in firing a field at a wrong time, thus occasionally proves disastrous. Wild animals, which have been sheltered by the high grass, are often driven precipitately from their lair, and Indians or travellers have sometimes been surprised by a conflagration, from which they have not escaped without the greatest difficulty. The wind not unfrequently spreads the flames faster than a man or even a horse can run, and then the safest way is, when possible, to plunge through the burning mass, and get to windward.

The Maiden's Rock.—This bold bluff rises from the banks of the Mississippi, at a point near the middle of the western boundary of Wisconsin, where it extends its breadth to two and a half miles, and bears the name of Lake Pepin. This rock is about four hundred and fifty feet in height, and the upper part forms a precipice of one hundred and fifty. A tragical tale is connected with it in an Indian tradition, from which it has received its name. The following is an abridgment of the story, as related to Major Long:—

In the village of Keoxa, in the tribe of Wapasha, once lived a young Indian woman named Winona, between whom and a young hunter existed an ardent attachment. Her parents opposed her wishes, having fixed their choice upon a warrior, whom they urged her to marry. Her brothers, however, resolved that she should not be treated with harshness, and endeavored to remove her objections to the warrior, by giving him valuable presents, which would enable him to make provision for his wife, if he should be absent on an excursion against his enemies. This encouragement from the family of Winona induced him to renew his suit: but she was as resolute as before, which provoked her parents to threaten her.

Maiden's Rock, on the Mississippi.

The hunter had already been driven into the forest, and she despaired of being allowed to lead a single life, and climbing to the summit of the bluff, seated herself upon the awful brink, and began to sing her death-song. Terrified at the prospect of her suicide, and repenting of their cruelty, the parents now strove to prevent her from performing her intention, and were seconded by their friends. Some climbed the rock to seize the desperate maiden, and the others took their stations at the foot of the precipice; but no exertions, protestations, or promises, would avail; and, throwing herself from the summit, she was killed by the fall.

The scenery between Lake Pepin and the St. Croix is not as lofty nor as picturesque as that below; but its interest is greatly enhanced by the greater number of Indians. The Red wing village is nearly midway between the two lakes mentioned, and contains about six hundred souls. A short distance from this village are two isolated mountains, where may be seen a most magnificent panorama of the wilderness. These mountains, from time immemorial, have been used as altars where Indian war parties have offered up their sacrifices, previous to going to battle. At the present time, however, their only inhabitants are rattlesnakes.

Lake St. Croix empties into the Mississippi, and its principal inlet is a river of the same name, which rises in the vicinity of Lake Superior. This is the valley through which the traders and Indians have been in the habit of passing, for a century past, on their way from the western prairies to Lake Superior, and from the lake back again to the prairies. The river is only distinguished for one waterfall of uncommon beauty. The lake is about twenty-five miles long, from two to five wide, and surrounded with charming scenery. The water is clear, but of a rich brown color, and well supplied with fish, of which the trout is the most abundant.

From St. Croix to St. Peter's, the banks of the Mississippi are steep but only about one hundred and fifty feet in height. The river is here studded with islands, whose shadowy recesses are cool during the hottest weather—and a more delightful region for the botanist to ramble can not be found elsewhere on the face of the earth. The water is clear as crystal, and its bosom is generally covered with waterfowl, from the graceful snow-white swan to the mallard and wood-duck. Isolated Indian wigwams are frequently seen here, pitched on the margin of the stream and at the foot of vine-covered precipices.

The Mines of Lake Superior.—Isle Royale is a portion of the territory ceded by the Chippewa Indians to the United States, by the treaty of October, 1842. So imperfectly known was the region thus acquired, that it was represented, in the instructions of the government to the first mineral agent, in the spring of 1843, as an "unexplored region—a newly-acquired country." This island had long been known to the Indians and fur-traders, as being rich in minerals, yet it was ceded by name, although clearly included in the general description. The consequence was, that after mineral locations had been made upon the island, in 1843, by Professor Locke, of Cincinnati, a portion of the Chippewas insisted that Isle Royale was not ceded by the treaty of 1842. The Indians were instigated to assert this pretended claim, by the "traders and designing men" who had obtained some knowledge of its great mineral riches. This pretended claim caused the suspension of mining operations on the island, and another treaty was made in 1844, whereby the Indians solemnly acknowledge the cession of the island by the treaty of 1842.

The owners of the locations on the island, after various delays, obtained the recognition of their rights, from the government, and in the spring of 1846, associated themselves together under the name of the *Isle Royale and Ohio mining company*, and proceeded at once to the island with an efficient force for mining operations.

Isle Royale is in the northwest part of Lake Superior, in forty-eight degrees north latitude, and eighty-nine degrees west longitude, extending northeast and southwest forty-five miles, and varies from three to five and eight miles in width. It is about one hundred and twenty-five miles in circumference, and has a greater number of harbors—larger, safer, of much easier access, and far more beautiful—than is within all the remaining territorial limits of the United States upon the lake. Rock harbor, upon the southeast coast of the island, is fifteen miles long, and from half a mile to a mile wide. Between the main land and the lake is a chain of islands for ten miles, between which are channels of deep water from the harbor to the lake. These islands are irregular elevations of rock covered with evergreens. Resting upon the transparent waters of the harbor, they present the most attractive feature in one of Nature's most enchanting pictures.

The next harbor of importance is at "Siskowit bay," eighteen miles southwest from Rock harbor. This harbor would afford safe anchorage for all the vessels of the upper lakes, and is at all times accessible through "Medary's entrance." Washington harbor comes next, at the west end of the island, extending inland about three miles. Then comes Todd's harbor, and M'Cargo's cove, on the north and northeast coast—both safe and beautiful harbors for vessels of any burden. Besides these, there are numerous inlets and indentations along the coast, except on the northwest shore, where perpendicular cliffs extend for fifteen miles. The northeast end of the island resembles a man's hand—the thumb being the point at the entrance into Rock harbor, and the fingers the four elevated ridges extending into the lake, with deep bays or inlets intervening, two, four, and six miles in length.

The lake around the northeast end of the island is thickly dotted with small islands of rock, from forty to two hundred and fifty feet high, covered with evergreens and white birch.

There are numerous beautiful lakes of pure water upon the island, from one to three miles in length, abounding in fish, furnishing streams of sufficient volume for saw-mills and all mining purposes. There are also many small prairies producing wild grass.

Isle Royale may be described as a mighty "up-heave" of irregular cliffs, bluffs, and mountains of rock—the elevation in many places being five hundred feet above the lake. The mountain ranges run nearly parallel with the island. There are also innumerable deep ravines or gutters, which are here called dikes, running parallel through the island, at the bottom of which metalliferous veins are invariably found, and to which the intervening veins or feeders usually lead.

The prevailing character of the rock on the different portions of the island is altered sand rock, underlaid with the true red sand-stone and conglomerate, which makes its appearance near Rock harbor, and continues along the southern coast. Green stone also shows itself frequently. On the northern coast, green stone, amygdaloid, sienite, and sienitic porphyry prevail; the mountain ranges are generally green stone also.

The island is thickly wooded, evergreens of small growth prevailing. The varieties are balsam, spruce, yellow and white cedar, white pine, tamerack, white birch, several kinds of poplar, black alder, mountain oak, a few black ash and maples, juniper bushes, and dwarf cherries. The pine and spruce are sufficient in number and size for boards and timber for the use of the island. The fruit consists of blue-berries, raspberries, wild strawberries, thimble-berries, and cranberries.

The animals are rabbits, red and gray squirrels, lynx, and carriboos (a species of deer). The fowls are ducks, loons, gulls, partridges, pigeons, night-hawks, jay-birds, owls, bats, &c. The fish are speckled trout, Mackinac trout, Siskowit trout, white-fish, mullet, pickerel, and herring.

During the summer months the climate is mild, healthful, and rejuvenating; the days not too hot for comfortable labor, and the nights just cool enough for refreshing sleep. In the winter the snow falls from two to four feet deep, and the weather is cold, without sudden changes.

The Great American Lakes.—We can n , perhaps, close the description of the latest cismontain state added to the confederation, more appropriately than by the following brief record of the depth, and width, and average extent of the great American lakes, two of which lave its borders. It is from the recent official report of the chief of the topographical bureau, and therefore may be relied upon.

"The great lakes of our country, which may justly be considered inland seas, are the following: Champlain, Ontario, Erie, St. Clair, Huron, Michigan, and Superior. These lakes are of great depth, as well as of great extent. The entire line of lake coast embraces about 5,000 miles, 2,000 miles of which constitute the coast of a foreign power.

Lake Champlain is	105 miles long.
Its greatest width	12 miles.
Its average width	8 miles.
Lake Ontario is	108 miles long.
Its greatest width	52 miles.
Its average width	40 miles.
Lake Erie is	240 miles long.
Its greatest width	57 miles.
Its average width	38 miles.
Lake St. Clair is	18 miles long.
Its greatest width	25 miles.
Its average width	12 miles.
Lake Huron is	270 miles long.
Its greatest width	104 miles.*
Its average width	70 miles.
Lake Michigan is	340 miles long.
Its greatest width	83 miles.
Its average width	58 miles.
Lake Superior is	420 miles long.
Its greatest width	135 miles.
Its average width	100 miles.

"These lakes may be considered as connected throughout their whole extent. Lake Champlain connects with Lake Ontario by means of the river Richelieu; the lock and dam navigation of St. Lawrence river; the Ottawa river and Rideau canal through Canada; and the Champlain and Erie canals of New York. Lake Ontario is connected with Lake Erie by means of the Welland canal through Canada, and by means of Oswego and Erie canals through the state of New York. Lake Erie is connected with Lake St. Clair by the deep and navigable strait of Detroit, twenty-five miles long. Lake St. Clair is connected with Lake Huron by the deep and navigable strait of St. Clair, thirty-two miles long. Lake Huron is connected with Lake Michigan by the deep and wide strait of Mackinaw, and with Lake Superior by strait of St. Mary's, forty-six miles long. This strait is navigable throughout except for about one mile of its length, immediately adjacent to Lake Superior, where from rocks and the extreme rapidity of the current, navigation ceases. These difficulties can, however, be easily surmounted by a canal of not more than a mile long, with locks to overcome a fall of about twenty-one feet. The only additional obstruction to this immense extent of inland navigation is in St. Clair lake, on approaching the St. Clair strait. This obstruction consists of an extensive bar, but not of great width, over which not more than seven feet of water, in depressed conditions of the lakes, can be counted upon. From an examination of this shoal, it has been found to consist of an indurated marl, leaving but little cause of doubt that if a channel were once dredged through, it would remain a durable improvement.

"Lake Champlain lies exclusively (except the strait near Rouse's point) within the states of Vermont and New York; the former occupying its eastern, the latter its western margin. It is not considered a dangerous lake to navigate; and the principal protection which its commerce requires, is in form of breakwaters, to shelter its open harbors."

The vast commerce of these lakes, and the great extent of coast, prove the necessity of the surveys through which this information is obtained, in order that we may possess an accurate knowledge of the bars, rocks, and shoals, to which this active commerce on so extensive a line of coast is imminently exposed.

* This does not include the extensive bay of Georgian, itself 120 miles long, and average 45 wide.

CALIFORNIA.

New or Alta California was discovered about 1542, by Juan Rodriguez Cabrillo, who explored the coast as far north as the forty-third degree of north latitude. Portions of the coast were visited by Sir Francis Drake in 1578, by Francisco Galli in 1582, and by Sebastian Vescayna in 1603. Vescayna discovered the ports of San Diego and Monterey, and closed the career of northern exploration which had originated with Cortez. In 1767, the Jesuits, by whom the settlement of Lower California had been accomplished, fell under the displeasure of the government of Spain, and were expelled from the peninsula. The Marquis de Croix, who was at that time viceroy of New Spain, replaced them by the rival order of the Franciscans, upon whom he strongly urged the *spiritual conquest* of the upper province. This enterprise the government considered more important than the settlement of the peninsula. The accounts which were current of the wealth of the country were very flattering, and political reasons induced them to lend efficient assistance to the adventure. Both France and England at that time evinced considerable interest in the islands of the Pacific, and the countries upon its coast; and the explorations of Bourgainville and Cook had begun to excite alarm. Russia also, with noiseless, but certain advance, was stretching her gigantic empire alone the western coast, and Spain recognised the necessity of preventing these dangerous intruders from obtaining a foothold in her American possessions.

Under these circumstances, the spiritual subjugation of Upper California was accomplished in a comparatively short time. The same career of privation and toil was run by the priestly pioneers as marked the settlement of the peninsula, but the missions grew up more rapidly, and the difficulties were, on the whole, fewer. The results were equally unimportant. Neither Mexico nor the colony was much benefited. The country offered great inducements to a profitable trade, and was believed to possess large deposites of quicksilver and gold; but the narrow and unwise policy of Mexico, both when an appendage of Spain, and an independent state, rendered the development of its resources impossible. The government fettered commerce. It imposed restrictions instead of granting facilities; levied onerous taxes, and stretched a barrier of customhouses across ports which a liberal policy would have crowded with profitable trade. The interests of the country were wholly disregarded; and California became a refuge for invalid soldiers, indolent priests, and pampered officials.

The missions, however, aided by large donations from the pious in Mexico, which were consolidated into what was styled "the California Pious Fund," rapidly grew in importance. They brought the mass of the native population into a condition of comparative vassalage, and gradually absorbed the valuable lands, almost to the exclusion of the white settlers. They existed in a state of almost total independence of Mexico; and although ordinary government establishments were kept up, as in the other provinces of the vice-royalty, the priests were virtually the owners of the soil, and the masters of the country. Affairs remained in this position until the occurrence of the Mexican revolution in 1824. This revolution, which separated Mexico from Spain, annexed California to that republic. The Californias were then erected into territories, not having sufficient population to entitle them to be federative states, and were each allowed to send one member to the general congress, who was privileged to take part in the debates of that body, but had no voice in its decisions. As territories, they were under the government of an agent styled the commandant-general, whose powers were very extensive.

The country has several times since the Spanish power was exterminated, suffered from revolution; and for the last ten or twelve years of its connexion with Mexico, the authority of that nation over it was very loose. Its distance from the metropolis would indeed tend to such a result. The people more than once declared themselves independent, and as often rejoined the confederacy. In 1846, on the breaking out of the war between the United States and Mexico, California was occupied by the United States forces; and, by the treaty of Guadalûpe Hidalgo, Feb. 2, 1848, the whole country was ceded to the United States.

In the latter part of the above named month, a mechanic, named James W. Marshall, was employed in building a saw-mill for Captain Sutter on the south branch of a river known as the American Fork. On Fremont's map, the river is called "Rio de los Americanos." While cutting a race for this improvement, Mr. Marshall discovered the scales of gold as they glistened in the sunlight at the bottom of the sluice. He gathered a few, examined them, and became satisfied of their value. He informed Captain Sutter of his discovery, and they agreed to keep it secret until the mill of Captain Sutter was finished. It however got out and spread like magic. Remarkable success attended the labors of the first explorers, and in a few weeks hundreds of men were drawn thither. Examinations were prosecuted at other points along the stream and almost everywhere with success. The result was extraordinary. Thousands flocked to California from all parts of the world, and a lively commerce was thus initiated which bids fair in a few years to become more extensive and valuable than all the present foreign trade of the United States together.

Previous to the discovery of the precious metals in California, the principal route to the Pacific coast of North America had been around Cape Horn. This long, perilous, and fatiguing voyage, consumed a period of from six to eight months, and sometimes longer for its accomplishment, and many of the earlier emigrants to California, reached there by this tedious route. But, previous to this period, however, arrangements had been entered into by government, under appropriations made by Congress for that purpose, for the establishment of a line of semi-monthly mail-steamers to California and Oregon by the way of the isthmus of Panama. This line was soon in operation; but though it proved entirely successful as a medium of rapid transmission of the mail to and from that distant region, shortening the period of transit from New York to California to less than forty days, it was still inadequate to the demand for passages of the thousands and tens of thousands, who determined to emigrate to the new El Dorado of the Pacific. To meet this demand, vessels were chartered in all the Atlantic ports for the conveyances of passengers to Chagres, on the Atlantic side of the isthmus, this being a far quicker and safer route than a voyage round Cape Horn. The passage across the isthmus was made in canoes up the Chagres river forty miles to Gorgona, and thence overland on mules, a distance of twenty miles to the city of Panama on the Pacific side of the isthmus. So immense was the number who chose this route, that the vessels on the Pacific side proved entirely inadequate to their transportation up to California, and soon several thousands were collected on the isthmus, many of whom had to wait months, ere they obtained a passage up the Pacific, though every possible sort of craft that could be pressed into the service, was made available to supply the demand for passage. The view of Panama, placed on the following page, shows a party of Americans converting canoes into vessels, in which to reach the golden land of their "hope deferred." The engraving is no fancy sketch, but was drawn by a gentleman residing at Panama, who witnessed their labors from the window of his hotel.

Additional steamers have, from time to time, been put upon the route, on both the Atlantic and Pacific sides, until this medium of travel can now accommodate all requiring a conveyance to or from the land of gold. A railroad across the isthmus is in rapid process of construction, which, when finished, will greatly facilitate, as regards both time and comfort, that most fatiguing portion of the journey. Another route, by the way of the river San Juan and across the lake Nicaragua, and about twenty miles by stage to the Pacific coast, has been established. This route is about a thousand miles shorter than that by the way of Panama; and the voyage, from San Francisco to New York, via Nicaragua, has been made in twenty-eight days. May we not hope that the day is not distant, when a railroad directly across the continent, shall shorten the passage between the Atlantic and Pacific metropolitan cities to one fifth of twenty-eight days; when the triumphs of science and art shall render them comparatively near neighbors, contributing to each other's prosperity, greatness, and happiness; and when, literally, from sea to sea, a continuous line of enlightened, civilized communities, shall greet the eye of the traveller, as he makes a rapid transit east or west across the American continent!

In September, 1849, in consequence of the disorganized condition of things, and the insecurity which generally prevailed, the people of California, by their delegates, met in convention, at Monterey, and formed a constitution, which was ratified by the people in November, 1849. The constitution being submitted to Congress, was ratified by that body, and the state of California thus admitted into the Union, September 9, 1850.

The intelligence of the reception of California into the Union was welcomed at San Francisco with expressions of universal enthusiasm. The steamer which bore the tidings was decked with flags and streamers of all nations, with a piece of canvass extending from fore to mainmast inscribed with the words "California is admitted." The salvos of artillery and the waving of flags soon spread the joyful news to every part of the city. All classes of the inhabitants shared the general hilarity, and with exchanges of mutual congratulations exulted in the accession of California as the thirty-first state of the federal Union. A more

Americans converting Canoes into Schooners, in the Bay of Panama.

formal celebration of this event took place on the 29th of October, in which the citizens generally participated with patriotic joy. A procession was formed in honor of the occasion, salutes were fired, banners displayed, an oration pronounced, a national ode sung, and the festivities closed with a ball and supper.

According to the terms of the constitution the legislative power is vested in a senate and assembly, called the legislature of California. Senators not less in number than one third, nor more than one half the number of members of assembly, are elected by the people in districts, for a term of two years, so classified that one half may be chosen annually. Members of the assembly are elected by the people annually, in districts. There shall not be less than twenty-four, nor more than thirty-six, until the population is one hundred thousand; and afterward, there shall never be more than eighty nor less than thirty. Senators and members of the assembly must be qualified electors in their districts, and be citizens and inhabitants of the state one year, and of their districts six months, before their election.

The executive power is vested in a governor, elected by the people for a term of two years. He must be over twenty-five years of age, a citizen of the United States, and a resident of the state two years next before the election. He may veto a bill, but two thirds of the legislature may pass it afterward. A lieutenant-governor is elected by the people at the same time, and for the same term with the governor, and must have the same qualifications; he is president of the senate, and in case the office of governor be vacant, he acts as governor. A secretary of state is appointed by the governor. A comptroller, treasurer, attorney and surveyor general, are to be elected by the people at the same time, and for the same term as the governor.

The annual election is held on the Tuesday next after the first Monday of November, and the sessions of the legislature are to be held annually, and commence on the first Monday in January. The place for the seat of government has been fixed at Vallejo. Divorces by the legislature, lotteries, banking charters, and paper-money, are prohibited.

In elections by the legislature, the members vote *viva voce*—by the people by ballot.

The judicial power is vested in a supreme court, district courts, and county courts; the judges of all which are elected by the people. The supreme court consists of a chief justice and two associates, elected for a term of six years. District judges are chosen for a term of six years. One county judge is elected in each county for four years. County officers are chosen by the people. A superintendent of public instruction is elected by the people of the state, for a term of three years.

Every white male citizen of the United States, and every citizen of Mexico under the treaty of Queretaro, twenty-one years of age, resident in the state six months, and of the district where he offers to vote thirty days preceding the election, is entitled to vote. Indians and their descendants may be permitted to vote in special cases, by a two thirds concurrent vote of the legislature.

Slavery, or involuntary servitude, except for the punishment of crimes is for ever prohibited.

A design for a state seal was adopted by the constitutional convention, an engraving of which, of the exact size of the seal, forms a part of the vignette at the commencement of this sketch, on page 601. It was designed by Major R. S. Garnett, of the United States army. Each region wished to be represented in the seal. The Sacramento district wanted a gold mine, with a miner at work; San Francisco, its harbor and shipping; the Sonoma members thought no seal would be complete without something from their ancient "bear-flag;" while those from Los Angelos and San Diego wished their corn, vines, and olives, to be represented. These several requirements were met, as far as possible, in the design.

Around the bevel of the ring are represented thirty-one stars, being the number of states of which the Union would consist, upon the admission of California.

The foreground figure represents the goddess Minerva, having sprung full-grown from the brain of Jupiter. She is introduced as a type of the political birth of California, without having gone through the probation of a territory. At her feet crouches a grisly bear, feeding upon clusters from a grape-vine, which, with a sheaf of wheat, are emblematic of the peculiar characteristics of the country. The sheaf of wheat and grape-vine add to the harmony of the design, as Ceres sat beside Minerva in the councils of the gods. A miner is engaged at work, with a rocker and bowl at his side, illustrating the golden wealth of the Sacramento, upon whose waters are seen shipping, typical of commercial greatness; and the snow-clad peaks of the Sierra Nevada make up the background. Above, is the Greek motto, "Eureka" (I have found it), applying either to the principle involved in the admission of the state, or the success of the miners at work. The remainder of the vignette, we will say, *en passant*, is a scene in the valley of the Sacramento.

California Alta, in its full extent, as acquired by the United States from the republic of Mexico, lies between the 32d and 42d degrees of north latitude, and between the 106th and 124th degrees of longitude west from Greenwich; and is bounded north by the territory of Oregon; east by the Indian territory and New Mexico; south by the river Gila, which separates it from the Mexican states of Chihuahua and Sonora, and by California Baja; and west by the Pacific ocean, on which it has a front of 970 miles. The area included within these limits is estimated at 500,000 square miles. California Alta is now divided into the state of California and the territory of Utah.

The boundaries of the state of California, as established by Congress, in its act admitting California into the Union, are as follows:—

Commencing at the point of intersection of 42d degree of north latitude with 120th degree of longitude west from Greenwich, and running south on the line of said 120th degree of west longitude until it intersects the 39th degree of north latitude, thence running in a straight line in a southeasterly direction to the river Colorado, at a point where it intersects the 35th degree of north latitude, thence down the middle of the channel of said river, to the boundary line between the United States and Mexico, as established by the treaty of May 30, 1848; thence running west along said boundary line to the Pacific ocean, and extending therein three English miles; thence running in a northwesterly direction, and following the direction of the Pacific coast to the 42d degree of north latitude, thence on the line of said 42d degree of north latitude to the place of beginning. Also all the islands, harbors, and bays along and adjacent to the Pacific coast.

This grand division of California (the only part, indeed, to which the name properly applies) is traversed from north to south by two principal ranges of mountains, called respectively Sierra Nevada, which divides the region from the great basin, and the coast range, running almost parallel to and a short distance from the Pacific coast. The main feature of this region is the long, low, broad, valley of the San Joaquin and Sacramento rivers, the two valleys forming one five hundred miles long and about sixty broad. Lateral ranges, parallel with the Sierra, make the structure of the country, and break it into a surface of valleys and mountains, the valleys a few hundreds and the mountains from two to four thousand feet above the sea. These form greater masses and become more elevated in the north, where some peaks, as the Shasti, enter the regions of perpetual snow. The great valley is discriminated only by the names of the rivers that traverse it. It is a single geographical formation. lying between the two ranges, and stretching across the head of the bay of San Francisco, with which a delta of twenty-five miles connects it.

Opposite the head of the bay of San Francisco and at the point where the Sacramento and San Joaquin river debouche, occurs the only break or gap in the range of mountains which forms the western boundary of the great valley, and (according to Fremont's map), run from the Oregon line to the 34th parallel, at an average elevation of two thousand feet. The portion of the valley which lies southeast of this point is called the valley of the San Joaquin. It is about three hundred miles long, and sixty broad, and presents a variety of soil, from dry and unproductive to well watered and luxuriantly fertile. Upon the eastern side, it is intersected by numerous streams from the Sierra which form large and beautiful bottom of rich land, wooded principally with white oak in open groves of trees, often six feet in diameter and sixty to eighty high. The larger streams only pass entirely across the valley. The low, or foot hills, of the Sierra Nevada, which limit the valley, make a woodland country, well-watered and diversified. This section of the valley is well adapted to the cultivation of the grape, and will probably become the principal vine-growing region of California. The rolling surface of the hills presents many sunny exposures, sheltered from the winds, and having a soil and climate highly favorable to this purpose. The vine thrives in California in an extraordinary manner. It is already cultivated to a considerable extent, and the wine produced is of very excellent quality. Intelligent cultivation alone seems needed to make wine in quantities sufficient both for consumption and exportation. The uplands bordering the valleys of the larger streams are wooded with evergreen oaks, and the intervening plains are timbered with the same tree, among prairie and open land. The surface is level, plain and undulating or rolling ground. The soil is rich, and admirably adapted to the cultivation of wheat, which yields enormous crops. The grasses are various and luxuriant; and oats grow wild, covering large tracts with a dense growth frequently as high as the head of a man mounted upon horseback.

Around the southern arm of the bay of San Francisco, a low alluvial bottom land, with occasional woods of oak, borders the western foot of the mountain ranges; terminating on a breadth of thirty miles in the valley of San José. This valley, in connexion with that of San Juan forms a continuous plain fifty-five miles in length, and one mile to twenty in breadth opening into smaller valleys among the hills. Shut in between the coast range and the lower hills upon the sea, with a soil of singular fertility, a pure, and dry atmosphere, and a soft and delicious climate, this valley, opening directly upon the bay of San Francisco, appears to unite more inducements to settlement than any other portion of California. It is wooded with majestic trees, covered with the richest grasses, brilliant with an endless variety of wild flowers, produces in profusion the fruits of the temperate and tropical zones, and breaks into secluded glens and wild recesses among the hills. All the tourists speak of it as a most attractive and beautiful spot.

North of the bay of San Francisco, between the Sacramento valley and the coast, the country is cut into mountain ridges and rolling hills, with many fertile and watered valleys. In the interior it is generally well wooded with oak; and, immediately along the coast, it presents open prairie land lying among heavily timbered forests, and frequently covered for miles with a dense growth of wild oats. To the eastward of this tract, and intermediate between the coast range and the Sierra Nevada, stretches from the head of the Sacramento and San Joaquin rivers to the mountains upon the forty-first parallel, that division of the country which is called the valley of the Sacramento. It is about two hundred miles long and sixty wide, watered by the Rio Sacramento and its affluents. It presents a diversity of heavily wooded plateaux, rich prairie land, fertile slopes, alluvial bottoms and strips of yellow gravelly soil. Many parts of it are well adapted to grazing, and its general character fits it in an eminent degree for the cultivation of wheat.

Upon the forty-first parallel, in a fork of the Sierra Nevada, is a tract of high table land, about one hundred miles in length, surrounded on all sides by mountains, which is called by Fremont the Upper Valley of the Sacramento. It is heavily timbered, and its climate and productions are greatly modified by its altitude and more northern position. The Sacramento river which rises in the mountains at its northern extremity, reaches the lower valley through a *cañon* on the line of Shastle peak, falling two thousand feet in twenty miles.

The largest river in Upper California is the Colorado, which after a course of a thousand miles, empties into the gulf of California about thirty-two degrees north. The name of this river is descriptive of its waters; they are as deeply colored as those of the Missouri, or Red river. It rises and flows through a region very little known, and inhabited by numerous tribes of savages, who manifest the most decided hostility to all who attempt to enter and explore it.

But by far the most important rivers of California are the Sacramento and San Joaquin. The San Joaquin rises in the Sierra Nevada, near the southern extremity of the valley. It is fed by many larger tributaries from the Sierra and empties into the bay of San Francisco after a course of about two hundred miles. It is navigable in some seasons during eight months of the year, and for a greater part of its length. The chief tributaries of the San Joaquin are the Reyes, the Stanislaus, the Javalones, the Merced, and the Cosumnes rivers. The Sacramento rises above latitude forty-two degrees north, and runs from north to south, nearly parallel with the coast of the Pacific until it empties, after a course of about two hundred miles, into the bay of San Francisco, in latitude thirty-eight and a half degrees north. It runs through an inclined alluvial prairie, and is described by all writers as a deep, broad, and beautiful stream. This river is destined to become a very important feature in the development of the country. It communicates directly with the bay, flows through a very fertile region and is already navigable for vessels of considerable draught as high up as the settlements at Nueva Helvetia. Its principal tributaries are the Rio de los Americanos and the Rio de las Plumas.

One of the most important features of California is the bay of San Francisco. It was discovered about 1768 by a party of Franciscan monks, who bestowed upon it the name of their patron saint. All writers unite in pronouncing it one of the most splendid harbors in the world. It is completely land-locked, and sufficiently capacious to meet the requirements of the most extended commerce. Approaching from the sea, the coast presents a bold outline. On the south, the bordering mountains come down in a narrow range of hills, against which the sea breaks heavily. On the northern side, the ridge presents a bold promontory, rising in a few miles to a height of three thousand feet. Between these two points, with abrupt and lofty cliffs upon each side, is a narrow strait about one mile wide and five in length, with a depth of water in mid-channel of forty to forty-five fathoms, which forms the entrance into the bay. This is called Chrysopolæ, or the Golden Gate. Beyond this gate the bay of San Francisco opens to the right and left, extending in each direction about thirty-five miles, having a total length of more than seventy miles, and an inland coast of two hundred and seventy-five in extent. Within, the view presented is of an interior lake of deep water lying between parallel ranges of mountains. Islands, some of them mere masses of rock, and others covered with grasses, and three to eight hundred feet in height, give its surface a picturesque appearance. It is divided, by projecting points and straits, into three separate bays. At its northern extremity is Whaler's harbor, which communicates by a strait two miles in length, with the bay of San Pablo, a circular basin ten miles in diameter; and this again at its northeastern extremity by another strait of greater length connects with Suissun bay, which is of nearly equal magnitude and form as that of San Pablo. Into Suissun bay the confluent waters of the Sacramento and San Joaquin rivers empty. The main bay of San Francisco lies to the southward.

The climate of California, as a necessary result of the configuration and extent of the country, presents marked contrast in the different divisions which have been described. With reference to the whole country, the year may be divided into the wet season and the dry. The wet season begins in November, and terminates in April. During this period the rain does not fall continuously, and frequent intervals of clear and beautiful weather occur for many days in succession. Rain sometimes falls without intermission for eight or ten days, followed by spells of sunshine; and frequently the weather is fine until the afternoon, when the clouds gather. The rain during this season is not continuously steady and violent, but warm and often drizzling. Usually from May until November no rain falls. There are exceptions, however, for rain sometimes descends in August. Apart from the mere physical discomfort, the sense of which is soon lost, the wet season is healthy and delightful, and during its continuance the country wears its most beautiful aspect. With the first rains in November, the grass, clover, and wild oats, spring up spontaneously; the trees are clothed with fresh foliage, the flowers display their rich colors, the comparatively arid soil is covered with diversified vegetation, and by Christmas the land in its broad extent is green and beautiful. Upon the coast and the shore of the bay, the climate is cooler and less agreeable than in the interior. This is owing to the northwest winds which frequently bring with them dense fogs which are cold relatively to the mean temperature. These fogs, however, are not of that raw and piercing kind that affect the constitution. They bear no seeds of disease. These characteristics of climate are perhaps more marked at San Francisco than at any other point, and the experience of nearly a century affords conclusive evidence that they do not injuriously affect health. It is seldom cold enough in the settled portions of California to congeal water. Snow rarely falls in the valleys, and the thermometer seldom sinks below fifty degrees or rises above eighty degrees. In the great valley bordering upon the lower slopes of the Sierra, the climate is peculiarly delightful. There are no prevailing diseases in the country, and the extremes of heat in the summer are checked by sea-breezes during the day, and by light airs from the Sierra during the night. The climate generally resembles that of Italy, and its characteristics are salubrity and a regulated mildness.

A stranger arriving at San Francisco in summer is annoyed by the cold winds and fogs, and pronounces the climate intolerable. A few months will modify if not banish his dislike, and he will not fail to appreciate the beneficial effects of a cool, bracing atmosphere. Those who approach California overland, through the passes of the mountains, find the heat of summer, in the middle of the day, greater than they have been accustomed to, and therefore many complain of it.

Those who take up their residence in the valleys which are situated between the great plain of the Sacramento and San Joaquin, and the coast range of hills, find the climate, especially in the dry season, as healthful and pleasant as it is possible for any climate to be which possesses sufficient heat to mature the cereal grains and edible roots of the temperate zone.

The division of the year into two distinct seasons—dry and wet—impresses those who have been accustomed to the variable climate of the Atlantic states unfavorably. The dry appearance of the country in summer and the difficulty of moving about in winter seem to impose serious difficulties in the way of agricultural prosperity, while the many and decided advantages resulting from the mildness of winter, and the bright, clear weather of summer, are not appreciated. We ought not to be surprised at the dislike which the immigrants frequently express to the climate. It is so unlike that from which they come, that they cannot readily apprecriate its advantages, or become reconciled to its extremes of dry and wet.

If a native of California were to go to New England in winter, and see the ground frozen and covered with snow, the rivers with ice, and find himself in a temperature many degrees colder than he had ever felt before, he would probably be as much surprised that people could or would live in so inhospitable a region, as any immigrant ever has been at what he has seen or felt in California.

So much are our opinions influenced by early impressions, the vicissitudes of the seasons with which we are familiar, love of country, home and kindred, that we ought never to hazard a hasty opinion, when we come in contact with circumstances entirely different from those to which we have all our lives been accustomed.

POPULATION.—Humboldt, in his Essay on New Spain, states the population of Upper California, in 1802, to have consisted of converted Indians, 15,562; other classes, 1,300; total, 16,862. Alexander Forbes, in his history of Upper and Lower California, published in London in 1839, states the number of converted Indians in the former to have been in 1831, 18,683; of all other classes, at 4,342; total, 23,025. He expresses the opinion that the number had not varied much up to 1835, and the probability is, there was very little increase in the white population until the emigrants from the United States began to enter the country in 1838.

They increased, from year to year, so that, 1846, Col. Fremont had little difficulty in calling to his standard some five hundred fighting men.

At the close of the war with Mexico it was supposed that there were, including discharged volunteers, from ten to fifteen thousand Americans and Californians, exclusive of converted Indians, in the territory. The immigration of American citizens in 1849, up to the 1st January, 1850, was estimated at eighty thousand—of foreigners, at twenty thousand.

Of the present permanent population of the state of California, it is not easy to form even an approximative estimate. While thousands of fresh immigrants are constantly arriving there, large numbers, whose residence has been merely a transient one, are constantly leaving. The returning tide, however, is far less than that which tends thitherward; and consequently, the permanent population of this young Pacific state is rapidly increasing, and may be set down at the close of 1851, as upward of two hundred thousand.

It is quite impossible to form anything like an accurate estimate of the number of Indians in the territory. Since the commencement of the war, and especially since the discovery of gold in the mountains, their numbers at the missions and in the valleys near the coast have very much diminished. In fact, the whole race seems to be rapidly disappearing.

The remains of a vast number of villages in all the valleys of the Sierra Nevada, and among the foot-hills of that range of mountains, show that at no distant day there must have been a numerous population where there is not now an Indian to be seen. There are a few still retained in the service of the old Californians, but these do not amount to more than a few thousand in the whole territory. It is said there are large numbers of them in the mountains and valleys about the head waters of the San Joaquin, along the western base of the Sierra, and in the northern part of the territory, and that they are hostile. A number of Americans were killed by them during the summer of 1849, in attempting to penetrate high up the rivers in search of gold; they also drove one or two parties from Trinity river. They have in several instances attacked parties coming from or returning to Oregon, in the section of the country which the lamented Captain Warner was examining when he was killed.

It is also impossible to form any estimate of the number of these mountain Indians. Some suppose there are as many as 300,000 in the territory, but it is not probable that there is one third of that number.

The small bands which are met, scattered through the lower portions of the foot-hills of the Sierra, and the valleys between them and the coast, seem to be almost of the lowest grade of human beings. They live chiefly on acorns, roots, insects, and the kernel of the pine burr—occasionally they catch fish and game. They use the bow and arrow, but are said to be too lazy and effeminate to make successful hunters. And they do not appear to have the slighest inclination to cultivate the soil, nor do they even attempt it—except when they are induced to enter the service of the white inhabitants. They have never pretended to hold any interest in the soil, nor have they been treated by the Spanish or American immigrants as possessing any. The Mexican government never treated with them for the purchase of land, or the relinquishment of any claim of it whatever. They are lazy, idle to the last degree, and, although they are said to be willing to give their services to any one who will provide them with blankets, beef, and bread, it is with much difficulty they can be made to perform labor enough to reward their employers for these very limited means of comfort.

Formerly, at the missions, those who were brought up and instructed by the priests, made very good servants. Many of those now attached to families seem to be faithful and intelligent. But those who are at all in a wild and uncultivated state are most degraded objects of filth and idleness.

It is possible that government might, by collecting them together, teach them, in some degree, the arts and habits of civilization; but, if we may judge of the future from the past, they will disappear from the face of the earth as the settlements of the whites extend over the country.

Previous to the occupation of the California territory, by the Americans, and the discovery of the rich gold deposites in the valley of the Sacramento, the principal towns in California, were Monterey (the ancient capital), San Francisco, San José, San Diego (a port in the south), and Los Angeles. None of these were of much importance, nor was their connexion with the commercial world, otherwise than very limited.

Since these great events, however, a new era has commenced, and the whole region has experienced one of the mightiest revolutions in the history of mankind. The old settlements above alluded to have become large cities, new towns have sprung up with almost fabulous rapidity, a living tide has inundated the country, from all parts of the habitable globe. Wherever a site eligible for commerce or trade is found, there we now see the germ of a future city or perhaps a city grown to considerable proportions. Everything is progressive; and where a few years ago the population could be numbered by thousands, it now numbers hundreds of thousands, and yet the tide flows on, and every week witnesses the arrival of enterprising immigrants, to become citizens of a state whose wealth and future position in the world bid fair to vie with those of Tyre in the days of its greatest glory. To attempt to describe the towns and cities of this young state in detail, while everything connected with them is in such a rapid transition state, were worse than useless; for what might be true today would be so far distanced, as to convey in effect a totally false impression to-morrow. Our notices, therefore, will be confined to a few of the more prominent cities; and even with them, with one or two exceptions, our sketches must necessarily be brief, and confined rather to the geographical position, and natural local advantages, than an attempt to portray the full measure of their present growth and prosperity.

San Francisco.—The city of San Francisco is situated on the west side of the bay of that name, and on the northern point of the peninsula which lies between the southern portion of the bay and the Pacific ocean. It is about four miles from the narrows or straits by which the bay is entered from the sea. The immediate site of the city is an indentation or cove in the western shore of the bay, directly in front of which, and at a distance of about two miles, lies a large island called Yerba Buena. From the water's edge the land rises gradually for more than half a mile, to the west and southwest, until it terminates in a range of hills five hundred feet in height at the back of the city. To the north of the city is an immense bluff (or rather three in one) more than five hundred feet high, which comes down to the water's edge, with precipitous sides of from twenty to one hundred feet in height. In front of this bluff is the best anchorage ground, the bottom being good and the high lands protecting vessels from the force of the westerly winds. Between this bluff and the above-mentioned hill, there is a small and nearly level valley which connects with a smaller cove about a mile nearer the ocean. The bluff forms the north-western boundary of the cove, while the eastern boundary is another bluff, called the Rincon, nearly fifty feet in height. To the south and southwest of this last-mentioned point there is a succession of low sand hills, covered with a dense growth of stunted trees peculiar to the country.

From the geographical position of San Francisco, its location immediately upon the bay, and its proximity to the gold regions, which must supply all the exports, it must eventually become the mart of an extensive commerce with Asia and the islands of the Pacific. Never in the annals of a nation has any city risen to importance at such a rapid rate as this. At the commencement of 1849, it was a mere village, composed of a few miserable-looking huts standing beneath the bleak and woodless hills. Now thousands of houses and stores, and evidences of the most civilized life are seen. Where, in 1848, but a single vessel might occasionally be seen in the harbor, now hundreds of vessels of every size and from almost every nation of the earth throng the noble bay. The following brief sketch of San Francisco, as it appeared in December, 1849, by Bayard Taylor, will give an idea of the rapid growth of this remarkable city. It is the more interesting, as it describes San Francisco at a period just anterior to the check its prosperity received by the occurrence of the first of those disastrous conflagrations which have since several times laid large portions of this unfortunate city in ashes:—

"Of all the marvellous phases of the history of the present, the growth of San Francisco is the one which will most tax the belief of the future. Its parallel was never known, and shall never be beheld again. I speak only of what I saw with my own eyes. When I landed there, a little more than four months before, I found a scattering town of tents and canvass-houses, with a show of frame buildings on one or two streets, and a population of about six thousand. Now, on my last visit, I saw around me an actual metropolis, displaying street after street of well-built edifices, filled with an active and enterprising people and exhibiting every mark of permanent commercial prosperity. Then, the town was limited to the curve of the bay fronting the anchorage and bottoms of the hills. Now, it stretched to the topmost heights, followed the shore around point after point, and sending back a long arm through a gap in the hills, took hold of the Golden Gate and was building its warehouses on the open strait and almost fronting the blue horizon of the Pacific. Then, the gold-seeking sojourner lodged in muslin rooms and canvass garrets, with a philosophic lack of furniture, and ate his simple though substantial fare from pine-boards. Now, lofty hotels, gaudy with verandas and balconies, were met with in all quarters, furnished with home luxury, and aristocratic restaurants presented daily their long bills of fare, rich with the choicest technicalities of the Parisian cuisine. Then, vessels were coming in day after day, to lie deserted and useless at their anchorage. Now scarce a day passed, but some cluster of sails, bound *outward* through the Golden Gate, took their way to all the corners of the Pacific. Like the magic seed of the Indian juggler, which grew, blossomed, and bore fruit, before the eyes of his spectators, San Francisco seemed to have accomplished in a day the growth of half a century."

It was but a brief period after the above sketch of San Francisco was penned, that that fated city was visited by the first of those calamitous fires, above referred to, which have six times desolated its finest streets, and proved a serious check to its growth and prosperity. The first of these took place on the 24th of December, breaking out in a gambling-house on Portsmouth square, and rapidly spreading to the adjacent buildings. In a short time, the finest portion

View of San Francisco from the Telegraph Hill.

of a large block of houses was burned to the ground. The fire presented a fearful spectacle. Fortunately the weather was calm, as the slightest wind would have exposed the entire city to almost inevitable destruction. The loss was estimated at one million and a half of dollars. With the genuine spirit of Yankee enterprise, many of the sufferers by the fire commenced business the next day in tents, and others on the same day prepared the site of the ruins for the erection of new buildings.

Another fire took place in San Francisco, on May 4th, 1850, which destroyed over two hundred buildings and property to the amount of over four millions of dollars. The fire commenced in the United States hotel, and spread with terrible rapidity in every direction. It was found impossible to arrest its progress, except by tearing down a large number of houses that presented materials for its fury. More property was consumed than could have been done within an equal space in any city of the world.

The third destructive conflagration which visited the city of San Francisco took place June 13th following, laying four large blocks of buildings in ashes, and consuming a great amount of valuable property. A portion of the district which had suffered from the previous fire was again burnt. With great difficulty the wharves and shipping in the harbor were protected from destruction. The total loss by this fire has been estimated at about $5,000,000.

A fourth disastrous fire was experienced in San Francisco, on September 20th, 1850, by which a loss of property to the amount of $1,000,000 was occasioned. The buildings consumed were mostly old and of an inferior order.

Several months now passed, without the recurrence of another fire, and it was hoped the precautionary preventive measures which had been adopted would prove effectual against such extensive conflagrations in future. But the hope proved a delusive one. On the night of May 3d, 1851, the anniversary of one of the great fires above recorded, another destructive conflagration occurred in this devoted city, by which a large portion of the business part of the town was destroyed. The number of buildings burnt amounted to over a thousand. The loss was estimated at ten millions of dollars. A number of lives were also lost. In one case six persons undertook the care of a store supposed to be fireproof; the iron-doors and window-shutters became expanded by the heat to such a degree that it was impossible to open them, and the inmates were all burnt to death.

Nothing excited so much surprise amid the many surprising things that occurred the night of this fire, as the little resistance that was offered to the progress of the flames by the splendid and substantial iron-buildings that had been constructed in the full conviction that fire could not harm them at least. Even when the insatiate flames were careering wildly elsewhere, laying low the fairest fabrics that man's ingenuity could devise to stay their course, those doing business in these iron-houses felt an abiding confidence that they should escape the general ruin. Others entertained the same idea, and rushed their costliest articles into those warehouses, and when the fire swept out of existence their own combustible houses, consoled themselves with the reflection, that a part at least of their property was saved. But never was confidence more misplaced. It is true iron will not burn, but destruction as total fell upon all such buildings as if they had been made of light wood.

The one seen in our engraving was an iron warehouse which failed to resist the devouring element. It was constructed of corrugated iron, seventy-five feet long, by forty feet wide, and twenty feet high. It was composed of plates of iron each eight feet long. It was manufactured in England, and cost previous to shipment, three thousand dollars. Corrugated iron has all the strength of brickwork, without its great weight; and, although it has proved to be not fireproof, at least on occasions of such overwhelming devastation as destroyed the houses we are speaking of, still it is peculiarly adapted for portable dwellings

Iron-House at San Francisco.

and storehouses, being very light, and packing so close, that the expense of freight is comparatively small.

The following description of the burning of two of these houses is from the San Francisco Herald :—

"We watched the fate of two elegant iron-houses—one situated at the corner of Washington and Sansome streets, and the other occupied by Messrs. Berthelot & Cronise, at the corner of Jackson and Sansome streets, and never was there a more complete wreck, when the fire had done with them. The zinc roof caught first and burnt as fiercely as if made of pine-knots. The flame was of a deep blue and looked most singular, beside that which rose up from surrounding frame buildings. But little smoke issued at first—but the heat was greater than that of a furnace. The iron pillars and plates glowed brightly, in a little while they warped, curled like crisp leaves, opened, let in the flames to the piles of rich merchandise stored within, and in a few moments all was over. With a tremendous crash they fell in ruins to the ground, and long after the wooden buildings around were reduced to ashes, these glowing heaps of iron threw out an intense heat that allowed of no approach. And, indeed, when we consider the fierceness of the heat that arose on that memorable night from hundreds of burning structures, and piles of costly goods—a heat that no one can conceive who was not present—it is not to be wondered at that even iron succumbed before its withering power. From the nature of the materials, however, a less degree of heat would have produced the same effect. Its expansibility will always open the interior of a house constructed of iron to the admission of the flames, and then it is not more secure than if made of wood. In the recent conflagration there were five elegant buildings constructed of plates of cast-iron, three stories high, destroyed, besides any number of corrugated iron-houses. The latter offered no check whatever to the fire. They went down as a matter of course. They have proven equally as insecure as wooden houses, and when burnt, more expensive, because in their case it does require some outlay to clear the ground of the wreck, while in the other nothing but a heap of ashes remains."

With energies undaunted by this fifth conflagration, more serious by far than any which had preceded it, the work of rebuilding was immediately commenced, and carried forward with such characteristic rapidity, that within ten days after the fire over three hundred and fifty buildings were in process of erection, and the greater part of them already occupied.

The sixth conflagration occurred on the 22d of June, just seven weeks subsequently to the one just described.

Thirteen blocks of buildings were consumed, and a number of lives were lost. The property destroyed amounted to from one to two millions of dollars.

These conflagrations, with many others of lesser note, some or all of them, are believed to have been the work of incendiaries. Indeed, previous to the last fire above recorded, it had become demonstrably evident that organized bands of malefactors, composed of convicts from the English penal settlements, and desperadoes from every quarter of the globe, were leagued together for robbery and plunder; who did not hesitate to commit arson and murder in the prosecution of their designs. The highest crimes were matters of every-day occurrence, not merely in remote districts, but in the towns and cities; in San Francisco especially. Under these circumstances, a large number of the most valuable citizens organized themselves into a committee of vigilance, for the purpose of securing the punishment of criminals, at all hazards. They opened a room, at which a certain number of the members, detailed for the purpose, were to be present day and night. When any offence came to their notice which, in their opinion, called for the interference of the committee, all the members were to be summoned by the ringing of a bell. The members all pledged themselves to carry into execution the sentence of the majority of the body so convened.

The committee soon had occasion to inaugurate their administration by a public execution, so deliberately performed, and so unflinchingly avowed, as to leave no doubt of their full determination to carry their designs into effect. On the 10th of June, an English convict from Botany Bay, who gave his name as Jenkins, or Jennings, was arrested in the act of carrying off a safe which he had stolen. He was brought before the committee, by whom he was tried, found guilty, and sentenced to be hung. This sentence was carried into execution the same night in the public square. The coroner's jury, who held an inquest upon the body, named nine members of the committee as specially and directly implicated in the execution. A card was immediately issued, signed by nearly two hundred persons, avowing that they, as members of the committee of vigilance, were all participators in the transaction, equally with those whose names had been given by the coroner's jury.

The committee went on adding to their numbers, and increasing the scope of their operations. Persons known as escaped convicts were ordered to leave the country within five days; and after a show of resistance, finding all opposition useless, they complied with the order. Vessels arriving from the English penal settlements were boarded in the harbor, and those on board who proved to be escaped convicts, were warned not to land. The committee went on to establish a central and branch offices, organized a patrol, and raised funds for carrying on their operations. Persons charged with minor offences were handed over to the public authorities, the committee taking care to keep in their own hands the adjudication of those cases which seemed to require a prompt decision, thus keeping up the *prestige* which they had gained by their first bold act. On the 12th of July, a Sydney convict named Stuart, was brought before the committee on a charge of robbery. He proved to be the ringleader of a gang of desperadoes, who had long infested the country. He was found guilty, and the tolling of the bell summoned the public to witness the act of execution. The criminal was brought out, pinioned, and escorted by more than five hundred members of the committee, and executed in broad day, in the presence of a great crowd, without show of tumult or resistance. Previous to his death he made a long confession of the crimes he had committed, and implicated a number of persons as accomplices.

Subsequently two Sydney burglars named Whittaker and M'Kenzie were arrested, tried, condemned, and sentenced by the vigilance committee to be hung. But a few hours before the period fixed for their execution they were rescued by the governor, with aid of the sheriff and his subordinates. The vigilance committee, believing that the authorities by this act, intended to shield them from all punishment, watched their opportunity, obtained access to the prison where the convicts were confined, took them forcibly out, and carried out their sentence against them, by hanging them upon the outer walls of the building in which their committee-rooms were located.

Several other criminals were arrested and as summarily executed under the direction of the vigilance committee, at Sacramento city, Monterey, and other places—but the details already given are amply sufficient to show the determined course of action pursued by this committee, to repress and punish outrages against person and property, by means they deemed more prompt and sure than those furnished by the ordinary administration of the law. And, although in the executions that took place, not a shadow of doubt existed of the guilt of the convicts—indeed, they all acknowledged the justice of their fate—yet, it is to be regretted that the trial and punishment of these miserable outcasts could not have been left to the legitimate, though perhaps imperfect and tardy process of the courts of justice. But at this distance from the scene of these events, so difficult is it to form a correct judgment as to the necessity that called for the organization of this self-constituted tribunal of justice—so impossible is it to fully appreciate the critical position in which life and property were placed by the congregating there of Botany Bay convicts, and desperadoes from all parts of the world, and who, through the inefficiency of the legal authorities, went "unwhipt of justice"—that we should hesitate before pronouncing condemnation upon the formation and subsequent action of a committee, numbering among its members some of the most respectable and valuable citizens of San Francisco.

Still, there is danger, that, as precedents for future guidance of bodies of men, less cool and unerring in their judgment, and more impulsive and less scrupulous in their proceedings, the formation and acts of this committee may lead to results far more injurious to the community, than a longer endurance of the evils which its measures were intended to eradicate. Heaven grant that the seed thus sown in that susceptible soil may not prove the germ of a bohun-upas hereafter to spring up and poison the moral and social atmosphere of that otherwise promising and thriving young Pacific state.

San Francisco has now (November, 1851), a population of about forty thousand, with one hundred miles of streets laid out, and sustains several daily papers. It has recovered entirely from the disastrous effects of the two great fires of May and June, the space burnt over having been completely rebuilt in far better style than before. Numerous fireproof and stone buildings have been erected, and the city in various respects is far better prepared to resist a conflagration than ever before.

The number of arrivals of steamers and sail-vessels from foreign ports during the past year was close upon two thousand, about half as numerous as those of New York, and much more numerous than those of any other port in the Union. There are now eleven steamers, regularly traversing the Pacific, in addition to five others in the Panama and Oregon trade. There are also about fifty steamers engaged on the river-trade, and over three hundred other crafts of various kinds navigating the rivers and bay. The amount of gold shipped from San Francisco, during 1850, was over forty millions of dollars. That of 1851 will be much larger.

The view of San Francisco, given on page 613, is taken from the foot of Telegraph hill, looking from Ringon point and Mission valley. The city is given boldly in the middle-foreground, while the harbor, with its imposing grandeur and beauty covered with a forest of masts, stretches away in the perspective. The foreground is characteristic and truthful of the neighborhood of the city, and the belongings of the gold country.

SACRAMENTO CITY.—The plan of Sacramento city is very simple. It is situated on the west bank of the Sacramento river, at its junction with the Rio Americano, one hundred and fifteen miles from

San Francisco. The town-plot embraces a square of about one and a half miles to a side. The site of the city was covered with oaks and sycamores of gigantic size, which have been cut down as far as is absolutely necessary to make room for buildings, and the trees that are left standing give the place an air not unlike that of one of the oldest and best-shaded towns of New England. It is laid out in regular right-angles, after the plan of Philadelphia, those streets running east and west named after the alphabet, and those north and south after the arithmetic.

The rapid growth of this "city in the woods" seems like the fabled productions of the magician's wand. In April, 1849, the town contained four houses. Six months later, the number of inhabitants, in tents and houses, was little short of ten thousand. At the present time, the population amounts to about fifteen thousand.

The aspect of Sacramento city on approaching it from the river is decidedly more novel and picturesque than that of any other town in the country. The forest of masts along the embarcadero (but which does not appear in our engraving, as it would intercept the view of the city) rivals the noble growth of the soil.

The city is settled principally by New-Yorkers, New-Jerseymen, and emigrants from the western states. In activity and public spirit it is not behind San Francisco, while its growth, in view of the difference of location is more remarkable.

In the month of January, 1849, a great overflow of the Sacramento river occurred, deluging the country both above and below the city of Sacramento, the flood extending in many places like an immense sea over the whole breadth of the valley. The course of the river was indicated only by the trees and shrubbery with which the banks were covered. A great number of horses and cattle were swept away by the flood and drowned. The wood-cutters and charcoal-burners on the banks of the river were obliged to climb into trees in order to save their lives. On the night of January 9th, the city of Sacramento was entirely submerged, and remained under water for several days. The streets in which the principal business operations were conducted were swept completely through by the raging torrent. Every description of merchandise was borne away in the mighty rush. Boats navigated the streets, taking passengers from the second stories of the dwelling-houses. The ridge of high land in the rear of the city was studded with tents, and man and beast, seeking safety in flight, were crowded together in dire confusion. Sutterville, situated a few miles below Sacramento city, was overflowed. The ranches back of the river suffered the same fate. A large amount of property was destroyed by this inundation, but it is believed that no lives were lost. A strong embankment has since been erected along the bank of the Sacramento, which will protect the city from a like calamity in future.

A serious disturbance occurred during the month of August, 1849, in the city of Sacramento, growing out of the disputes between the squatters and landholders. An armed body of the squatters proceeded through the streets of the city, and a collision ensuing between them and the authorities, several persons were shot and some mortally wounded. The city was placed under martial law, and it was several days before tranquillity was restored.

San Jose (pronounced San-hósa), the late capital of California, is sixty miles south of San Francisco, and nine miles from the south end of San Francisco bay. It is situated in a valley of rich land twenty miles wide by seventy long. It is an old Spanish town, and has some fine gardens, fruit-trees, &c. The climate is considered very fine. From eight o'clock in the morning to four in the evening the sun has great power, and the thermometer rises up to eighty and ninety degrees. The whole day a fine breeze is blowing, so that persons in the shade are very comfortable; but in the sun it is sometimes oppressive. After four o'clock it gradually becomes cool, sometimes making a fire necessary for comfort; indeed, generally a little fire after dark is pleasant. The nights

View of Sacramento City, from the River.

being cool, sleep is sound and refreshing. The sky is ever bright, except when fogs occasionally arise during the night; but when they do, the morning sun soon dispels them.

San José, from its pleasant and healthy locality, will probably become the residence of many wealthy families who do business elsewhere. Many gentlemen, merchants of San Francisco, have already purchased residences here. San José has daily communication with San Francisco, by stage and steamer. A railroad between the two places has also been projected.

MONTEREY, the ancient capital of Alta California, is about one hundred miles south of San Francisco. The situation of the city is admirable. The houses are built on a broad, gentle slope of land, about two miles from Point Pinos, the southern end of the bay of Monterey. They are scattered over an extent of three fourths of a mile, leaving ample room for the growth of the city for many years to come. The outline of the hills in the rear is somewhat similar to those of Staten Island, near the city of New York, but they increase in height as they run to the southeast, till at the distance of four miles they are merged in the mountains of the coast range. The northern shore of the bay is twenty miles distant, curving so far to the west, that the Pacific is not visible from any part of the city. Eastward, a high, rocky ridge, called the Tora mountains, makes a prominent object in the view, and when the air is clear, the Sierra de Gavilàn, beyond the Salinas plains, is distinctly visible.

The harbor of Monterey is equal to any in California. The bight in which vessels anchor is entirely protected from the northwesters, by Seagull point, and from the southeastern winds by mountains in the rear. In the absence of light-houses, the dense fog renders navigation dangerous on this coast, and in spite of an entrance twenty-five miles in breadth, vessels frequently run below Point Pinos, and are obliged to anchor on unsafe ground in Carmel bay. A road leads from the town over the hills to the ex-mission of Carmel situated at the head of the bay, about four miles distant. Just beyond it is Point Lobos, a promontory on the coast, famous for the number of seals and sea-lions which congregate there at low tide.

The trade of Monterey has rapidly increased since the territory of California was ceded to the United States. It contains about two thousand inhabitants.

From the salubrity of the climate and the cheapness of living at Monterey, it will be preferred as a residence by many of those who have retired with a competence from their golden labors. The pine-crowned slopes back of the town contain many sites of unsurpassed beauty for private residences.

With the exception, perhaps, of Los Angeles, Monterey contains the most pleasant society to be found in California. There is a circle of families, American and native, residing there whose genial and refined social character is in strong contrast with the popular idea of California life. In spite of the lack of cultivation, except such instruction as the priests were competent to give, the native population possesses a natural refinement of manners, which would grace the most polished society.

STOCKTON.—This city is situated on sloughs which contain the back waters formed by the junction of the Sacramento and San Joaquin rivers. The town was laid out, in 1849, by Mr. Weaver, who emigrated to the country seven years before, and obtained a grant of eleven square leagues of land from the government, on condition that he would retain settlers for the whole of it within a specified time. In planning the town of Stockton, he displayed a great deal of shrewd business tact, the sale of lots having brought him upward of half a million of dollars. A great disadvantage of the location is the sloughs by which it is surrounded; which in the wet season, render the roads next to impassable. There seems, however, to be no other central point so well adapted to supplying the rich district between the Mokelumne and Tuolumne, and Stockton will evidently continue to grow with a sure and gradual increase.

Stockton has been twice desolated by

fire. The first took place on the night of the 24th of December, 1849, the same night the first fire occurred at San Francisco. By this fire property was destroyed to the amount of a quarter of a million of dollars. Stockton was again visited by conflagration, on the 12th of May, 1851. Both of these fires were believed to be the work of incendiaries.

VALLEJO is a city yet in embryo. It is the site where the seat of government has been permanently located. Vallejo has a water front of about seven miles in extent affording a secure anchorage for vessels of the largest size. It is bounded on the west by Napa bay, on the opposite side of which is Mare island, recommended by the naval commissioners as the best location for the great Pacific navy-yard.

Although Vallejo is but in its infancy, yet many buildings have been put up, and many others are in process of construction. The statehouse, in course of erection, is a substantial building, one hundred feet long by thirty broad, and two stories high. The senate-chamber is in the upper story and the assembly-hall in the lower one, one immediately above the other.

The fine climate and healthy and otherwise advantageous location of the new capital, and the natural resources of the surrounding country, will render Vallejo a most attractive spot.

BENICIA, once thought to be a rival to San Francisco, is situated on the straits of Carquinez thirty-five miles from the ocean. It is a very pretty place. The situation is well-chosen, the land gradually sloping back from the water, with ample space for the spread of the town. The anchorage is excellent, vessels of the largest size being able to lie so near shore as to land their cargoes without lightering. The back country, including the Napa and Sonoma valleys, is one of the finest agricultural districts of California. Notwithstanding these advantages, Benicia must always remain inferior, in commercial importance, to both San Francisco and Sacramento city.

NEW-YORK OF THE PACIFIC, with its awkward but aspiring name, is located on a level plain on the southern shore of Suissin bay, backed by a range of barren mountains. The anchorage is good, but it will never be a large town.

SAN DIEGO is a seaport at the southern extremity of the state of California. It is situated at the foot of a high hill, on a sand flat, two miles wide, reaching from the head of San Diego bay, to False bay. A high promontory, of nearly the same width, runs into the sea four or five miles, and is connected by the flat with the main land. The bay is a narrow arm of the sea, indenting the land some four or five miles, and having twenty feet of water at the lowest tide. San Diego is considered one of the best harbors on the Pacific coast. Before California came into the possession of the United States, the principal trade of San Diego was hides, which were collected there for exportation.

Near San Diego, and within a day's march of the Pacific ocean, at the head of the gulf of California, ancient ruins have been discovered, which will interest the antiquary as much, perhaps, as the discovery of gold, has thousands of others. Portions of temples, dwellings, lofty stone pyramids (seven of these within a mile square), and massive granite rings or circular walls, round venerable trees, columns and blocks of hieroglyphics, all speak of some ancient race of men, now for ever gone, their history actually unknown to any of the existing families of mankind. In some points, these ruins resemble the recently discovered cities of Palenque, &c., near the Atlantic or Mexican gulf coast; in others, the ruins of ancient Egypt; in others, again, the monuments of Phœnicia, and yet in many features they differ from all that have been referred to. It is said the discoverers deem them to be antediluvian, while the present Indians have a tradition of a great civilized nation, which their ferocious forefathers utterly destroyed. The region of the ruins is called by the Indians "the valley of mystery."

There are many other towns and cities in California, but they are increasing so rapidly in numbers, extent, and population, that it is futile to attempt to describe them even had we room. Probably a week does not pass without witnessing the foundation of some new town or future city. Some idea may be formed of the extent of settlement in California, from the following list of post-offices already established, with the names of the towns and counties in which they are located. Those in *italic* are county-seats:—

OFFICES.	COUNTIES.	OFFICES.	COUNTIES.
Antioch,	Contra Costa	*Nevada,*	Nevada
Auburn,	Placer	Nicolaus,	Sutter
Benicia,	Solano	Oak Spring,	Tuolumne
Bidwell's Bar,	Butte	Park's Bar,	Yuba
Big Bar,	Trinity	Placerville,	El Dorado
Chico,	Butte	Quartzburg,	Mariposa
Colusi,	Colusi	Rough and Ready,	Nevada
Coloma,	El Dorado	*San Francisco,*	S. Francisco
Dobbin's Branch,	Yuba	*Sacramento,*	Sacramento
Double Springs,	Calaveras	Salmon Falls,	El Dorado
Downieville,	Yuba	Santa Clara,	Santa Clara
Foster's Bar,	Yuba	San Jose,	Santa Clara
Fremont,	Yolo	*Santa Cruz,*	Santa Cruz
Georgetown,	El Dorado	San Juan,	Monterey
Goodyear's Bar,	Yuba	*San Luis Obispo,*	S. L. Obispo
Hamilton,	Butte	*Santa Barbara,*	Sta. Barbara
Jackson,	Calaveras	*San Diego,*	San Diego
Knight's Ferry,	San Joaquin	*Shasta,*	Shasta
Lassen's	Butte	*Sonoma,*	Sonoma
Los Angeles,	Los Angeles	*Sonora,*	Tuolumne
Louisville,	El Dorado	Staple's Ranch,	Calaveras
Mariposa,	Mariposa,	*Stockton,*	San Joaquin
Martinez,	Contra Costa	Trinidad,	Trinity
Marysville,	Yuba	VALLEJO,	Solano
Mokelumne Hill,	Calaveras	*Vernon,*	Sutter
Monroeville,	Colusi	Volcano,	Calaveras
Moon's Ranch,	Colusi	*Weaverville,*	Trinity
Monterey,	Monterey	Wood's Diggins,	Tuolumne
Mormon Island,	Sacramento	Yuba City,	Yuba
Napa,	Napa		

MINERAL WEALTH OF CALIFORNIA.—The gold region of California is about six hundred miles long, and eighty miles broad, following the line of the Sierra Nevada. It embraces within its limits those entensive ranges of hills which rise on the eastern border of the plain of the Sacramento and San Joaquin, and extending eastwardly from fifty to sixty miles, they attain an elevation of about four thousand feet, and terminate at the base of the main ridge of the Sierra Nevada. There are numerous streams which have their sources in the springs of the Sierra, and receive the water from its melting snows, and that which falls in rain during the wet season.

These streams form rivers, which have cut their channels through the ranges of foot hills westwardly to the plain, and disembogue into the Sacramento and San Joaquin. These rivers are from ten to fifteen, and probably some of them twenty miles apart.

The principal formation or substratum in these hills is talcose slate; the superstratum, sometimes penetrating to a great depth, is quartz. This, however, does not cover the entire face of the country, but extends in large bodies in various directions—is found in masses and small fragments on the surface, and seen along the ravines, and in the mountains overhanging the rivers, and in the hill sides in its original beds. It crops out in the valleys and on the tops of the hills, and forms a striking feature of the entire country over which it extends. From innumerable evidence and indications, it has come to be the universally admitted opinion among the miners and intelligent men who have examined this region, that the *gold, whether in detached particles and in pieces, or in veins, was created in combination with the quartz.* Gold is not found on the surface of the country, presenting the appearance of having been thrown up and scattered in all directions by volcanic action. It is only found in particular localities, and attended by peculiar circumstances and indications. It is found in the bars and shoals of the rivers, in ravines, and in what are called the dry-diggings, and in all these localities is accessible to any man who has the strength to use a pan or washer, a spade and pickaxe.

The rivers, in forming their channels, or breaking their way through the hills, have come in contact with the quartz containing the gold veins, and by constant attrition cut the gold into fine flakes and dust, and it is found among the sand and gravel of their beds at those places where the swiftness of the current reduces it, in the dry season, to the narrowest possible limits, and where a wide margin is, consequently, left on each side, over which the water rushes, during the wet season, with great force.

As the velocity of some streams is greater than others, so is the gold found in fine or coarse particles, apparently corresponding to the degree of attrition to which it has been exposed. The water from the hills and upper valleys, in finding its way to the rivers, has cut deep ravines, and, wherever it came in contact with the quartz, has dissolved or crumbled it in pieces.

Gold-Washing at the Diggings in California.

In the dry season these channels are mostly without water, and gold is found in the beds and margins of many of them in large quantities, but in a much coarser state than in the rivers; owing, undoubtedly, to the moderate flow and temporary continuance of the current, which has reduced it to smooth shapes, not unlike pebbles, but had not sufficient force to reduce it to flakes or dust.

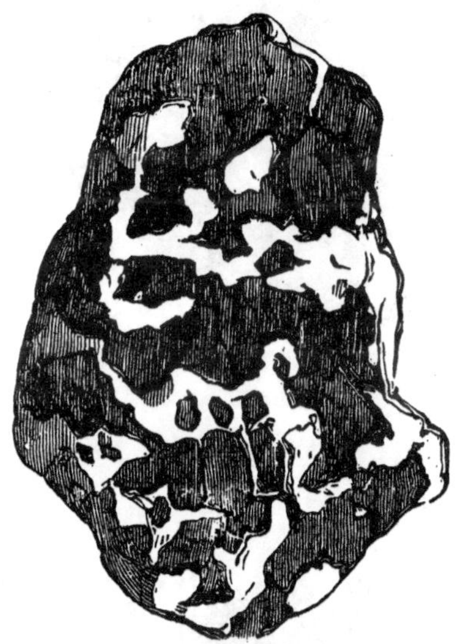

Rounded water-worn Pebble of Gold with Quartz.

The dry-diggings are places where quartz containing gold has cropped out, and been disintegrated, crumbled to fragments, pebbles, and dust, by the action of water and the atmosphere. The gold has been left as it was made, in all imaginable shapes; in pieces of all sizes, and from one grain to several pounds in weight. The evidences that it was created in combination with quartz are too numerous and striking to admit of doubt or cavil. *They are found in combination in large quantities.*

A very large proportion of the pieces of gold found in these situations have more or less quartz adhering to them. In many specimens they are so combined they can not be separated without reducing the whole mass to powder and subjecting it to the action of quicksilver.

This gold, not having been exposed to the attrition of a strong current of water, retains, in a great degree, its original conformation.

These diggings, in some places, spread over valleys of considerable extent, which have the appearance of alluvion, formed by washings from the adjoining hills, of decomposed quartz and slate earth, and vegetable matter.

In addition to these facts, several vein-mines have been taken, showing the minute connexion between the gold and the rock, and indicating a value hitherto unknown in gold-mining.

These veins do not present the appearance of places where gold may have been lodged by some violent eruption. It is combined with the quartz, in all imaginable forms and degrees of richness.

The rivers present very striking and, it would seem, conclusive evidence respecting the quantity of gold remaining undiscovered in the quartz veins. It is not probable that the gold in the dry diggings, and that in the rivers—the former in lumps, the latter in dust—was created by different processes. That which is found in the rivers has undoubtedly been cut or worn from the veins in the rock, with which their currents have come in contact. All of them appear to be equally rich. This is shown by the fact that a laboring man may collect nearly as much in one river as he can in another. They intersect and cut through the gold region, running from east to west, at irregular distances of fifteen to twenty, and perhaps some of them thirty miles apart.

Hence it appears that the gold veins are equally rich in all parts of that most remarkable section of country. Were it wanting, there are further proofs of this in the ravines and dry diggings, which uniformly confirm what nature so plainly shows in the rivers.

It is now a well-demonstrated fact that the gold found in the beds of the streams has been cut or worn from the veins in the quartz through which they have forced their way, and considering that they are all rich, and are said to be nearly equally productive, we may form some idea of the vast amount of treasure remaining undisturbed in the veins which

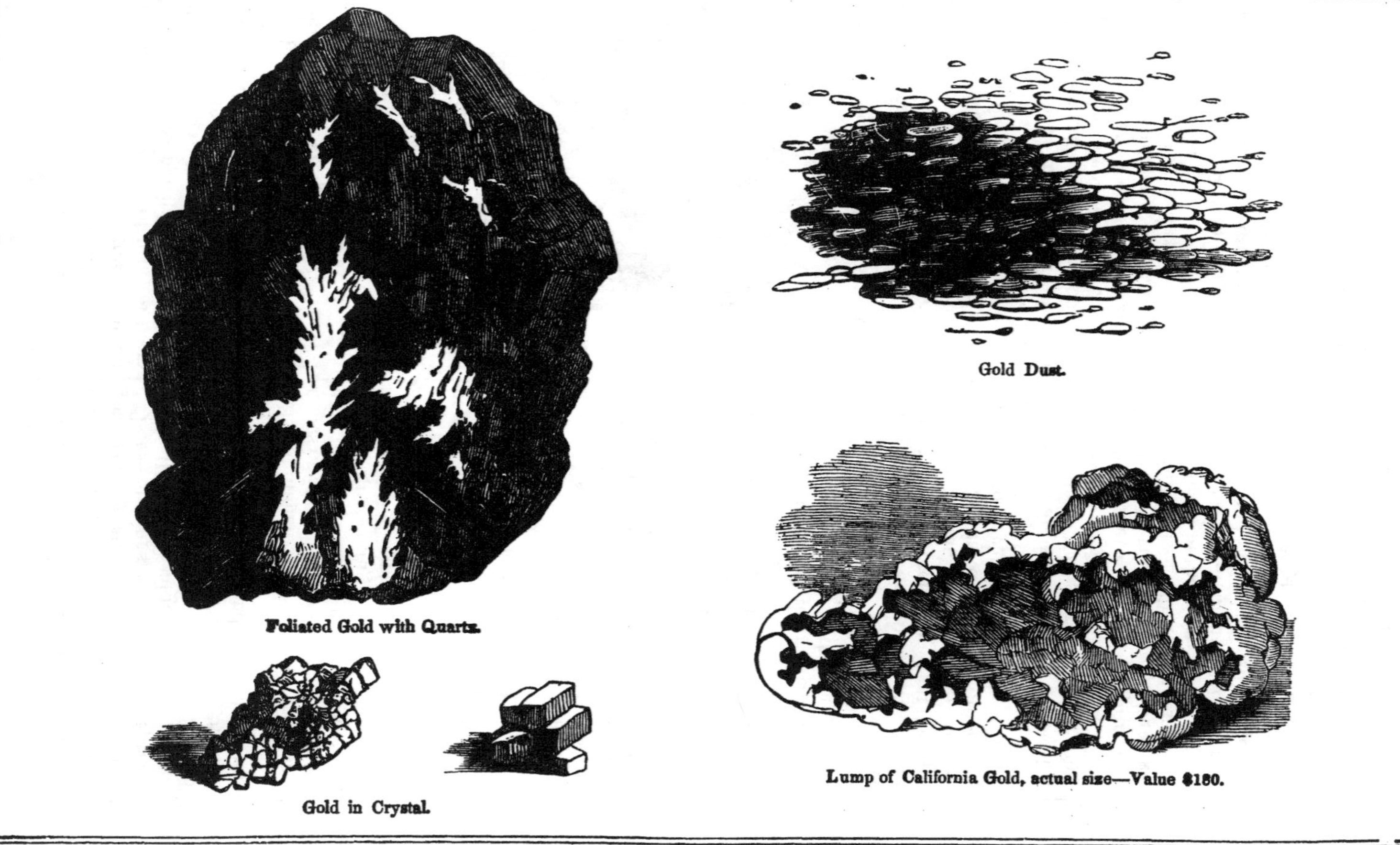

Foliated Gold with Quartz.

Gold in Crystal.

Gold Dust.

Lump of California Gold, actual size—Value $180.

run through the masses of rock in various directions over a space comprising nearly fifty thousand square miles.

If we may be allowed to form a conjecture respecting the richness of these veins from the quantity of lump or coarse gold found in the dry diggings, where it appears to occupy nearly the same superfices it did originally in the rock—its specific gravity being sufficient to resist ordinary moving causes—we shall be led to an estimate almost beyond human calculation and belief. Yet, there is no plausible reason why the veins which remain in the quartz may not be as valuable as those which have become separated from the decomposed rock. This matter is being satisfactorily decided by actual discoveries. These gold-bearing veins have, as yet, been pierced only at intervals, but the developments thus made, indicate that in her fields and ledges of auriferous quartz, California possesses an element of wealth, of incalculable extent and value.

The first experiments in quartz-mining were made in 1850, in Mariposa. An injudicious location and light machinery rendered this first trial in extracting gold from quartz comparatively a failure. The works were soon discontinued. Since then, improvements in machinery have been made, more eligible locations selected, and quartz-mining operations are being prosecuted with vigor and success.

The present great centre of quartz-mining is Grass valley, in Nevada county. This town is distant northeasterly from Sacramento city about seventy miles. The first quartz discoveries at this locality, were made about the month of November, 1850; but no machinery was erected until the latter part of the winter. So rich did the veins on "Gold hill" prove, even by the slow process of crushing in hand-mortars and washing in water only, that shafts were sunk on almost every hill for several miles around, in nearly every instance striking rich veins. There are between thirty and forty hills opened in the single township of Grass valley (four and a half miles square), and exhibiting incontestable evidence that extensive veins of gold-bearing quartz underlie them all.

The machinery for crushing the quartz rock is of course very expensive, and not nearly all of those possessing quartz claims have the means wherewith to purchase it; consequently, the principle of a division of labor commences to operate, and in the most favorable manner for the miner; that is, the miner gets out the rock from his claim, and then sells it to the parties owning machinery, who crush it and extract the gold.

There are now about eight mills in successful operation in and near the village of Centreville, in Grass valley township. Many others are in process of erection at the same locality, and still others in various parts of Nevada county. Centreville is already a thriving village of fifteen hundred to two thousand inhabitants, with some good dwellings, hotels, stores, markets, &c., and a saw-mill in active operation, turning out six thousand feet of lumber per day, which finds ready sale at eighty-five dollars per thousand.

Gold-mining may be said to be but in its infancy in California. The gold hitherto obtained, by individual effort, though amounting to over a hundred millions of dollars, has been gathered by no more effort than literally scratching the earth's surface, and will prove but an inconsiderable sum, when compared with the treasures which combined labor and capital, with the aid of efficient machinery, will yet bring to light.

The present condition of California is rich in hope and promise. While the mines continue to yield their golden tribute without abatement, many are turning their attention to agricultural pursuits, and large quantities of land have been taken up and placed under culture. Society is rapidly assuming a regular and permanent shape. The tide of immigration continues to flow steadily in filling the state with a hardy, enterprising population. Under the benign influence of a republican government, with life and property protected, and laws properly respected and efficiently administered, this latest child of our cherished Union can not fail to stride forward with giant-steps to the maturity of its strength, and the flush of consummate prosperity.

THE TERRITORIES.

TERRITORY OF OREGON.

Northwestern America is probably the largest portion of the world yet unsubdued by cultivation. Till very recently, in a region comprising more than four millions of square miles, two or three stations on the Pacific coast, and a few hunting-posts and missionary establishments in the interior, were the only points inhabited by civilized man.

A portion of this territory is the Oregon country, bounded on the north by the parallel fifty-four degrees forty minutes, on the east by the Rocky mountains, on the south by the Klamet range, or Snowy mountains, extending along or near the forty-second parallel, and on the west by the Pacific ocean. The British portion includes all north of latitude forty-nine degrees, while that belonging to the United States comprises all lying south of that parallel. It extends about five hundred miles north and south, and of average breadth of about five hundred miles—being narrower toward the north and broader toward the south, the Rocky mountains running in a southeasterly direction. It contains, therefore, about two hundred and fifty thousand square miles.

The Oregon territory is divided into three natural belts or sections, viz.: 1st. That between the Pacific ocean and the President's range, or Cascade mountains, called the *western section ;* 2d. That between the Cascade and Blue mountain range, or *middle* section; 3d. That between the Blue and Rocky mountain chains, or *eastern* section: and this division will equally apply to the soil, climate, and productions. All these divisions are crossed by the Columbia river; the main stream is formed, in the middle region, by the union of several branches flowing from the Rocky mountains, and receiving in their course several smaller streams, draining the intermediate sections.

The Cascade range runs parallel with the seacoast, the whole length of the territory, and rising in many places, in regular cones, from twelve to more than fourteen thousand feet above the level of the sea.

The distance from the seashore to this chain, is from one hundred to one hundred and fifty miles, and the ridge almost interrupts the communication between the first and second sections, except where the Columbia river forces a passage through it; there are a few mountain passes, but they are difficult, and only to be attempted late in the spring and summer. The climate of this section is mild throughout the year, experiencing neither the extreme cold of winter nor the heat of summer. The prevailing winds in the summer are from the northward and westward, and in the winter, from the southward, and westward, and southeast, which are tempestuous. The winter is supposed to last from December to February. Rains usually begin to fall in November, and last till March; but they are not heavy, though frequent. Snow sometimes falls, but it seldom lies over three days. The frosts are early, occurring in the latter part of August; this, however, is to be accounted for by the proximity of the mountains. Fruit-trees blossom early in April. The soil, in the northern parts, varies from a light brown loam to a thin vegetable earth, with gravel and sand as a subsoil; in the middle parts, from a rich heavy loam and unctious clay to a deep heavy black loam, on a trap-rock; and in the southern (the Willamette valley), the soil is generally good, varying from a black vegetable loam to decomposed basalt, with stiff clay, and portions of loose gravel-soil. The hills are generally basalt, and stone, and slate; between the Umpqua river and the southern boundary the rocks are primitive, consisting of slate, hornblende, and granite, which produce a gritty and poor soil; there are, however, some places of rich prairie, covered with oaks. It is, for the most part, a well-timbered country. It is intersected with the spurs or offsets from the Cascade mountains, which render its surface much broken; these are covered with a dense forest. The timber consists of pines, firs, spruce, oaks (red and white), ash, arbutus, arbor vitæ, cedar, poplar, maple, willow, cherry, and tew, with a close undergrowth of hazel, rubus, roses, &c. The richest and best soil is found on the second or middle prairie, and is best adapted for agriculture; the high and low being excellent for pasture-land. The climate and soil are admirably adapted for all kinds of grain—wheat, rye, oats, barley, peas, &c. Indian corn does not thrive in any part of this territory where it has been tried. Many fruits appear to succeed well, particularly the apple and pear. Vegetables grow exceedingly well, and yield most abundantly.

The Blue mountains are irregular in their course, and occasionally interrupted, but generally running in a northerly direction; they commence in the Klamet range, near the southern boundary of the territory; they are broken through by the Saptin or Snake river, at the junction of the Kooskooske river, and branch off in hills of moderate elevation, until they again appear on the north side of the Columbia river, above the Okanagan river, passing in a north direction, until they unite with the Rocky mountains, in latitude fifty-three degrees north. The climate of the middle section is variable; during the summer the atmosphere is much drier and warmer, and the winter much colder, than in the western section. Its extremes of heat and cold are more frequent and greater, the mercury, at times, falling as low as minus eighteen degrees of Fahrenheit, in winter, and rising to one hundred and eighty degrees in the shade of summer: the daily difference of temperature is about forty degrees of Fahrenheit. It has, however, been found extremely salubrious, possessing a pure and healthy air. No dews fall in this section. The soil is, for the most part, a light sandy loam; in the valleys a rich alluvial; and the hills are generally barren. The surface is about one thousand feet above the level of the western section, and is generally a rolling prairie country. The part lying to the north of the parallel of forty-eight degrees is very much broken with mountain-chains and rivers, consequently barren and very rugged. From the great and frequent changes in its temperature, it is totally unfit for agriculture, but is well supplied with game of all kinds that are found in the country. In the centre of this section, and near and around the junction of the Saptin or Snake and Columbia rivers, is an extensive rolling country, which is well adapted for grazing. South of the Columbia, and extending to the southern boundary of the territory, it is destitute of timber or wood, unless the wormwood (artemisia) may be so called, although there are portions of it that might be advantageously farmed.

The Rocky mountains form the boundary of the eastern section, and of the territory. They commence on the Arctic coast, and continue an almost unbroken chain until they merge in the Andes of South America. That part forming the eastern boundary of Oregon, extending north from the Great South pass, at latitude forty-two degrees north, to about the fifty-second degree, at the Committee's Punch-bowl pass, forms an almost impenetrable barrier, the few passes between being very difficult and dangerous. The climate of the eastern section is extremely variable. In each day there are all the changes incident to spring, summer, autumn, and winter. There are places where small farms might be located, but they are few in number. The soil is rocky and uneven, and presents an almost unbroken barren waste. Stupendous mountain-spurs traverse it in all directions, affording little level ground. Snow lies on the mountains nearly, if not quite, throughout the year. It is exceedingly dry and arid, rains seldom falling, and but little snow. This country is partially timbered, and the soil much impregnated with salts.

The Columbia is the great river of the territory. Its northern branch takes its rise in the Rocky mountains, in latitude fifty degrees north, longitude one hundred and sixteen west; thence it pursues a northern route, to near M'Gillivary's pass, in the Rocky mountains. At the boat encampment, the river is three thousand six hundred feet above the level of the sea (here it receives two small tributaries—the Canoe river, and that from the Committee's Punch-bowl), thence it turns south, having some obstructions to its safe navigation, and receiving many tributaries in its course to Colville, among which are the Kootanie, or Flat Bow, and the Flat Head, or Clarke river, from the east, and that of Colville from the west. This great river is bounded thus far on its course, by a range of high mountains, well wooded, and in places expands into a line of lakes before it reaches Colville, where it is two thousand forty-nine feet above the level of the sea, having a fall of five hundred and fifty feet in two hundred and twenty miles. To the south of this it trends to the westward, receiving the Spokan river from the east, which is not navigable, and takes its rise in the lake of Cœur d'Alene. Thence it pursues a westerly course for about sixty miles, receiving several smaller streams, and, at its bend to the south, it is joined by the Okanagan, a river that has its source in a line of lakes, affording canoe and boat navigation for quite a distance to the northward. The Columbia thence passes to the southward until it reaches Wallawalla, in the latitude of forty-five degrees, a distance of one hundred and sixty miles, receiving the Piscous, Y'Akama, and Point de Boise, or Entyatecoom, from the west, which take their rise in the Cascade range, and also its great southeastern branch, the Saptin or Lewis, which has its source in the Rocky mountains, near our southern boundary, and brings a large quantity of water to increase the volume of the principal stream.

The Lewis is not navigable, even for canoes, except in reaches. The rapids are extensive and of frequent occurrence. It generally passes between the Rocky mountain spurs and the Blue mountains. It receives the Kooskooske, Salmon, and several other rivers, from the east and west—the former from the Rocky mountains, the latter from the Blue mountains—and, were it navigable, would much facilitate the intercourse with this part of the country. Its length, to its junction with the Columbia, is five hundred and twenty miles. The Columbia, at Wallawalla, is one thousand two hundred and eighty-six feet above the level of the sea, and about thirty-five hundred feet wide; it now takes its last turn to the westward, receiving the Umatilla, Quisnel's, John Day's, and De Chute rivers from the south, and Cathlatate's from the north, pursuing its rapid course of eighty miles, previous to passing through the range of Cascade mountains, in a series of falls and rapids that obstruct its flow, and form insurmountable barriers to the passage of boats by water during the floods. These difficulties, however, are overcome by portages. Thence there is still-water navigation, for forty miles, when its course is again obstructed by rapids. Thence to the ocean, one hundred and twenty miles, it is navigable for vessels of twelve feet draught of water at the lowest state of the river, though obstructed by many sand-bars. In this part it receives the Willamette from the south, and the Cowelitz from the north. The former is navigable for small vessels twenty miles, to the mouth of the Klackamus, three miles below its falls; the latter can not be called navigable, except for a small part of the year, during the floods, and then only for canoes and barges. The width of the Columbia, within twenty miles of its mouth, is much increased, and it joins the ocean between Cape Disappointment and Point Adams, forming a sand-spit from each, by deposite, and causing a dangerous bar, which greatly impedes its navigation and entrance.

Frazer's river takes its rise in the Rocky mountains, near the source of the Canoe river, taking a northwesterly course of eighty miles; it then turns to the southward, receiving the waters of Stuart's river, which rises in a chain of lakes near the northern boundary of the territory; it then pursues a southerly course, receiving the waters of the Chilcotin, Pinkslitsa, and several smaller streams, from the west, and those of Thompson's river, and other streams, from the east (these take their rise in lakes, and are navigable in canoes, by making portages); and, under the parallel of forty-nine degrees, it breaks through the Cascade range, in a succession of falls and rapids, and, after a westerly course of seventy miles, it empties into the gulf of Georgia, in the latitude of forty-nine degrees and seven minutes north. The latter portion is navigable for vessels that can pass its bar drawing twelve feet water; its whole length being three hundred and fifty miles.

The Chikeelis is next in importance. It has three sources among the range of hills that intersect the country north of the Columbia river. After a very tortuous course, and receiving some small streams issuing from the lakes in the high ground near the head-waters of Hood's canal and Puget's sound, it disembogues in Grey's harbor; it is not navigable except for canoes; its current is rapid, and the stream much obstructed.

To the south of the Columbia there are many small streams, but three of of which deserve the name of rivers: the Umpqua, Too-too-tut-na or Rogue's river, and the Klamet, which latter empties into the ocean south of the parallel of forty-two degrees. None of these form harbors capable of receiving a vessel of more than eight feet draught of water, and the bars for most part of the year, are impassable, from the surf that sets in on the coast. The character of the great rivers is peculiar—rapid, and sunken much below the level of the country, with perpendicular banks; indeed, they are, as it were, in trenches, it being extremely difficult to get at the water in many places, owing to the steep basaltic walls; and, during the rise, they are in many places confined by dalles, which back the water some distance, submerging islands and tracts of low prairie, giving the appearance of extensive lakes.

History.—On the 7th of May, 1792, Captain Robert Gray, in the ship Columbia, of Boston, discovered and entered the Columbia river; to which he gave the name of his vessel. He was the first person that established the fact of the existence of this great river, and this gave to the United States the right of discovery. In 1804–'5, Captains Lewis and Clark, under the direction of the government of the United States, explored the country from the mouth of the Missouri to the mouth of the Columbia, and spent the winter of 1805–'6 at the mouth of the Columbia. This exploration of the river Columbia, the first ever made, constituted another ground of the claim of the United States to the country. In 1808, the Missouri fur company, at St. Louis, established a trading post beyond the Rocky mountains, on the head-waters of Lewis river, the first ever formed on any of the waters of the Columbia. In 1810, the Pacific fur company, under John Jacob Astor, of New York, was formed; and in 1811 they founded Astoria, eight miles from the mouth of the Columbia, as their principal trading post, and proceeded to establish others in the interior. A little later in the same year, the Northwest company sent a detachment to form establishments on the Columbia; but when they arrived at the mouth of the river they found the post occupied. In consequence of the exposure of Astoria by the war of 1812, the post was sold out to the Northwest company. At the close of the war, Astoria was restored, by order of the British government, to its original founders, agreeably to the first article of the treaty of Ghent. Various attempts have been made since the war to renew the fur-trade in Oregon. In 1821, the Hudson's bay and Northwest company, who had previously been rivals, were united, and since that time have greatly extended their establishment in the region of Oregon.

Astoria, on the Columbia River.

That section of Oregon watered by the Columbia river and its tributaries, was for a long time a subject of dispute between the United States and Great Britain. But by a treaty concluded at Washington, on the fifteenth of June, 1846, this long-pending question, which at one time seriously threatened to break the harmony existing between the two nations was put for ever at rest, by fixing the parallel of division between the respective portions, as given at the commencement of this description. There have been for some years several missionary stations at different points in Oregon, and since the settlement of the question of boundary, new ones have been established.

It will be almost impossible to give an idea of the extensive fisheries in the rivers, and on the coast. They all abound in salmon of the finest flavor, which run twice a year, beginning in May and October, and appear inexhaustible; the whole population live upon them. The Columbia produces the largest, and probably affords the greatest numbers. There are some few of the branches of the Columbia that the spring fish do not enter, but they are plentifully supplied in the fall. The great fishery of the Columbia is at the Dalles; but all the rivers are well supplied. The last one on the northern branch of the Columbia is near Colville, at the Kettle falls; but salmon are found above this in the river and its tributaries. In Frazer's river the salmon are said to be very numerous, but not large; they are unable to get above the falls, some eighty miles from the sea. In the rivers and sounds are found carp-soles, salmon, salmon-trout, sturgeon, cod, flounders, ray, perch, herring, lamprey-eels, and a kind of smelt called "shrow," in great abundance; also large quantities of shell-fish, viz., crabs, clams, oysters, mussels, &c., which are all used by the natives, and constitute the greater proportion of their food. Whales, in numbers, are found along the coast, and are frequently captured by the Indians in and at the mouth of the straits of Juan de Fuca.

Abundance of game exists, such as elk, deer, antelope, bears, wolves, foxes, muskrats, martens, beavers, a few grizzly bears, and siffleurs, which are eaten by the Canadians. In the middle section, or that designated as the rolling prairie, no game is found. In the eastern section the buffalo is met with. The fur-bearing animals are decreasing in numbers yearly, particularly south of the parallel of forty-eight degrees; indeed, it is very doubtful whether they are sufficiently numerous to repay the expense of hunting them. The Hudson's bay company have almost the exclusive monopoly of this business. They have decreased owing to being hunted without regard to season. This is not, however, the case to the north; there the company have been left to exercise their own rule, and prevent the indiscriminate slaughter of either old or young, out of the proper season. In the spring and fall the rivers are literally covered with geese, ducks and other water-fowl.

In 1848, a bill passed both houses of Congress, and was approved by the president on the 14th of August, by which Oregon was erected into a territorial government, and soon after the necessary officers were sent out, and the government organized.

Oregon City, the territorial capital, is situated about thirty miles up the Willamette river, and two miles above the Clackmas rapids, which prevent all navigation to the city. Few other places in the Union have such immense water privileges, and many large saw-mills are already in operation. The view we have placed on the opposite page, is from a drawing taken on the spot in 1847, since which time it has considerably increased. The population in 1850, was 702.

Portland, twelve miles below the falls may be considered as the port of Oregon City. Its trade with the Pacific towns, and also with those of the Atlantic, especially with New York, is prosperous and increasing. Population about 1,000.

Astoria, near the mouth of the Columbia, referred to on a previous page, has a good harbor, and many natural advantages for becoming eventually a great

Oregon City, on the Willamette River.

commercial dépôt. At present, however, there are but a few buildings in the place. Astoria is a port of entry.

FORT VANCOUVER, on the north bank of the Columbia river, one hundred miles from its mouth, is the principal trading post of the Hudson's Bay company, west of the mountains. Ships drawing fourteen feet water, can ascend twenty miles further up the river. The establishment consists of about hundred houses enclosed by picket-fences, and defended by armed bastions and a block-house. A catholic church is the only building of note. The inhabitants are chiefly South-Sea Islanders in the employ of the company. The establishment is on an extensive scale, and the centre of vast interests—all the company's Indian trade being conducted here. Extensive agricultural operations for the support of the traders, are carried on. The farm contains about three thousand acres. The stock of cattle and sheep is very large, and is rapidly increasing in numbers and improving in breed from the importation of European stock. The mixed breed of sheep yields from twelve to eighteen pounds of fleece. The mills and outposts of the fort extend several miles above on the river.

The upper colony from the United States is situated on the Willamette river, ninety-four miles from its entrance into the Columbia. It consists of about one hundred families, who raise considerable grain, and have about four thousand head of cattle, extensive fields of wheat, potatoes, peas, and vegetables, of all descriptions. They have hogs, poultry, &c., in abundance.

FORT WALLAWALLA is on the south side of the Columbia, ten miles below the entrance of Lewis river. On the Willamette river, fifty-five miles above its entrance into the Columbia, is M'Key's settlement, and twelve miles above, is Jarvis' settlement, which contain about twenty families.

FORT COLVILLE is on the south side of Clark's river, below the Kettle falls, just before it enters the Columbia. Here is a considerable farming establishment.

FORT OKANAGAN is at the entrance into the Columbia of the river of that name, one hundred miles below Clark's river. The Hudson's Bay company have several other trading posts in this territory.

FORT NESQUALLY, on Puget's sound, is occupied by the "Puget's Sound Agricultural Company." Their farms are very extensive, and are kept in a high state of cultivation. They supply provisions to the Hudson's Bay company's servants west of the mountains, and export largely to the Sandwich Islands and the Russian post of Sitka.

There are a few other small but thriving villages and settlements in Oregon.

Since the discovery of gold in California, a great demand has arisen for the agricultural products of Oregon, and, as a consequence, a commercial connexion has been the result. The export of lumber has been large. This incipient commerce will not be transitory—the demand for building materials is constantly on the increase, and that for breadstuffs and provisions will last as long as mining is the chief employment in California. Some commercial intercourse is maintained also with the Sandwich Islands and the Russian settlements on the north. But with all these fortuitous circumstances that have attended the first settlement of the territory, it must still remain much as it is—a mere agricultural and pastoral country, unless some means of easy and rapid communication can be maintained with the western states and the Atlantic coast. A railroad is the only solution of this difficulty. The one proposed by Mr. Whitney seems to have some claims to consideration, and by its means the shores of Lake Michigan would be brought into a juxtaposition with the mouth of the Columbia river. The details for the construction of such an avenue, chiefly through a country infested with hostile Indians, and through mountain passes almost inaccessible, have been laid before Congress, and are favorably spoken of; but to mature plans, and obtain capital for such a work, seems to offer almost insuperable difficulties even to its commencement. Still we trust the day is not far distant that will witness the triumphant completion of this gigantic enterprise.

TERRITORY OF MINNESOTA.

THE early history of MINNESOTA is involved in much obscurity, though Father Hennepin in 1680, and Baron La Hontan in 1689, both Frenchmen, visited that region, but subsequently gave narratives to the world, so strangely intermixed with the truth and seeming fable, that little reliance was placed on their statements. It would seem on investigation, that for several hundred years the possession of the land was fiercely contested by different Indian nations; mainly between the great tribes of Dakotahs or Sioux and the Algonquins or Chippewas. The latter, from their eastern location on Lake Superior, about the falls of St. Mary, and earlier intercourse with the French fur-traders, became first possessed of firearms, which gave them a superiority that enabled them to drive the Dakotahs from the rich midland hunting-grounds, rice and fish lakes, in the country about the head waters of the Mississippi.

The dispossessed bands of the Dakotahs moved westward, sweeping in their progress, the Sheans, the Iowas, and other tribes from their lands; until, in the course of time, the fugitive Dakotahs of the Upper Mississippi, became the fiercest lords of the vast buffalo-plains of the Upper Missouri. By a treaty negotiated under the protection of the United States, at Fort Crawford, near Prairie du Chien, in 1825, between all the different tribes of the northwest, their respective boundaries were defined; and thenceforward comparative peace ensued between them.

The name Minnesota is derived from the Indian name of the St. Peter's river, the principal local stream of the country. The Indians, living on its banks, called it thus on account of the different appearance of the waters from those of the Mississippi. At the junction of the two streams, the waters of the last-named river may be observed generally tinged of a chocolate color, derived from the extensive tamarac and pine swamps toward the north, in which it partly has its head springs; while the waters of the Minnesota are entirely different in appearance, being light-colored and clear. The name is compounded of two words, *minne*, "water," and *sotah*, "sky-colored." This poetical designation, "The territory of the sky-colored water," receives additional ornament in the Dakotah name bestowed on the junction of the river with the Mississippi, that of *Mendota*, or "Mingling of the Waters." This is also the appellation of the Indian trading-town at the mouth.

The United States had little authority over this region till 1812. In 1816, a law of Congress excluded foreigners from the Indian trade; and for the encouragement of our citizens the military post at Fort Snelling was established in 1819. Among the explorers of this country, the names of Pike, Carver, Long, Beltrami, Cass, Schoolcraft, Nicollet, Owen, &c., will ever be intimately connected with its history. The honor of verifying the sources of the Mississippi belongs to Schoolcraft.

Previous to the erection of Iowa into a state, all that portion of Minnesota west of the Mississippi was included in Iowa territory, and that part immediately on the river was embraced in the county of Clayton. The organization of Iowa into a state threw all north of 43° 30′ without the bounds of any organized government. Little, if any, inconvenience resulted to the white inhabitants in the excluded portion, as it was entirely Indian country, and under the control of the United States laws "regulating trade and intercourse with the Indians." But in 1848, Wisconsin was admitted into the Union; and her boundary on the north and northwest being the St. Croix, cut off the principal portion of two organized counties of the territory of Wisconsin—viz., St. Croix and La Pointe—comprising a considerable population, one county-seat, and important interests engaged in lumbering and trading. The people of this portion of the "Territory of Wisconsin," thus suddenly deprived of a judiciary, and the means of a proper administration of the laws, as the only remedy for the threatened evils of such a state of things, met in convention, and resolved that, inasmuch as the law establishing Wisconsin territory was not specially repealed by the erection of Wisconsin state, that their country was, *de facto*, said territory; and the acting governor of Wisconsin, Hon. John Catlin, secretary of the said territory, coinciding in this view, issued his proclamation for the election of a delegate to Congress. The people also memorialized Congress in regard to their condition, and instructed their delegate to ask the erection of a new territory, to be called "*Minnesota*." This was granted, by act of Congress, on the 3d of March, 1849. Shortly after, Alexander Ram ay was appointed governor. St. Paul's was made the capital, where the government was soon after organized.

The territory of Minnesota, thus created is situated between 43° 30′ and 49° north latitude, and 89° 30′ and 102° 10′ west longitude; and is bounded north by British America, east by Lake Superior and the state of Wisconsin, south by the state of Iowa, and west by Missouri territory. Of the immense territory included within these limits, 22,336 square miles belonged to the late territory of Wisconsin, and the remainder to the late territory of Iowa.

Throughout the whole of this territory scarcely an elevation that could be dignified with the name of mountain occurs. The surface is in general level or undulating, but varies considerably in elevation, and in the ascents and descents of its plateaux. In some parts, especially in the neighborhood of the Mississippi and St. Peter's, the ground is much broken, and their margins lined with high bluffs of various formations; while in others the rivers flow through deep channels, seemingly worn into the earth by the force of their waters.

Every portion of Minnesota may be reached by inland navigation. The traveller will meet constantly with springs and small lakes, the sources of mighty rivers, whose waters are discharged thousands of miles to the north into Hudson's bay, as many to the east into the gulf of St. Lawrence, or to the south into the gulf of Mexico. Springs are often seen within a few feet of each other, the sources of rivers whose outlets in the ocean are some six thousand miles apart! In almost every direction, canoe navigation, with short portages, is practicable by means of the numerous rivers, whose sources are nearly interlocked or connected by chains of lakes. The Mississippi has its source here, some three thousand miles from its mouth. Nine hundred miles of the length of this majestic river are embraced in this territory, and its numerous tributaries course through its fertile plains. The northeast portion is washed by the crystal waters of Lake Superior, which is of itself an inland sea for the prosecution of trade and commerce, and opens an avenue to the Atlantic. The Missouri, after having flowed nearly one thousand miles from the base of the Rocky mountains, sweeps along its whole western boundary, insuring navigation almost to Oregon. Its large tributaries, James and Big Sioux rivers, water valleys of great beauty and fertility. Extensive prairies, blooming with flowers, and covered with luxuriant grasses, afford sustenance to immense herds of buffalo, saying nothing of elk, deer, antelopes, and other small game. Red river, which discharges itself into Lake Winnipeg, has its sources near those of the Mississippi. Beautiful lakes of transparent water, well stocked with fish, and varying in size from ponds to inland seas, are profusely scattered over the territory. Forests of pine and other evergreens, orchards of sugar-maple, groves of hard and soft woods of various species, wild rice and cranberries, and various species of wild fruit, copious springs of pure water, a fertile soil, and water-power, easily improved and abundantly distributed, render this region peculiarly adapted to the wants of man. Add to these a salubrious climate, and Minnesota appears to enjoy eminent capacities for becoming a thriving and populous state. Its mineral resources are as yet but imperfectly known, but indications and discoveries have been made that certify its wealth in copper and lead

Building-stone of every description, limestone, &c., are found everywhere underlying the soil, while many valuable and precious stones are found on the shores of the lakes. For a country so overspread with lakes, and traversed by such a number of rivers, it is astonishingly free from marsh and morass. The land has a great elevation above the gulf of Mexico and the waters of the north and east, and, as a consequence, is easily and perfectly drained; and, moreover, the margins of the lakes and rivers themselves are generally surrounded by hills and bluffs, which protect their neighborhoods from inundation. The whole country is thus eligible for agriculture.

As yet, the settlements made in the territory are chiefly confined to the peninsula between the Mississippi and St. Croix on the south, and on the Red river on the north. Otherwise the country is inhabited only by the aboriginal hunters, the Chippewa and Sioux Indians. Their numbers are not ascertained, but may approximate to about twelve thousand. With some of the tribes treaties have been made for the purchase of their lands and for their removal, which, when fully effected, will open to the white settler immense tracts of rich and fertile soils, productive of every species of grain and fruits usually grown in northern climates. The hunting-grounds of the Indians are now chiefly confined to the vast prairies west of the Mississippi. The white inhabitants are from almost every portion of the world: the Canadian, the sons of New England and the middle states, with English, French, and Germans, are all intermingled; and not a few of the citizens consist of half-breeds, who chiefly reside on the Red river, and have settlements for some distance on both sides of our northern boundary. These are descendants of the original settlers at Lord Selkirk colony, and Indian women of the Chippewa family.

In the new settlements, the industry of the whites is almost entirely agricultural. They have mills on a number of the streams, and steamboats ply regularly on their waters. They are building roads, and, from the energy they exhibit in overcoming natural obstacles, the real prosperity of the territory seems to be insured. A large business has been already done by the steamboats that sail regularly between Galena and St. Paul's and Stillwater. The products of the chase and the fruits of the field are exported in considerable quantities.

With regard to immigration, the prospects are favorable. Farmers, laborers, and professional men, are daily ascending the rivers in search of a new home. The day, indeed, is not distant, when the forests will be laid low, and the flowery prairies be converted into fields and gardens, producing every necessary to the use and enjoyment of man. Earth, air, and water, abound in the prerequisites of man's happiness and enjoyment, and are only awaiting his advent to yield up their now-unused abundance.

So recent has been the organization of the government of the territory, that it is impossible to exhibit by statistics the resources of this new and almost untouched country. The first legislature, which adjourned after a session of sixty days, was chiefly employed in organizing the government, and dividing the territory into suitable civil districts, and appointing officers to enforce the laws. Among other important acts of the territorial legislature, are those establishing the judiciary, a school system, and those relative to the improvement of roads. All these will have a paramount influence over the future destiny of the country. Perhaps one of the most humane and politic acts of the legislature is the admission to citizenship of "all persons of a mixture of white and Indian blood, who shall have adopted the habits and customs of civilized men;" and not less politic is that law which requires the establishment of schools throughout the territory. The act of the general government organizing the territory, appropriates two sections of land in every township for the support of common schools. No other state in the Union has received more than one section in each township for such purpose. According to the census of 1850, the population of Minnesota was rising 6,000.

The territory was divided by the legislature into nine counties, in lieu of the counties of St. Croix and La Pointe, which constituted the remaining portions of the territories of Iowa and Wisconsin of which Minnesota was formed. The principal settlements are St. Paul's, Stillwater, Mendota, Fort Snelling, Pembina, &c.

St. Paul's, the capital, is situated on the left bank of the Mississippi, fifteen miles by water, and eight miles by land, below the falls of St. Anthony. The town is situated on a plateau terminating on the river in a precipitous bluff of eighty feet elevation above the water. The bluff recedes from the river at the upper and lower ends of the town, forming two landings, from both of which the ascent is gradual. The first store or trading-house was built in 1842. In June, 1849, the town contained one hundred and forty-two houses, all of which, with the exception of perhaps a dozen, had been built within the year previous : this number included the government-house, three hotels, four warehouses, ten stores, several groceries, two printing-offices—from which two newspapers are issued weekly—a schoolhouse, several mechanics' shops, &c. There was not a brick or stone house in the town. Since the period above mentioned, however, several churches and many durable houses, built of stone and brick, from materials in the vicinity, have been erected. The population, according to the census of 1850, was 1,135. St. Paul's is well located for commerce ; and from its being at the head of navigation below the falls of St. Anthony, must necessarily become not only the political but the commercial capital of the territory. In the neighborhood of St. Paul's there is an extensive settlement of Canadians, chiefly persons formerly employed by the Hudson Bay Company, called Little Canada. Its population is about 800.

Stillwater is situated on the west side of Lake St. Croix, near its head, on ground having a gentle ascent from the shore to a high bluff in the rear, which extends in the form of a crescent, and nearly encloses the town. The first settlement was made in 1843. It contains a courthouse, several hotels and stores, and many neat dwellings. Steamboats seldom ascend higher than this place. The environs consist of a beautiful prairie country, and are being rapidly brought under cultivation. Population in June, 1850, 636.

Marine Mills is a flourishing settlement on the St. Croix river, a few miles above its entrance into the lake. The precinct contains about 300 inhabitants. Its water-power, and the fine country which surrounds it, must speedily enforce its increase and prosperity.

Several villages on the Wisconsin side of the St. Croix river have been established, and are rapidly increasing in importance. Indeed, the resources of the vicinity on both sides are such as to insure to the villages considerable commerce.

Fort Snelling is situated on the high, rocky promontory, more than a hundred feet above the water, at the confluence of St. Peter's river with the Mississippi. The military works were commenced in 1819. The fort is in the form of a hexagon, and surrounded by a stone wall. From the river its appearance is imposing and seemingly impregnable. It is, however, within the reach of cannon from higher ground ; but the object for which the site was selected—the protection of the frontier from savage incursion—is well attained by its situation. The garrison usually consists of three companies of dragoons. The view from these fortifications is extensive. The military reservation of the establishment embraces an area of ten miles square, of which the fort is near the centre. The settlement in the neighborhood contains only about forty inhabitants. In the fort there were 267 males and 50 females in June, 1849.

Mendota, or St. Peter's, on the west bank of the Mississippi, south of the confluence of St. Peter's river, has been occupied for several years by the American Fur Company, as a dépôt for their trading establishments with the Indians of the northwest. Two stores and two or three houses constitute the village. It is, however, a fine town site ; and being situated at the junction of two great rivers, and near the head of steam navigation, its importanee in a commercial point of view has not been overlooked.

Whites are not allowed to reside here without special permission from the United States government, the village being in the military reservation. It will ultimately command the trade of the St. Peter's river. Population in 1850, 200.

Some other small villages exist in this neighborhood, but of their importance or present state little is known. KAPOSIA, from its situation near the point of land opposite St. Paul's, though yet little more than an Indian town, may ultimately become of consequence. SAUK RAPIDS, opposite the mouth of Osakis river, is on the eastern bank of the Mississippi; and higher up, on both sides of Nokay river, is FORT GAINES, the most northerly military establishment in the country. The supplying of these remote stations with provisions, &c., creates considerable traffic and travelling by both land and water. The return traffic consists of furs and peltry, with other Indian contributions.

The city of ST. ANTHONY, which is laid out on the east side of the Mississippi, directly opposite the cataract, is a beautiful town site. A handsome, elevated prairie, with a gentle inclination toward the river bank, and of sufficient width for parallel streets, extends up and down the river. In the rear of this, another branch of table land swells up, forming a beautiful and elevated platform. The inhabitants are chiefly from the state of Maine, and form an enterprising population.

The town of PEMBINA, situated on Red river, a short distance this side of the British line, contained, according to the census of 1850, 636 inhabitants: of these, 294 were males and 342 females. The men follow the chase, and engage in the pursuits of grazing and agriculture; and the women, besides attending to the usual domestic avocations, manufacture most of the woollen and linen fabrics necessary to clothe their families. Hardy and hard-working, prudent as the New England farmer, religious, brave, and intelligent, these half-breeds form no mean class in the general community. They trade with the southern settlers of the territory, exchanging furs and pemmican for the superfluities of the south. They have churches and schools, and many of the better class are educated at a collegiate establishment which has long been maintained among them. As a consequence, however, of their ostracized situation, they still retain many of the peculiarities of their original nations, modified indeed by the circumstances that surround them, and their connexion with savage life.

Minnesota embraces within its borders all the natural advantages necessary to a great state. Its water-power is inexhaustible. Mines of copper, lead, and iron, are abundant. It is doubtless destined to be one of the most powerful members of the confederacy. Its population is rapidly increasing, and in two or three years they will be knocking at the door of the Union for admission as a sovereign state.

The remaining portion of the United States territory east of the Rocky mountains is known as the Western territory, and is a part of the Louisiana purchase of 1803. It extends from the Nebraska or Platte river northward to the 49th parallel, and from White Earth and Missouri rivers westward to the Rocky mountains. The territory has an area of 579,584 square miles.

The greater part of this immense territory is watered by the Missouri and its numerous tributaries. The Yellowstone, the largest of these, extends its branches to the very base of the Rocky mountains, and to near the sources of the Nebraska. A mountain-ridge, which branches from the great Rocky mountains, in about 42° north latitude, traverses the country in a northeast direction toward Lake Winnipeg. In the east portion of the territory the country is partly covered with forests, but beyond this commences a vast ocean of prairie, almost level, and clothed in grass and flowers. As yet the whole territory is inhabited by Indians, but the time is not far distant when the pioneer will penetrate its wilds, and bring under cultivation the soil that from its creation has not been turned by the labor of man. The wild herds will be replaced by the ox, the horse, and the sheep; and golden crops will succeed the flowers and grasses that now bloom and wither without use.

TERRITORY OF NEW MEXICO.

The history of New Mexico lies very much in the dark. The Spaniards, it seems, received the first information concerning it in 1581, from a party of adventurers under Captain Francisco de Levya Bonillo, who, upon finding the aboriginal inhabitants and the mineral wealth of the country to be similar to those of Mexico, called it *New Mexico.* In 1594, the then viceroy of Mexico, Count de Monterey, sent the gallant Juan de Oñate, of Zacatecas, to New Mexico, to take formal possession of the country in the name of Spain, and to establish colonies, missions, presidios (forts), &c. They found a great many Indian tribes and settlements, which they succeeded in Christianizing after the usual Spanish manner, with sword in hand, and made them their slaves. The villages of the Christianized Indians were called *pueblos*, in opposition to the wild and roving tribes that refused such favors. Many towns, of which ruins only exist at present, were then established; many mines were worked; and the occupation of the country seemed to be secured, when, quite unexpectedly, in 1680, a general insurrection of all the Indian tribes broke out against the Spanish yoke. The Indians massacred every white male; and the then governor of New Mexico, Don Antonio de Otermin, after a hard fight, was compelled to retreat with his men from Santa Fé, and march as far south as Paso del Norte, where they met with some friendly Indians, and laid the foundation of the present town of that name. The insurrection lasted ten years, when Spain recovered possession of the whole province of New Mexico. Several other revolts occurred subsequently, but none so disastrous as the first. However, the deep rancor of the Indian race against the white has continued to the present time, and in all the frequent and bloody revolutions of later years in New Mexico, the pueblos have generally acted a conspicuous and cruel part.

This country followed the fate of Mexico after the revolution that overthrew the Spanish power, and since that period has been silently degenerating. The history of New Mexico, previous to the invasion by the Americans, has little to arrest attention. It is a continuous record of barbarism and tyranny. On the 8th of September, 1846, Santa Fé was captured by the Americans under General Kearney, and soon after several of the river towns were visited on his route to California. A civil government was now established. On the 19th of January, 1847, an insurrection broke out against the Americans, and in several pueblos many Americans were murdered, among whom were Governor Bent and Sheriff Lee. Taos, Arroya-Hondo, and Rio Colorado, were the chief scenes of strife. The battles of La Canada and El Embudo also occurred in this month, and in February the battle of Taos—in all of which the Mexicans were completely vanquished. Some few skirmishes occurred after these, but none of importance. From this period the United States authorities exercised exclusive jurisdiction and power. On the 2d of February, 1848, a treaty of peace and cession was signed at Guadalupe Hidalgo, by which New Mexico was assigned to the Union. It has since been erected into a separate territory, by act of Congress, which gave ten millions of dollars to Texas as an equivalent for the claim she preferred to that portion of the territory of New Mexico which lies east of the Rio Grande. The following are the boundaries of New Mexico, as established by Congress: "Beginning at a point in the Colorado river where the boundary line with the republic of Mexico crosses the same; thence eastwardly with the said boundary line to the Rio Grande; thence following the main channel of the said river to the parallel of the thirty-second degree of north latitude; thence east with said degree to its intersection with the one hundred and third degree of longitude west of Greenwich; thence north with said degree of longitude to the parallel of thirty-eight degrees of north latitude; thence west with the said parallel to the summit of the Sierra Madre; thence south with the crest of said mountains to the thirty-seventh parallel of north latitude; thence west with said parallel to its intersection with the boundary line of the state of California; thence with said boundary line to the place of beginning."

New Mexico is a very mountainous country, with an extensive valley in the middle, running from north to south, and formed by the Rio del Norte. The valley is generally about twenty miles wide, and bordered on the east and west by mountain-chains—continuations of the Rocky mountains—which have here received different names, as *Sierra blanca, de los Organos, oscura*, on the eastern side, and *Sierra de los Grullas, de Acha, de los Mimbres*, toward the west. The height of these mountains, south of Santa Fé, may upon an average be between six and eight thousand feet; while near that town, and in the more northern regions, some snow-covered peaks are seen that may rise from ten to twelve thousand feet above the sea. The mountains are principally composed of igneous rocks, as granite, senite, diorit, basalt, &c. On the higher mountains excellent pine timber grows; on the lower, cedars, and sometimes oak; in the valley of the Rio Grande, mezquite.

The main artery of New Mexico is the Rio del Norte, the longest and largest river in Mexico. Its head-waters were explored in 1807 by Captain Pike, between the thirty-seventh and thirty-eighth degrees of north latitude; but its highest sources are supposed to be about two degrees farther north in the Rocky mountains near the head-waters of the Arkansas and the Rio Grande (or the Colorado of the west). Following a generally southern direction, it runs through New Mexico, where its principal affluent is the Rio Chamas from the west, and thence winds its way in a southeastern course through the states of Chihuahua, Coahuila, and Tamaulipas, to the gulf of Mexico, in 25° 56′ north latitude. Its tributaries in the latter states are the Pecos, from the north, and the Chonchos, Salado, Alamo, and San Juan, from the south. The entire course of the Rio del Norte, in a straight line, would be nearly twelve hundred miles; but by the meandering of its lower half, it runs at least two thousand miles from the region of eternal snow to the almost tropical climate of the gulf. The elevation of the river above the sea near Albuquerque, in New Mexico, is about 4,800 feet; at El Paso del Norte, about 3,800; and at Reynosa, between three and four hundred miles from its mouth, about 170 feet. The fall of the water between Albuquerque and El Paso appears to be from two to three feet in a mile, and below Reynosa one foot in two miles. The fall of the river is seldom used as a motive power, except for running some flour-mills, which are oftener worked by mules than by water. The principal advantage which is at present derived from this river by the inhabitants is for agricultural purposes, by their well-managed system of irrigation. As to its navigation in New Mexico, it is very much doubted if even canoes could be used, except perhaps during May or June, when the river is in its highest state, from the melting of the snow in the mountains. The river is entirely too shallow, and interrupted by too many sand-bars, to promise anything for navigation. On the southern portion of the river, the recent exploration by Captain Sterling, of the United States steamer "Major Brown," has proved that steamboats may ascend from the gulf as far as Laredo, a distance of seven hundred miles. Although this steamer did not draw over two feet of water, yet the explorers of that region express their opinion that, by spending about one hundred thousand dollars in a proper improvement of the river above Mier, boats drawing four feet could readily ply between the mouth of the Rio Grande and Laredo. Whenever a closer connexion between this head-point of navigation and New Mexico shall be considered, nothing will answer but a railroad, crossing from the valley of the Rio Grande to the high table-land in the Mexican state of Chihuahua.

The soil in the valley of the Rio del Norte, in New Mexico, is generally sandy and looks poor, but by irrigation it produces abundant crops. Though agriculture is carried on in a very primitive way, with the hoe alone, or with a rude plough, made often entirely of wood, without a particle of iron, the inhabitants raise large quantities of wheat, Indian corn, beans, onions, and red peppers, together with some fruits. The most fertile part of the valley begins below Santa Fé, along the river, and is called *Rio abajo* (or the [country] down the river). It is not uncommon there to raise two crops within one year.

The general dryness of the climate, and the aridity of the soil, in New Mexico, will always confine agriculture to the valleys of the water-courses, which are as rare as over all Mexico—such, at least, as contain running water throughout the year. But this important defect may be remedied by Artesian wells. On the high table-land from Santa Fé south, at a certain depth, layers of clay are found, that may form reservoirs of the sunken water-courses from the eastern and western mountain-chains, which, by the improved method of boring (or Artesian wells), might be easily made to yield their water to the surface. If experiments to that effect should prove successful, the progress of agriculture in New Mexico will be more rapid, and even many dreaded *jornadas* might be changed from waterless deserts into cultivated plains. But at present, irrigation from a water-course is the only available means of carrying on agriculture. The irrigation is effected by damming the streams, and throwing the water into larger and smaller ditches *(acequias)* surrounding and intersecting the whole cultivated land. The inhabitants of the towns and villages, therefore, locate their lands together, and allot to each cultivator a part of the water at certain periods. These common fields are generally without fences, which are less needed, as the grazing stock is guarded by herdsmen. The finest fields are generally seen on the *haciendas*, or large estates, belonging to the rich property-holders in New Mexico. These haciendas are apparently a remnant of the old feudal system, and were granted, with the Indians and all other appurtenances, by the Spanish crown to favorite vassals. The inhabitants pay considerable attention to the raising of stock, and the great owners are possessed of large numbers of horses, mules, cattle, and sheep; these, however, are generally of small size. The pasturage in the uncultivated parts of the territory is extensive, and thousands of stock graze thereon throughout the year. The Indians prove the greatest enemies to the farmers, and frequently carry off numerous herds of cattle, &c.

The mines of New Mexico are very rich. Mining, however, has long been neglected by the native population, and many of the most valuable *placers*, which were formerly worked, have been wholly deserted. Gold, silver, iron, and copper, are plentiful in the mountains. Gold is found in the Sante Fé district as far south as Gran Quivira, and north as far as the Rio Sangre de Cristo. The poorer classes occupy some of their time in washing out gold-dust, which is largely deposited in the mountain-streams. The mines in the neighborhood of Santa Fé are the only ones worked at the present time. Silver-mines were worked by the Spaniards at Avo, Cerillos, and in the Nambe mountains, but operations have long since ceased. Copper is abundant throughout the country, and iron is equally so; but these metals are entirely overlooked by the Mexicans as useless! Coal has also been discovered in a number of places; and gypsum, both common and selenite, is found in large quantities. The common is used as lime for whitewashing, and the crystalline, or selenite, instead of window-glass. On the high table-lands, between the Rio del Norte and Pecos, are some extensive *salinas*, or salt-lakes, from which all the domestic salt in New Mexico is procured. Large caravans from the capital visit these in the dry season, and return with as much salt as they can conveniently carry. The merchants exchange one bushel of salt for an equal quantity of wheat, or sell it for one or sometimes two dollars a bushel.

The climate is generally temperate, constant, and healthy. Considerable atmospheric differences, however, are experienced in the mountain districts and in the low valley of the river. In the latter, the summer-heat sometimes rises to 100° Fahrenheit, but the nights are always cool and pleasant. The winters are comparatively of long duration, and frequently severe. The sky, however, is clear and dry, owing to the condensation of the moisture on the frozen hills. The months from July to October inclusive constitute the rainy season, but the rains are neither so heavy nor so regular in their returns as on the more southern part of the continent. Disease is little known, except some inflammations and typhoid fevers in the winter season. In taking the census of the territory in 1850, many remarkable instances of longevity were found among the native population, proving New Mexico to be one of the most healthful regions of the Union.

Population.—The whole population of New Mexico was, according to the census of 1793, 30,953; in 1833, it was calculated to amount to 52,360, and that number to consist of one twentieth *Gapuchines* (Spaniards), one fifth creoles, one fourth mestizoes of all grades, and one half of pueblo Indians. In 1842, the population was estimated at 57,026; and according to the census of 1850, it was by counties as follows: Santa Fé, 7,713; Taos, 9,507; Rio Ariba, 10,668; San Miguel, 7,071; Santa Ana, 4,656; Bernalio, 7,752; and Valencia, 14,207. Total, 61,574. This is exclusive of the independent tribes of Indians which still exist in the country. The *Navajoes* are a powerful tribe, inhabiting a fine country west of the Rio Grande, and numbering about 7,000; the *Eutaws* inhabit the northwestern frontier, and number 4,000 or 5,000; the *Apaches*, about 5,000, roam over the vast regions east of the Rio Grande and north of El Paso; the *Jicorilles*, a branch of the Apache family, 500 in number, are neighbors of the Eutaws on the northwestern frontier. To these must be added large parties of *Camanches*, *Arrapahoes*, and *Cheyennes*—perhaps 36,000 in number—which infest the borders to the north and east, and lay the unwary traveller under contribution—frequently committing the foulest murders, or carrying off women and children into captivity.

The chief city of New Mexico is Santa Fe, one of the oldest of the Spanish settlements. Its elevation above the sea is 7,047 feet. Santa Fé is about twenty miles east, in a direct line, from the Rio del Norte, and lies in a wide plain, surrounded by lofty mountains. A small creek, rising in the hills and flowing past the city, supplies it with water. The land around is sandy, poor, and destitute of timber; but the mountains are covered with pine and cedar. No pasturage is observed about the settlements, and as a consequence stock is driven to the mountains. The climate is delightful, and free from extremes; the sky is clear and cloudless, and the atmosphere dry. The houses are built of *adobes* (sunburnt brick), but one story high, with flat roofs. The streets are narrow and irregular. The *plaza*, or public square, is spacious, and one side is occupied by the official residence of the executive of the territory. The palace is, without being very grand, a good building, and exhibits two curiosities, viz., windows of glass, and *festoons of Indian ears.* Among the public buildings there are two churches with steeples, but of an ordinary construction. There are thirty or forty stores in the city, principally kept by Americans. The inhabitants, except the Americans, are Spaniards and Indians, and the castes sprung from an indefinite amalgamation of the two races. Society is in a deplorable condition. The native population spend their time in card-playing, drinking, smoking, and at *fandangoes.* They are expert thieves, and live in a miserable state of ignorance, superstition, dirt, and poverty. The city proper contains 4,000 or 5,000 souls, and about as many more are settled within its jurisdiction. Santa Fé is the dépôt of a considerable commerce carried on between northern Mexico and the western states, and is generally visited by the overland emigrants to California.

Las Vagas, seventy-five miles from Santa Fé, contains about 400 inhabitants, with a few American families. It is a military outpost, and has one company of about fifty soldiers. Tecalote, ten miles this side of Las Vagas, has about 200 souls, and a few American families.

San Miguel, fifteen miles this side of Las Vagas, has about 700 souls, but no Americans. San Jose, three miles farther on, has a population of about 300, all Mexicans. There are two or three other small villages, off the road.

Northwardly from Santa Fé, the first town of importance is Canada (*Canyarthan*), twenty-five miles distant. It is a place of considerable trade, and contains about 2,000 inhabitants. The town is located about one mile from the eastern bank of the Rio del Norte. The valley is thickly settled, and is said to be among the most beautiful and fertile portions of New Mexico. The river is at this place one hundred and fifty or two hundred yards wide, its current running seven or eight miles an hour. At low-water mark it is fordable. Proceeding on about forty-five miles farther, passing several unimportant places, you arrive at Taos, with a population of about 2,000 souls. This is a military station. There are no American families here, however. The entire Taos valley is populous, and the people are wealthy. There are about a dozen American families in the region, chiefly farmers.

Throughout this, as well as the valley of the Rio Grande, are to be seen mountains of the most singular shapes imaginable. Some of them appear like gigantic fortifications of very ancient date; others rise hundreds of feet in the form of pyramids, then surmounted by lofty towers of symmetrical proportions, with perpendicular sides. One high mountain, called the Sugarloaf, is seen north of Albiquin, resembling a truncated cone. Approaching Albiquin, the valley is under better cultivation, and more productive. This part of the valley is more thickly settled than that below.

Albiquin, one of the most northern military stations in the territory, is a small village, formerly an Indian pueblo, and is a romantic place. It is situated on a high bluff, and nearly surrounded by mountains. That part of the valley seen from the town is truly charming. The Rio Chalma runs through the centre of it, thus rendering irrigation easy. The Navajo and Eutaw Indians roam through this section of country, to prevent whose depredaticns a company of dragoons is stationed at Albiquin.

Southwardly from Santa Fé, the first town is Agua Fres (Cold Water), six miles distant, and containing about 200 inhabitants, with few or no Americans. Algodonis, forty miles distant, also has a population of about 200. Sandia, fifty-four miles from Santa Fé, is a pueblo Indian town, containing about 150 souls. Albuquerque, a large town seventy miles from Santa Fé, has a population of 1,500. This is a military station, with a few resident American families. Socora is an important military station about one hundred and twenty-five miles south. Zuni, about two handred miles distant, is an Indian town with a population of 2,000 or more. This is one of the most remarkable tribes on the continent, highly civilized in some respects; living in good, substantial two-story houses; obtaining their livelihood by agriculture; not warlike, yet able to defend thmselves against all their enemies. They are noted for their intelligence, universal benevolence, and kindness of heart. These Indians are now citizens of the United States. In the same vicinity are the *Mochins*, who are very similar to the *Zunians*.

El Paso, three hundred and twenty miles from Santa Fé, situated on the Rio Grande, has some 300 inhabitants on the American side of the river, including a few settled American families. A military post is established there.

Manners and Customs.—The manners and customs of the New Mexicans proper are very similar to those over all Mexico, so often described by travellers to that country. While the higher classes conform themselves more to American and European fashions, the men of the lower classes are faithful to their serapes or colored blankets, and to their wide trousers with glittering buttons, and split from hip to ankle, to give the white cotton drawers also a chance to be seen; and the ladies of all classes are more than justified in not giving up their coquettish rebozo, a small shawl drawn over the head. Both sexes enjoy the cigarito or paper-cigar, hold their siesta after dinner, and amuse themselves in the evening with monté (a hazard game) or fandangoes. Their dances, which are very graceful, are generally a combination of quadrille and waltz.

The principal ingredient in the Mexican race is Indian blood, which is visible in their features, complexion, and disposition. The men are, generally taken, ill-featured, while the women are often quite handsome. Another striking singularity is the wide difference in the character of the two sexes. While the men have often been censured for their indolence, mendacity, treachery, and cruelty, the women are active, affectionate, openhearted, and even faithful when their affections are reciprocated. Though generally not initiated in the art of reading and writing, the females possess nevertheless a strong common sense, and a natural sympathy for every suffering being, be it friend or foe, which compensates them in some degree for the wants of a refined education. The treatment of the Texan prisoners is but one of the many instances where the cruelties of the Mexican men were mitigated by the disinterested kindness of their women. Many of the evils of the present state of society in New Mexico will no doubt be eradicated by the contact of a more advanced civilization, and education will become an indispensable requisite in order to keep up with the progress of commerce, and the influx of an educated population from the east.

The New-Mexicans are a very devout, though, at the same time, none the less immoral people. Their devotion consists in all the forms, penances, confessions, and discipline, imposed by their church. All these are performed with undoubted sincerity and heartfelt devotion, and upon these observances and on these alone are based all their hopes of "eternal life." The New Mexican rising generation exhibit an aptness to learn, and are easily controlled and directed, and by no means want talent and capacity to become enlightened and independent in opinion. With a single exception, no really effective schools exist among them, though much desired by all composing the better classes. Could a general plan of education be established, much good might be expected to follow.

New Mexico, previous to the late war, as before remarked, was a state of the Mexican republic, and its rulers consisted of a governor and legislature *(junta departmental)*; but as the latter was more an imaginary than a real power, the governor was, in fact, despotic, and subject only to the laws of revolution, which, in this state, were very freely administered by upsetting the gubernatorial chair as often as the republic at large did the presidential. Well knowing the favors of fortune were at all times precarious, the governors, in general, while in office, plundered the treasury and provided against contingencies! The people, credulous and easily deceived, had to submit to every outrage; and should one, more courageous than his fellows, assert the profligacy of the government, his doom was as certain as speedy. Thus has New Mexico dragged on its existence—the sport of despots and the football of fortune. The judiciary was as dependent as the executive was independent, and all law succumbed to the dictates of one man. Besides these, the clergy, as well as the military classes, had their own courts of justice. In relation to the confederacy, however, New Mexico always maintained greater independence than any other of the states—partly from its distance from the capital, but more from the spirit of opposition in the people, who derived no advantage from the connexion, and suffered much from its taxation, without an equivalent protection. The supreme government never succeeded here in imposing upon the people the *estranquillas*, or monopoly of the sale of tobacco, and New Mexico was free from some other enormities. In the same way the people resisted the introduction of copper coin. This loose connexion with the central power will aid much in the assimilation of the people of this newly-acquired territory with the immigrants from other parts of the American Union, especially as the government of the latter will bestow upon them—what the former could not—stability, safety, protection, and the just rights which are enjoyed by all persons under the ægis of American republican principles.

TERRITORY OF UTAH.

THAT portion of Alta-California, now designated as the territory of UTAH, was never settled by the Spaniards, nor was it ever more than a nominal dependency of that nation or of the Mexican republic. Previous to the Mexican war, indeed, few white men, except those engaged in scientific explorations, had entered the country. About the period when that war broke out, the Mormons were driven from their city of Nauvoo, in Illinois, by mob violence; and shortly afterward a portion of them, under the leadership of Strang, removed to Beaver island in Lake Michigan, while the main body of the sect, directed by Brigham Young (who was regarded as their true "prophet" after the death of their founder, Joseph Smith, and in opposition to the "infidel" leader Strang), migrated to the borders of the Great Salt lake. Their settlements became prosperous and populous, and within two years after the first pioneers had entered the country, their numbers had increased to about 10,000. After peace had been ratified, they found themselves without a civil government, and without protection for their persons or property. To remedy this anomalous condition of things, they organized a temporary government under the style of the "State of DESERET." Under its sanction they elected officers to manage the affairs of the commonwealth, and made application to Congress to be admitted into the Union as a sovereign state. But Congress did not deem that this new settlement had arrived at that state of maturity which would justify its erection into a state, and passed a law authorizing its organization as a territory, with the following limits: on the west it is bounded by the state of California, on the north by the territory of Oregon, on the east by the summit of the Rocky mountains, and on the south by the thirty-seventh parallel of latitude. Congress reserved the right with Utah, as also with New Mexico, to divide it into two or more territories, or to attach portions of it to any state or territory in such manner and at such times as it shall deem convenient and proper.

Utah is one of the most singular countries in the world. The great basin in which it is situated between the Sierra Nevada and the mountains of New Mexico, is some five hundred miles in diameter every way, and comprises an area of 393,691 square miles. It is between four and five thousand feet above the level of the sea, shut in all around by mountains, with its own system of lakes and rivers, and without any direct connexion with the ocean. Partly arid and thinly inhabited, its general character is that of a desert, but with great exceptions—there being many parts of it very fit for the residence of a civilized people; and of these the Mormons have established themselves in one of the largest and best. Mountain is the predominating structure of the interior of the basin, with plains between—the mountains wooded and watered, the plains arid and sterile.

In the northern part of this basin lies the Great Salt lake. The waters of this sheet are shallow, so far as explored; though probably its central parts will be found very deep. Its waters are intensely salt, more so than those of the ocean—three gallons making one gallon of the purest, whitest, and finest salt. Southeast of this lake, shut in by the mountains, lies the Mormon valley, which contains their capital city. This valley is thirty miles long by twenty-two broad, connected with another valley which is about fifty miles by eight. These two valleys contain the principal body of the settlers, to the number of some 30,000 or 40,000. Explorers think that they are capable of supporting a population of a million. The Humboldt river is the principal water-course of the great basin, and possesses qualities which, in the progress of events, may give it both value and fame. It lies in the line of travel to California and Oregon, and is the best route now known through the great basin, and the one travelled by emigrants. Its direction, east and west, is the right course for that travel. It furnishes a level, unobstructed way for nearly three hundred miles, and a plentiful supply of the indispensable articles of water, wood, and grass. Its head is toward the Great Salt lake, and consequently toward the Mormon settlements, which must become a point in the line of emigration to California and the lower Columbia. Its termination is within fifty miles of the base of the Sierra Nevada, and opposite the Salmon Trout river pass—a pass only seven thousand two hundred feet above the level of the sea, and less than half that above the level of the basin, and leading into the valley of the Sacramento, some forty miles north of Sutter's fort. These properties give to this river a prospective value in future communications with the Pacific. The Rio Gila bounds the territory on the south, and the Rio Colorado traverses it in a southwest direction from the Rocky mountains to the gulf of California, into which both rivers empty by one mouth.

THE CITY OF THE GREAT SALT LAKE, tho capital of Utah, is beautifully laid out, within a short distance of the mountain forming the eastern end of the valley. It contains from 20,000 to 25,000 inhabitants, who are mostly engaged in agriculture, though a portion of their time is devoted to mechanical pursuits when understood. The streets of the city intersect each other at right angles, and each block is half a mile square, with an alley from east to west and north to south. Each block is called a ward, and has a bishop to preside over its government, whose duties are to act as magistrates, tax-collectors, and preachers, as well as street commissioners. The city and all the farming land are irrigated by streams of pure water which flow from the adjacent mountains: these streams have been, with great labor and perseverance, led in every direction. In the city they flow on each side of the different streets, and their waters are let upon the inhabitants' gardens at regular periods; so likewise upon the extensive fields of grain lying in the south of the city.

Fifty miles south of this city is the Utah lake and valley. Here lies the city of PRAVA, on the Prava river. The lake is of pure water, eight miles long by four in width, and abounds in fish. There is still another valley, one hundred miles farther south, called San Pete, where is also a settlement; and here are the hieroglyphic ruins, the remains of glazed pottery, &c., that indicate the former existence of the outlying cities of the Aztec empire.

Wheat, oats, and barley, yield abundantly in the great valley. Melons and all the vines grow in perfection, as also do vegetables; while hopeful efforts are making to raise the olive, orange, lemon, pineapple, tea, coffee, &c. The valley below produces tropical fruits, while the beach land or old lake shore, at the altitude of three or four hundred feet, brings forth all the productions of the temperate zones; and still higher up, the cedar, pine, juniper, and other evergreens of a northern clime, flourish. The pasturage on the plains, as well as on the beach land and side-hills, is luxuriant (the verdure reaching to the mountain-tops). equal for fattening qualities to that of California.

Utah abounds in minerals. A geographical survey has brought to light an inexhanstible bed of stone-coal, equalling that of Newcastle; iron ore, with a vein of silver running through it, which latter alone would pay for working; gold, in small quantities, and platina, are found; and traces of copper and zinc have been discovered. Its mineral springs are famous, little as they have been tried, and their analysis shows them to be equal to those most resorted to at the east.

The country only needs a thorough investigation, and hands enough to develop its resources, and the population will be independent of supplies from other quarters. In conducting the river Jordan by canal to the city of the Great Salt lake, a distance of twenty-five miles along the foot of the mountains, an immense scope of land is brought under the influence of irrigation, besides a vast water-power for machinery. The Mormons are already about to set up and finish their machines, furnaces, &c., for smelting ore, casting rails, and finishing engines, for manufacturing purposes as well as for railways to connect themselves with the neighboring country. A southern railway, to tap the Pacific at some practicable point, is a favorite plan with them; a road to Oregon is also contemplated; and the railway from the head of navigation on the Missouri to the Salt-lake valley will one day be as much travelled as any of our main thoroughfares are at present.

The whole character of the territory of Utah is singular. While its geographical position and features are unlike those of any other portion of North America, its origin and the manner of its settlement are no less strange. It is doubtful if it would have been settled for many years to come, had not persecution driven the Mormons to seek refuge and a home in its distant limits. They established themselves here, at first, with the idea that they would be cut off from the world by the natural difficulties of the contiguous territory and the peculiarity of their situation. Here they expected to form, in secrecy and silence, a great, peculiar religious empire; but the stream of California emigration discovered their trail and invaded their principality, and their territory is now the open, exposed half-way house to the Pacific. Its peculiar locality is and will continue to be of essential service as a stopping-place for the army of emigrants that, year after year, will seek California or Oregon by the southern pass; and when the Pacific railway is completed, it will prove of incalculable benefit as a great station-house on the route. The apprehension, however, is not altogether groundless, that in a community whose peculiar religious faith is made paramount to all other obligations, a spirit of disaffection may be engendered toward the United States government, which will result in an attempt to renounce their allegiance, and to place themselves beyond the protecting ægis of the Union. Indeed, such a feeling has already "cast its shadow before." It is to be hoped, however, that while all their natural and constitutional rights shall be properly respected, a wise and timely precaution will be exercised by the United States authorities to insure from them a due obedience to the constitution and laws of the Union. And however much we may regret to see a community, numbering a population of some 40,000 souls, so wedded to a religious faith which is little short of the wildest fanaticism, and among whose fruits is gross licentiousness, we can not but admire the enterprise, the industry and perseverance, which have laid the foundation of a future state in the deep recesses of our vast wilderness territory, and which are destined to transform that desert region into smiling gardens and fruitful fields. The foundation of Utah will stand on the page of history as coeval with that of California, and the record of its rise and progress will be regarded (though for far different reasons) as scarcely less marvellous and unprecedented.

Seal of the United States.

www.ingramcontent.com/pod-product-compliance
Lightning Source LLC
LaVergne TN
LVHW021052110826
845150LV00001B/51

* 9 7 8 1 4 2 5 5 6 7 4 5 3 *